CRIMINOLOGY

Longmans' Social Science Series

ERNEST R. GROVES, General Editor

RESEARCH PROFESSOR OF SOCIAL SCIENCE IN THE
UNIVERSITY OF NORTH CAROLINA

CRIMINOLOGY

BY

ALBERT MORRIS
ASSISTANT PROFESSOR OF SOCIAL SCIENCE
BOSTON UNIVERSITY COLLEGE OF LIBERAL ARTS

LONGMANS, GREEN AND CO.
NEW YORK · LONDON · TORONTO
1934

LONGMANS, GREEN AND CO.
114 FIFTH AVENUE, NEW YORK
221 EAST 20TH STREET, CHICAGO
88 TREMONT STREET, BOSTON

LONGMANS, GREEN AND CO. Ltd.
39 PATERNOSTER ROW, LONDON, E C 4
6 OLD COURT HOUSE STREET, CALCUTTA
53 NICOL ROAD, BOMBAY
36A MOUNT ROAD, MADRAS

LONGMANS, GREEN AND CO.
420 UNIVERSITY AVENUE, TORONTO

MORRIS

CRIMINOLOGY

FIRST EDITION

PRINTED IN THE UNITED STATES OF AMERICA

There are no crimes but criminals.

—*Ferri*

Le milieu social est le bouillon de culture de la criminalité, le microbe c'est le criminel.

—*Lacassagne*

PREFACE

THIS volume is a general text in Criminology. It purports to be neither original research nor a bald collection of facts garnered by others but a usable and suggestive arrangement and interpretation of important work already done in Criminology.

An attempt has been made to develop the subject matter logically by discussing in order the factors involved in the crime problem as they might touch upon persons from their babyhood until after their release from imprisonment. The table of contents is the author's outline of the possible natural sequence of events in the origin and treatment of criminals.

Throughout the book interest is centered upon personalities, especially those considered dangerous, rather than upon institutions. We are not so much concerned with crimes, courts and punishments as with criminals, policemen, prosecutors, public defenders, judges, wardens, and prison guards — people who commit crimes and those who attempt to control criminals. Only through persons do non-personal forces condition criminality. The problem is squarely one of human behavior.

An often neglected but important distinction is made between criminals and prisoners. Most prisoners are criminals. Few criminals are prisoners, but because the prisoners have been marked off from us in more or less dramatic fashion by prison walls they have attracted popular attention and have led people to picture criminals all too narrowly in terms of prisoners. The use of these terms as synonyms is an error and the common assumption that the information gathered about prisoners applies equally well to criminals is debatable.

The many factors that condition criminal behavior do not all exert their influence with the same force at any age level in the lives of human beings. There are age periods of

vii

greater or lesser susceptibility to them precisely as there are age periods of susceptibility or immunity to diseases. There are also differences in the length of the periods of incubation and in the duration of the effects of the factors making for criminal conduct. Some of them are apparently operative only during childhood and youth and they may have little to do with continuance in crime; others may exert an influence that persists through life; and still others may have shock effects that are vivid but temporary. This importance of the time element in criminogenesis has usually been glossed over or only vaguely apprehended. It is emphasized in the pages that follow, especially in the chapters that trace from conception to adult life the major factors in the genesis of criminal behavior that are operative at different age periods.

The possibilities of preventive work are considered in some detail as the first and fundamental step in the control of crime.

The author has incorporated in his picture of the field of Criminology the ideas of many persons whose works are quoted or referred to in notes and bibliographies. He has also been greatly aided by prisoners, policemen, prison officers, social workers and other friends who have contributed helpful facts and suggestions. To all of these who find their ideas incorporated in these pages the author gratefully acknowledges his indebtedness. Special thanks, however, are due Dr. Miriam Van Waters, Superintendent of the Massachusetts Reformatory for Women and Mr. Howard B. Gill, first Superintendent of the Massachusetts State Prison Colony at Norfolk for their careful reading of the entire manuscript and for their many helpful criticisms and encouragement; to my colleagues Professors Warren O. Ault, Frank Nowak, and Robert E. Moody who read and criticized parts of the manuscript; to Mabel F. Barnum, Librarian of Boston University College of Liberal Arts for her generous help in building up a file of current prison papers and journals; to the Hon. Sanford Bates, Director of the Federal Bureau of Prisons; Mr. Austin MacCormick, until recently Assistant Director of the Federal Bureau of Prisons and now Commissioner of Correction for New York City; Mr. Joel R. Moore, Chief of the Federal Probation Service;

Mr. Bennet Mead, Statistician of the Federal Bureau of Prisons; Miss Katherine Lenroot of the United States Children's Bureau; Hon. Joseph N. Ulman, Judge of the Supreme Bench of Baltimore; Dr. Vernon C. Branham, Deputy Commissioner of Correction of the State of New York; and Mr. Irving Halpern, Chief Probation Officer of the Court of General Sessions of New York for their suggestions for research which are listed in the appendix.

A special dept of gratitude is acknowledged to Professor S. Sheldon Glueck of the Harvard Law School, who also read the manuscript, for many stimulating discussions, for his helpful suggestions, and for many courtesies including the opportunity to use materials from his own studies before their publication; to Professor Ernest R. Groves, the editor of this series, not merely for his invaluable editorial aid but for his patience, his confidence, and his never failing encouragement; and to Dorothy, my wife, who in innumerable ways lightened the burdens and enhanced the joys of authorship.

ALBERT MORRIS

CONTENTS

PART ONE

CRIMINALS IN THEIR RELATION TO SOCIETY

PART TWO

THE NATURAL HISTORY OF CRIMINALS

PART THREE

THE PREVENTION OF CRIMINAL BEHAVIOR

CRIMINOLOGY

CRIMINOLOGY

PART ONE—CRIMINALS IN THEIR RELATION
TO SOCIETY

INTRODUCTION

THE FIELD OF CRIMINOLOGY

THE business of criminology is to understand criminals as a basis for preventing their appearance or for controlling them. It begins with a study of offenders and their relations to the great society of which they are such a sorry part. It involves an attempted appraisal of all of the forces, hereditary and environmental, that may contribute to their making and unmaking. It implies a critique of our present ways of dealing with criminals.

Who are these criminals? Strictly speaking a criminal is any person who, by due process of law, has been found guilty of committing a crime. Juvenile delinquents are not included. Malefactors, who are never convicted, are outside of the boundaries. Included, however, are a host of criminals like ourselves who have been fined for watching taillights instead of traffic lights. Just how long a convicted person remains a criminal may be a bit of a puzzle. Forever, though he commits only one offense? Until he has paid his fine or served his sentence? Until he succeeds on parole? Until he proves himself thereafter?

Criminology cannot draw a neat line about its subjects. Obviously its usefulness would be seriously curtailed if it confined its interest to legally defined offenders. Strange as it may seem criminology is really concerned, not with criminals, but with personalities considered dangerous in any particular place at any particular period in time. But at present it can only judge their dangerousness by their conduct as measured by contemporary standards. So it views them against our official list of socially harmful acts, known as the criminal law. The criminal law is the focal point of our attention. All those who seem likely to break its rules, as well as those who have done so, come within the criminologists' field of vision. The ultimate aim of criminology is to get a body of factual knowledge on which to build a successful technique for preventing their appearance or for controlling them.

That is a pious hope rather than an impending achievement. At present criminology, in common with all other social studies, is in possession of useful but incomplete odds and ends of information, which it is not certain just how to put together. However, it wants to develop its field as a science. Whether it can do so is open to question.[1] Possibly the ability to modify human nature can never be other than an art. In part the answer depends upon one's definition of science. Criminology deals with the understanding and control of human behavior which is too subtle a phenomenon to be described fully in comparable objective terms. Many useful facts about human conduct can be counted and measured statistically. Others are susceptible to reasonably precise definition. But many pertinent facts, that are no less real because they are intangible, defy all present efforts to use them for common comparison and analysis. The observations of a psychiatrist for example, may be made with scrupulous care and yet neither his understanding of what he has learned nor his technique may be transferable except by approximation to others. To date, criminology has acquired a small amount of genuinely scientific knowledge. It is persistently trying to gather more. Probably the major part of the work that has been done to date has reached untrustworthy conclusions because of lack of skill on the part of research workers in applying the methods of science in the field of criminological research. Nevertheless some criminologists such as Healy, Bronner, Shaw, the Gluecks, and others have successfully applied the scientific technique to problems in the field of criminology.

[1] See Michael and Adler, "Crime, Law and the Social Sciences" and the individual criticisms of this work by the members of a reviewing committee appointed by the Social Science Research Council and published in mimeographed form for an interesting and varied array of opinion about the present status of criminology and criminological research.

Science is, of course, neither dependent upon subject matter nor success, but upon method. It is only a name for a way of attacking problems, the best way that we have yet discovered. It involves making a working hypothesis, observing and recording facts, classifying and organizing the data so gathered, generalizing, the making and testing of new hypotheses, and the predicting of future conduct. Criminology is attempting to use these tools but it has barely made a beginning. Its scientific achievements lie chiefly in the future of hope rather than in the past of accomplishment. Very likely these tools of science may prove inapplicable to the gaining of certain very useful information in the field of criminology.

For the present, therefore, insofar as there is a grave lack of reliable, objectively stated, scientifically ascertained conclusions in the field of criminology it is necessary to examine the materials available critically and to pass a reflective judgment upon them. The method may not be ideal, but in the absence of scientific proof it is the only alternative to an indiscriminate easy acceptance of whatever seems plausible.

The student, therefore, should approach circumspectly both the facts and the interpretations presented by criminologists. More specifically the student should attempt to know and weigh the sources of the materials that he is considering, the extent and the quality of the samples presented ; and the abilities of the investigators, including their reputations for knowledge in the particular fields concerned, good judgment, precision, and the facilities that were available to them. Nor should the student neglect to question the validity of their interpretations of facts by holding them up against possible alternative explanations.

In spite of such possibly disturbing confessions of ignorance, there is no need to be dismayed because criminology is not yet a realm of blessed assurance. The science is yet very young. It has already demonstrated that it can grow. It offers ample opportunity for careful critical thinking. To anyone interested in scientific research it lifts a challenge worthy of the highest skill and extends the opportunity to further man's insatiable desire for knowledge into a field as yet little touched by able investigators.

In the chapters to come we shall try to chart the region that criminology has now explored and hint at the adventures that lie beyond for those who have an inclination for the quest. Our first task is to become acquainted with the legal boundaries of criminal behavior.

CHAPTER I
CRIMINALS AND THE CRIMINAL LAW

THE FUNCTION OF THE CRIMINAL LAW

THE criminal law defines crimes and assesses penalties for criminal acts. Crimes are acts that we consider to be such a menace to the public peace and security that we intend to protect ourselves against them as a sovereign group by legally limited force. The criminal law is our official list and description of those acts. It is the rule by which we identify criminal behavior and sort out of society for treatment those who are guilty of it. It is also the formula by which we classify crimes and distinguish one from another.

In primitive societies where groups are small, wealth is limited, and customs tend to remain unchanged, formal criminal laws are unnecessary. The law of custom serves in their stead. But in our complex society the absence of formal law is unthinkable. Our activities are so ramified, our ethical ideals so varied that without a sharply defined minimum list of prohibitions we should wander in chaos. There would be many honest differences of opinion. Meddlesome, ignorant or unscrupulous nuisances would add to our troubles. That handy and well-nigh inescapable conclusion, "There ought to be a law . . ." indicates how frequently we would interfere with each other if we relied upon our weird and conflicting ethical standards alone. No one would know what he might safely do without interference. So it is necessary that the boundaries of criminality be drawn with precision and established with a surety that will enable citizens to enjoy a satisfying measure of public protection without being placed in jeopardy of thoughtless or malicious interference. This the law attempts to do.

5

THE DEFINITION OF CRIME

How does the law define crime ?   If its Scandinavian root
may be trusted, a "wrong" is that which is awry, twisted, or
crooked.   Obviously many acts that are awry cannot be considered crimes.   Some are too trivial to warrant public
attention.   Others are too largely personal and individual in
their influence.   A sin, which is essentially a violation against
a divine authority, or a vice such as gluttony, which is a
wrong primarily against nature affecting oneself, may become
a crime only when it also results in acts of nonconformity to
the criminal law.   Even illegal acts are not all crimes.   Such
are the wrongs caused by one individual to another (except
those involving a breach of contract) which are recognized as
warranting a civil action between private parties but which,
theoretically, are not of public concern.   These are known
in law as torts.   They may include wrongs of the type done
by the truck driver whose machine skids into a store window,
or that done by the golfer whose ball, accidentally driven
askew, strikes and injures a person on a nearby public way.
Crimes, then, are only those illegal acts, or failures to act,
which violate a public right and are punishable under the
law by prosecution in the name of the sovereign ! [1]   The
New York Penal Law defines crime as : "An act or omission
forbidden by law and punishable upon conviction by (1)
death ; or (2) imprisonment ; or (3) fine ; or (4) removal
from office ; or (5) disqualification to hold or enjoy any
office of trust, honor, or profit under the state ; or (6) other
penal discipline."

Unfortunately, such a definition of crime does not help
us to recognize crime by its own characteristics.   In fact
many illegal acts straddle fixed boundaries.   As a result,
their labels are dependent more upon viewpoint and interest
than upon logic.   The keeping of pigs may be a commend-

---

[1] If Richard Roe is shot, the criminal indictment against his assailant
begins, *People* v. *John Doe*, and ends with the charge that the shooting
was done "contrary to the form of the statute in such cases made and
provided for and against the peace and dignity of the state."   The prosecution is in the hands of the district attorney who may press the case or
drop it without considering the wishes of Richard Roe.

able and wholly legitimate enterprise, a tort in the form of a private wrong to a property owner, or a crime in the guise of a public nuisance, depending upon the attendant circumstances. Private wrongs (torts), for example, indirectly affect public welfare, sometimes seriously. Conversely, public wrongs (crimes) concentrate their immediate effects upon certain individuals. Surely the person who has been grievously wounded by robbers has suffered more intensely than the community. In reality nearly all crimes are also torts and the criminal may legally be proceeded against in a civil action ; but in practice this is usually inadvisable because of the cost of bringing suit and because most convicted criminals, whose crimes involve torts, are propertyless. There are, of course, certain crimes, such as treason and mere attempts to commit crime, which do not injure private persons and which are, therefore, not also torts. As Sir James Stephen has aptly remarked, the question of whether an illegal act is a crime or a tort is much like the inquiry as to whether a man is a father or a son. He might well be both.

Moreover, the line between criminal and non-criminal acts is so sharply drawn that although most persons have a general notion of what acts are legally recognized as crimes, there is no way of telling whether a particular act is a crime except by discovering whether it is so considered by the law as interpreted by the courts. A hiker enjoying a winter stroll beside a river may sit down contentedly with his pipe to watch a stranger struggling to draw himself upon ice that had let him through, and even though the unfortunate adventurer should drown, the hiker who witnessed the incident without lifting a finger to save him would not be guilty of any illegal act. Yet the hiker would be guilty of a crime if he knew that the drowning person were his son. Obviously it takes more than intuition to tell us what is a crime.

Crime, then, is a legal concept, and a crime is any act which the law so labels. Since laws vary with the age and the state, crimes do also. There is no act, save possibly treason, that we now look upon with abhorrence as a crime that has not at some time or place been considered honorable.[2] The

---

[2] See W. Sumner's "Folkways" for an interesting and valuable discussion of the origin and evolution of moral codes.

killing of parents, the exposure of children, cannibalism, prostitution, adultery, polygamy, incest, nudity, slavery, theft, have all been permitted. On the other hand, many acts that we legally disregard, have been forbidden. It was a capital offense in ancient Egypt to cause the death of a cat, a vulture, or an ichneumon. The Code of Hammurabi prescribed death by burning for a votary not living in the convent, who opened a wine-shop or entered one for drink. Russia, Turkey and Persia have in times past forbidden the use of tobacco under penalty of mutilation or death. Confirmed bachelors were publicly scourged in Sparta. Detracting from the dignity of the sovereign, the crime of lese-majesty, was known to both Roman and English law. The death penalty was prescribed in colonial Massachusetts for children above 16, guilty of smiting or cursing their parents. Obstinate persistence in heresy, idolatry, witchcraft and blasphemy were other capital offenses in Massachusetts.

States at similar levels of culture by no means agree upon what practices are socially harmful. Prostitution is a criminal offense in our states but not in France. Nevada legalized public gambling in 1931. In other states it has not gone beyond the status of a privileged crime.

Apparently a practice is eligible for listing among the criminal statutes only when it is considered a public menace. The criminal law is an end result of our ethical guessing. It is a precise formulation of a belief that a certain practice is so dangerous that it must be stamped out. What will be considered dangerous depends upon the way in which the economic, religious, political or social interests of a group cause it to interpret and modify its ethical traditions. The reason we have only one universal crime is because no act, save treason, has always been noticeably harmful to the collective interests of society. Treason is our name for an act necessarily dangerous to the group as a whole. It is only when acts seem to menace the group (in reality become treasonable) that they are interdicted as crimes.

COMMON LAW AND STATUTE LAW

THERE are two types of law defining crimes, common law and statute law. The common law is an unwritten body of legal practices developed in England and largely accepted as authoritative in the United States today, except where replaced by specific statutes. The common law represents a slow growth and accumulation of precedents based upon ancient Anglo-Saxon customs. Age and common acceptance gave them authority. They were preserved in the decisions of the judges whom Blackstone described as "the depositories of the law, the living oracles who must decide in all cases of doubt, and who are bound by oath to decide according to the law of the land." The common law was made in the same way that a path is formed across a field. Someone passes through, others by accident or design follow the dim outline of the newly made trail until finally it has become a beaten path.

Statute law is the written law of the country enacted by legislative bodies but still rooted and grounded in the old common law. It is particularly useful for controlling acts that have only recently become harmful due to changes in the social order and in revising common law conceptions to meet the needs of modern times. At common law, for example, it was presumed that if a wife committed a crime in the presence of her husband it was done by his coercion, and that, if maintained, was a sufficient defense against the indictment. This position is so out of harmony with the requirements of the status of women in modern life that it has become necessary to make a specific revision of the old precedents by enacting statutes on this point.[3]

Many acts that are obviously harmful to the public cannot be precisely defined (common nuisance, for example), and it has, therefore, become an accepted principle of common law that any act which is obviously shocking, immoral, and harmful to the community is punishable as a crime. Statute law has added to these offenses many which are not inher-

[3] For example: "It is not a defense to a married woman charged with crime, that the alleged criminal act was committed by her in the presence of her husband." New York Penal Law, Section 1092.

ently evil but are crimes because they are forbidden for the sake of general social well-being, as in the case of a storekeeper selling tobacco to a child even though he is sure that it is really being bought for an adult.   Since legislators have found it difficult to provide in advance for every possible type of public wrong that might be committed, and, inasmuch as it is not advisable to leave gaps in the penal code, most states have retained the great body of common law as a filler to be drawn upon when offenses arise that have not been covered specifically by statutes.[4]

THE CLASSIFICATION OF CRIMES

UNDER the common law crime includes three grades of offenses classified as (1) treason ; (2) felonies ; and (3) misdemeanors.

In feudal times treason included a number of vaguely defined disloyal acts which were thought of as being on two levels : (1) petit treason which represented a vassal's violation of his allegiance due to his lord, and (2) high treason which was a direct violation of allegiance due the king. There was considerable confusion about what offenses should be adjudged treasonable until 1351 when the specific actions constituting the crime were set forth in the Act of 25 Edward III, c.2.   This statute reduced petit treason to three cases : the killing of a master by his servant, of a husband by his wife, or of a prelate by a priest owing him obedience.   In 1828 by the Act of 9 George IV, c. 31, s. 2, these acts were made simple murders and the crime of petit treason vanished.   High treason is, therefore, the only form known to modern law.   Seven forms of high treason were defined by the Statute of Treasons in 1351 and additional limitations have been made since, until now, in the United States, it applies only to two acts defined in the United States Consti-

---

[4] Several of the United States have abrogated the common law and replaced it entirely by statute law based largely upon common law precedents.   There are no common law offenses under the federal government.   It is interesting to note that the legal systems of Louisiana in the United States, of Porto Rico, the Philippines, and of the Province of Quebec in Canada trace their roots to Roman rather than Anglo-Saxon law.

tution, Article III, Section 3 in a form based upon the ancient statute of Edward III. This article provides that :

Treason against the United States shall consist only in levying war against them, or in adhering to their enemies, giving them aid and comfort.

Treason is, theoretically, the most heinous of all crimes because it strikes directly at the heart of social well-being by attempting to destroy the institution of government. Actually the traitor may be moved by the loftiest idealism and our final estimate of him may depend chiefly upon the success of his cause. George Washington would now be remembered as the traitor who was hung for leading a rebellion against the Crown if the colonists had lost their fight.

Felonies in England and Normandy were originally the gravest, the most despicable of common offenses. They included every act which entailed forfeiture of the felon's goods or land. Usually the felon also lost his life. Gradually the severity of the penalty was lessened so that relatively few felonies are now punishable by death. Nevertheless, acts that were felonies under common law are still felonies unless the statutes specifically provide otherwise, even though the penalty has changed. However, the characterization of felonies as crimes more serious than misdemeanors is now true only in a general way, and the distinction between them has become somewhat arbitrary. If a man steals $100 in New York he has committed a misdemeanor. If he steals $101 he has committed a felony. An offense that is a misdemeanor in one state may be a felony in another. An act such as the sale of a pint of gin when committed for the first time may be a misdemeanor and a felony if it is committed by the same person again soon after. The obtaining of goods by false pretenses may be a misdemeanor, whereas the obtaining of the same value by forgery may be a felony. At present the line between felonies and misdemeanors is sharply and arbitrarily drawn by some such provision as that in the New York Penal Law which states that :

Section 2. A felony is a crime which is or may be punishable by : (1) Death ; or (2) Imprisonment in a state prison. Any other crime is a misdemeanor.

In a few places violations of municipal ordinances such as those with reference to automobile parking are not classified as crimes but as "violations." This represents an attempt to protect citizens from having a criminal record for infringements of regulatory ordinances to which people do not ordinarily attach a stigma. However, in most places violations of city ordinances are still rated as crimes.

THE ELEMENTS OF A CRIME

Two elements are involved in crime : (1) Illegal conduct in the form of a voluntary, conscious act (or a neglect to perform an act which is a duty); and (2) an intent, which may be of two kinds : general, a so-called guilty mind (*mens rea*), and specific intent, which is an additional type that must be present in some crimes. These two elements, the act and the intent, are necessary to nearly every crime.[5] One of them alone is not sufficient. If a man who had been examining rings in a jewelry store should carry away one of them, mistakenly believing it to be his own, he would have committed the act essential to the crime of larceny, but inasmuch as the intent to steal was lacking he could not be convicted. If he had entered the store with the intention of confusing the jeweler and of substituting his own inexpensive ring for a valuable one and had, in his hurry to escape, actually picked up his own ring, he would also not be guilty of larceny since he would have committed no criminal act in spite of his intent to do so. Moreover the law requires that the act and the intent concur in point of time. If a man lawfully gains possession of an article belonging to another without at the time intending to steal it but later decides to convert the property to his own use he is not guilty of the crime of larceny although he might be proceeded against on other grounds.

Act and intent have been so carefully defined by court decisions that they have come to have technical meanings. A spasm is not considered an act since it is not willed. Nor is it an act if one stumbles over an obstruction and consequently

---

[5] There are minor exceptions. When an ordinance prohibits an act not otherwise wrong the mere doing of the act may constitute a crime.

bumps into and knocks down a fellow pedestrian. It has been held that mere possession is not an act. On the other hand, a word may be an illegal act, as is also inciting another to commit a crime.

The second element, the intent, might be difficult to prove were it not that the law presumes every man to intend what people would commonly expect to be the natural and probable consequences of such an act. The only requisite here is that the person commit the act voluntarily and with full knowledge of the surrounding facts. If a man should go out on a public golf course where people were playing to practise rifle shooting and should inadvertently kill someone he would very likely be guilty of manslaughter. We should say his intentions were good but his judgment was poor. The law would say that any reasonable man would know that he might kill someone if he went rifle shooting on a public golf course. In common presumption any man who shoots bullets across a fairway where people are playing intends to do mischief. The fact that this man did so warrants the presumption that he had the necessary guilty mind.[6]

It is also recognized that absence of knowledge that the act is forbidden by law does not prevent the holding of the necessary guilty mind. If a man not knowing that the law forbids it marries three wives with full knowledge that he is doing so and in accordance with his sincere religious conviction that he ought to do so, his lack of legal knowledge and the absence of evil intent in the popular sense will not excuse him. The fact is that he intended to do that which the law forbids even though his motive was most laudable. It has been held that a detective may not join in the actual commis-

---

[6] Notice that the law holds everyone up to a common standard. Although the presumption of intent is rebuttable the evidence must show that a reasonable man, not the defendant specifically, would not have intended the consequences that followed his act. See the interesting case of *Regina* v. *Machekequonabe* (28 Ont. Rep. 309) in which an Indian who was posted to help guard an encampment against an evil spirit in human form shot a man in the belief that he was shooting the evil spirit. Machekequonabe was found guilty of manslaughter. A reasonable man would not have held that superstition, but would have expected to kill a human being if he had shot at a running human form.

sion of a crime, even though he does it in order to apprehend the criminals.   On the other hand children and lunatics are held by law to be mentally incapable of harboring the necessary criminal intent.

Specific intent appears in crimes such as burglary, arson, and larceny.   For example, burglary at common law consisted in breaking and entering the dwelling-house of another in the night *with the intent to commit a felony therein.* Here it must be proved that the defendant in the particular case at hand did actually intend to commit a felony therein. It does not matter what one would ordinarily presume a man caught in similar circumstances to intend, but what the defendant did in fact intend.   An early application of this rule occurred at the assizes held at Buckingham in 1770 when

Joseph Dobbs was indicted for burglary in breaking and entering the stable of James Bayley, part of his dwelling-house, in the night, with a felonious intent to kill and destroy a gelding of one A.B. there being.   It appeared that the gelding was to have run for forty guineas, and that the prisoner cut the sinews of his foreleg to prevent his running, in consequence of which he died.

Parker, Ch.B., ordered him to be acquitted ; for his intention was not to commit the felony by killing and destroying the horse, but a trespass only to prevent his running ; and therefore no burglary.

But the prisoner was again indicted for killing the horse, and capitally convicted.[7]

SPECIFIC OFFENSES

IT is obviously impossible to give here a detailed list of the specific acts considered criminal by our several states.   Nevertheless the classification used by the Bureau of the Census in enumerating prisoners in 1923 will suggest the range of offenses.   A less detailed listing of offenses is to be found in the report on prisoners received in 1929 and 1930.   The figures on commitments are included to give an idea of their relative numerical importance :

[7] E. H. East, "Pleas of the Crown," Vol. 2, pp. 513-14, Edition of 1803.   Quoted also in F. Sayre, "Cases on Criminal Law," p. 203.

PRISONERS 1923 [8]

Offense	Commitments Jan. 1– June 30	Offense	Commitments Jan. 1– June 30
Total................	166,356		
Against the person........	8,101	Against public health and safety..............	16,273
Assault.................	5,893	Carrying concealed weapons................	2,609
Homicide, grave........	570	Illegal practice of profession..............	59
Homicide, lesser........	1,391	Nuisance..............	162
Threat to do bodily harm.	222	Violating city ordinances.	4,657
All other..............	25	Violating drug laws......	3,373
		Violating traffic laws.....	5,292
Against property, gainful...	24,626	All other..............	121
Burglary................	4,247		
Counterfeiting..........	109	Against sobriety and good order..............	80,168
Embezzlement..........	474	Disorderly conduct......	24,568
Forgery.................	2,010	Drug addiction.........	619
Fraud..................	2,224	Drunkenness...........	42,069
Having stolen property...	690	Vagrancy.............	12,911
Larceny................	12,825	All other..............	1
Robbery................	1,790		
Violating revenue laws...	130	Against public policy......	20,739
All other..............	127	Criminal anarchism or syndicalism..........	99
		Cruelty to animals......	205
Against property, other....	2,015	Gambling.............	1,858
Arson..................	114	Profanity..............	91
Malicious mischief......	307	Violating fish and game laws.................	125
Trespassing............	1,400	Violating liquor laws.....	18,239
Using another's property.	193	All other..............	122
All other..............	1		
		Against children and prisoner's family...........	2,353
Against sex morality.......	5,938	Contributing to delinquency..............	432
Adultery...............	544	Nonsupport or neglect of family...............	1,698
Bastardy...............	72	Violating education laws..	175
Bigamy and polygamy...	182	All other..............	48
Crime against nature....	143		
Fornication............	1,329	Unclassified and unknown..	4,901
Keeping house of ill fame.	431	Delinquency, etc........	166
Obscenity..............	556	Quarantine (venereal)....	99
Prostitution............	1,046	Violating labor laws.....	153
Rape..................	1,060	Violating parole.........	364
Securing and transporting women for immoral purposes.................	258	Violating U. S. postal laws, etc..................	410
All other..............	317	All other, specified......	2,750
		Unknown.............	959
Against the administration of government........	1,242		
Contempt of court......	497		
Escaping custody.......	287		
Falsely impersonating....	87		
Perjury................	95		
Resisting officer........	145		
Violating immigration laws	65		
All other..............	66		

[8] Bureau of the Census, "Prisoners 1923." Adapted from table 11, p. 28.

Definitions of these offenses vary and should be examined in the statutes and court decisions of each state. Nevertheless it may be helpful for us to review the essential characteristics of a few offenses whose precise nature is often misunderstood.

Assault and battery are generally linked together because it is not possible to commit a battery without also committing an assault. Yet these are two separate crimes. It is possible to commit an assault without a battery. An assault is a seriously intended threat to do bodily harm to another, as when an angry person tells a companion that he will punch him in the jaw. An assault does not involve striking another. The threat to do violence, the "leaping at" (*ad-salire*), constitutes the assault. A battery consists in using force upon the body of another in an angry or insolent manner, as by pushing or jostling a person rudely. It is the attack that frequently follows the assault. No matter how slight the injury done it may constitute a battery if done vengefully.

Homicide is the killing of any human being by another. It may be excusable, as when done in self defense ; or justifiable, as when done under a warrant of execution. The unlawful killing of a human being with malice aforethought is murder. "Malice aforethought" is a technical phrase including not only malignancy of spirit but any dangerous and unlawful act likely to cause death and indicative of a heart bent on mischief, regardless of the welfare of others. Murder may be divided into two degrees. First degree murder is committed with "*premeditated* malice aforethought." Second degree murder lacks the premeditation. Manslaughter is the unlawful killing of a human being without malice aforethought. It also may be divided into degrees. Since there can be no malice aforethought to the crime of manslaughter there can be no crime of attempt to commit manslaughter although attempts to commit murder are themselves punishable as felonies.

Adultery is usually defined by statute since it was not an offense at common law because it was taken care of by the ecclesiastical courts. New York defines adultery as the sexual intercourse of two persons, either of whom is married to a third person. Where adultery is made a crime, but is not defined, the courts differ as to its meaning, some holding that it can be committed only when a married woman takes part. This is on the old fiction that the blood of the family could only be adulterated by the act of the wife.

Rape is sexual intercourse with a female, not one's wife, by force and against her will. An important aspect of this crime is the fact that under a specified age a female is held by law incapable of giving her consent. Consequently, if in New York where the age of consent is 18, a young woman of 17 voluntarily has intercourse with a man he is guilty of rape, since the law says she is incapable of giving her consent. As it was held in California "In such case the female is to be regarded as resisting, no matter what the actual state of her mind may be at that time. The law resists for her." [9] Recognition of the lesser seriousness of technical rape has led in some states to a division of this crime also into degrees.

Larceny, which is the most common gainful offense against property, was at common law the unlawful taking and carrying away of the personal goods of another out of his possession with intent to deprive the owner of them. This ancient definition has been quite generally amended to include real property as well as personal goods. It is what we commonly call stealing. Usually it is divided into petty larceny which is a misdemeanor and grand larceny which is a felony on the basis of the value of the goods stolen. The line between the two grades is arbitrarily drawn and varies considerably from place to place.

Robbery is larceny from the person of another by means of force, violence and fear of injury.

Embezzlement consists in the fraudulent taking of property by one to whom it has been entrusted.

Extortion was originally the corrupt demanding or receiving of money by a person in office either in the form of taking a fee where none was due or a fee in excess of that provided by law. Some states have modified this by statute to include any persons who obtain property from others unlawfully but by their consent when it is gained through the wrongful use of force or through putting them in fear.

[9] People v. Vann, 129 Cal., 118.

Burglary at common law was breaking into the dwelling house of another in the night-time with the intent to commit a felony therein. Buildings outside of the yard of the dwellings were not mentioned since the charge was intended to protect persons rather than property. The intended felony did not need to be stealing. It might be an intent to burn the dwelling house or to assault its occupants with a deadly weapon or any other felony. On the other hand, if the offender unarmed intended merely to steal some intrinsically valueless object, perhaps for sentiment's sake, it would not be a burglary. Burglary is now defined by statute and sometimes extended to include buildings other than dwellings. Where this has been done burglary in the first degree is the old common law crime just described.

Arson, like burglary, was originally a crime against the inmates of a house rather than against property. It consisted in maliciously and voluntarily burning the dwelling house of another either by night or by day. This is still the law in some jurisdictions. In others it has like burglary been extended by statute to include buildings other than dwellings.

The foregoing is a rough sketch of the area of criminality as defined by law. It is like a wall-map of the world which gives only in barest outline the configuration of the continents without a hint of the countless bays and bluffs and islands that dot each coast. To understand these a local map is necessary. So the criminal law and the courts have gone on to define and to describe each act in minute detail in their effort to trace accurately and definitely the boundaries of crime.

What is a dwelling house in the crime of burglary? Must it be occupied? What is "occupied"? May the owner be away for the summer? Must it be completely finished, or may it be in the process of construction? How far along must the construction be? In what does breaking and entering consist? Must a window be forced or merely opened? Opened how far? Must one have his entire body within the house or is an arm sufficient? A hand? What is night-time? After sunset? After dark? At two o'clock in the morning?

In all of this careful outlining the law is concerned solely with defining the *acts* which men must not commit, and this is necessary unless "the courts undertake to exercise in one direction the full supervision of the Deity over men contrary to what is either practical or beneficial."[10] But then the law goes on to assess penalties for violations on the basis of the theoretical seriousness of these acts, and in so doing it does not take account of man's increasing knowledge of the forces involved in human behavior. It assumes that it is dealing with a free moral agent. Therefore it is not necessary to consider the actor. Yet it is obvious that the same crime may be committed by several persons with differing motives and in need of differing forms of treatment. One man may murder another who has seduced his daughter. A second may in sudden anger strike down one who has called him a foul name. A third murderer may be mentally defective or psychopathic, yet not legally insane, while a fourth may kill a policeman in an effort to escape from one who has surprised him in the act of committing larceny.

THE VIEWPOINT OF CRIMINOLOGY

CRIMINOLOGY is interested in the problems presented by these people. What is the importance of criminals in society? What effects do they have upon the non-criminal group? What had best be done with them? Can they be made safe and useful citizens? If not, what should be done with them? What forces brought such persons into being? Are those forces still at work producing a continuing stream of undesirables? What can be done to check, redirect, or lessen the influence of these forces? What is now being done in this field? How effective is it? How much is it wise to attempt?

To such questions criminology directs itself in an effort to secure and to lay bare the facts, whatever they may be, as the only reasonable basis for the establishment of a wholesome public attitude towards a problem about which every one, however uninformed, seems to be desirous of holding an opinion.

[10] J. Bishop, "New Commentaries on the Criminal Law," 8th Edition, Vol. 1, p. 25.

CHAPTER II

THE ECONOMIC COSTLINESS OF CRIMINALS

GUESSING THE COSTS OF CRIME

ESTIMATING the damage done by criminals seems to be the great American statistical pastime. Many attempts have been made to measure the economic losses that they cause. Insurance companies regularly report the sums lost through embezzlement, burglaries, bank robberies, and other crimes in which they are particularly interested. The annual reports of police commissioners, attorney-generals, city managers and other officials dealing more or less directly with the crime problem frequently fling out alarming guesses of the cost of the criminal menace. Courageous statisticians have not hesitated to attempt comprehensive appraisals of the economic burden of crime.

Historically interesting is the calculation of Eugene Smith made in 1900 that 250,000 persons in the United States made their living at least in part by crime at a cost of $400,-000,000 a year plus $200,000,000 additional, in taxes for their apprehension and punishment.[1] About the same time the Chaplain of the Prison Evangelist Society of New York placed the direct and indirect cost of crime in the United States at $1,075,000,000. Since then the figures have climbed. In 1910 Weir estimated the annual cost at $1,370,000,000. Lydston placed it at $5,000,000,000. A few of the more recently published figures on the yearly cost of crime are: Anderson, $912,500,000 (1923); Gillin, $3,000,000,000 (1926); Smith, $10,000,000,000 (1924); Enright, $11,800,000,000 to $13,000,000,000 (1929);

[1] E. Smith, "The Cost of Crime," an investigation for the International Prison Commission. House doc. 491, Government Printing Office, 1901.

Baumes Commission $13,000,000,000 exclusive of financial crime (1928); White House Conference on Child Health and Protection, $16,000,000,000 (1930); Reeve, $18,000,-000,000 (1931).

The implications of these more or less shrewd guesses are often made impressive by comparing them with other national expenditures. For example, the relatively conservative estimate of $13,000,000,000 by the Baumes Commission is more than six times as much as the cost of public school education in the United States for 1927-28, and nearly three times as much as the entire budget of the United States, the largest governmental budget in the world, for the fiscal year ending June 30, 1932. If the expense suggested by the Baumes Commission were to be apportioned directly the head of every family in the United States would receive an annual tax bill of approximately $464 for crime.

But the cost of crime is not limited to economic waste. Criminals are destructive of life as well as property. Frederick Hoffman notes in the insurance weekly *Spectator* that in 1931 there were nearly 12,000 murders, 6725 acknowledged suicides, and an estimated total of not less than 20,000 suicides, in the United States.[2] An unknown portion of the nearly thirty thousand automobile fatalities of 1932 was the result of criminal activities. Charles F. Carter notes that the 59,377 murders recorded for this country by the Chicago *Tribune* between 1912 and 1918 is 9050 greater than the number of battle deaths of American soldiers during the great world war.[3] How extensive are the non-financial injuries due to assaults, rapes, criminal libels and other offenses against the person remains unestimated for the country at large. Before someone attempts the task let us push figures into the background and consider just what we are attempting to measure by them, whether it can be done and if it is worth doing.

[2] F. Hoffman, *Spectator*, June 9, 1932, p. 10. Also March 30, 1933.
[3] C. F. Carter, "The Carnival of Crime," *Current History*, Feb. 1922.

THE MEANING OF "COST OF CRIME"

THE cost of crime may include the tragedy of wasted lives, the physical pain and the mental suffering that the activities of criminals entail. Obviously we have no adding machine that can calculate the destructiveness of criminals in these terms. We know no way to measure the increasing demoralization of the criminal himself, the shame felt by his relatives, the psychical reactions upon the victims of assaults, the loss to a family of the personality of a father who is murdered, the effects of obvious political corruption in a community and a host of other intangible evils that may be fully as important to society as the more definite economic waste due to criminals.

If we then limit our efforts to measurements of financial loss it is again necessary to ask what a loss is. When goods are stolen they merely change hands. They may be somewhat altered in appearance but their value may remain unimpaired. Are they then lost? Clearly the rightful owner or his insurance company has suffered a loss but society has not. On the other hand, the economic discrepancy between what a criminal produces and what he might have produced, were he not a criminal, is a social loss even though it is not felt by any individual. Recognizing this point, Dorr and Simpson in their analysis of the cost of crime for the National Commission on Law Observance and Enforcement[4] make a distinction between ultimate and immediate costs of crime.

By immediate costs they refer to transfers of wealth which place a burden upon individuals but do not constitute a loss to society. They include the expense of public and private protection against criminals, the administration of criminal justice, penal institutions, the support of the dependents of criminals, and of non-destructive crimes against property. These losses are felt as individual expenses in the form of taxes, wages or insurance premiums paid, protective devices purchased, or goods stolen. They are not of themselves an ultimate loss to society.

By ultimate cost of crime they mean the general economic

[4] National Commission on Law Observance and Enforcement "Report on the Cost of Crime." Ch. 2.

loss to society as a whole. For this country it would theoretically be the difference between the annual national income and the annual national income if there were no crime. It includes the loss of the potentially productive labor of criminals and of the public and private protectors against crime.

Although these are two distinct aspects of the cost of crime, they do in some measure overlap. When property is actually destroyed or persons are injured by criminals there is both an immediate loss to individuals and there may be a general loss to society as well. The loss due to arson, for example, is a loss to both the individual and the community.

CAN THE COST OF CRIME BE ASCERTAINED?

WITH these considerations in mind it at once becomes apparent that to render a bill for the total ultimate cost of crime for any important area is an impossibility. Until we know how many criminals there are and what capacities they have, and to what extent they are now unproductive, we cannot estimate the loss that they represent. We cannot determine how useful they would be, even were they law abiding. Nor can we estimate the contributions that law enforcement agents might make to society if they were in productive occupations. We shall simply have to admit that we cannot ascertain the ultimate economic cost of crime.

Theoretically, the immediate financial loss can be ascertained. Practically, it is a task too vast for our present research machinery. It would require studies of the cost of administering criminal justice by the federal government, 48 states, 3073 counties, 6252 incorporated cities and villages with a population of more than 1000 and 10,346 incorporated villages of less than 1000. In all of these places the expense of the criminal business of the courts and their associated agencies would need to be separated from the expense of their civil business. What part of the salaries of judges, attorneys, other court officers, clerks and janitorial staff should be charged to the cost of crime, and what part to civil business? What part of the investment in court buildings, equipment and running expenses should be allocated as a cost of crime? The same problems confront us in analyzing the cost of police protection, probation, parole, and the city, county and state institutions which sometimes house non-criminal dependents as well as criminals.

Private expenses due to crime include the cost of special police forces, watchmen, detective agencies, mechanical safety devices, and privately endowed institutions of a peno-corrective character. There is no central clearing house of information that can tell the amounts spent for these services. In addition to that handicap an investigator would again face the bugaboo of allocating costs. Should the salaries of watchmen be charged in their entirety against crime? Are not watchmen hired also to guard against fires, to sweep floors, tend furnaces and a host of other incidental tasks? Do not guards serve as porters and information bureaus? Are not private detectives hired frequently to secure evidence for use in civil actions? Are not bank vaults and safes for protection against fire as well as against criminals?

Any accurate analysis of crime costs should include a proper recognition of these non-criminal expenses. Private losses due to crime involve injuries done to persons, the criminal destruction or appropriation of property, and certain other crimes against wealth in the form of fraud and extortion. In spite of the fact that civil juries are constantly awarding damages to injured persons, no one supposes that their appraisals are economically accurate. Yet, except for similar crude estimates, it is not feasible to determine economic losses due to criminally caused injuries. The cost of medical and hospital care, of medicines, of wages, the loss of jobs, and the added incidental family expenses would all need to be included. Strictly speaking we do not know whether there has been a criminal injury or not until the responsible person has been convicted. Undoubtedly many criminal injuries are never reported to the police.

Likewise, many crimes against property and wealth are never reported. Losses due to fraudulent gambling games, blackmail and the extortions of racketeers have reached the proportions of a major but immeasurable economic activity in the United States. They are not reported. The loss due to insurance frauds is obviously unknown since if the frauds were detected there would usually be no payment. Losses due to credit and bankruptcy frauds are also impossible to ascertain. Often it is not possible to tell whether a loss is due to criminal activity or not, as in the case of fires, where the causes are frequently unknown. When property losses are reported, as in the case of thefts, owners are often unable or unwilling to set a fair value upon their property. The estimates of owners, police and insurance companies frequently differ. Only that small portion of the loss paid out by insurance companies can be definitely ascertained.

RESULTS OF THE STUDY MADE FOR THE NATIONAL COMMISSION ON LAW ENFORCEMENT

THE only study we have that frankly faces all of these difficulties is that made by Dorr and Simpson and their aides for the National Commission on Law Observance and Enforcement.[5] It has also the merit of being the broadest study yet attempted. But it is by no means all inclusive, the two most serious omissions being the costs of administration of criminal justice in counties and in cities and villages under 25,000 in population, and an adequate study of individual losses due directly to criminal acts. The Dorr-Simpson investigation carried out between 1929 and 1931, with the help of a large corps of field workers, involved a study of published and unpublished material already available, a nation-wide field study of the cost of criminal justice in 300 American cities, an examination of federal criminal justice costs, the collection of data relative to private expenses for crime protection, and an analysis of private and community losses. This report is worthy of careful study by anyone interested in the economic aspects of crime. Some of its more important findings are presented herewith.

The authors of the report agree that it is impossible to give a single lump-sum figure that will even reasonably approximate the aggregate annual economic cost of crime to the United States. Nor would precise knowledge on that point serve any useful purpose. The imperative need to reduce all of the wastes of crime is apparent without it. The values

[5] National Commission on Law Observance and Enforcement, *op. cit.*

of an economic study of crime lie chiefly in examinations of comparative costs. Certain figures that are of value as being reasonably accurate approximations are given as follows :

Federal cost of criminal justice	$ 52,786,000
State police forces	2,660,000
Cost of criminal justice in places over 25,000	247,700,000
State penal and correctional work	51,720,000
Private protective service	10,000,000
Armored car service	3,900,000
Fraudulent use of the mails	68,000,000
Insurance against crime	106,000,000
Loss of the productive labor of prisoners and law-enforcement officers	300,000,000
Insured losses due to crime	47,000,000

Their examination of the items that make up these totals leads them to suggest that :

1. The police are economically the most burdensome part of the machinery of criminal justice. They are admittedly inefficient. Active measures to make their effectiveness commensurate with their cost would be of marked advantage to the taxpaying public.

2. The great expense of penal institutions as compared with the relatively small cost of probation service indicates the need to consider whether the use of probation may be wisely extended.

3. The relatively small expenditure for prosecution raises the question of whether recognized inadequacies in criminal prosecutions might be partly overcome by larger appropriations for this purpose.

4. The costliness of enforcing statutes dealing with conduct not subject to effective legal action indicates that a thorough overhauling of our criminal codes is economically desirable.

5. Losses due to criminal acts are far greater than expenditures for the administration of criminal justice. Therefore it is clearly more important to increase the efficiency of the machinery for preventing and controlling crime than to reduce its absolute cost. Our objective should be the lowest possible cost consistent with the most effective reduction of losses due to crime.

As a means of approaching these ends the report recommends :

1. That an appropriate federal bureau compile and publish annual statistics on the cost of federal administration of criminal justice.

That a uniform system of state, county and municipal accounting for police, prosecution, court, institutional and parole expenditures be worked out and adopted.

That the Bureau of the Census compile and publish consolidated statistics based on the reports of the states and their subdivisions.

These recommendations are aimed to secure accurate, comprehensive and regular data of great value to students of criminology and public administration not now available.

2. The continuation of the study of municipal costs of administering criminal justice already begun by the commission.

This study gives promise of value in providing standards, now lacking, for judging the comparative efficiency of the administration of criminal law in different communities.

3. A scientific study of commercialized fraud and of racketeering and other forms of organized extortion to discover their extent, causes and means of control.

The work already done in these fields indicates the vital importance of these two branches of crime and the need to develop adequate measures for suppressing them.

4. That suggested measures be taken to reduce the economic burden now placed upon jurors and witnesses in criminal cases.

THE PROFITS OF CRIME

In view of the tremendous cost of crime we might well reverse the picture for a moment and ask what are its profits. If there are ultimate profits they are not ascertainable. The determination of immediate profits presents the difficulties already associated with the determination of costs plus the serious obstacle that records of the expense to criminals of doing their business are not available. Obviously, however, there are some immediate economic profits regardless of whether they are overbalanced as we are frequently told by the evils that trail in their wake. If the fruits of crime turn bitter in the mouths of criminals they nevertheless give physical nourishment. Three groups share the economic profits of crime: private and public agents hired to prevent, control or suppress crime; those who sell goods or services used in committing crimes, in protecting from crimes, or insuring against crimes; and criminals engaged in mercenary crimes. Obviously the first two classes reap legitimate profits. It is unfortunately true that illegitimate profits are often added thereto through traffic with criminals.

The cost of crime control itself, therefore, represents legitimate profits to someone, chiefly as salaries to enforcement agents, both public and private. The balance of the expense of battling against criminals is also diffused as profit amongst the makers and sellers of services and supplies used by enforcement officials. The earnings of companies on the sale of crime insurance or protective devices and services are also legitimate profits from crime. From the taxpayers' standpoint the earnings are made out of necessary but unproductive services.

What criminals get out of crime no one knows. We have long expressed, as a fact, the wish that crime shall not pay. Not long ago Warden Lawes made an address in which he pointed out that among a group of robbers the average haul was $30.74. He reported that 900 men committed to Sing Sing in 1927 made a total haul of $368,574 for which they received sentences totalling 12,389 years. The conclusion to be drawn was that crime does not pay.[6] If the wages of crime are low, are the wages of honest toil any higher?

Such statements made by men dealing with criminals are misleading when they are intended as a warning against crime. Presumably the sum of $368,574 represents the loot taken in the offenses for which these men were convicted. It is more than likely that the habitual criminals in the group had made many hauls for which the amounts were not reported. Nor will they actually *serve* 12,389 years since most of them will be paroled before the expiration of their sentences. The average time served in the state prisons of this country is now approximately three years.

The chief point to be noticed, however, is that figures of this sort deal with the earnings of *prisoners* who are but a portion of the criminal group. The fact that insured losses due to known direct crimes against property have amounted to an average of more than $47,000,000 a year for the years

[6] Anonymous, "Crime As a Business Proposition." *Literary Digest*, Vol. 101, p. 30.

1925 to 1929 gives a better hint of the gross immediate profits of crime to criminals, many of whom are not caught until they have been long at their business if they are caught at all. How deeply campaign contributions, bribes, gifts, lawyers' fees, bondsmen's fees, and other expenses cut into the aggregate gross profits of criminals it is not safe to estimate. It seems reasonable to believe that for individual criminals the economic profits of crime are as varied as they are among persons in legitimate occupations. Few amass the wealth of a Capone, but it is not unlikely that the income of criminals during their active careers compares favorably with that of honest wage earners throughout the country. For the present, however, we must remember that this is mere speculation. The entire subject of the income of criminals is an interesting but uncharted field waiting to be explored.

CHAPTER III

THE MORAL AND SOCIAL COSTLINESS OF CRIMINALS

THE CRIMINAL AS THE LOCUS OF INFECTION

THE old, old story of the boy who fell in with bad companions and was led into their way of life, although popularly used as an all-sufficient explanation of criminality, is so naïve in its assumptions that it cannot be accepted without careful examination. It does not tell us why the misguided one found evil company acceptable. It dodges the fact that it is often impossible to say of the members of a delinquent group, "This one is worse than that one." It neglects altogether the commonplace situation in which bad influences surround persons without turning them from their straightforward way. As a statement of what often happens, it is truth. As an explanation of the processes involved, it neglects all of the subtle forces that play about a personality and mold it for better or for worse.

In one sense criminals are the chief source of criminal suggestion inasmuch as they are the repositories of that part of the social heritage that has to do with crime. Theoretically, the socialized man impelled by a natural impulse to do this or that would be immediately and conclusively checked by the thought, "This isn't proper" or "This isn't right," if his intended course were contrary to the mores. He instills in his children a similar regard for the accepted ethical code. But the criminal, without being aware of his rôle, passes on from one social generation to the next a different set of attitudes. His legacy may be the equally conclusive assumption that if certain customs are in opposition to desires they are, as a matter of course, to be broken. The only real question is how to do it without suffering the pain and inconveniences of social displeasure. So he has in addition to his viewpoint developed some sort of a technique for carrying on his activities with a minimum of interference.

Criminals are, then, in a general way, the source of the suggestion, the encouragement, the stimulation to moral weaklings to commit crime. They are the chief source of those blighting influences that are continually gaining the mastery here and there among the forces appealing to men for the direction of their lives. *Criminals may, in this sense, be considered the locus of criminal infection.* It will be recognized that the influence in starting others along the criminal road may vary all the way from a near zero point, in the instance of the man who in rage attacks one who is calling him a liar, to the opposite extreme in the case of the criminal whose first job was doing "slow work" suggested and taught by a new-found pal.

The more obvious ways in which criminals act as a contaminating influence are fairly well known. Although Fagins are fortunately rare, there is ample opportunity for youngsters living in slum areas to see and to imitate criminal activities. The placing of slot machines in barber shops, the joys of "nigger pool," the visits to houses of prostitution, the "fixing" of policemen, and the exploits of adult gangs are not lost upon the inquiring street urchin living in the midst of such a life and chronically exposed to its corrupt standard of values. In spite of this situation, trustworthy evidence indicates that the seepage of demoralizing factors downward from the adult criminal to young people is slow compared to the expansion of those ideas among those of approximately the same age level. Once a member of the younger set succumbs to the lure of criminal ways, the spread of this knowledge horizontally is likely to be rapid. Furthermore this need not take place through an organized gang but merely through the mutual stimulation of acquaintances whose contacts may be quite casual and irregular, as among children meeting on the way to school.

The subtleties of diffusion and its consequences defy definite classification. They may be an immediate and direct imitation of what has been seen and heard; but frequently they will find expression by devious pathways leading to ends that have no obvious connection with their cause. The sight of disturbing things but vaguely understood may lead to worry, truancy, scholastic failure, vice, grudge formations, or to more grievous outlets for mental conflict such as stealing or sexual immorality.

Throughout the carefully recorded clinical studies of the Judge Baker Foundation (now the Judge Baker Guidance Center) ample evidence that criminals are the source of contamination in actual cases can be found :[1]

Case 2 : Winthrop Standen, Jr.: Charged with burglary and larceny of auto (Age 15 years, 8 months.)

"But he has also formed a very influential comradeship with one young fellow, somewhat older than himself, who is a notorious scamp, but who has succeeded in avoiding punishment because of the political influence of his family."

Case 5 : Douglas Darrant : Stealing (Age 12 years.)

Douglas said in response to a question as to how he so well remembered just when he first learned about sex affairs and stealing, " 'Because it was in the flour mill office. These fellows used to stay in there when Bob's father had gone out and talk over things with each other and they would talk about the girls. It was there the start of it all was. I know that.' (Is this all very clear in your mind ?) 'Yes. It was there that Bob opened the cash drawer and the fellows were standing around talking.' This intelligent boy is very mild in all of his statements and he evidently tries hard to be accurate." (Bob was four years older than Douglas.)

Case 6 : John Smith : Stealing (Age 16 years, 7 months.)

"At the time they moved, when John was 10 years old, he became acquainted with a boy named Mack, who was somewhat older, and who, the mother thinks, was John's undoing" . . .

"He never was in anything that was bad until they moved to a certain neighborhood in X. That's where he first knew Mack and through him he knew Wall."

" 'He (Wall) was a guy who was into everything, but he never got sent away. He is working in the X. bank now. I guess he's done better.' Then there was Mack. 'He got sent to the Island down in New York.' "

Case 9 : Matilda (Tillie) Mardon : Sexual delinquency (Age 13 years, 11 months.)

[1] "Judge Baker Foundation Case Studies," Series 1. Quoted by permission of the Judge Baker Guidance Center.

"Then when they moved to G. Avenue where they lived before moving to their present nice apartment, she met Mildred W. This girl talked to her much about boys and introduced her to 'some bums,' and through Mildred she also met Helen M., who had been out a good deal with men. The latter part of last summer Tillie had a chance, through the agency, to go out to the country for a vacation. . . There she talked a good deal to a girl who told her much about picking up sailors and soldiers.

"After she returned . . . met some sailors in the park . . . walked around with them . . . never made any real engagements . . . until . . . met Jim. She liked him. . . After she had known him . . . few weeks . . . spent the night with him . . . did so several times."

Case 16 : William Rybart : Stealing (Age 15 years, 2 months.)

"And then when he was about 10 and on a farm . . . an elderly man there gathered little boys down in a barn and drew for them pictures of bad things and told them stories about them. . . He began these habits very regularly, he thinks after his experience with the man on the farm and has had a great deal of temptation. . ."

Case 20 : Edward Somes : Stealing (Age 15 years, 2 months.)

"He sees his mother occasionally. At first he says he never worries about her, or wonders why she didn't raise him. But when asked if he ever thought that perhaps she was not a good woman, he answers, 'Sometimes.' And when asked if he ever thought she stole, Edward with averted face blurted out, 'I know it. . .'

"He knows that she stole at least twice. Just before he went to his uncle's he overheard the family talking about it . . . but it got on his mind after that. . . Just after this he went in the afternoon to meet her in the store where she worked. Then while he was waiting in the next aisle unseen by his mother or the manager, she was discharged, accused of stealing, and when she denied it the things were brought out from her locker. . . He thinks about this sometimes ; it makes him feel badly. These things happened before he ever took anything . . . but sometimes he feels so discouraged that he just doesn't care.

"She paid back the last $25 that he recently took. . . (Boy cries.) 'If I hadn't said I took it they would have blamed her.' He doesn't know at all that his mother is stealing now, but he thinks about what she did before and when he has an opportunity to steal he thinks of her and feels reckless, as if it didn't matter if he stole."

Of course when persons who have already exhibited unfortunate traits of character are brought into close contact in an institution with others whose habits of misconduct are already well-established the processes of contamination are accelerated. In detention homes, jails, industrial schools, reformatories, and prisons alike the more experienced offenders find more or less of an opportunity, depending upon how the place is managed, to tutor those less advanced and to foster in them a greater disregard for the law. Charles L. Clark, who has served sentences totalling more than 35 years in penal institutions, reports the common prison attitude in his autobiography:

"During my stay at Ionia I was given to understand by some of the old-timers that Society had no use for such as me, and that the only thing to do was to go out and get what I could, as the world owed me a living anyway. *Most people take this view on this subject. . ."* [2]

A delinquent boy of fifteen, speaking of his experience in a correctional school, said:

"It don't do you any good. You know how to crack a safe when you come out and lots of other things. Of course they watch you and you have to be careful because there are so many stools — pardon me, I mean talebearers. It's Saturday and Sunday afternoons that they do the harm ; that's when they talk. Every fellow tells the worst that he's done." [3]

THE CORRUPTIVE INFLUENCE OF ORGANIZED CRIME

BEYOND these devious ways by which the criminal blight creeps through the community lies the planned corruption of organized criminals whose activities constitute a "big business" that affects the well-being of entire communities. The extent of organized crime and its ramifications into the political, recreational and business life of our great cities can only be understood if the foundation upon which it

[2] Clark and Eubank, "Lockstep and Corridor," p. 13. Italics the author's. Quoted by permission of Earle Edward Eubank.

[3] "Judge Baker Foundation Case Studies," Series 1, Case 8, p. 26. Quoted by permission of the Judge Baker Guidance Center.

rests is clearly recognized. The underworld is in business for profit. These profits come from supplying illegitimately the opportunity for vicious recreation, gambling, and prostitution which the law forbids, but which respectable though unresourceful citizens demand (perhaps to give them surcease from their worries over the ever mounting costs of crime and law enforcement). Out of its earnings the underworld must subsidize those officials without whose connivance the game could not go on. The public demand for these forms of vice is great enough to make competition between rival dealers keen and to require some means of preventing unfair practices among them.

Lawful authorities cannot be appealed to for direct assistance here because of the danger of arousing a vigorous public revolt, and so private means of regulation and retaliation must be developed. Each company must have its own police force of gunmen to enforce its rights against the others. Gunmen will work only if they are shielded from prosecution. Employers can assure them immunity only by forming a symbiotic relationship with politicians which gives underworld business freedom from prosecution in return for the votes which it is able to command through wise distribution of a portion of its earnings among ignorant people who are needy, unemployed, or otherwise burdened. Only the partial disclosures that are made when a "Scarface" Al Capone is tried or a Rothstein is killed give an inkling of the lines that are thrown out from a criminal center to contaminate even those in high office and to exert sufficient pressure upon upright men to bring them into the machine or blot them entirely out of the picture.

The White Slave Traffic has long been known as a criminal enterprise. Field investigations recently carried out under the auspices of a committee appointed by the Council of the League of Nations remind us that this social evil still persists and is international in extent.[4] In spite of the absence of a formal organization of traffickers there are well developed trade routes, particularly between Europe, North

[4] League of Nations, "Report of the Special Body of Experts on Traffic in Women and Children." Geneva, 1927, Parts One and Two.

Africa and South America, and recognized centers where *souteneurs* and their allies gather to exchange information and make coöperative agreements. The United States, by reason of its strict immigration laws and its refusal to permit the licensed houses that flourish in many other countries, has been largely free from incoming traffic in recent years although there still appears to be some smuggling of Chinese slave girls on the Pacific coast. Outgoing traffic, however, continues, directed chiefly towards Mexico, Cuba, and Panama, and in some measure towards the few cities in Canada where prostitution is tolerated. Local recruiting in the United States has not, however, been stamped out.

Prostitution and drinking are inseparably linked together. In this country, where both have been illegal, a combined retail outlet was found in a variety of so-called "night clubs" catering to the demands of the sophisticated and opening possibilities to the curious innocent. The Committee of Fourteen which investigated 373 New York night clubs and speakeasies in 1927[5] found only 52 that could be called "respectable." They reported 806 women employed in the other 321 of whom 487 were admitted prostitutes. Some 418 additional prostitutes were allowed to seek patronage in them and 260 procurers were engaged in their business in these clubs. Their customers were young people out on a spree, curious adults from out of town, sophisticated patrons, college students, criminals from the underworld, some knowing the true nature of the resort, some anxious to find out, others quite unaware of the business, and all of them wittingly or unwittingly doing their bit to keep in business the syndicates dealing in women and liquor which represent one of the most powerful agencies of direct demoralization in our urban society. According to the evidence gathered by government agents for presentation to the Federal Grand Jury, the Capone beer syndicate had an annual gross income of $27,000,000. Capone's personal fortune from his combined ventures in prostitution, gambling, and bootlegging, was estimated by internal revenue agents at $20,000,000. However inaccurate that guess may be, when Al Capone was indicted for income tax evasion he offered to compromise

[5] The Committee of Fourteen, "Annual Report for 1927."

the case with the government by payment of $4,000,000.[6]

Labor and merchant racketeering is another criminal enterprise that has become well entrenched in many cities with all of the trappings of legitimate business. Racketeering is the exploitation of merchant or employee associations by violence for personal gain under the guise of building an apparently useful coöperative organization. It represents an alliance between business men or labor leaders and criminals protected by politicians. It has surged through several channels during its development. Shortsighted business men called in gangsters to stamp out price cutting among their competitors and then found themselves controlled by their hirelings. Occasionally the director of an established business association himself adopted strong arm methods of maintaining trade agreements.

Criminals were not long in discovering the possibilities in racketeering. By 1930 gangsters, anticipating a modification of liquor prohibition, were quite generally taking the initiative in foisting themselves upon legitimate enterprises as organizers. Regardless of the starting point of a racket the procedure is always to organize workers and trades-people, through terrorism, into unions on which the racketeer may levy tribute in the form of fees, fines, and dues. Those who resist are driven into line by slugging, arson, blackmail, bombing, murder, and other violent attacks.

An example of racketeering methods is given in the testimony of Morris Becker, president of an independent cleaning and dyeing company who told the grand jury:[7]

"I was introduced to Mr. Rubin by my foreman. I said, 'Oh, you are the Mr. Rubin [business agent for the Retail Cleansers' and Dyers' Association] I hear so much about.' He said, 'Yes, and you will hear a great deal more. I want to tell you something — you are going to raise prices.'

" 'The Constitution,' I replied, 'guarantees me the right to life, liberty and full pursuit of happiness.'

"He said, 'To hell with the Constitution. I am a damned sight bigger than the Constitution.'

"In that same spot a dynamite bomb was thrown three days later.

[6] *Time*, June 22, 1931, p. 17.
[7] Illinois Crime Survey, p. 987. Quoted by permission.

A few days later Abrams came to the store and I said, 'I want you to understand that these are our prices and we will stick by them.'

"He replied, 'If you do, Becker, you're going to be bumped off.'"

Within a few days a contribution of five thousand dollars to aid in maintaining cleaning prices was demanded of Becker. Indictments were secured against members of the association. Rubin and three others who were indicted for terrorism were powerful enough to secure their release on bonds totalling more than half a million dollars. Clarence Darrow served as defense attorney. Becker's testimony was insufficient to convict the defendants of the crime charged and they were found "not guilty." Later papers of incorporation were taken out which made Alphonse Capone and two of his professional bondsmen partners in the Sanitary Cleaning Shops, Inc., sponsored by Becker. Thereupon Becker boasted, "I have no need of the police or of the Employers' Association now. I now have the best protection in the world."

The shocking aspect of Becker's callous statement was its approximation of the truth. Before he lost his altercation with the federal government over the matter of his income tax, Alphonse Capone told Col. Robert Isham Randolph, then president of the Association of Commerce, that he had on his personal payroll about 185 ex-convicts and gunmen to whom he paid from $300 to $400 a week apiece. He offered to police the city of Chicago and guarantee that there would be no more gang killings, bombings, or spectacular crimes of organized violence if his liquor and gambling business were let alone.[8]

Since the stability of criminal syndicates depends chiefly upon immunity from prosecution, executives whose political influence is broad and powerful enough to spread across party lines are better able to weather political turnovers than those who lose their official friends when a new group takes office. Hence a process of natural selection gives power into the hands of a few lords of the underworld. Some of them have maintained their authority over a period

[8] Letter to the author from Hon. Frank J. Loesch, President of the Chicago Crime Commission.

as long as twenty-five years. As a result they have been able to build up a capitalistic business system engaged in syndicating vice on a large scale. Their political power, gained by playing the rôle of Robin Hood to ignorant voters and in late years by the impersonal force of their wealth, has kept them free from the control of the conventional machinery of justice and enabled them to set up feudal kingdoms of vassals and retainers who need fear only the competition of a greater lord than their own. In some cities vice lords and merchant racketeers have added force to their emotional appeal. Ballot boxes have been stuffed, votes miscounted, election officials intimidated, and nominees forced to withdraw at the point of a gun. Behind the altruism of criminal executives lies the brass knuckle, the bomb and the machine gun. What gratitude cannot accomplish the fear of death may bring to pass.

The funerals of the captains of underworld industry are enlightening spectacles for one who would understand their immunity to prosecution. It is on such occasions that friends, who might ordinarily prefer to keep their relations with underworld characters in the background, are impelled to brave the publicity attendant upon the payment of their respects to the departed. When Big Jim Colosimo, dictator of the old levee district, was killed in 1920, gangsters rubbed elbows with judges, opera singers, congressmen and aldermen as mourners at his funeral. According to the Illinois Crime Survey the long list of honorary pallbearers included: Judge J. K. Prindiville, Judge J. R. Caverly, Hon. Louis Behan, Congressman J. W. Rainey, Congressman Thomas Gallagher, Alderman J. O. Kostner, Alderman Dorsey Crowe, Tito Ruffo, John Torrio. At the funeral of Anthony D'Andrea, killed a year later, twenty judges served as honorary pallbearers. When Dion O'Banion was killed in 1924 he was refused the last rites of his church, but five judges, one former judge, and an alderman attended his wake, and Al Capone sent roses. Among the mourners at Angelo Genna's funeral in 1925 were two state representatives, a state senator, the city sealer, together with Diamond Joe Esposito and Al Capone.[9] More

[9] Illinois Crime Survey, p. 1033.

recently an aroused public opinion has frowned so noticeably upon the appearance of governmental officials at elaborate and ostentatious gangster funerals that there has been a noticeable decline in the practice. There is not much evidence that the reform has gone beyond a discreet drawing of the veil of publicity.

The political bosses behind the whole system, keep a guiding hand upon the activities of mayors, police officials, and judges, and hold their power, strange as it may seem, by virtue of their stability and trustworthiness. Elected officials may come and go. Many of them are merely puppets responding to powers behind their thrones. There is no assurance that their policies will be carried on by their successors. Political bosses retain power in their districts regardless of temporary election set-backs. Their policies are known. However unacceptable they may be to reformers the bosses may be depended upon to follow definite courses and to keep their promises as surely as any business man may be expected to follow the accepted practices of his group. The bosses are therefore supported not only by the criminal interests that need protection but by men in legitimate business enterprises who commonly place profits above ethics and who find it far more convenient to deal with a single person than with the clumsy and unstable machinery of government.

A great metropolis is not only a governmental unit but a great business corporation, spending millions of dollars annually for supplies and services. Those who seek city contracts are not apt to look with favor upon either red tape or reform. They will profit most by the success of those who see the reasonableness of awarding contracts and privileges so that all concerned (save the other taxpayers) may make profits out of the transactions.

A prerequisite to the bosses' continued power is an efficient organization able to deliver votes. Such a machine is founded upon the intimate contact work of district captains, each responsible for the votes of the people of his own neighborhood. Throughout the year he befriends them when they are in trouble. That is his job. Laborers and small tradespeople, sweating to keep body and soul together, know him as one who sends food to the hungry and aid to the sick; who gets lawyers and licenses and permits. On election day he collects his expected pay in the form of votes. Only a short-sighted ingrate would refuse him that favor. Successful political organizations may have the efficiency of machines but they certainly do not share their coldness. Tammany and other less famous or infamous bodies appeal to the warm aching heart of humanity, to the feelings of living toiling men and women. Reformers depend upon harsh reason. They appeal to the weaker force—intelligence. They do not stir the downtrodden because they offer, not bread, but vague and distant abstractions like righteousness and justice. As pain is biologically dominant over pleasure so underworld leaders in business or politics, who relieve immediate suffering or threaten sudden death, triumph over those who strive towards the joys of an apparently distant utopia.

CORRUPTION BY LEGITIMATE BUSINESS

SHADING off from those groups definitely committed to illegal enterprises are other borderline types sometimes found among great business corporations which, having power in their hands and being hampered by a multiplicity of legal restrictions, may attempt to circumvent, or, under unscrupulous leadership, to cut across the annoying barriers. The power of such a machine ruthlessly bent upon attaining its end regardless of consequences is entirely unsuspected until the flight or suicide of a financial giant reveals a trail of corruption unbelievable in its involvement of "respectable" persons in high places.

As Stuart Chase reminds us, it is a common scheme of directors to use their intimate knowledge of their companies' balance sheets to profit in the stock market. Purchasing agents are frequently bribed by sellers who want to outflank their competitors. Recently Congressman La Guardia placed before a senate investigating committee cancelled checks for large sums issued to financial editors of leading newspapers by persons desirous of publicity that would help to inflate or depress stocks in which they were interested.[10]

In his interesting reminiscences about his battle with the Peoples Gas Company, Donald Richberg recites the details of his own contact with a powerful organization determined to defraud the people of Chicago. His report of the methods of a legitimate business enterprise is enlightening:

"As soon as I had been named special counsel for the city (in 1915), a private detective agency was employed to shadow me, with instructions to report everything I did and everybody I saw — and particularly anything that might provide material for scandal or blackmail. This sleuthing was carried on in the clumsy way standardized by the best advertised agencies, so that I was soon aware of it. . .

"The conduct of the first judge before whom I appeared was so scandalous that I presented a petition to the entire Circuit Court of twenty judges, asking that this case be taken away from the feeble-minded old man who insisted on hearing it contrary to the rules of the court and in violation of settled principles of law. It was notorious that this judge was in his dotage and the gas company lawyers played on his eccentric ideas with scoffing disregard for a decent administration of justice. . .

"Meanwhile, by wire-pulling at the city hall, payment of all my accounts had been prevented — so that for nearly a year not a dollar was paid for the expenses or fees of myself or my associate counsel. . .

"My law partner refused to accept an annual retainer offered by Mr. Insull. But the 'former' (and future) partner of the head of the city law department drew $14,000 a year from the gas company. Then when the fight was hottest, this corporation counsel of Chicago (named Samuel Ettelson) attempted to 'discharge' me; and the mayor, 'Big Bill' Thompson (to whose election Samuel Insull had contributed $100,000), backed up the two Sams. . .

"During my long struggle with the gas company, I saw added to the company payroll a public utility commissioner, a corporation counsel, a United States senator, a justice of the State Supreme Court, a tax assessor, and a host of other former officials. I saw 'safe' aldermen elevated to the bench and 'unsafe' aldermen driven out of politics."[11]

[10] S. Chase, "A New Deal," p. 15.

[11] D. Richberg, "The Spoils of Normalcy," *Survey*, July 1, 1929, pp. 405-407. Quoted by permission of Survey Associates.

These tactics are not the isolated efforts of a particularly unscrupulous concern but are the all-too-common practices of aggressive and powerful companies. The scope of their control, the pervasiveness of their influence and the utter selfishness of their aims, no less than their sheer power and inaccessibility to regulation, make them a sinister force of no mean proportions. Since 1920 Donald Richberg has been participating in the drama at Washington. As chief counsel for the railroad shopmen during their strike he found merely a repetition of the tactics which he had fought in Chicago.

"Hundreds of private detectives were turned loose to spy, to provoke violence, to manufacture affidavits, to fill the newspapers with poisonous lies. The fictions about 'trains abandoned in the desert' were reprinted in newspapers and magazines long after this falsehood had been exposed under oath in the government injunction suit. I remember one dreadful photograph of a man 'tarred and feathered' which was introduced in evidence in that case and discredited as a palpable fraud. The 'victim' had been taken on a long train journey to be photographed before his 'sufferings' were relieved. Then there was an elaborate, malicious story printed concerning the trip of a labor chief to confer with a railroad president, in which the labor leader was described as traveling in the president's 'well-stocked' private car. It happened that I had accompanied this labor man to his train on that date and had examined and delivered to him his ticket and his *upper berth* reservation on a regular pullman. Hundreds of workers still believe that this man betrayed them for a small fortune — but I have known the exact state of his then bank account for years." [12]

Such is the nature of criminal contagion, involving not only the direct but limited marring of one personality by another but also the penetration of the criminal taint into the very marrow of our social structure so that its importance to the lay citizen is as close and as real as it is unrecognized.

CRIMINALS AND SOCIAL NERVOUSNESS

CRIMINALS not only undermine the moral tone of communities by contagion but they are a source of constant community

[12] D. Richberg, *op. cit.*, p. 427. Quoted by permission of Survey Associates.

irritations and disturbances. People have become criminal-conscious. Probably never before in the world's history has there been such widespread discussion about criminals and activity related to them as exists today. Exceedingly effective agencies of publicity have succeeded in arousing and stimulating a field of human interest that previously lay dormant in the public-at-large for want of information. The strength of the interest, once aroused, can best be judged by the willingness of men to pay in cash for its satisfaction. Newspapers run solely for profit have found it remunerative to extend their efforts in the gathering and reporting of crime news to a degree unheard of until recent years. Speaking of the work of the press in connection with the "Hall-Mills" trial, Silas Bent, a journalist of long experience, said:

"Not since Harry Thaw killed Stanford White has the American press found crime news so much to its taste as the Hall-Mills mystery. Tons of white paper have been covered with trivial details about clothes, with personalities and highly colored descriptions of individual deportment in the courtroom. Somerville, N. J., is by journalistic consent the news center of the world. The New York *Times* has already devoted to the trial (which is by no means completed as this is written) more words than Theodore Dreiser needed for the development of his monumental novel, 'An American Tragedy.' The others have not been idle. Enough words have been sent out of the Jersey village to fill nine volumes of the 'Encyclopaedia Britannica.'

"A giant telegraph switchboard, incorporating 120 'positions' has been rigged up in the basement of the courthouse. The daily capacity by Morse code is half a million words, and the telephone company has imported eight additional operators to help move the spoken load. A noteworthy aspect of this trial is the variety of 'trained seals' who are helping to report it. The daughter and widower of Eleanor Mills, one of the murder victims, are signing stories for a syndicate, but do not write them. Mrs. Henry Stevens, wife of one of the defendants, is writing for Cyrus H. K. Curtis's papers, which also have assigned to the case Dorothy Dix, their staff counselor and consoler of the lovelorn. The reverend fundamentalists, Billy Sunday and John Roach Straton, are moralizing for the public benefit on the sudden death of their fellow-clergyman, Edward W. Hall. For a time former Police Commissioner

Enright contributed stodgily to the Hearst String; but the brunt of this work is now being done by Rita Weiman, a playwright; Louella Parsons, a movie reviewer, and Damon Runyon, a sports writer. (Reporters are in the minority, apparently.) The Hearst papers are also represented by specialists on 'heart interest,' legal aspects, features, defense, prosecution, and so on. The number of employees, counting photographers and messengers, is seventeen. The *News*, which serves also its elder brother, the Chicago *Tribune*, has a staff of nineteen on the job, and is signing half a dozen names. The reams printed in the *Times* are ground out by anonymous drudges." [13]

Book publishers have also found it profitable to cater to the public taste for crime news. The records of by-gone days have been searched to furnish material for stories of famous murderers, famous criminals, and famous trials. Every month finds a new crop of mystery stories ready on the bookstands together with reprints of thrillers written half a century ago. Even cigar stores have become purveyors of mystery tales. The motion picture producers and those of the legitimate stage have seen fit to dramatize many of these offerings.

Definite reasons for the general eagerness to hear and to see reports of criminal activities are not easily uncovered. It seems improbable that many persons are concerned with the criminal because they live in fear of him, and the tendency to look to the journalist's element of "human interest" as an explanation is unsatisfying because of its vagueness. Perhaps the best available answer is that which dissects "human interest" in this particular problem into some of its lesser parts.

The criminal as a representative of the unusual, the mysterious, appeals to man's native curiosity about the unknown. Linked with this is a pleasurable titillation of the intellect through the puzzle element in crime which entices one to seek for an answer. Inasmuch as the solution need never be tested, it may always be convincing and hence mildly enjoyable to its originator. Criminals, guilty of magnificent frauds, whose careers are spectacular without being æstheti-

[13] Silas Bent, *The Nation*, Dec. 8, 1926. Quoted by permission of Silas Bent and *The Nation*.

cally disgusting, surely arouse in the public consciousness some worship of success, some hint of approval for a game well-played. Perhaps it is only when the successful criminal has been portrayed as the under-dog who has risen from below that such admiration is bestowed. Otherwise, there may be a sense of injustice because others can by unfair devices secure that which honest or timid folk also desire but may not have. The grumbling that appeared about the wealthy, who kept their cellars stocked with good liquor while the poor man thirsted or tempted the fates, may be an evidence of this.

\More disgusting crimes, like brutal murders or rapes seem to stir human emotions chiefly by the shock they give to habits of conduct held firm by their satisfying tinge of good feeling.\ The criminal who does that which we would not do, but might like to do, violates our consciences if not his own, for we unwittingly identify ourselves with him so that we rebel violently when he does that which we would not do in like circumstances. Undoubtedly, the criminal serves us as a scape-goat through whom we may relieve some of the tensions and irritations of life by becoming righteously angered. The myth of adventure and romance that glows faintly about the concept of the criminal also arouses the interest of those who seek an antidote for the drabness and conventionality of a too well ordered life, as did the student who plaintively remarked, "Ever since I was six I have known just what I was going to do, and to be, for the rest of my life, and just what steps I was going to take to get there. Sometimes I think that we miss a lot . . ."

It may be difficult to reconcile the seeking of vicarious adventure with an interest in the blundering and sordid existence of criminals unless we remember that the journalistic criminal is always colorful. He must be so, even if it is necessary to call him "The Lone Wolf" or "The Bobbed-Haired Bandit" in order to supply a picturesqueness that is usually lacking; otherwise he could not be allowed to usurp valuable newspaper space. Newspapers seek not facts, but a story. Stage criminals must always be vivid and capable of holding the attention of the audience. They are seldom disgustingly bad nor outstandingly stupid, but rather leave the impression that their failure and downfall is the author's perfunctory tribute to conventional morality. It need not prevent the audience from feeling an inward appreciation of the fact that the villain went long undiscovered and really made a clever fight against great odds.

Criminologists may object that the evidence does not indicate a widespread concern about criminals but only a lively curiosity about the fictional borderland of criminology. This is probably true. The significant fact, however, is that this mythical area supplies to people unacquainted with or unable to identify real criminals the connotation of crime, which, however distorted, is in large measure the basis for public sentiment and public action. Upon this criminal mythology rests a cult of fundamentalism in crime control that is one of our greatest obstacles to progress in dealing with criminals.

Just after the World War there went up a great cry that something be done about a much publicized "crime wave," the existence of which was a matter of grave doubt to those who knew the available facts. The criminal against whom the forces of the law were set was the habitual violent criminal as journalistically pictured. Habitual but non-violent or respectable criminals were generally beyond the range of either public or official vision. The result was a series of ostentatious efforts to rid our cities of criminals by means of round-ups, warnings, threats, and much smashing of doors. Police forces and district attorneys' offices were stirred into sporadic drives against crime. Legislators passed new and more stringent laws and attempted to put "teeth" into old ones. Many of the programs undertaken involved much running about to no other end than to convince people that their officials were doing something to curb the evil situation.

Although such wholesale round-ups of violent criminals have resulted in the capture of certain much sought individuals, their deterrent effect has been distinctly local and temporary; they have involved crimes on the part of those charged with enforcing the law; and they have led to a stirring up, not only of the underworld population, but of a much wider circle in the public at large. Laymen aware of the other side of the picture, the widespread and brazen connivance with favored criminals and the betrayal of public trust by so-called public servants, have often been tempted to disregard some laws themselves or they have had recourse to unhealthy cynicism, which is in itself a poor foundation for a decent personal attitude towards the law.

Another aspect of the general interest in mythical criminals is a certain degree of localized tension and social unrest when the criminal menace seems imminent. The newspapers of Boston recently gave publicity to the fact that a woman's coat had been slashed by someone while she was on an elevated train. Within the next few days several women reported that their coats had been similarly cut. The activities of the slasher made a good story for the papers with the result that many women were temporarily disturbed at the prospect of riding on the cars and the passengers in general became amateur detectives alert to catch the offender. It was subsequently reported that all of the coats slashed were of fur, and a Boston furrier who examined some of them suggested that the "cutting" seemed due to the effects of hanging the coats near hot radiators.

That the social disturbance engendered by the criminal as the public knows him and spread by the activities of emotionally irresponsible persons may result not only in a case of local social "nerves" but may also have specific painful results as well, is illustrated by the report of the Director of the Bureau of Juvenile Research at Whittier, California. He cites the instance of a twelve-year-old boy on whom the diagnosis "Hickman" was fastened by the community due to the exaggeration of harmless boyish activities by an excitable foster-mother who had been unwisely influenced by the publicity accorded the Northcott and Hickman cases.[14]

CRIMINALS AS BY-PRODUCTS OF SOCIAL CHANGE

ALTHOUGH criminals are unquestionably disturbing elements in the community, it must be remembered that they are, in another sense, products of social unrest. Their part in causing unrest represents but the feeble and perverted

[14] Norman Fenton, "The Diagnosis 'Hickman.'" *Survey*, June 15, 1929. For an illuminating discussion of the Hickman case see "Why Hickman Hangs," by Miriam Van Waters in the *Survey*, October 1, 1928.

"kick-back" of damaged personalities against the inexorable pressure of giant forces which have stirred up all mankind and which, in so doing, have been important factors in producing criminals. During the last fifteen years we have been in the midst of a social restlessness and discontent quite unusual in its frankness, its extent, and in its actual effects upon the structure of society. Man's unequal movement in various fields of endeavor has set up strains and stresses that have upset the habits and attitudes of people everywhere and have required a continuing process of adjustment to new conditions.[15] The relation between world-wide economic interdependence and war, production and distribution of wealth, urban living and family life, theology and the discoveries of science, morality and the needs of a new order, represents problems that we have not found the wit to meet with entire success.

The very strivings of the leaders, not all of whom have had the real interests of their fellows at heart, have often served to intensify the difficulties which they would solve, because their programs have been based upon insufficient knowledge of present facts or of future possibilities. The result has been a succession of political and economic upsets throughout the world that have trailed in their wake far reaching social consequences with an attendant shifting and mulling about in society more extensive than any that the world has previously seen. Criminality appears as part of the warp and woof of this social structure. The basic causes are to be found in the civilization of which it is a part — in this case a dissatisfied and bewildered civilization. It is simply one form in which man exhibits his failure to meet successfully the demands of living among his fellows in an environment which he has so largely remade.

There are some individuals who are physically ill-adapted to stand the mental strain of modern life. There are others who are unable to meet the requirements of economic competition. Criminals represent those who are maladjusted in particular ways, as to conduct. They may be physically well and economically self-sufficing but in a portion of the field

[15] See the Review of Findings in the Report of the President's Committee, "Recent Social Trends," Vol. I.

of conduct they do not meet the standards set up by the majority of their fellow human beings. Many persons who have become criminals in our society might have led acceptable lives under the pioneer conditions of an earlier day.

The influence of social discontent reacting upon criminals has appeared chiefly in opening for them new opportunities for wrongdoing. In an era of changing standards, when honest men disagree about the rightness of certain acts, selfish persons may more readily ally themselves with those whose interests are closest to their own desires and easily step across the boundaries of acceptable conduct without disturbing their consciences too deeply. So a state of flux in opinions about economic rights, sex mores, or personal liberty, may make possible a sufficient public toleration of fraud, sabotage, prostitution, or illegal industrial exploitation of workers or consumers, and so on, to make these activities reasonably successful for some persons. Beyond them, but allied with them, are the absolutely intolerable offenses.

But rationalization overcometh all things, and the process by which burglary becomes a proud profession far superior to the trade of pocket-picking is not different from the process that makes misleading advertising or the exploitation of unorganized workers superior to stealing. Criminals have approached the problem of living from an unusual and unacceptable angle. Their viewpoint cannot be condoned. It may be understood and faced.

PART TWO — THE NATURAL HISTORY OF
CRIMINALS

CHAPTER IV

*THE EVOLUTION OF THE CONCEPT OF
A BIOLOGICAL CRIMINAL TYPE*

THE POPULAR CONCEPTION OF THE CRIMINAL

IF THE havoc wrought by criminals is to be checked, the offenders, themselves, must be identified and understood.
This is an obvious and necessary preliminary to any effective
program for controlling them.

From the days of Homer's *Thersites* to Dostoevsky's
Lutchka, criminals have been thought of in terms of physical
characteristics that mark them off as a distinct and easily recognized human type.

> For of the soule the bodie forme doth take
> For soule is forme, and doth the body make.
> —SPENSER, *An Hymn in Honour of Beautie*

Their peculiarities of appearance have become imbedded in
the common speech. Beetling brows, bull-neck, sensuous
lips, and similar expressions are stock phrases to be applied
to criminals. Shakespeare has preserved a belief that still
finds expression among those who maintain that character
can be judged by the appearance of one's jaw or forehead:

> Let me have men about me that are fat,
> Sleek-headed men, and such as sleep o' nights:
> Yond Cassius has a lean and hungry look;
> He thinks too much; such men are dangerous.

Havelock Ellis has collected a number of proverbs that rest
upon the observation of oddities in appearance:

51

Salute from afar the beardless man and the bearded woman
Distrust the woman with a man's voice.
A pale face is worse than the itch.

Out of the gossip of the daily newspapers as well as from
the literature of the ages men and women have been able to
compound for themselves a picture of the criminal suffi
ciently definite to permit his assignment to a particular tim
and place. The 'kerchief covered, sombrero bedecked
desperado of the two gun type ; the gaunt, serious visaged
night skulking peterman ; and now the young, bold, cooll
murderous stick-up man can readily be placed in their prope
setting. Expressions like, "He is a born criminal," and "H
looks just like a thug," indicate that for the ordinary citizen
at least, there is a real criminal physiognomy.

THE CONCEPT OF THE CLASSICAL SCHOOL

For the scientist, however, the question of a distinct crimina
type different from other human beings has long been
mooted problem. Furthermore, the matter is of distinct im
portance, for if the criminal is born so, the entire program o
the criminologist must be shifted so that the emphasis will b
placed chiefly upon developing and applying to this probler
the principles of eugenics rather than those of environ
mental control and of education. In spite of what individ
uals may have believed, early treatment was based upon th
assumption that the criminal was simply an ordinary perso
who had *chosen* to do a legal wrong of a certain sort. Free
dom of the will was presupposed in every case. Even ani
mals were subjected to criminal trials. Beyond this littl
attention was paid to the criminal as such. The classica
statement of this thesis was made by Cesare Beccaria in hi
"Crimes and Punishments" published in 1764. Aroused b
extensive irregularities in the treatment of convicted persor
and influenced by the revolt expressed in contemporaneou
humanitarian writings, he so cleverly pointed the philosoph
of his day towards its application to his subject that his prir
ciples became the basis for extensive reforms in legal proce
dure and punishment.

Beccaria considered man a free moral agent who might choose to commit a crime. Crime deserves to be punished. That punishment should not depend upon the whim of the judge, but should be just severe enough to overbalance the pleasure derived from the act. All persons who commit the same crime should receive the same punishment. In summarizing his own work Beccaria said, "From what I have written results the following general theorem, of considerable utility, though not conformable to custom, the common legislator of nations.

That a punishment may not be an act of violence, of one, or of many against a private member of society, it should be public, immediate, and necessary ; the least possible in the case given ; proportioned to the crime, and determined by the laws." [1] Beccaria's ideas, put into practical effect in the French penal code of 1791, did much to correct the evil practices of his day, but the emphasis placed upon evaluating the crime pushed the criminal entirely out of consideration.

NEO-CLASSICAL THEORY

As classical theory faced reality it became apparent that the felon could not so easily be consigned to oblivion. Obviously children and lunatics were not responsible in the same degree as normal adults. Therefore, the conception of free will had to be modified and punishment conditioned by these differences *in persons*. Some thought had to be given to the one who committed the criminal act. Gradually rules modifying the degree of responsibility to be assumed by various groups of persons crept in. The French penal code of 1810 reveals the specific influence of the so-called Neo-Classical school which sought these changes. Yet, in spite of this beginning, the real criminal person remained virtually submerged and unknown.

[1] Marquis Beccaria of Milan, "An Essay on Crimes and Punishments," p. 133. Tr. from the French. Printed by John Exsham, Dublin, 1767.

ADVANCEMENTS IN BIOLOGICAL SCIENCE

THE century after Beccaria witnessed a remarkable increase in man's knowledge of himself. Biological science advanced rapidly during the eighteenth century. By the middle of the nineteenth century a few thinkers had so far followed Francis Bacon's advice to stop "tumbling up and down in their own reason and conceits" as to grope towards an objective study of human beings in their social relationships. Malthus horrified his friends by suggesting that automatic and nearly inevitable forces regulate population growth. Darwin and Wallace brought man within reach of the laws controlling the lesser creatures. The concept of evolutionary processes at work gained ground and the idea of causal relationships began to creep in with reference to human society. Spencer's influence spread these ideas. Quetelet, the founder of the science of statistics, added a new type of evidence which indicated that human conduct varies predictably in response to environmental conditions.[2] Apparently man's freedom of will was not altogether unlimited. Criminology needed only a thinker who could see the implications of this new knowledge for his field.

Already a few students in the embryo science of psychiatry had been groping towards that end. In France in 1857 Morel, building upon the work done by Pinel a half century before, developed his theory of the criminal as a degenerate type due to physical, intellectual and moral retrogression towards a primitive human stock. A little later (1868) Despine emphasized the psychological anomalies of the habitual criminal by noting their peculiar inability to feel remorse. It remained for English criminologists to round out the conception of the criminal as a distinct psychological type in which the intellectual capacity remains normal but in which the emotions are so irregular as to deprive the individual of his moral faculty ; in other words, the criminal is a person who is morally insane. Perhaps the most noted of those favoring the explanation of moral insanity was Maudsley

[2] The student will find it interesting to read portions of Ad. Quetelet "Physique Sociale," first published in 1835 under the title "Sur L'Homme et le Développement de ses Facultés."

who espoused the theory in his book "Mental Responsibility" published in 1873 and also added to it his concept of an intermediate area between crime and mental disease in which persons exhibit a greater or lesser tendency towards criminal conduct or insanity as they approach these extremes.

LOMBROSO'S CONCEPT OF CRIMINALS

CESARE LOMBROSO (1836–1909), an Italian physician, was the man destined to bring the meaning of these accumulating theories to a focus. He said the criminal is such because he is born so and cannot help expressing his nature ; a concept as far removed from that of the classicists as it could possibly be. Furthermore, Lombroso suggested that the criminal exhibited certain anatomical peculiarities by which he might be recognized. The little pamphlet in which Lombroso first expressed his ideas in 1876 grew to be a work of three volumes of which five editions were published.[3] In them Lombroso's reaction to his critics may be seen in the expansion and modification of his original thesis which unfortunately is still somewhat obscured due to ambiguities in his writing.

In 1870, when Lombroso was carrying on certain researches in the prisons and asylums at Pavia, he became suddenly aware that in the skull of a brigand which he was examining there were reproduced many of the characteristics of primitive men and of inferior animals. So he was led to study the evolution of crime among savages, animals and even plants, and also in children. As a result of this work Lombroso concluded that primitive people normally lived a life of crime. His study of contemporaneous criminals indicated to him that they possessed the characteristics of savages. Physically he discovered such anomalies as heavy eyebrow ridges, small skull capacity, retreating forehead and irregular development of the wisdom teeth. Physiologically, he discovered that criminals were much like primitive men in their insensibility to pain and to sensory stimulation in general. Psychologically, the criminal was found to be lacking in foresight, unstable, lustful, vain, and without pity.

[3] C. Lombroso, "L'Uomo Delinquente," 5th edition, published at Turin in 1896 by Fratelli Bocca.

Socially, he noted such primitive attributes as picture writing, tattooing and the use of a distinctive jargon. These results convinced Lombroso that the criminal was a reversion to a savage type due to atavism, a term used to denote the reproduction of primitive traits in a modern individual by inheritance from ancestors of the dim racial past.

He also noted a basic identity between the born criminal and the moral imbecile. Both exhibited the same characteristics but of the latter only those who chanced to come under the influence of unfortunate circumstances actually became criminals.

Lombroso's ideas met with sharp criticism and eventually Lombroso, himself, began to modify them on the basis of further research, which disclosed in certain criminals characteristics such as facial asymmetry, squinting of the eyes, meningitis and softening of the brain which could not result from atavism. While making a study of epileptic criminals, Lombroso came to realize that they combined the stigmata of degeneracy with those of atavism ; so he came to look upon epilepsy as the basis of criminality. Not content to rest here, he grew to sight beyond both atavism and epilepsy to those complex pathological factors in the human constitution that were the underlying causes of epilepsy which in turn he believed to be the direct stimulus to that primitive state of behavior called criminality. His final conclusion on this point has been neatly stated by the German criminologist Näcke in these words :

(a) the criminal, properly speaking, is *born* so ;
(b) the same as the *moral insane* ;
(c) on *epileptic* basis ;
(d) explicable chiefly by atavism ; and
(e) forms a special *biologic* and *anatomic* type.[4]

Lombroso's picture of the born criminal as a distinct type has aroused so much discussion that it has largely obscured his later recognition of three other classes of criminals : the insane criminal, the criminal by passion, and the accidental

[4] Quoted in C. B. DeQuiros, "Modern Theories of Criminality," p. 17 Reprinted by permission of Little, Brown and Co., publishers.

riminal. The first often exhibited the physical stigmata of degeneracy but were, nevertheless, not considered as born riminals. Definite crimes such as theft and incendiarism were linked with specific psychoses such as kleptomania and pyromania. In the criminals by passion physical stigmata were lacking but their mental states were indicative of epilepsy and insanity.

Lombroso recognized three groups of accidental criminals: the pseudo-criminal, the habitual criminal, and the criminaloid. The pseudo-criminal is he whose crime is due to extraordinary and overwhelmingly provocative circumstances or whose crime is merely a technical violation of the law without important moral significance. The habitual criminal is one of normal birth who has been chronically exposed from infancy to unfortunate environmental influences that have succeeded in warping permanently what might have been an honest life. In the criminaloid, Lombroso saw the forces of evil playing upon a nature tuned to the allurements of the criminal way of life but needing the actual thrust of an unfortunate occasion to drive them into it. The criminaloid would escape such entanglements had not the evil opportunity beckoned.

Of course Lombroso's ideas aroused criticism and further research has made them unacceptable to most modern criminologists. Possibly a desire to find proof for his theories tempered Lombroso's work more than the method of science can condone. For example, his psychological comparison of children and criminals led him to conclude that criminals were infantile in their lack of restraint and of foresight. Obviously so long as we assume that the viewpoint of society is correct, all those who move contrary to it will thereby, in our eyes, exhibit a lack of wisdom and judgment.

Yet Lombroso was a keen psychologist of the sort we sometimes label intuitive. His description of vanity, impulsiveness, and insensibility to pain among prisoners would strike a responsive chord in the minds of those who deal with criminals today. Lombroso's measurements were in some instances made upon a decidedly limited number of specimens. Although he started out bravely to use only measurable factors, he was forced to utilize also the method of quantitative description. His statistical analyses lacked refinement. His reference to socially acquired habits as inherited atavistic traits suggests either faulty biological knowledge or loose writing.

Lombroso's dogmatic literary style may have had a part in stirring up some of his critics whose own refutations of Lombroso have not been in all respects models of scientific impartiality. Modern writers have often been content to overemphasize and then tear apart Lombroso's concept of the born criminal as a preliminary to disposing of Lombroso with the patronizing suggestion that he deserves undying honor for arousing and focusing our interest upon the persons of criminals. In so doing they have failed to appreciate the breadth of the field which Lombroso opened up.

Lombroso recognized his criminal man as a function of two sets of variables. It is not the criminal's biological constitution itself that makes him a criminal but the fact that it operates in the wrong setting, namely, a highly complex modern culture to which it cannot by reason of its atavism adapt itself. Moreover, Lombroso like a true scientist continuously modified his theories in the light of additional and more refined evidence. He constantly broadened the field that he opened up. His discussion of criminal types leaves no room for doubt that as his thinking matured he was able to take into account a number of gradations ranging from the natural born criminal to the other extreme of the pseudo-criminal. In fact Lombroso finally estimated that the born criminal type, possessing five or more of the stigmata that he had described, represented about 25 per cent of a total criminal population which tended in its characteristics to cluster more or less closely about the born criminal type. Apparently Lombroso did more than apprehend the need for a new structure in criminology ; he drew its plans and built the framework upon which our later efforts to understand criminals rest.

GORING'S STUDY OF ENGLISH CONVICTS

THE most comprehensive and specific attack upon the concept of a distinct physical criminal type yet published is found in the work of Charles Goring, an English prison physician, and his assistants, who, following a suggestion originally made in 1901 by Dr. Griffiths of Parkhurst Prison, examined 3000 English convicts and, under the direction of the distinguished biometrist, Karl Pearson, tabulated the results.

Goring reached the conclusion that : "There is no such thing as an anthropological criminal type. But, despite this negation, and upon the evidence of our statistics, it appears to be an equally indisputable fact that there is a physical, mental, and moral type of normal person who tends to be convicted of crime." [5]

This is a shrewdly worded observation that at first glance seems to represent a quibble with Lombroso. However, a study of Goring's tables and his analysis of them amplifies his statement. It means that there are no inheritable characteristics apparent at birth which make it possible to predict an inevitable life of crime for their unfortunate possessor. [6] Goring recognized that "the forces of heredity, circumstance and chance" all played a part in determining the fortunes of men ; but his study indicated such a high degree of relationship between defective intelligence, defective physique and crime and such a trifling relationship between adverse environmental conditions and crime that he considered the hereditary factors to be by far the most important. His definite conclusion is "that English criminals are selected by a physical condition and a mental association which are independent of each other — that the one significant physical association with criminality is a generally defective physique ; and that the one vital mental constitutional factor in the etiology of crime is defective intelligence." [7]

Goring effectively disposed of the original Lombrosian criminal type characterized by the presence of numerous definite physical stigmata ; but he did little damage to Lom-

[5] C. Goring, "The English Convict," p. 370.

[6] It must be remembered that we are not here concerned with the *causes* of crime. We are interested only in finding out what sort of person the criminal is. Lombroso of course did not believe that the actual physical stigmata *caused* the crime, nor did Goring assume that crime was due to defective physique.

[7] C. Goring, "The English Convict," p. 263.

broso's later conclusions. In criticism of Goring's work it must also be noted that in spite of superior anthropometrical methods and of refined and adequate statistical treatment of his data, he was forced, like Lombroso, to use in parts of his work subjective judgments of unmeasurable characteristics and to depend upon a limited number of cases. In dealing with the mental traits of criminals, especially, Goring was dependent upon subjective impressions rather than objective measurements.

CRIMINALS AS A TYPE OF THE FEEBLE-MINDED

WHILE Goring was making his study of the English prisoners, increasing attention was being paid to the problem of feeble-mindedness. The development of mental tests following the work of Binet and Simon in France brought into being a yardstick for measuring intelligence that Goring lacked. In spite of disagreements over what psychometric tests actually measure, they are largely objective and the results are comparable. As soon as they were used in penal institutions it began to appear to many investigators that a great proportion of persons in confinement was feeble-minded. So extensive was mental defect among prisoners that Dr. H. H. Goddard saw in Lombroso's physical anomalies the stigmata of feeble-mindedness. Goddard's interpretation of the results of examinations given in sixteen penal institutions indicated that from 28 per cent to 89 per cent of the inmates were feeble-minded, and he was led to conclude that at least 50 per cent of all criminals are mentally defective. Said Goddard:

"The hereditary criminal passes out with the advent of feeble-mindedness into the problem. The criminal is not born; he is made. The so-called criminal type is merely a type of feeblemindedness, a type misunderstood and mistreated, driven into criminality for which he is well fitted by nature. It is hereditary feeble-mindedness, not hereditary criminality, that accounts for the conditions. We have seen only the end product and failed to recognize the character of the raw material."[8]

[8] H. H. Goddard, "Feeble Mindedness," p. 8. Quoted by permission of the Macmillan Co., publishers.

There were obvious errors[9] in the work of the early psychometrists but perhaps none more glaring than the naïve assumption that the normal intelligence level for the entire population had been determined by tests given to groups of school children. No adequate sampling of the general adult population had been made but it was believed that the norm could safely be set at sixteen years. Consequently those adults who could not pass the sixteen year tests were considered to be subnormal, and if they dropped below the twelve to fourteen year level, feeble-minded.

The testing of the draft army of 1,726,966 men gave psychologists their first definite information about the mental level of a great sample of the male population. They averaged less than fourteen years in mental age, and 46 per cent of them, under previous standards, would have been called feeble-minded. Whether psychologists revised their opinion of the normal adult mental age which would greatly decrease the number of criminals to be labelled "mentally defective" or whether they maintained their *a priori* standards and considered a great portion of the total population feeble-minded, the results would have been the same as applied to the mental status of criminals.

Hereditary feeble-mindedness could not account for criminality in any such sweeping fashion as some had assumed nor were the attributes of feeble-mindedness the distinguishing characteristics of criminals. Since the war Carl Murchison has made a comparison of the Alpha scores of the white draft army from several states with those of criminals from the same states, and although the level of intelligence[10] varied considerably as between various states, Murchison reached the tentative conclusion that:

"In terms of Alpha scores the criminal group seems superior to the white draft group. Not only is this true of a general comparison, but it is true if we make the comparison in separate units

[9] See C. Murchison, "Criminal Intelligence," Ch. 1, for a brief but efficient criticism of the work of Goddard and Goring on criminal mentality.

[10] Murchison means by *intelligence* "whatever is expressed quantitatively as measured by the Alpha test."

according to the states from which the draft quotas and criminal groups were drawn." [11]

On the other hand recent careful comparisons by Healy and Bronner, and by Slawson, indicate that there are from five to thirteen times as many mentally deficient children among juvenile delinquents as among non-delinquents. Thomas, summarizing these results,[12] suggests that the discrepancy between Murchison's data on adults and the results on juveniles here mentioned very likely indicates that the mental tests applied to adults are not satisfactory. However this may be, it is probably true also that some part of the difference may be due to the ability of intelligent adults to save their delinquent children from commitment to juvenile institutions with greater success than intelligent adults can protect themselves from the consequences of their own criminality.

THE CONCEPT OF CRIMINALS AS MENTALLY DISORDERED

As the attempt to explain criminality in terms of mental defect waned, Lombroso's criminal type made its appearance once more in the new guise of a psychopathic personality not vastly different from Maudsley's conception of the offender as morally insane. Goddard reports that 30.3% of 1034 clinical cases examined at the Ohio Bureau of Juvenile Research were psychopathic.[13] Dr. Bernard Glueck examined 608 prisoners admitted to Sing Sing Prison between August 1, 1916, and April 30, 1917, and found that "59 per cent of them were classifiable in terms of deviations from average normal mental health. . . Of the 608 cases 18.9 per cent were constitutionally inferior or psychopathic to so pronounced a degree as to have rendered extremely difficult, if not impossible, adaptation to the ordinary requirements of life in modern society. . . Of the 608 cases 12 per cent were

[11] C. Murchison, *op. cit.*, p. 57. Clark University Press, 1926. Quoted by permission.

[12] W. I. Thomas and D. S. Thomas, "The Child in America," p. 365, footnote.

[13] H. H. Goddard, "Juvenile Delinquency," p. 55.

found to be suffering from distinct mental diseases or deterioration." [14]

Other studies of the inmates of New York penal institutions made under the authorization of the New York State Commission on Prisons indicated that the following percentages of prisoners had definite nervous or mental abnormalities :

Auburn Prison 61.7
Clinton Prison 60.0
N. Y. State Reformatory 58.0
Auburn Prison (Women) 31.9 (feeble-minded only)
N. Y. State Reformatory
for Women .... 25.0 (feeble-minded only)

According to similar studies made in other states and mentioned in this report, from 57 to 82.1% of the population of the institutions included showed mental or nervous abnormalities. A more recent classification of 8475 male prisoners in six New York institutions indicates that 42.5% of them were normal, 25.5% feeble-minded, 29.6% psychopathic, and 2.4% psychotic or potentially psychotic. [15]

Between January 1921 and August 1924, as part of a study of the delinquent boy, John Slawson examined the children at three institutions for delinquents in New York State by means of the abbreviated psychoneurotic inventory questionnaire adapted by Dr. Mathews from the form used by Professor Woodworth during the war to select men from the army draft for further psychiatric examination. After comparing the results of his study of 834 delinquent boys with 516 unselected cases observed by Dr. Mathews, Slawson discovered an "overwhelming preponderance of psychoneurotic responses of the delinquent boys considered as compared with the responses of the unselected boys of Mathews. . . Only 15.6% of the delinquent boys in the three institutions in which the questionnaire was administered reached or ex-

[14] B. Glueck, "A Study of 608 Admissions to Sing Sing Prison." *Mental Hygiene*, January 1918, p. 86. Quoted by permission of the National Committee for Mental Hygiene, Inc.

[15] V. C. Branham, "The Classification of the Prison Inmates of New York State," p. 47.

ceeded the median performance of unselected school children, age for age." [16]

In spite of the mass of material about criminal personalities so carefully gathered, there still remains some doubt as to whether it should be completely accepted. The more frequent appearance among delinquents of a desire to run away from home or of a tendency towards fatigue may be more largely a reflection of environmental than personality difficulties. Furthermore we have yet to sample any considerable unselected group of adults as a means of determining their real norm. Perhaps when this is done the results may be as surprising as were those secured by testing the intelligence of the draft army. Our everyday experiences with our fellowmen certainly make it abundantly apparent that average mental and nervous traits are not synonymous with perfect mental functioning. Healy and Bronner have wisely observed that "Some of our more recent biographers have rendered an important service by revealing that even in the lives of those whom we consider great are to be found many of the traits commonly regarded as anti-social, commonplace and vulgar." [17]

CRIMINALS AS NORMAL PHYSICAL BEINGS

Not all modern students of criminology have accepted the picture of criminals as mentally abnormal individuals. Z. R. Brockway, the first superintendent of the New York State Reformatory at Elmira, Thomas Mott Osborne and Clarence Darrow are notable exceptions who look upon criminals as the product of the social environment. Osborne particularly emphasized his belief that criminals are the unfortunate products of circumstances that probably would have influenced in a similar manner anyone who happened to face them.

[16] J. Slawson, "The Delinquent Boy," p. 268. Quoted by permission of Richard G. Badger, The Gorham Press, publisher.

[17] Reprinted from Healy and Bronner, "Reconstructing Behavior in Youth," p. 14, by permission of and special arrangement with Alfred A. Knopf, Inc., authorized publishers.

THE FALLACY OF CONFUSING CRIMINALS WITH PRISONERS

No doubt part of our present confusion is caused by the varying connotations of the word "criminal." The studies previously referred to are studies of institutional groups. The adults among them are criminals. The juvenile delinquents, technically, are not. On the other hand most convicted persons are not sent to institutions but are fined or placed on probation. There are also those who have committed criminal acts, but who, because they have not been convicted, are not technically criminals. It would seem most useful in a sociological study to consider as criminals all those whether convicted or not who, intentionally and with the knowledge that it is legally forbidden or generally considered morally wrong, violate any statute other than a few quasi-criminal acts such as those dealing with minor traffic offenses not involving intent. Even repeated violators of minor regulations might well be added to the list.

Obviously those not apprehended cannot be examined. Yet there is ample evidence that there are many crimes committed for which no person is convicted or even tried. Hence our picture of the criminal is decidedly weighted by prisoners and unless they are representative of the uncaught as well as the caught, the composite picture based upon them cannot be accurate.

The Missouri Association for Criminal Justice reports the ratios of robberies committed to punishments, therefore, in St. Louis in a year as twenty-five to one ; in Kansas City twenty-eight to one. For burglaries the ratios for the two cities were twenty-five to one and one hundred and eighteen to one. Of 13,000 serious major crimes reported to the police of St. Louis from October 1, 1923, to October 1, 1924, only 964 resulted in criminal prosecutions and only 374 were actually punished.

In the absence of suitable means for a precise statement, even a casual comparison of property losses due to crime with the number of criminals found guilty of property offenses will make it clear that relatively few persons guilty of fraud, embezzlement and the like ever join the prison populations — certainly not more than one in twenty. What proportion are punished in other ways than imprisonment we cannot tell. Those committing offenses like attempted suicide, seduction, fornication, adultery, abortion, and perjury are not usually convicted. When Dr. G. V. Hamilton questioned two hundred married men and women of New York City about their lives 28 out of 100 men and 24 out of 100 women admitted that they had committed adultery. The number of illegitimate births in the United States is at least 70,000 a year. It is estimated conservatively by Professor East that there are 500,000 abortions performed yearly in the United States. Other estimates run as high as two million. These abortions frequently involve physicians in the criminal act of committing an illegal operation.

As against these evidences of criminality, the U. S. Bureau of the Census reports that there were confined in federal and state prisons and reformatories in the United States on January 1, 1931, a total for all offenses of 127,495 prisoners, and that during the year 1930 there were 78,866 prisoners committed and 71,270 discharged. If we add the short term prisoners sentenced to some 3500 county and municipal penal institutions who numbered 28,140 in the 2719 jails reporting on January 1, 1923, the last date for which jail figures are available, we should find present on any given day in all our penal institutions roughly 160,000 prisoners and total commitments during a year of perhaps 400,000.

The facts seem to indicate that our governmental machinery has sorted out for imprisonment chiefly the dull-witted, the unpleasantly eccentric, or the crude blundering operators who have aroused fear or hatred against them by their nastiness and violence, but has been neither so active nor so successful against the suave, the shrewd, the tricky criminals, who are among our friends, nor against those whose crimes have been limited in their direct effects and shielded from public view. That the mentally abnormal have a greater representation among prisoners than their proportion in the general population would entitle them to may be true although the available evidence is far from convincing. If true, it is not surprising.

The mentally defective, for example, who can be more

satisfactorily defined than other abnormal types, not only start with poor equipment to control the forces playing upon them, but, since they are likely to come of feeble-minded parents who consequently are both poor and ignorant, are frequently handicapped from childhood by unfavorable environmental influences. It may also be true that the mentally defective have less than their share of representatives among the uncaught criminals. The condition is analogous to that presented by a study of labor. The feeble-minded in good times would undoubtedly have a higher representation among the unemployed than among the employed. We have failed to recognize that the convicts we have studied are chiefly the day laborers and the unemployed and not the skilled and salaried workers.

The only certain difference that exists between criminals and non-criminals would seem to lie in the psychological ability of the former to disregard a certain part of that social mandate known as the criminal law, whereas the latter find it impossible to do so. Curiously enough, we have not noticed that the viewpoints of criminals are only peculiar to a very limited part of the field of conduct. The bank embezzler, who can so readily justify his act, is no more likely to commit a rape than the bank president whose reputation for honesty may be unimpeachable. The murderer by passion would be righteously indignant if he were suspected of being a thief. And, of course, criminals may be just as sensitive to group opinion in general as their legally upright neighbors and equally desirous of escaping the stigma of being thought liars, atheists, cowards, or dumb-bells. On the other hand, the non-criminal person who is duly sensitive to the wishes of his community regarding conduct that has been labelled "criminal" may have developed a peculiar disregard for the coercive efforts of his neighbors with reference to his religious beliefs or the conduct of his family life.

There seems to be no proof available that criminals caught and uncaught are fundamentally different from the general run of the population. They, like others, are the continuously changing product of an interaction between themselves as ever-growing physical and mental entities and their material and social environment. The resultant of these forces has been, in the case of the offender, a conduct variant of a type that the ruling authority has considered to be criminal. If the internal and external influences that weave their threads into the fabric of a developing personality could be identified and then watched, as they shuttle to and fro, perhaps we might discover why one pattern appears here and another there, so that some way of guiding the process might be found. That we shall attempt in some measure to do. The next chapter identifies, so far as is possible, the factors that go into the making of criminals. The four succeeding chapters trace the manner in which they seem to be woven into patterns of criminal behavior.

CHAPTER V

FACTORS CONDITIONING CRIMINAL BEHAVIOR

CRIMINAL BEHAVIOR, THE RESULTANT OF AN INTERPLAY OF FORCES

THERE is no cause of crime. Criminal behavior, like all other behavior, is a continuously growing pattern of activity drawn by the interplay of many forces within and without the criminal person. It cannot be too strongly emphasized that *for every man the combination is unique and the results are unique*. When we say that unemployment, poverty, mental defect and the like cause crime we are only partially right. If unemployment hits a particular person under just the proper circumstances it may be the determining factor in causing his crime. Like the last block in a jig-saw puzzle it completes that picture only when all the other blocks are there. As a matter of fact, we are well aware from common observation that when people are thrown out of work they do not usually become criminals. When unemployment is followed by crime, therefore, it is never *the* cause of crime although it may be the last, the most important, or the most spectacular element in a combination of factors producing crime *in this specific instance*.

THE NATURE OF THE FORCES CONDITIONING BEHAVIOR

IN every case of criminal behavior the factors involved are:

1. The criminal himself including his entire constitutional makeup, physical and psychic, inherited and acquired, at a given time.
2. His material environment both natural (geographical, climatic) and artificial (technic).
3. His social environment.

69

In any particular instance one of these elements may overshadow the others in importance, but always it is the interaction of all of these factors that produces the final result. One element has no meaning apart from the others. The time relation among them may also be of vital importance. The influence of some factors may persist over a long period of time. The influence of others may burst forth with such overwhelming brilliance as to make one morally blind for the moment and then fade away like a meteor disintegrating in the haze of the horizon. Factors that have much to do with the origins of crime may have little to do with its persistence. Bearing this in mind we may proceed to examine some of the forces conditioning criminal behavior.

GEOGRAPHICAL FACTORS

MANY studies have been made of the association between geographical factors and crime. Lombroso's survey of French statistics led him to believe that, except for rape, crimes against the person were most numerous in mountainous regions. Property crimes and rape were more prevalent in the plains. He explained this by saying that mountaineers lived in an invigorating environment and were exceptionally energetic. Their territory, too, permitted ambuscades. Level regions permitted the concentration of population and wealth and therefore invited property crimes and rape. A correlation also seemed to exist between soil conditions affecting mentality in the goiter belts of Italy and France and a lesser number of homicides, thefts, and sexual offenses than in non-goiterous districts.[1]

It has frequently been observed that crimes against the person tend to be more numerous in warm regions than in cold while property crimes are more frequently committed in cold areas. The notion that this is due to the effects of temperature upon the human nervous system remains unverified. A more likely guess is that people are out of doors together more in warm climates than in cold regions and are not in such dire need of clothing and shelter.

Seasonal influences on crime have long had popular recog-

[1] C. Lombroso, "Crime and Its Causes," p. 18.

nition. "Spring fever" is a perennial excuse for April restlessness. European criminologists, notably Lacassagne,
Chaussinard, Maury, and Aschaffenburg have recorded
seasonal fluctuations in crime in the form of crime calendars
showing the position of the major crimes for each month
and demonstrating a noticeable correlation between temperature and criminal behavior. Aschaffenburg, for example,
noted a steady increase in sex crimes correlated with rising
temperatures from March until June and of suicides until
July, but there the correlation ends inasmuch as the temperature continues to rise while the rate of these crimes does not.
Assault and battery were also linked with the temperature
curve.[2]

In this country Dexter's study[3] of weather influences in
New York City and Denver showed that arrests increased
with the temperature and with decreasing barometric pressure. Fair days brought more arrests than cloudy days.
Assaults were most numerous when the humidity was low.
Pugnacity reached its peak on days of light breezes. These
observations all link misconduct with bright invigorating
weather that is conducive to energetic behavior. Dull, depressing, enervating weather seems also to depress the
crime rate. Dexter noted that women seemed more susceptible to these influences than men.

Apparently geographical and climatic factors can be correlated to some extent with the crime rate but the nature
of the relation is indefinite. Whether they operate upon
the human organism directly as well as remotely we do not
know. Aschaffenburg believes that they do. Sydney Smith
once remarked that "it is impossible to feel affection above
seventy-eight degrees or below twenty. Human nature is
then either too solid or too liquid ; and lives only to shiver
or perspire."

It is certainly unwise for us to assume that geographical
conditions influence specific types of crimes. The inaccuracy
of our knowledge about the number of crimes committed and
the presence of complicating personal and social factors make
such attempts valueless except as statistical exercises. The

[2] See G. Aschaffenburg, "Crime and Its Repression," pp. 16-30.
[3] E. G. Dexter, "Weather Influences."

relation that exists between some geographical factors and crime may be simply one of parallelism. Regardless of this we may draw one advantage from these studies: insofar as we can predict increases and decreases in criminal behavior in accordance with the place, the season, and the weather we can prepare in advance to meet and check them.

TECHNIC FACTORS

TECHNIC factors are the man-made aspects of the physical environment. Since the industrial revolution they have come to exert a more powerful influence upon our behavior than factors that are purely geographical. We no longer live in the world of our fathers. Invention and the use of power have transformed it. The population of the world has tripled in the last 120 years. In 1930 the population of the United States was 31 times as large as it was in 1790. The goods we possess were valued at 362 billions of dollars in 1929 and 247 billions of dollars in 1932, while our annual national income has reached as high as 80 billions.

This enormous increase in population and property brings people and things together in closer and more frequent contacts. Opportunities for friction are multiplied and there is more portable wealth to be stolen. Persons and things may be more easily hidden. Anonymity is more easy to procure.

The possession of wealth insures its owner of considerable prestige regardless of its source. Ostentatious displays of wealth increase the hunger for it on the part of many who have somewhat less. Such effects are particularly marked in cities where extremes of poverty and wealth rub elbows and where advertising in its most vivid forms acts as a constant irritant. A wealthy country is a favorable *milieu* for piratical criminals who steal, not because they are poor, but because they have been inflamed and made greedy by the rewards and enjoyments that our society gives to those who manage somehow to get an abundance of money.

Wealth is unevenly distributed in the United States as in most civilized countries. One per cent of our people own fifty-nine per cent of the nation's wealth, the next twelve per cent own thirty-one per cent of it, while eighty-seven per cent of the people divide the remaining ten per cent, again unequally, amongst themselves. In a Bureau of Labor[4] study of the actual income and expenditures of 12,096 typical workingmen's families in forty-two states in 1918 and 1919 it was discovered that ninety-two per cent had an income of less than $2100 a year and fifty-six per cent received less than $5 a day. These figures represent not the wages of the father but the *total family income*. Some of these families were living on a yearly income of less than $900.

The fact is that in normal times more people than we are willing to admit are housed and fed like beasts rather than human beings. The struggle they must make is little realized by the somewhat more fortunate multitudes engrossed in their own struggle to make ends meet.

The direct criminal reaction to insufficient income appears in acts of mob violence directed against the economic order that permits such inequalities. The syndicalist I. W. W. represents in organized form the spirit of reform by direct and violent action. Sabotage and murder are the products of their bitterness.

Other effects of poverty upon criminal behavior are less direct but probably more important. Even when poverty is offset by other factors it is a tremendous handicap. When human beings are packed together like rabbits in a warren in ill-lighted basements and sweltering attics,[5] when young children, unable to sleep, roam the streets at night, when good and evil make their home within the same flimsy tenement walls there is little reason to hope that children can become, or men and women remain, civilized. It is to be expected that many of the submerged tenth will be unable to stand erect beneath so crushing an environment. As the people of the slums look about them they may well conclude that crime does pay, both in cash and prestige. The material

[4] "Cost of Living in the United States," U. S. Department of Labor Bulletin No. 357.

[5] There are more than 400,000 inhabitants per square mile in the 10th Ward, New York City, and more than a quarter of a million people living in each of four other square miles of New York's territory.

rewards of honest toil are certainly not over-impressive in
the slums. The child of the ghetto can look about himself
any day and see that only those who have a racket toil not
nor spin.

Yet these have both the power and the glory that the
miserable multitudes lack and it is a remarkable tribute to
the force of the mores that so many hold reasonably fast to
accepted standards of conduct under the demoralizing influences of the slum.

Another aspect of population and wealth has to do with
their concentration in cities. Cities are man-made mountains
lifting their peaks above the earth, the products of man's
technic achievements. Like Topsy they just grew, during
the nineteenth century. They were built for manufacturing
and trade, not for human beings to live in. The value of
space for these purposes has affected the city family. Space
in which to live and to play has been given grudgingly.
The kitchenette apartment cannot be the center of family
life. Its handicaps and the lure of the city lights outside
have destroyed that function. As a place of privacy and retreat it is impossible. That lack of privacy has probably
been no small factor in the delinquencies of girls who have
been unable to entertain their suitors decently at home.
Abnormal conditions of life in rooming house areas and the
contact of racial groups leading to crime are part of human
ecology in urban centers.

Recreational space is limited. The sidewalk is the lawn.
The city street is the ball-field. Yet youth in the crowded
city of commerce is the same eternal youth that leaps and
sings in sheer abandon of the world whenever space and more
fortunate circumstances permit. But here the walled streets
and narrow ways, restrictions to safeguard men and property, confine and distort the surging energy of childhood.
Small wonder then if it should sometimes break forth like a
spring freshet pushing aside the restrictions of its banks to
rush headlong in undesirable ways to freedom.

Shaw and McKay in a study of juvenile delinquency[6] in

[6] C. R. Shaw and H. D. McKay, "Social Factors in Juvenile Delinquency," being Vol. 2, "Report on the Causes of Crime," of the
National Commission on Law Observance and Enforcement. It is inter-

seven cities of the United States have supported with precise data the opinions long held by criminologists of the relations between city areas and delinquency. Their spot maps indicate graphically that juvenile delinquents are most numerous in the areas adjacent to the central business section or to industrial areas. These zones of delinquency are areas of poverty and poor housing where crime has persisted over a long period of time regardless of the racial composition of the population. The maps of Shaw and McKay also show that delinquency rates tend to decrease as the distance from the center increases. Yet even in the interstitial zones more than 90 per cent of the children are not delinquents, a fact which should give pause to those who are anxious to assume a crude cause and effect relation between slum areas and crime.

Rural regions are, of course, not altogether free from criminality although their rate seems lower than that of the cities. Such inconclusive studies as we have based upon commitments indicate that the crime rate increases in proportion to population density although there is some evidence that the crime rate reaches its very highest point in small towns.[7]

Anyone who has had experience in rural areas is aware that there are remote and isolated districts where entire communities have a hand in crime, especially in prostitution and the manufacture of bootleg liquor. To some extent organized bands of urban criminals have taken advantage of automobiles, aeroplanes and improved roads to use rural regions as their base of operations in rum-running, kidnaping, and counterfeiting. Rural regions near cities are often the scene

---

esting to notice that Alfredo Niceforo anticipated the ecological approach of modern criminologists in his "La Delinquenza in Sardegna" published in 1897 in which he recognized the existence of definite "zona delinquenta" (cf. Shaw's "delinquency areas") and discussed their characteristics in such terms as the distribution of crimes (using maps), successive cultural invasions, (cf. Shaw's "succession of cultural groups") delinquency rates, and the spirit of delinquency areas. See also Breckinridge and Abbott, "The Delinquent Child and the Home."

[7] See Sutherland, "Criminology," pp. 93-97, for a brief critical review of studies on rural-urban crime.

See also Children's Bureau Publication 32, U. S. Department of Labor.

of sex offenses committed by urbanites who have driven out into the nearby country to gain privacy. Farmers suffer from the depredations of ordinarily decent city folk whose notions of property rights fail them when they see ripe fruits and berries. Indigenous rural crime however seems to be essentially non-professional. Personal feuds leading to battery, arson, drunkenness, sex offenses, and petty thievery seem to be its characteristic forms.

BIOLOGICAL FACTORS

EVER since Lombroso tried to unveil the criminal menace resting upon an epileptoid base attempts have been made to find definite causal relations between biological factors and crime. Even Goring who demolished Lombroso's criminal man found quantitative differences between criminals and non-criminals for his figures reveal English offenders as a puny lot under the average of the general population in height and weight. Then he went on further to show that the tendency to criminality was itself inherited for he found a high degree of correlation ($+.60$) between the criminality of fathers and their sons. Since Goring had considered the influence of environmental factors in producing this result and found it slight he felt justified in concluding that hereditary factors were the dominant causes of criminal behavior.[8]

Criticisms of Goring's work have already been suggested. Here it is only necessary to recall that Goring is dealing not with criminals but only with those criminals who are prisoners. We must also consider the possible influence of occupational selection upon the physique of the English convict. Perhaps persons of slight build have a physical advantage over taller or stouter men who are too bulky or clumsy to make efficient thieves.

Germany, at present, is placing great emphasis upon the study of criminal biology. Recently Johannes Lange, with the assistance of the Institute of Criminal Biology in Bavaria, made an ingenious study of criminality among monozygotic and dizygotic twins.[9]

[8] C. Goring, "The English Convict," p. 369.
[9] J. Lange, "Crime and Destiny." Tr. Charlotte Haldane.

Monozygotic twins are the products of the fission of a single egg. Their physical inheritances are nearly identical. Their childhood environments also are apt to be very much the same. Dizygotic twins develop from two separate eggs and their inheritances are consequently no more alike than those of siblings. Their environments in childhood, however, are apt to be as nearly alike as those of monozygotic twins. Therefore if hereditary factors dominate behavior we should expect to find a close parallelism in the careers of monozygotic twins but not necessarily in the careers of dizygotic twins.

Lange investigated thirty pairs of twins of the same sex old enough to come into conflict with the law, and found a much greater agreement in criminal behavior among monozygotic, than among dizygotic twins. His results may be summarized as follows:

	BOTH TWINS IMPRISONED	ONLY ONE TWIN IMPRISONED
Monozygotic	10 pairs	3 pairs
Dizygotic	2 pairs	15 pairs

Lange therefore, while recognizing the complexity of causes in criminal behavior, concluded that inherited tendencies play the paramount rôle in the making of criminals.

Lange's study is not conclusive. It is an antidote to the claims of rabid environmentalists. His cases are few. They certainly suggest that if identical twins are placed in similar environments and one becomes a criminal it is a reasonable prediction that the other will become a criminal also. But suppose that identical twins were placed in different environments, would they behave alike? This question remains unanswered as to criminals, although non-criminal monozygotic twins, who have been brought up in different environments, varied noticeably in intellect and personality in spite of bearing closer resemblances to each other than is usual among brothers or sisters who are not twins.

Upon what do these inherited tendencies of Lange's twins rest? Out of what do they spring? To answer such questions some criminologists have taken a cue from the most enthusiastic students of endocrinology who assert that the ductless glands are the chief determiners of man's physical appearance, disposition, and emotional and intellectual capacities.[10] Schlapp and Smith have utilized glandular activity as the all-important explanation of criminal behavior. According to these authors all criminals are either feebleminded or of faulty mental or nervous constitutions and both conditions are caused by glandular abnormalities.[11] Dr. Grimberg concludes his "clinical study of five hundred criminals in the making"[12] by saying that most delinquents are constitutionally defective in mentality and emotions due to hereditary endocrine imbalance. In a statement to the Wickersham Commission's subcommittee on causes of crime Dr. Reynolds reported that 10 to 15 per cent of the prisoners he examined at San Quentin were obviously suffering from glandular dys-function. This proportion was noticeably higher than that which he had observed in the population at large. Many more showed stigmata of degeneration which Dr. Reynolds felt might be due to the passing on through several generations of an active glandular dys-function which would eventually result in individuals without glandular symptoms but "imperfectly put together."[13]

More conservative endocrinologists are quite unwilling to sponsor the theory of glandular imbalance as the cause of criminal behavior. They recognize the present impossibility of determining how the ductless glands do actually function in non-criminal persons. They find it difficult to account for the great number of glandular freaks whose behavior may amuse us at the circus or move us to pity in state hospitals but who never become criminals. Nor can they explain why people with obvious but less pronounced glandular disorders cannot be distinguished from the rest of us by their conduct. Substantial information may some day be garnered in this field by students of criminal biology. Their contributions to date comprise a group of interesting and suggestive theories that require further investigation. Their

[10] See L. Berman, "The Glands Regulating Personality," 2nd Edition.
[11] M. G. Schlapp and E. H. Smith, "The New Criminology," p. 119.
[12] L. Grimberg, "Emotion and Delinquency."
[13] National Commission on Law Observance and Enforcement, "Report on the Causes of Crime," Vol. 1, pp. 31-32.

efforts, like those of students in other branches of criminal biology, who believe that physical condition is a major cause of crime, will bear watching. At present our wisest course is to answer their claims with a Scotch verdict of "Not proven."

Most criminologists, who have studied the relation between physical condition and criminality, do not limit themselves to the consideration of hereditary factors. They are interested in the influence of the offender's physical condition whether it was inherited or acquired.

Cyril Burt, working in London, has found defective physical conditions one and a quarter times as frequently among juvenile delinquents as among non-delinquents from the same area. However in only 10 per cent of the boys and 7 per cent of the girls did their physical defects seem to be the major cause of their faulty behavior. The great majority of the defects observed were "mild physical weaknesses and irritations." [14]

Healy and Bronner found [15] that among 1000 Chicago delinquents, 27 per cent were in good physical condition and free from all significant defects or ailments. Among 1000 Boston delinquents 32.7 per cent were similarly free from defects. These delinquents compare favorably with 7698 school children of New York of whom 20 to 25 per cent were reported by Gulick and Ayres as free from physical abnormalities. Healy and Bronner note that more of their boys are above the norm for development and nutrition than below it while among the girls approximately 70 per cent are above the age-weight norm. These facts suggest that delinquency is often an outlet for an excess of physical energy. Among delinquent girls, overdevelopment is particularly prominent because of its rôle in making them sexually attractive to older males at an age when they can be most easily exploited.

The influence of mental condition upon criminal behavior is equally difficult to ascertain. Feeble-minded criminals are not hard to find but neither are feeble-minded persons who

[14] C. Burt, "The Young Delinquent," p. 239.
[15] Healy and Bronner, "Delinquents and Criminals, Their Making and Unmaking," Ch. 14.

are not criminals. That one group is more numerous than the other we cannot say. Feeble-minded persons are characterized by their lack of judgment and by their suggestibility. They are easily led. Where they are led depends upon the quality of the influences about them. Since many feeble-minded persons, particularly the morons who give the most trouble, are born of feeble-minded parents, they are apt to be brought up in poor social and material surroundings. On the other hand their defectiveness is likely to handicap them in becoming successful criminals and in evading capture and imprisonment for such crimes as they do commit. Their crimes are those of murder, arson and incendiarism without fraudulent motives, child rape, and unnatural sex offenses.

Mental disease is less frequently linked with criminal behavior than is feeble-mindedness although in specific forms its connection with crime is obvious. The law is just beginning to recognize the type of irresistible impulse that leads to the crimes of the kleptomaniac and the pyromaniac. That the system of morbid delusions, known as paranoia, has led to the commission of some of the most atrocious crimes on our records is well understood. These crimes are fortunately much less common than spectacular.

It is the psychopathic person, in that hazy borderland between mental health and mental disease, who causes the criminologist his sleepless nights. Because normal mental health cannot be defined any more satisfactorily than normal physical health, psychiatrists are not always agreed upon what constitutes psychopathy nor on when they have before them a psychopathic criminal. Figures of the amount of psychopathy among criminals or even prisoners are therefore untrustworthy. But even if the precise boundaries of psychopathy cannot be marked out it is possible for psychiatrists to select for membership in that group many who obviously are neither mentally normal nor clearly lunatics without falling into the error of assuming that criminality is itself evidence of mental abnormality. To cast aside the entire category because it is indefinable is like throwing out the baby with the bath. Do we not all recognize the type of physically ill person who is neither normally sound nor definitely diseased but who chronically "enjoys" poor health ?

Psychopaths are characterized by defects of emotion and will rather than of intelligence. They are unstable, poorly controlled individuals, flighty, impulsive, and temperamental. Mentally they may be normal or superior types, shrewd and keen minded but irresponsible. Among them are criminals who are reckless and wild-headed, spendthrifts and adventurers, astute swindlers with clever schemes for getting "easy money," pugnacious individuals who just can't keep out of trouble, and persons who make a single serious misstep and are sorry for it ever after. Their mental condition is not *the* cause of their criminality ; but neither does it represent a chance association with it. Rather it is a condition of susceptibility to criminal behavior which is all the more disturbing because it is so hard to detect and therefore is difficult to guard against.

ALCOHOLISM

ALCOHOLISM is a morbid physical condition and is extensively linked with criminality. Alcohol is both a food and a drug. Because of its pleasant physical and psychical effects it is widely used in the form of a beverage. Unfortunately the body has no mechanism for preventing an excess amount of it in the blood. Inasmuch as it does not go through a long process of digestion but is rapidly diffused its effects are quickly felt. Even in moderate doses alcohol is a mild narcotic and tends to destroy control in the highest level of the cerebral cortex. Self-consciousness is diminished, speech loosened, and emotional responses released. The bodily reaction becomes even more marked as the dosage is increased. Drunkenness results. Loquaciousness is followed by tremors increasing in coarseness until the inebriate staggers and sways. Accompanying this condition is a vivid and unrestrained emotional glow. Some drunkards become sloppily affectionate ; others pugnacious. Some are jovial ; others weep. Elation may alternate with despondency. Lack of judgment and of self-control is clearly discernible. Occasionally delusions of persecution arise. The spree may end with nausea, depression and actual paralysis followed by a stuporous sleep during which the alcohol is oxidized. The victim then awakes with a pounding headache due to severe nervous shock. Chronic alcoholics may suffer from delirium tremens during which they are tortured by terrifying hallucinations of ever moving human and animal grotesques. If too much alcohol is ingested complete mental disorganization and death from its acute toxic effects may ensue.

A relation between some of these states and criminality is obvious. Apparently also, the nature of the criminality is to some extent shaped by the degree of drunkenness. Neither the depressed nor the delirious alcoholic could successfully commit a robbery. Some students of the problem have found it convenient to distinguish between the criminality associated with drunkenness and that associated with a condition of chronic alcoholism. Simple drunkenness seems to be most commonly linked with street brawls, wife and child beating, malicious mischief, and sexual solicitations and assaults. Murder and other violent and brutal attacks seem more commonly to accompany the acute states of alcoholism. Sullivan's study [16] of alcoholism led him to believe that the ordinary drunkard is seldom involved in serious crimes except sex offenses. Aschaffenburg [17] supports this contention. Even slight intoxication makes any form of larceny difficult or impossible. However, the crimes of occasional drunkards are far more numerous than those of the habitual drinkers.

Some older students of alcoholism go beyond the mere statement that many criminals are drunkards and say that alcoholism is often the chief cause of their criminality. In an investigation carried on by the Committee of Fifty, [18] between 1893 and 1905, alcoholism was found to be the direct cause of the criminality of one-sixth of a group of 13,402 convicts from 12 states, a primary cause of nearly a third of the cases, and an element in the criminality of

[16] W. C. Sullivan, "The Criminology of Alcoholism" in T. N. Kelynack's symposium on "The Drink Problem."

[17] G. Aschaffenburg, "Crime and Its Repression," p. 74.

[18] Committee of Fifty for the Investigation of the Liquor Problem "The Liquor Problem."

half. Sullivan claimed that 60 per cent of the violent homicidal crimes and 82 per cent of the minor crimes in Great Britain were caused chiefly by alcoholism.[19] The Dutch criminologist Bonger[20] stated more discreetly that from a third to three-fourths of the crimes of violence in Europe were committed by offenders in a state of drunkenness. His conclusion is that the proportion of drunkards among criminals is so much greater than the general population that a causal connection is likely. Howard was led towards the same viewpoint by his discovery that 21,863 out of a group of 26,672 Massachusetts criminals were drunk when they committed their crimes. Said he, "Decidedly among the master makers of criminals in the United States, alcohol holds the highest rank."[21]

We are less certain today that alcoholism plays such a directly dominant part in crime causation. Obviously the sufferer from delirium tremens, because of his illness, may kill anyone who happens to be near by and an inebriate, who is in a state of deep dejection, may be led by his depression to attempt suicide. In the records of more common crimes, however, there is a grave possibility of inaccurate figures, due to the ways in which drunkenness is ascertained and the likelihood that prisoners may claim drunkenness as an excuse for their acts.

Quite apart from statistical error is the pertinent suggestion of the Freudians[22] that the real causes of crimes committed by intoxicated offenders are likely to be their neuroses of which alcoholism is a symptom. Stoddart finds alcoholism and drug addiction the means of getting relief from a mental conflict commonly due in alcoholics to an unbearable homosexual complex.[23] There is also the criminal who becomes deliberately intoxicated in order to destroy any opposing inhibitions operating against the contemplated act

[19] W. C. Sullivan, *op. cit.*, p. 192.

[20] W. A. Bonger, "Criminality and Economic Conditions," pp. 641-643.

[21] G. E. Howard, "Alcohol and Crime," *Amer. Jour. of Sociology*, Vol. 24, p. 66.

[22] See Alexander and Staub, "The Criminal, the Judge and the Public," for an interesting discussion of criminality from the psychoanalytical viewpoint.

[23] W. H. B. Stoddart, "Mind and Its Disorders," p. 357.

itself. In either case alcoholism is merely a means of submerging a conflict. Even arrests for drunkenness are no basically brought about by alcohol. There is little experimental support for this viewpoint as yet ; but, together with our probable errors of fact, it makes us wary of advancing the dogmatic statement that the use of alcohol is an important cause of crime.

What influence Prohibition had upon the relations between alcoholism and crime it is impossible to determine. The public saloon went for a time and with it the public invitation to drink distilled alcoholic liquors. In seaports, in cosmopolitan cities, and in sections where immigrants are numerous speakeasies and home-brewing plants flourished. In the Nordic areas of the rural northwest, in parts of the south and the extreme northeast drinking was not so common Bums had the time and the need to get their liquor whereve they were, even though they could only afford the doubtfu concoctions of the five-and-ten-cent stores. The well-to-do wherever they were, continued to buy what they wished Possibly their children took their liquor earlier and oftene because it was smart to be able to get it. But even wher hard liquor was sold openly it was not so convenient for th laboring man to find or to buy as when the swinging door opened from the sidewalk. Drunkenness, in large measure went off of the streets and with it the brawlings and mischie that make up the petty but common crimes long associate with drunkenness.[24]

DRUG ADDICTION

DRUG addiction is not so common as alcoholism but it pre sents a problem of much the same nature to the criminologis Estimates of the number of addicts being legally and il legally supplied with drugs in the United States vary fron

[24] See M. A. Bruere, "Does Prohibition Work" for the results of a interesting inquiry among social case workers throughout the country o how prohibition affected their districts. For an authoritative statemer of modern laboratory and clinical research into the effects of alcohol upo the human organism see, "Alcohol and Man," edited by Dr. Have Emerson.

88,964[25] to over one million.[26] Morphine and heroin, two opium derivatives, and cocaine, an alkaloid obtained from the coca plant, are the substances most commonly used. Since 1925 the use of marihuana, or American hemp,[27] long known to Mexicans, has become noticeably popular in the United States. Heroin because of its great potency, rapid absorption, and easy adulteration is more commonly used, at least in the Atlantic states, than morphine. Heroin is sniffed. Morphine is injected by means of a hypodermic needle. Marihuana is smoked in cigarette form. All of these drugs are exceedingly difficult and painful to drop once a tolerance for them has been acquired. The use of cocaine, however, may be discontinued with no greater effort than that required to break any habit. The use of cocaine apparently reached its peak about 1914 since when it has declined. It was widely used among the Southern negroes. Sometimes morphine and heroin addicts use cocaine as well.

Drug addicts involved in criminality are apparently of two kinds : criminals who have taken to the use of drugs as an addition to their list of bad habits ; and addicts who have turned to crime to satisfy their craving for drugs. The members of both groups are confirmed recidivists and are difficult to reform. Criminals who use heroin probably find it an easy means of getting into a state of reckless courage necessary to the violent crimes of the gangster. Genuine addiction, however, seems to be linked with petty hand-to-mouth stealing rather than with carefully planned or violent crimes.

After a study of addicts brought into the Boston Municipal Court in 1920, Dr. Sandoz conservatively estimated

[25] Estimate of the Committee on Drug Addiction, 1925-26.

[26] Estimate of a committee appointed by the Secretary of the Treasury in 1918. See the article on "Drug Addiction" by C. E. Terry, "Encyclopedia of the Social Sciences," Vol. 5, pp. 242-251.

[27] Indian hemp, another species found in the Orient, has long been known to drug addicts by its arabic name, hashish. As a means of spreading Mohammedanism, Hassan Sabah terrorized 11th and 12th century Persia through a secret band of murderers organized under the influence of hashish. Because of the use of the drug they were dubbed the Hashishin from whence through a corruption by the Crusaders has come our word assassin.

the cost of their daily dose of morphine at five dollars. Inasmuch as morphine is life's prime necessity for those enslaved to it, criminality in some form is assured when the addict's economic condition makes its purchase impossible. Dr. Sandoz found prostitution among the women and stealing among the men usual. In some cases male addicts exploit their women, even their wives, as a means of getting the purchase price of their dope.

As in the case of alcoholism, drug addiction seems to be a convenient way of escaping from a reality that one does not care to face. Addiction, itself, may therefore have its roots in some form of constitutional inadequacy. It rests upon an underlying weakness. This is borne out by Sandoz' observation: "That which I find most consistently in our cases is a defect of character which was present prior to addiction and which has probably been one of the main factors leading to morphinism." [28]

THE AGE FACTOR IN CRIMINAL BEHAVIOR

DEGREE of maturity bears some relation to criminal conduct but what is significant about the relation is difficult to discover. Children may be truants or thieves but they are not apt to be embezzlers, drunkards, nor rapists. Obviously levels of physical and social maturity affect in some measure the desires, the capacities, and the opportunities of persons to commit crimes. The age-offense correlations among prisoners are illustrative and suggestive of such influences.

Among the prisoners in state and federal prisons and reformatories in 1930 the lowest median ages were for robbery, 23.4 years; having stolen property, 23.6 years; and burglary, 23.7 years. The highest were for embezzlement, 35.3 years; violating drug laws, 35.1 years; and violating the liquor laws, 34.1 years. The median age of all prisoners committed was 26.5 years. [29] The number of pris-

[28] C. E. Sandoz, "Report on Morphinism in the Municipal Court of Boston." *Jour. of Criminal Law and Criminology*, Vol. 13, p. 40. Quoted by permission.

[29] Bureau of the Census, "Prisoners in State and Federal Penal Institutions, 1929 and 1930," table 29, p. 36.

oners in proportion to the number of the general population in the same age group in 1930 was highest for age 19 followed by age 20 as a close second. After age 24 there is a sharp decline in commitments.

The meaning of these figures is distinctly limited by the fact that they apply to prisoners rather than to criminals in general and they are introduced here for what they suggest rather than for what they prove. They intimate that as a person passes through the stages of maturation incident to a normal life the degree and manner of his response to the interplay of forces in and about him may vary considerably.

Recently the Gluecks, taking into account the fact that forces and situations involved in criminal conduct have their own life history, have been working on a study of three criminal groups consisting of 500 young men, 500 women, and 1000 juvenile delinquents who will be revisited every five years for a period of fifteen years to determine the influence of time and its accompanying changes upon the factors involved in criminality. "It is conceivable," says Sheldon Glueck, "that some of the criminogenic factors are of such a nature as to spend their energy, as it were, by the time the offenders progress from childhood to youth or adulthood; others are of such kind that their influence may well continue up to and considerably beyond the time when our men completed their sentences. Others may have continued to exert some influence down to today, still others may reasonably be expected to perpetuate their effect throughout the lives of the offenders, and a few may rationally be presumed to continue to work their mischief even in the offspring of the first, second or later generations of the prisoners." [30]

Evidence already accumulated lends support to this theory. In their study of the lives of 500 graduates of the Massachusetts Reformatory for Women,[31] carried through a period

[30] S. Glueck, "Individualization and the Use of Predictive Devices." *Jour. of Criminal Law and Criminology*, Vol. 23, p. 76. Quoted by permission.

[31] S. S. and E. T. Glueck, "500 Delinquent Women." The writer is indebted to Professor Glueck for permission to read this work in manuscript, and to Alfred A. Knopf, Inc., authorized publishers, for permission to take from it the following summarized material in this section.

of five years after their release from parole supervision, the Gluecks have separated the women into three groups : those who were not delinquent again after their release, those who persisted in crime (the recidivists), and those who were delinquent for a part of the post-parole period but who ceased their criminality at least a year before the end of the five years following their release from supervision. This last group they called "upgrade-delinquents."

Fifty-five per cent of all the women studied were delinquent during the period of their parole and 76.4 per cent were delinquent during the five year post-parole period. All of them : non-delinquents, upgrade-delinquents, and recidivists, resembled each other in some respects. In others the non-delinquents and the recidivists resembled each other but differed from the upgrade-delinquents. In still other respects the upgrade-delinquents fell between the non-delinquents and the recidivists. An analysis of the specific likenesses and differences suggests that the time of impact and the persistency of the forces involved are items to be taken into account both in understanding the genesis of crime and in making provision for its treatment.

For example, the factors in which the three groups most markedly resembled each other included : the extent of illiteracy among the parents, the size of families, the lack of savings prior to commitment, the lack of church attendance during adolescence, and the acquisition of venereal diseases during their minority. For some of these items comparable figures for the general population are lacking and they may have had nothing to do with the start of delinquency. The other items may have been related to the origins of delinquent behavior but without exerting a corresponding effect upon continuance in crime. This is possibly true of parental illiteracy and large families.

The upgrade-delinquents differed from the non-delinquents and the recidivists, who in turn resembled each other in several important ways. The upgrade-delinquents were considerably younger than either of the other groups. Proportionately more of them were under twenty when they were first arrested, more of them were under twenty when first committed to a penal institution, more of them had fathers who were skilled workmen, more of them were native born of foreign parentage, more of them had their first illicit sex experiences by consent (as opposed to rape), and more of them were single when committed to the reformatory. Fewer of them began work before the age of fourteen, fewer held any job more than a year, and fewer had any children, legitimate or illegitimate.

Possibly certain of these factors were causally related to the onset of delinquency but lost their controlling power over behavior later as, for example, the culture conflict in childhood suggested by the greater proportion who were native born of foreign parents. More marked, however, is the hint that the delinquencies of the upgrade women were peculiarly associated with the emotional stresses and instabilities of adolescence. The youth of these offenders, their voluntary sex experiences, their work mobility, their lack of husbands and children, are all suggestive of this. Immaturity, however, is normally temporary. Its accompanying maladjustments are apt to be short lived, at least as dominant factors in an adult life.

It was in fundamental and persisting qualities that the upgrade-delinquents fell between the non-delinquents and the recidivists. This is true of their physical and mental health and constitutions, the solidarity of their homes, the extent of their schooling, their arrests and penal experiences, their competency as homemakers, mothers, and industrial workers, and the type of environment in which they found themselves after the expiration of their sentences.

In other words the upgrade-delinquents were neither so mature nor so well-endowed as those who did not continue their delinquencies after their release. The criminality of the non-delinquents was not deeply rooted. Many of them might be called accidental offenders. Fundamentally they were sound. The upgrade-delinquents, however, possessed qualities that gave them an advantage over the recidivists in whom greater age was not sufficient to overcome the handicap of so poor an endowment and so deep-rooted criminality as was theirs. The unstable upgrade-delinquents, therefore, persisted in crime for a time but with increasing maturity their instability declined and the persisting effects of moderately good physical and mental equipment, schooling, and general competency became dominant in controlling their lives.

These interpretations of their data by the Gluecks, though resting upon the weight of statistical evidence of the rôle played by the several factors enumerated rather than upon an exploration of the actual rôle of each factor in each individual life, nevertheless suggest highly probable relations. They also indicate the great importance of research into the time relations of the factors conditioning criminal behavior and make it impossible for us, hereafter, to leave out age in any serious attempt to understand or control criminal behavior.

FACTORS IN THE SOCIAL ENVIRONMENT CONDITIONING CRIMINAL BEHAVIOR : THE THEORY OF DEMOCRATIC GOVERNMENT

THE government of the United States was founded by rebels anxious to escape from monarchical absolutism and eager for freedom. They were influenced by a growing belief in the rights of common men and they expressed their ideals quite definitely in the Declaration of Independence : "We hold these truths to be self-evident, that all men are created equal, that they are endowed by their Creator with certain unalienable Rights, that among these are Life, Liberty and the pursuit of Happiness. That to secure these rights, Governments are instituted among Men, deriving their just powers from the consent of the governed. . ." However, in spite of the certainty with which this doctrine of "unalienable" rights was enunciated, it is clear that any man may lose his right to life or liberty by breaking the criminal code. Rights, we have come to discover, are dependent upon the acceptance of corresponding duties. Yet in the history of the United States duties have not been emphasized. Always the insistence has been upon safeguarding our rights.

The colonists constantly and deliberately broke the laws

of Parliament as James Truslow Adams has pointed out.[32] When undeeded lands were set aside as the King's Woods, to save trees for the Royal Navy, the colonists invaded them because the restrictions were an interference with their rights. The laws intended to check the competition of colonial manufacturers with those of Britain were displeasing and therefore disregarded.

Nearly all of the merchants of New England were smugglers who were not averse to using violence when expedient and it was because the tax reduction on tea made it possible for the East India Company to undersell them that John Hancock, popularly known as the "prince of smugglers," organized the Boston Tea Party.[33] In the South, negro slavery brought about an unusual social condition. Many colonies forbade negroes to testify against white men. The rape of a slave negress was a mere 'trespass upon property.' Negroes involved in insurrections were lynched. After the Civil War lynchings, chiefly of negroes and chiefly in the South, occurred for a great variety of alleged offenses many of which were of a very trivial nature. Out on the Western frontier of the expanding nation the absence of legal machinery no less than the rugged individualism of the pioneers made every man a law unto himself.

The tendency in the United States of today is still for men to choose what laws they will obey. This policy is far more dangerous now when we rub elbows constantly with our fellows than it was in the days of our rural isolation. We cannot logically hold any rights that we are unwilling to grant our neighbors and our neighbors are now very much a part of our own lives. We do not like to have them keep pigs in their yards, nor send their sick children to school, nor drink their liquor and drive their cars upon the highway. Yet the tendency for us to do as we please persists and if society attempts to control our activities we are apt to look upon the effort as an infringement of our "unalienable" rights.

It is not *laws* that we lack but an *appreciation of law*. We

[32] J. T. Adams, "Our Lawless Heritage." *The Atlantic Monthly*, December 1928.
[33] A. M. Simons, "Social Forces in American History," pp. 61-64.

have great faith in laws to control other people. We write
about 13,000 laws a year on our statute books. Most of
them are of no concern to us. Some have gained our support because they seem likely to check the undesirable actions
of other men. Those that other men have passed to curb
us we are apt to disregard, with a complacent sense of
righteous resistance to an unjustified attack upon our liberties.
The proportion of perfectly reputable citizens who deliberately disregard traffic signals and speed laws when they are
"in a hurry and no one is coming" or when "it seems silly to
restrict a car to 35 miles an hour in a sparsely settled region
like this" would, no doubt, be appalling if it could be set
before us. And if we are caught our first thought is to find
someone who can fix up the "ticket" for us. These are
petty matters in themselves, but like the insignificant fungus
on a tree they are inseparably linked with the threads of
weakness and corruption that beneath the surface are rotting
the entire structure.

Disregard for law seems to be our pernicious heritage
from the political ideals of our rebellious forbears of the
eighteenth century. It has become imbedded in our traditions as a sort of national attitude of mind; an ideal of
liberty without responsibility. It seems to be a factor of
notable importance in helping us to understand the easy
contempt for law that so unfortunately characterizes the
people of the United States. We cannot measure its influence statistically nor even point out precisely how it operates.
Like the backdrop on a stage, it appears as a filler to complete every scene, yet it is not a recognized feature of any
of them.

ECONOMIC FACTORS

THE subject matter of economics lends itself readily to
statistical tabulation and analysis, so it is not surprising that
criminologists interested in economic factors have carried the
method over into their own field in an effort to be precise.
Unfortunately, safe conclusions from comparisons of economic and criminological data are not easily drawn because
other factors also are involved and because economic factors
are likely to work in a round-about way.

Morris Ploscowe, in a survey of the literature in this field,[34] has pointed out that investigations of economic influences have followed three main lines of attack. Older criminologists liked to compare the extent of crime and poverty in one country with the extent of the same conditions in another. Such geographical comparisons led to the belief that criminality increased directly with the extent of poverty. Facts that ran counter to this dogma were rationalized after the manner of Quetelet who, finding crime most prevalent in the wealthier provinces of Holland and France, said that poverty was relative and that criminality was likely to be common where great inequalities of wealth tempted and provoked the poor.

A second method is that of comparing the economic condition of criminals and non-criminals. Here again it is necessary to consider that economic distress may be relative to standards of living. Failure to agree upon what constitutes poverty has been the source of many disagreements. Baron Garofalo discovered that proprietors and proletarians in Italy contributed to crime nearly in proportion to their numbers, but Fornasari di Verce and M. Marro found the poor less numerous than Garofalo and hence found their crime rate high in proportion to that of the landowners. Dr. Foldes found that in Austria-Hungary the well-to-do were proportionately more criminal than the lower groups except in committing property crimes in which their rate was lower. Niceforo found this partly untrue in Italy where fraudulent crimes against property were most common among the comfortable and violent crimes most common among the poor.

As Ploscowe[35] points out these disagreements are due chiefly to the lack of an objective yardstick with which to measure economic status. The common reliance upon unchecked data furnished by criminals is also an untrustworthy procedure. Another flaw is the use of data on crimes *known* as a substitute for the unobtainable figures on crimes

---

[34] M. Ploscowe, "Some Causative Factors in Criminality," Ch. 5, in National Commission on Law Observance and Enforcement. "Report on Causes of Crime," Vol. 1.

[35] M. Ploscowe. *Op. cit.*, pp. 101-103.

committed on the unproved assumption that there is a constant relation between the two.

The most hopeful attempts to understand the relation of economic conditions to criminality have been the correlating of business cycles and criminal behavior. This path, like the others, is beset with thorns. A valid economic barometer is hard to find. Grain prices were used as a measure of the European economic situation until the Belgian economist, Hector Denis, applied the more satisfactory scheme of index numbers to the study of criminality. But even index numbers must be based upon facts that truly represent the whole economic picture. This presents an important difficulty in a country like the United States, with diversified economic activities, where economic changes may affect chiefly one or two elements in the population such as the growers of cotton and the textile workers, or where they may strike the farmers long before they touch industrial laborers. However, the growing industrialization of the world, which is affecting agriculture as well as manufacturing, has brought a sufficiently large proportion of the population of many countries under the sway of business cycles to make the line of study profitable.

Pioneers in the examination of grain prices and criminality found a neat correlation between the two. In good times property crimes decreased and crimes against the person increased. The increase was ascribed to more extensive recreational activities, including drinking, during easy times. In bad times the reverse of this picture appeared. Later students, Berg and Muller in Germany, Dorothy Thomas in England, and Emma Winslow in Massachusetts, using more precise indices, found little or no correlation between the economic situation and crimes against the person ; but all agree that the rate of property crimes moves up and down with the index of prosperity, although not at the same angle. A causal relation between economic cycles and crime is therefore strongly hinted at but not proved. Just how poverty or prosperity affects criminality we may however suggest in a sort of rough and ready fashion.

As business activities expand, property crimes tend to increase because of the greater opportunities presented by more numerous transactions involving portable and negotiable wealth. Here economic factors are not causal. They merely offer more extensive opportunities for predatory criminals to carry on their business of getting "easy money." It is part of their game of modern piracy. They probably could not carry on any business honestly. They simply can not grasp that viewpoint of business ethics which guides, however poorly, the majority of us.

Recruits all ready ripe will be added to the criminal crop through sheer want, through loss of resistance to temptation in unoccupied time, or through active rebellion against the apparent injustices of the economic system. Some of these are likely to remain criminals permanently if they achieve easy success or if imprisonment puts them under the tutelage of habitual offenders. Yet even here economic factors are not operating alone. The recruits must have been susceptible to a criminal way of life. One of the most obvious features of the recent economic crisis has been the manner in which literally millions of human beings pushed into economic dependency, bankruptcy, and want have never questioned the right of more fortunate people around them to hold their property inviolate.

Under conditions of chronic poverty whether due chiefly to individual incapacity or to a faulty economic organization arise effects in the field of criminality as real as they are immeasurable. The handicaps of poverty are heavy. Health, education, amusement, and good contacts are restricted. Interests are narrowed. Wholesome stimulation and opportunities are lacking. The poor of all sorts dropped into proximity by their penury continue to stew together in their own misery. For many the only way of escape is psychological. Vices flourish on poverty. Poverty flourishes on vices. It is not a matter for surprise if the milieu gives rise to more than its proportion of criminal lives.

EDUCATION : THE SCHOOLS

CRIMINAL behavior follows the manner of thinking and feeling rather than the matter. Viewed as a process of accumulating knowledge, formal school education is not of great importance in character formation, although the facts that are learned may indicate the advantages of a good life. Indirectly, however, since jobs are in some measure dependent upon knowledge, fact-gathering education may contribute to that degree of economic security which will make property crimes less likely. Against this must be set the possibility that information may arouse new desires that will call for satisfaction.

Facts, however, are seldom given in neutral fashion. The philosophy of the teacher unwittingly goes with them. Much teaching, especially in the lower grades, aims to inculcate definite ethical standards. Recently various programs of character education integrated with the entire contents of curricula have been adopted by certain school systems. The effects of such training upon delinquent careers remains unknown but it seems unlikely that character training as now organized, has any appreciable effect either in checking or producing tendencies towards delinquency. If anything, the unconscious formation of habits of thinking through the ordinary processes of school work seem more apt to be influential in shaping the behavior patterns of children.

The type of character formed in response to teaching depends largely upon the channels to which the child's receptive powers are attuned. It is quite possible for a dozen persons to hear the same speech or the same joke and go away with twelve different impressions of its import. Calvin Coolidge's unadorned phrase "I do not choose to run" presented a major problem in interpretation to editorial writers throughout the country.

It would seem therefore that formal education is essentially a neutral force neither conducive to delinquent behavior nor preventive of it. No doubt this is partly due to the artificial forced feeding methods of teachers and to the apparently necessary remoteness of subject matter from the more vivid everyday interests and real life situations of students.

EDUCATION : NEWSPAPERS, TALKING PICTURES, RADIO
BROADCASTS, COMMERCIAL ADVERTISEMENTS

THE schools, however, are not the only educative agencies in modern society. Pre-eminent among the educative forces in every community are the talking pictures, radio broadcasts, the newspapers, and commercial advertisements. Evidence of the extent, although not of the depth, to which these forces touch us is found in the vogue of catchy phrases introduced among us through motion pictures and cartoons and our common acquaintance with advertisers' slogans no less than in the white flood of letters that pours into editorial rooms and broadcasting stations in response to news items, editorials, and radio advertising.

"Publicity," as Andre Siegfried remarked, "is reduced to an exact science. . . In no other country can the public be so successfully manipulated by experts, or is it so liable to be carried away in times of excitement. In older nations where the civilization is more subtle, the currents of public opinion break down or wear themselves out against established institutions that have grown up like fortifications throughout the centuries." [36]

If it be granted that our behavior is influenced by powerful educative agencies outside of the school, the next step is to determine whether those agencies in any measure induce criminal behavior. Motion pictures and newspapers have frequently been charged with suggesting criminal acts, with making crime alluring, and with undermining the moral tone of patrons by publishing salacious material.

Thrasher [37] believes that picture shows are a possible source of delinquent behavior although the extent of their influence is unknown. He found that movies provide the gang boy with heroes and exploits to be imitated and they help to color his mental imagery. Burt [38] wisely points out, however, that often the portrayal of film situations by children is as innocently done as any make-believe and even when crimes are

[36] A. Siegfried, "America Comes of Age," pp. 244-245. Quoted by permission of Harcourt, Brace and Co., publishers.

[37] F. Thrasher, "The Gang," Ch. 6.

[38] C. Burt, "The Young Delinquent," pp. 138-139.

directly imitated it is the method of the criminal and not his aim that has been borrowed. The evil impulses have been "demonstrably" in existence before. Blumer and Hauser's study [39] indicates that children select from the motion pictures the themes or patterns to which they have become sensitized by their general social background. Harry Shulman [40] after a study of environmental factors in delinquency in Kings County, New York, concludes that the movie problem does not lie in the film program but in the social conditions under which the pictures are shown. Healy and Bronner report that it has been their regular practice to inquire into the effects of motion pictures upon their delinquents. Starting with contrary ideas they eventually came to believe that moving pictures have little to do with causing delinquent tendencies. [41]

How influential newspapers are in inducing criminal behavior is an equally moot question. It seems to be a common impression that newspapers, particularly of the tabloid variety, [42] offer powerful and unfortunate suggestions to people of low intelligence. Lombroso, Garofalo, Ferri, Tarde, Bonger and Aschaffenburg have all indicted the newspapers for inciting to crime. Child welfare agents have often noted the interest that certain weaklings take in whether their exploits have been duly recounted by the press. On the other hand, Dr. Healy, using much more satisfactory data than the European criminologists aforementioned, reports that he has not been able to discover a case in which newspapers were a strong cause of delinquency. [43]

The New York Crime Commission recently asked 616 law enforcement officials whether they considered the news-

[39] Blumer and Hauser, "Movies, Delinquency and Crime."
[40] "Report of the New York State Crime Commission," 1927, p. 263.
[41] Healy and Bronner, "Delinquents and Criminals," p. 181.
[42] A study made by Joseph Holmes for the New York Crime Commission between 1926 and 1928 shows that although the New York tabloids gave a greater proportion of their space to crime news, the larger conservative New York *Times* and New York *World* led all of the others in the number of inches of crime news printed. No doubt the manner of presentation also has a most important bearing upon its influence. See J. Holmes, "Crime and the Press," *Jour. Criminal Law*, Vol. 20, p. 28.
[43] W. Healy, "The Individual Delinquent," p. 58.

papers "in any way a factor in the present crime situation." The replies totaled 111.[44] Of these 42 were "Yes," 46 were "No" and 23 were noncommittal.[45]   There is obviously little agreement here even on so broad a question. Nevertheless some who answered cited examples from their experiences of ways in which they felt newspapers had been influential in causing crime. For instance :[46]

"Cases are difficult to ascertain, but boys in Children's Court frequently refer to notorious criminals and their methods in eulogistic terms indicating they have secured their facts and details from newspaper publicity. . ."

A Children's Court Judge.

"The hold-up business has been, and is, one of the best advertised businesses in the country. Every morning young men see headlines in the papers showing how jewelry, silks, pay-rolls, etc., worth many thousands of dollars have been secured apparently safely and in a few minutes. . . Several defendants, at the time of sentence, in answer to my inquiry, have stated that they committed the crime because of reading articles in the papers of other large hauls made successfully."

A Judge of the Court of General Sessions.

The weakness of the evidence here is apparent. We might again ask with Burt whether the newspapers created the criminal impulse or merely gave it encouragement and direction.[47]

[44] It is noteworthy that although the inquiry was made at the request of a commission created under the authority of Chapter 460 of the New York Laws of 1926 directed to examine into the crime situation, only 111 out of 616 judges, district attorneys, and police officials bothered to answer the two questions asked of them.

[45] "Report of the New York Crime Commission," 1927, pp. 323-324.

[46] J. H. Holmes, "Crime and the Press," *Jour. Criminal Law*, Vol. 20. pp. 48-49.

[47] That in itself is a serious charge for the newspapers to face. It must also be remembered that we are not here concerned with the part that newspapers may play in hampering officials in the detection of criminals, in arousing prejudice against the parties engaged in a criminal case, or in transforming the courthouse into a "big top." A forthcoming study on the relations of the press to crime made under the auspices of the Harvard Law School along lines suggested by Walter Lippmann gives promise of throwing new light on this entire problem.

Summing up the evidence on motion pictures and newspapers it would seem that:

Occasionally they directly incite persons of subnormal intelligence to commit crimes.

They induce much mental imagery among adolescents and when it is in the fields of sex or crime, mental conflict and relief through delinquency may follow. The path of the influence here is indirect and subtle yet clinical evidence would point to this type of influence as more common and more harmful than others less concealed.

They are a vivid and persistent part of our milieu. They contribute to the patterns of our lives. Insofar as the manner in which pictures or news is presented is chronically indecent, salacious, or on a low moral plane the general tone of the community is lowered and the moral threshold is dropped to a degree commensurate with the importance of pictures or the press as forces in any given community.

Against these effects must be set the check upon criminal behavior which these agencies exert through their more wholesome recreational aspects.

In the absence of definite evidence it may still be not unfair to guess that advertising may have a bearing upon crime causation at two points: it acts as an irritant by creating wants without regard to a person's ability to satisfy them, and it too, chiefly through its exploitation of sex, stimulates erotic phantasies which may issue in mental conflict and crime.

The radio, at least in the absence of television, makes a less vivid appeal than the press or pictures and is not restricted to those who can read. These factors have kept it relatively clean and innocuous as a direct stimulus to crime. Its programs, considered apart from the advertising that accompanies them, seem to be harmless and they may well replace other means of recreation that are not.

HOMES

HOME conditions are quite generally assumed to be major factors in the shaping of human behavior patterns. Common observation justifies that belief. The home has the child first and at a time when he is utterly dependent upon it. For many years it has a virtual monopoly of his time. It commonly demands a life-long share in his interest and affection.

Bad homes are therefore very likely to be of primary importance to us in searching for the genesis of delinquency and crime. Unfortunately we do not know what a bad home is. Many elements are blended in the home and apparently it is their peculiar product rather than the individual factors that counts. Moreover the influence of any set of home conditions is relative to the personality it touches. Crowding may be bad if there is poor parental oversight and children sleep in the same room with immoral strangers. It may be unimportant if the children are protected, the boarders are decent, and the family income is increased by their presence. Children may be initiated into the drunken sprees of their elders or they may be so repelled by them that they never want to touch a drop of liquor as long as they live.

Attempts to study the relations of home conditions to criminality have taken several forms. Delinquents' homes have been graded, often with emphasis, upon their economic base. The Whittier State School in California has made use of a highly mechanical score card [48] for grading homes objectively under five headings: necessities, neatness, size, parental conditions, and parental supervision. Fernald, Hayes and Dawley tried to rate the early homes of a group of women prisoners on three points: economic status, moral standards and parental supervision. On the basis of this survey they classified the homes as 8.3 per cent very poor, 38.1 per cent poor, 47.1 per cent fair, 6.0 good and .5 per cent very good.[49] But they failed to compare these homes with those of non-criminals, and so their results are of little value.

John Slawson more recently made a check-up on delinquent boys' homes that is more significant because a control group was used. He found abnormal home conditions in

[48] J. H. Williams, "The Whittier Scale for Grading Home Conditions." *Jour. of Delinquency*, Vol. 1, p. 273.

[49] Fernald, Hayes and Dawley, "A Study of Women Delinquents in New York State," p. 216.

the backgrounds of 45.2 per cent of 1649 delinquent boys but similar conditions were present in the homes of only 19.3 per cent of 3198 unselected school children.[50]

The methods used in these studies and others like them are open to much criticism and largely invalidate the conclusions to be drawn from them. Physical, social and moral conditions are lumped together as of equal importance. Much that experience tells us is weighty in family life is neglected because it is intangible. Yet imponderables are not unreal simply because they cannot be seen nor measured. Again these studies make the fallacious assumption that a home that is bad for one person is equally bad for another.

The practice of listing home conditions as arbitrarily "good" or "bad" is indefensible in a scientific investigation. As already pointed out, the effects of any set of home conditions is relative to the person affected. This fact is strikingly brought out in Healy's study of brothers and sisters of delinquent children. In 62 per cent of 2704 families where there was more than one child only one was delinquent. In only 4.4 per cent of the families were all of the children delinquent.[51] Yet delinquents and their nondelinquent siblings faced approximately the same home conditions as far as any ordinary investigation could disclose.

The best procedure yet found is to study what part homes have actually played in the making of criminal careers. This is the method pioneered by Healy and Bronner in the United States and by Burt in England. Their statistical tables look like any others, but the units in them represent facts carefully gleaned by numerous thorough clinical case studies. An interesting and potentially valuable variant of the case study is the attempt to secure from delinquents and criminals detailed autobiographies that will throw light upon the forces that have played a part in the development of their personalities.[52]

Basing their conclusions upon their searching inquiries into how the delinquents they studied actually came to "get that

---

[50] J. Slawson, "The Delinquent Boy," table p. 354.

[51] Healy and Bronner, "Delinquents and Criminals," table p. 104.

[52] See C. Shaw, "The Jack-Roller," and "The Natural History of a Delinquent Career." Also, Clark and Eubank, "Lockstep and Corridor."

way" Healy and Bronner have come to consider as the observable marks of poor homes : "poverty, great crowding or very insanitary surroundings, extreme parental neglect or extreme lack of parental control, excessive quarreling, alcoholism, obscenity, immorality, or criminalism, mother working, mentally diseased parent in the home." [53]   Assuming that all other homes were good they found a meager 7.6 per cent of 2000 repeated delinquents living under decent conditions.   There are no comparable facts about the homes of non-delinquents but it seems unlikely that the incidence of poor homes among them approaches any such proportion. Healy and Bronner found no other environmental factor so closely correlated with the extent of delinquency as bad homes. Burt's findings [54] are in essential agreement with those of Healy and Bronner.

Attempts to isolate the influence of any one condition such as poverty or broken homes have been inconclusive because, in the absence of comparable figures from non-delinquent homes, the incidence of any one factor in delinquent homes, though suggestive, is not sufficiently marked to constitute proof.   Only when the totals are in does the nature of the bad home become apparent.   So far as we can see, however, factors such as poverty and poor housing are of minor importance compared with broken homes, immorality, and faulty parent-child relationships.

Burt found poverty-stricken homes only a little more frequently among delinquents than non-delinquents but defective family relations were more than twice as common, defective discipline more than five times, and vicious homes four times as common. [55]   Again this suggests that the observable flaws in the home are merely symptoms of the presence of more subtle factors.   It is the interaction of personalities in the home and not the presence or absence of physical conveniences that counts.   It is the faulty social psychology of family life that is significant for our understanding of the rôle that the home plays in the genesis of

[53] Healy and Bronner, *op. cit.*, p. 129.
[54] C. Burt, "The Young Delinquent," Ch. 3.
[55] C. Burt, *op. cit.*, table p. 51.

criminal behavior. Our hope for understanding how conditions in both the home and the community foster delinquency lies in a thorough study of the complex social dynamics of many individual criminal careers.

CHAPTER VI

CHILDHOOD AND THE FOUNDATIONS OF BEHAVIOR

STUDENTS of criminology are becoming increasingly aware that the attack on crime must center at a new point. Criminals are not born so ; they are made. No new-born babe is predestined to become a criminal. If he becomes one it should be possible to find the starting point. Adult professional criminals are finished products. The only solutions of their problems — reformation, permanent segregation, or execution — are usually beyond the probability of attainment. Furthermore, they would not prevent damage — that has been done — but only make impossible additional damage. Recognition of these facts has led to an interest in juvenile delinquents which has enlivened the entire field. But delinquents also have arrived at a stage of conduct so undesirable as to call them to social attention. They, too, represent continuations and not beginnings. The place to begin our study is before birth. Then we may discover the genesis of crime.

Of course, not all criminals start off towards delinquency in childhood, nor do all who start towards criminality actually get there ; but ordinarily divergence from the wholesome pathway begins very early and progresses slowly. At its first stage it is not easily identified nor is it possible always to determine its real importance. The chances that children will become adults of good character are best for those whose behavior traits are healthy. Those whose antisocial behavior outruns that of the average child need attention, not for a grievous fault, but for dangerous though remote possibilities.

After behavior has become criminal there is little difficulty in distinguishing it from that which is considered proper ; but it is tremendously difficult then to remake it. Every bit of evidence we have points to the need of doing preventive work when the first signs of antisocial behavior appear. If those who deal with children could have at their disposal a trustworthy technique for detecting at the point of divergence those types which are starting in the wrong direction, society would have an effective means of checking crime. At present no satisfactory method of prediction is available because the effects of specific childhood traits upon adult behavior is not yet known. It may appear utopian to expect that science will ever be able to supply a useful means of forecasting adult character.[1] Yet studies[2] in the use of prognostic tables made during the past few years point to a future ability to say, at least, that given the presence of certain factors in any given case the odds against this person's escaping a criminal career, if unchecked by conscious social action, are such and such.

A considerable fund of information which may aid in originating such a prediction chart has already been amassed

[1] Lest the ever present query about the relative importance of heredity and environment should remain unanswered to plague the student through the reading that is to come, let it be said that inheritance, very likely, represents less a fixed determiner of life's course and more a limited but varied set of active possibilities striving to achieve their ends and in the process being continually stimulated, blocked or yielded to by other elements in that ceaseless interplay of forces that produces human behavior. Beyond this it is sufficient now to know that we understand so little about the working of heredity and environment in human life that both will warrant all of the study that scientists are able to give them. When specific problems arise they will indicate where the emphasis needs to be placed. The clergyman who is asked to marry two genuinely reformed criminals would like the eugenist to tell him whether their children are likely to inherit traits predisposing them towards criminality. The probation officer who must help a delinquent boy will be chiefly interested in his environment. That boy's inheritance can not be changed. At best it may be understood. The conditions under which he lives may both be understood and changed, and the alteration may modify that expression of his inner drives which we call behavior.

[2] See Bruce, Harno, Burgess, and Landesco, "A Study of the Indeterminate Sentence and Parole in the State of Illinois." *Jour. of Criminal Law and Criminology*, Vol. 19, Part 2, pp. 241-286; S. and E. T. Glueck, "500 Criminal Careers"; S. Glueck, "Individualization and the Use of Predictive Devices." *Jour. of Criminal Law and Criminology*, Vol. 23, p. 67; C. Tibbitts, "Success or Failure on Parole Can Be Predicted." *Jour. of Criminal Law and Criminology*, Vol. 22, p. 11.

by clinics making case studies of delinquents. The serious drawback is that such studies must deal only in a general way with the vital details of childhood history because they are recovered by tracing back through inadequate and faulty sources after the individual has grown up. Information about the earliest specific forces tending towards later delinquency is, therefore, lacking. On the other hand, habit clinics for children of pre-school age are gaining about all sorts of children who present behavior problems the kind of knowledge that would be most valuable to criminologists if it could be correlated with the after careers of the children who are examined.

Unfortunately it is not yet possible to say what proportion of the children who show behavior problems in infancy actually become adult criminals because of these early flaws. It is certain that many children who are never brought to clinics have markedly undesirable habits and that many, perhaps most of them, do not result in adult crimes although their ill effects may be expressed in other ways, equally injurious to the person, but less subject to public disapproval.

Dr. William Healy, who has for years been engaged in the study of juvenile delinquents, has repeatedly emphasized the primary importance of the child's mental life, his ideas and imagery, as a factor in producing delinquency. If a boy pilfers there must first come to his mind, however suddenly, the idea that he wants the thing that he steals and the impulse to take it. Why is it that one person who sees a pocketbook dangling from a woman's arm is obsessed with a desire to grab it while another who sees it never gives it a second thought?

This hint about the inescapable importance of the mental life in producing delinquency brings out sharply the values that will accrue to criminology through a more widely spread knowledge of the origin and expansion of personality in babies and young children and particularly of the conditions under which conduct abnormalities are likely to appear. Certainly criminal science must become thoroughly acquainted with personality deviations and the forces affecting them for its own better understanding of more serious conduct disorders.

Even though criminologists may not be actively concerned

with work among young children, they may find it wise to add their encouragement to agencies more directly concerned with the wholesome growth of young children, for in spite of the frequently repeated fact that the earliest years of life are most important for the setting of characteristics, few persons seem to know what it means in practice, especially as it applies to the child's mental health.

THE ORIGINS OF PERSONALITY TRAITS

THE human organism begins with the union of parent cells in the mother's body. In the fertilized egg that results lie all of the inherited potentialities of the individual. Growth occurs through cell division. As early as the second week the origins of the nervous system can be discerned. Long before birth neurone networks have evolved into functioning units. By the fifth month the neurones of the medulla have brought the heart muscles under control and the physician with his stethoscope can hear the rapidly beating fœtal heart. Shortly thereafter other independent body movements take place. The child within the mother kicks and moves. Its nervous system undoubtedly registers tactile impressions. Education, though not conscious, has already started before birth.

By birth the infant, helpless as it may be, has progressed from the original tiny fertilized cell about two-tenths of a millimeter in diameter to an exceedingly complex being, capable of performing such astounding feats of behavior as crying, sucking, grasping, kicking, and yawning. Its growth between conception and birth is greater than all it may achieve between birth and death.

As soon as the child is born it comes within the reach of powerful and insistent social forces that are determined to control the expression of innate impulses. The baby is not aware of this and they have him at a disadvantage. His world is still very tiny and confusing. The adult world is outside of his ken, for he does not yet know how to use his eyes and his ears, nor any of his sensory tools very well. Yet nature has cleverly equipped him from the beginning to satisfy his hunger, to protect himself from harm and even, conversely, to seek pleasure. His sensory equipment is designed to make the connections with the world through which alone these primary needs can be met, and as he begins to see, to hear, to smell, to taste, to feel, he gropes towards an understanding of his surroundings, which, however crude, soon becomes great enough so that he knows how to control parts of it and how to get along comfortably with the rest of it.

So the child explores and has experiences that may be drawn upon through memory to help him to conduct himself well as he goes on adventuring, building up mental images, a store of knowledge in the light of which he develops his own characteristic behavior which is the outward expression of his personality.

But while the child is growing, adults are busy trying to fit him to live among his fellows, for nature has not given him any direct means of meeting the intricate and often arbitrary demands of culture. He cannot escape living among his fellows, and so he must be trained to get along with them. If that training is faulty, his behavior will be classed as rude, eccentric, radical, or criminal, as the case may be, and he will suffer at the hands of others accordingly.

So there is a vivid interplay of forces in which the dynamic driving impulses of the child oppose, dodge, accept, reenforce, or submit to the pressures of the world about them. Gradually and very early in the midst of the tussle the outlines of personality begin to take shape. The new-born baby that cries when he is disturbed learns within a few days to cry instead for attention when he is left alone. Long before a child can walk he may wilfully oppose another's wish.

Barbara, aged 10 months, closes her lips tightly and shakes her head rapidly from side to side so that her mother cannot put a spoonful of carrots in her mouth. She stops her antics immediately if potatoes are substituted, and leans forward to receive them contentedly. She reverts to her former attitude if carrots are again presented, pushes the spoon away, and blows the carrots out of her mouth when her mother is successful in her attempt to feed them.

Susceptibility to praise and desire for recognition make their appearance just as early. A child soon learns to enjoy an audience. The humiliation of a scolding with its attendant loss of a parent's favor can be felt by a child not a year old. It is a commonplace observation that babies soon learn the weaknesses of their adult friends and play upon them by tears or smiles until they are bribed or rewarded to do that which they should learn to do as a matter of course. If a child is paid to behave he can hardly be expected to continue his good efforts unless his wages are regularly forthcoming, and he soon learns to go on strike at opportune times for an increased reward.

Charlotte Bühler placed 114 nursing babies together in groups of two or more and gave them toys to play with. As may be expected, the responses observed were of every conceivable variety. Some of the children appeared to be delighted, others to be bewildered. Some exchanged or displayed their toys. Others accumulated them. Still others explored. All of them exhibited positive personality trends.[3] In another study by Marjorie Walker, made at the Institute of Child Welfare, Minneapolis, under the direction of Anderson and Goodenough, children were put with others successively and their behavior was unobtrusively studied. Here again distinct individual traits appeared. One child tried pleading 200 times as a means of getting what he wanted. Another used that method with fewer than ten of his companions but instead commanded them frequently. Each of these children was getting twenty times as much practice as the other in subordination or leadership.[4] Professor Ernest R. Groves aptly describes this period of childhood as a battleground in which the child's desires, clamoring for satisfaction, are in conflict with the rigid facts of his surroundings consisting of people and things.

[3] C. Bühler, "Die ersten Sozialen Verhaltungsweisen des Kindes,' Sociologische und psychologische studien über das erste Lebensjahr (Quellen und studien zur Jugendkunde, 1927), pp. 1-102. Some of this work is summarized in W. I. and D. S. Thomas, "The Child in America," p. 518.

[4] See J. E. Anderson, "The Genesis of Social Reactions in the Young Child" in "The Unconscious : A Symposium." See also the illuminating and penetrating works of Jean Piaget : "The Moral Judgment of the Child," "Judgment and Reasoning in the Child," "The Child's Conception of the World," and "The Language Development of the Child," for a genuinely valuable picture of pyschological growth in children.

THE DELINQUENCIES OF YOUNG CHILDREN

THE acts of babies, of course, have no moral significance. Young children do not know that an act is right or wrong but only that their parents approve or disapprove of it, which is quite another matter. Even this latter concept may be only vaguely apprehended by the child. Because of the absence of the moral element in very young children, interest, for purposes of treatment, must be centered upon them rather than upon their acts. What they do is not nearly so important as *why* they do it. Yet inasmuch as adult criminals are treated for their acts rather than for their motives, the criminologists may be interested chiefly in those types of conduct in children which, if persisting, will be labelled criminal as soon as the age has been reached at which the law can impute the necessary criminal intent. The acts of this sort most often found among children of pre-school age are : swearing, temper tantrums, disobedience, assault and battery, destructiveness, pilfering, sex offenses, and lying. Usually they are found in combinations.

Their causes may be obvious or extremely complex and subtle. It is upon the nature of these underlying motives that the real meaning of the act depends. The little boy who is found distributing the contents of his father's change drawer to his kindergarten friends because a rotogravure picture of Mr. Rockefeller enjoying his custom of dispensing dimes appealed to him, needs to be taught the meaning of property. But his behavior offers far less cause for worry than that of the child whose tendency to dominate eventually led him to the point where he was forced to admit that, "Nobody in all the world wants to play with me." [5]

Mere lack of knowledge about right or wrong can easily be corrected in a normal child, but habits of excessive phantasy, self-assertiveness, or persisting immaturity expressed in the form of laziness, lack of initiative, cowardice, lying, stealing, temper outbursts, truancy and other conduct aberrations are difficult to break ; and in adults they need only a particular setting to reappear as the underlying causes of

[5] Blanton and Blanton, "Child Guidance," p. 265.

genuine criminal acts. General statements about the origins of undesirable conduct are of little value for understanding a particular problem for each child represents a unique individual in a unique situation. On the other hand certain elements appear so frequently as major or minor factors that an understanding of them can serve as a starting point for general preventive work.

The chief element in a case may be the child's inherited constitution. Children who are distinctly subnormal in mentality or in physique are likely to find the task of growing up a hard one. All too often parents exaggerate such conditions by an over-solicitous attitude that constantly reminds the child of his inferiority so that he comes to believe that his inadequacy is much greater than it really is. There are many ways in which children react to a position of inferiority and two of them are of particular importance because of their bearing upon early delinquency: the tendency to become irritable bullies among younger children or to force adults to recognize their prowess by violating taboos.

Emotional instability on an inherited basis may seriously interfere with wholesome development. This condition, also, is likely to be intensified because such a child may be unusually perplexing to those who have to train him. Inasmuch as the child in the home is protected from many of the possible effects of his inadequacy, his flaws may not be apparent to those near to him until he is pushed out more freely among his fellows at school age. A little boy studied by Dr. Healy illustrates this type of problem. At ten he was already notorious for his escapades which included running away and indulging in pervert sex practices. He had suffered from rheumatism and what was apparently mild chorea. His outstanding trait was his general nervousness and instability. Although of fair mental ability he was so erratic that the temporary diagnosis was neuropsychosis. Environmental conditions were poor. Suggested treatment was not carried out. After four years of disturbing behavior including petty stealing the boy got into serious trouble and was sent to an institution by the court.[6]

Superior mental ability or precocious physical development

[6] W. Healy, "The Individual Delinquent," p. 224.

may also complicate a child's early adjustments, although the important effects of physical over-development are more likely to appear at a later age with an early onset of puberty. The precocious child may be a joy to his parents or he may find that they are weaklings who can be made victims of his own clever wiles. In this event he becomes a tyrant and the family becomes his slaves.

Other inherited traits that need to be considered are the special skills that children sometimes exhibit. Children under two years of age may show an astounding ability as mimics. They may have unusual finger dexterity or other motor skill. These gifts are in themselves harmless enough, but if children who possess them are exploited by unthinking adults for their own entertainment, they may easily turn such abilities into destructive channels. Under poor environmental circumstances this is sometimes the unfortunate result.

Allowing a dextrous child to entertain adults by skilfully taking handkerchiefs from their pockets is one way of turning his abilities in the wrong direction. Giving a tiny mite of a street urchin a nickel for his "cute" imitation of a moving picture comedian is another. Naturally, if the children can get both pleasure and profit out of such experiences, it is likely that they will persist in them when they are no longer "cute." Sometimes children who are distinctly feeble-minded have special abilities which, correlated with low intelligence, may be used in whatever manner will bring them the most direct rewards. The feeble-minded verbalist may cause an endless amount of trouble when he grows up because of his lack of responsibility coupled with an unusual language facility.

The chief social factors influencing the pre-school child are, of course, the contacts within the family circle. Very often the problems of little children point directly to a general absence of positive directing within the family, a haphazard, hit-or-miss sort of home life, rather than to a specific evil. Even when physical factors like those already mentioned appear in the picture, the dominant influence of the home cannot be ruled out. Unquestionably, the overdose of unwise emotional attention that some short-sighted parents

give their children has much to do with their maladjustment
yet the existence of this evil should not blind us to th
equally harmful one of neglect of parental duties.

In nearly every form of delinquency occurring durin
the first five years of a child's life, the family situation is th
responsible element. Excessive and chronic displays c
temper may represent imitation of a chronically irritabl
adult. More often they simply mean that the child ha
learned how to gain an advantage over his short-sighte
parents. For example :

Harry, aged 5, would invariably cry and stamp his feet if he wer
crossed in his desires by his playmates or his parents. If he then g
what he wanted his heavenly smile returned. If they did not forth
with cater to him, Harry rolled on the floor and screamed and flaye
about him with hands and feet, knocking his toys in all direction
If scolded or spanked for his display of temper he would run to
corner and bump his head against the wall until his parents, fearfu
that he might injure himself seriously, kissed him and petted hi
and gave him what he wanted.

It is to be expected that children learning to talk wil
imitate swearing and obscene language as readily and in th
same way as they will follow adults in their more respectabl
conversations. A few unwise parents enjoy hearing childis
profanity but try to stamp it out when increasing age and th
lack of novelty make it no longer interesting. Unfor
tunately there are some homes in which profanity has becom
essential to conversation. The child in such an environmen
learns to swear as a matter of course. Queerly enoug
parents whose conversation reeks with filth so fluently spoke
that they are not aware of it, may notice the habit in thei
children and punish them violently for it. Of course, suc
treatment is ineffective in breaking them of the habit.

Children who talk in oaths soon become marked, b
mothers of children who do not, as undesirable playmate
Mothers impress it upon their children that they are not fi
to play with. A certain degree of social ostracism result
and the child is very early placed in the category of th
damned. It is not surprising that some "bad" boys attemp
to live up to their reputations as a revolt against the treat

ent they have received.   In such cases the poor home con-
tions that led to the habit of profanity have probably
fluenced their conduct in general so as to make it unaccept-
le.   In spite of parental warnings, children of this sort
e likely to have a few admirers who are charmed by an
parent boldness in the use of picturesque speech.   If their
terest stops with the imitation of an occasional bold curse
startle a group of companions or a milder oath mumbled
der the breath in the presence of an adult as a bit of
icy bravado, no harm may be done.

There is every likelihood, however, that children will hear
x words along with profanity from such a source, and in
e absence of better training than is now given about the
ysteries of life and death, these words, only dimly under-
ood, may set up an emotional conflict so disturbing as to
ad to repeated delinquencies.   Cases of this sort are
miliar to all clinicians, and in fact, nearly every one who
s worked with children has seen the results of such con-
ct without realizing the source because the resulting acts
e very often not sexual delinquencies but other forms of
isbehavior which are substituted for them as a way of get-
ng relief from the ensuing mental irritation.

A little boy, nine years old, examined by the Judge Baker
oundation, had been stealing, destroying property, setting
res, and riding about on street cars for several years.
Then he was only six years old he stole 19 pencils from
s classmates in the first grade and he was also seen rifling
e pockets of their coats.   When examined he was found
be physically normal, of average mental ability, and with
positive evidence of poor mental balance.   A combination
f poor parental supervision and bad companions leading to
ynamic mental associations and the formation of sex ideas
d habits were found to be the direct causes of his delinuencies.   The boy reported that his earliest companions
ere very "fresh."

"They talked bad and swore and they told him a lot of dirty
ords.   Harry repeats a number of the words and then, without
y special inquiry, he goes on to tell about sex affairs.   Even in
e first grade the boys would swear, and they did bad things to-
ther. . .

"It is what Ritto said that makes him feel like doing it to himself. 'Something gets in my mind to make me steal.'"[7]

Another illustration of this type of emotional disturbance is reported by Dr. Healy. Victor, twelve years old, was the son of a pleasant, intelligent widow. The boy lied, stole and was so stubborn in his misbehavior that no one could make any headway against his defiant attitude. Eventually Dr. Healy discovered that some neighbor boys whom Victor used to know when he was only seven or eight years old had told him about sex matters and had taught him to steal.

"He gave a very vivid account of how by night and day their teachings had been with him, and how he had never given way to doing the worst things they had taught him. . . He was particularly bitter about the case of a little girl . . . came to know she did bad things with other boys . . . has thought a good deal about this ever since. Sometimes he wakes up and thinks about it, sometimes he dreams about it, and dreams he was the one doing bad with her. States that in school hours it frequently came to mind what these boys told him."[8]

Victor's delinquencies were the result of his effort to get relief from his mental state.

In the instances just mentioned emotional conflict has centered around profanity or sex words but the delinquencies resulting have not been primarily sexual although that did enter into the problem. Sex problems may come from these or other sources. Curiosity about sex matters in children is as normal as curiosity about the new sled or the kittens. The first bit of the world with which the child tries to become acquainted is his own body. Children three or four years old, of both sexes, are quite likely to take an opportunity to examine each other. They will soon begin to ask questions about the differences that are observed and later other queries about the coming of babies may be expected. Such behavior is absolutely natural in a normal child and is distinctly no

[7] Judge Baker Foundation Case Studies, Series 1, Case 14. Quoted by permission of the Judge Baker Guidance Center.
[8] W. Healy, "The Individual Delinquent," p. 383. Quoted by permission of Little, Brown and Co., publishers.

evidence of a trend towards delinquency. The only un-
rtunate part of the situation is that parents may make it so.
Because of their own earlier training, parents seem to find
e task of sex instruction the most difficult part of their duty
d it is safe to say that most of them either evade the issue
blunder hopelessly through it. Sex curiosity in young
ildren is a fact. Parents have not the power to say
ether it shall be satisfied but only how. Deceit, evasion,
intense emotional displays about the matter only throw
intriguing halo of mystery about a normal interest so that
becomes intensified and perverted.

The child naturally begins to wonder what there is about
e subject that should make it so disturbing to adults, and
proceeds to investigate. Some children even delight to
ing such matters up purposely to watch the embarrassment
at it will surely cause. The parent loses the child's con-
dence and the way is open for some other person to
ntaminate the child with misinformation. The result may
disturbing thoughts or bad habits that may be repeatedly
ought into action by such ever present and usually harmless
imuli as magazine advertisements.

The results of evasion and poor oversight by parents may
indicated by the case of John and Mary, neighbors, five
d a half and five years old respectively :

Both of them had independently questioned their parents about
x and had been told that their inquiries were naughty, with the
sult that they next sought information of each other unsuccess-
lly. The apparent taboo mystified them. Finally, Mary inquired
a girl eight years old who used to pass her home when going to
d from school. The school-girl evidently gave a vivid and
tailed answer. Thereafter John and Mary repeatedly did bad
ings together over a period of several months until John's mother
came suspicious of their tendency to play in the cellar instead of
t-of-doors as they had previously done, and discovered the reason
r it. The parental treatment that followed, however, was dis-
nctly lax, their sex delinquencies continued intermittently over a
riod of several years and occasionally were with other children.
Vhen John was twelve his parents moved with him to another town
d he lost contact with Mary.

Now at seventeen, Mary has been obliged by her parents to marry

a man whom she does not love to prevent her child from being bor
out of wedlock.

John, living in another town, works as a mechanic and is con
sidered to be an intelligent, honest, and upright young man. Joh
shamefacedly admits that he has had a long and only partially suc
cessful struggle against bad personal habits. He has occasionally bee
sexually immoral with one or two girls in recent years. He says th
he sometimes runs upon passages in stories that he reads that exci
him, and some motion pictures have so disturbed him in the past th
he rarely goes to see any of them now. At one time John marke
his failures upon a pocket calendar as a means of shaming himsel
into improvement but the results were so discouraging that he thre
the calendar away. John still has a vivid mental picture of certa
scenes in his childhood that come back disturbingly to his mind. H
places their origin at the time when he was four or five years ol
because of various family happenings that are correlated with the
and because they occurred before he began school. This part of h
story agrees with the recollections of the mother, and it is unlike
that the corroboration is due to John's memory of his mother's wor
inasmuch as she thought his troubles were settled when they fir
occurred and she has not spoken to him about them since that tim
In spite of John's weakness and his faulty methods of gaining self
control, he is unquestionably sincere and his statements are honestl
given.

The seriousness of children's lies depends upon thei
causes. To a person of four or five many aspects of th
adult world are very confusing. Proportions are not th
same. A high school boy of sixteen is recognized as bein
very much older than a boy of seven, but adults of twenty
five and fifty seem to be of about the same age. One whos
time experiences extend over five years and whose geo
graphical experience has been limited to the radius of
Sunday automobile ride has as much difficulty in compre
hending adult time and space experiences as the geologis
the mathematician or the astronomer have in visualizing th
universe. How is it possible for Five Years to know tha
Jack-the-Giant-Killer was not the same kind of person tha
Julius Cæsar was? Childish stories that represent a con
fusion of unreality with reality are not harmful if they ar
gradually replaced by true perceptions as the child mature
However, some children persist in this habit beyond th

me when it may be expected, and their tales may be extremely exaggerated. Usually, this represents a defense
mechanism of the child by which he may escape from a world
that is too harsh for him into one that he can make to his
own taste. A habit of this sort inevitably leads to a poor
type of adult adjustment if continued. A slightly different
aspect of this defense reaction brings about the direct untruth
that is told to avoid impending punishment either because it
will be extremely severe or because the child has never
learned to accept a reasonable responsibility.

The relationship of this habit to adult crime may be seen
in any penal institution. It is almost impossible to find a
criminal who can squarely face his own responsibility for his
position. Like many adults, whose circumstances have not
been conducive to crime, these prisoners have from childhood
been able to place the blame for all of their difficulties upon
external circumstances, as did the boy, studied by the Blan-
ons, whose mother had been accustomed to say to him, "Do
not handle the old stick, dear; it might hurt you," or "Do
not handle the tin cans, dear; they might cut you" until the
child never thought of his own part in any matter, being
content to assume that *it* was always at fault.

There is also a distinct relationship between the habit of
lying and the crime of swindling which depends upon a suave
manner and a smooth tongue that does not concern itself
with making fine distinctions between fact and fancy. Perhaps some of the less ethical practices of over-enthusiastic
salesmen of legitimate goods are not far removed from this
easy untruthfulness. Beyond this is the type of pathological
liar whose startling accusations against persons of good character or even against himself may do great damage to innocent persons as well as cause endless trouble before the matter
is cleared up.

Stealing is a term that adults justly dislike to apply to
the acts of very young children, yet these same acts will be
treated as larcenies when the children are a few years older
simply because it will be assumed that they will then understand their meaning; an assumption which may be wrong,
if the children have not been taught the significance of
property.

Property depends upon ownership. Goods are property only when that relationship between them and a person is admitted and respected by other persons. In spite of the ease with which adults usually recognize property, the fringes of the concept remain ill-defined. Does the honest adult respect the railroad company's rights in the ticket which the conductor has forgotten to collect? Many a suburbanite, who would not for a moment think of cutting down one of his neighbor's trees for lumber, will cut one down for a Christmas decoration in December. This same type of relativity appears among children. Few of the youngsters who would take apples from a fruit stand would take them from the market basket of the customer standing beside it.

If respect for property of some sorts is so difficult for adults and older children to acquire, how much more so must it be for little tots not yet in school? Their entire idea of property may be as vague as some parts of it are for adults. The relation which it involves is not easy to see and must be learned. In the home the chairs, the radio, and the table silver may be used by anyone. Sister wears mother's new beads. Two Year Old must have Four Year Old's cart because he is only a baby. Dad takes forty cents from Four Year Old's bank to pay the paper boy who cannot change a five dollar bill. Under these conditions it is surprising that Four Year Old has any conception of property at all.

Of course, the child needs to have articles that are his very own. His rights in them must be rigidly respected by every one. In turn, he must have a chance to learn restraint towards the use of the property of others. The meaning of ownership can be readily grasped by one who has himself felt the heavy responsibilities of ownership.

There are many reasons for pilfering by young children that are more subtle. One little boy of six took milk bottles from a neighbor's doorstep and exchanged them for candy at the corner grocery store. The candy was distributed to the children on his street, and served to buy for him their attention and favor which had not been given to him before. From a neighbor's house a little girl of five stole articles that her well-to-do parents would gladly have bought her. For five years she had been the center of her parents' attention t with the birth of a brother and the consequent illness of e mother she was pushed suddenly and unthinkingly into e background. The father, who was much worried about s wife's condition, did not notice until later that his daugh-r had first begun to break dishes in an effort to gain atten-on. Not until she had gone so far as to steal from a ighbor was he aroused to her behavior, and then he became alarmed about his daughter's future that he called in a ychiatrist who explained to him the reasons for her con-uct. Of course, punishment without understanding would ave been a poor way to meet this problem.

Dr. Thom tells of a mother who was perturbed because er child bought candy with money given her as carfare for visit to the dentist. Only a few days before the mother d told the child she was taking her for an automobile ride hen in fact she was taking her directly to the dentist's office.[9]

These simple cases represent but a few of the variety of ctors that may lie behind pilfering in childhood. Some parently stubborn problems are resolved quickly once the use is found and removed. Perhaps the most alarming ses are those in which the child grows up without any sense property rights nor regard for them because of the laxity ith which property is treated within the family circle and en outside of it by family members. These are the cir-mstances which breed faulty habits of conduct.

There is ample evidence from the two hundred-odd child uidance clinics in the United States, as well as from those road, that too much stress cannot be put upon the child-ood origin of the causes of adult misbehavior. Healy and ronner, whose study of juvenile delinquents is outstanding, int unhesitatingly towards failures in training in the rliest years of life as a fruitful source of the more serious elinquencies of older boys and girls. Using data carefully llected and noted on their records they found that 40 per nt of a total of 4000 cases came from families in which treme and abnormal lack of parental control was an obvious ement. These authors also note for their Boston series 2000 cases) that extreme neglect, principally moral but casionally also physical, was a factor in 22 per cent of the

[9] D. A. Thom, "Everyday Problems of the Everyday Child," p. 249.

cases. Also in 12 per cent of their total 4000 cases there was *excessive* quarreling in the homes, which in spite of the absence of comparable figures for the homes of non-delinquents, seems to them unduly large.[10]

There is no way of escaping the conclusion brought by such evidence. Babyhood has for some time been thought of vaguely as a period of foundation building for adult life. In this sense criminologists have often referred to it as an incidental fact to be considered about criminals. Babyhood can no longer be dismissed in this off-hand fashion. Babies are not criminals but the habits of thinking and action that make criminality possible are established before the child becomes even a delinquent. Therefore the most fundamental preventive work that can be done in criminology will be learning to understand what experiences of childhood are really significant for later delinquencies and how to develop an effective means of putting that knowledge into conscious practice among the population at large, and more especially among those who seem now to have perfected the knack of influencing their children in the wrong way and at the wrong time.

[10] Healy and Bronner, "Delinquents and Criminals : Their Making and Unmaking," p. 125. Also table 31, p. 262.

CHAPTER VII

EXPANDING HORIZONS—MISADVENTURING INTO COMMUNITY LIFE

THE SCHOOL WORLD

At the age of five or six the child goes adventuring into the broader life of his community through school attendance. He goes from the home with a personality that has already taken a definite shape under the influences of the family that has been close to him during his earliest years. School life begins abruptly and it represents a sharp contrast to all that has gone before.

A new authority, the teacher, replaces the mother during school hours. She is not charmed by the peculiarities of individual pupils nor could she cater to them if she were because she must act as guardian to twenty-five or thirty wriggling children. Her viewpoint is that of a tutor rather than that of a parent. The child will respond to her authority with the devices with which he has met authority most effectively at home, be they unquestioning obedience, open rebellion, deception, or some other mechanism. Methods of defense that have already been learned are used and retained if they are still effective. Silence, alibis, countercharges, sulking, truancy, an air of injured innocence are common protective devices already available for use when the new world seems ready to overwhelm the weaklings. If the habits of conduct that the child has brought from the home do not suit his new position he must modify them quickly, for his success in group living depends upon his capacity to meet its demands readily.

However, the child can no longer depend wholly upon the well-learned behavior that has proved successful in dealing with parents, brothers and sisters. The school is a meeting place of personalities in the making. The teacher and the schoolmates are different. So a process of mutual scrutiny goes on accompanied by a testing out of strength and weakness, a sort of psychological shaking down process which eventually places each person in a particular niche.

When the child enters school the very routine of his life is changed. The supposed need for classroom order, even in the kindergarten, is for many the first restriction ever placed upon spontaneous activity. Occupational demands are new, and are set by the teacher rather than by the child's own whims. The assigned work is regular and progressive rather than haphazard. Often it must be done in coöperation with others. Usually it is competitive. It involves, in some way, consideration of the presence of others. Tasks often run contrary to the child's wishes. On the other hand, they often appeal to his strongest impulses, such as curiosity and love of prestige.

As a result of these rearrangements, hidden flaws of personality are uncovered and even intensified. They may represent emotional immaturity, an inability to find security and satisfaction away from the mother. They may be due to physical or mental handicaps that are first made clear by the spotlight of comparison. Sometimes they appear as products of poor training ; as the acts of those who are still unused to social responsibility. No one else will cater to these weaknesses as the family may have done and the children concerned are forced to meet that fact. So the shaping of the personality through crises goes on.

Into the same school to receive the same instruction flock endlessly different children : dull, superior ; aggressive, shrinking ; sensitive, callous ; poor, comfortable ; wanted, unwanted ; girls, boys ; naive, sophisticated ; all to go through the mill together. To some the new world that centers about the school offers their first glimpse of pleasant living. To others it represents the blocking of life by arbitrary and unjust demands. Now and then appear children who act upon their feelings and carry themselves beyond the conventions of the school group. They will not easily submit to its demands. These are the ones the schools call problem children. Mishandled through ignorance or carelessness they may become delinquents and criminals.

This statement of the relationship between troublesome school children and crime is necessarily a cautious one. Yet here is one point where crime begins, and one point where it can be prevented. It is our very inability to separate the beginnings of criminal conduct from other unusual forms of behavior that makes us usually disregard problem children as potential delinquents. We become deeply interested in some of them later after they have become confirmed criminals. Then our interest comes too late.

Of course, school life is but a part of the daily living of the child. Its effects may be overbalanced for good or for evil by outside interests. Intelligent handling of a troublesome pupil in school is not the only force preventing adult failure. Some children are turned from the dangerous path not by guidance but by the sheer force of chance that sends them to a different teacher, or a Saturday job.

It must also be emphasized that school failures and social failures are not identical. The schools, with a few progressive exceptions, concern themselves only with the intellectual life of their pupils. They have notoriously overlooked children who have given ample evidence of coming social failure but who have had a proper I.Q. and a respectful manner. On the other hand some spectacular classroom misbehaviorists have been exhibiting only a natural and even well-intentioned response to a real or an apparent injustice. Once more the conclusion is that these problem pupils are of concern to the criminologist not as predestined delinquents but only as the group likely to contribute most heavily to the numbers of adult criminals, a theory that sounds reasonable enough but for which satisfactory objective proof is difficult to give.

The failure of the school to discover the relationship between classroom work and the physical condition of the pupils may easily lead to troublesome behavior. Children who have never known good vision may be unaware of their defective eyesight and they may be treated as stupid or disobedient children by a teacher who is equally unaware of their handicap. Ear infection may not only be a source of chronic irritation but may cause the pupil to hear normally at one time and with difficulty another, leading to classroom behavior that the teacher is likely to treat as an attempt at wilful annoyance by the child. Speech defects accepted by parents as a little peculiarity to be outgrown may have much influence upon the child because of the manner in which they are greeted by schoolmates and teacher when expressed in public. Dr. Healy says that he has been tremendously impressed with the influence of speech defects upon the personality of certain delinquents studied at his clinic. He says that stuttering tends to make an individual highly anti-social. Persons so affected have been known to turn for comfort towards those who will overlook their disorder without comment, and who will demand little of them. Normal young fellows have made miserably inferior associations in this way and through them have been led into thieving, vagrancy and homosexual practices.[1]

Undernourished children who are easily fatigued may do a grade of work much below their potential ability. They appear to the teacher as lazy and shiftless or as mentally retarded individuals. Teachers are seldom aware that annoying behavior may be due to the inability of a tired child to control his actions as he normally can do. On the other hand unusually vigorous children may have a surplus of energy that breaks through the rigid routine of the classroom. The teacher of thirty children who is required to cover a definite number of chapters each term cannot allow interruptions that interfere with classroom progress, and she has little time outside for the study of individual children. Therefore she is apt to consider automatic obedience and goodness in her pupils as synonymous. Towards non-automatic behavior she is likely to react unpleasantly. The "bad" pupil may not only accept his label but he may proceed forthwith to improve his right to it.

The competition of the classroom soon throws into bold relief the more marked forms of mental abnormality that the home has so earnestly overlooked, but frequently it does not detect milder aberrations. Children in the upper reaches of feeble-mindedness, those who cannot be labelled

[1] W. Healy, "The Individual Delinquent," p. 221.

feeble-minded but who are unquestionably subnormal, those who have special mental disabilities, those classified as psychic constitutional inferiors, and even some with definite psychoses are all to be found in public schools unrecognized and uncared for except in the more progressive metropolitan centers. By no means all of these are involved in delinquency but they certainly represent a potentially dangerous group with the outcome usually dependent upon chance.

The dull child who is forced to repeat a grade, because of partial failure, may find his time during the second year so little occupied by assigned work that he escapes boredom only by annoying others or by playing truant. Phyllis Blanchard[2] has called attention to the type of subnormal child who struggles along repeating grade after grade because he cannot leave school until he has completed the age and scholastic requirements of his state. The school offers no industrial work suited to his needs and academic subjects are beyond his grasp. He can only wait until time and the wish of the teacher to be rid of a nuisance give him his freedom. Such pupils frequently become disciplinary problems, they form undesirable habits, and often they come into conflict with the law through truancy.

The constitutional inferior is characterized by unusual emotional reactions that constantly get him into trouble. He may be of normal intelligence but with little will power, easily shifted about, lacking in self-control, a creature of impulse, always intending to do better but never succeeding, frequently overwhelmed by the difficulty of living and reacting to the task by despair or childish rebellion. These pupils forced into a school system not adapted to their peculiar needs contribute to the group of frustrated, unhappy children whose delinquencies are but symptoms of their poor adjustment. Although children who suffer from disorders of emotion or intelligence can be detected by proper examinations, only two or three states have as yet made any provision for sorting them out or provided any regular form of treatment for them after they have been recognized. The results of their failure look like this :

[2] P. Blanchard, "The Child and Society," pp. 115-117.

Case 1. A seventeen year old high school girl of good parentage, working as a maid, strangled a year old baby because she disliked her employer and because the baby cried too much.

Case 2. A boy of nine, while bathing in an irrigation ditch, pushed his companion under the water and held him there until he was drowned.

Case 3. A sixteen year old boy sprang out of concealment and killed a woman who was walking by on her way to her home.

Case 4. A boy of nine stabbed another with a knife improvised from a pair of scissors after some other playmates had teased him.

Case 5. Eleanor, who had been told by her cooking teacher to wear a white apron, continued to appear in a dark one. When the teacher ordered her to obey her or report to the principal, Eleanor ran away. Later she became involved in delinquencies.

Case 6. Peter at ten was clumsy, irresponsible and made disturbing blunders but was excused by his teachers because he was so good natured. He pushed another boy who he knew could not swim off of a raft because the boy would not let Peter use his bathing suit.[3]

Of course, the weakness is not always within the child. The school too often starts delinquency. The physical condition of the school plant may be a causal factor, usually of minor importance. Poor lighting and ventilation, uncomfortable desks, and generally faulty equipment influence conduct. More important than these, especially in rural areas, are improper separation of the toilet facilities of the sexes and unsupervised play at noontime by children who carry their lunch to school. This combination particularly encourages vice.

Far more important than the school's material equipment is its classroom procedure. This has often been indicted for its artificiality and only a few schools have at all succeeded in removing the grounds for complaint. Recitations are stilted, formal. Questions aroused by the lesson cannot be discussed because the class must cover the requisite chapter a day. The study of civics, economics, religion, and ethics must be kept on a rarefied academic plane divorced from the

[3] Cases 1, 2, and 3 adapted from a Report of the California Commission for the study of Problem Children, p. 6. Cases 4 and 5 adapted from Miriam Van Water's "Youth in Conflict," pp. 39 and 96. Case 6, the author's.

realities or avoided entirely. The repressions of the classroom often seem to be arbitrary, pointless, and unjust. Considering the varied backgrounds of the pupils it is not surprising that they often lead to irritation or open revolt. Often the teacher suffers at the hands of the pupils as the representative of a system that is beyond her control. The teacher's attitude towards the pupils is of the greatest importance. Even the very youngest child rather shrewdly analyzes his instructor. Thirty children watching a teacher in school and knowing of her activities while away from it are not long deceived by classroom posing. Sympathetic insight, a reputation for absolute fairness, self-control, and an adequate fund of knowledge bring out responses of loyalty and respect. Undue severity, failure to appreciate the child's viewpoint, sarcasm, and dishonesty call forth bitterness and hatred. Personal peculiarities in dress, gestures, or voice as well as emotional flareups are weaknesses soon discovered and played upon by children to their own glory among their fellows.

Boy of eleven. "No, I won't recite for her. Just as soon as you start to read she makes fun of you. She wants you to speak each word out like this just — like — a — ba — by instead of natural. All the kids hate her. I hope her mother does die then maybe she will leave school."

Boy of eleven. "She said if we got eighty in arithmetic all week we'd get out at recess time Friday afternoon and Jim didn't get eighty so he said he'd come in half an hour late Friday noon and get his time that way. Then she happened to be in back of the room and saw him cutting across the railroad tracks, so when he came in she said she told us not to do that and there had been too much of it lately.— I guess she saw some of the other kids cutting across the other day.— So she said nobody could go early. Then some of the kids groaned and made noises out loud and she made the whole class stay till four. Boy, if I have her next year I ain't going to that school. She is always soaking us because one or two kids raise the deuce and we won't tell. Why don't she find out herself?"

Boy of thirteen. "Gee, what fun we had today. Downes was lazy or didn't know the lesson or something and he said we could have a study period, and Hank said let's hear him make his speech, so he spibbed a spit-ball right by Downes' head and sure enough he got up and put one thumb in his vest and pulled off his glasses and gave us the whole rigmarole about 'A Freudian psychologist would say' and ended up with 'A word to the wise is sufficient,' and when he finished Don said under his breath 'Very good. You may be seated.' You couldn't keep from laughing and Downes got sore and picked up a ruler on his desk and rapped and he hit a hunk of chalk and it flew up and hit him in the face. The whole class roared. Gee he looked funny."

Teachers of the sort pictured in these cases may swing their pupils towards misbehavior and delinquency as a reaction to the injustice or the artificiality of the schoolroom procedure.

Proof of the thesis that the failure of the schools to interest or control a goodly number of students fosters juvenile delinquency can be found in several recent studies based upon an adequate number of individual case records. Healy and Bronner found persistent truancy to be "second in degree of frequency among all offenses, each being engaged in by about 40 per cent of boys." [4] In their Boston series of 2000 cases these same investigators found after most careful study that school dissatisfaction was a *major* cause of delinquency in 9 per cent of the cases, the girls, however, showing only 2 per cent. [5]

Sheldon and Eleanor T. Glueck, in their study of 500 criminals paroled from the Reformatory at Concord, Massachusetts, found that the Reformatory group had far less schooling than the general population as represented by Boston public-school children. [6] In view of these facts the incidence of school retardation should interest the criminologist, especially if the facts are as startling as those printed in the University of North Carolina *News Letter* which reported that 202,232 white and 135,179 colored children were not promoted in 1927-28 out of a school population of 995,122 in North Carolina. [7]

[4] Healy and Bronner, "Delinquents and Criminals," p. 171.
[5] *Ibid.*, p. 181.
[6] S. S. and E. T. Glueck, "500 Criminal Careers," p. 133.
[7] *News Letter*, U. of North Carolina, January 29, 1930.

THE NEW WORLD OUTSIDE OF THE SCHOOL

SCHOOL age also brings to the child a new freedom and an increasing range of movement which he shares and enjoys with new-found companions. With them he goes in search of action, excitement, adventure outside of class hours. His new life brings to him new standards of values. Other adults view life differently from his parents. Other children follow different rules. Some may stay up until nine o'clock, or play ball on Sunday or go to the movies twice a week. Comparison begins. Old authorities lose their omniscience. Conflicts arise. Choices must be made. Independence is dimly perceived.

STREET LIFE

CLIFFORD SHAW[8] and his assistants have proved, what casual observation has long led us to believe, that delinquency and adult crime are both concentrated in areas where property deterioration and cultural disorganization have occurred due to the invasion of residential districts by business. In these transitional zones in our cities marked by poor housing and decreasing population, neighborhood standards disappear. The community as a social force ceases to exist. A vigorous public opinion upholding community standards of living is absent. Often the difficulty is enhanced by the presence of foreigners whose children are left stranded between the Old World code of their parents which they will not follow and the code of their Americanized friends which their parents oppose.

In such an area delinquency may not only be possible; it may become traditional. Into the streets of such a region goes the child, ready to enjoy the vivid concrete satisfactions that city life affords. Thrills and new experiences crowd upon each other in the normal happenings of the day. Now it is a fist fight over the possession of a precious bit of kindling wood, a fight enhanced in its satisfying value by the attendant crowd of boisterous onlookers. A fire, the bursting of a hydrant, the arrest of a "drunk," or an auto-

[8] C. R. Shaw *et al.*, "Delinquency Areas."

mobile accident contribute in rapid sequence to the experiences of the day. Always there is movement and excitement. The thrill of living is there. If the school is important in the expanding life of the child, these outside activities must have an infinitely greater appeal because they are so natural, so close to his interests, so directly appealing. It is not surprising that the school finds it hard to compete with them.

Adults are always to be found who will make street life pleasant for the roving youngster. Childhood has a distinct appeal for most grown-ups. Their sympathy or their applause can easily be aroused. The sobbing child who has "lost" the dime that was to take him into the movies can soon collect several more to take its place. The freckle-faced urchin who can do a clog-dance or yell a popular song can gain the admiring attention of strangers as he never could gain the interest of his teacher or his relatives. Here is pleasure without work or responsibility. The ways of the city are soon learned. Travel is easy. Rides are "thumbed." Turnstiles are "ducked." Small wonder is it that some children become habitual truants.

The results of this life neither the children nor the adults who make it possible can foresee. Failure in school work is both a cause and a result of truancy. The boy leaves school early with poor preparation for work. Periods of unemployment and depression will give him a precarious economic footing. The easy life of the street fosters poor habits, irregularity, lack of responsibility, the speech and manners that stamp him as outside of the society of decent people. His approach to life becomes twisted, unorthodox.

Profit and pleasure are easily combined. The city offers boundless chances for securing a precarious but alluring wage. Junk collecting on the dump, the gathering of coal from the railroad yards or of wood from store alley-ways may be done of necessity but it is work that offers definite satisfactions. The economic rewards are immediate and direct. New experiences are constantly met. The joys of success are tasted. Bootblacking or baggage-smashing bring returns in cash. Eventually a "regular job" as newsboy or messenger may entice the growing boy.

In themselves these commonplace activities carry no suggestion of delinquency but through them the slum child may be introduced to delinquency in ways that are subtle and irresistible. A home in which an uneducated mother is handicapped by poverty and the care of several children is not one in which there is either time or opportunity for teaching fine distinctions between what is mine and what is thine. Property rights are regarded crudely. The neighborhood standards are equally hazy. From such a background does the youngster go forth to gather his coal or wood. When he finds it he appropriates it as a matter of course either with or without the permission of the owner. This is the accepted mode of procedure. From that it is not a far step to the appropriation of any loose articles that may be lying around in the area-way behind a store or in the freight yards. Often the child is encouraged definitely by older members of the family to take anything of value which is unguarded. It is this unwholesome mental atmosphere of the slum rather than its physical condition that makes it such a fruitful source of evil.

The street trades present another danger to young people: frequent contact with adults of vicious character not only in the district of night clubs and cabarets but in the parks and cheap lodging house areas infested with tramps and hoboes. The courts are constantly forced to recognize this as a contributing factor in delinquency. The tramp population of the United States closely allied to the criminal group and consisting normally of approximately two million wandering and homeless men is steadily lowering its age level by the addition of recruits from the ranks of youth. Anderson conservatively states that fully a quarter of the tramp class is under twenty-one years of age.[9]

Delinquencies are rarely the acts of solitary children. They are committed by boys in groups. In 6000 cases of stealing studied by Shaw and Myers in Cook County 90.4 per cent of the cases were known to have involved two or more boys.[10] These groups may be fairly well organized

[9] N. Anderson, "The Juvenile and the Tramp." *Jour. Criminal Law and Criminology*, August 1923.
[10] Illinois Crime Survey, p. 662.

as gangs or they may be simply loose associations of neighborhood or school acquaintances. Much recent literature has emphasized the rôle of the gang as the unit involved in delinquency but it is questionable whether gangs are the most important delinquent group if the term is intended to impute to them a definite organization. Dr. Healy is one careful observer who has found the commonest form of association to be casual.

The power of the loosely-knit neighborhood group can best be understood against its environmental background. For reasons already mentioned the area of delinquency is one lacking in definite community opinion. The prevailing moral standards are low and they are reflected by the children as well as by the adults. The boy must drop down to the prevailing level of behavior or live in isolation. But to keep away from the other fellows and still live in the neighborhood is virtually impossible.

When a delinquent boy is sent home upon his sincere promise to do better, by what superhuman feat is he to escape the influence of the boys who live about him? He cannot inspire them, reform them, lift them up to new levels of conduct. He cannot shun them and live a tolerable existence. He cannot be with them but not of them without being constantly torn between pleading and persecution. Moral contagion is a process to be expected when unfortunates gather together looking for something to do. Their mere gathering together is a stimulant. The ensuing activity is likely to be undesirable, for deeds are not likely to rise above their source. While the slum area exists as it does threats and admonitions will not greatly change those who must continue to live in it. Nothing short of removing the slum from the boy or the boy from the slum is likely to have a noticeably good effect on his character.

More or less well organized gangs often evolve from neighborhood groupings of boys. The tendency to form compact units welded together under the magic of a gang name is particularly marked among boys during the earliest years of adolescence. In a study of 1313 gangs in Chicago, Thrasher found eighteen children's gangs with an age range between six and twelve years and 455 boys' gangs with an age range between eleven and seventeen years.[11] The gang provides a ready outlet for the boys' sense of loyalty. It is a meeting place of ideas. It arouses enthusiasms. It applauds his exploits. It becomes, in fact, his social world. It is doubtful if the boy who has tasted the joys of gang life would ever willingly exchange its stamping ground of alleys, dumps, or vacant lots for a supervised playground. Smoking and drinking are much heightened sensations when indulged in collectively. "Shooting craps," which has the attractiveness of any game of chance with the added merit of requiring little equipment, requires numbers. Pedler baiting, fighting, and marauding are essentially gang activities. As a gang member the boy becomes absolutely selfish, thoughtless, and irresponsible in his relation to the greater society about him.

The adventure that the gang seeks can be found only in the presence of danger, so the gang must be aggressive enough to create enemies who will make their ventures risky. The shopkeeper finds the gang a distinct nuisance, destructive of property, engaged in thieving, and dangerous to life. Railroads find it necessary to hire detectives to protect their property in the yards from gang raids. Pedestrians and autoists discover that streets converted into baseball fields or battle-grounds are not safe for travel. The result is open warfare between the gang and property owners or their representatives, their private detectives, the police, and the courts.

To the gang boy this conflict does not appear as a matter of right or of wrong. It is just the way life goes ; and you must play the game. In this battle the boys' immediate friends and usually their families support and shield them. In fact, they may be providing an outlet for any goods that the gang has stolen. Some gangs make regular expeditions into the shopping district and systematically engage in stealing. Newcomers are taught the art of placing a cap over an object and picking it up without attracting attention. There is no opportunity for correction at home. Gang life completely swallows the gang boy up so that by the time

[11] F. M. Thrasher, "The Gang," p. 74.

he reaches adolescence he is a hardened tough, sophisticated, precocious in the knowledge of all the evil that the street can teach. Every sentence that he speaks is polluted with the phraseology of degeneracy. His moral standards have become set on the lowest level and his viewpoint has become so warped that he can never see life eye to eye with his more favored brothers. If he turns away from the gang as he grows older it is not because he has found the predatory life distasteful, but because life sometimes tricks him into growing up. He falls in love ; and that interest overshadows all else. Its privileges are accompanied by restrictions : less time with the gang and more with the girl, a regular income, a safe job. Marriage comes and weights him with its responsibilities — and another member has been weaned away from the gang.

The boy who never meets this crisis or who dodges it when it comes may continue his gang activities into adult life, becoming part of that complex machinery of organized crime and shady politics that now foists itself upon our metropolitan centers.

CHAPTER VIII

ADOLESCENCE AND THE DIFFICULTIES OF A CHANGING LIFE

ADOLESCENCE is conventionally assumed to be one of the periods of strain in human life. Recent anthropological study has given us some reason to believe that adolescent conflict is chiefly due to the demands of civilization rather than to any innate difficulty in passing from childhood to maturity.[1] Be that as it may, it is unquestionably true that in our society adolescence is a period when conduct difficulties reach a numerical peak.

NEW INTERESTS : MATES, MONEY AND A THRILL

THERE are two great changes to be faced by youth in the teens. One is the physical and emotional expansion that characterizes the process of maturing sexually. The other is the task of assuming self-support which is a mark of social maturity. As youth meets these crises in his evolution a new pattern of interests shapes itself about them and colors all of his behavior during this period. The boy of twelve who considers girls to be worthless and who emphatically refuses to take part in any such ladylike pastime as dancing with his sister will be found at sixteen escorting a high school friend to a dancing class. Presently he may develop a definite and final "crush" upon a girl which is likely to be followed by a succession of equally final affairs before a life mate is chosen. The girl goes through nearly the same type of experience. This behavior is part of the outward expression of a profound intellectual and emotional reorganization. With it comes a new outlook on life, new demands, and new social and moral problems to be met.

[1] See M. Mead, "Coming of Age in Samoa."

Most young people go to work during their teens. Even among those who go on to college the need of self-support is not absent. Association now is chiefly with older persons rather than with those of the same age group. New work habits must be formed. The worker must find his place in a new social setting. The school was designed to cater to his welfare. The employer is interested chiefly in profits rather than in his employees. Wages bring a new incentive to labor. They bring also an elating sense of power and self-confidence. These new interests coupled with new power wean the adolescent away from the home. Less time is spent with the family and more with new-found companions. Daytime work consigns recreation to the evening hours. Parents are frequently unprepared for these changes in spirit and routine and they attempt to hold them in check. They are surprised and they sometimes become panic-stricken when youth challenges their authority. Family conflict ensues.

Out of the family confusion that often arises when children reach the verge of independence and out of the confusion of ideas and feelings, which is the adolescent's own mind, three demands seem to stand out. The adolescent wants a girl (boy friend), money for its power, and a thrill. These interests furnish the driving power for that tremendous activity which when misdirected is juvenile delinquency.

THE WORK-MONEY INTEREST

A GREAT proportion of young criminals are found guilty of larceny. In the majority of these cases it is doubtful if actual poverty or need caused the stealing. Instead there looms behind them a combination of such factors as failure to find satisfaction at work and inability to gratify ever growing wants with the wages earned. The industrial history of criminals is characterized by an aimless wandering from job to job. More than half (57.4 per cent) of the 500 Concord Reformatory cases studied by the Gluecks had held their longest jobs for less than a year.[2] It is only by

[2] S. S. and E. T. Glueck, "500 Criminal Careers," p. 135.

chance if young people, who knock about the industrial world so planlessly, find any work that gives them the hope of enduring satisfaction in their labor.

Unskilled laborers are easy to hire. When slack times come it is cheaper to dismiss them summarily than to keep them. So work continues off and on at various jobs interspersed with long days of idleness spent on the street corners. It is easier to stand there than to go home and confess the "lay off" to discouraged parents. Making the rounds of employment offices to ask for work is a painful process. At the corner will be found companions in misery ready to help each other rationalize their failures and also to while away the tedious hours in pointless and degraded conversation. It is difficult to overestimate the demoralizing influence of enforced unemployment in such surroundings. Idleness becomes a lecherous habit that slowly saps away the power to struggle on. Unoccupied time spent in the poorest of company cannot well be profitable and often it leads to definite criminal acts.

Dr. Van Waters has called our attention to the tendency of certain businesses to employ some young people, not for their efficiency as workers, but solely to capitalize the appeal of their youthful charm and vigor. Especially is this true of young women who serve as waitresses, manicurists, ushers, dance hall hostesses and the like, but it also applies in some degree to young men serving as bellhops, ushers in restaurants and theaters, and in other capacities where there is personal contact between employees and patrons.

At best, this means that youth is selling its personal attractiveness more successfully than age is selling its experience. Sex appeal is a recognized sales factor of great importance. Such employment brings attentions that are not always flattering. Against them a defense must be set up that will have the peculiar property of protecting the person while it also leaves both employee and patron so pleased that the position will not be placed in jeopardy. The psychological jiu-jitsu of flattery and cajolery by which youth accomplishes this feat cannot fail to leave the adolescent cynical, rebellious and shrewd.

Magazine publishers who shortsightedly teach droves of young people slick methods of getting into homes with camouflaged sales talks that sound at first blush like the self-introductions of a new neighbor are also stirring up dangerous possibilities. How much their efforts contribute to the education of future confidence men and to their own insurance rates against fraudulent crimes no one knows. It is certain that the unethical practices which they are teaching add to that low standard of public morality that makes crime control in our country unnecessarily difficult. Those who learn to confuse scholarships with commissions and votes with subscriptions are apt also to mistake bribes for gifts and possession for ownership.

At the other extreme such occupations definitely involve criminal activity. The following is a fair sample of many cases brought to light by one group of investigators :

Jean went to a booking agency for an opportunity to go on the stage and was placed as a night club hostess. She was required to be agreeable to the male customers and to get them to order drinks and food for her and in every way possible to get them to spend their money. Her pay was in tips. She presently discovered that she could keep her position only by going out with the guests after the club closed.

At the age of nineteen she gave herself up to the police for commitment to a reformatory as the only means of saving her nerves and her health from the ravages of drink and prostitution.[3]

In New York the number of night clubs had so increased by 1927 that they could not profitably sell liquor without the assistance of hostesses like Jean. By the fall of that year agencies and clubs had grown bold enough to advertise for recruits in one newspaper that was willing to accept the business. In the public press young women were offered an enticing but camouflaged opportunity to become criminals through the most disastrous sort of employment that could be given to them.[4]

[3] Abstracted from a case reported by G. E. Worthington, Secretary of the Committee of Fourteen of New York, *Survey*, January 1, 1929, p. 414.

[4] Committee of Fourteen, "Annual Report for 1927," p. 22.

The work of the adolescent appears to be quite frankly sought as a means to an immediate end. The ideal of working up in the business seems to be largely a folk-tale. It is sometimes a necessary process but it is not looked upon in practice as desirable. Many young people do not want to work long hours at little pay for the opportunity of rising to the heights. They would rather be paid now what they are worth, and they expect the sum to be at least sufficient to provide them with necessities.

But modern necessities are created by the tremendous pressure of high-powered advertising and they include fur coats, cars and vacations. In common with all who can look or listen young people are constantly bombarded with suggestions commanding, begging, enticing them to take unto themselves an endless array of offerings without which they can never hope to be completely happy. Every resource of modern psychology is enrolled to keep them in a state of constant longing for that which ever lies just ahead like the brick-red carrots dangled before the hopeful donkey's nose. It is this kind of pressure, not of poverty, but of created covetousness that breeds irritation, overreaching and reckless action.

A great desire in one who has little money may lead to theft, but it is not only in such a direct way that delinquency may occur. When advertising is combined with stupid credit selling that entirely neglects the economic capacity of the buyer the resulting evils may be quite as great as those that accompany a simple theft. It is pleasant to buy a fur coat on an easy payment plan but extremely annoying to find a collector waiting to take each week's wages as soon as they are received over a period of several months. Young people who have bought unwisely often find themselves unable or unwilling to pay their installments. Frightened by the insistence of the collector they change their lodgings, resort to subterfuges to keep their creditors from embarrassing them at their work, or even change their employment and name to escape the threat of legal difficulties.

The entire situation of being in debt is a puzzle to those who get into it. Desperate need leads to desperate remedies which may appear like this :

Helen, nineteen years old, worried over her indebtedness for clothes bought directly and on her aunt's account against the wishes of her father, met a friend who told her how she could make money by meeting men during her lunch hour.

Pauline an orphan of sixteen made her own living. She earned fourteen dollars a week. She bought new clothes costing more than a hundred dollars on credit. Unable to pay the required four dollars a week she became a fugitive. In an effort to avoid the collector she gave up one job after another, dyed her hair, changed her name, moved to a new boarding house and finally disappeared.[5]

The other side of this picture is one of calloused, sophisticated persons who buy what they want and use it without a quiver of conscience until the seller takes it back again. "Well, I had the use of it for three months, anyway."

These young workers face a perpetual struggle between wages and wants. They run constantly along the verge of an economic abyss and it is not surprising that some of them tumble over. One young man who is now imprisoned wrote naïvely, "I think that if I had plenty of money I would of never seen a jail."[6] How much they lack that necessary money is clearly shown in the Gluecks' study of 500 offenders. Of the 498 about which information was available, 479 (96.2 per cent) possessed no savings at all. Figures on pre-reformatory earnings were more difficult to get but in the 88 cases for which they were secured more than half (48) earned less than $15 a week and only ten earned more than $25. However the data on post-parole earnings in 248 cases indicate that the 88 cases are fairly representative of the entire group.

THE MATING INTEREST

The work-money interest of youth is only a means to the pursuit of pleasure. The adolescent increasingly seeks his recreation outside of the home. For its proper enjoyment the companionship of the opposite sex is necessary. Adolescence is the romantic age. Anyone who knows criminals

[5] Case of Pauline abstracted from M. Van Waters' "Youth in Conflict," p. 121.
[6] From a letter in the author's possession.

is aware that love is frequently the motivating power behind thefts.   The sensitiveness of the youth unable to give his girl what others are having, the lack of prestige that accompanies a chronically empty pocketbook, the need to meet the recreational expectations of women in the face of stiff competition from companions economically more fortunate have all been contributing factors in specific cases of youthful crime.

Adolescence is a period of experimentation and also of phantasy.   Lorinne Pruette's analysis of a group of adolescent girls showed that 90 per cent of them day-dreamed about courtship and marriage.[7]   Psychiatrists are often confronted with the problem of excessive sex phantasies in girls and many instances have come to light in which adolescent girls have kept detailed diaries of imaginary experiences with boys and have written letters to them.   This sort of idealism is not so likely to be found in boys whose interests under our social pattern are permitted a more direct expression.

Modern young people are living in a society in which sex is exceedingly prominent.   Lifted from its hiding place among the furtive shameful weaknesses of human-kind it has been thrust persistently upon us by those who have found cash profits in this once tabooed novelty.   Moving pictures, books, newspapers, magazines, poster advertisements overwhelm us with sex ideas.   Such a continuous bombardment of suggestion falling upon those who are in a period of unusual sensitiveness to them creates a stress that is abnormal in its intensity.

This sometimes leads to sexual delinquencies, but, whether it does or not, the actual physical contact is usually the least part of the difficulty.   It is the mental turmoil of the adolescent that brings disaster in its wake.   At every turn he bumps into sex suggestions which he cannot thrust aside. Pernicious ideas come to him in spite of his efforts.   Irritated beyond endurance by the conflict within himself he breaks out in delinquencies that have no obvious connection with his emotional restlessness.   Stealing, fighting and other apparently malicious misconduct are often traced back by

[7] L. Pruette, "Women and Leisure," Ch. 8.

clinics to emotional disturbances over sex problems. The present hopeful frankness of young people and of some parents about sex may become an effective preventive of mental conflict on that score.

There is a minority of adolescents who become involved in sexual delinquencies quite directly and often, no doubt, without any ensuing mental upheaval. Freedom of discussion has removed the mysteries of sex from youth but it has also made them aware of its pleasures and desirous of tasting them. An unwarranted confidence in their own ability to take care of themselves makes this possible. For them, sex stripped of its shame has lost its halo, too. They are frankly experimentalists. The resulting delinquencies of this group are directly expressed and may be followed by little or no mental disturbance. If a chain of escapades does follow it is more likely to represent an attempt to cover up or escape social disapproval than to be an emotional purgative.

The criminologist is interested in both aspects of the sex problem as here presented. First, illegitimate coitus is itself a crime although generally undetected and unpunished even among adults. Secondly, ideation about sex matters, with or without physical intimacies is often the basis of other forms of delinquency. Individual case studies furnish ample evidence of these facts. However, it is not possible to measure the statistical extent of sexual delinquency in the general adolescent population nor its effects in producing secondary offenses. It is possible to note that 397 (78 per cent) of the Concord parolees studied by the Gluecks admitted that they had illegitimate heterosexual experiences before entering the reformatory, chiefly between the ages of 14 and 17. What the relationship is between these experiences and their other crimes cannot be determined, but the extent of the admitted irregularities among these Concord boys very well indicates the difficulty that young people of poor social and economic status have in making a socially acceptable adjustment to their awakened sexual interests.

THE RECREATIONAL INTEREST

The adolescent demands his recreation with a thrill. Commercial amusement agencies give it to him. Their success in appealing to young folks will be vouched for by anyone who has watched a holiday crowd waiting to buy tickets for a roller-coaster ride or who has seen a Saturday noon ticket line at a popular motion picture house.

The Educational Research Committee of the Payne Fund which in 1933 completed a thoroughgoing four-year study of the effects of motion pictures upon young people reports a weekly attendance of 27 million children and adolescents out of a total weekly audience of 77 millions. Those between the ages of eight and nineteen attended an average of 52 times a year during which time they saw 156 films in which love-making, other aspects of sex, and crime were the features emphasized. Messrs. Lehman and Witty checked the frequency of 200 play activities among boys and girls and found that automobiling and movies ranked third and fourth among sixteen, seventeen and eighteen year old boys, and third and fifth, second and fourth and second and fifth, respectively among sixteen, seventeen and eighteen year old girls. Having dates ranked sixteenth, fourteenth and fourteenth among the boys and sixteenth, sixteenth and tenth among the young women. The importance of dates increases in the later years of adolescence for both men and women. The importance of the position of these leisure time activities is even more impressive when it is remembered that they are included in a list of approximately thirty games indulged in by more than 25 per cent of those in any age group and that this list included such common activities as chewing gum and reading the funny papers.[8]

Naturally it is during the pursuit of pleasure that adolescents are most apt to fall into delinquency. Yet it is difficult to indict business directly for their downfall. Hotels are sometimes conveniently unaware of the intent of some of their patrons. Managers of motion picture houses sometimes forget laws that are intended to protect adolescents.

[8] Lehman and Witty, "The Psychology of Play Activities," pp. 52-54.

These are sins of omission. They do not incite a person to become delinquent; they merely provide a convenient opportunity which otherwise would very likely be found elsewhere. The crux of the matter, however, lies not in such specific faults but in the general unwillingness of these enterprises to assume any social responsibility for their influence upon their patrons. They feel that their business is to sell what people will buy, and not to decide what is best for them. They have become a part of the modern industrial machine with a standardized technique for exercising human emotions with the same unholy and depressing efficiency that a mechanical horse exercises the human body.

Only New York and New Jersey forbid unaccompanied children under sixteen at all movies and even in these states the law is but feebly enforced. Six others prohibit unaccompanied children during the evening and school hours. Forty states have nothing but a few flimsy and inadequate regulations to keep children from unsuitable pictures at unsuitable times.

What the adolescent's recreation will do to him, of course, depends largely upon what he seeks in it. For those who want, at little cost, some escape from the endless routine of the mill, some measure of adventure in a drab world, the cinema presents as no other medium can, a glimpse of the world of dreams. It makes true the land of romance which is so very far from the crass reality of his daily life. About its stars the motion picture industry has built up a glamorous ambivalent theology — demonology compounded of hero worship and sex appeal by publicity at the rate of eight or nine thousand words a day. Unfortunately, the pictures exhibited at the cheaper theaters are (perhaps only less so than in the more pretentious houses) those of life's crudities and impossibilities exaggerated and woven into themes not on the highest ethical plane. The press notices of popular shows abound in phrases of this sort:

" . . . See how talkies are made. See studio happenings the camera never dared show!"

"Story of a Primitive Love-Hungry Child of the Tropics."

"It will catch you in the current of mass emotion . . . sweep you on the shoulders of its surging mobs into profligate palaces where a people drunk with the new wine of freedom trample the dead glories of kings in abandoned bacchanalia and voluptuous debauch."

Pictures of romantic or passionate love are definite sexual excitants to a considerable proportion of adolescents. Some of them consciously turn this power of the motion pictures to their own uses. It is a not uncommon practice of some young men to seek out plays that will sexually arouse young women whom they wish to entertain in order that they may be led more easily into caresses or to direct sexual relations after the show is over. Much of the sex play of adolescents, the phrases, mannerisms, and methods of dress are imitations of the techniques of motion picture lovers. In one selected group of 252 delinquent girls between the ages of 14 and 18 studied by Blumer and Hauser, 25 per cent declared that they had had sexual intercourse with men due directly to the arousal of their sex impulses by love pictures; 48 per cent stated that they usually "felt like having a man make love to them" after seeing such pictures; and 40 per cent admitted that they imitated ways of kissing, flirting, or of acting with a man that they had learned from photoplays.[9]

Some factual evidence can be brought forth to support the oft repeated contention that some motion pictures induce youthful observers to commit crime directly through suggestion and imitation, and young people, particularly boys, are indirectly stimulated at times to beg or steal as a means of securing the admission price, but the chief harm in such shows is in their distinctly low tone which opens up and continually emphasizes new and unworthy ideas. There is also a constant stimulation to a life of pleasure-seeking and a desire to gain wealth and affluence quickly and without effort. Observers who have little experience upon which to base their judgment, gain therefrom distorted views of life and its meaning. In producing these effects rather than in teaching criminal methods the cheap movie must

[9] Blumer and Hauser, "Movies, Delinquency and Crime," Chs. 4 and 5. See also H. Blumer, "Movies and Conduct," Chs. 3 and 7. Both of these works report numerous illustrative cases.

admit its guilt.　Connected with this problem is the oppor
tunity for mischief afforded by the darkened halls and th
intermingling of strangers, especially in those houses tha
are poorly managed.

The effects of the motion picture upon young peopl
particularly because of the sale of American pictures abroad
has become a problem of international scope and was con
sidered of sufficient importance to warrant attention by th
delegates to the Ninth International Prison Congress a
London in 1925 in the adoption of a resolution favoring
an effective film censorship in every country, with the pri
mary object of protecting youth.　Even here, however, i
fairness, it must be remembered that the theater provide
a vicarious outlet for energies which might without it, or
substitute, be expended in ways even more disastrous t
youth.　Those who are harmed might find even mor
vicious outlets were this channel blocked while those wh
are firmly anchored to good tradition can survive a con
siderable shock.

Cheap fiction has basic effects similar to those of the pic
ture shows.　It, too, offers a happy escape from realit
accompanied by stimulation, distortion of life, and a lo
moral tone.　It frankly caters to the adolescent's sexua
curiosity.　Yet, much of the risquéness of current chea
fiction extends no further than the covers between whic
the reading matter is trite and unalluring enough.　Stuar
Chase says that the editor of a highly successful Confessio
Magazine advises his authors to write of the eternal triangl
with the shadow of the bed, but only the shadow, on ever
page.[10]

The automobile is the most convenient means of secur
ing actual excitement and adventure for the modern youth
Because of its expense it has not until recently become com
mon enough to affect recreation among the poorer classe
but the extent of its sale has now so reduced the price an
so spread a knowledge of its mechanical principles that eve
the poorest workers can secure and repair some kind c
used car.　The menace of the automobile is, therefore, quit

[10] S. Chase, Essay on "Play" in "Whither Mankind," edited by C. A
Beard, p. 350.

real.   The quickness of movement which it allows makes it an efficient aid to thievery.   In its duplex rôle as a medium of quick travel and as a parlor chair, it presents acceptable opportunities for mixed parties to carry on an unsupervised courtship away from all of the conventional restrictions of society.   When used for such purposes, often in combination with liquor, the automobile becomes one of the very worst factors in the demoralization of city youth, particularly through sexual delinquencies.   Its influence is seen among young people with careless or bewildered parents regardless of the economic level of their homes.

Dorothy, 16 years old, presents a typical picture of unfortunate youth and a car in search of excitement.   She was arrested for driving fifty-three miles an hour in a 15-mile zone.   She had done it before.   Dorothy told the court that she wished she had been going really fast and not simply poking along.

Her respectable family was shocked because she was detained with common offenders.   The parents admitted that they knew nothing about the affairs of their daughter who drove her own car, had a latch-key and spent her time with friends unknown to the family.[11]

THE NEW PLEASURE PHILOSOPHY AND THE OLD ASCETICISM IN CONFLICT

THE pleasure philosophy of life has been accepted wholeheartedly by youth.   Self-denial is no longer a virtue, nor is self-abasement successful as a technique.   The genius of the country lies in its industrial and commercial achievements, and these color the social background with which individual lives must blend.   Their advancement is accelerated by vivid, constant self-assertive publicity, the herd appeal working day and night to promote ideals and habits of conduct that will make good business whether or no they lead to wise living.   It is no longer good form to be poor but honest.   Esteem is not likely to be bestowed upon those whose clothes are threadbare but neat.   Honest one should be.   But possessed of the outward indices of prosperity one *must* be.   It is essential to a tolerable existence.

[11] Abstracted from M. Van Waters', "Nineteen Ways of Being a Bad Parent." *Survey,* January 1, 1927, p. 436.

The pressure behind this attitude may result only in topsy-turvy living which requires one to have a car at the expense of health or training; which requires one to drive that car one hundred and fifty miles before lunch in order that one may get back again by supper time; which requires one to dine upon a cup of coffee and an éclair because one's pay is already portioned off for clothing "one simply must have"; and all of this at a terrific nervous cost. But a few, bound less closely to the orthodox rules of conduct, or pushed more fiercely by the irritations of the system, meet their needs by methods outside of the burdensome restrictions of conventionality. They steal. They become bootleggers, sellers of shady stocks, gamblers. They marry "money." They become prostitutes by avocation. They join the ranks of the gold diggers.

The conflict between pleasure and Puritanism has led to mutual attacks, chiefly between those of different generations, with the natural processes of birth and death favoring youth. Debunking life has become a type of recreation. Its truthfulness appeals to realists in rebellion. However, an honest desire for truth does not insure its complete attainment. Those who believe only in what can be seen and touched, may misinterpret any situation. Youth has pierced much of the camouflage of life and found stark reality beneath it. The shock that has come from contrasting earlier ideals with present actualities has bred in some a cynicism that has led them to feel that "anything is right if you can get away with it." Rare indeed is the criminal who cannot sincerely justify his own needs, even though he may be well aware of the wickedness of the deeds of others. The whole world is playing the same game, but some men have better lawyers, greater influence, or more luck than others.

Youth, living between the beckoning opportunities of its own generation and the worried pleadings of the one to which affection links it, faces a problem of adjustment that requires a heroic willingness to face the facts. This is youth's perennial task, but the rapidity of recent social changes has made the dilemma more pronounced. Parents sometimes persist in thinking that a code of conduct differing from their own must be undesirable and disgraceful. On the other hand, if children fight to be unconventional, it may be only because they dare not defy their group convention that demands this fight.

The code of conduct of modern youth must meet the conditions of a new metropolitan culture that is so recent that even their parents did not have to face it until their philosophy of life had become fairly well set. In nearly every urban community there are men now living who were born when the center of our population was in Virginia. Ninety years ago Florida was still a territory. The covered wagon had not yet lumbered across the western plains. Men were still puzzled about how to get a ship across the Atlantic Ocean wholly by steam. There were no telephones, no electric lights, no automobiles — just a generation ago.

Overnight we have become an urban civilization. The tempo of life has increased. We see and hear many times more than our fathers did with less time to find out what it means. Speed and numberless hurried contacts amidst a continuous barrage of eye and ear suggestions are two prime characteristics of the metropolitan era. Age may partially avoid their effects by digging in behind old established habits of action and thought. Youth, not so entrenched, must openly meet the new world of kaleidoscopic change. Only a conception of what this means to the befuddled adolescent can make his behavior understandable.

CHAPTER IX

THE CRIMINAL HABIT

A CLASSIFICATION OF CRIMINALS

ONE of the most difficult tasks of the criminologist is to define what he means by a criminal. It must be obvious to us by now that no clean line can be drawn that will separate criminals from non-criminals nor mark off nicely the varying degrees of criminality. As we have seen, for sociological purposes the legal concept of the criminal is unsuitable. Technical offenders who break laws that require no criminal intent or that have little moral significance are not apt to have the criminal nature that demands our interest. The criminologist would like to leave these pseudo-criminals aside and consider only real criminals. Not all of these are of equal importance. Occasionally men of previously good behavior are overwhelmed by a crisis too great for them to conquer. It may never recur and they may never relapse. The defect may be chiefly within themselves (the psycho-neurotic offender) or in their environment (unusual provocation). These men may lack steadiness but they have not the criminal habit.

Among the real criminals, then, it is the habitual offenders who are truly important. Many of these may be thought of as delinquents grown older and more experienced, for men who have lived upright lives for twenty years are not likely to change their habits overnight. The causes of their criminality are written in the history of the forces that played through them during their childhood and youth. Their lives are the normal products of a faulty past. As naturally as other men have become salesmen or lawyers these men have become criminals. They are not even aware that their viewpoint differs from that of their fellows until the contrast is brought sharply to their attention. So far as they can see all men are playing the same game in one guise or another. The criminal life has indeed become a habit, accepted as a matter of course. There is no more need to justify it than there is to justify the career of any artisan.

We must recognize, however, that the unfolding of criminal habits does not proceed at an even pace from childhood on through adult life. Not all criminals pass through all the phases of delinquency that we have outlined. As some youngsters shoot up suddenly in physical stature at fourteen while others seem destined to remain undeveloped until at seventeen they too begin to grow rapidly, so others who have never been troublesome begin suddenly to exhibit undesirable types of behavior. Many seventeen year old delinquents have never been in difficulty with the law before. In Massachusetts only four per cent of these seventeen year old delinquents are guilty of serious offenses. The forces that begin to operate at that age may, however, turn them quickly into habitual criminals. Under our present system, for example, the experiences of arrest, possible jail detention, and subsequent reformatory sentence may for the first time definitely assure the continuance and extension of their criminal behavior. In other words, there are age points that are critical for delinquency and crime even as there are age points at which we are most susceptible to specific illnesses.

CRIMINALS OF THE UPPERWORLD

It may be convenient now for us to think of habitual criminals in two main groups : those of the upperworld and those of the underworld.

The phrase criminals of the upperworld is suggested to define that numerous but never clearly identified group of criminals whose social position, intelligence, and criminal technique permits them to move among their fellow-citizens virtually immune to recognition and prosecution as criminals. Between them and their upright fellow-citizens there is no chasm, but only a broad gray zone that shades insensibly into the black and the white on either side of it. In this shadow-land are non-criminals whose ethical standards are more or less debatable, and among these many near criminals who, although keeping within the law, operate in a manner that would suffer by comparison with the open law breaking of pickpockets or prowlers. Some idea of the range and importance of the activities of the criminals and near criminals of the upperworld may be gained from the following samples which are illustrative rather than exhaustive :

1.   Usurers, such as pawn brokers and loan sharks charging interest illegally at rates varying from 250 to 5000 per cent a year on loans totalling well over a billion dollars a year. The businesses of legitimate small loan associations which charge high, but legal rates of interest are not included in these figures.[1]

2.   Operators of bucket shops who take their customers' money for the purchase of securities, but who frequently do not buy them at all. When the market reaches strategic points they notify their customers that they have been sold out.[2]

3.   High pressure stock brokers who sell good stocks by telephone or through slick salesmen to people living at a distance and then shift their customers' holdings with or without their consent to worthless stocks on which the brokers receive high commissions.[3]

4.   Bankers who peg prices to maintain them at unwarranted levels until securities can be unloaded upon a gullible public.

5.   Speculating manufacturers who lift the price of their stocks by postponing legitimate operating expenses so that their net earnings may appear high and insiders may sell stocks advantageously. Later when the addition of postponed and current expenses apparently depresses earnings they may repurchase their stocks at bargain prices.

6.   Operators who pyramid stocks through holding companies to the point where the paper value of the securities [sic] issued is many times the actual value of the basic property.

7.   Investment bankers who organized investment trusts to buy securities for their stockholders and who then proceeded to play both sides of the market with excessive and unstipulated profits to themselves and with loss or ruin to the stockholders of the investment trusts for whom they have bought the speculative stocks which they, as investment bankers, were marketing. John Flynn reports as one sample of these operations the instance of a banking house that

[1] See A. M. Murphy, "Small-Loan Usury," in MacDougall (Ed.), "Crime for Profit."

[2] See D. H. Jackson, "What are Financial Rackets," in MacDougall (Ed.), *Ibid.*

[3] *Ibid.*

received $200,000 for reorganizing a corporation but made an estimated $15,000,000 out of its operations incident thereto.[4]

8. Directors who use inside information to make profits at the expense of the stockholders in whose interests they are presumed to be working. Flynn cites an instance illustrative of this practise: a board chairman persuaded his co-directors to go into the market and buy the stocks of another company in order to effect a merger. Empowered by his board to name a purchasing committee he delayed a few days until he could purchase 60,000 shares for his personal account. When the committee then began its purchasing with a resulting rise in the price of the stock, the chairman sold his own shares to his own company at a profit of $165,000. When a stockholder who got wind of the operation complained to the board of directors they considered the matter and reported that no wrong had been done.[5]

9. Investment bankers who sell bonds advertised as backed by first mortgages on property worth twice their value when they know that the real value of the property does not exceed the mortgage.

10. Manufacturers, of whom Stuart Chase reminds us,[6] who take advantage of a virtual monopoly control over natural resources, processes or inventions to gouge consumers to the limit of their willingness to pay.

11. Manufacturers who sell goods such as cosmetics, toilet articles, preserves, patent medicines, some of them useless, adulterated, or harmful, at many times their value through clever but misleading high pressure advertising.

12. Grafters in business : for example, purchasing agents who must be well paid before they will place orders with concerns desirous of making sales through them or employees who pad expense accounts.

13. Grafters in political offices who seek and receive pay for doing a thousand and one legitimate and illegitimate favors.

14. Corporations that exploit the people of small unstable nations in which they do business.

15. Employers who exploit the labor of women and children in industry contrary to law.

16. Theater managers who wink at the admission of children to motion picture performances contrary to law.

17. Working girls who add to their earnings by part time prostitution.

---

[4] See J. Flynn, "Financial Racketeering," in MacDougall, *op. cit.*
[5] *Ibid.*
[6] S. Chase, "A New Deal," Ch. 1.

18. Storekeepers and managers of amusement resorts who sell goods or services illegally on the side: for example, narcotics or opportunities for prostitution, or gambling.

19. Contractors and builders who substitute materials inferior to those called for in their specifications in order to increase their margin of profit.

20. Law enforcement officials who break laws in order to enforce others, as, for example, the common use of the so-called "third degree" as a means of securing evidence or confessions.

21. Organized bodies active in depriving citizens of their political rights, as for example, under amendments 5, 14 and 15 of the Constitution of the United States.

22. Government officials who deliberately use untruthful, misleading, and fraudulent propaganda to stir the people to a particular course of action, as for example, the manufacturing of false evidence against a nation to induce citizens to desire to declare war against it. Such activities are analogous to the sale of fur coats, oil stock, or patent medicines by the use of clever but false and misleading claims.

23. Governments that with deliberate malice aforethought disregard international law when it is expedient for them to do so.[7] Probably no great nation has been altogether free from actions of this sort. The seizure and appropriation of neutral vessels with cargoes consigned to neutral ports, the seizure and search of neutral citizens, and the forceful taking of territory from peaceful nations are examples in point. The remark of Premier Asquith that "We are not going to allow our efforts to be strangled in a network of judicial niceties . . . under existing circumstances there is no form of economic pressure to which we do not consider ourselves entitled to resort"[8] expresses precisely the attitude, if not the words, of many individual criminals of the underworld who have not been able to get what they want by legitimate means and who finally have been pushed into a tight corner by their illegitimate activities.

These are but a few examples of the criminals of the upperworld.[9] In many instances the complexity and privacy

[7] See H. E. Barnes, "Mercenary Crime and International Relations," in MacDougall, *op. cit.*

[8] Quoted in *ibid.*, p. 321.

[9] For others see such books as: J. T. Flynn, "Investment Trusts Gone Wrong"; *Time*, January 30, 1933, p. 45 and April 17, 1933, p. 34; J. T. Flynn, "Graft in Business"; F. Perkins, "The Cost of a Five Dolla Dress," *Survey*, Vol. 22, p. 75; S. Chase, "A New Deal," Ch. 1; Chas and Schlink, "Your Money's Worth"; E. D. MacDougall, Ed., "Crim

of their dealings makes a fair identification of them difficult. It is not always easy to evaluate their motives and their methods. This is especially true if our general ethical notions are befogged or dulled by the near universality of sharp, if not illegal, business practices. Yet it needs to be emphasized that the criminals of the upperworld are genuine, not metaphorical, criminals. They may not be recognized as such because we have fallen into the unjustifiable habit of limiting that appellation to the obstreperous, socially inferior denizens of the underworld; the day laborers in the field of crime.

Unlike the criminals of the underworld, the permissive criminals of the upperworld have never been marked off and dramatized as a distinct group upon which public disapproval could be focussed. They have never been rounded up by the police nor gathered together in a prison where they could be examined, crushed into some semblance of uniformity, and talked about as a special type of human beings. Instead they have been scattered among us as friends and fellow members in clubs and churches. They have contributed to organizations for the treatment of juvenile delinquents and have served in legislatures passing laws to check crime.

They differ from their more upright brethren only in being ethically less sensitive at certain points due possibly to nature and their persistent closeness to their own particular type of crime. It is doubtful if they look upon themselves as criminals. Their attitude is not likely to be self-critical and they may accept quite naïvely the happy opinion that others hold about them. Failure to be caught and brought to account keeps many of them from being jolted out of their complacency. Their conduct becomes apparent in its true light only when a crisis brings to light the details of their methods.

Possibly there are among the tolerated acts many that ought not to have been placed on the statute books as crimes. Passing a law is not always the wisest way to prevent undesirable conduct. Some acts are not easily controlled by the machinery of law enforcement. Is it possible, also, that we

for Profit"; Amer. Medical Ass'n, "Nostrums and Quackery," 2 vols.; D. T. Lynch, "Criminals and Politicians."

have been inveigled by idealists to write into the statutes an ethical code in some respects higher than that by which we care to live? Is it a guilty public conscience that prevents the rigid enforcement of laws, lest our own movements be uncomfortably restricted? Ought we to limit the criminal law to the control of antisocial acts of a crude physical sort and use different methods to control other socially undesirable activities? There seems to be little likelihood of a successful encounter with upperworld crime until issues of this sort are squarely faced.

Obviously, as the facts now stand before us, the criminals of the upperworld are real, numerous, and near at hand. It is likely that they are more costly in an economic sense than those of the underworld. They may well turn out to be more of a menace to society in every way than their less pleasant counterparts, the underprivileged criminal class. Certainly the matter of upperworld crime deserves serious study as an authentic part of the crime problem. Possibly little can be done with it short of fundamental changes in general social attitudes such as, for one example, a new economic perspective in which the competitive struggle for wealth will be secondary and will seem less desirable than a coöperative struggle for human welfare.

CRIMINALS OF THE UNDERWORLD

WE have much more data about criminals of the underworld because we have focussed our attention upon them. We cannot say that they outnumber the others nor do we know that they are more destructive. Most of our penitentiary inmates are of this group. Others who have not been convicted of serious crimes are known to the police. Their victims have given information about them. Their methods have been studied.

They drop naturally into two classes. One is the professional type composed of those who have adopted a specialized form of work with a definite technique and standards. The other consists of underworld business executives, salesmen, and general workers who are part of the machinery of organized crime. Each group has its own peculiarities based upon its work. For instance a study of persons listed in the "Who's Who of Organized Crime in Chicago"[10] discloses these interesting facts about their criminal occupations.

Nearly all of the pickpockets are Ghetto Jews, born in Russia or New York. Their average age is forty-three and they began their recorded crimes at twenty-two. Their careers are probably so long because their crimes are not of the sort that arouses hot pursuit and a clamor for vengeance. Their larcenies are small and they are discharged from the police court more frequently than other occupational groups. They travel about extensively, seldom turning their hands to other forms of crime. Pickpocketing may be an individualized occupation carried on by an operator working alone.

Other activities such as railroad and bank robbery involve small groups. The unit includes an expert safe-blower, one or two experienced individuals to do the planning and make any necessary local contacts, and perhaps also one or two apprentices. The safe-blower must be a skilled workman versed in the use of explosives. Captain Matheson of the San Francisco detective squad tells of a safe-burglar who was found with a complete formula and set of diagrams for opening safes worked out to a sixteenth of an inch. These gangs commit their crimes in widely separated spots. They rarely try other forms of crime.

Forty-five prominent criminals in the Chicago Who's Who specialized in stealing automobiles. This group is the youngest in the list, their average age being twenty-six. The known span of their criminal careers is six years. Its members are a conglomeration of nationalities from every section of the city. Apparently the larceny of automobiles is frequently but an aid to the commission of other crimes for many of these auto thieves are known as robbers and gunmen.

The twenty-six racketeers listed in the Chicago survey are a mixture of Irish, Jewish, Italian and German stock. Their average age is thirty-four and their recorded criminal careers average ten years. Many of them have never been punished and others have paid fines or escaped with light sentences to the House of Correction. Undoubtedly this is

[10] "Illinois Crime Survey," Part 3.

due to the influence of the local organizations of which they are a part. Railroad robbers, who work as isolated units and who deal with a federal rather than a local administration of justice, receive notably heavier sentences.

THE NATURE OF THE UNDERWORLD

It is clear that the habitual underworld criminal moves in a milieu that has definite characteristics of its own. Primarily it is a man's world. Its emphasis upon physical force keeps women out. Moreover those who trust in masculine strength are likely to be extremely conservative about accepting women as business partners. Male prisoners outnumber women prisoners from eight to ten times, and men are arrested perhaps fifteen times as frequently as women. To be sure women are employed as professional prostitutes and they engage in crimes like shoplifting, but their number is relatively small and their range of activities is restricted because of lack of physical vigor, agility and strength. Moreover their general background is usually such as to keep them sheltered, to restrict their opportunities, and to make them less aggressive and venturesome than men.

The criminal is usually a single man. He cannot risk home ties. His alliances are informal. He is on record and must be free to shift about from place to place. So he becomes a denizen of rooming houses and cheap hotels.

The criminal is likely to be a young man. A surprising number have not yet attained physical maturity. Those committed to institutions are probably representative of the general criminal group with a tendency to minimize the importance of the youngest groups because they are less likely to be arrested or sentenced. Even with this allowance the Bureau of the Census finds that commitments in proportion to population reach an early peak in the age period twenty-one to twenty-four and thereafter drop with advancing age. There is a sharp decline above the age of forty-five.

The spirit of youth is apparent in the boldness of modern crime. Unlawful acts are constantly committed with a reckless audacity that older persons would not dare to imitate. The escapades of modern desperadoes continually suggest a desire for action, an incautious approach, an impulsive attack. Crimes must more often be committed against the person since science has made the mechanical safeguards of property well-nigh invulnerable, so that the criminal must have recourse to deception or bold attack when goods are in transit. The older criminal is at a disadvantage before this type of competition. Gang warfare seems to shorten the careers of those who are part of the feudal system. Longer prison sentences for those who have records still further weed out all but the few who have been successful enough to act as directors rather than laborers in the field of underworld crime.

Criminals, wanderers on the frontier of society, are like other nomads, propertyless. Lawyers do not want to take their cases. Saving is not one of the criminals' habits. The lack of regularity that characterizes their whole lives appears as would be expected in their handling of funds. Their earnings come in lumps. What else can they do with their takings but spend them? Real estate investments and bank accounts are ties that bind their restless persons too closely, and they will lose them if they are caught. From their standpoint a penny spent is a penny earned. They are apt to be good cash customers for, of course, they must satisfy many of their wants by honest purchase. A pickpocket is no more likely to steal a suit of clothes than a barber is to cobble his own shoes. The opening of charge accounts invites inquiries that a criminal prefers to avoid. Unpaid bills also lead to disturbing investigations. The moral is obvious to criminals : buy only for cash.

The underworld of the criminal has its own definite organization. As a man drifts into the University Club or the Y.M.C.A. expecting to find people of a certain type so does the criminal meet his friends in his own haunts without prearrangement. He has tradesmen who will sell him tools and guns. He has an outlet for the goods he steals in the "fence" who will take them quickly off his hands for a fraction of their value and dispose of them later as best he may. Very likely the "fence" will give him a loan on the security of his word when he needs money quickly. The criminal knows which officials can be bribed, which bondsmen to get,

which lawyers are "right guys." There is nothing mysterious about these underworld connections. The criminal
learns of them and uses them as naturally as a building contractor learns where to buy his materials to advantage, which
bank will give him the largest loan, and which agent can
most satisfactorily sell his houses.

The criminal community has its own customs, different
from our own, but definite. Caste lines are rigidly drawn
even in prisons. Safe-blowers and pickpockets are on entirely different levels, and a first class stick-up man looks
with contempt upon a bag-snatcher. Each of these professions has its own technique and definite grades of skill are
recognized. Working partners must be chosen carefully for
freedom and even life may depend upon their acts. The
spoils must be divided in accordance with the risk assumed
and the ability required. Property rights within the group
must be respected. Bills must be paid. Help in the form
of loans, lies or concealment must be given against the time
that help will be needed. It is the criminals' sole basis of
credit. So it comes about that in the absence of material
securities in the form of property, criminals, dishonest and
treacherous in the eyes of their victims, magnify, among their
own kind, the virtue of loyalty. The criminal's behavior
must be his bond among his fellows. To break faith within
the group is to court disaster. It is not only treachery to be
abhorred and avenged, but it is business suicide. To be sure
criminals, like non-criminals, do sometimes violate their own
code. They become informers when their freedom hangs
upon their value to the police. However, the severity with
which such transgressions are frequently punished among
criminals only emphasizes how important loyalty is to their
safety and welfare.

How tightly this world of insecurity and force binds its
members can be surmised by anyone who has tried to escape,
even for a brief vacation, from his own. Jack Black, a former criminal, has painted for us a vivid picture of his own
struggle to free himself from obligations, squarely incurred
within the criminal community that he could not honorably
disregard as a man nor legally repay as a citizen. On several

occasions since he renounced the criminal life he has found himself not wholly free from its entanglements. Once he was called upon to shield from the police a desperately wounded fugitive who needed medical attention. This same man had previously risked his own life to take Jack Black out of jail when he was so ill with tuberculosis that he could barely walk. Now he was faced with the choice of turning his respectable back upon a criminal or of breaking the law to pay a debt in the only way it could be paid to the man who had befriended him. In this instance he chose to hide his friend until he regained his health. On other occasions his non-criminal friends have helped him to repay his debts to the underworld in legitimate ways. The criminal who is trying to go straight, and who has not yet established himself with others, has no recourse but to disregard past favors or to repay them in kind.

THE RELATION OF THE UNDERWORLD TO THE GREAT SOCIETY

IN trying to picture the characteristics of underworld criminals and their world we have emphasized peculiarities rather than similarities. Their peculiarities are most important for they determine our attitude towards them. Similarities are more extensive, for it must be remembered that the conduct which we call criminal is only a part of their nature. Likewise, the criminal community whose standards they accept is not a wholly isolated group. It borrows its customs from the great society of which it is a part and adapts them to its own needs.

In other words, we cannot think of society *and* the criminal as though the two were separated by a chasm. Criminals are an integral part of society and they carefully follow most of its rules. They may be as easily horrified by anything improper as the ordinary law-abiding citizen. They are self-supporting in their illegal way. They may have made entirely satisfactory religious adjustments. They may resent atheistic or fundamentalist propaganda. Certainly the dictates of fashion and the ceremonies of social intercourse are as binding upon them as upon non-criminals of equal intelligence and education. The following excerpts are from letters written by three different prisoners : [11]

"I may be known as a crook but not a drunk or a smoker."

"Please excuse this writing for I never could write anyway."

"One must remember that he is a gentleman, you know, keep the mud off the ladies, Sir Walter Raleigh, etc."

The natural pride of the craftsman is not absent among criminals of the professional types. A western pickpocket explained very earnestly to Lincoln Steffens that he was putting the watch *back* when he was caught. He had promised not to work in New York and he intended to keep his word ; but the sight of a new wrinkle in watch guards was an irresistible challenge to his ingenuity. His fingers itched to see what he could do with it. They won. He got the watch and was returning it to the owner's pocket when two rival New York thieves saw him and caused his arrest.[12] Another artist whose skilful safe-cracking disturbed the police of Portland, Maine, in the fall of 1932, was finally captured because he was so pleased with his exploit in opening a particularly difficult safe that he could not bear to have the feat remain anonymous. A scrawled note tacked onto the wall beside the opened strong box read,

"I opened this safe in 1 hour and 10 minutes."
"Boston Johnny" [13]

When we picture criminals as lacking in foresight or imagination, as impulsive and thoughtless, as having a satisfying ability to justify their wrongful acts, we must remember that in the criminal these traits stand out noticeably because what they fail to consider is glaringly obvious to us and what they are able to justify is shockingly improper to us. How fearfully perverted is the viewpoint of the criminal who wrote, "If I was trusted I could go straight but if I went out and got a job and I found out that the boss was suspicious of me why I would steal anything I got my hands

[11] From letters in the author's possession.

[12] L. Steffens, "Autobiography," pp. 226-229.

[13] *Boston Herald*, October 27, 1932.

on, *why shouldn't I*." [14] Yet this satisfying process of rationalization itself is not confined to criminals, nor is impulsiveness nor lack of foresight. In any factory, office, or college yard, you will see the same characteristics differently expressed in accordance with the training and opportunities of a different environment.

Only with reference to a corner of their behavior do criminals differ from non-criminals. They have not adjusted their conduct with regard to property or personal security in accordance with the socially accepted code. Insofar as this failure has also served to place them in a special class with others whose difficulty is a similar one, they develop, in addition to general social mores, a set of habits peculiarly fitted to meet the needs of their group, in the same way that physicians or lawyers add to their conduct as social human beings a code of behavior suited to their peculiar professional needs.

We fight criminals so fiercely because they, of all our social rebels, thrust straight at two of our most vulnerable points, life and property. That attack is a menace to our immediate welfare which we cannot condone. To meet it we must strip the mystery from the criminals who force it and recognize them for what they are, twisted souls that have not had the wit or strength to face the job of living squarely. They are failures of an age that hurls man a greater challenge than ever he has faced before. Opportunities, stimulations harmful and helpful pour upon him in a deluge. College deans have frequently commented upon the superior preparation and seriousness of purpose among college undergraduates of the present. The same social forces that have brought these young people to a hopeful and early intellectual maturity have made possible the youthful sophistication of those whose energies are being misdirected. Their criminality is simply one form in which man manifests his failure to meet successfully the demands of living amidst the powerful forces of the civilization which he has created.

Here is a sample of what we have been talking about :

On May 6, 1931, an automobile nosed into a blind lane at Merrick, Long Island. In it was a girl of sixteen and a

---

[14] From a letter in the author's possession. Italics, the author's.

young man whose engagement ring she had returned. He had stolen the car in order to visit her. A policeman who saw the car turn in walked up to the driver and asked to see his license. The driver reached into his coat pocket to get it. His fingers touched a revolver. Whipping it out he sent three bullets into the policeman's body. Then getting out of the machine he took the policeman's own gun and fired a last shot into his prostrate form. The murderer was New York's notorious "Two-Gun" Crowley.

Turning the car he rushed towards New York. On the way he abandoned the machine and transferring from one taxicab to another covered his retreat to a hideout on Ninetieth Street. The girl went with him. A jealous mistress tipped off the police. They came 150 strong armed with automatics, tear-gas bombs, and machine guns. For two hours he shot it out with them while crowds gaped and news cameras turned. He was taken to Bellevue Hospital still alive boasting proudly, "Anyway you didn't kill me." Inspector Sullivan had called nineteen year old Crowley "one of the most dangerous criminals at large." He was tried and found guilty of murder. In 1932 he was electrocuted at Sing Sing.

"Two-Gun" Crowley was a criminal ; the sort of criminal we yearn to stamp out ; the sort that assumes the proportions of a heroic menace in our newspapers. He makes us forget all that we have learned about unwise marriages, temper tantrums, truancy, and adolescent urges. We are not apt to link his dramatic career with such prosaic, unromantic problems. Yet "Two-Gun" Crowley and his ilk are the very persons we have been talking about throughout these last four chapters.

Crowley was the illegitimate child of a policeman and an immigrant servant. From the age of one month until he was nearly three years old he lived in a licensed boarding home. Then his foster mother, Mrs. Crowley, became ill and he was transferred to an institution for another three years. At six he was sent to school, promptly played truant, and again removed to an institution. Three years later he was given another try at public school but had to be removed. Then he ran away to his old foster home. After more truancy and some window breaking at school he was taken into juvenile court and placed on probation. Unable to get on in his regular classes he was sent to a printing class. Not until he was over fourteen was it discovered that Crowley had an I.Q. of 76, the mental rating of a borderline defective. Crowley left school at seventeen unable to read or to write simple sentences.

At seventeen he went to work as an apprentice lathe-hand. When work was good he earned a peak wage of $44 a week of which he gave half to Mrs. Crowley. He did not attend night school with the other apprentices because he was "no good at books." Small and weighing only a hundred pounds he nevertheless managed to secure the companionship of girls by stealing cars in which to take them riding. Eventually he was arrested for larceny of a car but released upon the plea of his employer who took him back into his shop. Twice after that he was arrested and dismissed. On a third occasion he was placed on probation, became involved in a shooting affray, and fled to Philadelphia to escape arrest. There he bought revolvers, blackjacks, brass knuckles and ammunition. In a run-in with the police he wounded a detective. After a brief imprisonment he came out and began a career as a "stick-up" man. He was living with a mistress but carrying on an affair with another girl who turned him down because of his bad companions. Hearing that she was in Merrick he stole a car and went out to effect a reconciliation. It was while Crowley and his girl were parked at Merrick that patrolman Hirsch asked for Crowley's license and was shot, thus starting the final spectacular chain of events leading to Crowley's arrest, conviction, and subsequent electrocution.[15]

Crowley's career is not unlike the careers of other professional thugs who menace our cities. Most of them look like pretty sorry stuff to the clinical examiner however frequently they may reign as "czars" or "master-minds" in our journals. They are dangerous; not, however, because they are able but because they are weak and warped. Many of them can be detected as dangerous personalities and checked before

[15] Abstracted from I. S. Wile, " 'Two-Gun' Crowley *vs*. The People." *Survey*, February 1, 1932.

they reach adult years. Able criminals do not use physical violence. They do not wish to thrust their businesses into the foci of our attentions. Consequently they are apt to be pleasant fellows to meet socially, as the Crowleys are not. They are more difficult to identify and check in the making. Yet among both groups our chances of prevention seem considerably brighter than our hope of turning any appreciable number of adult offenders away from their course. We might well have diverted Crowley's energies into useful channels if we had the machinery for making our present knowledge applicable to such cases. It would therefore seem wise for us to make a valiant attempt to recognize and build up among us those agencies likely to prevent the emergence of criminals in our society.

PART THREE — THE PREVENTION OF
CRIMINAL BEHAVIOR

The punishment of a crime cannot be just, (that is, necessary) if the laws have not endeavored to prevent that crime by the best means which times and circumstances would allow.—MARQUIS DE BECCARIA

C'est sur l'enfance et la jeunesse qu'il faut agir. Toute measure pénale qui ne commence pas d'abord par l'amélioration de l'enfant est nutile.—A. LACASSAGNE

CHAPTER X

THE PREVENTION OF CRIMINAL BEHAVIOR: GENERAL METHODS

THE IMPORTANCE OF CRIME PREVENTION

IF every criminal in the country were executed today, even that unthinkable act would only temporarily and incompletely check crime. The same processes that brought those unfortunates into being would create a new crop of wrongdoers to take their place. Penalties for crime are necessary, but we must also remember that they are negative. Treating crime by punishing criminals is like bailing out a leaky boat ; the more water that is thrown out the easier it is for more to pourt in. The sensible remedy is to plug the holes as well as may be — and still continue to bail the boat. It is not the water that needs attention, it is the hole.

Exactly the same reasoning can be turned upon this problem of crime. The pain of the criminals' presence first called our attention to them but we could not discover what makes criminals until we followed their histories. Once their sources are known the way to combat criminals is to prevent their creation. But it is difficult to arouse interest in something that has not happened. It takes the event itself to win our belated attention. A half dozen people may view a demonstration of fire prevention, but half the town will turn out to see a fire.

Preventive methods may be thought of as general and specific. In this chapter we shall consider only general methods.

Any movement that lifts the level of human conduct in some measure touches and reduces crime, and therefore merits the criminologist's encouragement. His own efforts, however, will need to be concentrated on those factors that most directly build up criminal habits of thought and action. It is from our study of criminals-in-the-making that we have garnered the evidence, however inadequate, to direct the development of preventive work.

CRIME PREVENTION AND FAMILY LIFE

WHOLESOME family life is unquestionably an important factor in preventing the appearance of criminals. The first step in achieving it is the prevention of unwise, hasty, and ill-considered marriages. We do not yet know enough about human beings to predict in every case what unions should be forbidden and therefore it is necessary to be conservative in our interference with the lives of others. Yet proceeding with all due caution it is still possible to throw about the marriage relation better safeguards than we now have.

Common law marriages based upon mutual consent, followed by cohabitation, are still valid in 24 states. Such marriages are not solemnized in any regular form and the state has no record of them. Twelve states allow the marriage of girls at twelve, and thirteen allow the marriage of boys at fourteen with parental consent. That parental ignorance or indifference does in fact permit and even arrange such marriages, chiefly among girls, is to be seen in the fact that not only are there more than 12,000 married girls of fifteen in our population but there are some who were married, contrary to even our low legal standard, as early as eleven years of age.[1]

[1] See Richmond and Hall, "Child Marriages," and "Marriage and the State," for detailed figures and illustrative cases.

In general, state supervision of marriages is lax and the legal standards of marriage are low. There are no adequate checks upon the marriages of children or the mentally or physically sick. Hasty marriages and ill-considered marriages are common. People marry on the spur of the moment when they are drunk or out on a lark. They marry because they are frightened or because they have been dared. They marry partners they have known for two days or two hours and later find them to be burglars, prostitutes, or bigamists.[2]

Fifty per cent (as contrasted with 11.2 per cent in the general population) of 500 inmates of the Massachusetts Reformatory for Women recently studied by the Gluecks were married under eighteen years of age and 12.3 per cent (as contrasted with .4 per cent in the general population) were married between twelve and sixteen. In 31.2 per cent of these cases the husbands were "pick-ups" and in 29 per cent casual acquaintances. More than 13 per cent knew their husbands less than a month. In more than a third of the cases the marriages were "forced" by parents, clergymen, or others to save convention (at what grievous cost!). The resulting conjugal relations were poor in more than four-fifths of these marriages.[3]

The effects of this state of affairs in producing poor homes, broken homes, unwanted children, exploited children and similar evils is obvious. The relation of these factors to crime has already been emphasized. Here is one point at which general preventive work needs to be done. The methods and specific remedies that seem most promising have already been outlined by workers in the field of marriage reform. The first step is for the welfare agencies that are acquainted with these facts to make the public aware of them and of their significance. Intelligent interest in each community will itself serve to improve many conditions with-

[2] See Richmond and Hall, "Marriage and the State," for cases and for an illuminating discussion of this entire problem based upon field studies done under the auspices of the Russell Sage Foundation.

[3] Data taken from S. S. and E. T. Glueck, "500 Delinquent Women." The writer is indebted to the authors for permission to read this study in manuscript, and to Alfred A. Knopf, Inc., authorized publishers, for permission to take from it this summarized material.

out a resort to new legislation. Necessary laws may be passed later when education has made them possible as a free expression of public sentiment against the few who will only respond to coercion.

After a new family has been founded the relations between parents and children are of the greatest significance to the criminologist. Birth itself is frequently an injustice. All too often children are born to parents who for reasons of health or economics do not want or should not have them. Some married people in good health who can afford children do not like them even though they may have one. It is an unfortunate trick of fate that brings a child into such homes. In all of these cases the circumstance that is likely to lead towards delinquency and crime is not the poverty or lack of care, although these may enter, but the child's own feeling that he is not wanted and does not rightfully belong in the family circle.

The remedy for this evil is to make contraceptive information available to all married persons who wish to use it through their family physicians. Science has not yet discovered a perfect means of controlling births within the family but clinics now working in the United States, as well as those abroad, are on the way towards that discovery. In the meantime it should be made possible for doctors to diagnose the individual needs of their own patients and to prescribe for them from among the methods that have already proved highly successful in clinical practice. Permission to do so would simply give to families that want it a greater mastery of their own destinies. Those who would use their new knowledge to have the children they want come when they are able to receive and care for them properly would benefit inestimably. It is doubtful if those who would use it to remain childless would be any great loss as parents. The plea that it would increase immorality is difficult to justify.

Those who worry about the spread of power to irresponsible young people must remember that bootleg information is available to all intelligent adolescents today. Because of psychological factors and differences in the frequency of intimacies the faulty methods popularly used seem to be more efficient in preventing conception outside of marriage than within. Furthermore young people are apt to have such unwarranted confidence in their own knowledge that they emulate the fools who step in where angels fear to tread.

When children have arrived, any means of helping parents to meet their responsibilities successfully will also prevent the development of delinquents and criminals by giving the children a better chance to form good habits of thought and action during their formative years when the family influence dominates them. The fact that some children respond to evil forces indicates a plasticity that invites good influences to take their turn.

Professor Groves has spoken of homes as good, bad and bewildered. Most American homes seem to fall into the last class. It is unquestionably true that the rapid change from a rural to an urban way of life has brought parents face to face with so many new problems that they really want aid in meeting them. Common sense and good will is not enough. Whatever sound advice child guidance clinics can give them directly or through books and magazines about child training in general and more specifically about the prevention and care, of behavior disorders in children, if applied, should be a potent preventive of crime.

The United States Children's Bureau, state divisions of child hygiene, public health, and education, state universities, habit clinics, and child guidance clinics now numbering over 600 in this country are resources for parents to draw upon. Institutes of family relations, capably manned, to give premarital advice and to counsel with family members about problems of family adjustment may come to be of great value in the maintenance of wholesome behavior. The fact that perplexed parents frequently visit probation officers, and other court attachés, clergymen, teachers, and physicians, for help with family problems involving children, is evidence of the service that trained, sympathetic, and trusted institute staffs might render. In 1934, New York City, Dayton, Los Angeles, Cleveland, Detroit, and Washington had centers devoting their entire efforts to family relations problems.

Unfortunately knowledge alone, however extensive, will

not make good parents. Fears and prejudices, loves an
hates may do damage that all the world's logic cannot undo
A child whose parents are bitter and defeated may reflec
these moods so that he can never face the world squarely
The only hope for this evil is that experiences outside wil
somewhat offset those of the home to the benefit of th
second generation if not of the first.

Of course, information, no matter how valuable, will no
solve problems. Only persons can do that. There is n
substitute for courage and common sense in the parent
The responsibility of sorting out and applying proffere
ideas to their individual difficulties rests squarely with then
The modern deluge of psychological theories about chil
care may even become a curse to homes that indiscriminatel
accept hypotheses and verified data alike as the words of
scientific Jehovah. The popularization of psychology seem
to have sorted out families into three groups : those wh
can profitably use the new knowledge ; those who ignore
through ignorance ; and those bewildered but determine
who can confuse labelling with explanation and accept ex
planation as excuse until the home becomes a positive menac
to the adult adjustment of its children. The slow stead
effort of every honest educational agency is needed to hel
us to increase the proportion of real knowledge in that mix
ture of good common sense, diluted science, superstition
normal affection and misunderstood psychology by whic
children are now brought up.

Some families are so disorganized by sickness, poverty
crime and ignorance that they are not capable of proper self
management. They contribute more than their quota t
the population of our penal institutions. Family welfar
societies, that are doing heroic work in rebuilding such home
and in connecting them with the social resources of thei
communities, are making an energetic flank attack on crim
The case of "Emmy" reported by the Family Welfare Sc
ciety of Boston is but one example in many of an agency'
recovery of a family failure :

"Emmy, at ten years old, was a child after the good Victoria
own heart. Her pigtails hung to her waist ; her woolen dresses ha
tight, buttoned bodices and long, full skirts in an era when fashio

escribed for little girls Dutch cuts and the briefest of muslin ruffles
ove bare knees.

"'Don't you think you ought to dress Emmy more like other chil-
en?' The Family Welfare Society visitor asked her mother.

"Mrs. Stone was offended.

"'Emmy's all right,' she insisted. 'She's happy. As for her
othes — her pa likes 'em as they are. He's always had a hanker-
g for sewing, and when we took Emmy . . . yes, we took her
ght after her own ma died. We were gettin' along in years an'
e'd always wanted a baby . . . well, as I was sayin', the first thing
er pa did was to make her a dress. I always remember him layin'
e baby on the floor so's to cut out a pattern by her. (He uses the
me pattern still, only bigger.) I'll show you the dress some day ;
's a real handsome shade of purple. She's so fair, she looked awful
retty in it. He was that proud of her ! . . Her pa and me, we
now what's best for Emmy — he has lots of ideas an' I do what he
ys. We want her to be a steady child.'

"Neighbors said of the Stones, 'They're queer as they make 'em !'
Ir. and Mrs. Stone were past middle age, old-fashioned, slow of
nderstanding, and distrustful of all new ideas. The visitor saw
em often, for Mr. Stone had serious heart trouble, and his wife
epended upon her for advice and help during his frequent illnesses.
inally he had to give up work, and the Society arranged for an
llowance from the city to support the family.

"Every one used to worry about Emmy, bubbling over with en-
usiasm and allowed none of the pleasures her schoolmates had.
Ier parents walled her off from the world, and expected her to
end her time caring for them and playing with the cats and the
og, who was like another child in the family. Nothing could make
em see that protection from temptation was not enough, that they
ust fill her life with interests absorbing enough to take the place
f the fun they denied her. It was clear enough to every one else
at Emmy intended to have fun ; and there were disquieting stories
the neighborhood about her way of finding it. Attempts to talk
ings over with Mr. and Mrs. Stone were in vain, for they resented
ggestions. Summer camp, vacation in a carefully chosen home,
embership in a Home Library group, recreation through the church
— each proposal was vetoed by Mr. Stone. Only twice did he re-
ent — once to let Emmy go to the circus with the minister, again
permit her to go to *Peter Pan* with the visitor.

"Things changed after Mr. Stone's death. Gone were the long
raids and the long skirts ; but there, as far as Mrs. Stone was con-
erned, the change ended. Her husband's prejudices still ruled her
fe.

"Emmy, however, was restive. Apparently demure at home, outside she did much as she pleased, secure in her belief that her mother would never know what was going on or do anything about it if she did know. Her teachers liked her, but complained that she made little effort to do well, and that she showed poor judgment in choosing her friends. Perhaps she had no choice, for she was not allowed to bring boys or girls to her home, even those whom she met in the dancing class and the club which the visitor, backed by the minister, had finally persuaded her mother to let her join. The street corner offered companionship without criticism ; and she made up for her lack of an allowance by using the money intended for the Sunday School collection, covering her action by a series of ingenious fibs. After this theft was discovered, Mrs. Stone yielded and sent Emmy to a church camp for a month — a month of happiness undermined each week by letters reproaching the child for leaving her mother alone in the city.

"A year ago the crash came. Repeated misbehaviour, involving several boys and girls, brought Emmy into court. For a time it was feared she would be sent to a state training school — a solution which, curiously enough, her mother favored, on the ground that she had heard such schools were 'lovely places where girls have music lessons and never have to lift a finger.' After listening to what Emmy had to say, however, and consulting the Family Welfare Society, the minister, and the worker from the children's agency in whose charge she had been placed when she last ran away, the judge offered her a chance to make a fresh start.

"Emmy is now a ward of the children's society to which her mother had more than once been urged to trust her. She writes affectionately to her mother, but she is happier away from her, living with friendly people and earning her room and board and a little money by caring for a child that she loves. Last fall she entered high school with colors flying, and her teachers all speak well of her. It is hard, now and then, for her to realize that it is not necessary to scheme and deceive in order to enjoy legitimate fun, but she feels that making good is worth the effort." [4]

PREVENTING CRIME THROUGH THE SCHOOLS

THE latent opportunity to do preventive work against criminals through the schools needs also to be explored. The public school system is the first social agency that is in a

[4] *Family Welfare*, April 18, 1932. A weekly bulletin of the Family Welfare Society of Boston. Quoted by permission.

position to identify all of our physically, mentally and socially defective children and to sort them out for appropriate treatment. Certainly the schools offer a far more promising point for handling the crime problem than the courts or our penal institutions that must wait until the weaklings mature into full-fledged social liabilities.

Clinical facilities for the thorough study of every child upon his entry into the school system and for checking his condition thereafter would prove to be a wise and economical investment. Traveling clinics could serve the smaller schools. In Massachusetts such clinics regularly examine all school children three or more years retarded. The staff consists of a psychiatrist, a psychologist and a social worker who are assisted by a teacher and the school nurse. The nurse takes the family, personal and economic, social and moral history of the pupil before the clinic arrives. The psychiatrist makes the physical examination and also takes the clinical history of the child. A complete psychological examination is made by the psychologist.

Upon the basis of findings in ten fields of inquiry the staff makes its final recommendations. The labelling of pupils is avoided. This is the sort of analysis that might be extended to all children with profit to themselves, their families, and to society. It would bring to light not only the personality defects of the child but also any environmental factors that might be a hindrance to his success. There is surely as much reason to check the condition and capacities of a child facing the world as there is to check the condition of an automobile before sending it out on the road.

If the work of a diagnostic clinic is to be made most useful, facilities for the care of those who need definite treatment must be at hand. Means of remedying physical ailments can usually be found. Institutional care for the feeble-minded, who need commitment, is becoming more generally available. It is for the eccentric, worried, morose, defiant, excessively shy, and slightly subnormal children that adequate care is lacking ; and also for those whose social background is a detriment to their welfare. For them some provision will have to be sought. Chicago made a start in this field through the establishment, during 1929 and 1930,

of special day schools for behavior problem children, manne
by special staffs supplemented by regular psychiatrical aid

The visiting teacher movement whose work was starte
in 1906–1907 in New York, Boston and Hartford simu.
taneously, by private aid, is one promising means of helpin
children whose difficulties come to the surface in schoo
The movement has since spread into ninety centers in fiftee
states and has become, in most of them, a part of the cit
public school system. It might easily be linked with th
work of a diagnostic clinic.

The majority of the visiting teachers, now working, ar
former instructors who have had special training and ex
perience in social work. Their knowledge of school re
quirements and of teachers' viewpoints on the one hand
and of family and neighborhood conditions on the othei
makes them exceedingly useful liaison officers between th
home and the school. Children are referred to the visitin
teacher because of maladjustments in scholarship, advers
home conditions, misconduct, and irregular attendance, c
because they are gifted and need special opportunities. Th
work is not limited to the poor but cuts across economic line
as do the problems with which it is concerned. The visit
ing teacher is expected to do a thorough piece of social work
calling to her assistance whatever community resources ma
be available in an effort to understand and remove the caus
of the trouble. In practice the visiting teacher seems t
have two main tasks. One is to gain a real insight into th
personality of the child as a basis for intelligent schoo
training. The other is to remove or minimize the influenc
of adverse social conditions such as bad companions, parenta
neglect, lack of recreational opportunities and so on.

In towns that have little likelihood of getting such profes
sional aid much might be done in solving persistent conduc
problems in school by a standing committee composed per
haps of the school principal, a clergyman, a policeman, th
school nurse, and a member of the board of overseers o
the public welfare. The effectiveness of such a committe
would, of course, depend not upon the offices represente
but upon the interest and intelligence of its member
Granted these qualities in fair measure, this group coul

ring the full resources of the community to bear upon each
ase. Incidentally, the leaven that each member of this
ommittee would carry back into his own field of work
ould broaden and interrelate the viewpoints of every wel-
are group in town with a corresponding improvement in
heir usefulness.

One factor sometimes neglected in a study of maladjusted
children in school is the teaching staff. Habit clinics soon
became aware that the disturbing conduct of pre-school children is most often caused by unwise parents. We have as
et hardly noticed that the problem child in school may in
ome measure be due to the problem teacher.

Every college instructor is aware that many graduates
ach year accept teaching positions because they do not know
hat else they can do. Some of them find that they like
he work. Others hate it and long to escape from it. Many
f them unfortunately for their pupils "don't mind teach-
ng."

In many school systems married women are not permitted
o teach. No one can deny the benefits that children have
ained from the devoted services of those who have not
xperienced motherhood but it is unwise to overlook in
hose who have not made the natural transferences of affec-
on incident to growing up, the possibilities of emotional
isorders sufficient to handicap them, particularly as high
chool teachers.

Miss Lehrer, a high school teacher, admired from afar a local
minister whom she had met but once. She detected in his reading
f the scripture a subtle way of expressing his affection for her.
One of his sermons was interpreted as a promise of marriage at the
nd of the school term. At that time Miss Lehrer visited him to
et the matter settled and was overwhelmed by his ignorance which
he felt was dishonesty.

Later Miss Lehrer went to a summer conference and faced a
imilar experience with a lecturer whose remarks to his audience
ere taken by her to have a personal reference. Her disillusion-
ment was followed by deep depression which gave way to activity
nd high enthusiasm with the reopening of school activities into
which she plunged with vigor. During the year she disagreed
with the school authorities over teaching methods in the town. She
esigned at the end of the term to study for her master's degree.

There are other teachers who have suffered during thei
college years from the conflict between earlier beliefs, fos
tered by their parents, and the content of their colleg
courses. These students have revolted against the cor
spiracy of silence that left them vulnerable to such a shocl
Religion and sex, in particular, are likely to be their wea
spots. Our schools employ them as teachers whose joy
is to expound the truth, let the weaklings fall where the
may. Yet so eager are they to destroy absurdities that the
work becomes an emotional campaign to crush misconcer
tions, rather than a studied plan for the wise guidance c
their pupils. Like the "professional lad" of whom Frank
wood Williams speaks they are attempting to grow u
themselves but have not quite succeeded and they ar
responding subconsciously to their partial failure. "See m
long pants. Why don't you ask your mother to get yo
some long pants? You don't like long pants. Aw, you'r
such a kid!"[5]

Many pupils are saved because they are intellectually ir
capable of being touched by the barbed evangelism of suc
teachers. Others understand but rebel against any log
that threatens their established beliefs. But a considerabl
number turn against those who have hurt them by witl
holding from them the truth and attempt to break the cod
that ignorance was expected to safeguard.

The remedy here is to have the schools manned by whole
some, vivacious teachers, married and unmarried, who enjo
their work. This will require a much more thorough ex
amination of applicants than is now made with emphas
upon the personality of the teacher rather than upon lengt
of experience. Teachers who can get their classroom wor
done in an atmosphere approaching that of life outside ar
to be preferred to those whose pupils behave like autom
atons. It might be well for any teacher who consistentl
has trouble with her pupils to seek the counsel of a psy
chiatrist about her own condition.

As mental hygiene clinics become an accepted part of th
services of a college to its students, perhaps those who ar
notably unfitted to teach will be steered away from tha

[5] F. Williams, "Putting Away Childish Things," *Survey*, April 1, 192&

profession before graduation. A brief course in psychiatry would be a positive advantage to prospective teachers as a means of equipping them, not to treat but to recognize, when they see them, the truly important symptoms of conduct maladjustment. At present their perspective upon behavior traits is distinctly out of line with that gained by psychiatrists through clinical experiences.[6]

Of course, the community cannot expect to get $5000 teachers for $1000, nor to receive the greatest service from those employed if they are bound by salaries that will not permit them the books, the study, and the travel that they need to insure their continuous growth. The work of the teacher is far more exacting and important than that of the average business man (parents who cannot manage two children think it easy for teachers to manage thirty) and cannot safely be entrusted to mediocre persons. A poor teaching staff in the finest of modern school plants cannot hold a candle to a group of wholesome, capable, interesting teachers in an old and worn-out shack.

Curriculum changes may seem far removed from the problem of crime but in reality their importance as a preventive is altogether too great to be overlooked. Our attention has already been called to the number of children who escape from the tedium of the classroom as soon as the law will allow without any definite means of earning a living, but still able to want automobiles, movies and girls. To them, and to others who do not escape but are graduated unfit to make their own way, the school owes a duty.

Many voices have been raised within the last few years to proclaim that a course of studies designed for genteel folk living in an earlier day is not suited to the masses in this urban age, but the task of remodeling the curriculum thus far has presented so many difficulties that change has consisted chiefly in crowding in new courses on top of the old. This cannot go on indefinitely. The times await a leader with sufficient courage, wisdom, and influence to start a movement for determining the objectives of modern public schools as a basis for a complete curriculum revision.

It would be foolish to predict the changes that would be

[6] See E. K. Wickman, "Children's Behavior and Teachers' Attitudes."

found necessary but a hint of some apparent needs may throw light on the way in which they would be a preventive of criminal careers. The objectives of the new school, shared to some extent with other agencies, might look like this :

1. To establish the health of pupils and to teach them how to maintain it.

2. To teach pupils how to be self-supporting. The fact that correspondence schools get a million and a half new students each year, about five times as many as are registered for degrees in the colleges and universities of the country, indicates that training to earn a livelihood is a widespread need of adults.

3. To prepare children for wholesome marriage and family life. Since 1890 the percentage of the population that is married has steadily increased. Eighty per cent of persons between 35-45 are married. Of the other twenty per cent some are widowed or divorced. Divorces are 15 times more numerous than in 1870 in a population 3 times as great.

4. To prepare pupils to take an active intelligent interest in their government.

5. To prepare pupils for a wise enjoyment of their leisure time. Increasing leisure seems to be one of the certainties of the future.

Under such aims algebra might disappear from the high school. Biology, sociology and art in several forms might come well to the fore. A minimum of academic training and a maximum of real industrial work would need to be provided for the mentally subnormal and perhaps certain other types. Some vocations would be taught even in the grammar school so that those pupils who do not go to high school may not be thrown unto the world altogether un-equipped to earn a living. Whatever the changes might be the result would be a school so close to the child's real needs and interests that the ordinary pupil would want to receive its instruction. Misconduct in and out of school would decrease. Truancy would become less frequent. Children would be better prepared to meet life squarely and to enjoy living it honestly.

A further development of the school's work has already appeared in the vocational guidance movement through which the more progressive institutions try to discover the aptitudes of their pupils and to acquaint them with fields of

ork that offer a real promise to them. It is an obvious
ut generally disregarded truth that parents and friends
re constantly turning young people towards their first jobs
ithout any consideration of their opportunities or of the
pplicants' fitness.

Conversations with young people at work will soon make
lear that a particular job was accepted because "my brother
orks there," "the boss is a neighbor of mine and he said
e'd get me in," or "I heard that they needed a boy." Even
ollege graduates are not usually aware of the variety of
obs that men and women actually do, the preparation and
ualifications required, their rewards, nor whether they have
he necessary aptitudes to meet these conditions.

No one would be so foolhardy as to say that it is possible
o predetermine the life work of one who has not been
ested outside of the classroom, but it is possible to give to
pupil who leaves school at any age a more thorough in-
ght into his own aptitudes and the chances for their use
han young work-seekers usually get. The ever present
anger that vocational guidance may harden into a sort of
ocational predestination must always be guarded against by
broader knowledge of a person's background and a deeper
sight into human motives than any standardized tests can
ive. The square peg in the round hole is always an irri-
ated misfit whether placed there by chance or by careful
isdirection.

Yet, in spite of the harm from a possible overzealous ap-
lication of green knowledge, alluring values seem to lie
n making it an inherent part of the school's job to show
hose about to go to work the multitude of ways in which
en earn a living; and then not only to gauge for each
dividual the chances that surround his self-expressed in-
erests but also to help him by encouragement, counsel and
onnections to attain them.

CRIME PREVENTION THROUGH IMPROVED INDUSTRIAL RELATIONS

NOTHER favorable point at which to make a flank attack
n crime is in the field of business relations. The part

played by industrial conflict, unemployment, unwholesome employment, and irresponsible business practices in producing criminals has already been discussed. If these unsatisfactory conditions could be removed without allowing greater evils to slip into their places another set of criminal breeding influences would be destroyed.

How the fundamental problems accompanying industrial change can be met is a question still to be solved. Economic facts cannot be avoided. Evils are not all man made. Yet there lingers the suspicion that great improvements in human relations could be made in the working world if industrial leaders and workers shared a greater measure of social responsibility. As R. H. Tawney points out in his stimulating book, "The Acquisitive Society," strikes, lockouts and wage disputes persist because industry denies any purpose but the satisfaction of those who take part in it. Each group gets what it can, subject to no limit except that imposed by economic laws. Wealth is distributed not only for work performed but also in even greater measure for the accident of birth, social position, and inherited wealth. Rewards are out of all proportion to services rendered. We worship riches regardless of their origin and not because they are just reward for services rendered. The man who makes a million dollars is a success whether the goods he sells are honestly made and represented or not.

The remedy Tawney suggests is easy to understand, and difficult to apply : make the chief aim in business, as in the professions, the performance of a function. Doctors are expected, first of all, to be interested in service. If physicians increased their prices during an epidemic they would be unhesitatingly condemned. Why should the man who sells coal to a hospital get all that he can for it while the physician who works in the hospital is expected to measure his income by services performed and then take less if those who need his help cannot afford to pay for them ? Those who would sincerely seek a remedy for industrial warfare will need to give serious consideration to the idea that industry is a social agency and can only justify those parts of its code that contribute to the general welfare. The need of commercial amusement agencies to recognize a social esponsibility to keep their places from becoming standing nvitations to those who are seeking opportunities for delinuencies is another aspect of this same problem.

Recent economic history has given us more than a hint nat there is need for us to ponder a bit over the objectives f an economic system. Our sense of values needs drastic evision if we are to control industrialism for the benefit of nan rather than sacrifice our well-being to our lust for gold f which crime is, in so large a measure, merely a distorted eflection.

Short of a fundamental change in our economic system, list of business improvements that would have a part in ecreasing crime might include:

1. The use of scientific methods of determining the qualificaons of job applicants and the assignment of men to their tasks.

2. The development of a genuine coöperative program beween industry and the schools.

3. An adequate number of ably managed free government mployment agencies such as the department of labor has been atmpting to establish.

4. The reduction of seasonal and technological unemployment irough improved management aided by the building of previously lanned public works to take up the slack in times of depression.

5. The development of unemployment insurance and unemoyment reserves.

6. Progress in coöperative worker-employee management.

7. The development of programs of interstitial employment nd craft training.

8. The enforcement and improvement of the laws regulating ie work of women and children.

9. Education of the public and of retail sales-organizations in re proper use of credit buying and selling.

10. Minimum wage laws, at least in certain industries.

11. Some means of counteracting the deadening monotony of ainutely standardized work with interest and self-respect.

GOVERNMENTAL AGENCIES OF CRIME PREVENTION

EVERAL governmental agencies, apart from those dealing /ith the administration of criminal justice, are important in the field of preventive criminology. The National Congress and the state legislatures are constantly enacting regulatory laws, not aimed at criminals, that nevertheless are of decided importance to the criminologist. The restriction of immigration by federal law and the enactment by most states of some form of a Mothers' Pension Law designed to prevent the breakup of homes are examples in point.

The United States Children's Bureau, established by Congress in 1912, is constantly studying many aspects of child life and its bulletins serve to keep every social agency aware of the facts about child welfare in the United States and alert to dangers that must be confronted. Facts disclosed by the Children's Bureau have been the basis for federal, state and private activities designed to protect children and to conserve home life.

Governmental interest in matters affecting the general welfare is likely to grow as urban life decreases man's isolation. In 1920, 1,437,783 children in the United States between seven and thirteen years of age were not in school. Most of them were child laborers working in those states where callous industries and ignorant parents are still allowed to make future handicaps for society. In the depression year of 1930 there were still 667,118 children between the ages of 10 and 15 employed in gainful occupations. Under the National Industrial Recovery Act child labor except under very restricted conditions was temporarily forbidden. A movement to give the federal government the constitutional right to control child labor is now under way. This is one manner in which governmental interest in the welfare of young people may act as an important general preventive of crime.

COMMUNITY AGENCIES OF CRIME PREVENTION

COMMUNITY organizations that try to influence human conduct are legion. Their methods overlap considerably but, nevertheless, fall roughly into five groups. Some like the Church School, rely chiefly upon exhortation. Americanization groups, civic leagues, mental hygiene societies and the like depend upon education. The Y.M.C.A., Boy Scouts nd the like rely upon guidance. Schools for subnormal children control through habit training and supervision. Planning boards and housing associations influence persons by changing their physical surroundings.

The point of attack as well as the method varies. The Church School, the Boy Scouts and the Y.M.C.A. approach the child himself. Americanization classes and mental hygiene brochures teach adults who must deal with children. Housing associations attack environmental influences that may harmfully affect conduct.

It is difficult to estimate the extent to which these organizations help to prevent crime. Unlike the home or the school they touch directly only a part of each community and very likely the groups that they influence are those who least need their help. Organizations like the Boy Scouts, Y.M.C.A., Y.W.C.A., Boys' Clubs and Church Schools attract but a small proportion of the normal young people of a neighborhood, and they generally turn away the troublesome and disturbing children who are of most importance to the criminologist.

In New York about 2 per cent of the girls of scout age are actually members of the Girl Scouts. The Boys' Club Federation reports that 79 per cent of the boys in Chicago remain untouched by any community organization. In a Brooklyn area studied by a subcommittee of the New York Crime Commission, 51 churches, 4 schools having playgrounds, 2 regular playgrounds, 4 settlements and 14 Scout troops together served a total of only 5166 children out of a total population of 49,846 young people under 21 years of age.

On the other hand, we have had enough experience to know that any provision made for the wholesome use of a child's energy and talents may keep those who are actually reached away from influences strong enough to turn any ordinary child towards damaging habits. It is not possible to accept the exaggerated claims sometimes made by playground directors and others of startling success in decreasing misconduct but it is undoubtedly true that the delinquency rate tends to be lowest in those areas that are best served by supervised play spaces. Where boys' clubs have been able to corral boys' gangs and turn their energies and interest into constructive channels, their delinquencies, at least, hav been minimized. Individuals who have seemed surel pointed towards criminal careers have been redirected int better paths by the efforts of social workers who have happil linked them up with wholesome local movements.

The effectiveness of any of these groups depends so muc upon specific local conditions such as the quality of leader ship, type and proportion of the population influenced, co operation with other welfare agencies, and so on, that it i hazardous to attempt to rate them in the order of thei importance in preventing crime. In general, however, i seems safe to say that insofar as they reach potential delin quents, groups that actively assist children in making rea adjustments to real situations are much more important tha those that rely upon abstract teaching or ethical appeal However, adolescents undoubtedly need help in formulatin a philosophy of life which will be satisfying and which wil give them a faith in that which is beyond reason to cling tc The church here has an opportunity to come to grips wit a vital human need. Man must have the strength that i rooted in a faith compatible with his knowledge. Adoles cents particularly challenge the church to help them to fin a stabilizing faith.

PUBLIC OPINION AS A PREVENTIVE FORCE

APART from the expression of community spirit, through it many organizations, the general cast of public feeling in community is a force that cannot be left out of our reckor ing. Previously we have noticed that in those city area where a transient population makes a well-defined publi opinion impossible delinquencies reach their peak. W recognize the influence of local sentiment every day as w see the trend of the news from staid New England town wealthy, restless New York, Southern mountain commun ties, Mexico-bordered El Paso and mushroom cities lik Detroit and Los Angeles. Careful observers have ofte noticed in passing from town to town that areas having abou an equal number of inhabitants at the same economic leve differ markedly in civic pride and in capacity for self-government.

Two New England towns bordered a manufacturing city in which most of the men worked as factory hands. The houses in both communities were wooden box-like affairs. In Alpha the small lawns were trimmed and every house had its little backyard garden in which the men could generally be found after suppertime. The boys played ball in a nearby field. In Beta the lawns were unmowed and the yards were strewn with rubbish. A knot of men, young and old, could always be found in the town square. Women disliked to walk through the center at night because of the comments openly made about them as they passed. Shopkeepers suffered from vandalism. Although the young men played baseball here, as in Alpha, a group of them could always be found shooting craps behind one of the stores. Four members of this group were eventually committed to juvenile correctional institutions.

Just what causes such differences, when wealth and educational opportunities are not factors, is hard to say. Perhaps communities, like persons, may be thought of as having temperaments compounded out of the intelligence, training and traditions of their members, and once the tone of a community is established it attracts to it those who can be comfortable in its atmosphere and repels those who would find its way of life distressing.

There are other towns, fewer in number but more spectacular in their influence, that are little better than moral sewers due basically to the repeated inbreeding of degenerate stocks. Out of them come poverty, crime, illegitimacy and a host of lesser evils. Few states have been able to escape the burdens arising from such groups as the Pineys, the Nams, the Jukes, the Kallikaks and the Hill Folk whose wretched careers have been so destructive of all human values.

Probably there is no specific remedy for low community standards. Degeneracy due to defective stock can be overcome by the improvement of marriage requirements along eugenic lines and by social service work that would include the breaking up of such village units by the segregation of those who are commitable in institutions. Communities where the evils are not so vividly marked will probably change little until the expansion of neighboring populations forces new blood upon them sufficiently aggressive to upset old traditions and institute new standards.

This method of improvement might be brought about consciously and with greater speed if a spot map showing the crime rate for an entire state were made and then used by public and private welfare agencies as a basis for concentrating their efforts where they are most needed. If the many organizations, now doing constructive work with young people, were to see their opportunities through the eyes of the criminologist and were to take the initiative in placing their resources strategically where they are needed, although not requested, the agencies more directly interested in crime prevention would gain a powerful ally.

Also there is great need for an enlightened public opinion upon the subject matter of criminology to replace the prejudice that stamps delinquents and criminals as bad without reference to the chance happenings that bring them to court. There is need for the public to accept the viewpoint that criminality is understandable and can be treated rationally. It is no more mysterious, no more an act of God than an epidemic of influenza. Our only hope to eradicate either crime or influenza lies in the willingness of the public to support with confidence and patience those agencies that are laboriously searching out causes and experimenting with promising cures.

CHAPTER XI

THE PREVENTION OF CRIMINAL BEHAVIOR: SPECIFIC METHODS

A PERMANENT STATE DEPARTMENT OF CRIMINOLOGY

DIRECT methods of preventing crime can succeed only insofar as they fight real criminals and real sources of crime instead of mythical bogies. Yet every organization that has tried to get the facts that will enable them to prevent crime has discovered how tricky current information is. One reason for this condition is that the agencies dealing with particular parts of the crime problem disagree whole-heartedly about methods, aims and basic assumptions. They have no common philosophy with respect to crime control. Police departments, juvenile and adult courts, lawyers, psychiatrists, penal administrators are all striving to reach independent ends. The word "criminal" has a different connotation to each of them and stirs up a variety of conflicting emotions. As a result, our agencies of crime-control work in a discouraging mess of cross-purposes, getting in each other's way and sometimes consciously thwarting one another for the sheer glory of disconcerting the other fellow. There is an urgent need for some means of welding them together into an integrated, coöperative, workable, combination for the prevention and control of criminal behavior.

It is also true that facts about crime are not static. They change day by day like the conditions in the textile industry or the automobile business. We need to take an inventory and establish a comprehensive and permanent accounting system in criminology. Of course police departments, courts, penal institutions and the like have long kept records, but their work has been done so inadequately as to be unreliable and not useful for comparative purposes. Fortunately, recent publicity has aroused some interest in this difficulty and several organizations have appointed committees to outline uniform methods of recording data. However, each set of figures would simply illumine one corner of the problem.

This defect has been met recently by a series of crime surveys made under various auspices throughout the country. These have attempted to lay bare a cross-section of facts about the administration of criminal justice in the region studied and several of them, notably those made in New York, Missouri, Massachusetts, Illinois, and Cleveland have been capably done. But they will be out of date in a few years. To some degree they are even now untrue to present facts.

I) What is needed then is a permanent Department of Criminology in every state with powers of regulation and control roughly comparable to those of a state department of public health. When one stops to think of the importance of crime control in a modern society it seems astonishing that such departments have not everywhere come into being as the obviously sensible tool by which to attack criminality.[1]

The major tasks of a state department of criminology would be :

(*a*) To serve as the central authority directing or supervising, and coördinating the management of all of the official state agencies concerned with the control of crime such as the state police, the probation service of the criminal courts, the state penal and correctional institutions, and the parole service. Presumably it would assume its more obvious functions first and gradually gain other powers at present so frequently scattered among isolated boards and individuals. The department would make recommendations to the state legislature and work in close coöperation with the criminal courts which might also be better organized under a state ministry of justice. The department of criminology should gain regulatory

[1] Illinois centers its efforts through the office of state criminologist. California has a state department of penology in which are included six divisions, namely : prisons and paroles, criminal identification and investigation, pardons and commutations, narcotic enforcement, women's institutions, and criminology. The division of criminology is the California Crime Commission which has been made a permanent body. The Massachusetts Department of Correction includes a bureau of research.

and supervisory powers over county jails and houses of correction, police lockups, municipal police forces, and other governmental subdivisions of the state dealing with criminals.

(b) A state department of criminology would maintain a permanent bureau of research to gather and interpret the facts about crime and its treatment that are essential to effective crime prevention and control. It would keep its finger continually on the pulse of crime. It would constantly check the effectiveness of state agencies concerned with delinquents and criminals.

Only a permanent research bureau can maintain the continuity of crime accounting long enough to show not only a critical, up-to-the-minute picture of affairs but also the trend of events through a period of time. There is also considerable evidence in the experience of the many private and officially organized crime commissions that have appeared in recent years to show that the recommendations of an official state bureau would be much more likely to produce any needed action than the suggestions of a private committee.

A properly conducted bureau of criminal research should never be a mere depository of carefully filed records. It should be a powerful dynamic force in the field of crime prevention. It could serve every agency working against criminals as a sorely needed friendly critic of their daily work. It could help to prevent unwise use of money and time in crime prevention programs not based on good evidence of probable success. As an informational center it would coördinate criminal work throughout the state by furnishing to each the same facts as a basis for their programs and also by keeping each acquainted with the actual practise of others. It would go far towards lifting the administration of criminal justice to a high level.

The living core of a state department of criminology would be its bureau of research. That would be the fruitful vine that would support its other activities. Research would keep it alive and give it the power to pile fact upon fact continuously until those whose methods were indicted by them would be forced, in self-defense, to shape their programs to fit the evidence. Its publications and its press releases ought to be an educational force of great usefulness in shaping public opinion to recognize and support good work in crime control.

(c) A state department of criminology would through its research bureau foster and conduct experiments in the prevention and control of crime. The state police, the correctional and penal institutions and other agencies could all be used as experimental laboratories without hampering their daily work. New programs and new techniques would be tried out in a corner of each field leaving the routine undisturbed. For example, exploration and experimentation in a possible method of crime prevention by the police might be made by a specially selected police squad in a limited area ; or a group of delinquent boys, possibly one in every ten or twenty of those committed to a state correctional school might be sorted out for intensive study and treatment.

The great objection raised against a research bureau of crime is its cost. When a crime wave frightens us we are anxious to appoint commissions to investigate it and we clamor for reports with definite recommendations quickly. If the problem of crime were so easily met, we should have solved it long ago. We have only just begun to understand the motives of human conduct, and we have much yet to learn before we can control them. The forces that modify human behavior are often subtle. In the nature of things a research bureau that intends to build safely must gather momentum slowly. It took years for the United States Public Health Department to discover why cholera ravished our Atlantic seaboard every ten years. But in time it conquered and banished the scourge. Gone also are yellow fever, smallpox, and scurvy. In every field except that of remedying his own behavior man recognizes the value and economy of this sort of work based upon laborious research. It seems only a matter of time before we shall see also that a permanent bureau of criminalogic research, far from being another drain upon our income, is the most economical as well as the most logical foundation upon which to rest our entire program of crime control.

REGIONAL COÖRDINATING COUNCILS FOR CRIME PREVENTION

A SECOND step in crime prevention is to coördinate the work of the other state and private welfare agencies now fighting crime so as to make more effective use of their joint resources. Social work agencies long ago discovered that they could maintain their independence, prevent duplication of work, and still serve their communities more fully by the simple device of the social service exchange supplemented, perhaps, by a council of members.   Although there may be an efficient working arrangement between some agencies in the field of crime, such as the police and the district attorney's office, no such coöperative spirit can usually be found between police and family welfare associations or courts and the Y.M.C.A.   Yet any well founded program of crime prevention calls for a clearly defined working arrangement of every welfare agency in a community.

In the United States the coöperative idea, as it affects crime prevention, has been most fully carried out in Berkeley, California, which has long been noted for its progressive police department, built up by August Vollmer.   There under the leadership of Dr. Virgil E. Dickson, Assistant Superintendent of the Berkeley public schools, a group of welfare executives were called together in 1925 to consider ways of helping maladjusted children.   Out of that conference came the Berkeley Coördinating Council, through which the health department of the public schools, the Berkeley Health Center, the city health department, the Berkeley Welfare Association, the Bureau of Research and Guidance of the Berkeley public schools and the Berkeley police department are linked in a coöperative enterprise to increase the effectiveness of their child welfare work.

Once a week the chief of police, a police woman, the city health agent, the director of social service of the health center, the executive secretary of the welfare association, the agent of the charities commission, the director of research and guidance of the public schools, the director of elementary education, the visiting teacher, and the chief executive of the Boy Scouts meet to discuss cases of delinquency in the community.   This Berkeley plan has proved so desirable that the California Commission for the Study of Problem Children has suggested that the legislature consider the appointment of a state coördinator acquainted with the procedure of the Berkeley Coördinating Council to introduce similar systems throughout the entire state.[2]

A check of the cases handled by each of the associated agencies showed that in many instances two, and in some

[2] "Report of the California Commission for the Study of Problem Children," p. 42.

cases four or five, organizations, had been dealing with the same problem independently. A master list now eliminates this overlapping and focuses their combined resources through one channel. Spot maps of truancy and delinquency have revealed sources of infection and have made it possible to treat faulty conditions. A continuing series of city studies helps the council to know what local conditions are in fact contributing to the maladjustment of children and also what influences seem to be shaping their conduct for good. The council clearly sees that welfare work involves the encouragement of wholesome activities as well as the destruction of those that are harmful. Public school teachers report each year to the council upon each child who has become a problem because of his inability to adjust himself to the normal group educational plan of the school system and also upon every child who has some special skill or interest. The nature of the difficulties that would require a report under the first head are pointed out to the teacher in a suggestive list which includes, "retardation, truancy, sex difficulty, stealing, fighting, lying, nervous instability, cruelty, reticence or any behavior that deviates from the normal." For the second group attention is called to the possibility that special talents may be either general or specific and may be expressed in a variety of forms, including social activities as well as intellectual ability or physical skill. The teachers' reports are made the subject of regular follow-up work by a traveling clinic through whose aid proper handling is secured for each case.[3]

There seems to be no reason why a similar coördination of welfare activities could not be developed through regional councils for the prevention of delinquency and crime wherever public and private social agencies are sufficiently unselfish and enlightened about the true objectives of their work.

[3] See V. E. Dickson, "The Berkeley Coördinating Council," *Mental Hygiene*, July, 1929, and A. Vollmer, "Coördinated Effort to Prevent Crime," *Jour. of Criminal Law and Criminology*, Part 1, August, 1928, for concise statements of the organization and work of the Berkeley Coordinating Council.

NEIGHBORHOOD COUNCILS FOR CRIME PREVENTION

As a corollary to the idea of a regional coördinating council, the New York Crime Commission in 1930 recommended that smaller neighborhood councils for crime prevention be set up under the auspices of community-wide councils.[4] Their suggestion was based upon the fact that neighborhood areas, defined by reasonable definite social and geographical boundaries, include all of the primary agencies affecting children. The home, the school, the street, the gang, and the recreational centers are all within the limits of the neighborhood area. Therefore, it would be large enough to include practically the whole life of the growing child while yet remaining small enough too so that the primary forces affecting character formation could be seen and dealt with.

The proposed neighborhood council would comprise neighborhood leaders from the fields of business, politics, social work, and the professions. It would be housed in permanent quarters as a visible sign of its functioning, and be directed by a capable, professionally trained executive aided by a small but able staff. Its expenses would be met by public funds provided for possibly in the budget of the police department's crime prevention bureau.

The purpose of a neighborhood council would be to build up a clear, continuous picture of the neighborhood delinquency situation, to coördinate the efforts of the neighborhood welfare agencies in a program of crime prevention, to register all neighborhood problems conducive to delinquency about which something should be done, together with a plan of action to be carried out towards them, and to act as a clearing house of information about the forces working both for and against good citizenship in that neighborhood. The expense of the program should easily be met out of the savings in crime costs to the municipality. It should be recognized, however, that the mobility of criminals will be a partial handicap to all such programs until they become general in the breeding places of crime throughout the entire country.

[4] New York State Crime Commission, Report, 1930, pp. 173-180.

SCIENTIFIC INDIVIDUALIZATION OF TREATMENT

ANOTHER movement of much promise in the prevention of crime is that for the scientific individualization of treatment of young offenders. The trend now is all away from the old method under which the learned judge had only to read the prescription for each *act* duly set forth in the law, quite without regard for the circumstances surrounding the particular culprit who stood before him.

We must be careful not to be blinded by the possibilities that lie in the separate handling of each case. Individualization, itself, may be good, bad, or indifferent. What we are after is a particular kind of individual attention that is based on scientific study and understanding, rather than on the erratic foundation of unchecked personal prejudice and mere guesswork. It is this sort of individualization, based upon the best knowledge clinical practice has developed, that offers the most reasonable chance for re-directing delinquent conduct into acceptable rather than into criminal channels.

A constellation of official and semi-private agencies, that has grown up during the first quarter of the twentieth century with the juvenile court movement, has pioneered with varying success towards the attainment of this ideal. It is to the juvenile court and its associated agencies of probation service, psychiatrical clinics, junior republics, and training schools that we must turn for an understanding of some of the most promising facilities available in our society for the specific prevention of crime.

JUVENILE COURTS AND ASSOCIATED DIAGNOSTIC AND TREATMENT AGENCIES

FOREGLEAMS of the modern juvenile court appeared in the nineteenth century as modifications of the traditional criminal procedure in the trial of young persons, notably in Massachusetts and Illinois. Special hearings for children, the assignment of special magistrates to hear children's cases, privacy, and release on probation were part of the evolution of the juvenile court. In Australia, courts that were, in a sense, children's courts were established by ministerial order in 1890 but the procedure was still the same as in the adult courts.

In 1899 Illinois established in Cook County a specially organized children's court which is usually thought of as being the world's first juvenile court, although the progressive Judge Ben Lindsey at Denver, Colorado, had already assumed the authority to hold juveniles separately under a school law passed by his state two months before the Illinois law. Colorado later organized a regular juvenile court and also indicated its progressiveness by passing the first law for the punishment of persons who contribute to the delinquencies or dependency of children. The idea of the modern juvenile court at first spread slowly, but today only Maine and Wyoming have failed to establish them. Even these states have laws designed especially to safeguard children.

The new element in the treatment of young offenders that has given the juvenile court its real opportunity to enroll as a crime prevention agency is a complete break with the spirit and methods of adult criminal trials. Unfortunately many juvenile courts still cling to the archaic practices of the criminal courts, but those that have attracted the hopeful attention of students are courageously breaking new ground under a procedure by which the state as *parens patriæ* takes the place of the father for the purpose of shielding the child from a career of waywardness.

This procedure is in no sense a trial for an offense but is, in fact, designed to save the child from becoming a criminal. It was boldly borrowed for the treatment of delinquents from an ancient feudal equity practice, by which the crown assumed control of the property of minors in order to protect the rights of the overlord. As the feudal system disappeared, this practice gradually became established as the king's conventional duty towards all children in cases involving property. In practice, actual jurisdiction over minors was delegated to the chancellor's court. In time judges came to decide that the chancery court acting for the sovereign had authority to assume the guardianship of any minor subject. On this basis our states have assumed the right to exercise parental control over delinquent children through the juvenile courts.

While this chancery procedure was evolving children were still tried before the adult criminal courts, for delinquency was a concept unknown to common law. Persons over fourteen were treated exactly like adult offenders. A less rigorous formula applied to younger children. Those under seven were conclusively presumed to be incapable of forming the criminal intent necessary to the commission of a crime. Those between seven and fourteen were also presumed incapable of forming the necessary criminal intent but that presumption might be shown by the evidence to be false.

Modern juvenile court acts pushed this tendency to modify the law for children a step further by devising separate hearings for juveniles and by including within that term all persons up to the age of seventeen. Then the best of them revived the old chancery procedure to replace the regular criminal trial, making the whole process protective rather than punitive.

As the guardian of the child, the juvenile court faces a human rather than an abstract legal problem. Here is a child that is running astray. Why? What is the remedy? Has he qualities that can be redirected to become a positive advantage to him? The aim of the process is to discover real difficulties and by removing them to direct the wayward child towards wholesome behavior. To accomplish this end, the juvenile court movement has attempted to thrust aside the trappings of the criminal courts. Indictments, pleas of guilty and not guilty, prosecuting and defending attorneys, strict rules of evidence, juries, public trials, are all believed unnecessary.

Instead, a thorough investigation into the heredity, present condition and environment of the child is intended as a necessary preliminary to an understanding and treatment of each case. At present this work is limited to the efforts of probation officers, sometimes aided by child study clinics. The court hearing is private and quite informal. In several states the law specifically requires the judge to proceed as a parent would. The judge sits down beside the boy and talks to him and tries to understand what should be done in his interests. The court may also talk with the boy's parents, companions and other interested persons. Then on the basis of his own conversation, the information gathered by the probation officer and any other agency that has been consulted, the court decides upon the treatment of the case. When girls are brought before the court as delinquents, they are usually heard by women referees, who are appointed by the judge, and who report their recommendations to him for a final decision. Frequently moral suasion rather than force is used to bring about the necessary adjustments. The National Probation Association found that fifty to seventy-five per cent of the cases heard in cities of more than one hundred thousand population were handled in this informal fashion.

Inasmuch as juvenile courts are created by statute their procedure and jurisdiction are arbitrarily defined and are not the same in all states. Some are separate from all other courts, some are held as special sessions of the regular court, others are family courts handling juvenile and domestic relations cases together. Not all of them have the desirable equity or chancery procedure. Some still retain the trappings of the criminal sessions. In a few states, juveniles who have committed felonies must stand trial in the adult court. At present, the only federal juvenile court is at Washington, D. C., although some other federal judges find grounds for referring delinquents to the state children's courts. In general only large cities with a population of more than one hundred thousand are adequately served by juvenile courts, while in four-fifths of the rural areas their services are not in practice available.

Much of the value of juvenile courts obviously depends upon the skill and wisdom of the judge and his probation officers. Not all legally trained men are happily blessed with the insight, objectivity, and firmness necessary in those who would deal with troublesome and irritating young people. It is much easier to determine what penalty an adult should receive (if in effect the law allows any choice) than to outline a wise and extended course of treatment for a wayward boy.

Judges need the regular help of child study clinics to guide them in the disposition of their cases. Although the courts of our larger cities do make use of the services of clinics or individual psychiatrists to a greater or less extent, more than that is needed. A child study clinic should be an integral part of every sizeable juvenile court with the judge and his probation officers actively participating in the making of findings and in the shaping of treatment programs.

Probation officers whose work and personality is the very heart of the treatment may be progressive, socially minded workers or ward-heelers holding an easy job. Probation work may vary all the way from an A1 piece of social work through which the officer, with firmness and wisdom, works with family, friends, neighborhood, and welfare agencies to link youth up with every helpful community resource, to a matter of brief, routine, office interviews and worse than useless treatment. One reason why good results do not show up more clearly is because probation work in practice is still too often carried on like this :

John, aged 12, returning from a ball game in an unfamiliar part of the city, saw some boys take a short-cut across the railroad tracks and followed them. He, with the others, was captured by railroad police, who took their names. A few days later, John's father brought him to court in response to a summons. The probation officer, without questioning or investigation, assumed that John had been with the other boys who were known to the police, and proceeded to give him a crude, threatening lecture, after which he turned to the father and told him to take the boy home and "lambast him proper. You wallop him sufficient." The effect of this contact with the practical working of the law was to knock to bits the ideal conception of his government that this intelligent youngster and his own friends, who heard about his court experience, had built up.

Unfortunately, probation work, as a living influence that can stand behind a wayward child, guiding, helping and encouraging him towards better things is still an ideal rather than an achievement in most cities. In many courts probation staffs are so under-manned that officers have one or two hundred children to supervise. Such barriers remove any hope of proper case study or effective supervision. Only a few children's courts yet meet the minimum requirements of separate hearings, regular probation service, and adequate legal and social records.

Naturally there is much controversy over the value of juvenile courts as agencies for the prevention of adult crime, although in some quarters their usefulness in this respect is assumed. Actually it was not until 1934 that the first trustworthy study[5] of the effectiveness of a juvenile court was published and that disclosed the startling fact that 88.2% of a group of 905 boys dealt with by the Boston Juvenile Court aided by the Judge Baker Foundation were recidivists during the five years following the end of their official treatment and 70% of them were involved in serious offenses.

Inasmuch as the Judge Baker clinic and the Boston Juvenile Court are recognized as among the leading agencies in their respective fields the Gluecks' functional analysis of their work should furnish a clue as to the possibilities inherent in the juvenile court-guidance clinic method of dealing with delinquents. The Judge Baker clinic is privately endowed and studies problem children sent to it by private agencies and persons as well as by the Boston Juvenile Court. About half of its clients however come from the juvenile court. For the purpose of making a study of cases during a five-year period after the conclusion of treatment the Gluecks selected cases studied before and after the year 1919[6] until 1000 cases were secured.

The Gluecks followed through with meticulous care the history of these boys. The dealings of court and clinic with them were gained through case records and interviews with staff members. A thorough investigation by competent field workers who interviewed the young men, their relatives and friends disclosed their activities following their release from official care.

[5] (S. S. and E. T. Glueck. "One Thousand Juvenile Delinquents: Their Treatment by Court and Clinic." Harvard University Press, 1933.) The writer is indebted to Dr. Sheldon Glueck for his courtesy in permitting the writer to read this study before its publication.

[6] 1919 was midway between the year when the clinic was started and 1922 the last year that would permit a five-year post-treatment study at the time this work was begun. The average age of the delinquents when examined by the Judge Baker clinic at the request of the juvenile court was 13 years, 5 months.

The boys whom the clinic tried to help were not a promising lot. In 86% of their families one or more members were mentally diseased or defective or suffering obvious psychological abnormalities. Of 918 families 773 (84.2%) included parents or siblings who were delinquents or criminals and in 23 more near relatives were delinquent. In 195 instances one or both parents had committed criminal offenses. In 70 per cent of the homes discipline ran to extremes of laxity or harshness. Of 971 cases, 850 (87.5%) were being aided by welfare agencies. Some 352 families (36.2%) had been helped by five or more agencies. A more discouraging background of unsatisfactory heredity, unwholesome family life, poverty, immorality, and criminality it would be difficult to find.[7]

The clinic procedure of diagnosis, prognosis and recommendations to the court follows the lines standardized by the better grade clinics and is outlined elsewhere.[8] The judge of the Boston Juvenile Court accepted the recommendations of the clinic and acted upon them as he saw fit. The clinic staff itself does not, except in rare instances, undertake to carry out its own recommendations although it does ask reports of the institutions and agencies dealing with cases and may meet their workers for conferences. Occasionally follow-up studies made for research purposes after a case has been closed may lead to treatment action by the clinic.

One striking finding of the Gluecks' study was that in spite of clinical studies ably made and reported to an intelligent socially minded judge more than half of the recommendations made were never carried out. Summarizing this situation the Gluecks say:

"Considering these recommendations *in toto* (2246), 56.3% of them were not carried out at all, 9.2% were partially followed; 30.4% were fully carried out within the treatment period; and 90 more (4.1%) though carried out, were not instituted until after the end of the original treatment period."

"The foregoing analysis indicates that the vocational recommendations of the clinic were most frequently followed by the court, and

[7] See S. S. and E. T. Glueck, *op. cit.*, Ch. 5, for tables on which the figures are based.

[8] (See pages 210-11.)

those having to do with changing family and living conditions least frequently. Slightly less than one-third of the clinical recommendations pertaining to health, educational adjustment, disciplinary and supervisory control, other types of constructive effort, and further study of the offender were followed by the tribunal ; about one-fourth of the recreational recommendations were put into effect." [9]

The reasons noted by the Gluecks for the lack of compliance with the clinic's recommendations suggest the nature of some of the defects which must be remedied before even the best of our juvenile courts can become generally effective instruments for the prevention of crime. Among the reasons for not following clinic suggestions were : [10]

Legal obstacles, such as age and residence limits on institutional commitments, lack of clear jurisdiction, lack of authority to commit children to specialized institutions such as schools for the feeble minded, that sometimes stood in the judge's way.

Lack of parental coöperation—due to irresponsibility, ignorance, failure to assist in supervision, or to carry out the bargain as to health treatment.

The refusal or *inability* of various social agencies to help the court in placing delinquents.

Lack of coöperation by delinquents, in the form of escapes, and runaways.

The failure of other public institutions to coöperate, as when an industrial school releases a boy on parole though prolonged incarceration was recommended.

The limited skill of probation officers and other social workers.

The paucity of community facilities, as for example the lack of special classes in school.

Unrealistic or experimental recommendations by the clinic.

Too rapid development of events.

Hesitancy of the judge to take drastic action in view of family difficulties.

Yet in spite of the repeated inability or unwillingness of the court and its agents to follow the advice of the clinic, the Judge Baker Foundation still was not informed of the facts

[9] S. S. and E. T. Glueck, *op. cit.,* Ch. 7. Quoted by permission of S. S. and E. T. Glueck and the Harvard University Press.

[10] S. S. and E. T. Glueck, *op. cit.,* Ch. 8.

and the reasons for them. It therefore continued to make recommendations that were destined not to be followed. So in spite of thoughtful consideration of cases by the court and able, costly study by the clinic a great portion of the efforts of both have been dissipated for want of close integration of these units such as would obtain were the clinic an integral part of the court with the staff of clinic, court, and treatment agencies all participating in the solution of their common problems.

As the Gluecks suggest, staff conferences "will never produce the best results until the judge and probation officer become active participants therein, and point out to the clinic any legal or other obstacles to the carrying out of the recommendation for treatment, put forward alternative suggestions, obtain more specific details about the case, and in general get a better comprehension of the possible etiologic factors involved and the implications and limitations of the suggested plan of treatment."[11]

The records of the boys dealt with by the Judge Baker Foundation and the Boston Juvenile Court and the associated treatment agencies during the five years following the conclusion of official oversight were discovered to be as follows: Of 923 cases in which adequate information could be secured, 798 were delinquent, 107 not delinquent, and 18 had no opportunity to be delinquent. In 568 cases there were convictions for serious offenses and 167 for minor offenses; 12 arrests for serious offenses and 12 for minor offenses; 11 serious offenses and 13 minor offenses were not brought to the attention of the authorities; 2 warrants were out for minor offenses, and there were 13 desertions or dishonorable discharges from army or navy.[12]

Where clinical recommendations were carried out, somewhat better results were obtained than when they were not, as the following table indicates. Although the difference was not great it is noticeable and encouraging.

[11] S. S. and E. T. Glueck, *op. cit.*, Ch. 4. Quoted by permission of S. S. and E. T. Glueck and the Harvard University Press.
[12] S. S. and E. T. Glueck, *op. cit.*, Ch. 9.

Degree to which clinic recommendations were carried out	Number and percentage of Delinquents	Number and percentage of non-delinquents [13]
Fully	133 (82.1%)	29 (17.9%)
Partially	540 (88.2%)	72 (11.8%)
Not	124 (95.4%)	6 (4.6%)

As a result of their study it is not surprising that the Gluecks are led to remark, "It is high time, therefore, that someone should ask these blunt questions: Why should we assume that a large part of delinquency and criminality can be 'cured' at all, with the methods at present available? May it not well be that the fiber of criminality is much tougher than we have thus far believed and that its tangled roots lie deeper than we have over-optimistically assumed?

"Is it not time that the enthusiastic clinical criminologists stopped hunting for a pot of gold at the end of the rainbow they have constructed? Great humility on the part of all concerned with this colossal problem is called for. We need less exaggerated claims of 'success,' less optimistic expectations from the various proposals daily made for the reduction or elimination of criminality, less newspaper 'solutions of the crime problem' and we cannot have too much thoroughgoing research into fundamentals." [14]

Part of the answer to this query lies in the fact that in spite of our meager knowledge of the roots of human behavior and our limited ability to control it we have only two alternatives, either we must continue to examine and probe and theorize and experiment and reflect, and modify our beliefs, knowing that all human knowledge has been acquired by the same slow painful process ; or we must be willing to spend our money and risk our safety from crime upon hunches and the vagaries of chance.

The best of our juvenile courts and their associated clinics are experimental. They are less bound by the hoary rigidi-

[13] *Ibid.*, Ch. 10.
[14] *Ibid.*, Ch. 13. Quoted by permission of S. S. and E. T. Glueck and the Harvard University Press.

ties encrusted in the criminal law than most other agencies concerned with the treatment of crime. Dealing as they do with the early years of delinquency rather than with the later years of the criminal habit they are slowly learning facts about human behavior that may yet be of inestimable value to society in the prevention of crime.

Not only are the juvenile courts and their clinics gathering information about delinquents, but they are also marking out with increasing clarity the environmental sore spots associated with the breeding of delinquency in our communities. They are also finding out what facilities that communities ought to have are lacking. Sheldon Glueck has suggested that it would further this end if clinics would set down both the desirable and the possible treatments in each case the better to indicate what needed facilities are lacking that a civilized community should maintain.

As educational agencies in the community the better juvenile courts and clinics may well be having a most desirable although immeasurable effect. The contacts of parents, ministers, teachers, and employers with the viewpoint of an understanding juvenile court judge or with the findings, interpretations, and suggestions of a trained clinic staff are very apt to be a leaven of considerable potency in improving the methods of lay persons in dealing with the behavior problems of young people.

Finally, in spite of the suggested low record of even the best of our courts and clinics in actually preventing recidivism there are still apparently some good results of the contact of delinquents with agencies of this caliber. The improvement of the health of delinquents through proper medical care and more especially treatment for contagious diseases may be of advantage to both the delinquent and the community even though he persists in his misbehavior.

Although it is sheer speculation, there may in some instances be improvement in ethical standards and in conduct beyond that which may result were these boys subject to cruder and less intelligent management as delinquents. Moreover although the number who cease their delinquency is relatively small, nevertheless some do straighten out. Again, whether this is due to the work of court and clinic it is difficult to say although the slightly better record of those in the illustrative study who were treated according to clinic recommendation at least suggests that in other instances of success also the contact with the clinic and an intelligent judge may have helped towards that end.

The inevitable conclusion is that in spite of doubtful claims of considerable success in checking delinquency, notably in Denver and Cincinnati, the juvenile courts cannot justify themselves on the ground of noteworthy present achievements of that specific type. Non-success may be largely due to the failure of practice to equal the ideal of juvenile court procedure. It may also be true that even in the best of juvenile courts human knowledge has not yet reached the point where it can successfully treat the more complex cases of misbehavior. Yet unless we are willing to throw aside altogether the well-founded belief that cause and effect relationships are effective in human conduct it is only logical to assume that in an intelligent and critical attempt to improve the technique of the juvenile court lies a way of great promise.

At present the greatest obstacle to that improvement lies in the manipulation of the juvenile courts for political ends that is made possible by public indifference or ignorance. In some states the juvenile court movement has become so frankly political and inefficient that some of its originators and stanchest supporters feel that the juvenile court as it now exists had better be abolished.

CHILD STUDY CLINICS

The work of child study clinics is fundamental to any program of crime prevention. Often the real stimuli to misconduct are covered up. The causes of misbehavior may be complex, subtle, difficult to overcome. If the work of the juvenile court is ever to be thoroughly curative it must rely heavily upon clinical study to guide it towards a wise disposition of each problem. The first step towards a cure must be intelligent diagnosis.

Pioneer work in studying conduct problems in children was begun in 1909 by Dr. William Healy with the founding of the Juvenile Psychopathic Institute at Chicago; a privately supported clinic designed to handle cases sent to it by the juvenile court and by private agencies. This clinic proved to be so useful that in 1917 it was taken under the wing of the state government as the Institute for Juvenile Research. The change in name means that its experience had already overturned the earlier theory that misconduct revealed a psychopathic personality.

Between 1917 and 1919 other clinics were established in Ohio, Massachusetts, California, Michigan, Pennsylvania, and New York. In addition many city courts secured less extensive facilities for child study by arrangement with private agencies or individual psychiatrists. The clinics established to aid the juvenile courts still maintain their earlier connections but they are constantly expanding their services to the community at large. Since 1921 when the Commonwealth Fund for the Prevention of Delinquency began its demonstration clinics, progressive communities have caught the importance of child study work and have provided directly for them as centers not especially to handle court cases but as resources available to all who need their help.

Child study clinics are a living demonstration of our belief that human conduct is subject to the laws of cause and effect. Proceeding on that assumption they study carefully and in detail every aspect of a child's life in an effort to trace the evolution of his present condition and to manipulate forces to his advantage. An outline of the study made by such a clinic would be essentially like the following:

    I.   Problems involved, immediate and general.
    II. Study of background
         1. Heredity: The Family
            (a) Father
            (b) Father's family
            (c) Mother
            (d) Mother's family
            (e) Brothers
            (f) Sisters
         2. Developmental History
            (a) Birth
            (b) Health history

    3. Home and Neighborhood Conditions
    4. Home influences
       (*a*) Including such items as :
          Home atmosphere
          Family interests
          Discipline
          Routine
    5. Boy's (girl's) own habits and interests
       (*a*) Recreation
       (*b*) Work
       (*c*) School
       (*d*) Eating and sleeping habits
       (*e*) Other
    6. School history
       (*a*) Scholastic record
       (*b*) Conduct
    7. Court history
       (*a*) Sentences
       (*b*) Behavior on probation
       (*c*) Record in homes and institutions
III. Study of the Individual
    1. Physical examination
       (*a*) General appearance
       (*b*) Details of examination
    2. Mental examination
       (*a*) Results on extensive psychological tests
       (*b*) Mental balance
       (*c*) Personality traits
    3. Boy's (girl's) own story
       (*a*) Life story
       (*b*) Story of delinquencies
       (*c*) Own explanation of reasons for his troubles

Each part of this inquiry is carried on by specialists. Their separate findings are brought together at a staff meeting at which time the case is discussed from every angle. The result of the conference is a summary of the case and a statement of the probable causes of maladjustment and of the outlook for the future, followed by specific recommendations for treatment. If the clinical study has been made at the request of a juvenile court the findings and recommendations are turned over to the judge for his guidance.

This form of procedure offers by far the best basis that

we have for straightening out the kinks in a boy's or girl's career but we must not look upon it as a mystical formula by which we can precisely and finally dispose of each problem. Practical difficulties arise. It may not be possible to find the right family for a particular troublesome child when just such a foster home is needed. It may not be possible to get a boy out of high school and into an industrial school in the middle of a term. Delay may lead to a continuation of truancy, stealing or other delinquencies. Teachers, neighbors, the judge may become pessimistic about improvement and withdraw their support. Then the task of treatment has to overcome a new load of antagonism.

Proper handling of problem children nearly always involves a continuing series of adjustments. It is not often possible to take one final step that will settle the issue for all time. Treatment that is good at first may be outgrown. Cases, therefore, cannot be handled in accordance with any rigid formulæ. Constant but unobtrusive oversight by persons sensitive to the progress of the child and courageous enough to try new programs when old ones fail is a necessary part of the method of successful child welfare agencies.

And again it is necessary to emphasize the fact that in spite of a little progress, especially in helping those who are desirous of understanding and improving their own behavior, our ability to redirect the lives of those who are brought in voluntarily for treatment is still quite naturally limited.

The achievement of child study clinics in general as preventers of crime cannot yet be told with statistical accuracy, although the Gluecks' study already discussed would suggest that in preventing recidivism their success is limited. Healy and Bronner who have been carrying on an analysis of their own work published in 1926 a study and comparison of 400 cases of delinquency handled by them in Chicago and Boston.[15] It included the records of :

(*a*) 920 delinquents studied in Chicago between 1909 and 1914 whose after careers were checked through special research between 1921 and 1923.

[15] Healy and Bronner, "Delinquents and Criminals : Their Making and Unmaking." See also Healy, Bronner, Baylor and Murphy, "Reconstructing Behavior in Youth."

(*b*) 400 boys who were studied for the Boston Juvenile Court between 1909 and 1914, whose careers were checked again in 1923.

(*c*) 400 boys studied in Boston during 1918 and 1919, whose later behavior was known through a regular follow-up system established by that time.

All of these individuals were of juvenile court age when first studied and well above it when the follow-up check was made. The outcome was considered successful if the person was not a known detriment to the community where he lived and was not engaged in criminal activities. Cases were recorded as failures if the person involved had been convicted in an adult court or were known to be distinctly harmful to society because of vagrancy, alcoholism or gross immorality. A few outcomes had to be classified as indifferent.

Of the Chicago series of 920 it was eventually possible to check as successes or failures 675 cases. Of these 39 per cent of the boys and 54 per cent of the girls appeared to be successful. Of the first Boston group of 400 boys studied between 1909 and 1914, 79 per cent seemed successful ; and of the second group of 400 boys studied between 1918 and 1919, 74 per cent seemed successful. However, these figures are so at variance with the later results disclosed by the much more rigid follow-up investigation in the Gluecks' Boston study already summarized that it seems unsafe to take them at their face value. No doubt the most useful part of the Healy-Bronner study is the light which it throws upon the factors entering into the making of criminal careers.

It must be reiterated, however, that in spite of the slight measure of success that may have been achieved, thorough study of the nature of the delinquent personality seems to be the intelligent way to learn how to control delinquent behavior. Lack of success in preventing recidivism is obviously not due to the ineffectiveness of the clinic alone but in part, possibly in large measure, to the disconnectedness of the chain of police, court, diagnostic, and treatment agencies ; to their lack of realistic coördination in dealing with what are really unit problems.

Child study clinics are new. Their union with the juvenile courts and associated agencies is not perfected. In the brief span of time since Healy and Bronner began their work at Chicago they and others in the same field have learned much and have shown a commendable willingness to modify their techniques in the light of their experiences. In this persistent, able type of experimentation and improvement lies the hope that we may steadily increase our ability to cope successfully with delinquent behavior in young people. It is a slow, painstaking, unspectacular method, but it is the only sensible procedure for an intelligent civilization to follow.

THE USE OF FOSTER HOMES

SOME psychiatrists believe that problem children can best be helped if treatment is carried out in the midst of a normal family life. This would seem to be particularly true of children whose difficulties are due largely to their own faulty homes. The use of foster homes for certain types of delin-quents has, therefore, been much favored by some guidance clinics, although as yet no facts are available to prove the merits of foster homes as compared with institutions *for the same type of offender*. Cincinnati has made the interesting experiment of placing many of its juvenile delinquents on probation in their own homes.

California, Virginia, and Massachusetts have splendid records in the foster placement of children. In Massachu-setts it has become almost a tradition that wholesome family life is the necessary setting for the proper development of the child. Institutions are only for those among the feeble-minded, epileptic, mentally diseased and delinquent who would be dangerous in the community or who need the spe-cial facilities of a hospital for their care. Instead the use of substitute homes for orphans, delinquents on probation, and for the feeble-minded on parole has been extensively devel-oped. The idea has become so well entrenched that public sentiment supports it as a correct procedure. As a result twelve thousand approved foster homes stand ready to re-ceive children from public and private welfare agencies each year.

Long experience has made the placement workers discerning in selecting and supervising the work of foster families. Their oversight is, in general, intelligent and rigid. Exploitation of children is guarded against. With such a background it is not surprising that Massachusetts and in particular the central Juvenile Court at Boston has sought the aid of foster parents in improving the conduct habits of the children who are brought before it.

Doctor Healy and his associates have recently made a careful examination of the results obtained during the period of treatment with 501 juvenile delinquents who were placed in foster homes upon the recommendation of the Judge Baker Foundation of Boston.[16] These young people were not simply annoying, they were genuinely delinquent. In spite of that, so earnestly has the public learned to accept the idea that behavior can be reconstructed that homes were found for all of them.

Viewing the results of discriminating placement and care of delinquents in foster homes with the result obtained by the chance disposition of cases that usually occurs is like walking out of darkness into sunshine. Of the 501 cases placed, only 355 were actually analyzed in the Foundation's study, because the placement work of some public agencies proved unsuited for rigid comparison with that of the private agencies that were used. In 16 cases outcomes could not be definitely determined. Hence 339 comparable cases were finally used.

The results give ample proof that the lives of many delinquent and problem children can be successfully modified under controlled conditions. Moreover, the chances of success were dependent little or none upon such features as kind of offenses, number of delinquencies, sex, age, illegitimate birth, or poor heredity that are popularly considered to be of the gravest importance. On the other hand the mental health of the child was found to be a distinctly vital element. It is between those of normal mentality and those of abnormal mentality or personality only that significant differences appear. Eighty-five per cent of the delinquents of normal mentality stopped their troubling upon placement but only

[16] Healy, Bronner, Baylor and Murphy, "Reconstructing Behavior in Youth."

forty per cent of the delinquents with mental abnormality were equally successful.

These results are direction pointers. They show that skilled workers can achieve a high rate of success in checking delinquency through placement in the special, controlled environment of a foster home. If we add to this the fact that 86 per cent of these delinquents who did well in foster homes appear to have continued their good behavior after discharge from agency supervision often in the face of a return to poor conditions, it becomes clear that the intelligent use of foster family resources may become an important device in the prevention of crime. However in view of the extreme difficulty of discovering the actual behavior of persons once they are released from supervision the chances are that a more rigid investigation would require a reduction in the ratio of success among these delinquents after their discharge. Sometimes it happens that children who have regained their balance through treatment outside of the home are upset by the adjustments incident to their return to it. Dr. Healy's recognition of this problem has led him recently to emphasize direct therapy in the home whenever possible even though it involves the modification of the environment as well as the child. There seems to be no valid reason why we may not in the future learn how to follow this logical procedure effectively.

JUNIOR REPUBLICS

ANOTHER interesting agency that might be so modified as to become a genuine aid in the treatment of certain types of delinquents is the Junior Republic. The first of these was organized in Freeville, New York, in 1894. There are now several. In 1908 the National Association of Junior Republics was established in New York. The Little Commonwealth at Dorsetshire and the Sysonby Village Colony in England were experimental colonies patterned after the George Junior Republic. Both of these were discontinued after auspicious beginnings due to lack of funds.

The parent organization grew out of a most informal charitable enterprise begun in 1890 when William George, a man with an insatiable interest in young people, rounded up a group of the toughest slum children he could find and took them out to the country at Freeville, New York, for a vacation. Friends assisted George in his altruistic work by supplying them with food and clothing. The Freeville Fresh Air Camp grew and in the immediately succeeding years an increasing number of unfortunate children were given a vacation and then sent home loaded with gifts. But when youngsters began to come to Mr. George and say, "De lady what we wuz by last year gave us a good many more t'ings dan youse are givin' us, and we had a good deal gooder time der dan we're havin' here ; See !" he began to have serious doubts about the value of his work. The children were expecting gifts as a right. They were being pauperized.

When another box of clothing arrived Mr. George refused to distribute the contents freely but instead offered a natty suit to the boy who would earn it by five days of ditch-digging. The boys at first rebelled but presently one of them offered to work for it. In a few days he was the only chap in the crowd who had a new suit and he was so proud of it that he borrowed a flat iron from Mr. George so that he could crease his trousers. It was not long before other fellows were working for new clothes.

Gradually Mr. George began to shape a different policy. Nothing was given away. Food, clothing, lodging, and amusements had to be earned and bought. Money was therefore needed in the village as a medium of exchange. A bank was required for its safekeeping and as a source of loans. Those who accumulated property gained a new idea of its meaning. They valued what formerly they had destroyed. They sought protection for it. That required a police force. Culprits had previously been whipped by Mr. George. But now, why should he punish them ? They were not taking his property. So they were turned over to their own group for judgment and sentence.

Soon Mr. George saw that his village was reproducing exactly the social and economic problems of the adult world outside. Why not apply the social and economic organization of the United States Republic to this youthful community, a republic in miniature, a Junior Republic ?

The movement grew until the George Junior Republic became a laboratory of training in citizenship. To it are sent problem children of both sexes to learn by practice the rights and duties of social living. The Republic has its own schools, industries and governmental organization. Citizens are employed and dismissed exactly as adults are anywhere. Those who are capable and aggressive accumulate wealth. Others drop to the point of requiring public relief. The Republic has its own currency. The need to earn whatever they own gives Republic citizens a real interest in the protection of property and develops in them a sense of civic responsibility. A governmental organization has therefore developed.

The laws of the United States and of the State of New York are enforced within the Republic, and in addition there are local statutes passed by vote of the citizen body. The machinery of law enforcement is similar to that in any community and includes a police force, a court presided over by a citizen judge, and lawyers organized in a bar association. Their business is seriously assumed and law violation is perhaps more responsibly treated than outside.

In spite of the establishment of several republics similar to the present institution at Freeville, the idea has not yet made great headway and must be thought of still as in an experimental state as a preventive of crime. Little can be done in the Junior Republics for those whose problems are the result of mental abnormalities. No check has been made upon the after success of Republic graduates as yet, although efforts are made to keep in touch with those who go out. A few outstanding successes are known, as well as some failures. What part Republic life played in these cases awaits further research.

CRIME PREVENTION BY THE POLICE

THE police are in many respects strategically situated to do preventive work. The policeman who patrols a neighborhood day after day for many months becomes intimately acquainted with its life. He is in a position to see specific cases where the loss of a job, the operations of a bootlegger, or the beginning of a companionship are breeding crime. He is, for many people, the impersonation of the law and the basis of their respect for it. As he appears in their eyes, so do the commands of the law. His presence in a district may count for much or little, good or bad, to the folk who live there. It is always fraught with possibilities.

Arrests are filled with social implications that extend beyond the person arrested, for he is always a son, a daughter, a father, a brother, a boarder, an employee, or the like. His arrest may turn savings into lawyers' fees, make relatives ashamed to face their friends, take a brother out of high school and send him to work, please a gang whose member has beaten up a cop, shift the attitude and activities of the police towards others, and so on. The police who make the arrests are the first ones to be aware that others are going to be affected. They are in a position to start whatever welfare machinery is available to prevent harmful consequences from trailing in the wake of their arrests. The very manner in which a juvenile is first arrested and detained may be the critical factor that will thrust him headlong into criminality or snatch him back from its allurements.

Very often the police are the first persons interested in young people from a protective point of view who see them running head-on into danger. They see youths working at illegal hours or out late in bad company. They have the first opportunity to make them or their parents aware of their danger and to call to their assistance the constructive agencies of the community. Furthermore, the suggestions of the police in cases of near delinquency and crime are likely to be unusually effective in stirring people to assume their responsibilities.

Properly carried out, the crime prevention activities of the police might become the most valuable part of their jobs. Unfortunately, in this country, apart from the growing policewoman's movement, police interest in crime prevention has appeared only sporadically and, even then, has been short lived. European police systems pay much more attention to preventive work and are far ahead of us in this respect. Dr. Sheldon Glueck, who recently made a first-hand study of

European police departments, reports that Paris is the only large Continental city not stressing preventive work.

The Hague, for example, has a children's police composed of male detectives and policewomen under a woman sergeant. They visit cafés and amusement resorts, picking up juvenile delinquents and others who are in danger. They handle problems brought to them by parents whose children keep questionable company, come home drunk, or otherwise endanger themselves beyond parental control. They also investigate and act on complaints of neglect or mishandling made against parents.

Each day the children's police sort out of the list of arrested persons all under twenty-one and all men who are bread-winners. The women police immediately visit the homes of these prisoners to see if the arrest will cause a serious social problem. They work in close coöperation with the social agencies of the city. A thorough social study is made of each case that they handle. A special children's attorney prosecutes all cases involving minors.

Prague has a special social police force of ex-patrolmen which has made an enviable reputation for the excellency of its case work. When a regular patrolman makes an arrest that is likely to leave social effects, he at once reports the case to the social police. To them also are referred cases of truancy, vagrancy, neglect, and the like. The social police do not treat cases but instead refer them to proper agencies after diagnosis.

Vienna has an elaborate social police force which is particularly concerned with the question of alcoholism, which it considers of much importance. Special clinics established at each precinct station offer voluntary treatment on the basis of an individual case study to all persons whose alcoholism is an element in their crimes. There is also a juvenile police force which has initiated a voluntary society interested in the protection of young people. A system of blank forms and envelopes that need not be stamped is used to notify the juvenile police of cases needing attention.

Rome and Berlin are much concerned with crime prevention. Berlin handled more than 15,000 cases involving social problems in 1924. In Switzerland welfare work is done by a branch of the municipal government housed in the police station.

In the United States, the work of Vollmer at Berkeley and of Col. Arthur Woods during his brief term as police commissioner of New York from 1914 to 1917 are the most outstanding examples of progressive ingenuity in police administration.   Their work serves as an illuminating exhibit of what can be done.   Here and there a few police departments have timidly gone a very little way in following their lead.

Woods did not put into effect any preconceived plan. His technique evolved, day by day, as his alert mind met new experiences in police administration.   He assigned carefully chosen men to keep a protective oversight of the boys in certain troublesome districts and to ferret out the temptations that were leading them astray.   Certain streets were closed to traffic each afternoon and made into play areas. He organized a uniformed and drilled Junior Police force of 6000 boys from eleven to sixteen years old under the command of regular police captains.   The result was a marked decrease in juvenile delinquency in the 32 precincts that had Junior Police forces.

Fully realizing the connection between poverty and criminality, Woods endeavored to meet it by making his police organization a voluntary employment agency through which more than 3000 persons got jobs during his régime.   He went up to Sing Sing and told the prisoners that the police would not hound them but would help them to go straight. Then he acted upon his promise by getting jobs for 176 ex-convicts, of whom 130 were still working when he left office.   Under Woods' directions the police reported all destitute families to relief agencies and sometimes provided immediate aid from a fund established by policemen, themselves, for that purpose.

Woods made an interesting attempt to improve the relations between police and public by holding Christmas parties in each precinct house for the neighborhood folk.   The police captain acted as Santa Claus.   Forty thousand children enjoyed these Christmas parties in 1916.   Through such a program, alike unconventional and unsentimental in its attack, Woods made clear his belief that although regular police work is essential and must be carried on, the most promising place to smother crime is at its source.

The international policewoman's movement is a direct step towards crime prevention. Whenever children, girls and women are involved in police cases, the services of a policewoman are likely to be useful. It has been estimated that 65,000 girls disappear each year in the United States, many of them no doubt voluntarily.

Every large city has its disturbing quota of abandoned babies. Runaway adolescent girls, ignorant of pitfalls and at the mercy of exploiters, get into endless difficulties in their quest for freedom and a livelihood. Every city has its spots of moral infection dangerous to the well-being of youth. Wherever women have been used successfully, they have been assigned to protective and preventive work amidst problems of this nature. Their international organization is now busy lifting the standards of the profession, marking out the boundaries of its usefulness and unifying its members. Through it the work of the pioneers in this country has grown from a novelty to a movement that is beginning to assume a major place in police work.

Unfortunately, women have sometimes been appointed to police forces because it seems to be the thing for a modern city to do and not because anyone could see tasks that they might be peculiarly fitted to handle. Under such conditions utterly ridiculous attempts have been made to train women to do a man's work, even to swinging a night stick. There is no need to seek a substitute for men. It is equally foolish to train men to do well what women may do better.

Already individual policewomen, here and there, have done splendid work, sometimes without the full coöperation of their departments. In 1921 New York established a Women's Precinct under the direction of patrolwoman Mary E. Hamilton. The atmosphere of prison coldness was removed from an abandoned station house on the West Side by a little ingenious renovating, and the inviting attractiveness of a woman's center took its place. It was designed to be an informational center where women could freely come for any proper police aid or advice from members of their own sex. A detention house for women was planned here contamination of the wayward by the hardened offenders would be minimized and self-respect salvaged. The precinct house was also to be a model home for girls in which detention would become for them an opportunity for work and education under the direction of nurses and teachers. A training school for women protective officers was also projected. Mrs. Hamilton was transferred before she had a chance to put some of her ideas into practice and thereafter the precinct slumped into the form of a conventional complaint office.

Prevention work by the New York police took a new lease on life in June, 1931, when a Crime Prevention Bureau was established in New York City and placed under the direction of a Sixth Deputy Police Commissioner. Henrietta Additon was appointed to that office. The Bureau has had the cooperation of prominent citizens as a lay advisory committee on crime prevention. The new Bureau referred 1002 cases to other social agencies for follow-up in 1931, and received their references to the number of 631. Altogether 9846 cases were handled by the new Bureau during 1931, of which 650 were new. Some 2497 cases were closed as satisfactorily adjusted. During 1932 there were 13,139 cases under the care of the Bureau of which 10,391 were new. Clearances are regularly made through the social service exchange.

Especial attention has been given to persons and conditions contributing to the delinquency of minors, to securing improved and adequate treatment for young offenders, and to the control of juvenile gangs. An example of this work is the break-up of a group known as "The Forty Thieves," which was involved in annoying acts of destruction, in stealing from trucks, and in breaking into stores. Their delinquencies were so serious that it was thought wise to disperse the gang. Its members were identified. Seven of the most serious offenders were arrested as a warning to the others that laws must be respected. Other members are now under police supervision in their communities. Some have been turned to more desirable amusement. Jobs have been found for several. Others were sent to school. Parental aid has been sought. Some of the boys have responded satisfactorily ; court action will be taken against those who do not.

In another instance, some boys were believed to be responsible for breaking street lamp bulbs and for throwing bottles from roofs. They were organized into a hiking club. The membership grew to include 36 boys between the ages of 9 and 15. They have taken 26 hikes during which the crime prevention officer has taught them woodlore, including the precautions taken to guard against fire. The bottle breaking stopped after the second hike. The streets of that district are no longer covered with litter thrown about by the boys.

Seven girls, aged 16 to 18, of respectable families, attended a dance given by a boys' club in their headquarters in an apartment house cellar. The boys drank and gambled. One was arrested at the dance. Five of the girls had jobs. The others were induced to join vocational training courses. They were also directed into church social activities and membership in a women's educational and recreational organization. The boys' club has dispersed.[17]

At the Flatbush Boys' Club the following Police Night program was presented in December, 1931, as a means of securing the interest and coöperation of the boys in the police department and its work :

POLICE NIGHT[18]
FLATBUSH BOYS' CLUB
December 17, 1931
8 P.M.

To further strengthen the ties of friendship between the boys and Policemen this affair has been arranged tonight. Anything that can be done to develop better understanding between guardians of the law, on the one hand, and boys who must be depended upon to uphold the law, on the other, is building good citizenship, so the Flatbush Boys' Club feels.

Boys need to know that Policemen are their friends and that law and order are essential to the proper conduct of society. When this is understood there will be less willingness to disobey, disregard and to act regardless of offense to one's neighbor.

[17] Police Department, City of New York, "Annual Report, 1931," pp. 97-103.
[18] Ibid., p. 106.

The officials of the New York City Police Department concur in this expression and graciously offer their services as proof of their friendliness. The Flatbush Boys' Club appreciates this attitude and so do its two thousand members.

FLATBUSH BOYS' CLUB

Band Selection, 7 : 45 o'clock

Master of Ceremonies.................Mr. E. A. Delmhorst

Assisted by

COMMITTEE MEMBERS AND MR. CHARLES E. WHOWELL

Welcome on Behalf of Flatbush Boys' Club...Master Eli Wallach

INTRODUCTION OF GUESTS

Selections by Members of Band of Police Department,
New York City

Vocal Numbers by Glee Club of Police Department

Remarks by Commissioner Henrietta Additon

and

Inspector Louis F. Costuma, Crime Prevention Bureau

Drill by New York Police Department Recruits

Calisthenics   Jiu Jitsu Wrestlers   Boxing

GLEE CLUB

Band Leader......................Lt. William M. Mahoney

Director, Glee Club......Acting Lieutenant Patrick Fitzgibbons

TEAMS

Drill   Calisthenics   Jiu Jitsu   Boxing

Under the direction of Acting Dept. Chief Insp. John J. Noonan,
School of Recruits

Concluding Numbers by Members of the Band

Program arranged through the courtesy and cooperation of
Edward P. Mulrooney, Police Commissioner, New York
City.

"If you want to do anything permanent for the average man, you must begin before he is a man. The chance of success lives in working with the boy, not the man."—Former Police Commissioner Theodore Roosevelt.

Eventually our entire police machinery must turn more imaginatively towards preventive work than it has yet been able to do. This would involve a thorough understanding and coming to grips with basic neighborhood conditions breeding crime, such as ganging, bootlegging, racial and cultural conflicts, suspected houses of prostitution, and other defective conditions.[19] Our present attacks are dramatic but empty of permanent results. They stun but do not sterilize.

There is a need for the police to know and to utilize more fully the social resources of the community. They can hardly be expected to do family case work, but every police-man should have a taste of social work theory in his regular training so that he may see and bring to the attention of social agencies the sore spots needing disinfection. There should be a social service department as an integral part of the police organization, here as in Europe, to which cases having serious social ramifications might be immediately reported.

The six hundred policewomen, more or less, now asso-ciated with police organizations in this country might become an entering wedge for this advance. There is no reason why the police should not make use of the social service ex-change as a basis for reference nor in every way utilize exist-ing agencies for tying up disorganized groups and individuals with their neighborhood life. Such coöperation would in-crease police effectiveness in supervising public places and of maintaining a constructive contact with delinquents and criminals who are on probation, parole, or discharged in the community. A not impossible shift in the conventional police viewpoint would give every sizeable city a trained force of several hundred men linked up with every agency in the community in a coördinated effort to prevent crime.

[19] See A. Vollmer, "Coördinated Effort to Prevent Crime," *Jour. Crim. Law and Criminology*, August 1926, Part 1, p. 196.

PART FOUR—THE APPREHENSION AND CONVICTION OF CRIMINALS

CHAPTER XII

THE POLICE

No program of crime prevention, however well conceived, can wholly prevent the appearance of actual offenders. Police forces are therefore necessary. They are the front line troops in the attack upon criminals in action. The police are expected to preserve order and to maintain the general security of life and property through preventive work, through the deterrent effect of their presence in a community, and through the apprehension of offenders.

The term "police" is elastic. It applies alike to the one man, part time police force of a rural community and to the complex police organization of a great city. It includes state game and fire wardens, federal agents of the Department of Justice, the secret service of the Treasury Department, the Customs Border Patrol, and the Immigration Border Patrol, and so-called private police such as the railroad police or the unique Coal and Iron police of Pennsylvania. The town marshal, the town or township constable, and the county sheriff are all policemen.

RURAL POLICE

SOME of our rural districts still depend for protection upon these last named officials whose offices and powers are an outworn heritage of Anglo-Saxon and Norman England. Our town constable has derived his office from the constable of Norman England who absorbed the old Anglo-Saxon tithingman. Justices of the peace were English peace officers who became really chief constables in charge of the watch which was established by the Statutes of Westminster in the days of Edward I (1100-1135). The elected marshal of our small towns harks back to the reign of Edward II (1327-1377) when the title, borrowed from a medieval dignitary in charge of the royal stable, was first given to a court officer whose duties included the custodianship of prisoners. The position of county sheriff which carries both criminal and civil powers can be traced back to the Anglo-Saxon shire reeve who, as the royal representative, was usually the most important officer in the county and had broad civil, judicial, and administrative powers.

Modern counterparts of these ancient peace officers have been shorn of many of their original duties and brushed to one side by the pressure of newer police organizations that have grown up around them. Nevertheless they still carry on, outgrown, and performing only passably well the tasks that are left to them, like a horse-drawn vehicle in the midst of city traffic.

The duty of the sheriff is still to pursue and arrest all criminals, but in practice he disregards this part of his job and concerns himself with his civil duties and with the administration of the county jail. He has neither time, money, man-power, nor training to undertake the pursuit of criminals. The constable, now fast disappearing, has also the power to arrest and detain those who are charged with crime. The marshal is still found in some small towns as a part-time policeman.

Inasmuch as this attenuated group of men is not equipped to do modern police work, many rural areas that depend upon it have, in practice, no police protection at all despite the fact that the automobile is increasing the necessity for it. Beginning with the organization of the Texas Rangers in 1901, eleven states, Connecticut, Maine, Massachusetts, Michigan, New Jersey, New York, Oregon, Pennsylvania, Rhode Island, Texas and West Virginia, have attempted to meet the police needs of rural communities by creating state constabularies patterned after such successful forces as the Canadian Northwest Mounted Police, the Royal Irish Constabulary, and the British South African Police. Twenty-four others have forces whose work is in practice limited to traffic control and another five have small supervisory staffs. A state police force brings to rural areas a well-organized, trained and properly equipped police service that they could never provide for themselves. They have the advantage of mobility which makes possible their rapid concentration when they are needed in an emergency and allows them to cover a wide territory quickly in coping with offenders who make use of automobiles.

Opposition to the development of state police forces has been made by trade unions on the ground that they are used by capitalists to break strikes and hinder the success of workingmen. Their claim is just. State police have been so used. The Pennsylvania State Constabulary, organized originally to cope with labor troubles in the coal and iron industry, has in the past been an agency of intimidation used to defeat strikers by methods bordering on terrorism. Illegal interference with strikers, however, is not an evil peculiar to state constabularies. City police have frequently used unwarranted methods to break strikes. The trade union argument is, therefore, not a valid indictment of a state police organization but rather of the improper direction of any police force.

The police of small towns have sometimes opposed state patrolmen as outsiders not sensitive to local conditions. Behind this attitude there is probably a bit of wounded pride because the success of a state officer in their district may seem to reflect upon their own ability. Minnesota recognized this problem and tried to meet it in 1927 when it created, not an independent state constabulary but a state police bureau of broad powers to assist and coördinate the work of the local police. The bureau is to maintain a central identification and record office, conduct police schools, and perhaps also provide trained detective service to sheriffs. Zone training schools to give effective police instruction to small town forces have recently been established in New York.

Louis N. Robinson suggests that we may yet need to change our conception of the state police as an independent force to that of a staff whose duty it is to stimulate and coördinate local police forces.[1] This would seem to be a valuable function of the state police but it would probably be inadequate in itself as a substitute for their patrol work inasmuch as the local police would still be handicapped by poor pay, lack of suitable recruits, poor equipment, and the limitations of town boundaries. Such a bureau in conjunction with a state patrol might raise the level of village police work and break down antagonism between the state and local officers. Regardless of the type of organization used the future is apt to see an extension of statewide coördination of police work either through the establishment of more state police forces equipped to handle any aspect of police work or through the increasing use of state police supervisory and training bodies.

URBAN POLICE

OUR city police have evolved from the old colonial town-watch, directed by a constable after the precedent of the motherland. In Boston

"The watch that the constables were required to order was an unpaid company composed of men of the town who served turns as a night patrol from May to October. All male inhabitants, except certain officials, were required to serve or to hire substitutes. The watch, in charge of a constable or his deputy, went on duty at ten in the evening and patrolled the town until daybreak.

"As early as July 20, 1631, the Court of Assistants ordered '. . . a watch of sixe & an offi(cer) kept every night att Boston, 2 whereof are to be of Boston, 2 of Charlton and 2 of Rocksbury.' Later eight persons constituted the watch. Watch houses were set up at various points at different times, the first one being near where the present Union Street enters Dock Square. At one time (1664) the east end of the town cellar under the staircase was assigned to the use of the watch. From these houses the patrol went out walking two by two 'a youth allwayes joyned with an elder and more sober person.' It was their duty to make discreet inquiry about the burning of any lights after ten o'clock, and to see that they were put out. If they heard any noisy disorderly

[1] L. N. Robinson, "The Relation of the Courts to the Crime Problem," p. 16.

conduct in any dwelling they were first to admonish the house-holder and, if the disturbance did not then stop, to tell the constable. All noises in the street were to be silenced, and any persons behaving themselves 'in any ways debauchedly' were to be arrested. If any persons 'not of knowen fidellitie' were found on the streets after ten o'clock, they had to explain to the watchmen why they were abroad." [2]

As colonial towns grew, the night watch became inadequate. In 1736 Boston appointed a committee to find more effective means of policing the town. The will of Stephen Girard provided Philadelphia with the money and the incentive to establish a day watch of 24 men in addition to 120 night watchmen by an ordinance that was repealed in 1835. An independent day watch was formed in Boston in 1838. New York and Cincinnati followed suit soon after. In the meantime, in 1829, England, led by Sir Robert Peel,[3] established the first modern police organization, the Metropolitan Police of London. In the United States a series of riots that occurred between 1835 and 1844 made clear the utter inadequacy of independent day and night watchmen and led New York, in 1844, to replace the obsolete watch system with a single twenty-four-hour police force of 800 men under a chief of police. During the next decade the other large cities of the country followed New York's example.

The new police of the 40's and 50's were far from being efficient. They were in the grip of the spoils system and so dependent upon the success of political parties for their jobs that they became the tools of bosses rather than the impartial guardians of the law. When Baltimore's police force was organized in 1857 it became chiefly a means by which the Know-Nothing party exercised the terrorism necessary to their control of the elections. In New York, police lawlessness under political protection was habitual. Policemen assaulted their officers, refused to patrol their beats, released prisoners from custody or blackmailed them in utter disregard of their duties. Throughout the country the police looked upon uniforms as a mark of servitude and

---

[2] A. Morris, "Crime in Old Boston," *Bostonia*, January, 1930.
[3] After whom the police were nicknamed "Bobbies."

refused to wear them. Even the requirement of a badge was bitterly opposed. The police organizations in such a state of anarchism were neither feared nor respected. Riots continued. Street fighting on Sundays and the burning of houses for loot were common sports among the rougher element.[4]

Faced with unbearable police disorganization in New York City and the equally intriguing opportunity to help the Republican party, the New York state legislature in 1857 created a Metropolitan Police District controlled by five commissioners appointed by the Governor. Other states took this hint and before long nearly every large city in the country had a state-controlled police force. But the legislatures did not limit their interest in cities to municipal police systems. They extended their control to other city departments throughout the closing years of the 19th century, finally going so far that a wave of opposition to their dominance rolled up and they were forced to retreat before a rising demand for home rule. Under its influence police control in most cities reverted to the local authorities.

Throughout their history police organizations in the United States have been closely allied with political parties. The police have sometimes been little more than the henchmen of political bosses. Changes in police administration have been for the good of political parties. Until recently most cities having police boards required them by law to be bi-partisan, a frank recognition of the political position of the police.

With such hampering affiliations it has been impossible for police forces to keep everlastingly pointed towards the goal of becoming highly efficient units for the control of crime. Politicians have diverted their efforts and robbed them of incentives. Frequent shifting of executives has put them in the position of a football team that has its coaching staff changed each year.

Recent surveys have clearly indicated that the alliance of police and politics still persists with unfavorable effects upon the qualifications of appointees, their tenure of office, and

---

[4] See R. B. Fosdick, "American Police Systems," pp. 68-71, for a more extended account of this interesting period.

their independence.   The commissioners of the Metropolitan Police of London have had an average term of fifteen years in office.   In New York City the commissioner's average term is one year and seven months ; in Chicago, two years ; and in San Francisco, one year.   The morale of the men in the ranks is injured by the feeling that promotion depends upon influence rather than merit.   The incentive to keep in the good graces of political favorites is powerful. A patrolman can soon be made to see that his advancement will be proportionate to his knowledge of when to forget that he is a policeman.

Summarizing the results of a detailed examination of certain police organizations by the Missouri Association for Criminal Justice, Bruce Smith speaks of the Kansas City, Missouri, department as "riddled with politics," that of St. Joseph was not much better, while St. Louis is improving although with no assurance that the gain will continue under the next board.[5]   These cities are not alone in their difficulty.

When it is possible to "fix" cases with higher officials in the police department or the courts, a policeman, however honest, has little incentive to prosecute offenders, especially, as often happens, if he is punished for his zeal by being transferred to an outlying district.   Instead, the pressure is all in the direction of making him play the same game.   The man who performs his duty conscientiously must look with bitterness upon a system that rewards the unworthy in preference to the competent.

POLICE ORGANIZATION

THE organization of police departments varies considerably from place to place.   Municipal control is the rule although the police of Boston, Baltimore, St. Louis, and some lesser cities are under state control.   The board of commissioners has given way to a single head in about four-fifths of the large cities of the country.   Occasionally the police are under the direction of a commissioner of public safety who has charge of several supposedly related city units such as the police, fire, health, and building inspection departments.

[5] "The Missouri Crime Survey," pp. 40-41.

Civilians without police experience are preferred in the United States as commissioners. Chicago alone, of all our large cities, appoints its police head from the ranks. The reason is that police work has become a great business demanding skill in organization and control quite unrelated to success in the ranks. Twelve cities in the United States have an annual police budget in excess of one million dollars. The successful administration of a business of this size, which involves contacts of an unusually delicate nature with the community, requires an administrator of wide experience able to order the relations of the police to the public in harmony with a wise and far-sighted policy. Patrolmen are not likely to have such qualifications, and there is nothing in patrol work itself which would fit an otherwise inexperienced man to become a police commissioner.

Theoretically the aim, then, is not so much to gain a civilian police head as it is to extend the range of choice so that the most capable men may be chosen regardless of their connections. Unfortunately, the selection of civilian executives, also, has been hampered by factors of residence and political affiliations quite out of harmony with that ideal. Cleveland's recent directors of public safety have included a minister, a roofing salesman, two lawyers, and a jeweler. Salt Lake City has appointed a plumber, an insurance agent, a tea and coffee salesman, a livery keeper, a stagecoach operator, and a fire insurance adjuster. New York, Philadelphia, Detroit, Los Angeles, and other large cities can boast of equally democratic and heterogeneous lists.

By way of contrast, European police heads, who are also usually chosen from outside of the ranks, are ordinarily high officials trained as jurists, army officers, or executives in other branches of the governmental service somewhat related to police work. Appointments are divorced from political considerations. The one requirement is fitness. Once a good man is found he is secure in his office against any political changes about him. A new municipal council would no more think of replacing him than a business house would consider discharging a competent executive.

The chief-of-police serves as the technical advisor of the commissioner and has direct supervision of the routine work of the police force. In the United States there is no fixed standard of training or ability to which police chiefs must conform. They may vary in ability all the way from the competent and progressive August Vollmer to the ignorant and untrained chief-of-police of a small New England city who could not even fill out routine office papers without assistance. In Ohio, New Jersey, and Massachusetts, and in a few individual cities elsewhere, attempts have been made to improve police leadership by putting the office of chief under civil service control. This prevents the frequent removals from office that are associated with political turnovers and gives a man a chance to build up definite standards of police work. It is significant that Milwaukee with perhaps the cleanest record with respect to crime in the country has had only two police chiefs in 46 years, and has permitted them unparalleled freedom from political control.

On the other hand, until it is possible to gauge an individual's qualifications for office better than can be done with present civil service examinations, inefficient men may not only become police chiefs but they may also be secure in their positions against removal.

The organization of the main body of a police force depends upon the size and special needs of a city. Obviously an inland community will not have a harbor police. Roughly, a city police force comprises two bodies of uniformed men, the traffic police and patrolmen; and a non-uniformed detective service which, in turn, may include men and women engaged in general criminal investigation and numerous special groups, such as the vice, pawnshop, and pickpocket squads.

Men join the force either by direct appointment or through passing civil service examinations. Appointed police forces have long been the treasure chest of politics, serving as the most ample source of rewards for political aid available. Those under civil service have partly avoided this trouble but have not yet succeeded in finding the sort of men that a police organization needs, because the civil service examinations do little more than select men with a certain minimum amount of general knowledge. As yet no examination has been devised that will sort out men with the intelligence, courage, moral stamina, and tact that are desirable in a policeman, although the United States Civil Service Commission is now trying to devise scientific and practical methods of police selection. Many improvements in selection have already been made and the resulting trend is definitely upwards.

Ideally, policemen ought to have the combined virtues of soldier, lawyer, parent, and diplomat; but their wages are those of an unskilled laborer. The cities of prosperous New York State in 1926 paid their patrolmen a minimum wage that varied from $1200 a year in Canandaigua to $1950 in White Plains, and a maximum wage that ranged between $1380 in Harwich to $2500 in New York City. The country over a patrolman's pay probably averaged $150 a month for full-time work during our most prosperous years.

The result is that diplomats and lawyers do not join police forces. Instead the majority of recruits are everyday workingmen; former store clerks, truck drivers, factory hands, mechanics, and the like, who have been attracted to police work by the lure of a steady outdoor job, summer vacation with pay, and retirement with a pension. Some of them are apt students of police methods and become skillful in doing regular police work. Most of them have no conception of the crime problem as a whole nor even of police work beyond their immediate jobs. Twenty-five per cent of the police force of Kansas City, Missouri, twenty-one per cent of the police of Cleveland, and fourteen per cent of the police of Los Angeles were found in recent surveys to be in the low average, inferior, or very inferior grades as represented by a score of 45 or less in the Army Alpha Test. Mr. Amsden, Civil Service Examiner at Los Angeles, says that he has learned from experience that it is useless to appoint as patrolman any candidate who cannot score 120 in any one of the Alpha tests.[6] If this is a reasonable minimum, and the scores actually made by policemen in several large cities are representative of the ratings of policemen in

[6] National Commission on Law Observance and Enforcement, "Report on the Police," p. 61.

general, more than 75% of the policemen of the United States are not intellectually able to perform their work.

Some of our largest cities have welded their police forces into passably effective units by establishing training schools for recruits. New York City gives each new man 148 hours of intensive training, correlated with field work during an eight weeks' course in everyday police work, such as methods of dealing with parades, accidents, fires, arrests, use of fire-arms, and knowledge of the criminal law. Berkeley, California, has a three-year course which meets one hour a day and includes a wide range of basic subjects not taught in other American police schools and including criminology, anthropology, toxicology, psychiatry, and micro-analysis, in addition to the conventional courses. Louisville, Kentucky, has an interesting police school not limited to recruits but offering also a seminar course for officers. Cincinnati has an effective course which particularly emphasizes legal training, drill, and target practice. St. Louis and Milwaukee are now giving much attention to the improvement of their training programs. These are the outstanding police schools of the country.

These schools, however, are the exception and not the rule. Most cities have no training course worthy of the name. As late as 1927 Schenectady, with a population of 92,786, gave its recruits a ten days' course. Utica, a city of 101,604, required every member of its department to take six to eight hours of instruction in criminal law each year.

The investigators for the Wickersham Commission asked 745 communities with populations over ten thousand what training they gave their police. Of the 383 that took the trouble to reply only 78 reported that they gave any training at all, and not more than 15 had reasonably adequate courses.[7] Police training all too commonly leans toward the method used by the commissioner of public safety of a large New York city who told the investigators of the New York Crime Commission:

---

[7] National Commission on Law Observance and Enforcement, *op. cit.*, p. 71.

"I say to him (the recruit) that now he is a policeman, and I hope that he will be a credit to the force. I tell him that he doesn't need anybody to tell him how to enforce the law ; that all he needs to do is to go out on the street and keep his eyes open. I say : 'You know the Ten Commandments, don't you? Well, if you know the Ten Commandments and you go out on your beat and you see somebody violating one of those Commandments you can be sure he is also violating some law.'"[8]

POLICE WORK

THE duties of the police in England and the United States are mainly to preserve order, apprehend offenders, and regulate traffic. In Continental Europe the police have broad powers covering nearly every governmental function not definitely lodged with some other department. Ten of the twelve divisions of the Berlin police organization deal with matters such as food inspection, health and fire protection, preparation of road construction plans, and supervision of building construction, which in England and the United States are in charge of separate municipal departments. The limited scope of police work in the United States is quite in harmony with the English dislike of minute and detailed supervision by an organization with summary police powers.

The actual work of the American police may most easily be thought of as comprising five lines of activity : traffic regulation, patrolling, criminal investigation, preventive control of criminals, and general crime prevention.

TRAFFIC REGULATION

THE extensive use of the automobile in cities whose streets were never planned to care for these innumerable swiftly moving vehicles has made traffic regulation an important function of the police and has called for the establishment of a special group of men to care for it. Although traffic violations are crimes they are usually technical rather than true criminal offenses, and hence the main part of the work

[8] "Report of the New York State Crime Commission, 1927," p. 213.

of the traffic police is thought of as only incidentally bearing upon crime control. To be sure, they may stop cars whose occupants are wanted for serious offenses or capture a criminal who causes an open disturbance in the neighborhood; but in practice their attention is largely confined to controlling the movements of vehicles and pedestrians about them.

2. PATROLLING

PATROLLING, in spite of its routine nature, is an essential and valuable police task. It serves to keep within the law a considerable body of persons who are kept within the bounds of good conduct, especially with reference to property, only by the presence in the community of an organized repressive force. What may happen in a normally law abiding city when the police are withdrawn was well attested by the looting of stores and rioting that occurred in Boston at the time of the police strike in 1919.

The police patrol also acts as the eyes and ears of the department. A knowledge of what is going on in a city is absolutely essential to good police work. The policeman daily covering a given area absorbs a mass of detailed information about a city neighborhood and what the people in it are doing that is highly useful to the department.

Furthermore, to many people, particularly aliens, the policeman on the beat is the direct representative of government from whom they will gain their impression of its characteristics. He needs to give them a worthy conception of the authority that he represents.

In spite of the importance of patrol work, the police are doing less of it each year. A rapid increase in the volume of traffic has required the steady enlargement of traffic squads. In the face of this new demand it has been difficult to get cities to appropriate enough money to provide adequate patrolling. In addition, the number of special demands for police service at dance halls, ball parks, district attorneys' offices, the homes of public officials, and the like all decrease the number of men available for street duty.

The New York Crime Commission has concretely illustrated the vanishing patrol by the situation in the Buffalo police department which they found to be "so common among the police forces of this State as to be almost typical." [9] Out of a total force of 1162 employees, of whom 813 were patrolmen, the Buffalo police department, in 1925, had 310 men available for street work during any average twenty-four-hour period. However, inasmuch as Buffalo is under the three platoon system which fixes a normal day of eight hours on duty, there were only about 100 men actually patrolling Buffalo's 700 miles of streets at any one time. Moreover, this represents a decrease of 30 per cent in the course of six years although the number of police employees was increased by 7 per cent during that period.

Patrol work really offers a greater scope for administrative ingenuity than is usually given to it. The rapid growth of our cities, shifts in their racial character, the transformation of residential areas into business districts, the discontinuance of car lines, the decentralization of banks and a host of other changes make frequent shifts of patrol beats advisable. Regularity of patrol is advantageous to criminals who are thereby enabled to predict the movements of the police. In spite of this, the tendency in the United States is for each man to patrol a regular beat every day in routine fashion.

In England and on the Continent flexible patrol systems have been devised which provide adequate protection for each area while keeping criminals in a constant state of suspense about the movements of the police. One European type of patrol calls for several men to cover a given area simultaneously by different prearranged routes which may be changed each day. A variant of this plan requires several men to patrol the same route in succession starting at irregular intervals. In Berlin, these precinct patrols are supplemented by an overlapping patrol that starts out from headquarters and covers several precincts, sometimes immediately after the local patrol. England has successfully used a decentralized box system devised by Chief Constable Crawley of Newcastle-upon-Tyne, under which both sergeants and constables report for duty and receive orders and messages at booths placed on their beats. The points at

[9] "Report of the New York State Crime Commission, 1927," p. 218

which the men are to begin their duties are changed daily according to a schedule.

All of these plans make it unnecessary to concentrate the patrol force and leave a city unprotected two or three times a day when new men are relieving those who have completed their tour of duty. They make flexibility possible and consequently make police appearance uncertain and their patrolling more effective as a deterrent force.

The modern tendency is to use means of rapid transit in residential areas and reserve the foot patrol for congested districts. Berlin uses the automobile patrol, but the men get out to make rapid foot surveys as they go along. The Hague prefers bicycles. Berkeley, California, and Kansas City, Missouri, were pioneers in the use of automobiles in the United States. Berkeley's patrol is completely motorized. Every patrolman drives his own car. This, combined with radio on the instrument board for receiving signals, has made a noteworthy contribution to the recognized efficiency of the Berkeley police. Both in Kansas City and in Berkeley the extensive use of automobiles has proved effective and economical, and other cities are now falling rapidly into line.

New York and Detroit have experimented successfully with the use of patrol booths and signal systems. Detroit established its first booth in 1918 and found it so useful that thirteen more were promptly added. This system requires two men equipped with a motorcycle or automobile at each post. One stays at the booth while the other patrols. The district then has the advantage of constant mobile protection and at the same time is always able to call immediate police assistance in an emergency. This plan is particularly useful in extensive residential areas.

The value of effective communication in police work is attested by Detroit experience. In 1929 the police made 22,598 broadcasts resulting in 1325 arrests within an average time of 1 minute 42 seconds. Often offenders were caught in the act. Fifty cities now use radio-equipped patrol cars and regional police broadcasts are rapidly becoming common. The teletypewriter, originally used for interdepartmental communication has also been extended. New York,

Pennsylvania, and New Jersey now have interstate teletypewriter communication and these three will soon be linked
with a network covering the New England states. Yet the
Wickersham Commission was forced to report in 1931 that
with two exceptions not a single police force in cities with
populations over 300,000 has an adequate communication
system.[10]

The use of dogs in patrol work is a European feature that
we are not likely to imitate because of an adverse public
sentiment. Yet the movement is growing rapidly in Europe
and the Continental police seem to have much faith in it.
The dogs are of several breeds and are highly trained for
special types of work. When put into service each dog is
assigned for the regular use of one man with whom he lives.
They have been found useful in parks, along the water-
front, in wooded districts, and in residential areas. A man
aided by a police dog is generally considered the equal of
four men. Col. Arthur Woods brought some of them to
the United States but found them unsatisfactory under
American conditions. Yet the possibilities of a limited but
important use for them in warehouse districts and along
waterfronts might be worthy of study by police administrators.

CRIMINAL INVESTIGATION

CRIMINAL investigation is carried on by detectives operating
either from headquarters or from station houses, assisted
sometimes by regular patrolmen assigned to special duty because of their original discovery of the crime and knowledge
of the attending circumstances. Every large city organizes
its detective force into special details, such as the homicide,
pawnshop, forgery, and pickpocket squads. By this means
the men are able to become rather fully acquainted with the
methods and whereabouts of habitual criminals in a limited
field. Possessed of this knowledge, they may be able to
make a fairly shrewd guess as to who committed a crime as
soon as they know the details of it.

[10] National Commission on Law Observance and Enforcement. *Op
cit.*, p. 5.

The technique of American detectives is not at all mysterious but quite matter-of-fact. They have no special training but may have personal attributes, such as an excellent memory for details, that will contribute to their success. In some departments, patrolmen may serve a sort of apprenticeship on special assignments. When called to the scene of a crime, the detective informs himself of its nature and the circumstances surrounding it. He inquires into the habits and associates of the victim, interviews witnesses, considers the whereabouts of criminals likely to commit such acts, notes the presence in the neighborhood of strangers or released prisoners, trails relatives and pals, and in general seeks to uncover every fact that may throw light on the case.

In such investigations the great fund of miscellaneous information that the regular patrolman has about neighborhood happenings may be very helpful to him. Detectives also lean heavily upon "stool pigeons" or informers who can be pressed to give them valuable hints. Every successful detective knows where he can put his hands on those who have close connections with the underworld. His job is not only to pursue criminals but to make alliances and effective compromises with them.

Once a suspect is caught, the methods used to induce a confession vary all the way from shrewd quizzing to physical torture. An ordinary citizen who may come into the hands of the police for questioning is not likely to meet with untoward treatment,[11] but suspected criminals or obviously uninfluential wretches may be manhandled with unbelievable brutality, especially if they are not in touch with an attorney. Some of these victims are actually guilty, but by no means all of them. Silence seems to be the supreme refuge of society's unfortunates. It is the easiest way to avoid trouble. Fear of retaliation closes the mouths of witnesses. Under such handicaps the police may find it difficult to get the evidence necessary for conviction even when they know that their prisoner is guilty. In these circumstances their aim is to get a confession. There is also the likelihood that even if their prisoner is convicted he may escape adequate punish-

[11] Although prosperous citizens have been manhandled.

ment. If they can give him a dose before he goes in court, so much the better. At any rate, they feel that crim nals are tough customers and the police, who risk their liv to capture them, feel that they cannot be expected to tre them as guests.

The tortures of the third degree depend upon the seriou ness of the offense in the eyes of the police. Physic brutality is common. Drug addicts may be forced to ta by depriving them of drugs. Other prisoners may kicked, beaten with a rubber hose, or a telephone book th does not leave too obvious marks, whipped, deprived sleep and water, jumped on, given the water cure, partial suffocated, or even more horribly maltreated until they a willing to admit their crimes. Protracted questioning men in relays, threats of death or other violence, and illeg detention of persons *incommunicado*, so that they cann notify friends or attorneys, are other types of third degr pressure.

Between 1920 and 1930, 67 cases of the use of third d gree methods were proved in three federal courts and the appellate courts of twenty-six states. Including 39 oth instances in which there was evidence of the third degr insufficient to constitute legal proof, there were 106 cas from thirty-one states and four federal courts. In only of these cases was there proof that the victim had a crimin record. New England was the only section of the count not included.[12] These instances merely hint at the extent its use. They exclude all of the cases thrown out the trial courts and all those that are never mentione either by the police or their victims. Beyond a doubt t third degree is a characteristic police method in the Unit States.

Yet in spite of the reliance that the police place on it t third degree undoubtedly hinders their efficiency, caters laziness, and discourages adequate investigation of case Its victims are embittered and its perpetrators brutalize It often introduces irrelevant issues into criminal cases ar leads to acquittals on the ground of coercion when leg

[12] National Commission on Law Observance and Enforcement, Report on Lawlessness in Law Enforcement," p. 21.

idence might have been secured that would lead to con-
ctions. It has demonstrably led to fake confessions of
uilt. Apart from any humanitarian considerations and
urely in the light of its results, the use of the third degree
utterly unjustified and intolerable as a modern police
ethod.

American detectives make very little use of scientific
evices and frown upon the *technique policiére* of the Euro-
eans, although they do turn to experts in ballistics or
athology in special cases. Although municipal police de-
artments have photographic and other identification equip-
ent, few police laboratories in the country are properly
quipped to make routine blood analyses, examine stains,
air, dust, or tools, detect counterfeiting of bank notes,
amps, or documents and identify gunpowder or bullets,
though some cities have made notable progress in their
ientific work since 1920.[13] Occasionally outside assistance
sought but the police do not regularly and as a matter of
ourse make use of the available facilities of university
boratories.

An essential element in criminal investigation, and also
successful prosecution, is a workable method of criminal
lentification. At least as far back as 650 A.D. the Chinese
sed fingerprints for this purpose. Europeans, however,
ere not aware of their value until the end of the last
ntury. They depended upon human memory until the
evelopment of photography made the establishment of
gues galleries possible. These became the basis of the
rst police methods of criminal identification. The pictures,
owever, were a crude device that did not provide a positive
ethod of identification because men's features change with
ge, they may be easily disguised, and because of the danger
f mistaken identity when two persons resemble each other.

In 1882 Alphonse Bertillon perfected a method of identi-
cation which became famous as the Bertillon system. It
volved :

[13] The Scientific Crime Detection Laboratory recently established at
orthwestern University now offers police of the country its excellent
boratory service. In addition in 1931 it began to give resident courses
crime detection. In 1932 it instituted its first course in police training.

1. Certain anthropological key measurements on parts of th body not likely to change after maturity. On the basis of the measurements the photographs to which they referred were classifie

2. The *potrait parlè*, a description of the person examine recorded in standardized fashion on a printed form.

3. A record of the presence and location of peculiar mar such as moles, scars, and tattooes also recorded on a standardize form.

4. Fingerprints, which were unfortunately unclassified.

5. A front and right profile view of the subject.

The Bertillon system caught hold in Europe and later i the United States, where it was frequently installed in polic departments by legislative fiat. Its deficiencies soon becam apparent. Immature and very old persons could not b identified by it. The maintenance of Bertillon recorc seemed a bit too complicated for small departments. Th taking of photographs and measurements required a specia skill. Finally, the most disturbing problem of all was th fact that the success of the system depended upon the ac curacy with which extremely fine measurements were mad and it was not long before it was discovered that even skille operators were apt to measure the same person differentl

The Bertillon system has therefore been discarded in favc of fingerprint identification although metropolitan police de partments still keep their old Bertillon records for th identification of old criminals.

Dactyloscopy, or fingerprinting, is the most satisfactor method of identification yet devised. It is now used b police departments in every civilized country. There some disagreement as to who should receive the credit fc first devising a practical system of fingerprint identificatior although it is quite apparent that in its present form dactylos copy is the product of many minds. The Chinese an Japanese cite the use of fingerprints as proof of identity i their literature as early as 650 A.D. and 702 A.D., respectivel Sir William Herschel, in 1858, while serving as an adminis trative officer in Bengal, began to use fingerprints to prever the fraudulent impersonation of government pensioners. I 1880 Dr. Henry Faulds, an Englishman working in Tokic wrote of his experiments in the practical use of fingerprint their work, however, did not include any system of classifying fingerprints that would make large collections usable. Sir Frances Galton is usually given the credit for devising the first usable method of fingerprint classification in 1888, although recently discovered documents seem to show that a German veterinarian, Wilhelm Eber, had in the same year unsuccessfully offered his government a proposal for the use of fingerprinting that embodied many procedures later developed by others. Shortly after this Juan Vucetich of Argentina actually made a criminal identification by means of fingerprints. The system of classification now used generally throughout the United States is a modification of one developed by Sir E. R. Henry of Scotland Yard and introduced in England in 1901. In 1930 New Scotland Yard adopted a new Battley system of classifying and filing single fingerprints and fragmentary impressions to supplement the Henry system which is based upon the prints of all of the fingers.[14] Single fingerprints are now taken and used successfully by nearly all European police departments and by a handful in this country.

Dactyloscopy is based on the diverse ridge pattern of whorls, loops, and arches that are found on human fingertips. The form of these patterns around two points known as the core and the delta serve as a means of classifying every print so that it may be filed in an individual but easily ascertainable position on the basis of its own characteristics.

Fingerprinting has the merit of being simple and positive in its operation. No complicated apparatus is necessary, ink and paper being the essential equipment. Any normally intelligent person can learn to *take* fingerprints properly in an hour. Fingerprints left on objects are usually dusted with powder and photographed. Even that method has now been simplified. In 1932 Dr. Lunge, Assistant Director of the technical laboratories of the Lyons police department, announced the invention of a method of taking fingerprints that eliminates photography. The object on which the fingerprints have been made is dusted with "animal black" over which a mixture based on collodion amylacetate, acetone, and ether is poured. In a few seconds

[14] H. Battley, "Single Fingerprints."

this results in a transparent film on which the fingerpri
impression is perfectly recorded. The film can be easi
lifted and carried about like a photographic negative. Th
possibility of error in making fingerprint identifications is s
slight as to be no hindrance to their use. It has been est
mated that the chance of duplication is one in thirty billio

Twenty-four states now have fingerprint bureaus. I
1924 a National Division of Identification and Informatio
was established within the Department of Justice at Wash
ington. It exchanges and furnishes identification for a
law enforcement agencies and is an important factor in de
veloping nation-wide coöperation in its field. Use of th
bureau is entirely voluntary and police departments are no
obliged by the federal government to send fingerprin
records to it, although some states have made coöperation b
their police departments mandatory. The bureau also ha
exchange arrangements with major nations throughout th
world.

To cite an example of their usefulness: Alfred Bral,
Belgian, was committed to the U. S. Disciplinary Barrack
at Alcatraz, California, for helping a prisoner to escap
His prints were sent to the federal identification burea
which promptly forwarded a copy of them to Belgium. Th
Belgian identification service reported that Bral had serve
a two-year sentence for desertion and two briefer terms wit
a fine for abuse of confidence. In another instance th
fingerprints of Frank Alaimo charged with robbery in Colo
Panama, were forwarded to the U. S. Bureau of Investiga
tion with the result that Alaimo was recognized as Alfons
Travali, wanted by the police of Buffalo for robber
Negotiations for his return to Buffalo to face charges we
then begun.

On September 1, 1933, the federal identification burea
had 3,870,910 fingerprint records on file. During the ye
ending May 31, 1932, the bureau made 204,220 identifica
tions and 2383 fugitives were apprehended as a result.[15]

Although fingerprints are recognized as the surest aid w
have for identifying criminals we have not yet learned ho

[15] J. E. Hoover, "The United States Bureau of Investigation." *Jou
of Criminal Law and Criminology*, Vol. 23, p. 439.

gain full value from their use. If fingerprints are found
the scene of a crime, the one who left them can be identi-
:d only if his fingerprints have been taken before. If a
iminal is caught and gives a false name, the record of his
evious offenses may be ascertained if his prints happen to
: at the federal identification bureau or a state bureau with
hich those who catch him may communicate. Even then
s true identity may be concealed under a string of aliases.
ll this could be obviated if the fingerprinting of all persons
iring school years were carried out as a routine matter.
ich a procedure would not only make certain the identifica-
on of criminals but also of persons who have committed
iicide, who have been seriously injured, or who are suffer-
g from mental disease. Furthermore, the first record of
ich person would be taken at an age when his true name
id connections could be noted so that whatever aliases he
ight assume later or however much of a wanderer he might
:, his real antecedents could be established with assurance.
ingerprinting on such a grand scale might interfere to some
tent with the speed with which a central bureau for a
untry as large as ours might operate. In that event, it
ould no doubt be possible to provide several regional
ireaus to cover the country instead of one. Very likely
ich bureau would be able to make a considerable proportion
f the identifications required in its own district. For other
ises there would be needed at most a correspondence with
:n or a dozen regional bureaus.
Dr. Robert Heindl has suggested that the fingerprint
:cords of all young persons be filed in their home towns in
phabetical order according to the name of each individual.
'his would simplify the task by making it possible for any
erk to file the prints without the services of one skilled in
ngerprint classification. Then when a man is arrested he
ould be asked where his record is on file. If it cannot
ien be found, that would be sufficient proof of falsification
f name and the prisoner would remain in custody until
e chose to be truthful.
Buenos Aires tried an identification system in 1917 that
roved so useful that this so-called Argentine System was
iade compulsory in 1921. Every person is there required

to carry a numbered booklet containing his signature, pho
graph, thumb print, and his brief description. A dupli
is on file at police headquarters. These credentials are
handy for establishing identity in business dealings and
commonly used as references in business transactions
only criminals are disturbed by the requirement.

Germany and Austria make use of the Meldewesen s
tem under which every person is registered and his mo
ments recorded from the cradle to the grave. In Germ
every person must report his arrival and departure
mediately to the local police. If he changes his reside
he must present a certificate of character to the police fr
those of his previous residence. The Meldewesen laws
strictly enforced throughout Germany. The police
therefore able to locate any person, whose name is kno
without difficulty. The larger centers publish weekly l
of men wanted and their names are recorded by neighb
ing police departments in red ink in their Meldewesen fi
When any wanted person registers in a city he is discove
at once through the red-letter card already in the fi
Falsification of name is well-nigh impossible because of
rigid police check on the entire sequence of individ
records.

Another means of identifying criminals known as
Modus Operandi plan was devised by Sir Llewelyn Atche
while he was chief constable of the Yorkshire Constabul
It is based on two assumptions: that criminals are creatu
of habit and that there is no crime without a clue. A cri
nal may be identified, therefore, by his manner of work
The details of a crime are classified according to a plan wh
makes a comparison of methods possible. So far it
been applied chiefly to property crimes. The schedule to
filled out is as follows:

1. CLASSWORD .. nature of property attacked —— hotel, dw
   ing, etc.
2. ENTRY ...... place of entry —— cellar window, backd
   etc.
3. MEANS ...... what tools were used —— ladder, key, etc.
4. OBJECT ..... kind of goods taken —— furs, diamonds, etc
5. TIME .... dinnertime, church time, etc.

6. STYLE .... whether the criminal pretends to be a plumber, gas man, etc.

7. TALE .... any information given by the criminal about himself.

8. PALS .... whether alone, with confederates, a woman, etc.

9. TRANSPORT ... whether on foot, in automobile, etc.

10. TRADEMARK .. individual characteristics of the crime — leaving a sarcastic note, eating a meal, etc.

Each item in the schedule is clearly defined and numbered so that a complete description of a crime can be telegraphed in code. This assumes the establishment of clearing houses with which information can be exchanged.

The Modus Operandi system is psychologically sound. Professional criminals do have a definite method of procedure which they are not inclined to vary. Each man or gang develops a particular style of attack which is repeated both because it is successful and because change would involve the effort of learning a new way and also dangerous experimentation with what is untried. One man prefers to break into a house when he is sure everyone is in bed. Another prefers to do his work in the daytime, first making sure that no one is home by ringing the door-bell. Each develops a characteristic mode of attack. Perhaps a clearing house receives word that a man representing himself as a stocking salesman has taken deposits on orders directed to a company which he does not represent. If the game is an old one, the bureau police may have the records of several men who have played it in the past. A check up of their whereabouts may show that of half a dozen possible thieves, two are in prison, one is on probation and known to be at home when the series of thefts was committed. So the list of suspected persons narrows down to one or two individuals for whom the police may then begin a direct search.

The Modus Operandi plan at first made headway slowly in England until Scotland Yard adopted it and increased its usefulness during the World War. August Vollmer brought it to the United States but it has not yet come into general use among American police forces although it is now rapidly gaining ground. A sector system for recording both the places of residence and the operating methods of criminals has improved the Modus Operandi system by limiting the necessary scope of investigations.

Other improvements in methods of police investigation that have recently appeared include : Schemes for classifying handwriting, the use of the Dewey decimal system for recording stolen and recovered property, the development of effective laundry mark files, better laboratory equipment including microphotographic equipment and special types of microscopes, the use of the so-called "lie detector," better record keeping, including the use of a uniform crime report schedule, a uniform police chiefs' annual report, and system for following through and recording the disposition of all complaints.

4) PREVENTIVE SUPERVISION OF CRIMINALS

SPECIALIZED crime prevention is given only a minor place in the work of the American police, probably because of our unwillingness to tolerate interference with any man until he has actually done something. Ex-prisoners are more or less under the eye of the police. Vagrants are sometimes run out of town, which of course means into another one. Only in special and rare instances is anything more done. The Chicago police, however, report when and where they have observed known criminals and what conversations they may have had with them to a vagrancy section which uses the information it accumulates to obtain warrants against those who have no legitimate means of support.

Some European cities have made an attempt to do more. In Prague discharged prisoners are divided into three classes: those who are given complete freedom, those who must be reported to the police before release, and a third class called for and returned to their homes under police supervision. German prison officials notify the police of the time when all important prisoners are to be released. Rome, however, carries this work to its most rigid point by its vigilance system. This scheme allows ne'er-do-wells to be placed under police supervision for two years by the authority of a special judge. Men who are placed under police vigilance re required to live according to rules set by the police with eference to the company they may keep, the time they must e home at night, and similar details. More dangerous indi- iduals are placed under special vigilance the terms of which re enforced by a plain clothes force of about 150 men. Men under special vigilance are confined to a specified area nd their liberties are otherwise seriously curtailed. They re required to carry a book listing the requirements made of nem. Men under special vigilance are subject to summary rrest if they are found out of their districts and their full eriod of supervision begins over again.

Another phase of police protective work that is likely to ave more attention in the future than it now receives is the ducation of the public in methods of safeguarding them- elves against criminals. It has been the traditional task of atrolmen to see if store doors are properly locked. In ome cities patrolmen are now taught to make specific sug- estions to storekeepers about night lighting of shops and lleys and to help them in other ways to secure their estab- ishments against criminal entry.

The San Francisco department assigns men to teach hotel nd lodging house keepers how to protect their buildings gainst entry by burglars and how to protect themselves gainst other types of criminals that are apt to prey upon hem. Occasionally police departments advise householders hrough the public press to keep their window shades up, eave a key with a neighbor, and notify the police when they re to be absent from their homes for any great length of ime. The New York police department, under former Commissioner Enright, published and distributed pamphlets nstructing business men and householders how to guard hemselves against specific types of criminals. Vollmer eports that in Pomona, California, business men displayed igns informing purchasers that checks would be accepted rom unidentified customers only after their fingerprints had een impressed upon them. Some European police depart- nents, notably in Germany, have shown brief interesting notion pictures to audiences in the regular cinema theaters nforming them specifically and in detail how to circumvent he activities of criminals.

It seems as though it should be possible to give American audiences lessons in self-protection as vivid and unforgettable as those we now offer on the techniques of gangsters. The entire field of coöperative protective work between the police and the public against criminals has barely been touched. Means and devices to develop it await discovery by able and imaginative police officials.

5) GENERAL CRIME PREVENTION

As indicated in the previous chapter, the possibilities of preventive work by the police have remained quite in the background in the United States, except for the constructive work of August Vollmer and the short but enlightening régime of Col. Arthur Woods. The speed with which Woods, the ablest police commissioner New York has had, was turned out of office when a new city administration came into office indicates how little the people appreciate and support this type of police activity.

Throughout the country at large policewomen are the only group in the service who in any way emphasize preventive work. Appointed to police forces often because it appeared to be the fashion to have them about, policewomen began their work with women and children, gradually enlarging police functions in that special field until they made the woman's bureau a definite crime prevention agency. Now 200 cities have from one to one hundred policewomen. Altogether they handle many thousands of cases each year, many of which are clearly indicative of wide opportunities for preventive work.

THE PROSPECTS OF AMERICAN POLICE WORK

In performing their duties the American police are seriously handicapped, in comparison with their European brethren, by lack of authority. Continental policemen, as representatives of the Sovereign, have powers and privileges not shared with private citizens. Their activities are national in scope. They may detain persons even though they are not suspected criminals. They may legally subject accused persons to extensive questioning. The power of seizure and search is largely at their discretion. In Germany and Austria the police register all inhabitants and require a notification of every change of address. In other Continental countries the police register all foreigners. In general the European police are immune to prosecution by private citizens.

The police of England and the United States are entirely lacking in such privileges. We prefer to handicap them rather than to break down the ancient bulwarks raised to safeguard personal liberty. So far has this tradition been carried that the police of England and the United States have only slightly more power than any other citizen. For example, in the highly important matter of arrest, private persons have the same authority as policemen :

(*a*) To make an arrest upon the authority of a warrant issued by a magistrate.

(*b*) To make an immediate summary arrest of any person committing a misdemeanor amounting to a breach of the peace in their presence.

(*c*) To arrest, without a warrant, any person who has committed a felony or who is reasonably suspected of felony if a felony has been committed.

Only at one point does the policeman have authority not shared by other persons : He may arrest anyone whom he reasonably believes has committed a felony although in fact no felony has been committed. In some states this general law of arrest has been modified by statute.[16]

In practice, of course, private citizens rarely exercise their police powers, even if they are aware of them, preferring to leave the disagreeable task to the police who are hired and equipped for that purpose.

Unfortunately, the limitations of police authority in the United States place them in a difficult position. The plain fact is that they cannot control criminals and keep within the law themselves. If they exercise only their legal force, criminals escape and the police are charged with inefficiency. In practice, however, the police constantly exceed their rights,

[16] See article on "Arrest," by F. B. Sayre in the *Encyclopedia of the Social Sciences*, for an excellent, concise statement on arrests.

arresting persons on suspicion, rounding up men in wholesale fashion, and applying pressure upon them to make them talk.

One metropolitan police executive recently ordered his men to arrest the relatives of the men they were seeking if they could not find the persons they wanted. Probably more than half of the arrests made by the police are technically illegal ; but because those who are arrested are either uninfluential loafers or actual criminals, release is a sufficient compensation for the inconvenience of detention. The police constantly settle neighborhood squabbles and personal differences that should never get into the courts only by assuming powers that they do not legally possess.

Such unlawful activity by the police places them constantly in danger of prosecution if they unwittingly run afoul of the wrong person. It leads the police to break down legal barriers raised to protect individual liberty, with the result that their methods are as high-handed as expediency allows. Where they are responsible for prosecuting as well as apprehending offenders, that duty tends to interfere with good police work. The disturbing spectacle of a law enforcing body continually engaging in lawless acts is not likely to breed a respect for law in those who come in contact with its methods for the first time, nor does it give any citizen the comforting assurance of justice if, perchance, he should innocently arouse the attention of the police.

Handicapped by deficiencies in organization, training, and authority, the police of the United States face a task far more difficult than that of their European brethren. In the United States criminals can travel from state to state throughout a country more than three million square miles in area with never a customs barrier to cross. The use of privately owned automobiles, to an extent elsewhere unknown, makes it possible for them to run through several states in a single day without attracting the slightest attention. Yet the numerous uncoördinated police organizations are limited in their reach by budgets, laws, and policy. Contrasted with this situation is the small area, the limited mobility of people, and the carefully watched boundaries of European nations. Germany is a trifle larger than California. France is smaller than Texas. Italy is almost precisely the size of Nevada.

Not only is the territory of the United States large and easily traversed but its 125 million people are a heterogeneous lot, including 14 million aliens and 12 million negroes. The cities especially are a polyglot mixture of peoples and cultures. In New York, Boston, and Chicago from two-thirds to three-quarters of the population is of foreign parentage. New York has within its limits more Jews than ancient Palestine, more Germans than Hamburg, more Irish than Dublin, and more negroes than Birmingham, Alabama.

Furthermore, these people are living in a country where the theory of democracy has a daily influence. The idyll of the poor boy who rises to wealth and affluence is more than a pleasant tale to school children. It is accepted dogma. "Any boy in this class may become president of the United States." The effect is to make every man feel the equal of his neighbor. A tremendous premium of approval is placed upon conspicuous success. There is a drive towards higher social and economic levels that turns to irritation in the face of arbitrary obstacles. Restrictions upon conduct are resented. It is with this temper rather than with the European attitude that recognizes horizontal levels in society and leads a man to accept the position into which he was born, that the police in the United States must deal.

In view of this spirit, the seemingly boundless American faith in laws as a means of regulating the conduct of others is a curious anomaly. Perhaps thirteen thousand laws are added to the statute books in the United States every year. Many laws indicate a confusion of morality with æsthetics. Often that is forbidden which is noisy, rough, or in poor taste, while more important problems run unattended because they are superficially proper though inwardly admittedly rotten. As urban relations become more and more complex, the law forbids an increasing number of acts that are bad merely because people are crowding together and becoming ever more interdependent. Such laws are not re-enforced by a deep sense of public morality. Both because of their number and their nature it is an absolutely impossible task for the police of any great American city to enforce all of the statutes applicable in it. Sporadic attempts to enforce customarily neglected laws are useless and frequently aggravate the evil by antagonizing an already unsympathetic public.

As might be expected in view of the conditions outlined, our police are appallingly incapable of doing their work well. Criminals may therefore go about their business with considerable assurance that they will not be molested. In New York State, although many stolen cars are recovered, arrests are rarely made in more than ten per cent of the cases reported.[17] The following ratio of arrests to certain crimes known to the police in England, Wales, Canada, and in several American cities further emphasizes the limited success of the police in catching offenders.[18]

Place	Burglary	Embezzlement	Forgery	Larceny	Manslaughter	Murder	Robbery
	%	%	%	%	%	%	%
England and Wales [I][a]	25[II]	47	37	59	100	64	80[III]
Canada [b]	84 per cent Average for all Indictable Offenses						
Baltimore (Md.) [c]	21	73	31	25	62	74	47
Buffalo (N. Y.) [d]							3
Cleveland (O.) [e]	35[IV]			47	96	73	49[V]
Kansas City (Mo.) [f]	5					72[VI]	23
New York (N. Y.) [d]	14						
Rochester (N. Y.) [d]	12						30
St. Louis (Mo.) [f]	8	17	8	6		32[VI]	11
Schenectady (N. Y.) [d]	17						
Syracuse (N. Y.) [d]	7						10

I. The figures for the American Cities relate to the year 1924 ; those for England and Wales for 1925.
II. Burglary, Shopbreaking and Housebreaking.
III. Robbery and Extortion.
IV. Burglary and Larceny ; Housebreaking and Larceny.
V. Robbery and Assault to Rob.
VI. Murder and Manslaughter.
a. Judicial Statistics, England and Wales, 1925. Police Returns, Table XVIII, pp. 104-107.
b. Forty-eighth Annual Report of Criminal Statistics, 1924, Canada. Police Statistics, pp. 318-321, Table XVI.
c. Baltimore Criminal Justice Commission. Third Annual Report, 1925 ; Table, p. 5 (1924).
d. Report on Police Administration in New York State, by Bruce Smith, "Municipal Police Administration," p. 7.
e. Cleveland Association for Criminal Justice. Fourth Quarterly Bulletin, Dec., 1924, Table 2, p. 10.
f. Missouri Crime Survey, 1926 ; Tables pp. 543-545.

[17] "Report of the New York State Crime Commission, 1927," p. 39.
[18] L. N. Robinson, "The Relation of the Police and the Courts to the Crime Problem," p. 6.

Although the defects of American police systems cannot easily be overcome, there is no reason to suppose that the difficulties of police work are in themselves insurmountable. In fact, they are not greatly different from those which are met with considerable success in other activities. Great business enterprises, such as news gathering organizations, daily meet the need of coördinating the activities of a varied personnel operating over far-flung boundaries under conditions demanding speed, precision and adaptability. Social agencies accept as routine work the task of dealing intimately with the conduct of persons in alien culture groups without the implied authority of a uniform. Business leaders long ago found it wise to choose employees carefully and to train them adequately to meet their tasks. Even in some branches of the public service the bugaboo of political interference has been removed when people have realized the direct and vital importance to them of a particular department, like that of public health administration.

Yet in police work these same difficulties have not been mastered because their roots are thrust deep into a set of basic social attitudes that cannot easily be removed. On the one hand are those who are selfishly interested in police work and are constantly using pressure to have it done so as to further their own interests, legitimate or illegitimate. Lumped together in this group are criminals who want to escape interference, taxicab companies who want special privileges, politicians who want to increase their power, business corporations and labor unions who want to win strikes, and the like. All of these interests are organized. They pull strings to get what they want. They disregard the result of their demands upon the general efficiency of the police service.

On the other side is the great public, unorganized and uninformed. Its attitudes vary from apathy to anger ; from a cry for action to a complaint of officiousness. The side of police work that ordinary citizens usually meet is traffic regulation. The nature of that contact is likely to breed in us an unsympathetic feeling towards the whole service. With its protective work we are not familiar. Urban living has pushed the problem of police administration entirely out of our ken. We simply know that the police organization is there. When our immediate neighborhood is frightened by a series of thefts we call for police protection. When we want to buy a lottery ticket we resent police interference. Beyond that the bald fact is that we are not vitally interested in crime nor in criminals and we feel no genuine responsibility for the crime situation. Our verbal battle against crime is little more than a means of exercising the pleasant emotion of self-righteousness. We complain of police corruption when gangsters go unpunished, but we give gambling houses the money with which the police are bribed. We are overwhelmed with compassion for the family of the policeman shot by rum-runners but we continue to patronize the liquor store they were supplying.

Few adults have the good sportsmanship to accept punishments justly deserved. Instead, "seeing some one who can fix it" is a matter of course even for respectable people, and he who knows no string to pull is considered unfortunate.

Inasmuch as policemen are appointed by a community from among its citizens, the police merely reflect the ideals of the city they serve. There is no alchemy in a uniform that can transform an everyday man into a personification of wisdom and virtue. Whenever there is a vigorous and well-defined public opinion expressed in a community, the police are sensitive to it. Unfortunately, public attitudes are so often illogical and unpredictable that police organizations must either disregard them or exist in a state of confusion and indecision of policy that destroys their efficiency. Wherever the citizens of a community are in general agreement about what conduct they will or will not tolerate, the police are assured of a support of inestimable value.

The direction of police improvement is much more certain than the possibility of its early attainment. Generally stated, progress requires the professionalization of the American police with all of the changes in viewpoint and method that professionalization involves.

A good police system requires capable, trained, imaginative leadership. There is no adequate substitute for competent executives. The police of Vienna have been under the direction of a former chancellor. One Commissioner of the Metropolitan Police of London was formerly the Governor-General of Canada. Public opinion in the United States has not yet reached the point where it will induce men of comparable qualifications, the Secretary of War for example, to become the heads of our larger police departments. In Paris the prefects are nearly all university men. European police laboratories are directed by such eminent jurists and scientists as Dr. Gustave De Rechter of Belgium, and the late Dr. Siegfried Türkel of Austria. Men of this stamp bring into police work not only adequate technical knowledge but a thoroughly scientific attitude that lifts police work to a high level of competency and insures its continuous progress. Police leadership of this sort could leaven the entire organization with a new spirit, a new pride in its work. It could lift the level of honesty. It could create an *esprit de corps* that would vivify and improve even routine patrol work. In its wake one might hope to see such improvements as the establishment of adequate police training schools, scientific police laboratories, the appearance of professional police journals of high standing,[19] and coördination of the work of the many state, federal, and municipal police bureaus. When these changes begin to appear, we may expect better things of police work in the United States. The association of many police organizations of the United States with those of other countries through the International Association of Chiefs of Police, the International Police Conference and the International World Police is already helping to spread throughout this country as well as others a knowledge of advanced police methods. Their application depends upon whether a majority of the voting public can become genuinely desirous of police improvement to the point of seeking and supporting scientific rather than political leadership in police administration.

[19] There are many local police magazines published in the United States, but they contain matter of little value except for entertainment, and they fall far short of being professional journals. The first number of the *American Journal of Police Science*, published not by the police but by the newly created Scientic Crime Detection Laboratory, affiliated with Northwestern University, appeared in January-February, 1930. In July, 1932, it was fused with the *Journal of Criminal Law and Criminology*.

CHAPTER XIII

THE ADMINISTRATORS OF CRIMINAL JUSTICE

THE ORIGIN OF ENGLISH COURT PROCEDURE

THE outlines of our present judicial system first took definit
shape in twelfth and thirteenth century England. Befor
the Assize of Clarendon in 1166 there was a great variet
of tribunals, such as church courts, moots, baronial courts
and the courts merchant. Only very slowly as the king'
courts increased in power did the people turn to them as th
safest guardian of their rights.

Since there were no king's police, each town was require(
to appoint four to six watchmen to follow wrongdoers im
mediately and to summon the townspeople who, if they wer
above fifteen years of age, were also obliged to follow hu
and cry. When a felon was caught red-handed by such
posse, he was killed then and there.

Men of fighting age — but not women, children, nor ol(
men — could bring a charge, called an appeal, against a sus
pect who was not caught in the act. Only the victim ha(
this privilege, which he might exercise only in good fait!
and within a year and a day from the occurrence of the al
leged crime. If a person so appealed (charged) failed t(
appear he might be outlawed. If he came to court he migh
take exceptions to the procedure. If they were not grante(
the court then set a date for trial and required pledges fo
the appearance of the contestants.

Trials were of several kinds ; all of them being quite un
like their modern successors. Trial by battle was originall
a fight to the death between the plaintiff and the defendant
If the accused person was not vanquished before the star
came out he was acquitted and his accuser was put in prison

Trial by compurgation was another means of deciding a case. Compurgators were originally kinsfolk who were ready to fight in a sort of legally sanctioned feud. Later, compurgators were simply required to offer a sworn denial of the guilt of the principal in accordance with a set form. If a defendant on his oath formally denied the accusation against him and could get a sufficient number of compurgators to support his oath he was acquitted.

Another type of trial supported by the prevailing belief in miracles was the ordeal, of which there were three forms: ordeal by cold water, ordeal by boiling water, and ordeal by red-hot iron. All of these forms were solemnly carried out in accordance with an elaborate ritual of fasting, communion and prayer which preceded the test itself. Those who were tried by cold water were bound with the knees drawn up to the chest and with the hands clasped in front of them. A rope was fastened about them and a knot made in it above the head at a distance equal to the length of the hair. The accused were then let gently down into the water. If the water received them to the depth of the knot they were drawn up and freed. If it rejected them and they floated, they were found guilty.

In the ordeal by red-hot iron accused persons were required to carry a glowing rod of iron a distance of nine feet. The hand was then kept bandaged for three nights, after which the wound was examined. If it was clean defendants were innocent; if unhealthy they were guilty.

Somewhat similar in plan was the ordeal by hot water, in which accused persons were required to grasp a stone suspended in boiling water at a depth of one palm in the single proof, or up to an elbow in the triple proof. The arm was then sealed and examined at the end of three days, as was done in the ordeal by iron.

In 1166 the Assize of Clarendon seized upon an old Norman form of inquest, rarely used, and evolved from it a tribunal of twelve men in each hundred or four in each township to report, on oath, those persons who were commonly believed to be guilty of certain crimes. Their task was simply to give definite consideration and form to what was already a matter of current rumor. Persons named by this group of men were then tried by ordeal, compurgation, or battle. Such was the original form of our grand jury.

Just fifty years after the Assize of Clarendon, the Lateran Council (1216) abolished trial by ordeal. Trial by battle still remained, in fact was not legally abolished in England until 1819, but it became an increasingly unsatisfactory means of achieving justice. In its place qualified persons were required to attend the courts to serve on a petit jury which had assumed the task of determining the guilt of those who were accused. Jury trial was not made obligatory until 1772, but its convenience and success as well as the pressure put upon defendants by the courts made its use common. By the end of the thirteenth century the basic elements of modern English and American criminal administration had been fairly well laid down.

MODERN COURT ORGANIZATION IN THE UNITED STATES

THE machinery of criminal justice in the United States centers about the systems of federal and state courts which are entirely independent of each other. The federal courts have jurisdiction over all matters arising under the Constitution of the United States, the laws of the United States, or treaties made under their authority. Inasmuch as the federal government has only the powers specifically delegated to it by the Constitution, it cannot recognize common law offenses. The authority of the federal courts includes both criminal and equity cases.

The federal court organization consists of the Supreme Court of the United States, ten Circuit Courts of Appeals, and ninety District Courts. The Supreme Court has a limited original jurisdiction and receives most of its cases from the lower federal courts. The Circuit Courts receive cases from the District Courts on appeal. Like the Supreme Court, they function without a jury. The District Courts are usually served by one and a jury. They have a wide original jurisdiction.

Separate from the courts but prosecuting cases in them is the government's legal force in the Department of Justice.

The chief of this branch is the Attorney-General, who represents the government in cases in which it is interested. Under him in each federal judicial district is a district attorney acting as his representative. These officials as well as the federal court judges are all appointed.

The states also have higher and lower courts that vary considerably in their titles but that are essentially alike in their organization. There is a state Supreme Court served by a varying number of justices who may be either appointed or elected. Beneath it are Appellate Courts that receive cases on appeal from the lower courts or that assume original jurisdiction in important cases. The County or Superior Courts served by a judge and jury have a wide original jurisdiction. The preliminary hearings and examinations are held in Magistrates' courts, variously known as police courts, municipal courts, or justices' courts, which also have summary powers in petty cases.

The law officers in charge of the state's legal interests consist of an Attorney-General elected by the people, his assistants, and county or district attorneys elected by the people of the county.

Private persons engaged in litigation in the courts need not employ attorneys but ordinarily do so except in petty cases. Attorneys employed to conduct the affairs of clients are not only bound to protect their interests but are also legally officers of the court, sworn to conduct cases in a seemly manner and solely on their merits.

CRIMINAL COURT PROCEDURE

A CRIMINAL case may start with the arrest and subsequent complaint against a person caught in the act of committing an alleged crime, by the making of a complaint before an inferior magistrate who then issues a warrant for the accused person's arrest, by indictment or presentment of a grand jury, or in some jurisdictions by a charge, known as an information, prepared by a prosecuting attorney. In cases of a trivial nature the accused person may be allowed to appear in court, without arrest, in answer to a summons. Except in some capital cases arrested individuals may be admitted to bail at once by proper authorities, if they can get sureties, so that they need not be confined while awaiting a hearing or a trial. Prisoners have the right to consult counsel or friends.

Within a few hours after arrest accused persons are brought before a magistrate. In most states in trivial cases, like traffic offenses or breaches of the peace, the justice hears the evidence and passes judgment on the issue at once. When the offense charged is more serious, the magistrate conducts a preliminary hearing which is not a trial but is simply to consider whether the accused could be convicted if the evidence presented were found to be true. Ordinarily, only the evidence for the prosecution is heard. If the magistrate believes there is sufficient cause, he holds the prisoner for the grand jury or for trial.

The prosecuting attorney, who is often not represented at the preliminary hearing, then prepares a carefully worded indictment setting forth the charge and the facts to be proved and presents it to the grand jury. The modern grand jury may consist of from twelve to twenty-four persons, frequently twenty-three, who consider the evidence put before them by the prosecutor. They do not hear the accused person nor his witnesses. If a majority of the grand jury is satisfied that there is valid ground for prosecuting under the indictment, they return a "true bill" to the court. Otherwise they ignore it and the accused is discharged.

In an attempt to expedite proceedings, eighteen states allow prosecuting attorneys to bring a person to trial upon a properly worded charge, called an information, made up by themselves without recourse to a grand jury.

After a person has been indicted, on the date set for the trial the defendant is brought into court to answer to the charge made against him. There are several possible pleas, the most common being "guilty" or "not guilty." The former admits the charge and allows the judge to pass sentence at once. A plea of "not guilty" leads to a trial.

In a few jurisdictions, notably in Maryland and Connecticut, defendants may waive trial by jury and have their cases disposed of by the judge alone. The usual procedure in other states is to impanel a jury of twelve men selected from the tax or voting lists to hear the evidence and render a verdict upon it. Both the prosecuting attorney and the defense attorney have the right to challenge a limited number of jurors without assigning a reason. Persons so challenged are not permitted to sit on that jury. In addition any number of jurors may be challenged for any cause that would unfit them for their duty. Each side, of course, tries to get jurors likely to favor its case.

The function of the judge is to preside over the trial, to decide all questions of law that may arise, such as whether evidence may be admitted or excluded, to give an explanation of the law in the case (a charge) to the jury at the conclusion of the trial, and after hearing the jury's verdict to pass sentence.

The prosecuting attorney opens the case for the state by a speech to the jury briefly setting forth what he intends to prove. He then proceeds to examine the witnesses for the state. After he has ended his questioning of a witness the defendant's attorney may cross-examine him and the district attorney re-examine him if he wishes to do so. At the conclusion of the state's evidence the defendant's counsel may ask to have the case dismissed on the ground that, even were the evidence true, guilt has not been proved. If this motion is refused the defendant's counsel proceeds to examine his witnesses, who in turn may be cross-examined by the prosecutor. Upon the conclusion of the evidence the district attorney and counsel for the defendant, in order, make a shrewdly worded, often vividly emotional, appeal to the jury, setting forth the merits of their cases. A skilful lawyer may often win his case through the strength of his final address to the jury.

The judge then explains to the jury the law referring to the offense that has been charged, instructs them how to analyze the evidence, and tells them what must be proved to warrant a verdict of "guilty." In practice in the United States it is customary for counsel on both sides to turn in to the judge the instructions they want him to give to the jury. The judge accepts those that are in accordance with the law, edits them, and delivers them to the jury as part of his charge. The clever within-the-law wording of instructions by partisan counsel are, of course, not intended to insure impartial and transparent information for the jury.

After the judge's charge the jury retires until it reaches a verdict or discovers that it cannot agree upon one, in which unfortunate event a new trial must be held. When a decision is reached the jury returns and announces the verdict. Then, unless the court grants a motion for arrest of judgment or for a new trial on the basis of error, the judge may place the case on file or pass sentence of fine, imprisonment, or both, in accordance with the law. After sentence the judge may also suspend it and place the convicted person on probation under the care of a probation officer. During the entire trial the defendant must be present in court, although he need not testify, and his presence must be noted in the records. Appeals to a higher court may be taken by the defendant on the basis of exceptions noted during the trial and in accordance with the rules described by law. The result of this procedure is, theoretically, justice.

The criminal courts dispose of men's dearest possessions, money, liberty, and reputations. To save them, men will fight, plead, pay. The whole process is emotional and spectacular. Public sentiment is aroused. Those in authority face conflicting waves of influence. They have opportunities to exploit the situation. A host of human interests not remotely connected with justice are involved. As a result, the courts in action differ from the courts in legal blueprint, as a man differs from his skeleton. They are alive with human strivings. They can only be understood through an examination of the human factors in their conduct.

THE PUBLIC PROSECUTOR

THE king-pin of the entire scheme of criminal procedure, an official who exercises more power than either judge or jury, is the public prosecutor. When a magistrate binds a suspect over for the grand jury the prosecutor may refuse to present the case, although he has no common-law right to do so. When he does come before the grand jury with his recommendations the jurors can do little but rubber-stamp his requests. They have no legal training. They ordinarily hear only such evidence as the prosecutor lays before them. If the district attorney wishes to drop a case in which there has been no preliminary hearing, without assuming any responsibility for doing so, he may offer such inconclusive evidence to the grand jury that they will refuse an indictment. Prosecutions initiated by information are entirely in the public attorney's hands. The prosecutor also has the power to enter on the record a *nolle prosequi*, which means that he will not prosecute the defendants in that case. Such action on a valid indictment absolutely prevents further proceedings. The district attorney may accept a plea of guilty to a lesser offense in preference to trying a defendant on a more serious charge. When a case actually does come to trial the effectiveness and fairness of the prosecution rests largely with the district attorney. In populous districts prosecuting attorneys receive thousands of complaints from citizens each year by telephone, letters and personal calls. With the prosecutor rests the decision as to whether to ignore them, investigate them, dispose of them informally by bargaining, bluffing, or threatening, or to initiate formal proceedings.

A striking example of the real power of the public prosecutor appears in the records of felonies made by the Missouri Association for Criminal Justice covering a period of two years in the county districts and one year in St. Louis, Jackson, and Buchanan counties. Arrests were made and warrants applied for in 8637 cases. Of these cases, 400 were found guilty after trial, 1832 pleaded guilty, and 6135 cases on which action was started were not prosecuted by the state.[1] In the face of a record like this the power of judge and jury dwindles into insignificance. That of the public prosecutor seems nearly unlimited.

Unfortunately for the good of the office, the responsibility of the public prosecutor is by no means comparable to his power. Under urban conditions much of his work never comes to public attention. Much of it is office work not subject to public scrutiny. Cases are numerous and the prosecutor's office rarely has adequate facilities for investigating and preparing them. He must therefore choose whether to try them or to dispose of them informally.

[1] "The Missouri Crime Survey," pp. 121-122.

Cases in which the accused has died or is in prison, cases in which essential witnesses cannot be found, old forgotten cases discovered in the files of a previous attorney, are obviously best handled by nolle-prossing. Other cases in which there is a chance of conviction may sometimes better be handled informally.

It is because many cases are rightly dropped with only the prosecutor and his assistants in a position to pass judgment on them that the nolle-prossing power is open to abuse. Some jurisdictions have tried to curb it by requiring the concurrence of the judge. Unfortunately he has no facilities for investigating the cases that the prosecutor wishes to drop, especially when an attorney may bring blanket nolle prosses several hundred in number. In the Cleveland survey one instance appeared in 1920 when "nolles in 410 cases were simultaneously presented to the court and entered." [2]

Actually the *nolle prosequi* has been freely used and subjected to such abuse that courts and crime commissions have called attention to it and laws have been passed to curb it. Over 11 per cent of the indicted cases in Cleveland in 1925 were nolle prossed, over 10 per cent of those in St. Louis in 1923-1924, over 28 per cent of those in Minneapolis in 1923, and over 25 per cent of those entering the trial court in Chicago. [3] New York has abolished the formal *nolle prosequi*, but the court upon motion of either the district attorney or the defendant's counsel dismisses about the same proportion of cases as are elsewhere nolle prossed.

In cities where the free use of the *nolle prosequi* has been criticized, prosecutors have apparently become more discreet, since the proportion of "nolled" cases has declined. However, the practice of accepting pleas of "guilty" to lesser offenses than those charged is now so extensive that a prosecutor still has ample liberty to use his own judgment in the disposition of cases. In Chicago in 1926, out of 2449 convictions secured on felony charges, 594 were on the crime originally charged and 1855 were for lesser crimes than those charged. In New York State in 1926, pleas of guilty *of another offense* were made in 37.5 of all of the cases

[2] Cleveland Foundation, "Criminal Justice in Cleveland," p. 182.
[3] R. Moley, "Politics and Criminal Prosecution," p. 152.

arraigned, and in New York City pleas of guilty to another offense were accepted in 52.5 per cent of all of the cases arraigned.[4]

The acceptance of a plea of guilty to a lesser offense is only a part of a more extensive bargaining process that goes on between prosecutors and defendants. Pleas of guilty to the offense charged may also be the result of an understanding between the attorneys for the state and the defendant that the prosecutor will plead with the judge for leniency or help the prisoner to get an early parole. Prosecutors defend the practice because of the need to clear a crowded docket of unimportant cases and because the court is often unable to consider surrounding circumstances that, in justice, require a disposition not open to the judge. However, the proportion of felony cases settled by a plea of guilty is so great that their alleged lack of importance becomes questionable. Undoubtedly the offender's background merits extra-legal consideration, although there may be a difference of opinion as to whether the prosecutor is the proper person to do social case work.

On the other hand, the value of being able to "point with pride" to a long list of convictions at election time is certainly not a forgotten element in the mind of the prosecutor in the practice of informal compromise, while the judge who escapes all possibility of reversal by a higher court, and the defendant who drives a good bargain in terms of money and punishment both gain by pleas of "guilty." The only loser is the taxpayer, who pays for a protection that he does not get.

Obviously an office with such wide and unregulated powers as that of the public prosecutor is extremely useful to politicians. Influential members of the community, corporations, and organizations may be impressed and made grateful by the prosecutor's energetic attacks upon their foes or by leniency towards their own failings. Through the public prosecutor party leaders may grant favors, punish political irregulars, and prevent interference with their programs by reform agencies. Consequently the office is often managed in accordance with political expediency and the public prose-

[4] R. Moley, *op. cit.*, table, p. 169.

cutor is more likely to shine as a political strategist than as an officer of justice.

Assistant prosecutors are characteristically young men recently admitted to the bar who quite naturally look upon their office as a stepping-stone to more important positions. Their hope is to gain experience and prestige. Sensational trials cleverly handled make good newspaper copy. The successful prosecution of such cases wins votes. Consequently the state is more likely to find itself running a training school than a capably staffed prosecutor's office. Of nearly one hundred members of the Cleveland bar who individually expressed their opinions of their municipal and county prosecutors, ninety-two declared them incapable of properly performing the duties of their offices.[5] A chief assistant in the Los Angeles prosecutor's office stated that less than one in ten of the assistants who receive appointments to that office has more than one year's experience at the bar.[6] It was found that 40 per cent of the prosecutors in Missouri are not law school graduates and many of them have a limited preliminary education.[7]

The work of the prosecutor's office is also frequently handicapped by inadequate equipment. Although efficient offices like that of New York County may be adequately housed, have the services of medical, photographic, and engineering specialists, and the facilities of a law library of 42,000 volumes, most prosecutors can only look upon such an organization as a dream. Away from the great cities library facilities are altogether inadequate. The county prosecutor must act as a jack-of-all-trades able to do the neglected work of coroner, sheriff, and detective as well as that of his own office. Records are so poorly kept as to be well-nigh useless. Expense appropriations are skimpy. In some states there is not even an allowance for clerical assistance. Salaries are low even in large cities compared to the professional earnings of other members of the bar, ranging from $400 a year in some Nebraska counties to a maximum for the country of $15,000 a year in Cook County, Illinois.

[5] Cleveland Foundation, *op. cit.*, pp. 133 and 167.

[6] R. Moley, *op. cit.*, p. 67.

[7] "The Missouri Crime Survey," p. 157.

In Vermont salaries range from $450 to $1700 a year, in Wyoming, $1200 to $2000 and in Nebraska, $400 to $4000. The maximum actually paid in only one or two counties in Pennsylvania and New Jersey is $12,000, in Indiana, $10,000 and in Massachusetts $9000.[8]

When the tremendous power of the prosecutor's office is considered it would seem that only politicians and criminals have paid sufficient attention to it. Yet it remains the most vital part of the entire machinery of administering criminal justice ; an office upon which the full glare of an intelligent public interest should be centered in order that men of the highest talent and of unimpeachable integrity may be elected to it, and thereafter safeguarded by a thorough recording of the disposition of all cases and the specific reasons therefor.

THE MAGISTRATE

In actual practice, second in importance only to the prosecutor, stands the examining magistrate of our municipal courts. To the multitudes charged with petty offenses, the usually peaceful citizens who violate traffic ordinances, drunks, vagrants, ne'er-do-wells involved in disorderly conduct, the magistrate is *the* judge. In a great city his court is crowded every morning with these unfortunates whose cases he hears and disposes of summarily. Rarely do these petty offenders have lawyers. They are prosecuted by the policemen who arrested them or by an officer detailed to handle police cases. Often the defendants make no attempt to examine witnesses against them. The judge finds them "not guilty" and dismisses their cases, or "guilty" and assesses punishment.

Few municipal courts live up to the layman's conception of a hall of justice. In part this is due to the conditions under which such courts are held. The dockets are crowded. Cases must be disposed of with reasonable speed. The records of repeaters are not usually accessible. Certain types of offenses and offenders reappear with such frequency that a particular method of handling them becomes habitual, and

[8] De Long and Baker, "The Prosecuting Attorney." *Journal of Criminal Law and Criminology*, Vol. 23, p. 943.

they are given the routine useless dose that they have swallowed without improvement many times before.

The practice of electing judges, which forces them to look to a political machine for support, also makes them amenable to suggestions from political workers whose constituents get into trouble. There is a good deal of visiting with judges in chambers and of subdued conferences at the bench that cause friendless defendants to suspect that Justice can wink. In this atmosphere the ignorant petty offender before the municipal court is more likely to gain an impression compounded of confusion, indifference, and bewilderment than of dignity, firmness, and justice. The more intelligent citizen guilty of a technical crime is likely to leave with a feeling of disgust.

Since this is the prevailing form of introduction to our courts and the only type of court experience that most persons have, their respect for the entire judicial process is transmuted into a mild cynicism towards anything that savors of lawyers and courts.

Another distinctly different sort of prisoner that is brought before the magistrate is neither overwhelmed nor angered by court procedure. This group comprises the habitual felons facing preliminary examinations to see whether they shall be held for the grand jury or dismissed. These disciples of Machiavelli are well acquainted with the practicalities of court procedure and they intend to profit by its failings. To them the magistrate's court represents the first, and often the easiest, opportunity to escape the uncomfortable grip of the law. Sophisticated, represented by attorneys whose chief qualifications are their political connections, they intend to take full advantage of the flaws in the magistrate's court. That weaknesses abound is undeniable.

Although the abilities of magistrates vary so greatly that it would be unfair to characterize them in blanket fashion as incapable, magistrates as a group tend to be of inferior caliber. Lack of experience and of legal knowledge is too common a characteristic among them. The standards set for the office are low. In Philadelphia magistrates need not be lawyers. In Chicago only fourteen of the forty judges elected to the Chicago Municipal Court since 1917 have had any college training whatsoever. The judges of the Cleveland Municipal Court were characterized by Smith and Ehrmann in the Cleveland Survey as "inferior in quality and ineffectual in character."[9] Probably "ineffectual character" marked by a lack of courage and resourcefulness is a greater handicap to a magistrate than a lack of legal scholarship. After all, the municipal court deals more largely with human emotions than with legal abstractions and, if necessary, it can be managed passably well with a rough and ready knowledge of the law if it is based upon sincerity and a genuine insight into human nature.

The chief reason for unsatisfactory magistrates is unsatisfactory aims in the political factions that secure their appointment or election. Any magistrate, however strong, finds it difficult, particularly in an elective office, to escape political influence. Unfortunately, it seems that many of them gain their offices in the first place because they have been judged unlikely to resist pressure from their friends. According to the *Chicago Tribune* of April 20, 1928, sixteen out of the thirty-seven judges of the Chicago Municipal Court were away from the city in attendance upon the two political conventions then in session at Springfield. Several of these magistrates are local political bosses.

The recent exposures of corruption among the *appointed* magistrates in New York City indicates fairly well that the governing ideals of the party that elevates them to the bench is a better gauge of the quality of magistrates than the methods of attaining office. In March 1930 a New York grand jury submitted a report sharply criticizing the New York magistrates for their political activities, for the habit of holding conferences in chambers, for permitting improper practices by court officers and attendants, and for general lack of consideration for persons having business in the court. Following this in the winter of 1930-1931 came the exposure of a ring of corruption in the lower courts involving magistrates, attorneys practising in the courts, and police, which resulted in the resignation or disappearance of several magistrates.

These very conditions that preclude the possibility of

[9] Cleveland Foundation, *op. cit.*, p. 253.

justice for the uninitiated furnish the means by which shrewd offenders can escape. Faulty record systems make it difficult to uncover their histories. Their attorneys are political workers capable of exerting pressure where it will be useful. They are part of the inside courthouse ring able to use every device of friendship or profit to gain advantages for their clients.

The importance of these conditions in the magistrates' court lies in the proportion of serious cases that are terminated there. Magistrates' examinations have never attracted much attention and have been thought of frequently as a means of eliminating obviously faulty cases, and as time-wasting preliminaries to indictment and trial. So well accepted is this notion that such hearings are often not attended by any representative of the prosecutor's office. Yet the records from every American city for which facts are available make plain that this casual neglect of the preliminary hearing is based upon an utterly fallacious assumption. The examination is not an inconsequential proceeding. Often it is not preliminary to indictment and trial. Instead, in a large proportion of cases it represents a complete settlement through the dismissal of the charge and the release of the prisoner.

In 1926 in New York 58.7 per cent of the felony cases were dismissed or discharged in the preliminary hearing. The proportion of cases similarly eliminated in 1926 in Chicago was 48.8; in Milwaukee 17.3; in Philadelphia 78; in St. Louis 34.7; and in Cleveland 38.6.[10] In view of these facts magistrates' courts might well be afforded some of the attention hitherto lavished upon the later but less influential points in the judicial process.

THE TRIAL JUDGE

THE trial courts have captured popular interest because their proceedings are public and the drama of the trial is often spectacular. Cases that have aroused the emotions of the people and have been made vivid by extensive newspaper accounts of the crime, escape, and detection of the criminal

[10] R. Moley, *op. cit.*, table, p. 26.

are not easily dropped by the wayside, but are forced into an open trial. Hence the courts that hear these cases receive an attention not vouchsafed to other parts of the criminal procedure.

In spite of obvious failings the trial judge stands out as one of the most hopeful figures in the entire scheme of criminal justice. He has been less besmirched by the corruption about him than other officers. He still retains a large measure of that public confidence that prosecutors and criminal lawyers have lost. The measure of scorn that has been heaped upon judges who have been implicated in corrupt dealings is itself evidence that conduct, more or less expected in some public servants, cannot be condoned in those who have assumed the judicial robe.

The tendency is to recognize the judge as the most likely hope for court improvement by increasing his powers. It has often been said that in the state courts, judges are little more than umpires. True, it is recognized that a strong judge may by his manner and actions in the courtroom noticeably affect the outcome of the trial, particularly in his influence upon the jury. Nevertheless, his legal powers have been exceedingly narrow. Now there are signs of a change.

The rise of probation has given the judge the machinery for exercising discretion in sentencing convicted prisoners. Six states have followed the lead of the federal courts in giving judges the power to comment on the weight and credibility of the evidence before the court. Far more important than this in its implications is the provision made in several states for the waiver of a jury trial and the submission of the entire case to the judge for determination. Maryland has long given the accused this privilege. Connecticut, Wisconsin, and Michigan have more recently followed Maryland's example. Several other states have provided for the waiver of a jury trial in certain types of criminal cases.

In view of the increasing power of the judge it is essential that he be wisely selected and thereafter adequately protected from interference. The present scheme of electing judges to office is not satisfactory. Under urban conditions it is absurd to believe that voters can be aware of the qualifications of the men who seek the office. The way is open for small organized groups, who have a definite interest in the personnel of the courts, to elect the man they want. Inasmuch as the criminal and quasi-criminal elements have the most vital interest in the courts, it is their influence that is organized. Their political machine picks the people who are to run. In Chicago the 28 circuit and superior court judges are nominated by ward committeemen of the political parties who make up a union ticket. At one time Al Capone claimed control of 25 of the 50 ward committeemen in Chicago.

The elective system may cause judges to indulge in disgusting self-publicity both in court and out. It makes it necessary for them to advertise their qualifications and to cater to the prejudices of racial, religious, labor, and fraternal groups. They must be socially amenable and willing to make a gracious handshaking appearance at endless social functions. They must see to it that their names appear frequently in the newspapers. The utter importance of the name is a commonplace to every political observer who has seen unknown men, or candidates rejected by their own party, elected to office because they bore a name similar to that of a popular nominee. Electioneering of this sort is decidedly harmful to the judicial office and makes impartial trials impossible. It is not pleasant for the judge who leaves himself open to thrusts from conflicting groups. It invites harsh and spectacular sentences to gain public favor and quiet lenience in chambers to satisfy the requirements of political lawyers.

The investigators for the Cleveland Survey found the police court using a "motion in mitigation" of sentence in such a manner as to make a farce of the entire judicial procedure. Fines totaling $101,650 in 314 liquor law cases originating in one month were reduced by $42,135 through motions in mitigation made in 193 cases and allowed in 114.[11] Subterfuges of this sort are hardly consonant with the expected character of judicial proceedings.

Attempts to remove the evils of the elective system have

[11] Cleveland Foundation, *op. cit.*, p. 286.

taken many forms. The Chicago Bar Association has moved a timid step forward in polling its members on the nominees of the ward bosses and in some cases it has campaigned for the desirable ones. In Cleveland the judges are elected on a non-partisan ticket and the Bar Association has assumed the task of campaigning for the candidates it favors.

Whether appointed judges will be better than elected judges depends upon the manner of their choice. If the mayor or the governor simply appoints the nominee of the political boss in the section to be served, the method has nothing to commend it in preference to a popular election.

Suggestions for improvement include modifications of both the elective and appointive systems. The following three methods were recommended for Cleveland in order of their preference and possibly also in the inverse order of the probability of their achievement:

1. The appointment of judges for a limited term with the provision that they run for election at the end of that time, not against another candidate but against their own record in office.

2. The election of a Chief Justice who would appoint his associates.

3. The election of judges for a short first term with possible reelection for progressively longer terms on the basis of their own records, the question before the people being simply "Shall this judge be retained?" [12]

A good non-partisan civic league or an alert bar association might wield a tremendous influence in the nomination and election of suitable candidates or under an appointive scheme they might prepare a list of nominees from which the governor or mayor might make an appointment.

THE ATTORNEY FOR THE DEFENSE

WITH few exceptions criminal lawyers can only build up a regular, remunerative patronage among those whose vocation is crime. Success depends upon gaining acquittals or reductions of sentences. This in turn, in view of the conditions surrounding the office of prosecutor and examining

[12] Cleveland Foundation, *op. cit.*, p. 276.

magistrate, requires influential political connections. Hence, successful specialists in criminal law work in the gray borderland between crime and politics, using the tactics of both fields. Knowledge of the underworld and political influence are far more important to them than legal skill.

It would be quite unfair to assume that every attorney who defends a criminal case is of this sort. However, inasmuch as a civil law practice is infinitely more profitable than legitimate criminal law practice, more impersonal, and more interesting to those who enjoy solving questions of law rather than in dealing with persons amidst the emotions of a court drama, it has attracted the best legal minds and has become more respectable than criminal law. This in turn exercises a selective effect that favors the civil branch. Only 12 out of 386 members of the Cleveland Bar who answered a questionnaire took criminal cases regularly. As a result, those engaged in defending criminal cases fall roughly into some such categories as these :

1. Lawyers recently admitted to the bar who will take what work they can get for the sake of experience and a small fee.
2. Poor incapable lawyers who frequent the courts in the hope of being appointed to defend a client who has no attorney.
3. Good civil lawyers who occasionally handle an easy criminal case for a friend.
4. Capable lawyers such as an ex-prosecutor or a law school professor engaged or appointed by a judge to defend the accidental or single-offender type of criminal charged with a serious crime.
5. Successful attorneys whose business is largely the defense of clients in criminal cases.

A rule of thumb classification of their clients would show the new attorneys, the incapable, and the civil lawyers taking the minor cases of ignorant or technical offenders, the capable lawyers of the fourth class handling a few spectacular cases, often of single offenders, and the regular criminal lawyers defending the professional and organized criminals whose acts are of greatest social importance.

Judged by the number of cases disposed of out of court or by pleas of guilty in court, the successful criminal lawyer is seldom found in action at a trial. His work involves little law. It consists chiefly of keeping on good terms with the "boys" around the courthouse, of "seeing" the right persons, of bargaining with the prosecuting attorney for the best possible terms, and of getting the case heard before the right judge. Since one judge may have the habit of putting on probation men who have committed a particular crime while his brother on the bench gives every such offender the maximum sentence, apart from any matter of influence, it makes a world of difference what judge presides over a case.

The federal Constitution and the constitutions of the several states give defendants the right to legal assistance, hence it is necessary for the judge to assign counsel to defendants who are unable to afford a lawyer. However, since only ten states provide counsel fees for all such cases and nineteen make no allowance except when a capital crime is charged, the men assigned to the defense of the poor are frequently inexperienced, unsuccessful or unscrupulous attorneys brought into the case too late to take part in any of the vital preliminaries to the trial. The best they can do is to steer their client through the technicalities of the trial and go through the motions of conducting his defense. Under these conditions, justice to the poor and the friendless is a doleful fiction.

THE PUBLIC DEFENDER

A RECOGNITION of this unhappy fact has given rise in some jurisdictions to the office of public defender, known in several European countries and dating back even to ancient Rome. Although the form of this office varies, its aim is everywhere the same : to provide an adequate legal defense for impecunious clients.

The public defender, as a paid public official, was first made possible in this country in Los Angeles County, California, in 1913, by a charter which provided for an official who, upon request, would defend and advise without cost all persons charged with offenses in the Superior Court. In 1915 defenders were assigned to the lower courts and since then the legislature has given all counties authority to appoint defenders to be paid a fixed salary out of public funds. In 1915, Omaha, Nebraska, created the office of defender in its superior court. Connecticut has provided for a public defender in each county, to be appointed by the superior court of that county from among attorneys with five or more years of experience. The defender submits a reasonable bill for services, which the court considers and allows. Minnesota and Virginia have public defender laws.

Another type of public defender early represented in Houston, Texas, is the retired lawyer who volunteers his services to needy clients. In other places this form of philanthropy has flowered into a privately supported agency for the defense of those without means. In New York County the Legal Aid Society has assimilated the Voluntary Defenders Committee as its criminal department, which now has a staff of four full-time lawyers, four investigators, a social worker, and two secretaries, as well as the assistance of attorneys who volunteer their services to the organization.

Although a favorable conception of the public defender seems to be spreading, there is some criticism of the office as unnecessary, socialistic, sentimental, and costly. The prosecutor is, of course, a judicial officer, charged with the duty of preserving the defendant's rights as well as the state's. Why pay another attorney to do his work? In theory, this argument is logic tight, but it is questionable whether the defendant in practice will get his rights unless he has his own lawyer to see that he does. Business men who consider a public defender unnecessary usually prefer to have a competent legal staff to care for their own interests.

Actually there has been such collaboration between the prosecutor and the defender that the expense of maintaining the new office is less than the cost of assigned counsel. Defenders looking after the personal social problems of their clients and prosecutors guarding the public interests have frankly faced the issue before them and have come to an agreement satisfactory to all parties. This practice has eliminated useless delays and greatly reduced the costs of trials. In Cleveland in 1920 assigned counsel handled 528 cases at a cost of $32,500, while in Los Angeles in 1917 the office of the public defender handled 522 criminal cases as well as

8000 civil cases for less than $25,000. In other jurisdictions the work of the public defender is proving equally efficient and in every case far superior to the unfortunate system of assignment of counsel. Our chief concern now is to see that the caliber of our public defenders does not decline when the newness of the idea has gone and public interest begins to drop off.

THE TRIAL JURY

THE process of trial by jury has long been the subject of extensive and often vitriolic criticism. In recent years there has appeared a vigorous sentiment for its outright abolition.[13] The features of the jury method that draw the fire of critics are :

1. The method of selecting juries excessively delays and harms the administration of justice. In the famous Calhoun case in San Francisco ninety-one days were spent in selecting a jury. When Shea was tried in Chicago 4821 jurors were examined in order to secure a panel of twelve men. In contrast with this, Justice Ridell of the Ontario Supreme Court after thirty years of judicial experience says that only once has he seen it take more than half an hour to select a jury, and in that one exceptional case the process took forty-eight minutes.[14] When the infamous Crippen was tried in England a jury was impanelled in eight minutes.

The most obvious reasons for the greater efficiency of the English in securing juries seems to be :

(a) The spirit of the court proceedings. The aim of both prosecutor and defense attorney in the English courts is to uncover the truth. Facts are reported openly and without quibbling. In America the trial is a battle of wits. The end desired is not truth but victory. Hence fact-finding jurors are not wanted. Each side tries to put on the jury those whose passions and prejudices lean in its favor and to exclude all others.

(b) The English jurors are selected for character and intelligence and are freed from the sharp, sometimes insulting, quizzing

---

[13] See H. E. Barnes, "Trial by Jury," in the *American Mercury*, Dec., 1924, for a sample of sharp writing on this subject.

[14] R. Moley, *op. cit.*, p. 117.

of contending attorneys. In America jurymen are likely to be th
least promising of citizens.

2. The second criticism of the jury system is, therefore, tha
jurymen are incapable, unintelligent, and unqualified to do the wor
required of them. The law seems determined to weed out most c
those persons who by training and intelligence would make goo
jurors. Professional men such as clergymen, physicians, lawyer
and teachers are exempt from jury duty. So also are fireme
policemen, and members of the National Guard. Business me
whose interests would be injured by jury service are frequent
excluded by statute. New York exempts among others editors an
reporters, engineers, pharmacists, optometrists, conductors and eng
neers (except on street railways), telegraph operators, undertake
and embalmers. In addition to the groups exempt by law, busine
men and tradesmen, who are called for jury service, are frequent
excused by the judge because their business would be damaged
their absence. Still others, who do not want to serve, gain their d
missal by the convenient device of having a definite opinion about t
issue to be tried. Smith and Ehrmann, writing of the situation
Cleveland, said that to be called for jury service was a kind
mild disgrace. One judge who served in Cuyahoga County sa
"I have held court here two months and have never seen a busin
man on one of my juries." [15]

The end of this selective process is to leave available for ju
service the less fortunate members of the community who are usua
also among the least competent. Frequently a few men, who fi
even the small jury stipend satisfying, appear repeatedly on juri
The problem is not so much one of higher or lower ethical standa
as one of capacity to meet the demands upon attention, psychologi
insight, and range of experience that jury service needs. Few jur
have the technical equipment for weighing conflicting evidence pla
before them nor for safeguarding themselves against the stage sett
of a trial. More than one defendant has lost any possible adva
tage from the presumption of innocence in his favor because he
been marched into the court-room by several burly attendants a
obviously guarded to give the impression that he was a danger
criminal. No doubt also the properly timed appearance of a we
ing mother or wife has induced juries to neglect facts.

3. A third criticism of the jury system is that too many ext
neous factors influence jury decisions. Men who have been loc
up for several hours in a jury room get tired of discussing the is
particularly since they are not usually accustomed to that kind

---

[15] Cleveland Foundation, *op. cit.*, p. 340.

mental effort. Tiredness leads to violent haggling on the one hand or disinterestedness on the other. Men are anxious to get home. Under such conditions a determined minority may persuade a weary majority to change its votes to secure its own freedom. One juror discussing the procedure of his panel said, "We just took a first vote to see what most of us thought and then we all voted with the majority. We didn't give a damn whether they were guilty or not. Anyway, his Honor seemed to be satisfied." The *Boston Herald* of February 5, 1931, carried this report of the jury proceedings that led to a disagreement in the Garrett trial :

> "Although members of the jury were so fatigued last night after their long confinement that most of them sought a bath and a bed as soon as possible, some of them paused long enough to give newspapermen a clear picture of what went on during their arguments.
>
> "The first ballot taken, after the jury went to their room, just after 3 P.M. Tuesday, showed four of the men voted for acquittal, and half a dozen more ballots showed no change.
>
> "Then came the first of many furious arguments, which became more and more heated as the hours wore on. At no time did any of the jurymen come near to blows, but lack of sleep and the persistence of some of the men, put the nerves of all on a fine edge.
>
> "One of the jurymen who held out for acquittal did not seem to have followed the evidence at all, according to Juryman Herman G. Swan of 12 Osceola street, Hyde Park. 'He finally agreed to the others that he couldn't grasp the evidence,' said Swan.
>
> "Finally, at about lunchtime yesterday, one of the four men who had been holding out for acquittal suddenly announced that he was 'disgusted with the whole business,' and shifted his vote to one for conviction.
>
> "The three left refused to change their stand from the one taken at the first, and to the end they voted to acquit the three defendants.
>
> "Foreman Albert I. Fishel of 9 Egremont road, Brighton, said: 'It was practically impossible to get that jury to agree. From midnight Tuesday until Wednesday morning about 9 : 30 most of the jurors were apathetic and were too tired to listen to the discussion. I think in such cases the jurors should be allowed to go to bed at midnight and resume their discussion when they are refreshed with sleep in the morning.' " [16]

[16] *Boston Herald*, February 5, 1931. Quoted by permission.

The Garrett jurors listed their occupations as follows:

Salesman	Janitor	Shipper	Painter
Salesman	Plasterer	Chauffeur	Clerk
Clerk	Janitor	Electrician	Machinist

Undoubtedly some improvements could be made in the rules of procedure affecting jury trial, but the weaknesses of human nature bulk so large in its failings that the importance of such reforms seems likely to be slight. The real point to be noticed is that juries receive a sentimental interest not warranted by their extremely limited influence. They are a minor factor in the administration of criminal justice and completely overshadowed by the power of the examining magistrate and the prosecutor. In the entire state of Illinois in 1926 only 4.45 per cent of the cases of arrests for felonies reached juries for trial. In practically all of the cases of arrest for felony (95.5 per cent) the juries of Illinois had not a word to say.

Elimination before trial has pushed the work of the jury into the background, and the growing practice of allowing defendants to waive jury trial in favor of being heard by the judge alone is causing the jury to fade nearly to the vanishing point. Public sentiment still favors the use of the jury as an assurance that the common man has his place in government. No doubt in certain types of cases it will not soon be replaced, but it is moving towards extinction. In Maryland, which has always permitted the waiver of jury trial in criminal cases, defendants have shown their preference for trial before the judge alone in no uncertain terms. More than 90 per cent of the criminal cases in that state are tried without juries. Connecticut, with a more recent provision for waiver of a jury trial, finds about 70 per cent of its criminal defendants choosing to place their cases before the judge. Several other states have very recently passed legislation making jury trial optional in most criminal cases. Their experiences are too brief to permit evaluation, but with the exception of Washington, these states are meeting the same response noted in Maryland and Connecticut.

PROFESSIONAL BONDSMEN AND THE BAIL SYSTEM

ONE regular but unofficial attendant of the court is the professional bondsman. Unlike judge, jury, and attorneys, he has no official status, yet he often works in close alliance with attorneys, the clerk of the court, and other attachés. His business is to give bond to act as surety for the appearance at their trial of persons admitted to bail. For this service the bondsman charges a fee that may or may not be proportionate to the amount of the bond. There is nothing inherently wrong in this procedure. In fact, except in rural communities where everyone is personally acquainted with everyone else, some such practice seems inevitable. Unhappily, much of the business has fallen into the hands of shysters of questionable ethics, whose sole interest is profits. Often the bondsman is merely a disreputable salesman who, for a consideration, brings together a large property owner, who is willing to make some easy money, with a prisoner who most of all wants his liberty.

The success of the professional bondsman, like that of the criminal lawyer, depends upon familiarity with criminals. In St. Louis, where about 33 per cent of the bonds are signed by professional bondsmen, several of these men themselves had lengthy police records. Obviously such persons are not fit to assume custody of a prisoner. The Missouri Crime Survey uncovered little difference between professional and non-professional bondsmen in actually producing their defendants in court, but the attempts of professionals to tamper with the program of their cases makes it doubtful if the public is as well protected during the period of the bond whether the defendant appears or not.

Faulty organization of records makes a judge helpless to determine to what extent the property of a bondsman has been accepted as surety in other courts. In New York there are 110 places where bonds are accepted. This favors the unscrupulous tradesman who can do a great volume of business on inadequate security. One St. Louis bondsman with a police record of twelve arrests was allowed to become surety to the amount of $670,295 on real estate worth

$24,100 that was mortgaged for $31,500.[17] The chances of recovering a bond in the event of forfeiture under such conditions is slight. No doubt the customary lack of prompt action to secure judgment has much to do with bail bond losses. However that may be, of $292,400 forfeited in one year in Missouri, $1572 was actually collected in two rural counties. Judge John R. Caverly of the Cook County Criminal Court has estimated that bail bonds totaling between three and four millions of dollars remain uncollected in Chicago.

Dr. Raymond Moley, whose wide experience in fact-finding crime surveys makes him an excellent judge, has listed as the objectionable features of professional bondsmen:[18]

1. Poor character
2. Close relations with the underworld
3. Excessive charges for services
4. Evasion of responsibility
5. The pledging of property in excess of its value
6. Improper relations with public officials

An unfortunate aspect of the bail system is its marked tendency to favor the professional criminal much more than the less dangerous defendants, to the direct disadvantage of the community. The regular criminal has no trouble in finding a professional bondsman to secure his release while awaiting trial. Bondsmen have been known to appear at the police station before the police have arrived with their prisoner. Instances have been observed in which criminals, out on bail, have committed crimes to get the money for their defense, while their lawyers have made every effort to delay trial. In other cases criminals have used their freedom as an opportunity to escape after apparently making arrangements with their bondsman to insure him against loss if the forfeited bail should be collected.

On the other hand, friendless and unsophisticated prisoners are frequently unable to secure bail because they are unknown and unprofitable risks. So they go to jail to await

[17] "Missouri Crime Survey," p. 212.
[18] R. Moley, "Bail Bonds" in "The Missouri Crime Survey," p. 207.

court action. In order to relieve possibly innocent persons of confinement, jail cases are tried before the others. This again turns nicely to the advantage of the professional out on bail, for the chances of securing a conviction dwindle perceptibly if the trial takes place long after the offense. Witnesses move away. Their memory of the facts becomes faulty and confused. Public interest dies out. The criminal knows that time is on his side and he uses every available means to gain its help. Bail procedure reaches the peak of absurdity when a complaining witness, essential to the prosecution, is held in jail while the defendant is out on bail. Sometimes it is advisable to hold important but unfriendly witnesses, but it is hardly necessary to imprison a man who has been robbed for 106 days while the robber, eventually convicted, is at liberty on bail, as was done in Cleveland.[19]

Recognizing the evils of the bail system, many cities have made attempts to improve it. Cleveland and Baltimore have appointed bail bond commissioners. In 1927 a bail bond department was formed in the Chicago Municipal Court in charge of one of its judges. Through the efforts of the Chicago Crime Commission a Bail Bond Bureau has also been set up in the state attorney's office to investigate the records of defendants seeking bail and of bondsmen doing business in the criminal court. Recommendations for the guidance of the court are made on each case.

New York has made bail jumping a crime and has seriously restricted the ability of professional criminals to secure bail by requiring all persons charged with a felony or with certain misdemeanors linked with professional crime to be fingerprinted and their records checked and submitted to the proper official before they may be admitted to bail. In addition, persons previously convicted of a felony or twice convicted of certain misdemeanors cannot be admitted to bail by a magistrate but only by a county judge or a supreme court justice.[20]

As might be expected, the first changes to be made in the bail system have been intended to set thorns in the way of

---

[19] Cleveland Foundation, *op. cit.*, p. 314.

[20] "Report of the New York State Crime Commission, 1929," p. 13.

professional criminals and bondsmen. The other side of the difficulty is now in need of more careful attention. Professor Beeley, after a careful study of the bail system in Chicago, has made it clear that many who are confined in jail might safely be released on their own recognizance. Persons who had lived at least a year in Chicago comprise about 90 per cent of the samples of the unsentenced jail prisoners whose records were studied in 1923 and 1924. Many of them had families in Chicago. They had references from employers, clergymen, and social workers attesting their reliability. Authentic information about them was easy to secure. They were known in the community. Beeley's conclusion after an intensive study of 225 prisoners selected at random was that at least 28 per cent of them were needlessly imprisoned.[21]

If these findings are any indication of the workings of the bail system in general, it defeats its own purpose. A device for insuring the presence of persons in court when they are needed, without imposing upon them the stigma and discomfort of imprisonment, is so administered as to confine the least vicious and most trustworthy defendants (not yet found guilty) who happen to be poor, and to allow freedom to habitual criminals who know how to manipulate the system.

The remedies suggested for this aspect of the bail problem are :

1. *The more extensive use of the summons* [22] *in minor cases.* In England this is the customary and entirely satisfactory method of securing the attendance of defendants in all except the most serious offenses. Although it is not fair to compare conditions in England directly with those in the United States, there is ground for believing that it might well be used here in cases of technical crimes and petty misdemeanors. The successful experiences of Detroit and New York with the summons bears out this contention. Since a great proportion of persons arraigned in the magistrates' courts are arrested, detained, and then discharged as soon as they are given a hearing, it would seem the part of both economy and justice to

[21] A. L. Beeley, "The Bail System in Chicago," pp. 158-159.

[22] A notice issued by a court commanding the appearance of a person at court.

replace the needless arrests with the less wasteful process of summons.[23]

2. *Extension of the practise of releasing prisoners on their own recognizance without sureties.* Although this is now done in a very few petty cases, it would seem possible to extend the practise with safety to many reliable defendants who are now committed to jail because of their poverty. Successful use of the personal recognizance will depend upon a knowledge of the prisoner's character and background. Perhaps the probation staff might add to its functions the business of preparing a report to the judge on persons seeking release from custody.

3. *A more careful determination of the amount and nature of the surety required, with a possible increase in the use of cash deposits for petty crimes.* At present the amount of bail for each type of offense is fairly well standardized by judicial custom. Such automatically determined bail assessments insure speed without economy or justice. The character of the prisoner is largely disregarded. Inasmuch as the purpose of requiring bail is to insure the presence of the person at court, the chief factor to be considered should be the prisoner himself.

FUNDAMENTAL DIFFICULTIES IN THE ADMINISTRATION OF JUSTICE

BENEATH the conditions that characterize the administration of justice in America lie certain fundamental difficulties that have nowhere been better described than by Dean Roscoe Pound in his contribution to the Cleveland Survey: [24]

1. *Any system of rules is general and more or less mechanical in operation.* Injustice in particular cases is bound to follow their rigid and automatic application. The method used to escape the inflexibility of law is to permit some discretion to those who administer it. But so far as freedom is allowed it involves uncertainty as to what the law may or may not sanction and also affords opportunity for the perversion of justice. The chance unevenness of justice is one of the outstanding irritations of our system. One court

[23] Of 162,190 persons brought into the Municipal Court of Chicago in 1921 for felonies, misdemeanors, or for violation of ordinances, 101,206 (62.4 per cent) were discharged. See table III, A. L. Beeley, *op. cit.*, p. 18.

[24] R. Pound, "Criminal Justice and the American City," Part 8 of the Cleveland Foundation, "Survey of Criminal Justice in Cleveland."

may sentence a vagrant to serve 10 days and another court 2 years. A man taken in adultery may get 6 months while the woman participant in the same offense receives a five year sentence.

2. *The law lags behind public opinion and tends to be out of joint with it.* Not until public opinion is fairly well settled can it be crystallized and made law.[25]

3. *The American feeling that legal administration is a simple thing* leads to ill-founded criticism and to the barrier of a hostile public opinion.

4. *The increasing complexity and interdependence of men in an urban society involves a growing amount of restraint upon individual freedom of action.*

5. *The limitations of human ability sometimes make the attainment of justice impossible.*

(*a*) The testimony of witnesses in criminal cases is frequently untruthful. Even when witnesses are sincere the flaws in human observation and memory may make it impossible to ascertain the truth.

(*b*) It is often impossible to prevent subtle injuries that may be serious in their effects or petty irritations that may do much harm because they are chronic. For example, the ability of the law to prevent a man from flirting with another's wife is doubtful.

(*c*) The operation of the law is dependent upon the willingness of persons to start its machinery. It can not begin its work until some one is sufficiently interested to initiate proceedings.

6. *Americans have a tendency to overburden the criminal law by using it as a cure-all for human ills.* We suffer from the naïve faith that every difficulty can be resolved by passing a law against it. As a result both the nature and the volume of law is beyond the capacity of our legal machine. The law can not be stretched to solve all social problems. There is a limit to its effective action.

A recognition of these obstacles to the easy administration of justice makes it obviously true that the simple expedient of arousing public sentiment to vote out bad men and vote in the good will not cure all of its sad defects.

Improvement requires attention not only to the caliber of the men who administer the law, but also to the rules and machinery by which they proceed, and to the social setting in which they do their work.

[25] The American Law Institute, organized in 1923, is now engaged in the stupendous task of restating the principles of the common law, both civil and criminal.

BASIC SUGGESTIONS FOR IMPROVEMENT

THE present requirements, both of training and character, for admission to the bar could be lifted several notches without making the profession too exclusive. Both the law schools and the bar associations face a responsibility here. Any progress towards the training of honest and socially responsible lawyers acknowledging their primary duty to the public would remarkably raise the level of procedure by changing the legal process from an ordeal by battle of wits to a straightforward effort to establish the truth. Pre-law school requirements of study in sociology and psychology are needed to develop within the profession the viewpoint that is essential to a socially progressive legal group from which much of the impetus and direction for necessary but difficult legal reforms must come.

Law, itself, is merely a set of rules that may be used with as little moral or ethical responsibility as a crowbar which may serve as well to open another's strong box as to lift an automobile from the back of an injured man. Lawyers need technical skill in the use of law as a tool but unless it rests upon a broad base of knowledge and a sincere interest in the general human welfare they are not fit for admittance to the bar. No doubt some attention could profitably be given to devising a more specialized form of training and apprenticeship for those looking towards a judicial career as is done in some European countries. Perhaps it would not be amiss also to seek ways of acquainting the public more generally with the basic principles and theories of the law, as well as to lay bare their own responsibility for the legal evils they decry.

At present the courts are not well organized for the work they are trying to do. As the Cleveland Survey points out, the fundamental trouble is the persistence of rural methods in an urban environment. Absence of system interferes little with the attainment of justice in a village court where everyone's actions are public, but it makes municipal courts impotent to perform their duties. Yet our courts still try to work independently of each other and in the dark. No improvement is more needed than carefully planned organization of our state courts, prosecuting, and administrative agencies under a responsible head. Such a program involve adequate cross record and audit systems, efficient assignmen of work, and proper facilities for handling quasi-crimina traffic offenses and petty crimes. It implies a utilization by the courts of the reasonably tested knowledge of the socia sciences, particularly psychiatry.

Steps towards unification have already been taken in a few courts, notably in Detroit in 1920 and in the federa courts in 1922. Massachusetts has taken the lead in the use of psychiatrists as a routine procedure. The American Ju dicature Society is advocating a conservative plan for merging state courts into a unit under control of a judicial council The ultimate success of the movement seems inevitable even though its first steps are timid and halting.

Beyond court unification lies the need to coördinate the tasks of law making and law enforcing. Early in the nine teenth century Jeremy Bentham advocated a committee charged with the duty of examining and evaluating the effect of laws. A little later Lord Chancellor Westbury proposed a Department of Justice to superintend the administration of justice, prosecute legal amendments, and help in the busi ness of current legislation. In recent years Lord Haldane Dean Pound, Dean Wigmore and Justice Cardozo have recommended what Dean Pound calls a juristic general staff a responsible body to keep an eye on the whole legal system

Although modern jurists are not clear about the exact limits of its authority, a state ministry of justice could per form an inestimably valuable service in examining the suc cess of present laws, comparing proposed laws with similar enactments, and their results in other states, and by recom mending needed legislation. The work of state bureau might still farther be increased by coöperation with a federa ministry of justice. A scheme of this sort would eliminate much needless and ill-considered legislation. It would re lieve the police and courts of many unenforceable laws. I would give some semblance of logical direction and con tinuity to the efforts of legislators.

Another suggestion, which is yet but little more than an intriguing idea in the minds of a few observers, would limi the function of the courts to the determination of guilt.[26] After that is done, treatment would be prescribed on the basis of a clinical study made in a receiving and diagnostic prison by a staff with opportunties for observing and studying offenders rather than by a judge with neither training nor facilities for determining how best to treat the criminal and to protect the public. The program would be administered by trained penal workers with power to modify the treatment of each case from time to time as circumstances might warrant. The conditions and duration of each prisoner's sentence would depend upon his needs and his progress in fitting himself to live in freedom among his fellow-men. Some legal safeguard would be needed to insure individuals against arbitrariness on the part of those in charge of their sentences.

The jurist sees in this scheme the breakdown of necessary legal principles and the destruction of individual safeguards. The layman looks askance at "treatment" as an escape from a just punishment. By it the deterrent effect of punishment is nullified and law-abiding citizens are left at the mercy of thugs. The professional criminal dislikes the indeterminate sentence. He wants to know in advance just what it will cost him for any given crime if he is caught, and when convicted he would like to be sentenced under definite rules, so that he may arrange to pay his bill and return to business. Nevertheless, the idea of so limiting the judicial function is likely to persist and to spread. The newer methods of penology already give progressive administrators of modern institutions much leeway in adjusting the conditions of imprisonment to the needs of individuals.

A still more radical idea is to eliminate the entire contentious system and make the trial a legal and social investigation rather than a contest. The work of the courts is to determine whether an act has been committed; if so, who did it and what should be done with him. This is a clear-cut problem which can best be solved by an impartial scientific investigation within the limits set by the law. It requires neither jury nor counsel nor antiquated procedure, but only

[26] Mexico, however, has already so limited her courts by statute.

a judge acting as a chairman to safeguard rights and to accept responsibility for the conduct of the inquiry.

This suggestion has the merit of being eminently reasonable in theory, but it assumes that all parties to the proceedings will have an honest desire to uncover the truth and meet it squarely. Under present conditions nearly everyone connected with the trial, including the judge, is affected personally to some extent by its outcome. That is why criminal trials are hedged about with procedural rules.

There might be less likelihood of bias if the idea of a contest were eliminated, yet undoubtedly some limits would need to be drawn by rules. Yet rules are in opposition to the spirit of individual case study and diagnosis. However, if the ideal of replacing trials by impartial investigations is good, the difficulty of achieving it should not frighten us away from attempting to reach it. Regardless of how far we may be able to travel along that road, we certainly have reason to believe that we can strike a better balance than now exists between the stability that is desirable in the criminal law and the equitable handling of criminal cases.

We shall have to come by this improvement gradually. The work of some juvenile and domestic relations courts has already given us an entering wedge. Their success with the method of social investigation will do more to further a similar evolution in the adult criminal courts than any arguments that can be advanced. It is in the juvenile courts, where powerful interests are not involved, that the technique of the new procedure may be evolved. In time we may come to see that there should be no difference in principle in the administration of justice between young persons and adults; that the distinction between the delinquent and the criminal is largely artificial, except for the longer experience of the latter, and must, therefore, inevitably break down, making possible the application to both groups of the method that proves best fitted to survive.

PART FIVE — THE TREATMENT OF CRIMINALS
CHAPTER XIV
MINOR PUNISHMENTS

FINES

A FINE is a pecuniary penalty for the violation of the criminal law. It is related to the ancient Germanic *wite* which
it eventually replaced. A man guilty of a breach of the
peace had to make *bot* with the outraged victim and *wite* with
the king. About the twelfth century damages assessed by
the courts replaced the *bot* and money penalties replaced the
wite. Criminals however were not at first fined by the
courts. Instead, they were in certain cases permitted to fine
themselves as a substitute for the penalty set by the courts.
That is, a misdemeanant made an end, *finem facere*, to his
imprisonment by paying a sum acceptable to the judges.
Fines as original penalties assessed by the courts were unknown to the common law. They did not develop in England until the sixteenth century. Our own present system
of fines is based upon statutory enactments.

Fines are our most common penalty. They have become
an important type of punishment both in Europe and America
where their use yearly becomes more extensive. Fines constitute numerically possibly 70 or 80 per cent of all of the
penalties imposed by our courts today. They serve as sup-
plements or alternatives to imprisonment as well as substitutes. Generally some judicial discretion is permitted
through the legislative device of setting minimum and maximum limits to fines although this is not always done. Excessive fines are prohibited by our state constitutions. If a
prisoner is unable to pay his fine he may be imprisoned and
credited a fixed sum each day until his debt to the govern-

ment is cancelled ; a practice that completely reverses the original purpose of the fine. However, with the extension of probation the practice of putting offenders on probation and permitting them to pay their fines in installments is becoming more and more common.

Widespread consideration has been given to the system of fines in recent years, particularly in Europe. Its advocates claim for it many advantages. Fines are an economical punishment far less burdensome upon taxpayers than the maintenance of penal institutions. In fact, they provide a source of governmental revenue. They are presumed to be flexible and easily adjusted to either the seriousness of the offense or the condition of the offender. Fines are ideal penalties when it is not desirable to attach to the violator the stigma that goes with imprisonment. Moreover, fines are the only punishments that are completely revocable if an error has been made. They do not involve the contamination of minor offenders by older hands at crime. They avoid the unintended hardships of lost jobs or lost pay that often accompany the imprisonment of petty offenders. They are the only means we have of punishing legal persons such as corporations which we cannot subject to corporal punishments.

There is also inherent in fines the possibility of compensating directly the immediate victims of criminals without obliging them to seek damages in well-nigh hopeless civil suits while the government pockets the full amount of the fines. Several European states now use fines as a means of getting direct reparations for the victims of criminals. Our only recourse is a civil suit unless the judge induces the criminal to make restitution.

Not all of these presumed advantages remain unchallenged and there are some serious disadvantages. Although fines do represent revenue their total is an inconsequential part of the income of the states or of the federal government. They may, however, be an important item in the finances of small municipalities. Fines are condemned also because they discriminate against the poor more than other forms of punishment. It is well recognized that although fines are theoretically flexible, in practice the courts adopt what

mounts to fixed price lists for petty offenses. Judges drone
ut the same penalties day after day for the same offenses
pon all comers without regard to differences in their in-
omes.   If the guilty ones cannot pay their fines imprison-
ient becomes a penalty for poverty and the state assumes
he unwarranted expense of boarding its victims. The
emedy for this, already introduced in some places, is an
rrangement for the payment of fines in installments under
he supervision of probation departments.

The deterrent effect of fines is sometimes questionable.
Habitual offenders are not apt to be reformed by fines.
Drunkards continue to get drunk. The spectacle of alco-
olics being alternately fined and jailed over and over again,
en, twenty, thirty and forty times with utter seriousness by
nimaginative judges would be humorous were it not such
drain upon our pocketbooks. Drug addicts, prostitutes,
nd pickpockets, far from being deterred by fines, are often
timulated to increase their activities to recoup their losses.

The flaw in our technique seems to be that we apply fines
s we do all other penalties to a certain class of crimes with-
ut bothering to discriminate among the criminals who com-
nit them.   Obviously fines have a place, but they are not a
ure-all for misdemeanors. Perhaps their most useful func-
ion is to serve as a penalty for selfish or careless technical
riminals to whom we usually attach no moral stigma. What
ve ought to do, of course, is to set about devising a rational
cheme for the use of fines as penalties.

LOSS OF RIGHTS

CRIMES that cause infamy carry in addition to other punish-
nent a loss of some important rights. The specific rights
f which an infamous convict are deprived vary from state
o state. Nearly all of them include the loss of the right
o vote, to hold public office, and to practise certain profes-
ions such as law or medicine. Other rights and privileges
nay be curtailed. Aliens may be deported or refused natu-
alization. In any subsequent criminal proceedings the
resumption of innocence may be lost. Facts about an in-
amous offender may be used to impute his credibility as a

witness. In all but five states conviction of an infamo
crime is a ground for divorce.

Which crimes are infamous is a moot question unclarifi
by the courts. Usually infamy is thought of as depende
upon the type of punishment suffered. Death, bodily i
jury, hard labor, and imprisonment in a state prison ha
been thought of as making criminals infamous in the ey
of the public. The sentences must actually be passed up
the guilty persons in order to impose civil disabilities. The
is some ground for believing infamy is in part due to t
nature of the crime itself and not solely to the punishme
suffered since civil rights are not necessarily restored wh
the infamy of punishment is wiped out by a pardon.

Deprivation of civil rights acts as a mild form of banis
ment by pushing infamous criminals in some measure o
of association with decent citizens. Its chief failing is th
it loses sight of the individual against whom it is effectiv
As an accompaniment of imprisonment it is probably justifi
though of slight importance. As a form of ostracism up
release its value depends entirely upon the needs of ea
prisoner released. As a general policy it would seem wis
to make a man shoulder his responsibilities in the communi
than to start him out from the beginning as an outcast. U
der a penal system designed to prepare prisoners for co
munity life and authorized to keep them in custod
indefinitely until they appear fit for release this scheme wou
have a better chance to produce good results than it can fi
at present.

CHAPTER XV

PROBATION AND ITS ADMINISTRATORS

THE MEANING OF PROBATION

PROBATION is a voluntary arrangement between the state and a defendant intended to bring about the defendant's good behavior without committing him to an institution. It is usually initiated by the court immediately after conviction, although in certain instances a person charged with crime may be placed on probation. The ordinary procedure is to suspend either the imposition or the execution of the sentence and to place the prisoner in the care of a probation officer.

Probation is sometimes loosely referred to as "giving a man another chance." That choice of phrasing is a bit unfortunate. If probation means turning an offender loose once more to see if he can resist the same sort of temptation to which he has just succumbed, it is an absurd practice.

As a matter of fact, however, probation was never intended to be a discreet form of leniency. Its essence is a well-considered plan for selecting and socializing in the community defendants who seem likely to be safe and more responsive to treatment there than in confinement. It involves rigid but well-planned discipline. The probationer must accept and live up to a definite standard of behavior among his fellow men under the scrutiny of a probation officer. Properly administered probation makes a man prove his fitness for freedom by shouldering the normal responsibilities of life of which prison would relieve him. Since the conditions of a probation period involve regular work and a thorough surveillance of the probationer's daily activities by an officer, its punitive effect may be more severe than that of a prison sentence.

Probation is often confused with parole. Therefore it may be well to notice that these are two distinct forms of treatment. Probation takes place immediately after the trial is ended and without commitment to an institution.[1] Parole refers to the early conditional release from prison of one who has served a portion of his sentence. Probation officers are generally appointed by the justices of the courts they serve and their departments are adjuncts of the courts. Their jurisdiction is limited. Parole is administered by an independent state board whose agents have jurisdiction throughout the commonwealth. The power to place an offender on probation almost always rests with the judge. The power to place prisoners on parole rests with parole boards. The number of persons on probation, where it exists, is many times greater than the number on parole.

Probation work has three major aspects :

1. Investigation of cases pending in the courts in order that the judge may have before him a complete and trustworthy social history and psychological analysis of the defendant. This information is absolutely essential to the court if it is to act wisely in passing sentence, placing an offender on probation, or in making other disposition of the case.

2. Personal supervision, discipline, and guidance by trained officers of persons placed on probation in accordance with a carefully worked out coöperative plan for readjusting probationers to society.

3. Informal advising of perplexed individuals, often parents who come to the probation officer for aid in handling relatives, friends, and neighbors whose behavior is troublesome.

Good probation procedure now rests upon the principle of social case work of which it is a specialized branch. It is the application to a particular type of behavior problem of the techniques already recognized and applied in dealing with maladjusted human beings in general. It involves interviews with the probationer, home and neighborhood studies, school and work histories, and a clinical examination of the physical and mental health of the probationer. I

[1] Occasionally judges impose short terms of imprisonment as one of the conditions of probation although their legal right to do so is questionable. More certain is the right of a judge to impose a term of imprisonment for one offense followed by probation on others when an offender is simultaneously convicted of several offenses.

alls for an intimate knowledge and utilization of the social
esources of the community on the part of the probation
fficer. Upon the basis of this knowledge must be built
or the probationer a new plan of life that has his confidence
nd his active coöperation.

THE HISTORY OF PROBATION

\T common law, courts had the right to suspend sentences
emporarily. In the United States some courts developed
he practice of suspending sentences indefinitely as a means
f extending judicial clemency when there were extenuating
ircumstances that could not otherwise be recognized. This
entimental and probably illegal disposition of certain cases
s not a scheme of probation, but it paved the way for it.

Near the middle of the last century an altruistic Boston
oot-maker, John Augustus, became interested in a young
lrunkard who was arrested in his city. Augustus persuaded
he judge to continue the case and release the prisoner on
ail in his care. He successfully helped the young man to
ontrol his unfortunate appetite so that he became a tem-
erate and diligent citizen. Thereafter Augustus, much to
he annoyance of the judges, pushed his services upon them,
roviding bail for offenders out of his own pocket in order
o secure their custody.

In this way, during the period from 1849 to 1864, John
Augustus extended his benevolent offices to several hundred
nen and women. Soon other volunteers appeared in the
ourts, among whom was Father Rufus W. Cook, chaplain
f the Boston jail. During the 70's he repeatedly investi-
ated cases and acted as a friendly guide and counselor to
hose whom the judges placed in his charge. It is to the
umanitarian practices of these counselors rather than to
he foresight of the courts that probation owes its inception.

Glimmerings of probation first appeared in the law in an
ct passed by the General Court of Massachusetts in 1869
nd amended in 1870 authorizing the Massachusetts State
3oard of Health, Lunacy and Charity to investigate the cases
f juvenile offenders and to undertake their placement and
are. Although the term "probation" was not used, the act

really permitted probation for juveniles. In 1878 Massachusetts added the word "probation" to the criminal law by an act defining the duties of a probation officer and authorizing the Mayor of Boston to appoint one for Suffolk County. Two years later similar permission was given to every city and town in the Commonwealth, but the idea of probation was then so strange that few followed Boston's example.

Yet by 1891 probation had so well commended itself that the legislature replaced the privilege of municipal option by a law making probation service mandatory in every lower criminal court and placing the power of appointment in the hands of the judge. The extension of probation to the superior court in 1898 made that service available to every Massachusetts criminal court. By the turn of the century three other states, Maryland (1894), Vermont (1898), and Rhode Island (1899), had passed probation laws unrestricted as to age, and three states, Illinois, Colorado, and Minnesota, enacted juvenile probation laws in 1899 in connection with the juvenile court movement which was then rearing its head.

Now thirty-two states and the District of Columbia have adult probation laws and all of the states except Wyoming have made provision for juvenile probation. In 1916 the Supreme Court of the United States rendered a decision in the famous Killits case[2] which put a stop in the federal courts to the practice of suspending sentences indefinitely and induced Congress to give serious consideration to the need of a federal probation system. Such a system was finally established in 1925. By July 1932, 61 of the 85 United States districts had salaried probation officers and new appointments are being made steadily. The number of probationers under supervision increased from 4222 on July 1, 1930, to 28,419 on March 1, 1933.

In the meantime a restricted form of probation had appeared in England under the Probation of First Offenders Act of 1887. England modernized her procedure under the Probation of Offenders Act of 1907, which removed the restrictions as to age and first offense and provided for paid probation officers. The Criminal Justice Act of 1925 made the appointment of probation officers mandatory in each of

2 *Ex parte United States*, 242 U. S. 27, 1916.

1031 Petty Sessional Divisions in England and considerably strengthened the probation service by financial aid and by the appointment of supervisory committees.

On the Continent probation has steadily gained ground. The presence or absence of certain features of treatment makes it difficult to tell in every case whether or not a system of treatment should be labelled "probation." However, assuming two necessary elements : (1) a probationary period to demonstrate good behavior and (2) supervision by a probation officer, Trought[3] was able in 1927 to list nineteen out of thirty-one European countries as having a probation system, with the possibility that two or three others should be included. Canada authorized paid probation officers in 1922. Japan has a well-established system. Latin America and South Africa have made beginnings.

Coincident with the spread of probation has come an improvement in the facilities for good probation work. In the United States the establishment of the Juvenile Psychopathic Institute in Illinois in 1909 under Dr. William Healy's direction marked the beginning of the clinical study of delinquents as a necessary preliminary to treatment. Five years later the Boston Municipal Court extended clinical study in modified form to adults by adding a psychiatrist to the probation staff. In 1921 the Recorder's Court at Detroit incorporated for the first time in an adult court the service of a fully equipped clinic.

The use of psychiatric services by adult courts has not yet become common although it has been rapidly extended since 1922. No court yet makes routine examinations of convicted offenders. Usually the persons to be examined are selected by judges or probation officers. Of 1168 adult and juvenile courts replying to an inquiry in 1927, 110 courts in 31 states reported some form of regular psychiatric service.

Although the boundaries of probation work have pushed ever onward since its inception, its forward line has not been thrust ahead equally far in all states. Many jurisdictions limit probation work seriously. The National Probation Association[4] reports that eighteen states and the District of

[3] T. W. Trought, "Probation in Europe," p. 185.
[4] The National Probation Association, organized in 1907 and incor-

Columbia forbid probation to those guilty of a specified lis
of offenses ; thirteen states refuse probation to persons pre
viously convicted of felonies or imprisoned for crime ; an
many other restrictions often illogical are found less wide
spread than these. For example, Iowa forbids probatio
to persons who have a venereal disease while North Carolin
permits probation only to persons who are venereally dis
eased or are guilty of second degree prostitution. Onl
eight states, Massachusetts, Maryland, Vermont, New Jersey
Virginia, Oregon, Colorado, and Utah, have unlimited pro
bation within the discretion of the court.

Since probation work is under the control of individua
uncoördinated courts, probation departments throughout th
country have tended to develop their own standards. Thes
have varied so widely that practices running all the way fron
infrequent and perfunctory checking of an offender's pres
ence in the community to thorough clinical study an
constructive, detailed, active supervision are labelled "proba
tion." As the result of a painstaking investigation and re
port by an able investigating commission, New York earl
came to see the folly of permitting each probation office t
grow in a haphazard manner.

A State Probation Commission was therefore authorizec
in 1907 to supervise, not to administer, probation worl
throughout the state. The following year Massachusett
created a supervisory Commission on Probation (since 192(
the Board of Probation). In 1914 it began a system o
gathering and exchanging records for the courts of Suffoll
County. This service has been magnificently expanded s
that today every criminal court in the Commonwealth re
ports its disposition of cases daily to the central record offic
at Boston. There the complete court record of every of
fender is available, together with his parole history, if any
and, for county prisoners, the findings of the psychiatrist
who have made the routine examinations for the state De
partment of Mental Diseases. The central office of th
Board of Probation has therefore become a great clearing
house of information containing a file of 750,000 names

porated in 1921, has done yeoman work in raising the standards o
probation work in this country.

receiving records at the rate of 610 a day, and answering approximately 180,000 inquiries a year.

Following the lead of Massachusetts and New York, twenty-two states have developed state agencies to supervise and coördinate probation work. In four of them, Rhode Island, Vermont, Utah, and Wisconsin, probation officers are state employees. The 1931 Directory of Probation Officers lists 3955 probation officers for the entire United States. Salaries have been improved and although many probation officers receive far less than a living wage, the average annual salary of probation officers, excluding chiefs and deputy chiefs, in 1931 was $2094. This is far too low for the type of personnel needed but it compares favorably with what other social workers receive.

THE PRESENT STATUS OF PROBATION

PROBATION finds its stanchest advocates in those jurisdictions that have most thoroughly tested it. There it is recognized, not as a cure-all, but as a method of brightest promise and one that has proved itself good enough to gain an accepted standing.

New York places about 20,000 adults and 7000 juveniles on probation each year, and the proportion of offenders placed on probation steadily increases. Massachusetts has for many years placed approximately 30,000 persons on probation annually. About 9 per cent of them are women. In 1932 for example the probationers numbered 33,993 of whom 4085 were juveniles and 29,908 adults. Included in these figures are 353 girls and 2412 women.[5] The offenses represented cover a wide range of crimes, felonies as well as misdemeanors. Only habitual and determined criminals are regularly excluded from its opportunities. The test is in the possibilities of probation as a method of handling each particular case. One of the interesting features of probation in Massachusetts is the uniformity with which it is used. Year after year from 22 to 25 per cent of the total number convicted are placed on probation. Only ten

[5] Commonwealth of Massachusetts, "Annual Report of the Board of Probation for the year ending September 30, 1932," p. 6.

per cent are committed to institutions. Other cases are
disposed of by fines and suspension of sentences. England
places about 80,000 persons on probation annually.

Several merits of the probation system may be cited. It
is preferable to imprisonment for young and first offenders
because it keeps them from that intensive course in crime
that they are bound to take if they are forced into daily
companionship in prison with criminals steeped in the ways
of the underworld. They escape, also, the abnormal and
degrading atmosphere characteristic of prisons. On the
other hand, probation makes them accept the responsibility
of living a normal life under normal social conditions under
a carefully worked out plan and with the assistance of a
probation officer.

Probation is obviously a good substitute for the absurd
practice of sending a man to jail for non-support or because
he was unable to pay his fine. As Herbert Parsons has so
aptly remarked, because a man did not support his family the
state put him in jail where he could not support them and
then undertook the task for him. Then, on top of that, it
required him also to accept board and room at the taxpayers'
expense. Or, when a man owed the state a fine of fifteen
dollars which he could not pay, the state clapped him into
jail for thirty days, gave him food and lodging there, looked
after the welfare of his family, paid him fifty cents a day
for his trouble, and at the end of his sentence, cancelled the
fine with the fifteen dollars due him for staying in confinement.

Now under probation, a man is given an opportunity to
earn his fine or is required to support his family and himself
as well, under the eye of a probation officer. In Massachusetts in the lean year of 1931 probation officers collected
$1,517,151 in non-support cases, $148,374 for restitution,
$287,209 in suspended sentence returns, largely fines, and
$13,766 in miscellaneous collections ; a total of $1,966,500
which was somewhat less than previous recent totals. In
1932 the total amount collected was $1,645,669.[6] New

⁶ Commonwealth of Massachusetts, "Annual Report of the Board of
Probation," year ending September 30, 1931, and year ending September
30, 1932.

York has collected upwards of $24,000,000 from probationers since 1907.

These figures point to another advantage of probation, its economy. Not only are probationers required to assume their own financial responsibilities which otherwise the state would take over, but the expense of supervising them while they do it is less than the net cost of their institutional care. Roughly, the cost of probation supervision is $15 to $30 a person and of their prison maintenance $300 to $600 a person annually. The latest figures available for New York give the exact annual costs per person as $29.20 on probation and $440.52 for state institutional care.

When it comes to a question of the success of probation in turning criminals and delinquents away from crime and into acceptable ways of living the evidence with which to give an accurate, truthful answer is lacking. Throughout the country the percentage of probationers who are believed to have come through their terms satisfactorily is commonly reported as close to 80 per cent. In New York the proportion of adult cases discharged as successfully terminated since 1907 is 78 per cent. In Massachusetts eight out of ten persons are reported as completing their terms of probation satisfactorily. One out of every ten is a known failure.

Encouraging as these assumptions are, they must not be allowed to lead us into an unwarranted optimism, as they often do when they are contrasted[7] with figures indicating that "between 50 per cent and 60 per cent of all persons in our jails are repeaters." No doubt the behavior of prisoners while they are in jail is quite as satisfactory as the behavior of probationers while they are on probation is believed to be. In fact it is more apt to be so since prisoners are under actual supervision while probationers, in many instances, are seldom seen by probation officers. As a result they violate the terms of their probation and even commit crimes unknown to their supervisors and are still discharged as successful. Moreover, if prisoners fail so obviously after their discharge, perhaps it would be interesting to see how well

[7] See the statement by the Hon. H. G. Cochran, "1929 Year Book of the National Probation Association," p. 13.

probationers behave after the prop of supervision has been removed from them.

On this point little is known. One suggestive study is an "Inquiry into the Permanent Results of Probation" made by the Massachusetts Commission on Probation in 1923.[8] The cases investigated were those handled during the first half of 1915 by a group of courts selected as representing a fair cross section of the state. The inquiry was carried on during the period from July 1, 1923, to March 15, 1924. It thus attempted a checkup on the condition of the offenders about eight years after they were placed on probation. The survey covered 2114 cases classified as follows:

Juvenile		312
Boys	296	
Girls	16	
Adults		802
Women:		
General offenses	205	
Drunkenness	37	
	—	
Total		242
Men:		
General offenses	383	
Non-support	157	
Illegitimate Child	51	
Non-support of Parents	9	
Vagrants	74	
Drunkenness	216	
Confirmed Drunkenness	105	
	—	
Total		995
Unclassified by Sex:		
Suspended fines, drunkenness	209	
Suspended fines, general offenses	211	
Suspended fines, violation of ordinances and motor vehicle laws	76	
Unsupervised (ordered to leave jurisdiction)	36	
Information received too late for tabulation	33	
		2,114

[8] Commonwealth of Mass. Senate Document No. 431, "Report of the Commission on Probation on an Inquiry into the Permanent Results of Probation."

By far the most important test of probation in this study is the response of the 383 adult males who were on probation for general offenses. The first point to be noticed is the obvious exercise of discretion by the courts. Although the offenses represented by these probationers covered a wide range, only twenty-five cases were of extreme offenses and in these the circumstances permitted confidence in the probationer's future. One hundred and twenty-nine had previous court records.

On probation, 227 (59%) of this group of 383 men presumably completed their term satisfactorily, 68 (18%) showed no improvement, 50 (13%) disappeared, 36 (9%) were surrendered to the court and committed to institutions, and 2 (1%) died.

Of this same group *after their period of probation,* 165 (43%) had no subsequent court record, 136 (36%) had a court record, and in 80 cases (21%) information was lacking. Not all those who completed their probation period satisfactorily maintained their good record, although they did far better than those who had previously failed. Fifty-five (24%) of the probation successes had later court records, as compared with 60 (74%) of the 81 unresponsive souls. Obviously those who fail on probation are poor risks thereafter.

Another point to be noticed about this group is the high rate of post-probation failure (65%) among those with a previous court record who were placed on probation, as compared with the failures (33%) among those believed to be first offenders.

Eight years after these men were placed on probation it was possible to secure detailed information about the condition of 168 out of the original 383 cases. Of these 126 (75%) were non-drinkers, 24 (14%) drank moderately, and 18 (11%) drank to excess. An inquiry into their work habits disclosed 139 men (83%) working regularly and 29 (17%) irregularly. The investigators believed that these facts might fairly represent the status of the entire group of men.

Of the women general offenders, 88 (44%) had no court record after probation, 59 (30%) had no ascertainable record, and 51 (26%) are known to have had a subsequent court record. As among the men, repeaters failed on probation more frequently (twice as often) than supposed first offenders.

Of the boys placed on probation 114 (39%) of the 294 cases tabulated had no court record after probation, 52 (18%) had no ascertainable record, and 128 (44%) had later court records.

The condition of 219 of these boys was also ascertained eight years after they were placed on probation. Twenty-two of them were in the army and navy, twelve of them having acquired court records prior to their enlistment. The 197 civilians included 171 (87%) abstainers; 10 (5%) moderate drinkers, and 16 (8%) excessive drinkers. Of this same group 153 (78%) were regular workers and 44 (22%) irregular. Comparative information about neighborhood conditions in 124 cases indicated that 75 (60%) continued to live in the same kind of neighborhood, 10 (8%) had moved to less desirable ones, while 39 (34%) were living in a better section.

This Massachusetts study, which is not altogether reliable, probably presents an example of the best state-wide probation now being done. It tends to interpret facts in the light most favorable to probation. It was assumed throughout that persons for whom no court record could be found should most likely be included among the successful. In view of the mobility of habitual criminals, the absence of routine interstate identification, and the small proportion of court records in proportion to crimes committed, this procedure seems unduly optimistic. Yet in spite of it, this very lenient check indicates that 36% of the men, 26% of the women, and 44% of the boys had *known* court records *after* probation. The real record of non-success is very likely much higher. This rather knocks askew some of the exaggerated claims of those who have represented probation as a semi-miraculous panacea for crime. It is unfortunate that probation is still laboring to keep its face in the light of inflated claims quite out of line with the results of this study and of the follow-up studies of the best juvenile clinics.

Probation has nothing to lose from facing the facts as they are. It is still experimental. So are the older methods of dealing with criminals. It has been moderately successful and its degree of success seems much greater than that to which penal institutions may safely lay claim.[9] Moreover, probation as a technique is still young and growing. Its weaknesses are those of youth rather than old age. It has the means of great improvements already at hand. The ideal of probation is excellent. Its practice is poor, in part because of the subtleties of its task but more especially because of the present poor qualifications of probation officers and their lack of facilities. Only as the public comes to appreciate and support real probation work will its true value be known. Its present claim to support must rest primarily upon the fact that it is a logical and intelligent device to add to our present penal equipment.

Clearly realizing this, His Eminence, Cardinal Hayes, in 1925, authorized the expansion of the work of the Catholic Charities Probation Bureau in the Court of General Sessions in New York County as a two-year demonstration of the possibilities in good probation work. Adequate facilities for establishing the highest possible standards were provided in an attempt to build a model probation service that could be copied and in the hope that the state would see the value of continuing the work at the same high level at the end of the demonstration period.

Edwin J. Cooley, a chief probation officer of long experience and a former president of the National Probation Association, was placed in charge of the bureau. Minimum salaries of $3000 a year for probation officers were established. With adequate pay it was possible to employ a high grade personnel. Every probation officer on his staff was a college graduate, chosen with careful attention to personality. All were experienced in social work. They were all given additional special instruction in probation work.

The finest standards of social work were maintained.

[9] We must however remember that penal institutions have to deal with the failures of the probation system as well as those considered such poor risks that they are never placed on probation.

The case load was limited to fifty. All cases were cleared through the social service exchange with the result that 60 per cent of the cases were found to be known to other agencies. Rigid investigation of all cases before they were placed on probation eliminated poor risks and assured the community of its safety. One officer was specially detailed to investigate criminal records to discover whether the offenders were repeaters. This selecting of cases was so carefully done that only 19 per cent of 3053 delinquents investigated were actually placed on probation, as compared with 35 to 40 per cent previously.

The supervision of probationers was done with equal care and thoroughness. Strict discipline was enforced. A carefully planned program fitted to the needs of each probationer was developed, with the aim of restoring him to normal citizenship. That plan, intelligently conceived and applied, involved not only a working adjustment to the world round about but an inward change in the probationer's mental set. Obviously a probationer's ability to grow towards a finer viewpoint, a greater self-control, a higher ideal of conduct, depended nearly as much upon the character and personality of his leader as upon his own basic capacities. Hence, the wisdom of Cooley's insistence upon probation officers of positive and suitable personalities as contrasted with the general disregard of an officer's personal characteristics. As much as a probation officer needs the wisdom of the gods, he needs even more the qualities of sincerity, humanness, assurance, firmness, and patience.

The work of the Catholic Charities Probation Bureau, now taken over by the Court of General Sessions, became admittedly the best probation work for adult offenders in the country, and the most convincing demonstration of the meaning of probation work that has ever been made. The Bureau, after a careful check upon its own work, came to the conclusion that 85 per cent of its probationers gave promise of permanent adjustment in their communities. Therein lies a reason to believe that as the ideals of probation elsewhere come to be equally well understood and the service more generally attains professional standards based upon adequate resources and equipment, it bids fair to become one of our most useful means of reshaping twisted lives.

THE PROBLEMS OF PROBATION

IF probation is to be brought to its point of maximum efficiency it must face its problems squarely. The key fact about probation is that its basic assumptions are out of harmony with those of the judicial system to which it is linked and within which it must function. Probation accepts the viewpoint of the social sciences that human conduct is the understandable result of complex factors within and without the person which can, to a useful degree, be uncovered and directed, in this instance, towards the conquest of criminality.

The law, on the other hand, assumes that man is a creature of unexplainable whim who freely chooses to do what he will and who must be punished, if he wills to do wrong, as a means of expiating his sin and of deterring himself and others from further misbehavior. Judges trained in the classicism of the law but touched by the popularization of the social sciences, and sensitive to the conflicting opinions of lay citizens, approach their tasks with objectives vague and confused but with methods dogmatic and assured. Police departments and district attorneys' offices are primarily interested in convictions and punishments rather than in reformation and social protection. Legislators, who determine the basic conditions under which probation departments must operate and whose appropriations are essential to the service, are moved by many extraneous considerations and rarely have an adequate conception of what the probation service might be.

The public generally clamors for punishment but looks upon probation as a means of extending lenient treatment to juveniles or adult offenders who have managed to arouse sympathy. This is the incongruous network of which the probation service is a part and in coöperation with which it must function. The primary responsibility for developing effective coöperation between the probation service and the other elements of the system rests with probation officers.

The first need of probation departments is therefore for men of a stature equal to their important tasks.

THE PERSONNEL OF PROBATION DEPARTMENTS

THE basis of successful probation is an able well-trained personnel. The probation service is no fit place for retired political wheel-horses who must end their days in easy jobs. Neither is it a place for sentimentalists who have a kindly feeling towards the fallen and who yearn to help them up. It is altogether too important to be entrusted to many who are now engaged in it. Crime, like disease, is a major menace to human welfare. Crime, like disease, needs to be met by men and women who are able, impartial, and trained in the skills of their profession and who are possessed of a genuine but intelligent humanitarianism.

Probation work should be a creative art based upon scientific knowledge. The problems of probation officers and their opportunities for public service are quite as great as those of physicians or teachers. They need, as an absolute minimum of preparation, a high school education plus a year of supervised social work training. Preferably they should be college trained and graduates of recognized social service schools. Regardless of the extent of their formal training they should be acquainted with the elementary facts of biology, sociology, and psychology, particularly as they are applied in the fields of physical and mental hygiene, domestic relations, vocational guidance, and social case work. The attitude with which they approach their work is of the highest importance. They need to be wholesome and honest in their own personal relations and able to get and maintain the confidence and respect of their charges. As Dr. Van Waters has aptly put it, they should be social physicians having respect for the worth, dignity, and integrity of the human personality, using knowledge rather than force, and believing in the possibility of reconstructing human lives.

At present probation officers are not chosen by any such standards, although a very few of them could be measured favorably against them. Usually the indefinite requirement is that an officer shall suit a judge well enough to secure his approval and appointment. In some states sheriffs or policemen act as probation officers. Eight states make no provision for salaried probation officers for adults. In six states some probation officers are selected through civil service examinations. In some others, state welfare boards or local boards appoint, or approve the judicial appointment, of applicants. Rarely are specific qualifications made or published, although in 1928 New York went so far as to provide that probation officers in that state should be between the ages of 21 and 60, physically, mentally and morally fit, and with the equivalent of a high school education.

There is an obvious need here for the development and general acceptance by appointive bodies of reasonably definite and workable qualifications for probation officers which can be improved as the service is built up. Judges might then make their appointments from lists of eligible applicants. At present an added difficulty lies in the dearth of capable applicants for probation positions. As yet probation work has not interested college men and women greatly. Either it has been an unknown field to them or has had the reputation of being essentially a police job. Its somewhat unsavory political entanglements have led to a slightly snobbish aloofness rather than to a desire to improve a vital public service. Moreover, other branches of social work have been largely pre-empted by women with the result that trained women social workers outnumber men ten to one. Few professionally trained men are therefore available for immediate entry into probation work.

Fortunately, however, a better conception of the intent of probation is spreading and college men are beginning to give serious attention to the opportunities of the probation service. Many colleges now offer uncoördinated courses in criminology, criminal law, abnormal psychology, clinical psychology, the family, community organization, mental hygiene, social case work, vocational guidance, physiology and personal hygiene, and others that could be built into a vocationally useful program by liberal arts students who might plan to enter probation work or allied fields. The University of Notre Dame now offers a definite course, including field work, for advanced undergraduate students and graduates leading to a certificate in probation work. The Institute of Criminal Law of the Harvard Law School also offers a two-year professional course for graduate students designed to train men for executive and semi-executive positions in penal work, including probation. Other universities are now considering the development of professional courses along these lines. A few probation departments in the larger cities have undertaken to give their staffs definite professional instruction within their own organizations.

When probation officers more generally have training commensurate with the importance of their work, the attributes of a profession will appear in the probation service. Instead of being clerks or snoopers, probation officers will know how to analyze the problems represented in the men with whom they deal ; how to think through the facts of a case so that the core of the problem will be illuminated rather than lost in a maze of details. They will know enough about their charges and about their communities so that they can draw up workable programs for the readjustment of probationers and carry them out.

This means that probation work cannot be desk work as it frequently is at present. It is not enough that the probationer should arrive at the probation office once a week, announce that he has behaved himself, and depart with an admonition to continue to behave. It may well be that the probation officer's chief problem, if he but knew it, centers not in the probationer but in his wife and family. Perhaps there is little that can be done for the probationer but much that can be done to protect the family and prevent it from becoming a community burden. Perhaps the important factor in the case lies in the subtle elements in the probationer's work situation. To discover these things probation officers must make useful contacts with those whose lives influence those of their probationers.

Cooley's standard for his office was a minimum of two home visits and one employment visit a month plus contacts with other people when indicated. A standard of this sort presumes a case load of not more than fifty probationers, which social work experience in other fields has indicated to be the maximum requirement permitting adequate supervision under ordinary conditions. It is, of course, not a rigid figure but subject to modification in the light of special duties, the nature of the area served, whether rural or urban, the types of offenders, the age of offenders, and possibly other factors.

In practice, probation staffs are numerically inadequate to their tasks, so that probation officers frequently carry a burden of work that makes proper supervision impossible. In New York State the case load often runs as high as 200 to 250 per officer with the result that visits to probationers' homes are limited to one or two a year. In 1925 three officers in Milwaukee County were trying to care for 839 men. Investigators found a superman in Flint, Michigan, responsible for 881 adults, 67 juveniles, 180 mother's aid cases, and 409 alimony cases. Probation under these conditions exists in name only.

Another essential of good probation work is a wise selection of those who are to receive its advantages. Certain types of persons are poor risks. They are not fit subjects for probation and departments should not be burdened with them. They are a menace in the community. Their failures injure the service. They waste time and money that could more profitably be expended on others.

The selection of those to receive probation cannot logically be made on the basis of their offenses. A thorough investigation of every defendent who is before the court, regardless of his crime, is the only adequate criterion for determining whether an offender should be placed on probation. However, to do that is a practical impossibility because of the overwhelming case load that it would entail until such time as probation offices are properly manned. As one way out of the difficulty Sheldon Glueck suggests that a test study of all offenders be made in a given area over a sufficient period of time to determine what types of offenders are most in need of a thorough-going examination. Thereafter these types would invariably be intensively investigated while others would receive the less detailed examination. In the absence of such tests it would seem at present as though it would be unwise to grant probation to chronic offenders, drug and alcohol addicts, feeble-minded and psychopathic offenders except under unusual and carefully considered circumstances.

One fact is certain, probation work cannot be successful if judges continue to place on probation persons who give no indication that they can profit by it. Adequate investigation to provide judges with all of the pertinent information relative to a defendant is an absolute prerequisite to rigid selection of those who are to be placed on probation. Beyond this the judges must be able and willing to interpret a properly prepared case history and to apply the resulting conclusions to the case with the greatest possible measure of scientific impartiality.

If eventually judges can supplement their own conclusions based upon facts and their experiences with scientific aids such as the prediction tables that are now the object of much experimental research, probation officers may some day find themselves dealing only with the types of offenders with which their service was designed to cope.

Whether the duties of investigation and supervision should be combined in the same person is a question that has given some concern to those charged with probation administration. Some administrators believe that if a probation officer has charge of every aspect of a case his supervision will rest upon the most intimate knowledge available. The resulting continuity of case study and control is also cited as an advantage. Linked with that is the supplementary fact that those with whom the probation officer works are not irritated by the need of making adjustments to two workers.

On the other hand, those who feel that investigation and supervision should not be entrusted to the same persons believe that the process of getting information about a prisoner whose case is to be heard in court is likely to arouse antagonism against the officer among the very persons whose coöperation he will need if the defendant is later placed on probation in his care. It is also felt that the type of person who makes a good investigator may not be so well suited to the task of supervision. In city practice it is also a fact that probation officers inherit supervisory cases from other officers who have left the service or who have been transferred and that offenders who have been investigated in one district go home on probation to another. Therefore it is impracticable for one officer to combine the duties of investigation and supervision. Cooley, whose successful experience entitles him to speak with authority, says that the most potent argument in favor of separating these two functions is that both are full-time jobs and full-time effort in either of them is essential to good work.

THE JUDGE

THE judge as a factor in probation work is frequently overlooked. Actually his importance in the scheme is difficult to over-emphasize. Probationers are wards of the court and under his ultimate jurisdiction. The probation staff is under his control. Obviously the man who appoints probation officers and decides whom to place on probation, who disciplines probationers and revokes probations, holds a key position. If he cannot assure successful probation work he can certainly ruin all chances of it by his failure or unwillingness to understand and support it. That few judges make effective use of their opportunities with probation is not surprising in view of the traditional insulation of the law in which they have been trained from the realities of social living.

Nothing in the ordinary legal training of judges fits them to guide probation work. Day after day they dispose of cases as though they are dealing with absolutely plastic beings who are to be cast into a mold, there to be set in the form which the judges have decreed so long as they shall live. And judges do this with little knowledge about the offenders that is fundamental and with equally little knowledge at close range of the actual workings of the agencies into whose hands they entrust offenders for that purpose. Instead their prescriptions for the rehabilitation of prisoners depend largely upon habits and hunches grounded in their experiences and their prejudices, and they are issued as though the court were an all-powerful agency instead of just one link in a chain of forces affecting those who are brought before them.

The judge has the power to send a man to prison or put

him on probation but no power to determine the subtle ways in which either experience will affect him nor to guarantee that a convict will be either reformed or frightened into keeping out of future crime merely because the judge has decreed a sentence for that purpose. There is more than a little food for thought in the fact that among six New Jersey judges passing sentences on similar types of offenses in 7442 cases in one county one judge gave jail sentences in 55.7 per cent of his cases while another gave them in 33.6 per cent of his, and that one judge suspended 15.7 per cent of his sentences while another suspended 33.8 per cent of his.[10]

If they are to support probation work effectively, judges themselves, no less than probation officers, need the new outlook of the social physician. One of them, Judge Ulman of the Supreme Bench of Baltimore, has remarked that "there is greater need for a sense of social responsibility on the criminal court bench than for nicety of definition of the judicial function."[11] In part, as Judge Ulman suggests, the mere use of probation by a judge has a tendency to draw him out of his judicial insulation and entangle him with the continuing process of which his acts are a part.

However, it seems sensible to expect as a prerequisite to appointment to a judgeship that candidates should receive an adequate training better adapted to the social requirements of their work than they now have. That judges, no less than probation officers, need to know at least the elementary facts of biology, psychology, sociology, and mental hygiene, as well as to gain a truer perspective on the place of their work in the total scheme of dealing with criminals, seems so apparent that it is surprising that special training involving the social science disciplines has not already become a necessary qualification for the judgeship.

Another attribute of the judge which affects the advancement of probation work is his courage. As yet the public has not accepted the ideal of social protection through reformation as excluding the desire for vengeance. The judge

[10] Gaudet, Harris and St. John, "Sentencing Tendencies of Judges." *Jour. of Criminal Law and Criminology*, Vol. 23, p. 816.

[11] J. N. Ulman, "The Trial Judge's Dilemma : A Judge's View," being Ch. 6 of S. Glueck, (Ed.) "Probation and Criminal Justice."

must be sensitive to that public opinion for his position is vulnerable. It is therefore not easy for him to use probation wisely when he is under the constant scrutiny, through the press, of a public that is anything but logical in its attitudes towards the treatment of offenders. As a result he may send a man to jail who is "a typical case for the wise and proper use of probation," as Judge Ulman did because "he believed that Baltimore, in the year 1931, was neither the place nor the time to do what he thought was wise and proper,"[12] or he may put on probation a man who ought to be in prison simply because a misguided public is convinced that the prisoner is a persecuted martyr.

THE PROFESSIONALIZATION OF PROBATION

LIKE other professional agencies probation departments will need to insure their progress as well as may be by constant checking of their work to determine its effectiveness, to uncover and correct its weaknesses, and ultimately to decide after a sufficient trial whether it should be retained as a method for dealing with criminals. If the facts do show that probation is a valuable method of dealing with some types of criminality then the facts so gathered will be the most effective means that probation departments may have for gaining public support for it. Bennet Mead, Statistician in the United States Bureau of Prisons, has already suggested a possible technique for evaluating the results of probation through a progress record applied to case studies.[13]

The continuous growth of staff members in personal knowledge and skill is also a requisite of a professional probation service. This would be brought about by such commonly accepted devices as regular staff meetings for the discussion of probation problems, the self-advancement of staff members through the reading of professional journals and books, and possibly by attendance upon formal training courses or university courses of study. In sparsely settled areas less frequent district conferences would probably be

---

[12] J. N. Ulman, *op. cit.*, p. 116.
[13] B. Mead, "Evaluating the Results of Probation." *Jour. of Criminal Law and Criminology*, Vol. 23, p. 631.

necessary substitutes for staff meetings and extension courses or specially planned reading courses would be used instead of university instruction.

Another necessary function of probation departments is to take the initiative in interpreting their work both to the judges and to the public at large, not in terms of successful cases but in terms of its function and techniques. Until probation is understood and supported at least as well as the work of health departments or public schools it will be necessary for probation departments and for professional organizations of probation workers to carry on a persistent but dignified campaign to gain the intelligent coöperation of the public for their work.

CHAPTER XVI

CORPORAL PUNISHMENTS: THE BLOOD LETTING STAGE

Punishment — A penalty inflicted by a court of justice on a convicted offender as a just retribution, and incidentally for reformation and prevention.— WEBSTER'S NEW INTERNATIONAL DICTIONARY.

METHODS of punishment have grown up as part of man's social code. No one knows how early human groups began to assess formal penalties against criminals. A glance at the practices of contemporaneous primitive peoples gives us the hint that by the time our ancestors had begun to live a settled life in early neolithic times they had definite penal customs. Something akin to legal punishment certainly occurs in primitive tribes now at a neolithic level, although differences in their organization and psychology make it difficult for us to understand the motives that lie behind it. The principles of justice among them are hazy and their forms of punishment ill-defined and dependent more upon personal whims than legal formulæ. The elements of family vengeance, religious sacrifice, and protection from evil spirits all enter into the picture, perhaps to the exclusion of the idea of criminal justice.

Ellsworth Faris believes there is good reason to doubt whether any homogeneous primitive group ever formally punished its own members. That could have occurred only when there were three or more groups, one of which could act as an impartial umpire in the best interests of all parties.[1] However, a crystallized public opinion may well have supported one person against another of the same group. The question at issue seems not to be whether primitive man pun-

[1] E. Faris, "The Origin of Punishment," *International Journal of Ethics*, Vol. 25, p. 54.

ished members of his group, but whether that punishment was a penalty for crime.

Among the Eskimos, who have a very informal social organization, the family of a murdered man may privately avenge his death. Side by side with this procedure, any man who feels that the welfare of his village will best be served by the death of a notorious character, a sort of public enemy, may properly venture his opinion to the other members of the group. If they are unanimously of like opinion, he may kill the offending member without fear of retaliation by the family of the criminal.[2]

Among the natives of the Trobriand Archipelago in Melanesia, Malinowski witnessed the following incident : Namwana Guya'u, the favorite son of a Melanesian chief, wounded his cousin, Mitakata. According to the system of mother-right there prevailing, the chief's son did not belong to the father's clan ; the chief's nephew did. Bagido'u, elder brother of Mitakata and heir to the chief, came to the door of the hut where Namwana Guya'u was brooding and uttered the ceremonial words, "Go away. We chase thee away." Failure to comply with such a ritual request is unknown among the natives. During the night, Namwana Guya'u left his father's house forever.[3]

Howitt reports that among the natives of Australia, when a man has committed a major crime a posse, known as a pinya, is organized by the council of head-men to hunt down the offender and kill him or arrange a suitable payment of goods by barter.[4]

Although these penalties are not inflicted by formal courts of justice upon convicted criminals, the incidents recited are at least suggestive of an early origin of penalties inflicted in the public interest by a socially approved method. They support our belief that from the very earliest days petty criminals have suffered loss of social prestige or loss of po-

---

[2] F. Boas, "The Central Eskimo," 6th Annual Report of the Bureau of American Ethnology, p. 582.

[3] B. Malinowski, "Crime and Custom in Savage Society," pp. 101-105.

[4] A. W. Howitt, "Native Tribes of South-East Australia," pp. 295-341. Reprinted in W. I. Thomas, "Source Book for Social Origins," pp. 764-787.

litical rights while more serious offenders have been exiled or put to death. Later, payment for crime in goods or money came to be an acceptable substitute for the removal of criminals. All of these types of punishment have persisted in one guise or another throughout the ages.

HISTORICAL FORMS OF PUNISHMENT

MODERN penal methods have evolved through several well-marked stages each of which has contributed to the forms of modern punishment. Prior to the thirteenth century, imprisonment as a regular means of dealing with offenders was unknown. Punishment was chiefly in the form of direct bodily injury ending in the death or mutilation of the offender.

THE DEATH PENALTY

THE devices men have used for legally killing their troublesome brothers have been so cleverly varied that it seems as if inventive genius must be inspired by the thought of human blood. Twenty-nine forms of capital punishment were listed by Wines in his classic work on "Punishment and Reformation." Hanging, beheading, and burning have been among the most common forms of execution in the past. Many times they were carried out with fearful elaborations. The Persian king, Sefi II, devised a method of killing by piercing the body with burning wicks. Medieval Europe seemed to rely upon the purging influence of fire. Burning at the stake was the medieval punishment for a host of crimes including heresy, witchcraft, poisoning, and arson. Roman slaves guilty of theft were flung from the Tarpeian rock. Parricides were sewed up alive in a sack with venomous serpents and thrown into a river. Crucifixion, strangulation, and flogging to death were preferred methods among the ancient civilizations of the near Orient. The Hebrews considered stoning a particularly disgraceful death. It was not unknown among the Nordics for in the tenth century Æthelstan ordered male slaves guilty of theft to be stoned by their fellows. Criminals have been thrown to lions (Rome), to crocodiles (Siam), or to serpents (Rome).

They have been dragged to death behind horses (Germany), or trampled under the feet of elephants (China). The Athenians forced some of their criminals to drink poison.

To this list of forms must be added drowning, burying alive, boiling, impaling, drawing and quartering, breaking on the wheel, starving, and squeezing to death, to say nothing of the many artistic variations upon these penalties devised by inspired kings and nobles for special occasions. After the invention of firearms, shooting was added, and still more recently have appeared electrocution and death by lethal gas.

In modern times the death penalty had its most extensive use in England from the sixteenth to the close of the eighteenth centuries. Seventy-two thousand persons were reported executed during the reign of Henry VIII. As late as 1780 there were 240 crimes punishable by death in England. Yet, in spite of this determined blood-letting, criminals are said to have rushed to the gallows after hangings in order to pull the hand from the corpse in the belief that certain of its bones were charms that would open any door. Pickpockets filched from the crowds at every hanging, although picking pockets was one of the capital offenses. John Price, hangman for the city of London in 1714 and 1715, was himself executed for the murder of Elizabeth White. His successor in office, William Marvel, hangman from 1715 to 1717, was transported for stealing ten silk handkerchiefs. John Thrift, public executioner from 1735 to 1752, was found guilty of privately killing David Farris without bothering to get legal sanction, and for this murder he was sentenced to die. He was actually imprisoned, however, instead and later he received a full pardon.[5]

Perhaps Lord Eskgrove, judge from 1784 to 1805, was a bit uncertain whether simple murder warranted capital punishment for in passing the death sentence upon a prisoner he carefully pointed out:

"Prisoner at the Bar, not only did you murder your victim, whereby he was bereft of his life, but you did add to your crime

[5] See H. Bleackley, "The Hangmen of England," for an interesting record of England's eighteenth and nineteenth century "finishers of the law."

by thrusting and projecting, or pushing or propelling or piercing the lethal weapon through the belly-band of his regimental breeches, which said breeches were the property of his Majesty, the King." [6]

In colonial America death was prescribed for only ten to eighteen offenses. Hanging was the usual form of execution. Under a charter wheedled out of Charles II by William Penn the Quakers in Pennsylvania reduced the number of capital offenses to one, while among the West Jersey Quakers treason and murder alone were punishable by death. When the code of the early Quakers was set aside by Queen Anne the old punishments returned but the influence of the Quaker code persisted. In 1788, Ohio limited the penalty of death to murder. The Quakers also had begun again after the Revolutionary War to reduce the severity of their laws. Eventually a complete revision of Pennsylvania's criminal code permanently discarded capital punishment for every crime but first degree murder.

Since that time the United States has diminished the importance of execution as a punishment for crime to a nearly inconsequential point in line with the tendency to discard it that extends wherever European civilization is found. In Norway, Sweden, Latvia, Lithuania, Austria, Holland, Portugal, Belgium, Esthonia, Finland, Denmark, Hungary, Czechoslovakia, Russia, Rumania, San Marino, Guatemala, Brazil, Ecuador, Venezuela, Nicaragua, Peru, Costa Rica, Argentina, Uruguay, Colombia, Honduras, Mexico, five states of Germany, and in fifteen Swiss Cantons legal capital punishment has been abolished. Italy abolished the death penalty, but restored it to limited use in 1926. During the last half of the nineteenth century eight of the United States abrogated it entirely. Twelve more have limited its use to murders only. Delaware and Virginia alone have retained it for as many as six offenses. In 1892 the federal government made capital punishment applicable only for treason, murder, and rape.

In other ways, also, capital punishment is being hedged

---

[6] Quoted by the English criminologist, Sir Horace Wyndham, "Criminology," pp. 30-31.

about by restrictions that are slowly smothering it. Of the forty states that are holding it as a last defense in a limited number of cases, thirty-four permit the courts to substitute life imprisonment for execution at their discretion. That this is in line with a widespread public sentiment is suggested by the observed reluctance of juries to bring in verdicts of guilty in cases where the death penalty is mandatory. It is doubtful, however, if it is yet the prevailing opinion among jurors that the death penalty should be abolished, as some would have us think. More likely it means that there are frequently one or two persons on juries in such cases whose sentiments incline them against it.

Another evidence of the decline of the death penalty is the suppression of public executions. Legal hanging as a common spectacle has disappeared, although some critics feel that modern tabloid newspapers have provided an effective substitute for direct observation. Florida now holds the dismal honor of being the only state where public executions may legally be held.

The sweeping nature of the trend is obvious. For more than a century and a quarter capital punishment has been markedly on the wane while most of us have been unaware of the fact. Through outright abolition, reduction in the number of capital offenses, the substitution of permissive for mandatory laws, and through attempts to make executions secret and painless capital punishment has been cut down towards the vanishing point. These factors in combination with the difficulties we have in apprehending and convicting criminals render the death penalty in the United States today statistically of relatively little moment. In a population of 125,000,000 persons among whom the annual number of killings by automobiles now average more than 30,000, and among whom the number of homicides annually is now about 12,000, our quota of 155 executions in 1930 does not seem to be a major item for the concern of either criminals or criminologists. Yet impelled by a justifiable interest in the principles involved in man's judgment of death, associations have been formed to accelerate its passing. It is known that innocent men have been put to death.[7] That in

[7] See E. M. Borchard, "Convicting the Innocent," for specific cases.

itself justifies the abolition of capital punishment in the eyes of those who feel it wiser to stop with life sentences for the worst criminals rather than permit the probable execution of an occasional innocent person. A mistake in a life penalty can in some measure be remedied. A capital penalty is irrevocable.

On the other side surety companies, assuming that the efficacy of the death penalty can best be judged by crimes that they believe are not committed on account of it, have tried to stem the tide. An endless number of debating societies still marshal the arguments. Such efforts may give the public an earlier opportunity to express itself than might otherwise come, but beyond that they seem likely to be of little practical effect, except, as Sutherland has suggested, in making clear the fundamental issue between those whose aim is vengeance and those whose aim is scientific control of criminals. Two points seem clear : First, capital punishment is now used so infrequently that it can make no great difference to either the public or to criminals whether it is abolished or not ; and second, the drift of public sentiment that has been carrying the death penalty steadily towards oblivion will ultimately abolish it entirely or will retain it only as a permissive method for exceptional cases.

If we ever reach the point where the treatment of criminals is intelligently determined, it might be wise for us to retain the right to execute criminals as a carefully guarded permissive procedure to be applied to offenders for the public good on the basis of their imminent dangerousness and potential incorrigibility instead of on the basis of the seriousness of the particular offense of which they happen to be guilty. Logically, if on the basis of a thorough scientific case study we become convinced beyond a reasonable doubt that a criminal is unfit to live and is irreformable, we should accept the responsibility of killing him as decently and painlessly as possible. Practically, there are at least two objections to this scheme. One is the difficulty of devising the standards and assembling the knowledge by which to pass a scientific judgment of death. Here, to console us, we have the likelihood that such decisions would need to be passed infrequently and would be, at the worst, less fallible than those we now make. The second obstacle is that we are so touched by our emotions in these matters that such coldly reasoned killings by the state might do more damage to the public than the living but imprisoned person of the criminal.

MUTILATION

CRIMINALS fortunate enough to escape the horrors preceding ancient executions still had to suffer the pains of bodily mutilation. With an eye to poetic justice, rulers and their aides seem always to have approached the Mikado's sublime object of making the punishment fit the crime. Persons guilty of assault and battery were sentenced to have their hands cut off, forgers lost their fingers, blasphemers' tongues were slit, and sexual delinquents were castrated. King Canute mercifully desiring to reduce the number of capital offenses, ordained that minor offenders should lose only the hands, or feet, or both, according to the seriousness of the offense. For greater wrongs the eyes were to be put out, the nose, ears, and upper lip cut off, or they were to be scalped.[8] Such punishments in ancient days were inflicted at wholesale by rulers in spite of the fact that powerful voices like that of the Emperor Constantine, who forbade such barbarisms, were occasionally raised against these inhumanities.

Gradually, however, the most horrible disfigurements disappeared. Branding was perhaps the last form of mutilation to be forbidden. In England and her American colonies it persisted until the reign of George III. Branding consisted in printing the emblem of a sovereign (early) or an initial description of the crime (later) upon the body with a hot iron. Usually the mark was impressed in some conspicuous place such as the forehead or the fat of the thumb, although the shoulders, legs, or buttocks were sometimes marked.

A modern variant of mutilation appeared in some of the first sterilization laws passed in the United States. Since 1907 twenty-three states have passed sterilization laws applicable to various types of mentally diseased and defective persons, including some who have been adjudged criminals. In the beginning some of these laws were frankly punitive

[8] F. H. Wines, "Punishment and Reformation," pp. 71-72.

nd aimed with poetic justice at the castration of those guilty
of certain sex crimes.   Much litigation ensued, usually resulting in the declaration that such punishment was unconstitutional.   Modern sterilization laws have avoided punitive
features.   Instead they are intended to protect the public
welfare by preventing the reproduction of defective children.
They apply to non-criminals as well as to criminals.   The
constitutionality of sterilization laws on this basis was upheld
in 1927 by the Supreme Court of the United States.[9]

Flogging or whipping, although not intended to cripple or
mark an offender permanently, has often had that effect.
As a punishment it was known in all of the ancient civilizations where it was often carried out with the utmost brutality.   In modern times it has been used throughout Europe
and America, but with decreasing frequency and severity,
although in Russia flogging with the knout whip,[10] which
was replaced by the cat in the nineteenth century, probably
equalled any other ancient method in its cruelty.   Whipping
was common in the colonies, especially for wife beating and
for violation of the blue laws.

It is still permissible under Anglo-Saxon common law, and
in Virginia, Maryland, and Delaware is authorized by
statute.   In Virginia it is authorized only for juvenile delinquents and in Maryland its use is restricted to wife beaters ;
but in Delaware it may be applied for some twenty-five
offenses.   Canada, Great Britain, and, to some extent, continental countries still use flogging as a punishment for some
crimes against the person.   As a means of disciplining prisoners, it is commonly used in many of our prisons, especially
in the southern states.

From time to time citizens, who are disturbed by a seeming
coddling of criminals, call for a revival of the whipping post.
They are answered by those who feel that flogging in any

[9] See "*Carrie Buck* v. *J. H. Bell*," 274 U. S. 200.
[10] As described by John Howard, who saw a man and a woman flogged
with it, the knout consisted of a wooden handle to which several thongs
were attached, twisted together into a cord, to the end of which a single
tough thong, eighteen inches long, was fastened in such a way that it was
"capable of being changed by the executioner, when too much softened
by the blood of the criminal."   J. Howard, "The State of the Prisons,"
p. 76.   Everyman's Library Edition.

circumstances is barbaric and inhumane. Actually, the severity of this form of punishment depends upon how it is administered. One of its chief flaws is the fact that the pain of ten or twenty lashes cannot be standardized. But for that matter, a year's imprisonment is of vastly different import for different prisoners.

Perhaps it would be easier to standardize whipping through the use of a mechanical device than to equalize the pain of imprisonment. Proponents of whipping claim that it is economical and an effective deterrent. The experience of Delaware belies the last claim as applied to those who are punished, for many persons have been whipped two and three, and some four and five times. The ultimate economy of whipping, also, depends upon its relative effectiveness as a deterrent when it is contrasted with other forms of punishment.

It would seem that modern penologists cannot afford to overlook the possible values in the whip. As an undiscriminating outlet for social or individual anger it can have no place. As a form of treatment prescribed for a particular individual to secure a particular result, it may warrant a widespread but carefully used and guarded revival.

EXPOSURE

Many methods of exposing criminals have been devised for their punishment. Few of them were in themselves physically painful. They were not intended to be. Their object was to degrade and shame petty offenders by making of them a public exhibition. However, the public had the right to make them the targets of something more substantial than ridicule, and often took advantage of that right to pelt prisoners with decayed vegetables or stones, not only to their added discomfort, but to their serious physical injury. Forcing prisoners to sit for a time in a public place, their legs in the stocks or their heads and wrists in the pillory, were the most common methods of exhibition in England and the American colonies. Occasionally the ears of a pillory prisoner were nailed to the head board. Drunkards, who could not manage their legs, were often thrown on their backs with their feet clamped together in the air at right angles to the body in the sliding shackles of the bilboes.

The ducking stool, a chair fastened to the end of a lever, balanced like an old-fashioned well-sweep, was used for immersing scolds and nagging persons in a pond or river. The ducking stool was considered an especially effective means of cooling off husband and wife after a family disagreement. The brank, a wire helmet put on over the head and equipped with a piece of flat iron placed in the mouth so as to hold the tongue down, was also a favorite device for chastising scolds. Placarding an offender with the initial letter of his crime was a common penalty. Even the dead did not escape the disgrace of exposure, for the head might be thrust upon a pole in the public square, or the entire corpse might be hung up in an iron frame, so made as to support the skeleton until the body had completely decomposed.

On the Continent the *carcan* made stocks and pillory unnecessary. It consisted simply of an iron ring locked about the prisoner's neck, and attached by a chain to a post. Criminals were sometimes led through the streets of European cities dressed in a Spanish mantle, a heavy tub-like vest with an iron frame around the neck. Dragging a prisoner through the mud, though less common than other punishments, was not unknown in Europe.

During the first quarter of the last century, punishment by exposure began to drop into disuse, coincident with a wave of penal reform that led to the building of new jails for misdemeanants and prisons for more serious offenders. France abolished the *carcan* in 1832 ; England the pillory in 1837. The corpse of a bookbinder, named Cook, hung in a frame in Leicester in 1834, was the last body to be exposed in England. That year hanging in chains was forever prohibited.

TRANSPORTATION

EXILE as a punishment for crime has been known since our primitive days. In the guise of systematic transportation of criminals it first appeared in England in 1619. In Russia it was first mentioned in 1648 as a means of removing crippled offenders. France proposed to transport second offenders to Madagascar in 1791, but her war with England interfered with the plan. Sixty years later France established her first penal colonies in Algiers and Guiana.

An increase in crime in England and a demand for laborers in America were the complementary forces that led England to think of transportation.

Fifteenth and sixteenth century England struggled through the crisis of a series of fundamental changes that completely transformed her social and economic life, and marked her transition from medieval to modern times. Serfdom, manor courts, landlord farming, gilds, and the power of local governments waned rapidly. In their stead rose a powerful central government, free laborers, an industrial class, textile manufacturing, and foreign trade controlled by Englishmen. As might be expected, maladjustment in the form of poverty and crime accompanied the shakeup.

When landlords, finding sheep-herding more profitable than agriculture, enclosed their lands and let them turn to pasture, hundreds of tenants were forced off of the farms they rented and crowded out of work. A run of bad harvests between 1527 and 1536 added to their misery. Silver flowing in from the New World, as well as debasement of currency by the government at home, made it impossible for many to earn a living. Great numbers of people were in abject poverty. Several insurrections were harshly suppressed by the Crown.

A rise in crime was the inevitable outcome of unalleviated misery. Crowds of rogues and vagabonds wandered about the countryside begging, cheating, and stealing. Pike, the English historian of crime, described the odd assortment of wretches in an Elizabethan house of correction as a reflection of life outside. Among them were to be found

"practisers of unlawful games — the forerunners of our modern skittle-sharpers, welshers, and gaming-house keepers. There were persons who 'used physiognomy, palmistry, or other abused sciences, tellers of destinies, deaths or fortunes.' There were 'minstrels not belonging to any honorable person of great degree,' unlicensed buyers of rabbit-skins, sellers of aqua vitæ, petty chapmen, tinkers, pedlers, jugglers, bearwards, fencers, unlicensed players in interludes. There were begging sailors pretending losses at sea and unable to show a license from two justices living near the place where they landed. There were Irishmen and Irishwomen 'of the sorts aforesaid,' who lived by begging. There were hedge-breakers and petty pilferers of wood. There, too, were scholars of Oxford or Cambridge that went about begging, 'not being licensed by the Chancellor or Commissary.'" [11]

Overrun with these miserable creatures, and without an established system of institutions, England looked towards the new lands of the west and thought of the double blessing to be gained by colonizing her undesirables.

Exile, as a punishment for Englishmen, was forbidden by Magna Charta. Astute advisors to the Crown found a way out of the difficulty. In 1596 a statute was passed, giving rogues and vagabonds leave to depart from England for the good of the country. During the reign of Charles II transportation to his Majesty's American colonies was authorized for felons sentenced to die. Such felons were then given a pardon if they would consent to be exiled. In 1718 all felons sentenced for more than three years were offered the substitute of transportation for the term of their sentences.

Penal transportation clearly resembled the slave trade. Prisoners were carried to the colonies by private shipowners under contract. Often a third or more of each shipload died en route. The right to the prisoners' labor might be sold to anyone, including the criminals themselves. Convicts were auctioned off in the colonies by the regular slave auctioneers. Usually American planters bought their services. High-minded citizens in the colonies frankly condemned the scheme, but some planters were glad to get laborers of any sort, and England needed the outlet that her dominions provided. Four or five hundred prisoners were shipped to Maryland each year. Others were sold in Virginia or Jamaica, and Barbados.

By 1775 England was transporting about a thousand criminals annually. Many of the prisoners were of the kind that in our day would be considered as victims of overwhelming circumstances. Given a fair chance, they had no desire

[11] L. O. Pike, "A History of Crime in England," Vol. 2, p. 75.

to do wrong. The new land gave them the opportunity they needed. It was rich in resources for the ambitious, and at the same time lacking in the chances for criminality that abounded in the Motherland. Prisoners who were shipped to the colonies had the advantage of being placed as servants in families. Their social contacts were normal. They were separated from other offenders who were bought and taken away by planters in need of their services. The number of criminals was small relative to the number of colonists.

America was an easy land to leave in those days and many of the worst offenders escaped and found their way back to England soon after they arrived here. Others went back at the expiration of their time. Furthermore, under the practice by which contractors sold the services of their prisoners, criminals who could afford their own purchase price, or who had friends to raise it for them, were released sometimes before the transport left England. The privilege of purchase thus changed the whole complexion of transportation, making it a penalty for poverty rather than for crime. Then, too, although many who landed in America became worthy settlers, others continued their nefarious practices, and they became an increasing burden to the new country.

When the African slave trade became well established, convict transportation was so unprofitable to shipowners that the government gave them £5 a prisoner to carry them away. Mandeville ironically suggested that England offer her convicts to the Barbary States as slaves to recompense them for negroes taken by the English, thus exchanging "lazy, cowardly thieves and incorrigible rogues for brave, laborious and useful people."[12]

The American Revolution forcibly stopped transportation. England tried to divert the traffic to Sierra Leone, but was obliged to abandon her attempts to establish a penal colony there by an unbearable climate. There was no other suitable outlet; a prison system did not exist. Forced to do something with her convict population, England turned to the use of hulks and for nearly thirty years, following an act passed in 1776, the prisoners who could not be trans-

[12] S. and B. Webb, "English Prisons Under Local Government," p 44 ff.

orted were quartered under unspeakable conditions in ancient frigates or merchantmen moored in the harbors and
rivers of England. The use of hulks was not entirely discontinued until 1858. Although some of the prisoners
worked ashore during the daytime, the close confinement in
the hulks at night, the vice and moral contamination that
accompanied the crowding together of young and old men
(and sometimes women), lunatics and the feeble-minded, the
unbearable monotony of the life, especially for those who
did not work ashore, all coupled with the free use of the
whip, made the era of the hulks the blackest in England's
penal history.

John Howard, sheriff of the county of Bedford, who knew
more about penal institutions in Europe than any other man
of his day, paid several visits to the hulks. These are extracts from his reports:[13]

Hulks on the Thames

". . . from August 1776 when the convicts were first put aboard
the *Justitia,* to 26 March 1778, out of six hundred and thirty two,
one hundred and seventy six had died."

The conditions on the *Justitia* were finally improved following a parliamentary inquiry into the management of the
Thames hulks.

The Hulk at Plymouth

"10 November, 1787, the convicts at Plymouth dock were on
board the hulk of the *Chatham,* a seventy-gun ship, and were healthy
and well ; but the *Dunkirk,* which is more commodious, was repairing for them. Their bread, beef, and beer were good ; but the
bread allowance of 4lb. a day to six men, is not sufficient. There
were among them many fine young fellows, who all lived in total
idleness, though some useful employment might here easily be found.
There were ninety-two men and one woman : nine more convicts
were coming on board from the gaol at Glamorgan.

"28 June, 1788, there were three hundred and sixty-six convicts
in the *Dunkirk,* which was fitted up with several separate rooms. In

[13] J. Howard, *op. cit.*

one of the rooms, fifty-seven feet by eighteen, and six feet high there were sixty-eight.   Such a room, at night, when the hatches are down, must be very offensive.   At one end, there is a room called the infirmary, and a recovery ward ; in the former were seven convicts, and in the latter thirteen.   The meat was sweet, but the bread not good, and the beer thick.

"The prisoners were all in total idleness, except six or seven who were making a boat for the captain.   One ingenious man had made a small inkstand (which I have by me) out of a bone of his meat but his knife was taken from him.   I saw some with Bibles in their hands ; but there is no chaplain, nor any religious service.   Here also some of the keepers, by their profaneness, set a bad example to the prisoners.

"Three miserable objects, for attempting to break out, were let down into a dreadful, dark and deep hole at the bottom of the ship where they lay, almost naked, upon a little straw ; but, having been thus confined for some weeks, upon their earnest entreaties, obtained their release."

The Hulk at Gosport

". . . Here were several to be transported for life and some whose sentences were for a short term : among them were boys of only ten years of age."

The Hulks near Portsmouth

"At Langston harbour, near Portsmouth, are three hulks.   In *La Fortunee* (formerly a French thirty-six gun frigate) there were 8 July, 1788, three hundred and thirty-eight convicts.   In the *Ceres*, which was the receiving ship at Woolwich . . . were two hundred and nineteen convicts. . .

"Both the ships were clean, particularly the *Ceres*.   The *Fortunee* had few sick in that part called the hospital; but the *Ceres* had many more sick than the hospital part could contain.   Several had the gaol-fever, and a few, petechiae.   Six out of ten that went from Bedford were dead, and two of the others were very sickly and dispirited.   The convicts lie two on a straw bed, with one blanket ; and after one is taken ill, his companion soon sickens."

If the American Revolution turned England to the unfortunate makeshift of the hulks, it drew her attention forcibly, if unpleasantly, to the state of her penal institutions, and gave Howard, Blackstone, Eden and their fellow reformers the bludgeon they needed to secure parliamentary action.   Under a Penitentiary Act of 1779 England intended to build suitable prisons for her convicts.   The administration of the project, however, was so bungled that the proposed prisons were never built.   In the meantime Captain Cook went avoyaging to Australia, and so intrigued his countrymen by its possibilities that all eyes were turned towards another new world.   Among those who saw the possibilities of Australia were the advocates of penal transportation.

In 1787 a fleet of eleven convict ships under Commodore Alfred Phillip, newly appointed governor of New South Wales, set out for Australia.   Aboard were 564 male convicts, 192 female convicts, and a troop of soldiers to act as guards.   Horses, cattle, seeds and tools were included in the cargo.   Eight long months later a few of the sick were disembarked at a barren spot euphemistically called Botany Bay, while the others pushed on to Port Jackson, now Sydney, Australia.   Nine men and six women were placed a thousand miles northeast of Sydney, on beautiful Norfolk Island, later to become England's largest and most notorious penal colony.   (Out of Norfolk came, however, an influence that left a favorable mark upon our modern reformatory systems.)   Later, in 1804, Hobart Town, Tasmania (then known as Van Diemen's Land) was founded as a penal colony.   England continued to ship prisoners to the region of Australia for more than three quarters of a century.   Not until 1857 was the word "transportation" dropped from the statutes and even then the practice continued until 1867, when England sent out its last shipment of convicts.   During this second period of transportation, something like 150,000 criminals had been sent to penal colonies.

England's second venture with transportation was even less successful than her first.   The convicts sent out with Commodore Phillip found no settlers ready to receive them. They were unwilling and incapable pioneers, with no one to teach them how to wrest a living from the virgin soil of Australia.   Scurvy and smallpox swept through the encampment ; the aborigines were hostile ; and the death rate of the

colonists was appalling.   After two and one half years of
discouraging hardships the survivors were on the verge of
starvation when a second fleet of prisoners arrived with provisions after a voyage of terrible suffering under the mishandling of contractors schooled in the African slave trade.

Free colonists lured by the possibilities of the new land
began to arrive, often without equipment, to make their
homes.   About 1791 the sentences of some of the prisoners
began to expire.   Many of them got back to England by
hook or by crook.   Others accepted the governor's offer of
free land, tools, seeds, and rations for eighteen months.
Some who stayed spurned the chance to earn an honest living.   Far from being reformed, they were an evil menace,
aiding and abetting their fellows in constant conspiracies
against the authorities.   Murder, incendiarism, drinking,
gambling, and sex offenses were committed with impunity.
Among the free settlers arose a sharp feeling of hostility
towards the released convicts.   About 1793 a scheme of leas-
ing convicts to planters as clearing gangs added to the irritation.   More dangerous criminals were used about the
countryside in chain gangs on government work.   In spite of
heavy leg irons and confinement in barracks at night, many
of them escaped into the bush where they united as brigands
to ravish the countryside.

The difficulties of managing gangs of rogues at large, as
forced settlers in a distant land, were well-nigh insurmountable.   The disproportionate numbers of men and women
led to unspeakable moral conditions.   Incoming ships smuggled liquor into the colony.   The split between the "eman-
cipists" who favored convict participation in the government,
and the "exclusionists" who bitterly fought penal colonization grew even wider.   In 1830 a league of free settlers
was formed, and by 1835 the exclusionists were vigorously
campaigning to stop transportation.   In 1837 their persistent
efforts were rewarded by the appointment in England of a
Parliamentary commission to examine their complaints with
the result that assignment of convicts to settlers was replaced
by a so-called probation system under which prisoners were
managed in chain gangs by the government.   By good con-

duct prisoners might in time secure transfer from the road gangs to service with private individuals. In 1840 the transportation of convicts to eastern Australia was stopped. Thereafter they were sent in greater numbers to Van Diemen's Land under an extension of the probation system by which convicts might, through good behavior, work their way upward through several stages from strict confinement to eventual freedom.

With the victory of the free settlers in 1840, transportation as a penal policy began to disappear. A growing awareness of its evils to Englishmen led to its condemnation there. The yearly expense of more than two and a half million dollars for transportation induced humanitarian sentiments in others. A new scheme for handling convicts in great cellular prisons was coming into vogue. In 1857, in name, and in 1867, in fact, transportation from England stopped.

Elsewhere transportation still has a limited use. In 1863 France established a new colony for incorrigible prisoners at New Caledonia in the southern Pacific which is still in use. An annual death rate of a quarter to a third of the prisoners shipped to Guiana led France to stop the shipment of European prisoners to that colony, but it is still used for convicts from French colonial possessions in the tropics. Russia shipped in the neighborhood of 865,000 convicts to Siberia between 1807 and 1897. In 1869 the island of Sakhalin was made a penal colony. After 1900 the Russian policy was greatly modified, and since that time only political and religious offenders have been transported. The Soviet Union still uses transportation to Siberia, especially for political offenders. Since 1857 India has maintained a penal colony on the Andaman Islands in the Bay of Bengal. Italy, under the code devised by the late Enrico Ferri, provides for the banishment of prisoners to varying distances from the region where the crime was committed. In the United States, particularly in the southwest, the custom of giving undesirables a few hours in which to leave town is still prevalent. This practice of the police and the courts of "floating" offenders is also a modified and particularly useless form of transportation by which one community gratuitously drops its problems at the back door of another, and is rewarded by a similar gift from another town that has undesirables to float.

Transportation has proved to be an expensive and unsuccessful scheme. It has been the experience of every government that has tried transportation that prisoners who have served their time will go back to their old haunts as soon as they are able. They will not colonize the land. Heindl[14] found that only 1% of the released prisoners in New Caledonia and the Andaman Islands had permanently settled there. The few who do settle down to a new life object to the continuance of transportation as creating an unfit environment for their families.

[14] R. Heindl, "Penal Settlement and Colonization," *Jour. of Criminal Law and Criminology*, Vol. 13, p. 56.

CHAPTER XVII

HUMAN IMPRISONMENT: A HISTORY OF CONFLICTING PRACTICES

IMPRISONMENT as a common punishment for crime is a nineteenth century experiment, not a matured and proved formula of the ages. The dungeons of ancient times bore not the faintest resemblance to the prisons of today either in construction or purpose. They were merely separate rooms in a palace or fort for the safekeeping of persons awaiting trial or punishment, or subtle substitutes for the slaying without trial of those whom a ruler dared neither to kill outright nor to release. We are told that Jeremiah was first scourged and then "put in prison in the house of Jonathan the scribe: for they had made that the prison." Later the princes took Jeremiah "and cast him into the dungeon of Malchiah the son of Hammelech, that was in the court of the prison. And in the dungeon there was no water, but mire: so Jeremiah sunk in the mire" where he would have died had he not been rescued by Ebedmelech the Ethiopian.[1]

The famous Bastille of Paris was originally the city gate, Porte Saint Antoine, made over into a fortress in the fourteenth century and into a prison in the early part of the fifteenth. The notorious *oubliettes*[2] in the Bastille were constructed with hidden trapdoors through which prisoners were dropped into deep pits of mud, water or wheels set with knives by means of which unfortunate wretches were unostentatiously killed. The name of the Conciergerie, a prison in Paris, preserves the idea of its original use as the home of the royal porter at the palace of Paris whose duty, as Wines

---

[1] Jeremiah 37 : 15 ; 38 : 4-13.
[2] Derived from the verb "oublier," because the prisoners placed in them were to be conveniently forgotten.

reminds us, "was to keep people in as well as to keep them out." [3]

THE ORIGIN OF JAILS

GRADUALLY in old England as the authority of the king increased the parochial or manorial authorities lost the power of summary punishment of prisoners and they were forced to hold suspected persons for the quarterly visits of the king's justices. In order to keep prisoners for trial lawful places of detention had to be provided. These were the common jails of which there were some two hundred in sixteenth to eighteenth century England. They were originally solely for the safekeeping of prisoners ; not for their punishment.

Theoretically they were the king's jails. Actually only those at Marshalsea and the Fleet, the Tower of London for political prisoners, and the military prison at the Savoy Palace were directly administered by the national government. The others were under the control of various local powers. Counties, municipal corporations, and other governmental subdivisions had their own jails. In addition bishops, lords, and similarly powerful individuals owned and maintained jails because of the income they provided. Jail keepers rarely received salaries but instead paid the owners a fixed sum for their concession and earned their own living by charging the prisoners fees.

In 1748, for example, a schedule of payments to be met by the prisoners at Southwark was drawn up. This included charges for admission, for detention in a special part of the prison, for a bed, for a common mattress, for a feather bed, the use of bedclothes, for putting on and taking off the irons, for a copy of the commitment papers, and for a variety of other privileges. [4]

Almost any building might serve as a jail, and since the safekeeping of prisoners was a commercial enterprise for the jailers, little money was spent on elaborate quarters. Often the jail was a room or two in a castle, a market house, or even

[3] F. H. Wines, "Punishment and Reformation," Revised Edition, p. 111.

[4] S. and B. Webb, "English Prisons Under Local Government," p. 6.

in the jailer's own home. Chesterfield jail belonged to the Duke of Portland to whom the jailer paid £18 12s a year for the concession. This jail consisted of "one room with a cellar under it ; to which the prisoners occasionally descend through a hole in the floor."[5] The jail at Halifax was owned by the Duke of Leeds. Masters-side debtors were imprisoned in "four rooms in the keeper's public house. Through this you pass to a court about fourteen yards by seven : at the farther end of which is a sizeable room on the ground-floor for common-side debtors, it is called the low gaol ; over it a chamber (the low gaol chamber) where prisoners pay one shilling a week. The whole prison greatly out of repair : it rained in upon the beds : the rooms were clean. Keeper, no salary : he pays the Duke £24 a year : and pays window-tax for the gaol."

THE ORIGIN OF THE HOUSE OF CORRECTION

DURING the sixteenth century another institution that came to take on many of the characteristics of the common jail originated in England as an outgrowth of her developing poor relief policy. This was the house of correction. It was specifically originated to restrain the troublesome poor, and the multitude of sharpers, petty thieves, gypsies, beggars, and vagabonds who were then such a nuisance about the English countryside. In 1552, the mayor, the bishop and other prominent citizens of London besought the Privy Council to help them to control these wandering rogues. As a result of their plea the King gave the city of London the palace at St. Bridget's Well[6] as a municipal charitable institution, for the care of several groups of idle persons. Here untrained children were to be taught a trade, the aged and infirm were to be given a home, and vagrants were to be confined and forced to work. The London Bridewell proved to be such a happy way of meeting the needs of these special groups that in 1575-6 Parliament passed "An

[5] J. Howard, "The State of the Prisons," Everyman's Library Edition, p. 206.

[6] Corrupted to "Bridewell" whence the name still commonly applied to Houses of Correction.

Acte for the setting of the Poore on Worke, and for the avoyding of ydleness," requiring every county to provide a house of correction.

Under the law the house of correction remained a combination hospital, training school, and place of compulsory industry for idlers. Raw materials furnished by regular manufacturers were made into finished goods in the houses of correction and returned to the manufacturers for sale. The county received a fixed price for each piece of work done. Since Bridewells were at first looked upon as institutions essentially for the relief of the unemployed, the inmates in many of them were paid regular wages.

Within the century after its establishment, the English house of correction was gradually transformed from a poorhouse into a penal institution. Inmates were no longer only the idle poor for many judges had adopted the practice of committing petty offenders to the Bridewell, and occasionally incorrigible rogues were committed to the house of correction for life.

In 1609 the use of the Bridewell as a place of punishment rather than correction was recognized by statute. Incidentally the growth of workhouses[7] for the unemployed decreased their numbers in the Bridewells. The county justices of the peace who were originally responsible for poor relief in the houses of correction quietly shifted their burden to keepers who ran the Bridewells as private enterprises. As the poor in the Bridewells were replaced by petty criminals, the keepers, faced with a decreasing income from the work products of the inmates, sought the privilege of exacting fees from them after the manner of the jail keepers.

[7] In the United States today some houses of correction are known as workhouses. The original workhouses, however, were in no sense penal institutions. Under the English system of poor relief goods were distributed to needy families by the pound to be made up into finished goods in their homes. So much material was lost in this way that distribution of goods to families in their homes was replaced by congregate work in factory established by the parish or municipality. Here the unemployed who could not get other work might come. Some parishes farmed out their unemployed poor to private contractors who owned their own work houses.

Although the fee system never became universal in the Bridewells the practice was permitted by the justices in many of them. The extortions common to the jails also crept in. Bridewells and jails coalesced until the beginning of the eighteenth century when they had become, for all practical purposes, identical. The principle of imprisonment as a punishment had appeared in England. It was limited, however, to petty offenders.

THE STATE OF THE JAILS

THE conditions under which prisoners were confined in jails and Bridewells were as bad as anyone would care to imagine. Those presumably innocent awaiting trial and the guilty awaiting punishment were thrown in together and frequently those who had been adjudged not guilty were carried back to jail because they could not pay the keepers' fees. Men and women, young and old, were lodged together in a common room. Debtors, prostitutes, thieves, and apprentice boys consorted freely with each other. Discipline was unknown. The prisoners evolved their own rules. Newcomers were forced to pay "garnish" or be stripped of their clothing. The money thus secured was used in treating the prisoners to liquor from the prison tap. Prostitutes plied their trade with greater ease in jail than outside, and even virtuous women sold themselves to keep from starvation. Jail keepers not only permitted licentiousness for a fee but encouraged it in order to increase their incomes. Madames seeking prostitutes visited the jails to look them over and paid for the release of those they hired. Men from outside frequently used the jails as brothels while the petty officers exploited the female prisoners as they pleased.

No adequate provision was made for feeding or clothing the inmates of the jails. Many of the unfortunates were unable to buy food for lack of money and the county allowance, sometimes as little as a penny a day, was insufficient. Rags served them as clothes. Bed straw was reduced to powder by continual use. Devonshire increased the allowance of its prisoners in 1608 because a number of them had starved to death. Friends, who could afford it, helped others. In some places prisoners were allowed on certain occasions to go out onto the street to beg.

Jail buildings were poorly constructed, damp, drafty, and without fireplaces. Some were so flimsy that prisoners had to be securely fastened at night. The Bishop of Ely was obliged to rebuild his jail in 1768 because Judge Collyer complained of his methods of securing prisoners who were chained every night to the floor by spiked iron collars about their necks and a heavy iron bar across their legs.[8] Sanitary arrangements were conspicuous because of their absence. Sick and well were housed together. Few jails had baths or an infirmary. Open sewers ran through the courtyards. Water was difficult to secure. The stench of the jails was so nauseating that the prison reformer, John Howard, traveled on horseback on his trips of inspection so that he might not subject the coach passengers to the odor of his clothing.

Dr. William Smith, an eighteenth century English physician who often witnessed the treatment of prisoners, wrote that thirty or forty wretches were commonly squeezed into one dark ward to spend the night together half naked, their rags in motion with vermin, and their bodies covered with scorbutic and venereal sores.[9]

As might be expected, it was easy to die in jail. Malignant typhus, the so-called "jail fever," was prevalent in every prison in England. John Howard was fully convinced that many more prisoners were destroyed by it, than were put to death by all the public executions in the kingdom.[10] Assizes had to be adjourned because of jail fever. Communities were infected by jail inmates. It is said that about three hundred persons present at the Assize at Oxford Castle in 1577 died within forty hours as a result of jail fever among the prisoners. Several hundred died of typhus brought from Ivelchester jail to the Lent Assizes in Taunton in 1730. Discharged prisoners were another source of infection. Some who were impressed for service with the

[8] J. Howard, *op. cit.*, Everyman's Library, p. 200.
[9] S. and B. Webb, *op. cit.*, p. 19.
[10] J. Howard, *ibid.*, p. 6.

army or navy carried the disease among the troops where for a time it caused more deaths than were due to all other causes combined.

REFORM MOVEMENTS ASTIR IN THE EIGHTEENTH CENTURY

DURING the eighteenth century several forces converged to bring about reforms in imprisonment. A spirit of revolt against the out-worn barbarisms of a previous age was sweeping Europe and America. It was the age of Beccaria, Montesquieu, Voltaire, Tom Paine, Blackstone, and Jeremy Bentham. It culminated in the revolutions of America and France.

Montesquieu (1687-1755), in his "The Spirit of the Laws," indicted the penal methods of his day and advocated punishments less harsh than execution and mutilation. In 1764 Cesare Beccaria (1735-94), published his "Dei Delitti e delle Pene" (Crimes and Punishments) which summed up the revolt of his contemporaries against the current arbitrary and irrational criminal procedure and made him the leader of a new school of criminologists. It set forth as a major principle that punishment should be limited by the social need, and suggested that imprisonment replace more severe penalties. In England, Jeremy Bentham thundered against the atrocities of the English system (or lack of it) and devised, with the assistance of his architect brother, the Panoptican, a circular prison, so planned that every cell could always be seen by an inspector from his station at the center.

More directly influential than Bentham was John Howard, a nonconformist squire who in 1773 was appointed to the semi-ceremonial office of sheriff of Bedfordshire. Unlike his predecessors, Howard took the duties of a sheriff seriously. The distress and injustice that he found in his jail led him to visit those in neighboring counties to discover how to improve his own institution. Everywhere he went, Howard saw only horror piled upon horror.

Thoroughly aroused by the evils uncovered Howard devoted the remainder of his life to prison reform. For seventeen years he worked with untiring industry and high courage to replace the abuses of the jail system with rational methods of jail management. He inspected every jail in England two or three times, and in addition made two journeys throughout Europe to examine the penal institutions of other countries. On a leaf of one of his memorandum books appears a detailed account of the extent of these journeys. They total 42,033 miles. Beneath his figures Howard wrote, "To God alone be all praise! I do not regret the loss of many inconveniences of life, but bless God who inclined my mind to such a scheme."

In 1777 Howard's "The State of the Prisons" was first published, followed by second and third editions in 1780 and 1784. In 1789 his description of European prisons appeared. Howard's writings were free from emotional diatribes. Instead they were astoundingly impressive by the sheer weight of the facts piled up in them. With the precision and style of an engineer Howard examined and listed the numbers, age, and sex of prisoners, the area and cubical contents of their apartments, the quantity and quality of food and water, the manner of sewage disposal, the methods of securing prisoners and the fees required of them.

Facts spoke for themselves with an authority that colorful phrases could not approach. Intelligent citizens were stirred out of their apathy by them. The consciences of legislators were aroused and they betook themselves to the task of jail reform. Parliament heard of Howard's extraordinary zeal even before his first book appeared, and he was summoned there for examination. Faced with Howard's incontrovertible facts Parliament was bludgeoned into passing, in 1774, the first of a series of bills aimed at the improvement of conditions in the local jails and Bridewells. The eyes of men had been opened to the need for a new penal system. In 1780 Burke said of Howard, "I cannot name this gentleman without remarking that his labors and writings have done much to open the eyes and hearts of all mankind."

Howard died on the shores of the Black Sea from a jail infection contracted in the course of his work. Carved on his tomb so far away from his native land are these words:

JOHN HOWARD
*Whoever thou art, thou standeth
at the tomb of thy Friend*
1790

THE RISE OF PRISONS IN EUROPE

HOWARD struck his blows at an opportune time. While he was awakening England to an interest in her jails the War of the Revolution put a temporary stop to penal transportation to America. England had no choice but to find another disposition for deportable criminals. The immediate answer was the hulks, previously described, but the idea of imprisonment as the ultimate solution came rapidly into prominence.

Fortunately England had influential workers of the caliber of Sir William Blackstone and Sir William Eden. Grasping the full import of Howard's work they drafted a bill providing for the administration of a national penitentiary based upon Howard's major recommendations that :

Prisoners be comfortably, safely and cleanly housed. The aim of imprisonment should be reformation through diet, work, and religious instruction.

The prison administrators should be paid salaries instead of fees.
Prisoners should be regularly examined by impartial inspectors.

Blackstone and Eden's bill was passed in 1779 but so inefficiently did the government move that the prisons authorized by the act were never built. Nevertheless, the ideas set forth in it left their impress upon succeeding prison legislation.

In Italy Pope Clement XI had preceded the reformers in putting their theories into practice by nearly a century. In 1703 he organized a papal correctional prison for juveniles as part of the great charitable institution of San Michele at Rome. In 1735 correctional quarters for women were added. Unique for its day was the architectural scheme of individual cells in the juvenile quarters in place of the common room. Yet in an institution managed by the Church it was an almost inevitable adaptation of the long established monastic system of seclusion and penitence. It was the world's first cellular penitentiary. In it the boys were housed separately in their cells at night, but they worked together in silence during the daytime. Reformation rather than punishment was Pope Clement's avowed aim for San Michele. In its corridor were inscribed these words: "It is of little advantage to restrain the bad by punishment unless you render them good by discipline."

Actually the régime fell far short of its conception. Discipline was harsh and mechanical. The hours of work were long and the tasks arduous. Moral training was of a formal and apparently useless sort. The good really achieved is questionable. Yet in attempting to apply this ideal at San Michele Pope Clement suggested the first positive use of imprisonment. Unfortunately the papal prison was not widely known even after it was visited and described by Howard, and it seems to have had little influence upon succeeding prison experiments.

In Flanders, the Deputies of the Estates, confounded by hordes of wandering thieves and vagabonds, similar to those that plagued England, called, in 1771, upon the ingenious and public spirited Hippolyte Vilain XIII for advice. He suggested a reformatory prison. The idea was approved, and under his direction the prison of Ghent was begun. It was never completed but while still unfinished it received its first occupants in 1773. As at San Michele, a constructive program of reformation rather than a negative scheme of repression was adopted. Vilain's ideas were decidedly progressive for his day. In his institution prisoners were separated on the basis of age, sex, and seriousness of offense. Useful work combined with trade instruction intended to fit prisoners to earn a living upon discharge was the chief means of reformation. Inmates worked together in the prison shops but were housed in separate cells at night. Vilain anticipated the modern prison wage movement by paying his prisoners a percentage of their earnings. He foresaw the disadvantages of both excessively short and life sentences as affecting the reformation of prisoners and sought instead a minimum sentence of one year and the power to recommend convicts for pardon.

Vilain's work was well-nigh destroyed by the stupid intervention of Emperor Joseph the Second of Austria, but not before the persistent Howard had examined its features and commended them to the world.

THE RISE OF PRISONS IN THE UNITED STATES

In America, the Quakers took the lead in prison reform. Violent physical punishments were incompatible with their religious convictions and in 1786 the Pennsylvania legislature substituted "continuous hard labor publicly and disgracefully imposed" for the capital punishment of some felons. The sight of these wretches marching through the streets brought the question of prison reform before intelligent people more vividly than all of the tomes that could have been written. In May 1787, a group of citizens organized the Philadelphia Society for Alleviating the Miseries of Public Prisons of which Bishop White of the Protestant Episcopal Church was the first president. Stimulated by the zeal of Friend Roberts Vaux and his son, Richard, the new prison society became the most influential agency for reform in America.

The decline of the death penalty left an ever increasing number of criminals to be cared for under the new laws. The old jails which in America, as in England, were breeding places of evil and unfit for human habitation, would not serve the purpose. The legislature therefore influenced by the new prison society, converted the old Walnut Street Jail into a prison in 1790, by coincidence the year of John Howard's death, and provided for the building of a new wing of thirty individual cells instead of the conventional common room for the solitary confinement of "hardened and atrocious offenders." In practice an attempt was made to classify prisoners in accordance with their offenses, and the less hardened ones were placed in large rooms rather than in solitary confinement. Legal provision was made for the employment of every prisoner but in practice those in solitary confinement had no opportunity to labor. The others worked together in the shops during the day.

The separate and solitary confinement of felons in the Walnut Street prison was an innovation to America although it had already been tried in Europe. In introducing it to this country the prison society had the support of Howard with whom they had corresponded and the example of the newly erected reform jail at Wymondham based upon Howard's suggestions. "Solitude and silence are favorable to reflection," said Howard, "and may possibly lead them (the prisoners) to repentence." [11] To the growing conviction abroad that separation of prisoners would prevent mutual contamination the Quakers added a fervent belief in the reformative value of meditation and communion with God.

It was because the Friends lifted up a clear cut objective and moved unwaveringly towards it that their program came to exert a world-wide influence. They were trying to set up, not a mere prison, but a true penitentiary. Today the terms are synonymous but the Quakers used them with precision. Their idea of a penitentiary harked back to the ancient "pénitences" of the Roman church by which both crime and sin could be expiated through labor and meditation in solitude. As in the monasteries of the Middle Ages penitents worked and fasted in seclusion, so the Quakers intended to bring criminals to repentance through solitary labor and fellowship with God.

THE PENNSYLVANIA SYSTEM

THE hopes of the reformers were never realized at the Walnut Street Jail because it was utterly inadequate in size to care for the prisoners committed to it. By 1816 as many as thirty men were locked together in a room eighteen feet square. The administrative difficulties that ensued caused the legislature in 1817 to authorize one penitentiary at Pittsburgh and one at Philadelphia which should be so large and so well built as to house every prisoner in effective solitude. The Pittsburgh penitentiary, first to be built, was designed by William Strickland with a circular arrangement of cells. That at Philadelphia designed by Edward Haviland, built in radial form with outside cells, became a model for later prisons and has been widely copied.

In the meantime several states, including New York,

[11] J. Howard, *op. cit.*, p. 21.

Massachusetts, Maryland, and Virginia, followed the plan of the Walnut Street prison in their classification of prisoners. In all of them the evils of confinement in idleness had disastrous effects upon the mental and physical health of the prisoners. The experiences of Auburn prison in particular caused Pennsylvania, then in the process of building the Cherry Hill penitentiary for eastern Pennsylvania, to make sure that labor was actually provided for prisoners. The number of occupations available for solitary labor in cells was necessarily very limited, although it must be remembered that individual craftsmanship without the aid of machinery was much more common then than at the present time. The trades practised by inmates of Cherry Hill were chiefly weaving, tailoring, shoemaking, and carpentry. The work seems to have been eagerly accepted as an antidote to the almost unbearable monotony of solitary life in cramped quarters.

Even religious services were not permitted to break down the isolation of the prisoners. Instead a curtain was drawn across the cells of each tier and then a slide in each cell door was opened so that the preacher might be heard by all while the rule of no communication between inmates was effectively preserved.

Such was the reformatory scheme that came to be known throughout Europe and America as the Pennsylvania system, sponsored by the Quakers and believed to offer in its system of solitude a rich opportunity for the improvement of those who could not escape the searchings of their own consciences during long weeks of silence. Two foreign observers, De Beaumont, and De Toqueville, who were evidently much impressed by the advantages of the Pennsylvania system wrote,

"Nothing distracts, in Philadelphia, the mind of the convicts from their meditations ; and as they are always isolated, the presence of a person who comes to converse with them is the greatest benefit, and one which they appreciate in its whole extent. When we visited this penitentiary, one of the prisoners said to us : 'It is with joy that I perceive the figure of the keepers, who visit my cell. This summer a cricket came into my yard ; it looked like a companion. When a butterfly or any other animal happens to enter my cell, I never do it any harm.' If the soul is thus disposed, it is easy to conceive what value the prisoners must attach to moral communications, and how great must be the influence of wise advice and pious exhortations on their minds." [12]

THE AUBURN SYSTEM

IN 1816, the year before Pennsylvania authorized the building of its penitentiaries, New York created the Auburn State Prison. At first New York received its prisoners into the new institution under the old congregate plan, grouping ten or more convicts together in large rooms. It was soon apparent that discipline could not be maintained under such conditions and New York began to cast about for a solution of its problems. Faced with differences of opinion about prison methods, New York tried an interesting experiment. The prisoners at Auburn were divided into three groups. The first, comprising the most hardened offenders, was housed in solitary confinement without work. Less vicious prisoners were confined three days a week, while those who were amenable worked together and lived in groups.

Complete solitary confinement was quite as unsatisfactory as congregate living. Five of the solitary prisoners died during their first year of confinement. Another went insane. Others were so affected in body and mind that cellular isolation was abandoned. In its place appeared a compromise scheme consisting of separate confinement in cells at night; common meals and congregate work in absolute silence during the day. Rigid discipline harshly maintained by Warden Elam Lynds with the help of a ready whip started the Auburn system on its triumphant way.

THE BATTLE OF THE PENNSYLVANIA AND AUBURN PLANS

As the prison policies at Auburn and Philadelphia began to crystallize into distinct and different schemes of prison administration a vigorous dispute sprang up as to their relative

[12] De Beaumont and De Toqueville, "On the Penitentiary System in the U. S.," p. 51.

merits which was destined to shape the prison policies of Europe and America to this day. Those who favored the Pennsylvania system found in it five advantages:

Ease of controlling prisoners in cells.
Provision for prisoners in accordance with their individual needs.
Freedom from the influence of fellow prisoners and restriction to beneficial contacts.
Opportunity for meditation and repentance.
Relative anonymity upon discharge.

It is doubtful if all of these advantages were in practice secured for, in spite of the elaborate devices that have been used in some institutions to prevent communication among prisoners, no practical barrier has yet been found against signalling by taps on floors, walls, or water pipes. The needs of prisoners for exercise and instruction are difficult to meet under the solitary plan. In addition, isolation brings the evils of physical and mental decay, solitary vices, and a social retardation that makes normal life upon discharge difficult if not impossible. The scheme is the practice of cruelty under the principle of reformation. To these disadvantages must be added that of greater costliness.

Under the Auburn system prisoners could be offered a much wider range of trade opportunities, due to the system of congregate work. Very likely, however, the ease of administration that attended steady uninterrupted work, and the emphasis placed upon a good financial report tended to make the opportunity for learning a trade only incidental to the necessity for keeping up production. The contract system, generally in force, also interfered with vocational training. In fact, the great appeal of the Auburn system lay in its economy. The state had learned how to make its prisoners pay a part of their own keep. Inmates under the Auburn silent system were no more fitted for discharge than those sentenced under the Pennsylvania plan. They were as much subject to vice, and more schooled in deceit and evasion. The silent system no more prevented communication than solitary confinement.

The issue between the two schemes of prison management

was made sharp and clear by the crusading activities of the country's two powerful prison societies. The Philadelphia Society for Alleviating the Miseries of Public Prisons fervently defended the Pennsylvania system. The Prison Discipline Society of Boston led by Louis Dwight urged the merits of the Auburn plan. Both societies carried on a bitter, unscrupulous, partisan campaign to prove their cases. Their controversy spread abroad. France, England, and Prussia, among others, sent commissioners to America to make first-hand investigations. In general European observers favored the Pennsylvania plan. Belgium, Sweden, Norway, Denmark, Holland, and France adopted it. England modified it for use at Millbank. In America the Auburn system by reason of its apparent economies forged rapidly into pre-eminence and even those states that had originally copied the reforms at the Walnut Street Jail turned to the Auburn plan. Finally, Pennsylvania itself came to permit the congregation of prisoners, in the Western Penitentiary in 1869 and in the Eastern Penitentiary in 1913.

PRISON POLICIES IN CONFLICT

THE dispute over the merits of the Pennsylvania and Auburn systems simply marked the center of a more extensive storm of controversy that was occupying prison reformers in America and England. The rise of prison reform societies both here and in England kept the issues alive and made divergent theories stand out in sharp relief. England, with a more compact population and feeling the full effects of the industrial revolution, faced a more insistent prison problem than America. Experiments in prison methods, therefore, went on in England at a feverish rate.

Agitation by the influential Sir Samuel Romilly led England in 1810 to appoint a commission to study penal methods which vigorously recommended "a system of imprisonment not confined to the safe custody of the person, but extending to the reformation and improvement of the mind, and operating by seclusion, employment and religious instruction." [13]

[13] From the First Report of the Committee, May 31, 1811, quoted in S. and B. Webb, *op. cit.*, p. 48.

The efforts of the commission, under the chairmanship of George P. Holford, led to the building of a costly national penitentiary completed as the model prison at Millbank in 1821. There the national government introduced a modification of the Pennsylvania plan known as the Separate System which differed from permanent solitary confinement only in supposedly allowing the prisoner generous opportunity to talk with the prison wardens.

EXPERIMENTS IN PENITENTIARY ADMINISTRATION

IN 1812, the wealthy and zealous Quaker, Elizabeth Fry, had begun to sense the horror and hopelessness of imprisonment through visits to Newgate. Much impressed, she began a philanthropic movement among her friends to provide food, clothing and religious instruction to prisoners who would try to mend their ways.

Between 1817 and 1827 there arose a number of Ladies' Prison Committees devoted to charitable and religious work in prisons. Organized presently into the Society for the Improvement of Prison Discipline they were able to exert pressure upon legislators. They sought educational opportunities for prisoners and regular religious services. They favored the transformation of prisons into cheerful workshops, and were successful in getting their devices adopted in the reformed jails.

The reform movements were in flat contradiction to the older notions of penal treatment. Violent arguments about prison policies resulted. Reformers talked about making prisons into hives of industry. Conservatives railed about the need to make prison work hard and distasteful. Reformed jails were organized like workhouses. Others drove their convicts until they dropped of exhaustion from walking the treadwheel or turning the crank. Reformers called the treadwheel exhausting, injurious, torturesome, useless, inhuman. Its advocates called it a cheap, flexible well-deserved punishment and an efficient deterrent. Opponents of the treadwheel and crank pointed to the economy of useful productive prison industry. Outside manufacturers objected to the unfair competition of prison labor. Disputes arose over the merits of flogging, of prison education, of religious services, of various diets, of contract labor as opposed to government labor.

Finally in 1835, after a searching investigation that brought to light a state of near anarchy in the local prisons, Parliament passed an act bringing the penal institutions of England and Wales under the control of the Home Office. Experimentation and dispute continued but with growing uniformity throughout the country. National supervision became increasingly detailed and exacting and in 1877 the entire administration of English prisons was placed under the direction of the Home Secretary working through a body of prison commissioners.

With painful slowness reforms came about. By the beginning of the twentieth century, prisoners after an initiatory period in solitary confinement were allowed to work in association followed by conditional release. The crank and the treadwheel were abolished. Prison-made goods were used in the prisons themselves or were of a sort, like mailbags, that could be used by other governmental departments. The starvation diet was replaced by one adequate in content if not in variety. Extreme and arbitrary cruelty was reduced. Prisoners were given an opportunity to pass through progressive stages characterized by decreasing severity of confinement and to earn marks entitling them to their discharge earlier than the time set by their original sentence. These were the essential features of English prisons by 1900. They were paralleled by similarly meager and uninspiring accomplishment in America. In both countries, except in a few institutions, they represent the essential features of prison life today.

CHAPTER XVIII

THE REFORMATION OF PRISONERS: THE GROWTH OF AN IDEA

ONE of the chief characteristics of the early prisons was the mechanical régime under which they operated. Once the prison doors closed behind a convict his identity as a person was lost. He became another automaton going through the prison routine. Nothing that he could do might in any essential way change the nature of his confinement, nor improve his condition. He might never be considered as an individual with unique personal characteristics. He was put through the prison process as a log would be run through a sawmill. He was just another piece of raw material to be run through the machine.

So long as the accepted means of protecting society was by permanently segregating offenders and by frightening potential criminals, the only objection to be made to the prison was a humanitarian one. That in itself was not a sentiment to be casually put aside as humanitarians had already demonstrated in bringing about the substitution of costly imprisonment for cheap executions. As life imprisonment for felons was replaced by shorter sentences, a new objection arose. Prisoners were being restored again to freedom after the expiration of their terms. What happened to them in prison, therefore, became of much concern as it made them more or less fit to be at large.

A few progressive workers, here and there, grasped the fact which is not kept in mind by most of us even today: *unless prisoners are to be killed or permanently incarcerated, their reformation prior to release is as essential for social protection as their imprisonment seems to be after their conviction.*

363

EARLY JUVENILE REFORMATORIES

As might be expected, the possibilities of reformation were first seen in juvenile offenders whose condition pulled most easily at the heart-strings, and whose immaturity permitted the hope of improvement. At San Michele, in 1703, Pope Clement XI had separated juveniles from adults in a special wing, over whose doors were written these words:

"For the correction and instruction of profligate youth, that they who when idle are injurious, may when taught, become useful to the State."

In 1813 the "Society of Friends in Need," founded by Johannes Falk, established in Weimar, Germany, an industrial school for delinquents and for the children of criminals. Later, when the institution was moved to Duesselthal, farming was added to its curriculum. Similar schools were founded in Erfurt, Aschersleben, Breslau, Danzig, Memel and Berlin prior to 1830. In England, the Marine Society and the Philanthropic Society, organized in 1756 and 1788 respectively, became active in caring for the children of convicts. Sometimes boys who had been sentenced to exile were placed in their care under a conditional pardon. So effective was their work that the government tried the unsuccessful experiment of using reformatory methods with the juvenile offenders in Parkhurst Prison.

The first juvenile reformatory in the United States was opened in January 1825, as the New York House of Refuge, on a county site now forming part of Madison Square, New York. Boston opened a House of Reformation in 1826, and Philadelphia, a House of Refuge in 1828. These three were the only juvenile institutions for delinquents in the United States until 1845, when New Orleans built a municipal reformatory for boys only. They were founded by reform societies and maintained by private funds. Not until 1847, when Massachusetts, prodded by a gift of money from ex-mayor Lyman of Boston, established the first state reformatory school for boys at Westborough (now the Lyman School) was a national movement for juvenile reformatories begun.

Another type of penal institution that began to appear just

before the Civil War was the truant or parental schools which were an outgrowth of the new requirement of compulsory education. A Massachusetts law of 1850 made truancy punishable by confinement in an institution. Other states passed similar laws. At first truants under this law were placed in jails, almshouses, or almost any convenient establishment. Later, as a result of public opposition to such treatment, special schools for truants were provided. Some of them began to accept children guilty of other delinquencies. Commitment might be either by school authorities or the courts. Always juveniles were sent to them for an indefinite period, although it was sometimes specified that it must not extend beyond the age of twenty-one. This was the first regular use of an indefinite sentence in the United States.

In the early New York, Boston, and Philadelphia Houses of Refuge, definite correctional training was instituted. Work, study, and religious instruction, re-enforced by a scheme of rewards and punishments were the means of reformation. De Beaumont and De Toqueville, recording their visits to these institutions, said : [1]

"In every house of refuge the inmates are divided into good and bad classes. Their conduct makes the children pass from one into the other. The good classes enjoy privileges which the bad ones are denied ; and the latter are subject to privations which the former have not to undergo.

"Eight hours, at the least, are assigned every day to labour in the workshops, where the children are occupied with useful arts, such as shoemaking, joiner's work, cloth-making, carpenter's work, &c. Four hours daily are spent in the school. After rising, and before going to bed, prayers are offered. Three meals take half an hour each ; in short there are about fifteen hours of the day occupied with study, labour, &c., and nine hours with rest."

At the Boston House of Refuge a limited form of self-government was set up. Methods of punishment were decided by vote of the children. They elected their own monitors, and each child kept in a book his own marks of

[1] De Beaumont and De Toqueville, "On the Penitentiary System in the United States," p. 115.

merit and demerit. Corporal punishments were not permitted. Delinquents accused of certain offenses within the institution were tried by a jury of their fellows. During the superintendency of the remarkably competent Mr. Wells, the Boston institution attracted favorable comment from impartial observers,[2] but its features were too progressive for the City Council, which presently dismissed Mr. Wells.

These juvenile reformatories that started so auspiciously under the able leadership of men like Hart of Philadelphia and Wells of Boston soon went into a decline. They took on all of the outer, and most of the inner, characteristics of adult prisons. In some cases they were merely wings of adult institutions set apart for children. In other cases they were separate institutions built in true prison style, with locked cells, barred windows, and a wall-enclosed yard. The labor of juveniles was sold to outside firms for whom they made brooms, shoes, cigars, clothing, and furniture. The life was one of monotony and exacting routine. Little attention was paid to the physical, mental, or social needs of the delinquents. The aim was punishment; the method, repression.

MODERN CORRECTIONAL SCHOOLS

SLOWLY, painfully the juvenile reform schools have been climbing out of the slough of short-sightedness. They are still far from perfection, although here and there, particularly during the last decade, certain schools have accomplished noteworthy reforms. Since the turn of the century there has been a marked tendency to drop the prison-like features of juvenile reformatories. The first hint of regen-

[2] De Beaumont and De Toqueville were much impressed by it during their tour of the penal institutions of the United States, as was also Charles Dickens, who visited it a few years later. The Inspectors of the State Prison in their report to the Honorable Senate and House of Representatives of the Commonwealth of Massachusetts, May 26, 1830, were moved to digress a bit to say, "There is one Establishment in this vicinity, the House of Reformation for Juvenile Offenders in South Boston, which has attained so high a character in this respect, [reformation] that there is said to be no difficulty whatever in procuring places for those who have been confined in it."

eration appeared when congregate living in walled fortresses began to give way to the so-called cottage type of housing suggested by the industrial school at Hamburg, Germany, and by the much discussed agricultural and industrial school for boys at Mettray, France.

The cottage scheme was introduced to the United States in the first separate Industrial School for Girls at Lancaster, Massachusetts (1854) and in the Boys' Industrial School at Lancaster, Ohio (1856). The Massachusetts commissioners in establishing a state reform school for girls recommended a village of homes without walls or fences in which the unit of organization should be that of a family of eight to twelve persons. As it was actually built the school cottages housed from twenty-five to forty girls, the older ones in single rooms, the younger ones in dormitories. In those schools where the cottage system now prevails, the houses are likely to be fair-sized brick dormitories instead of homes. And, of course, thirty or forty delinquents of about the same age living together with a master and matron as supervisors is not a family. Nevertheless, such an organization offers infinitely better opportunities for influencing juveniles than can possibly obtain in a great congregate prison.

Along with the change in organization has come a better conception of reformatory training. Most of the correctional institutions are now midway between a school and a prison, but the best of them have frankly become schools. They recognize that training fails if it does not prepare young people for normal living. Emphasis is placed upon vocational training in school and in shop. Agricultural work has become an integral part of the reformatory process and not simply a means of reducing expenses. The notion that behavior can be understood and modified is coming to be accepted as a basic working principle.

In the girls' reformatories, which have come into existence since the new viewpoint has gained favor, the attempt to approach the conditions of wholesome family life has met with its greatest success. The Home School for Girls at Sauk Center, Minnesota, Samarcand Manor, North Carolina, the Girls' Training School at Gainesville, Texas, and the Glen Mills School (Sleighton Farms) in Pennsylvania are examples of the more progressive type of schools.

An English visitor, Mary Gordon, late His Majesty's Inspector of Prisons recently said :

"In America I have only seen a few places of detention, and among them were the best and the worst I have seen anywhere.

"But the Sleighton Farm School for girls and young women is a model of what an educational establishment for young women could be if the 'prison' element were taken out of it. I do not think discipline is absent from this institution by any means ; I think there may be, in one sense, more than even we are accustomed to, but my impressions were rather casually gathered and are not worth much. But I visited this place accidentally on a holiday, and saw several hundreds of girls giving a party to their friends, and amusing themselves. Boys from a neighbouring school had brought a band. There were field sports, and exhibitions of cookery, and sweets and needlework, and prizes for these, and a delightful procession in fancy dress took place in which the girls' fancies had free play. The tone of the institution was . . . well there *was* a tone and there were good manners, and there was spontaneous gaiety, and interested play.

"All the girls were in pretty frocks, and the houses they lived in, and all else, bore more relation to a high class school in this country than to a reformatory. Again I envied the conditions for prisoners at home ; there was so much that mitigated discipline, and that provided outlet, and conduced to development. They were prisoners — but could, and some did, go on from their place of detention to colleges and universities — places that I have known Borstal girls deeply interested in hearing about." [3]

Few juvenile reformatories are yet able to merit this description. Nevertheless, all of them have in some measure been swept along by the tide that has set to change the juvenile reformatory from a prison into a home ; from a factory into a school ; and to set for its goal, not punishment, but reformation.

There is a growing belief now that some juvenile delinquents at least, can best be corrected by good home life cor-

[3] M. Gordon, "Penal Discipline," pp. 219-220. E. P. Dutton and Co., Inc., publishers. Quoted by permission.

related with associations and responsibilities in a normal community. It is recognized that no institution, however well-managed, can duplicate the conditions which juveniles will have to meet when they are released. Recent advances in the field of individual clinical study of problem children plus the rise of social work as a profession have made possible the practice of this theory to some extent in the form of placement of delinquent children in carefully selected and supervised foster homes. Casual and questionable methods of putting neglected and dependent children in foster homes have long been known in Europe and America, but the idea of placing *delinquent* children under scrupulously studied conditions still meets with resistance. Germany, however, has for some time included juvenile delinquents in its noteworthy practice of placing children in selected rural foster homes. In this country Massachusetts has had considerable success with the placement of carefully studied delinquents. It seems probable that as clinical facilities for individual case studies improve, it will be both possible and advisable to relieve juvenile reformatories of the care of many problem children who could be handled successfully in foster families.

EUROPEAN EXPERIMENTS WITH ADULT REFORMATION

THE application of definite reformatory principles to adult prisoners was first made in Europe from whence its influence spread to America. From 1830 to 1842 the Bavarian prison of Kaiserslautern was in charge of a courageous and progressive governor, Obermaier, who labored constantly to improve prison methods. When he was transferred in 1842 to control the prison inferno at Munich where some six to seven hundred sulky and rebellious convicts were kept in a mere semblance of order by chains, weights, and a heavy guard of soldiers, Obermaier so successfully gained the confidence of the prisoners that he was able to remove their chains, dismiss most of the soldier-guards, and to appoint inmates as shop superintendents. Aided by the Bavarian practice of sentencing men for indeterminate terms and by a well-organized system for helping and supervising discharged men, Obermaier's program was outstandingly successful. Although we may doubt the accuracy of the claim that "only about seven per cent of those at Kaiserslautern, and ten per cent of those at Munich, relapsed into crime after their discharge,"[4] it is evident that Obermaier accomplished wonders.

In Spain, Colonel Montesinos was at the same time developing a reformatory régime at the great prison of Valencia of which he was made governor in 1835. Montesinos was an exceptionally capable administrator possessed of a keen understanding of men. He organized the prisoners in military companies under inmate leaders. Every prisoner had an opportunity to attend school and to learn a trade. His avowed object was "not so much to inflict punishment as to correct, to receive men idle and ill-intentioned and return them to society, if possible honest and industrious citizens."[5] He made decent behavior in prison worth while by permitting convicts to reduce their sentences by as much as one-third for good conduct.

Like Obermaier, Montesinos saw a marked reduction in recommitments as a result of his policy. Montesinos resigned, and his scheme failed when reactionaries passed a law requiring prisoners to serve the full term of their sentences.

THE MARK SCHEME OF MACONOCHIE

IN 1840 England appointed Captain Alexander Maconochie of the Royal Navy as superintendent of the penal colony at Norfolk Island. Maconochie had previously served as secretary to the Governor of Van Diemen's Land, and had written constructively on convict management out of his experience in penal establishments. Norfolk Island was a most difficult field for reformatory work because two-thirds of the prisoners there were men who had been convicted

[4] F. H. Wines, "Punishment and Reformation," Revised Edition, p. 203.

[5] From a pamphlet by Colonel Montesinos quoted in F. H. Wines, op. cit., p. 202.

wo or three times of committing crimes in other Australian
oenal colonies while serving time for previous convictions in
England.

At Norfolk, Maconochie introduced a mark system as the
chief means of bringing order to a turbulent and ill-managed
group of prisoners. The idea of the mark system first came
o Maconochie in 1837 when he was in Van Diemen's Land
and was derived from Maconochie's reflections over the use
of the mark system in education.[6] Maconochie knew that
prisoners who were sentenced for a fixed term had no incentive
o work or to improve themselves since their sentences would
oe neither increased nor decreased by their behavior. He,
therefore, sought to make conditional freedom as well as
esser privileges dependent, not upon the passage of time, but
upon the satisfactory completion of a fixed amount of work.
The fundamental principle of the mark system was the substitution of a task sentence for a time sentence. In order
o achieve this end, he debited each arriving prisoner with a
number of marks proportional to the seriousness of his offense, and made them redeemable in terms of good work.
When the original assessment was paid off the prisoner was
eligible for conditional release. By means of marks which he
earned a prisoner also secured his food, supplies, and special
privileges. By means of fines in terms of marks a prisoner
was punished for misconduct. The record of each prisoner
was kept on a card similar to the following :[7]

Grade	Earnings	Marks
(marked on a	Prisoner's name and number	
scale of 0 to 5)	Entire sentence in marks	
	Present accumulation	
	Personal demeanor	
	Kinds of labour	
	Diligence in labour	
	Efficiency in labour	
	Chaplain's report	
	Schoolmaster's report	

Total earnings . . . .

[6] A. Maconochie, "The Mark System of Prison Discipline," p. 12.
[7] A. Maconochie, op. cit., p. 5.

Grade	Forfeitures and	Marks
	Expenditures	
	Food	
	Kinds of indulgences	
	Charge for indulgences	
	Kinds of offenses	
	Fines for offenses	
	Imprisonment in days	
	Total expenditures	
	Balance	

The entire scheme was intended to develop responsibility in the prisoners instead of enforced submission; to develop voluntary, internal effort, rather than external compulsory obedience.

Maconochie's scheme was handicapped by his limited authority, which did not permit him to give prisoners their complete release from Norfolk Island regardless of their behavior. He could only reward improvement with local privileges. Nevertheless, Maconochie amply demonstrated the value of his ideas during his four years at Norfolk Island by turning a veritable riotous hell-on-earth into a well-governed community.

Appointed in 1849, to be the first governor of the new Birmingham jail in England, Maconochie continued his experiments until his enforced resignation in 1851. There he extended his mark system so as to train prisoners in social responsibility by permitting small units of six or eight prisoners to pool and share their earnings of marks equally.

CROFTON'S IRISH SYSTEM

FORTUNATELY, the principles of Obermaier, Montesinos and Maconochie were not lost when their limited experiments came to an end. Instead, they were mastered by a great prison organizer, Sir Walter Crofton,[8] who in 185

---

[8] See the pamphlets by W. Crofton, "A Few Remarks on the Convic Question," published in 1857. "A Few Observations on a Pamphle

became Chairman of the Directors of Irish Convict Prisons. Through the administrative ability of Crofton the work of these reformers was adapted to the prevailing penal system which consisted of two grades of imprisonment followed by conditional release.

Under Crofton's régime new prisoners entered Mountjoy penitentiary for eight or nine months of solitary confinement. During the first three months of the period they were fed on limited rations and kept in enforced idleness as a means of bringing them to appreciate the joys of working.

After passing this first stage, prisoners were transferred to work prisons where they progressed through four grades, not including a probationary class for some, in accordance with the number of marks they were able to accumulate through industry, school progress, and good conduct.

Then instead of receiving tickets-of-leave, prisoners under the Crofton plan were required to go through a new third, or intermediate stage of at least six months' duration to test their fitness to be at large. Intermediate prisoners were housed in portable unlocked huts. They, and a few unarmed guards, worked together on land reclamation projects. The number of intermediate prisoners in a colony was restricted to a maximum of one hundred in order that teachers and prisoners might come to understand each other so that good influences might be given their fullest scope.

ORIGIN OF THE ADULT REFORMATORY IN THE UNITED STATES

IN the 60's a group of American penologists including Sanborn, Wines, Dwight, Hubbell, and Brockway, aroused by the possibilities in Crofton's scheme, began to consider its adaptability to prison systems in the United States. Their enthusiasm for the so-called Irish system became so marked that in 1867 the New York legislature, which had been considering a new penitentiary, upon recommendation of the New York Prison Association, passed an act establishing, not a new prison as had been intended, but an adult reformatory

Recently Published by the Rev. John Burt on the Irish Convict System," published in 1863. "The Present Aspect of the Convict Question," published in 1864.

to be built at Elmira. It received its first prisoners in 1876.

Zebulon Brockway, an ardent believer in the Irish system, was its first superintendent. In common with Wines and Dwight, Brockway had urged upon the legislature the need of indeterminate sentences; of committing men to prison until they had reformed, rather than for a fixed term. He looked upon the indeterminate sentence as an absolute essential in any reformatory scheme on the ground that a motive for improvement is essential and that the love of liberty is the strongest and perhaps the only desire capable of arousing the interests of prisoners.

In line with this belief Brockway, with the approval of the Elmira Board of Managers, included a wholly indeterminate sentence clause in a bill which he drafted and presented to the New York State legislature for the governance of Elmira. However, fearful that the legislature would not approve it, Brockway subsequently modified it to permit young first offenders to be sentenced to Elmira until reformation, except that their imprisonment could not exceed the maximum term provided by law for the offense of which they were guilty. Brockway's judgment of the temper of the legislators was a momentous one for American penology because his indeterminate sentence law became the model for the country. If, as Superintendent Scott believed,[9] the bill could have been passed just as well in the original draft, it was unfortunate that Brockway lost the chance to introduce the wholly indeterminate sentence which penologists are still struggling to get in the United States nearly sixty years after Brockway's decision.

Brockway built his program for Elmira upon the belief that criminals could and should be reformed. By means of the limited indeterminate sentence and promotion or demotion in grades through marks, he placed a large measure of responsibility for their own welfare in the hands of the inmates. He was not content, however, to permit the state to avoid its own duty towards its prisoners. Insisting that reformation is fundamentally an educational process, Brock-

[9] Joseph F. Scott, one time Superintendent of Reformatories for New York in C. R. Henderson (Ed.), "Penal and Reformatory Institutions," p. 94.

way developed at Elmira the means by which labor, education, and religious influences might contribute to that process. Under his management Elmira acquired facilities for training prisoners comparable to those in outside schools. According to Brockway,

"The list includes a gymnasium, with steam baths and massage; manual training for prisoners who are exceptionally defective; trade classes for the technical training of every prisoner; a school of letters graded from the elementary to academic studies; a lecture course; with the institutional newspaper; military training as thorough if not as comprehensive, as that of the national Military Academy; and religious ministrations. It is intended to provide in these reformatories all commonly approved means for developing and cultivating good citizens and to secure their best use. The course of education is not optional or elective with these prisoner pupils, but is prescribed and enforced. The system, when it is most thoroughly administered, places the entire conscious life and conduct under unceasing direction. There must not be — there are not — idle hours for the prisoners, nor merely superficial occupations." [10]

The Elmira conception of the reformatory process spread into other states, and is at present found in modified form in many penal institutions. It has had an influence, not only upon reformatories for young and supposedly less vicious offenders, but also in state prisons and penitentiaries.

PERVERTED REFORMATORIES

THE original intention was to send to Elmira only "male felons between the ages of sixteen and thirty not previously convicted of any crime punishable by imprisonment in a state prison." Other reformatories similarly were expected to receive only first offenders. Under existing methods of criminal identification and recording, however, it was impossible to tell who were first offenders. Hardened criminals were, therefore, given reformatory sentences.

At present it seems likely that most reformatory inmates have been at odds with the law since childhood, and that

[10] Z. R. Brockway, "Character of Reformatory Prisoners," in "Extracts from Penological Reports of New York State Reformatory, 1926."

many of them have had institutional experiences. In studying the inmates of Concord Reformatory whose sentences expired in 1921 and 1922, the Gluecks found that 433 out of the 510 offenders involved were known to have been arrested for offenses prior to that for which they were sentenced to Concord. These men committed a known total of 1944 offenses followed by convictions in 1688 cases.[11] It seems likely that this unique study pictures facts representative of other reformatory inmates throughout the country.

The adult reformatories now in the United States have, therefore, taken on more and more the characteristics of the older prisons. In age and length of sentence reformatory prisoners are barely distinguishable from state's prison convicts. They are housed in cells and subject to the poor housing, faulty ventilation, overcrowding, and deadening routine that are characteristic of the prisons. Methods of discipline are similar in both institutions. Usually the system is repressive. It does not arouse the desire of prisoners to behave. It bribes them. It does not instil in them a sense of group responsibility. In short, the high ideals of its founders have not been realized. The modern reformatory has, with a few progressive exceptions, become essentially a prison.

Fortunately, some reformatories aroused, particularly since 1930, by several illuminating commentaries on their work,[12] have stirred again with an encouraging new life. A thorough understanding of the nature and capacities of each prisoner is coming to be recognized as an essential preliminary to reformatory treatment. The need for an adequate academic and vocational program of education is being given some attention. Again Elmira Reformatory, though not alone in its interest in these matters, seems to be setting the pace for other male reformatories. Following the recommendations of the New York State Commission to Investigate Prison Administration and Construction (the Lewisohn Commission) appointed in 1930, a psychiatric clinic was established at Elmira to gain immediately upon commitment

[11] S. S. and E. T. Glueck, "500 Criminal Careers," pp. 140-144.
[12] Notably studies by Austin MacCormick, the Gluecks in Massachusetts, and the Lewisohn Commission in New York.

the information necessary to proper assignment and treatment of offenders, and to introduce them by a carefully planned series of steps to the institutional régime.[13]

Integrated with the work of the classification clinic are the academic and trade schools of Elmira reorganized along the lines suggested in MacCormick's study of prison education published in 1931.[14] MacCormick pointed out that effective educational work with adult prisoners requires individualized instruction and a curriculum that can arouse the interests of adults of varying capacities. Elmira has undertaken to discover the value of applying these principles.[15] A competent school administrator has been secured to direct Elmira's educational work. Educational assignments are determined by the needs and capacities of prisoners as judged by the classification clinic. The clinic psychologist aids in school adjustment problems and in general serves as a liaison officer between the clinic and school staffs. Prisoners are given a chance to inspect the reformatory plant, note the vocational opportunities available, and to express their work preferences. Assignments are then made on the basis of clinic data, the inmates' expressed preferences for study, post-reformatory placement possibilities, the work distribution of the general inmate population at the time, and the maintenance needs of the institution.

The School of Letters is organized in three divisions instead of the customary grades. The Preparatory Division includes classes for illiterates and for those whose achievements are comparable to those of first, second, and third grade students ; the Intermediate Division carries the work through grade six ; and the High School Division cares for those above grade six. The classroom procedure is an adaptation of the Dalton and Winnetka plans. Groups are small and their membership is determined by the intelligence ratings of the students. The project method of instruction is

[13] See J. L. McCartney, "Introducing the Offender to Institutional Routine," *Jour. of Criminal Law and Criminology*, Vol. 24, p. 584.

[14] A. H. MacCormick, "The Education of Adult Prisoners."

[15] The writer is indebted to F. L. Bixby's article, "A New Education Program at Elmira Reformatory," The Osborne Association News Bulletin, April, 1933, for the description of the new educational set-up at Elmira.

used and each student goes ahead as rapidly as he is able. The content of each course is determined by the ability and needs of the one who is taking it. School study is carefully linked with the work of the vocational shops where the project method is also used.

In the reformatories for adult males in half a dozen other states similarly hopeful, though less comprehensive trends towards the building of better educational programs, both academic and vocational, have begun to make headway recently. The women's reformatories as a group, as distinguished from the women's prisons, have maintained and improved upon the early reformatory ideal somewhat more effectively than the men's institutions. In general their task is intelligently conceived as one of socializing their charges through broad educational programs designed to fit them for decent living in their communities after their release. Considerable effort is made to arouse and provide for the assumption of responsibility by prisoners within the institutions. Emphasis is placed upon normal living as nearly as it may be achieved by those confined in a correctional institution. Frequently handicapped by inadequate appropriations the women's reformatories nevertheless manage to express a degree of ingenuity and willingness to experiment in their treatment of crime that is sadly lacking in the reformatories for men.[16]

[16] See E. Lekkerkerker, "Reformatories for Women in the United States," for a comprehensive description of these institutions by a capable foreign observer.

INTERLUDE

INTRODUCING THE PENAL INSTITUTIONS OF THE UNITED STATES TODAY

THE penal institutions of the United States now comprise a heterogeneous, uncoördinated maze of more than 125 major federal and state prisons, farms, camps, and reformatories, and more than 3400 federal, county, or municipal jails, houses of correction and chain gang camps for short term offenders.

FEDERAL PENAL INSTITUTIONS

THE federal institutions consist of civilian penitentiaries at Atlanta, Georgia, Leavenworth, Kansas (2), Alcatraz Island, California, McNeil Island, Washington, and Lewisburg, Pennsylvania; the Federal Industrial Institution for Women at Alderson, West Virginia; the U. S. Industrial Reformatory at Chillicothe, Ohio; the Federal Reformatory Camp at Petersburg, Virginia; the Federal Correctional Camp at Fort Eustis, Virginia; four Federal Prison Camps, and three jails. In addition the federal government had under construction in 1933 a Hospital for Defective Delinquents at Springfield, Missouri, a Reformatory for Young Men at El Reno, Oklahoma, and two more Federal Jails. Pending the completion of adequate facilities the federal government also houses some of its convicts in state, county, and municipal institutions. All federal penal institutions and prisoners are controlled by the Department of Justice through a bureau headed by a Director of Federal Prisons. In addition to these civilian institutions there are three naval prisons and two army disciplinary barracks maintained by the Army and Navy Departments in the United States.

STATE PENAL INSTITUTIONS

Nearly every state now has at least one prison of the sort made famous by Sing Sing, San Quentin, and the motion picture producers, as well as specialized institutions such as reformatories, industrial schools, and women's prisons. Penal institutions are most numerous in populous industrial states and in the South where white and black prisoners are separated. In the South where a mild climate permits farming the year around an extensive development of prison farms has taken place. Texas has a huge area, 76,461 acres, in prison farms. Mississippi has 28,750 acres; Louisiana, 15,600 acres; Florida, 17,000 acres; and South Carolina, 4168 acres in convict farms. More recently in the North there has been a decided tendency to take prisons away from the city and build them out in the country. Pennsylvania has acquired 5000 acres of land, Wisconsin more than 2000 acres, and Minnesota, nearly 1000 acres for prison use. Massachusetts is building its new state prison on the outskirts of the little village of Norfolk.

COUNTY AND MUNICIPAL PENAL INSTITUTIONS

Of the 3000-odd jails and workhouses in the United States, four-fifths are county institutions and the remainder except for five federal jails are administered by municipalities. County road gangs have flourished in the South where highway construction is possible throughout the year in a climate permitting convicts to be housed in portable camps. While most of the chain gang prisoners are serving short terms there are among them individuals sentenced for the most serious offenses. In North Carolina where ten prisoners are committed to camps, now under state control, for every one sent to state prison, convicts may be sentenced to a maximum of ten years on the county roads. In Georgia, except for disabled prisoners, all male convicts are worked in county road gangs numbering twenty to one hundred and fifty prisoners.

THE PRISON POPULATION

At any given time about 150,000 prisoners are serving sentences in all of these institutions. Nearly 400,000 commitments are made to them each year. The number of individuals sentenced, however, is less than this since many unfortunate souls are convicted more than once during the year. The average time actually served by all prisoners is slightly more than two years. Prison terms average about three years; those in county institutions, six weeks; and in municipal jails, seventeen days.

For every man who enters the prison world another leaves it. About 96 per cent of those who are imprisoned are released again. About 60,000 inmates from reformatories and penitentiaries and 300,000 jail prisoners are released among us every year. They do come back. Therefore it is of the utmost importance that we should know the nature and degree of the influence that modern penal institutions have upon their inmates. Gun-men, burglars, swindlers, sex offenders and the like, are committed to prison. What manner of men are they when they return? How has prison life affected them? Are they prepared to live in a socially acceptable manner? Are they more dangerous than ever? In either event is it because of what happened to them in prison or in spite of it? It is against such questions that modern penal institutions must be measured in greater detail.

CHAPTER XIX

JAILS AND THE JAILED

THE UBIQUITOUS JAIL

COUNTY jails are not only our typical short term prisons; they are the country's most common penal institutions. They outnumber prisons and reformatories thirty to one. Of the 3469 short term institutions listed by the Bureau of the Census in 1923, nearly 3000 were jails. To them during the first six months of 1923, were sent over 58 per cent of all the prisoners committed to penal institutions in the United States. In that year together with the local workhouses, farms, chain gangs, and stockades, they received nearly seven out of every eight persons committed to prisons throughout the country.

In addition to these institutions, used for both punishment and detention, there are more than 10,000 police jails or lockups in the country in which arrested persons are detained until they can be taken before a magistrate. During the first six months of 1930 more than 1,350,000 prisoners were locked up in police jails in the United States.[1] That is more than fifty times the number committed to state and federal prisons in a similar period of time. Although the time of detention in police lockups is short they occupy a strategic position since they receive offenders immediately after the shock of arrest and at a time when they are flustered and pliable.

Unfortunately, our police lockups have not been designed to take advantage of their opportunity. Many are appendages to town halls, fire stations, or other public buildings. Thousands of them are firetraps. Inadequate sanitary ar-

[1] H. H. Hart, "Police Jails and Lockups," a special report to the National Commission on Law Observance and Enforcement appended to their "Report on Penal Institutions, Probation and Parole."

rangements are still further strained by the practice of furnishing overnight lodging to dirty, vermin-infested vagrants and sick drunkards. Generally little housekeeping is done. Proper separation of young and old, men and women, diseased and well, witnesses and offenders is rare, although in Akron, Cleveland, Philadelphia and New York women are housed in separate buildings.

Only New York, New Jersey, Minnesota, and Oklahoma have state supervision of lockups and New York alone publishes reports of its inspections. Pennsylvania inspects upon complaint and Alabama apparently supervises some police jails in cities of more than 10,000. It has been the experience of New York and Minnesota that regular lockup inspection by a state commission with power to condemn unsuitable quarters brings excellent results in ridding communities of institutions that are often a menace to community health, fire protection, and morality. There is ample need for other states to consider the wisdom of a similar form of supervision.

THE DETENTION OF JUVENILES

THE psychological effect upon juveniles of the procedure following their arrest is so important in its bearing upon the treatment of their cases that it should always be a matter of thoughtful, competent decision by trained, socially minded workers rather than a matter of routine. Ordinarily, however, it is merely an unstudied step in the handling of supposed delinquents.

Somewhat more than half of the boys and girls detained in the United States are cared for in their own homes until their cases can be heard by the courts. Public detention homes, private children's institutions, jails, and police lockups house most of the others, although hospitals, almshouses, boarding and foster homes care for a few. In a study of juvenile detention in 141 areas in 38 states and the District of Columbia,[2] Warner found that of 118,772 juveniles detained during the fiscal year 1929-30, 77,809 were held in public detention homes, 18,659 in private shelters, 16,493 in jails and police stations, and the remaining cases in other

[2] F. M. Warner, "Juvenile Detention in the United States."

types of institutions or homes.[3]   The ratio of boys to girls in jails was four to one and in public detention homes seven to three.   Some 44,218 of these juveniles were under sixteen years of age.   Of 16,759 children for whom the period of detention could be ascertained a little less than half were detained for a period varying from one day to one week.   A few, 109 (2 per cent) girls and 126 (1.1 per cent) boys were detained for more than a year.[4]

The conditions in jails built for adults are not satisfactory for the accommodation of juveniles.   In many public detention homes the environment is no better.   Private detention homes seem somewhat superior to either.   Boarding home placement appears to be generally preferable to institutional commitment.

Warner's study includes sixty-three public detention homes in twenty-eight states and the District of Columbia.   In eleven of these Warner found the children in virtual solitary confinement.   In fourteen no schooling whatever was provided and in others it was restricted to certain students or carried on in the most perfunctory manner.   Five homes had not even a book for the children to read.   Six permitted no free play indoors ; twenty-seven had little indoor play space ; eighteen with space had no playthings ; twelve had indoor play space and some equipment.   Thirteen institutions forbade outdoor play ; thirty-one permitted it ; and the others allowed outdoor play with restrictions.   A few homes allowed their children to use community facilities such as the Y.M.C.A. and the public playgrounds.[5]   In Juvenile Hall, Los Angeles, for the detention of boys two and one-half to sixteen years of age and of girls two and one-half to twenty-one years of age the educational work is organized as a regular branch of the city schools, resident medical and psychiatric service is provided, two full-time recreational directors are employed, and a branch of the county library is maintained. Group activities and clubs are encouraged.   It stands as an example of the few adequately equipped and properly managed juvenile detention homes.

[3] F. M. Warner, *ibid.*, table II, p. 16.
[4] F. M. Warner, *ibid.*, p. 139.
[5] F. M. Warner, *ibid.*, pp. 62-63.

COUNTY CONVICT ROAD GANGS

NEARLY every state has statutes permitting and regulating the work of convicts on public highways and lands. In the North road gangs have not been common although the use of convicts on public reclamation projects seems likely to increase. These units, however, are comprised of selected honor prisoners from state institutions working under state supervision.

In the South, where convict road gangs are county units,[6] they have become the typical penal institution comparable to the jail in northern industrial states. The gangs are composed of half-a-dozen to a hundred unselected prisoners guilty of all sorts of offenses from poverty and vagrancy to rape, robbery, and attempted murder. In North Carolina, which had 2500 prisoners in county chain gangs on October 1, 1926, about two-thirds of the offenders were negroes and one-third whites. Their sentences ranged from fifteen days to ten years. Among 1500 of these who were the object of special study[7] the most common sentence was one to two years.

A larger percentage of negroes than whites was serving short sentences, presumably because they could not pay fines or court costs. The chances of getting a road sentence of more than three years also "favored" the negro two to one. Negroes received lighter sentences than whites for offenses against morality. About half of the chain gang prisoners had never married. One-fifth of them had not reached their majority. A sixth of the whites and a third of the negroes were totally illiterate. Three-fourths of the entire group could not read a newspaper.[8]

The counties that control this human wreckage are small, independent, and relatively poor governmental units. They cannot provide proper equipment for the care of their charges nor train the guard personnel in penal management. They see no reason to spend money on criminals. In fact chain gangs owe their existence to their supposed economy

---

[6] Except in Maryland and Virginia, and since 1931 in North Carolina.
[7] Steiner and Brown, "The North Carolina Chain Gang."
[8] *Ibid.*, Ch. 8.

and the hope for profit. Prisoners are sinners delivered into the hands of county agents for punishment through exploitation. No consideration is paid to the possibilities in individual prisoners nor to the wisdom of reforming offenders before they are given their freedom.

The aim of guardianship with economy therefore dictates the conditions under which county prisoners are maintained. Convict stripes, shackles, chains, and spikes are common. Armed men maintain continuous close watch over the prisoners. Sleeping quarters vary in form but are commonly of flimsy construction so that a bull chain is necessary to prevent escapes at night. Some convict gangs are housed in portable steel or windowless wooden cages that look like box cars. Others are kept in portable camps or cheap frame shacks not vastly different from those provided for free construction gangs except that the latter are not crowded together in chains at night. The possibilities in auto transportation have induced some counties to provide decent permanent central housing for their road gangs and the tendency, perhaps temporarily, is slowly towards the extension of that practice.

The crowded housing of ignorant men, sick and well, in flimsy temporary camps presents a major sanitary problem that is by no means properly met in spite of the inspections of county or even state health authorities. A recent official report of the Board of Public Welfare of North Carolina, one of the most progressive of our southern states, gives this picture of health conditions in a convict camp:

"Three of these men were sick men, another one the cook and a fifth man assisting around the camp. Two of the sick men were confined in one cage, the third one was in an old house that is used as a bunk house at night instead of the cages. The two sick men in the regulation cages have tuberculosis. They have each been in bed a month; one has ten months still to serve, the other eleven. No sleeping garments are provided them. They have on the regular convict stripes. The third man has running syphilitic sores on his legs. The tubercular patients have not receptacles to expectorate in, consequently they use the ground, the floor of their cage, and anything that is convenient. There are no screens in the cages or in the kitchen to protect the food. Flies are swarming everywhere. The kitchen is only a short distance from the cage where the sick men are confined ; and even nearer the cage than the kitchen is a block of wood on which meat is chopped. When we visited the camp the meat was lying on the block of wood exposed to the flies and dust. The filth of the bedding and the sleeping quarters of this camp is indescribable. The sick negroes were asked how frequently they got clean bed clothes. One negro replied that he had been in bed a month and no clean bedding had been given him. From the appearance of the bed I could well believe this to be true." [9]

Discipline in chain gang camps is usually in charge of ignorant men no better in manners nor in morals than those whom they rule. Modern ideas of penal purposes and management are foreign concepts to them. Force is their only tool and their only weapon. Instances of physical torture are common. Occasional killings, which still occur, emphasize the extent of lesser brutalities.[10] One may judge of the caliber of the keepers by the complaint of one that "I have been here twelve months and ain't had no chance to shoot a prisoner yet." [11]

Obviously county chain gangs are completely out of joint with modern penological knowledge. They survive as an anachronism through the indifference of a public steeped in the shortsighted tradition that a sure cure for crime is the exploitation of criminals. Fortunately, enlightened public opinion is beginning to sense the foolishness of rehearsing men to behave like beasts and then setting them free to find out what they will do. Economic facts are helping towards

[9] *Biennial Report*, North Carolina State Board of Charities and Public Welfare, 1920-1922, p. 85. Quoted in Steiner and Brown, *op. cit.*, pp. 77-78.

[10] On October 15, 1932, George W. Courson, a guard, was found guilty of manslaughter following the strangulation of a convict in the "sweatbox" of the Sunbeam prison camp in Duval County, Florida. The convict had been placed in a small windowless confinement cell, the "sweatbox," neck chained to the roof, feet clamped down by heavy stocks, and left without food for at least twenty-four hours before he died. See also the disturbing photographs and documentary exhibit of the horrors of convict camps in the Black Belt collected by John L. Spivack in the appendix to his 1932 book, "Georgia Nigger."

[11] Steiner and Brown, *op. cit.*, p. 100.

this change of viewpoint. In spite of shaky cost accounting there is a growing opinion that county road gangs are a doubtful financial asset to a county. Effective work is impossible with less than twenty-five men in honor camps or thirty-five where guards are required. Varying lengths of sentences also add to the difficulties of management.

More and more it is coming to be realized that restricted gangs are unprofitable on road maintenance and light construction work where labor mobility is necessary nor can they compete where machines can be used. Only in heavy construction work under conditions where mules must replace machines do the convict gangs clearly show up to advantage.

The slow but inevitable trend is apparent. Virginia and Maryland have abolished county controlled road gangs. Faced with the need to reduce taxes the North Carolina legislature in 1931 transferred to the state highway commission the care of 46,000 miles of local roads together with the 3700 burdensome county prisoners with sentences of 60 days or more. The state was organized in 5 divisions of 5 districts, each in charge of an engineer. In 1933 the state was caring for 4500 prisoners in 45 remodeled county camps and 24 new ones. Under state care the control of the former county prisoners has been greatly improved. A physician has been assigned to each camp. Vegetables are being raised on camp truck farms. Work under decent conditions has replaced idleness. The cost of prisoner maintenance is charged to the state prison department and the prisoners' labor value is credited to it at current wages. The counties have been relieved of a burden, and the state is acquiring improved roads.[12] In West Virginia only a quarter of the counties now have camps and most of these are not operated during the entire year. In Louisiana 53 out of 64 parishes have abolished their chain gangs. There are signs that other sections of the South may cast aside a system that in the light of modern penology seems not only barbarous but useless. The wonder is that the southern county chain gang and its ailing sister, the northern jail, have managed to survive for so long.

[12] P. W. Wagner, "State Succeeds in Highway Business," *National Municipal Review*, Vol. 22, p. 59.

THE JAIL POPULATION

THREE types of prisoners are held in jail: unconvicted persons detained as principals or witnesses awaiting trial, misdemeanants committed because they cannot pay their fines, and offenders sentenced for short terms. Houses of correction generally receive misdemeanants only after conviction and they at least make the gesture of putting them to work.

About half of our jail population consists of persons awaiting trial. They are held anywhere from a day to a year or more. During that time they are presumed to be innocent. Many of them, possibly, a third to a half, are subsequently discharged without being convicted. Among those who will later be convicted are habitual criminals who will be sentenced to prisons and reformatories. While in jail the innocent and the guilty receive about the same treatment. Those eventually found "not guilty" have no redress for their loss of time or money short of special legislative action.

Of the *sentenced* prisoners committed to the jails and workhouses of the United States between January and June, 1923, more than half (52.9 per cent) were imprisoned because they were too poor to pay their fines. In other words they were imprisoned for debt, a debt owed to the state. Such prisoners are maintained in virtual idleness by the county, given their board and room, and credited a fixed sum of money each day for their presence until they have earned the amount of their fines. Four-fifths of those imprisoned for nonpayment of fine are committed for a month or less. About 2 per cent of them are sentenced for a year or more in jail. One-fifth are released within ten days. Persons economically more fortunate, found guilty of similar offenses, pay their fines and go their ways.[13]

Convicted prisoners serving sentences in jail are a heterogeneous lot. Less than 7 per cent of them are women. As a group they are older than the inmates of prisons and reformatories. Of 30,465 prisoners over 45 years old committed between January and June 1923, 28,557 (93 per cent) were sent to jails and workhouses and 1908 (6 per cent)

[13] Bureau of the Census, "Prisoners 1923," p. 35.

to prisons and reformatories. On the other hand only 51 per cent of jail inmates are under 35 whereas 66 per cent of those in prison and 92 per cent of those in reformatories are under age.

Among the younger prisoners in jail, however, are a few juveniles serving time as well as a goodly number of boys and girls under 18 held in jail awaiting a court hearing. The federal government detained 2066 boys and 177 girls 18 years of age and under in county jails during the six months ending December 31, 1930. Of these 3 boys and 1 girl were under 12, 9 boys were 12, and 8 were 13 years of age. Over a fourth of the juveniles were detained in Kentucky and Texas.[14]

Consequently, jails do not act primarily as feeders for long-term prisons as is frequently suggested. Instead they seem to be the catch-basins into which the social misfits for whom no special provision has been made, eventually drift. They become the temporary resting places of the chronic drunkards, the vagrants, the feeble-minded and psychopathic misdemeanants, the driftwood of society. In 1923, 71.6 per cent of all convicted prisoners sent to the country's jails and workhouses were committed for drunkenness, disorderly conduct, violation of the liquor laws, vagrancy, and petty larceny. In 1910 these same offenses accounted for 77.7 per cent of the jail population.[15]

Many jail inmates are old-timers who have been drifting in and out of police lockups, municipal courts, and jails for years. Life for them has been a series of inevitable confinements interspersed with the stupid sprees that cost them their freedom. The courts, lacking both facilities and imagination, have periodically fined, discharged, put on probation or sent to jail these weaklings.

Those who are sentenced to imprisonment in jail are committed for longer periods than those who are in for nonpayment of fine. About 55 per cent of those sentenced to imprisonment are committed for a month or less and over 7 per cent are committed for a year or more.

[14] National Commission on Law Observance and Enforcement, "The Child Offender in the Federal System of Justice," pp. 38-47.

[15] Bureau of the Census, "Prisoners 1923," p. 35.

More than four out of every hundred prisoners sentenced to jails and workhouses in the United States during the first half of 1923 were known to have been previously committed *ten or more times*. Forty five per cent of the men and 58 per cent of the women sent to jail had been previously committed one or more times. In view of our practical inability to determine whether a man sent to jail by one court has previously served time somewhere else, the amount of recidivism reported by the Census Bureau is very likely less than the actual amount.

No nationwide study has been made to throw light upon the personalities of jail inmates although local studies of varying importance have been made. Early studies suggested a high proportion of feeble-mindedness and psychopathy among jail prisoners. Later studies have forced a modification of these figures. A study of an Ohio house of correction in 1917 indicated that only 10 per cent of its 147 inmates were normal.[16] On the other hand the percentage of inferior prisoners in the St. Louis jail in 1921 was less than that for the Missouri draft army.[17] In the Cleveland workhouse white prisoners were of somewhat lower mentality than whites in the draft army while negro inmates were considerably inferior to colored recruits who were drafted.[18] A survey of Wisconsin jails in 1920 disclosed that 55.4 per cent of the prisoners were normal, 16.4 per cent feeble-minded, and 15.2 per cent psychopathic.[19]

It is not therefore possible to say with assurance just how the mental condition of jail inmates compares with that of the general population although it seems likely that the percentage of feeble-mindedness among jail prisoners is somewhat higher than that among the general population and also higher than that in prisons and reformatories.

An interesting and valuable psychiatric study of jail prisoners carried on by the Division for Examination of Prisoners

[16] S. A. Queen, "Passing of the County Jail," p. 59.

[17] St. Louis, Director of Public Welfare, "Report of Mental Hygiene Survey of Delinquency and Dependency Problems," 1922, p. 16. Quoted in E. Sutherland, "Criminology," p. 107.

[18] "Cleveland Survey of Criminal Justice," pp. 55-57.

[19] Wisconsin Mental Deficiency Survey, 1920, p. 17. Quoted in J. L. Gillin, "Criminology and Penology," p. 553.

of the Massachusetts Department of Mental Diseases has thrown considerable light upon the personalities and needs of jail prisoners in that state. Their classification in 1928 showed a distribution of types as follows: [20]

Classification	Approximate per cent	Treatment recommended
Chiefly problems of alcoholism	31	Long period of care, training and occupation in institution for alcoholics.
Psychopathic delinquents, intelligence good but emotions undiciplined	9	Long term segregation in special institution.
Mentally diseased or epileptic	4	Special institution.
Defective delinquents	5	Special institution.
Feeble-minded, not essentially delinquent	3	Special institution.
Self-correcting after sentence	14	No further treatment.
Hopeless	4	Do not yet know how to deal with them.
Can be helped in the community	28	Need supervision and friendly help after discharge
Aged or sick	few	Infirmary care.
Miscellaneous types	4	Deportation, transfer to reformatory, etc.

It seems obvious that the county jails and allied local penal institutions still remain as in ancient days the dumping ground for all sorts and conditions of persons who run afoul of the law for lesser offenses. They are not usually youthful delinquents just starting upon a career of crime. They are not professional criminals. They are not shrewd and unscrupulous lawbreakers. They are the community's

[20] E. L. Simmons, "Psychiatric Signposts," *Survey*, April 15, 1928, p. 104.

weaklings and misfits aptly described by penologist Gates of the Massachusetts Department of Correction as "a most mediocre colorless lot of mutts." [21]   They would represent a perplexing problem for any institution to deal with.   What does the jail and its administrators do with them ?

THE JAIL HOUSE

THE institution to which this motley crowd of persons is sent has consistently aroused observers to most vivid and unpleasant descriptions of its character.   Joseph F. Fishman, for many years the only federal inspector of prisons, describes 85 per cent of the country's jails as unbelievably filthy institutions that support thousands of able-bodied men and women in idleness while giving them a thorough grounding in every sort of viciousness and crime.

Dr. Louis N. Robinson, an authority on penal conditions in the United States, says :

"Most jails are insanitary.   It is impossible even to keep them clean.   Their walls are rough and provide hiding places for vermin. The disposal of sewerage is difficult ; the insanitary buckets are still used in many jails.   The heating is often poor, and as a result the windows are kept closed.   Men are thrust into cells reeking with filth and vermin.   Some of this wears off or creeps off and is left to torment the next comer who may be, perhaps, an innocent man not trained in the best manner of fighting fleas and bedbugs, or versed in the method of remaining clean and unspotted in the midst of refuse accumulated in the gutter." [22]

The eminent German penologist, the late Dr. Moritz Liepmann of Hamburg said, "There are no words to describe the almost medieval conditions in the county jails of the U. S."   The National Commission on Law Observance and Enforcement (The Wickersham Commission) reported in 1931 that "The United States county jail is the most notorious correctional institution in the world."

The besetting evils of the county jail may be summed up as :

---

[21] C. A. Gates, "Dubs and Dollars," *Survey*, April 15, 1928, p. 103.
[22] L. N. Robinson, "Penology in the United States," pp. 41-42.   John C. Winston Co., publishers.   Quoted by permission.

1. Indiscriminate mingling of young and old, innocent and guilty, first offenders and habitual criminals, healthy and diseased, and in a few places fast disappearing, of the sexes.
2. Atrocious sanitary conditions breeding and spreading disease.
3. Poor and unhealthful food.
4. Overcrowding in some jails.
5. Lack of occupation for inmates.
6. Lack of any positive program of improvement.
7. Costliness and wastefulness.

THE PROBLEMS OF JAIL MANAGEMENT

ONE basic factor in the sad condition of the county jail is the viewpoint of political rings which have the peculiar notion that the chief function of the jail is to serve political patronage. The commissions and fees that surround the office of sheriff or jail keeper as a hangover from the days when they were private profit-making institutions, often make it one of the most luscious plums that a political party can offer. In some instances it approaches, in its economic rewards, at least, the office of president of the United States. The sheriff of Fulton County, Georgia, not long ago had a net income of $20,000 a year which was several times the pay of the state governor. In 1916 New York County paid its sheriff $12,000 in salary and an additional $60,000 in fees.[23]

A major item in the sheriff's income is the profit in feeding prisoners. In olden days the prisoner's board was chiefly supplied by his friends. Later the sheriff provided food out of money appropriated by the county. In 18 states out of 22, for which information is available, the administrative officer of the jail is still paid a fixed sum each day for feeding prisoners.[24] The opportunity for abuse here is obvious. If the sheriff can feed his prisoners for less than their allowance the difference is his profit. Since the office is a political reward it is natural to expect its incumbents to take out of it whatever they can get ; and that is just what happens.

A California sheriff contracted with a restaurant to supply

[23] University of North Carolina Record, Extension Series No. 25 Oct., 1917, pp. 54-55. Quoted in L. N. Robinson, *op. cit.*, p. 42 ff.

[24] L. N. Robinson, "The Relation of Jails to County and State," *Jour. of Criminal Law and Criminology*, Vol. 20, p. 413.

meals at 52½ cents a day for which he was paid 67½ cents. Similar practices have been observed in Pennsylvania and Illinois. At present, Texas, Ohio and North Carolina allow sheriffs 75 cents a day for maintenance, Nebraska and Minnesota allow 70 cents, and Indiana 60 cents. In the absence of accepted dietary standards the fee system results in a poorly balanced and inadequate diet, excessive cost of maintenance to taxpayers, resentment and a sense of injustice on the part of prisoners, and in some instances it stimulates unnecessary arrests and detentions for the sake of securing fees.

Most counties are of course too poor and too thinly populated to need or to be able to support a modern penal institution. They could not hire competent managers if they would, nor provide them with the equipment they would need. Many jails stand empty of prisoners from time to time. In 1923 the Census Bureau reported 2719 jails with an average population of less than 11 prisoners. A local jail for a dozen prisoners is an expensive joke on the taxpayers.

The rapid turnover of the short-term jail prisoners makes it difficult to find suitable occupations for them. Of course, unsentenced prisoners detained for trial cannot be made to work. As a result jail inmates spend their time in idleness, hanging about the corridors, swapping stories not learned in Sunday School, or resorting to vicious practices in an effort to relieve the tedium of their existence. Some counties have even gone back to the old scheme of selling the labor of inmates to outside manufacturers as preferable to keeping them in the physical and mental stagnation of idleness.

Discipline is generally lacking. Jailers are not likely to interfere with prisoners unless there is an open disturbance. Jail keepers *are* keepers, and nothing more. Sometimes they are less than keepers. The federal government has been obliged to remove its prisoners from some county jails because they have been permitted to attend races, county fairs, and in one instance a World Series game (practices however not bad under certain circumstances) or to hold drunken orgies in jail. Such leadership as does appear crops out among the prisoners who still in many jails carry on the ancient practice of "garnish" through an informal institution of self-government called the "Kangaroo Court."

An illuminating evaluation of county jails is now being carried out by the Federal Bureau of Prisons which in 1930 was charged with the duty of assuring suitable quarters for approximately 11,500 federal prisoners who are being boarded at federal expense in local jails. In pursuance of this task the Bureau of Prisons has increased its inspection force, devised a scheme for rating jails, and established a sliding scale of payments based upon the ranks achieved. By the end of June 1933 some 2578 institutions had been inspected by federal agents. Of these only 3 ranked above 90 per cent while 1027 failed to attain even the low grade of 50 per cent.[25]

Jails were scored on the items listed in the following table which also indicates the ratings they achieved on each item :

JAIL RATINGS FOR ITEMS
CLASSIFIED
Based On Inspections Made From July 1, 1930, to June 30, 1933

Classification	90–100	80–89	70–79	60–69	50–59	40–49	30–39	1–29	0	Total
Administration and Discipline	198	582	1004	542	148	47	19	28	11	2579
Building and Equipment	168	387	578	575	354	219	98	184	16	2579
Cleanliness and Sanitation	174	556	645	574	302	143	56	111	18	2579
Employment and Industries	15	11	21	11	38	47	84	545	1807	2579
Food	157	785	984	567	57	16	3	2	8	2579
Hospital Facilities	24	25	40	16	26	16	38	65	2329	2579
Medical Service	73	116	341	207	631	193	43	912	63	2579
Personal Hygiene	106	416	778	409	397	132	115	146	80	2579
Personnel	185	611	992	528	166	43	20	23	11	2579
Rehabilitation	12	6	6	7	14	11	4	40	2479	2579
Religious Instruction	25	28	141	53	93	82	95	480	1582	2579
Ratings of Jails Permitting Kangaroo Courts	...	...	28	136	300	130	21	10	...	625
Sanitary Courts	...	...	5	40	79	32	7	1	...	164

The table on the opposite page shows the inspection ratings of the jails by states up to June 30, 1933.

[25] The two tables that follow have been supplied by Miss Nina Kinsella, Executive Assistant to the Director, Federal Bureau of Prisons. See also N. Kinsella, "County Jails and the Federal Government," *Jour. of Criminal Law and Criminology*, Vol. 24, p. 428.

JAILS AND WORKHOUSES INSPECTED
July 1, 1930 to November 30, 1933.

State	LATEST INSPECTION RATINGS									Year Ending June 30, 1933
	90–100%	80–89%	70–79%	60–69%	50–59%	Under 50%	Total Insp.	Counties in State	Jails Used	Daily Aver. Fed. Pop.
Alabama			1	3	53	47	104	67	24	303
Arizona				2	15	1	18	14	20	126
Arkansas				2	20	56	78	75	13	72
California			1	20	30	10	61	58	54	333
Colorado		2	5	14	15	25	61	63	9	107
Connecticut								8	8	20
Delaware	1			1	1		3	3	1	14
Florida				1	38	27	66	67	22	201
Georgia				6	92	88	186	161	30	389
Idaho	1	1		3	27	9	41	44	31	175
Illinois		2	9	19	41	31	102	102	38	596
Indiana				17	55	18	90	92	14	196
Iowa		1	6	30	34	33	104	99	22	74
Kansas			1	3	8		12	105	9	68
Kentucky			2	4	57	63	126	120	80	324
Louisiana			3	5	28	38	74	64	16	108
Maine								16	7	53
Maryland			4	8	11	3	26	24	20	196
Massachusetts								14	7	58
Michigan			1	7	58	15	81	83	28	278
Minnesota	1	3	3	16	44	9	76	87	39	407
Mississippi				4	25	46	75	82	18	342
Missouri			2	3	36	63	104	115	52	333
Montana				1	20	30	51	56	39	155
Nebraska			1	6	7	19	33	93	12	61
Nevada				1	2	2	5	17	12	59
New Hampshire				6	1	1	8	10	2	36
New Jersey								21	7	96
New Mexico			2	4	10	12	28	31	26	74
New York		2	2	1			5	62	56	148
North Carolina				6	66	56	128	100	71	255
North Dakota				3	20	29	52	53	15	19
Ohio		2	4	9	60	34	109	88	34	297
Oklahoma			1	14	41	15	71	77	31	770
Oregon			1	4	11	22	38	36	9	42
Pennsylvania			2	24	37	13	76	67	42	171
Rhode Island								5	1	10
South Carolina				2	20	25	47	46	28	197
South Dakota				6	23	32	61	69	14	61
Tennessee			3	4	37	56	100	95	50	404
Texas		1	3	14	95	133	246	254	36	746
Utah		1			4	21	26	29	3	33
Vermont								14	7	36
Virginia			1	26	48	54	129	121	38	102
Washington			1	7	23	7	38	39	24	105
West Virginia			1	10	33	46	90	55	44	298
Wisconsin			3	13	48	8	72	71	20	270
Wyoming				5	15	1	21	24	17	23
	3	15	63	334	1311	1196	2922	3096	1200	9236

NOTE: This table includes a few state reformatories and training schools which have been inspected; and also a few county and city institutions other than jails and workhouses. A number of the above jails have had more than one inspection, but each jail is counted only once in this table.

Inspections made by inspectors of the Bureau of Prisons, Washington, D. C.

A RATIONAL PLAN FOR CONTROLLING MISDEMEANANTS

THIS mulling about of all kinds of persons in the conditions of physical and moral filth that characterize our jails is a picture that no civilized nation can long afford to ignore. What should be done is fairly well agreed upon by penologists. How to do it is another matter. The proposals generally advanced for improvement are the following:

1. *Use jails for the detention of persons awaiting trial only. The eventual substitution of detention homes for jails.*
2. *Decrease the proportion of persons detained by:*
   (a) More intelligent use of bail privileges.
   (b) The release of selected persons on their own recognizance.
   (c) The development of some means of universal identification along the lines suggested by the Argentine system to make escape difficult.
3. *Develop facilities for the case study of offenders by probation departments as a basis for intelligent disposition of each case by the judge.*
4. *Reduce the prevailing extreme commitments for nonpayment of fines through:*
   (a) Provision for payment of fines in instalments.
   (b) The use of suitable agencies to collect fines.
   (c) The placement of fined prisoners on probation until they have paid their assessment.
5. *Extend probation to many prisoners now sentenced to short terms.*
   This involves also the extension and professionalization of the probation service beyond the point it has now reached. Adequate probation supervision for a year would be far more effective than a month in jail for most offenders.
6. *Apply state control to all convicted misdemeanants.*
   The ancient distinction between felons and misdemeanants has largely broken down. Prisoners now sentenced to county jails have usually broken state laws. There is no reason to suppose that the thief who steals $150 needs state care more than the thief who takes $50. In these days of easy travel the menace of even the petty offender is not restricted to his own county. He is a danger to a wider community and should be handled with the facilities of the state.

7. *Commit indicated types of prisoners to state farms and to special institutions for defective, psychopathic, and alcoholic delinquents.*

Physical work on farms is suitable for most prisoners and will at least reduce demoralization from idleness, decrease the chances of contamination, reduce the costs of maintenance, and send the inmates out physically in good condition. In some states workshops would be needed in the winter time.

Prisoners whose problem is fundamentally one of mental defect or mental disease should have medical treatment in state hospitals. Suitable provision for chronic alcoholics is not yet available except in a few private institutions. These cases require a long period of care with medical treatment correlated with habit training and occupational guidance.

8. *Extend the indeterminate sentence to misdemeanants.*

Short sentences are recognized as being ineffective in improving prisoners. The time served should depend upon the prisoners' demonstration of their probable fitness to be released.

9. *Extend the parole system to include misdemeanants.*

They need assistance and supervision in reestablishing themselves in the community as well as felons. It is an added assurance that the prospects of good behavior that have led to their release will actually be realized under normal conditions. For parolees it means needed assistance in reestablishing themselves. Both of these possibilities require great improvement in the parole services now existing.

THE INTRODUCTION OF NEW METHODS

SOME parts of this program are already in effect in a few places. Many cities and some states now permit persons to pay fines in instalments under the oversight of probation officers. Under this scheme a man is not relieved of his responsibilities but is forced to assume them. He supports his family and pays his fine instead of accepting free lodging for himself and aid for his family at the state's expense. He escapes the influences of the jail. He feels the full deterrent effect of paying for his misdeeds with the sweat of his brow. Wherever the practice has been tried it has proved workable, economical, and more nearly just than imprisonment.

The use of state farms for misdemeanants has been tried with success both in Europe and America but only recently has the plan begun to gain widespread recognition. In 1870, Belgium established an industrial and farm colony for vagrants and beggars at Merxplas with the idea of holding them for an indefinite period until they could be given proper habits of life. In 1895, the Canton of Bern established a world famous penal farm at Witzwil, Switzerland. In this country Indiana has demonstrated the advantages of state care of misdemeanants on its 1600-acre farm at Greencastle which receives all offenders sentenced to thirty days or more as well as others at the will of the judge. Virginia which built its first state institution for convicted misdemeanants in 1926 expects eventually to remove all convicts from its jails to farm or industrial institutions. A few other states make greater or less use of state farm facilities for misdemeanants.

Massachusetts and New York have developed special institutions for defective delinquents. Some other states send defective prisoners to schools for the feeble-minded. Existing hospitals and colonies for the mentally diseased and epileptic are used to some extent but it is still common for mentally ill and defective delinquents to be housed in jails. Special provision for psychopathic or alcoholic misdemeanants has not been made in the United States although such institutions are being considered.

No state has as yet been bold enough to end imprisonment in county jails although the Crime Commission of the State of New York in 1928 recommended that "County jails should be abolished except for commitments for the briefest terms and for prisoners awaiting trial. In their places district penitentiaries and state industrial farms for misdemeanants should be established and equipped for vocational training and other useful outdoor labor." [26]

The chief obstacle to a rational plan for controlling misdemeanants is the vested interest of local political rings in these anachronisms called county jails. Their power can best be broken down by a gradually increasing amount of state regulation. Great Britain long ago went through this process which culminated in the successful transfer of all

[26] "Report of the New York State Crime Commission, 1928," p. 185.

rights and responsibilities in local penal institutions to the national government in 1877. In this country Rhode Island alone has complete control of her jails. Seven other states have sufficient control to dictate minimum standards of care to the local authorities. Sixteen states exercise no supervision whatsoever over county jails. The other twenty-four approach the sixteen rather than the eight in their powers. A desirable objective for them is indicated in the Wickersham Commission's report on penal institutions in these words : [27]

"Each state ought to have certain powers over county jails, and the other institutions for short term offenders ; for example, power to :

(a) Inspect and publish reports of such inspection.

(b) Prescribe standards covering food, sanitation, clothing, exercise, work, and living conditions.

(c) Close an institution when conditions therein fall so far below the prescribed standards as to justify such action.

(d) Transfer prisoners from one institution to another at the expense of the local unit, when it appears that the interests of the community and the welfare of the prisoner require such transfer.

(e) Compel local authorities, both county and municipal, to submit for approval plans for new buildings.

(f) Require uniform accounting and the making of reports in prescribed fashion.

"With all these should go, as we say, evolution of district jails and the development of state farms for misdemeanants. The short term offender should be taken out of dirt and idleness, removed from neglect — and given whatever chance his nature affords for improvement and the building up of physical health."

In the meantime, the Federal Bureau of Prisons is now cleverly taking advantage of its power to supervise the care and treatment of federal prisoners housed in local institutions to bring about the improvement of jail conditions. First, it is constructing a few federal jails which will serve as examples of what architecturally and administratively adequate

[27] National Commission on Law Observance and Enforcement, "Report on Penal Institutions, Probation and Parole," pp. 278-279.

jails might be like. Secondly, it is using the powerful lever of its payments for the housing of federal prisoners in county jails to induce county authorities to improve their institutions so that they may retain federal patronage and receive the highest possible pay for it. All federal contracts with jails include a clause providing that :

"It is expressly understood and agreed, however, that inasmuch as it has become the duty of the Federal Government to supervise the care and treatment of all Federal prisoners whether in Government institutions or otherwise, the Government hereby reserves the right under this contract to enter upon the jail premises herein referred to at reasonable hours for the purpose of inspecting the same and determining the conditions under which the prisoners are boarded." [28]

Payments to local jails for boarding federal prisoners are then made on a sliding scale which provides for payment of :

$1.05 per prisoner per day for jails rating 90 to 100 per cent [29]
.80 per prisoner per day for jails rating 80 to 89 per cent
.70 per prisoner per day for jails rating 70 to 79 per cent
.60 per prisoner per day for jails rating 60 to 69 per cent
.50 per prisoner per day for jails rating 50 to 59 per cent

Local officials are notified by the federal government of the results of their inspections, suggestions for improvements are made to jail officials, and a list of approved jails is given to United States marshals and judges. The result, especially where jails have been put in low income classifications or where federal payments have been stopped because of the removal of federal prisoners from low standard jails, has been to arouse considerable local interest and coöperation in the removal of poor conditions. Many sheriffs and jailers have shown a commendable desire to coöperate to meet federal standards within the limits of their abilities and of the funds available to them. Where jail officials have been handicapped by lack of funds, lack of authority, ignorance,

[28] N. Kinsella, "County Jails and the Federal Government," *Jour. of Criminal Law and Criminology*, Vol. 24, p. 430.
[29] N. Kinsella, *op. cit.*, p. 430.

or unwillingness to respond public-spirited citizens or civic organizations have in several instances taken steps to bring about indicated improvements.

Pressure of the Federal Bureau of Prisons may induce favorable changes in the administration of county jails more rapidly than any other force now at hand. However, it must be remembered that the extent of the improvements is still limited by the comparative poverty of county governments, by inherent difficulties in the use of the jail as a catchall in the absence of other facilities, by lack of parole service for misdemeanants, and by the general lack of integration that characterizes our entire scheme of administering criminal justice. These fundamental defects in our technique of caring for convicted misdemeanants will apparently for some time require our thoughtful attention.

CHAPTER XX

REFORMATORIES, PRISONS AND THE IMPRISONED

THE PRISONS

THE typical state prison of the United States today is a walled fortress of stone and steel. Cell houses, workshops and an administration building enclose prison yards and exercise grounds. Outside may be a prison farm. Within the walls from 300 to 4000 prisoners live. Nearly half of our prisons and reformatories house 1000 or more men. In an equal number of prisons a few women are confined in separate wings behind the same wall that restrains the men.

Within the drab cell houses cleft with narrow barred windows are the cell blocks which house the prisoners. Four-fifths of the prisons were built upon the model set by old Auburn in 1819. The cells within are placed back to back, from two to six tiers high down the center of the prison house facing its bare stone walls from which they are separated by corridors.

The cells are small; as small as a "good sized grave stood on end," and give the impression of being hewed out of solid rock. In some prisons the cells are made of steel. The cell door may be barred or made of solid iron pierced with vent holes, in which case, light enters only through the grated windows. In many cells it is not possible for a prisoner to stretch his arms across the width of them nor straight above his head without touching the wall. A five-foot width, eight-foot length, and eight-foot height is a fair size. Only the newer cells are larger. Some are smaller. The cells in the old section of Sing Sing are three feet, six inches wide, seven feet long, and six feet, seven inches high. Ninety per cent of the prison cells in the United States have

404

less than the *minimum* air space of 600 cubic feet now required for *outside* cells for new federal prison construction, a fact that indicates both an evil and a growing awareness of it.

The furnishings of a room may consist of an iron cot bed and bedding, a locker, small table, and chair. Not every prison offers as much. Artificial light is necessary, since only a little indirect light from the corridor can filter through the cell window. Prisons recently built are better planned so that every cell may be touched by sunlight for a few minutes a day. Where the cell walls are of stone and the heating pipes are outside in the corridors the whitewashed or painted walls are likely to be damp and conducive to rheumatism which is a common prison malady.

Rough damp surfaces make vermin control difficult, although considering the obstacles results are reasonably good. Running water and toilets in many prisons have been a chief factor in overcoming a major sanitary problem. That evil, however, is by no means abolished. In the older prisons and reformatories, buckets numbered in the hope that each man will get his own, are used for toilet purposes. Fourteen of our largest prisons today have no other toilet facilities. In them the use of the bucket is not only an unhealthy practice but it is an æsthetic nuisance of more than ordinary psychological importance in prison where several hundred men are locked up in cells, side by side and tier upon tier, twelve to fourteen hours every night in ill-ventilated cell blocks.

The evils of faulty housing have been aggravated in recent years by the persistent crowding of our prisons, due to such factors as increasing length of sentences and conservatism in granting paroles. In 1927 the number of prisoners confined in all of our penal institutions was one-fifth more than their original capacity. Several prisons were caring for twice the proper number of prisoners. As a result cells, not large enough for one prisoner, have been equipped with double-decked bunks and made to house two. In some cases a mattress on the floor takes care of a third prisoner. Some prisons have placed strings of cots down the length of their corridors as beds for the inmates. The added strain of such overcrowding upon already inadequate heating, ventilating, feeding and sanitary arrangements has made conditions in many institutions perilous, illegal, and insufferable.

The workshops built within the prison walls are similar to the older type of factory in the outside community. The goods manufactured vary from place to place. San Quentin's chief industry is the preparation of jute fiber. Stillwater, Minnesota, has modern factory buildings for the manufacture of binder twine and farm machinery. Other prisons are less specialized in their industrial work but employ men at a variety of tasks such as those at Sing Sing which include the making of shoes, brushes, hosiery, knit goods, mattresses, sheet metal goods, printing, and the use of some men at road work and new prison construction. Clerical work in connection with these industries is cared for by prisoners. The general maintenance of the institution, laundry work, food preparation, and general housekeeping are also inmate tasks. Nearly all prisons now run a farm worked by prisoners who are sometimes housed outside of the prison walls.

The other features of prison equipment are a hall or chapel used both for religious services and entertainments, school rooms, a library, hospital, mess hall, recreation yard, and a room where prisoners may meet visiting relatives under the eye of a guard. The level at which these facilities are maintained varies greatly. The library may be an uncatalogued collection of ancient ill-assorted books and without funds for the acquisition of useful literature, or it may be a collection properly installed by trained librarians and offering to inmates planned reading courses, trade journals and other educational services. The school may be held in a regular classroom reasonably well equipped or in the lower corridors of a cell block.

PRISON ROUTINE

Sentenced prisoners brought in by the deputy sheriff are first examined by the prison record clerk, who secures a brief history of the criminal and his offenses and lists him on the prison books. The newcomer is then taken to the dressing room where he is stripped, examined carefully for the possession of drugs, and given a shower bath. A suit of prison gray is given to him based on an estimate of his size. His civilian clothes are burned, stored or sent home. Trinkets and money are listed and kept until the prisoner's release. From that point on the newcomer is to outward appearances just one more inmate, stripped of all individuality like a summer bather in a municipal bathhouse costume. He is taken at once to a cell where he remains for a few days during which time he may be examined by the deputy warden, physician, chaplain, and other officials. Usually he is assigned to an intermediate conduct grade from which he may move up or down, depending upon his behavior. Some attention having been paid to his health, intelligence, past work experience, the presence of criminal rivals, and the needs of the institution, the prisoner is given a place in the prison industries.

The prison day begins with a rising bell at about six o'clock in the morning. Guards count the men in their cells. The men dress, tidy their rooms, and march in line to the mess hall for breakfast. At a given signal they sit down to eat. In some institutions knives and forks are not allowed and the men get on as best they can with spoons and the tools Nature gave them. When prisoners need more food or drink they get it by means of a primitive sign language. Watchful guards stand about them as they eat. Twenty minutes is the customary time allowance for each meal.

The work period runs from eight until four or four-thirty with a brief intermission at noon for dinner and recess. Reasonably quiet communication is usually permitted during work hours although in some prisons the old silence rule is still in force. Usually the men do not work at top speed for one of the major problems of prison administration is to find enough work to keep the prisoners busy. Moreover, in the absence of some positive incentive to work, prisoners who cannot very well be discharged for inefficiency are likely to become clever at doing only enough work to avoid punishment.

After work, prisoners may be allowed in the recreation yard to play ball, or mill about and converse for half an hour to an hour. After supper they are returned to their cells. There they may read, mend, or make knick-knacks. Some attend evening classes, usually of grammar school grade. Those who earn the privilege may attend weekly motion picture shows. Usually all may attend religious services on Sundays. All prisoners are returned to their cells and lights are turned out about 9:30. One of them speaking of the conventional prison routine has said:

"Day after day we find that prosyness, inertia, stolidity, weariness and dejection are the prevailing qualities of our lives. The escapes and murders — the exciting things — are so infrequent as to be practically nonexistent. . . Every minute of the day, all the year round, the most dominant tone is one of monotony.

"Four o'clock. Yard time. Recreation. . . We go from the stuffy shop to the colorless yard. In it is no blade of grass, no tree, no bit of freshness or brilliance. Gray walls, dusty gravel, dirt and asphalt hardness. We walk about, or during our first few months or years manage to throw a ball back and forth and in some degree exercise our bodies. The longer we stay here, the less we do. At last we merely walk at a funeral pace, or lean against a wall and talk.

"We always talk. During the working hours, but even more so during the cell hours, we store up facts, reflections, broodings, so that our minds are overflowing. And every chance we get to unburden them, we avail ourselves of it. We talk *at* each other. We do not converse ; we deliver monologues in which we get rid of the stored-up bubblings. We try to live through words and self-dramatization. Our essential need is for actual tangible living, which we cannot have ; so we try to live by pretending to live in tall stories based on how we'd like to live, how we long to live. . .

"Four-thirty. Yard time is over. We march to our cells, taking with us the evening meal. The shop has been so enervating, so weakening, so downright devitalizing, that we are glad to go to our cells. We think, 'Well, here's another day done. Another day nearer home. God, but it's good to get back to the cell !' In our hearts, however, we know that the cell is even worse than the shop ; and that in the morning we'll be saying, 'God, but it's good to get out of that damned cell !' "[1]

[1] V. F. Nelson, "Prison Days and Nights," pp. 15-16. Boston, Little, Brown and Co., 1933. Reprinted by permission.

REFORMATORIES

REFORMATORIES, which in the late nineteenth century represented a distinct break with the penitentiary methods of their day, are now essentially the same as the old line prisons in architecture, routine and type of prisoners. They have slipped away from their original level into the rut of conventional prison practice. Much of their zeal for reformation has died out. The increasing use of probation for first offenders has left them to care for prisoners who, though youthful, have run afoul of the law before.

Prisons, on the other hand, have come to apprehend reformation as one of their functions. Their prisoners, also, are young. The age of felons sentenced to prison closely approaches the reformatory level. Fifty-six per cent of all the inmates in thirty-two prisons in 1930 were under thirty years of age, and twelve per cent were under twenty. In 1928, forty-five per cent of those admitted to our prisons were between twenty and thirty years of age as contrasted with forty-seven per cent of that same age group admitted to reformatories. Reformatory sentences served average about two years; prison sentences three years. The régime in prisons and reformatories is similar. In every basic respect they are alike. The exceptions are the great prison farms in half a dozen southern states and the women's reformatories of the country.

PRISON FARMS

SOUTHERN prisons are characterized by their emphasis upon agriculture rather than industry. The large number of negro convicts is another factor peculiar to the South. As a result there are many more prison units in proportion to the prison population and they are scattered about over a wide area. The walled fortress type of prison is here replaced by units of smaller farm buildings, industrial plants and dormitories. Some buildings are of wood. Others, as at Kilby, Alabama, are of excellent modern construction and design.

In Mississippi, which stands as an illustration of the use of the agricultural prison, four farms are utilized. The largest of these at Parchman covers 16,000 acres. This is divided into thirteen sections on each of which is a separate camp unit in charge of a sergeant. Two of the camps are for whites, ten for colored men, and one for colored women. Each camp consists of a collection of farm buildings and long one-story cell-less dormitories of frame or brick surrounded by a barbed wire fence. Nearly all prisoners are occupied during the day in farm work outside of the enclosure.

In Arkansas, Mississippi, and Louisiana and to some extent in Florida trusties are used as guards both within the enclosure and out in the fields. The work overseers who accompany the field gangs are free white men, usually mounted, but unarmed. Although this practice has been freely criticized it seems in practice to work reasonably well. Those who favor the scheme point out that trusties are not likely to abuse their authority at the risk of losing their privileges of extra pay and "good time" nor are they likely to permit escape since they are adequately rewarded for performing their duties. Disturbances under this system have occurred but not more frequently than when paid guards were employed. Of course, the economy of the scheme makes it appealing to administrators.

Work in the open fields is probably more healthful than semi-idleness in antiquated prison factories, and it is well suited to the needs of the rural South. Perhaps the relative docility of southern negroes and possibly of agricultural laborers in general helps to make their employment on farms feasible. In the North where ninety per cent of the convicts come from industrial centers, farms have developed only as minor adjuncts to the prisons. Few northern prisoners could make use of farm training and it is doubtful if many convicts that come from urban centers could be properly managed on farms.

WOMEN'S PRISONS AND REFORMATORIES

PROVISION for separate prisons for women in this country was first made by Indiana in 1869 followed by Massachusetts in 1874. The reformatory ideal was first applied to women by New York which authorized a reformatory for women at Bedford Hills in 1892. Nineteen states now have separate state penal institutions for women. Seven or eight of them together with a handful of men's prisons represent the progressive element in American prisons today. Here and there a few capable leaders have been appointed. Superintendents like Dr. Katherine B. Davis of the New York State Reformatory, Dr. Mary B. Harris of the Federal Industrial Institution for Women, the late Mrs. Jessie D. Hodder of the Massachusetts Reformatory and her successor, Dr. Miriam Van Waters are internationally known for their work in penology. Under them and others of their kind a few women's reformatories have been willing to experiment constructively and courageously.

As in the better men's prisons they have worked on the assumption that prison life must come as close as possible to duplicating the duties and responsibilities which inmates must face upon discharge. The normal life is their ideal. Under it has appeared the tendency to replace fortresses with cottages. The need for careful understanding and individualization of treatment has been recognized. Particular attention has been paid to the health requirements of the women, of whom many are diseased. The values of farm work for women are being exploited. Educational work is broadly construed. The community organization of women prisoners has come to be recognized as a vitally important element in the development of social responsibility. Much attention is being paid to the establishment of satisfactory relations with their families on the outside.

Unfortunately the majority of women's reformatories do not fit this description. On the contrary, in many of them the disadvantages of male prisons appear in intensified form because of the restricted range of occupational and recreational interests available to women. At the bottom of the entire prison list must be placed the wholly undesirable women's wings in which women are housed under the control of the men's prison wardens in many of our state prisons. Few male institutions can equal their barrenness. Kate O'Hare's description [2] of her confinement in one of them is

[2] K. O'Hare, "In Prison."

a revealing as well as a vivid picture of one of these anachronisms.

For obvious reasons, women's prisons have never attracted so much attention from the public as the men's prisons. Reformers have likewise given them little more than a passing glance. Perhaps the notion that prostitutes who form a large part of their populations are hopeless has been in some measure responsible for their attitude. It is questionable whether this judgment of prostitutes is warranted. As Dr. Warren Stearns has pointed out, prostitution is an economic rather than a sex problem. It is analogous to larceny among men and is not the result of biological impulses difficult to modify but of factors susceptible to understanding and correction.

THE PRISONERS

THOSE whose world is for a time bounded by prison walls are nearly all men ; 98 per cent of those in prisons and 87 per cent of those in reformatories. They are youthful, one-third of the prison inmates and three-fourths of the reformatory inmates being under 25 years of age, and only 13 per cent of the prison inmates and 3 per cent of the reformatory inmates being over 45. Single prisoners are proportionately twice as numerous in prison as in the general population. The proportion of divorceés in prison is also overgenerous. Half of the offenders committed to prisons and reformatories are known recidivists, or repeaters, but the chances are that the real proportion is higher. The Gluecks' thorough study of 510 men at Concord Reformatory, disclosed that 433 of them (84.9 per cent) had been previously arrested a total of 1944 times and convicted in 1688 cases.[3] Almost four-fifths (79.7 per cent) of the Massachusetts State Prison population in 1929 had previously been convicted of criminal offenses.[4]

Although it is not possible to speak with precision about the mental condition of prisoners in general, specific studies

[3] S. S. and E. T. Glueck, "500 Criminal Careers," pp. 140 and 144.
[4] F. Loveland, Jr., "A Statistical Analysis of the Inmate Population of the Massachusetts State Prison on September 30, 1929."

indicate that a high percentage of prisoners, perhaps more than 50 per cent, have recognizable mental and nervous ailments ranging from feeble-mindedness and definite psychoses to marked psychoneurotic traits such as extreme impulsiveness, suggestibility, and the like.   How common these traits are among the general population outside of prisons we unfortunately do not know, although casual observation suggests that the incidence of the lesser mental and nervous disorders is high.   To be more definite about the prison populations, it appears safe to say that among male prisoners in state institutions about 40 per cent are psychologically normal, possibly 25 per cent are neuropathic, an equal proportion feeble-minded, and possibly 2 to 10 per cent definitely psychotic (insane).   Among women prisoners the proportion of normal prisoners is apt to be much lower and the proportion of feeble-minded and psychopathic prisoners higher. No doubt the tendency to give normal women opportunities for adjustment outside of prison coupled with the fact that the crimes for which women are imprisoned tend to attract unstable or unintelligent types accounts for the difference.

Alcoholism amounting to a psychopathic state is limited to a small proportion of our prison populations, possibly 5 to 8 per cent, although users of alcohol are, of course, much more numerous than this.   However, such great variations exist in the extent of its use that it is difficult to classify prisoners with reference to their drinking habits and still more difficult to judge how they compare in that respect with the non-prisoner population.   In addition to its alcoholics, the prison population includes a small, but exceedingly troublesome, proportion of drug addicts and sex perverts.[5]

These figures apply to the prison and reformatory populations of a state as a whole.   Whether they will hold true for any particular institution depends upon whether a state houses all offenders in one type of institution or whether it classifies its prisoners and sorts out the insane, the feeble-

---

[5] See "Men Without Women" and "Drugs and the Criminal," being chapters 6 and 7 of V. F. Nelson, "Prison Days and Nights," for a picture of prison conditions with reference to sex and drugs as observed by a prisoner.

minded, and others needing special attention and deals with them in specialized institutions, as is done in some measure by a few states, notably New Jersey, New York, Illinois, and Massachusetts. Another point to be kept in mind is that an alcoholic prisoner may also be psychopathic ; a drug addict may be feeble-minded ; or an epileptic may be feeble-minded or superior in intelligence. In other words these categories are not mutually exclusive.

As a specific example of prison types from a psychiatric standpoint the following classification of the prison population of six New York institutions in 1930 is illuminating. The institutions represented, whose populations made up the total of 8475 men were : Sing Sing, Auburn, Clinton, Great Meadow, Elmira, and Napanoch. The classification was based upon direct personal interviews by psychiatrists in accordance with the standard scheme of the American Prison Association.[6]

PSYCHIATRIC CLASSIFICATION
AMERICAN PRISON ASSOCIATION CLASSIFICATION [7]

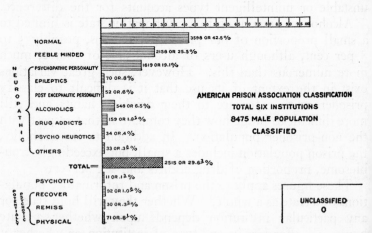

The intelligence ratings of these same men as determined

[6] American Prison Association, "Classification Handbook and Statistical Guide."

[7] Dr. V. C. Branham, "The Classification of the Prison Inmates of New York State" Supplemental report to the Commission to Investigate Prison Administration and Construction, p. 47. Chart reproduced by permission of Dr. V. C. Branham.

by standard psychometric tests given by competent examiners was as follows : [8]

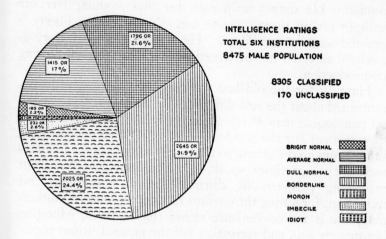

INTELLIGENCE RATINGS
TOTAL SIX INSTITUTIONS
8475 MALE POPULATION

8305 CLASSIFIED
170 UNCLASSIFIED

1796 OR 21.6%
1415 OR 17%
185 OR 2.2%
1 OR 1.4%
232 OR 2.8%
2645 OR 31.9%
2025 OR 24.4%

BRIGHT NORMAL
AVERAGE NORMAL
DULL NORMAL
BORDERLINE
MORON
IMBECILE
IDIOT

THE PRISON ADMINISTRATORS

THE state penal institutions in Connecticut, Indiana, North Carolina and Pennsylvania are under the authority of unpaid local boards of trustees. Elsewhere centralized control is exercised either by a state prison board of some sort as in thirteen states or more commonly by a single paid commissioner. The executive officer in immediate charge of each prison is the warden who is assisted by one or more deputy wardens, guards, stewards, shop and school instructors, chaplains, physicians and in rare instances by social service and research workers. Inmates are often employed as clerks, school instructors, and, in some places, as guards.

THE WARDEN

THE warden is the general manager of the prison responsible for its policies. He is expected to be an efficient jailer, a skilful reformer, a capable educator, and a successful business man. Usually he is a first class politician. Yet his subjects are admitted social failures whose number, type, and

[8] Dr. V. C. Branham, *op. cit.*, p. 56. Reproduced by permission of Dr. V. C. Branham.

length of stay he has no power to regulate. Inevitably under present conditions the separate aspects of his work conflict. He cannot train men for their coming freedom without giving them some to use. Yet so far as liberty is granted security is reduced. He can not run his factory as a school to teach inexperienced men trades without slowing up production.

Happily for the old-line wardens they are generally unconcerned about the real difficulties of their jobs. Theoretical penologists may worry about the inconsistencies in prison management but the wardens, who actually run the prisons, suffer from no disturbing conflicts. When questioned by laymen they sometimes speak, a bit unconvincingly, about reforming prisoners by discipline, work, education, and recreation, forgetting the obvious fact that in their institutions discipline is for convenience rather than reform, education is a meagre sop, and recreation for the general prison population is unorganized, limited, and nearly valueless. But when the wardens gather together at their annual meetings there is an appalling unanimity as to the nature of their tasks ; and rehabilitation of prisoners is not one of them. Instead their major objectives seem to be :

(*a*) To hold prisoners in safety during the length of their sentences.
(*b*) To make the prisoners work.
(*c*) To make the prisons as nearly self-sustaining as possible.
(*d*) To hold their own jobs.

These tasks present many difficulties, of course, but they do not run counter to each other. Moreover they seem to be quite in line with the wishes and expectations of uninformed laymen.

However, if we think of the wardens' work in terms of social protection, which involves not only keeping dangerous persons in custody but in making them as little dangerous as possible before they are freed, it is difficult to think of a task that offers a greater challenge to human ingenuity. As an opportunity for men who enjoy matching wits against obstacles it might easily attract capable, scientifically grounded, socially minded persons with executive ability into the prison field.

In practice, unfortunately, the warden's office is not an exalted one. Neither in pay nor prestige is it generally accorded proper rank. Special training for the office is not yet considered necessary although the recent establishment of schools for prison officers suggests that it may be soon. Usually the warden works up to his position from that of a guard. Former sheriffs or policemen are considered suitable appointees. Less frequently army officers or business men receive such positions. The real trouble all along the line is that loyalty to a political party rather than fitness for the warden's job is the basis of appointment. All too often each political upheaval brings a replacement of wardens. Against this absurd practice may be set the commendable and apparently growing tendency in some quarters to appoint as wardens men of unusual capacities.

The chance to secure such men, even where they are desired, is hampered by the aura of distastefulness that hovers about the warden's duties as conventionally understood no less than by the low salaries paid for the caliber of men required. It has been aptly pointed out that:

"The prison is looked upon not as a professional problem of the highest complexity, requiring men of great knowledge and ability; not as an institution having three or four thousand young people needing educational interest and activity, but rather as an institution for the repression and control of the dangerous, and for that purpose the higher type of individual is not available. Not until we recognize that a prison is a great opportunity for broad educational endeavor will we attract the kind of administrator who is needed. That is one of the first needs of the prison — a new type of institutional head, a type of administrator who could be called as the president of a great educational institution. Until then we shall make progress slowly, if at all." [9]

THE DEPUTY WARDEN

THE deputy is the executive officer in immediate charge of the prison routine. He assigns prisoners to their work and determines the disciplinary action to be taken when rules are

[9] National Commission on Law Observance and Enforcement, "Report on Penal Institutions, Probation and Parole," p. 43.

broken. The prison guards are under his direction. He is a key man upon whose wisdom, courage and ability to manage men a large measure of the prison's success rests.

Conditions affecting the warden's office are likely to be repeated in that of his subordinate. The deputy travels the same road as his superior but is a step behind him in pay, prestige, and authority. Usually he is appointed by the warden.

THE GUARDS

PRISON guards have one of the world's most unattractive jobs. The pay is low, the hours long, the chances for advancement virtually non-existent. Out of 86 prisons and reformatories for which figures are available 37 pay their guards a maximum salary ranging from $600 to $1300 a year. Seventy per cent of these same prisons work their guards from 10 to 16 hours a day. The labor turnover of guards is excessive. The New York State Crime Commission reports that at Sing Sing it is sometimes as high as 50 per cent in a year.[10]

While guards are on duty they are imprisoned as effectively as the men. The conditions under which they work are irksome and confining. What they may carry in and out of the institution is carefully circumscribed. Their persons may be subject to search in the enforcement of this rule. They may not leave prisoners unwatched. Conversation with inmates is often limited to essential directions. Ordinary human relations with them are forbidden.

The tension under which guards work is unremitting. Resulting cases of insanity among keepers is not unknown. They are constantly on the defensive against the prisoners who tend to go just as far as their courage and the rules will permit. As strict discipline is considered essential to the safe custody of convicts, rules for their conduct are numerous, arbitrary, and detailed. It is the duty of the guards to enforce them. For so doing they often incur the enmity of their charges. Opportunities for friction abound. Ill-feeling simmers underneath the surface. In the jumpy

[10] "Report of the New York State Crime Commission, 1929," p. 146.

atmosphere of fear that ensues two sorts of responses are observable. Some guards know only one effective weapon — hard-boiled repression. Assumed, at first, as the easiest and most obvious means of control it becomes a habitual attitude bordering in some cases on sadism.

The other type, whom Howard B. Gill has called "near prisoners," slumps to the level of the men they guard. Complete acquaintance begets forgiveness. Through living with convicts their own moral standards get to be blurred and fuzzy. They become good-fellows among the men and traitors to their fellow-guards, willing to condone forbidden acts to curry favor with the prisoners. The slump is physical as well as moral. In the end they become unrespected, shifty, evasive apologies for men. Quite naturally, no doubt, they become like those with whom they live so large a portion of their lives.

Ignorant ill-paid guards are excellent subjects for corruption. Prisoners and their friends are often eager seekers after favors. Sometimes the pressure that they can exert is considerable. The graft may run all the way from the profits on forbidden cigarettes sold to prisoners at a nickel a piece to considerable sums of money for smuggled messages, drugs or connivance at an escape. These activities are not lost upon the general prison population which soon learns which of its keepers are playing the game and cynically adapts its behavior to its knowledge.

Improvements in the way of more pay for fewer hours of duty are suggested by these facts. Genuine progress, however, is not likely to come until the functions and opportunities of prison guards are broadened to attract a different type of personnel. Probably the paternal and police functions of keepers should be modified and completely separated from each other. In place of the guard there should be on the one hand a prison police force, uniformed, trained, and out of direct, intimate contact with prisoners, and on the other hand house officers able to do social case work with the men in their care in correlation with the prison school teachers, chaplains, and physicians.

A dawning recognition of the need for definite minimum

standards in the selection and qualification of line men in prisons made its active appearance in Europe [11] in 1925 when England organized a training school for prison officers at Wakefield. Since then several other European countries, and the United States have established similar schools. Following a lecture course for prison workers given by the Massachusetts Department of Correction in 1926-27, Commissioner Patterson of New York organized the first Keeper's Training School in the country in 1928. One of the first acts of the Hon. Sanford Bates, when he was appointed Superintendent (now Director) of Federal Prisons in June 1929, was to develop plans for a federal prison officers' school in which the first course was given from January to April 1929. In 1931 New Jersey opened a training school for prison officers at Rahway Reformatory. Massachusetts is permitting a few serious students of penology to gain experience as internes in its penal institutions. Harvard University now offers a two-year professional course to qualified students intended to fit them for executive positions in prisons as well as in other branches of criminological work. About sixteen American Universities give one or more courses designed primarily to prepare students for practical work in criminology.

This is as far as we have gone. The movement is still in its infancy but is catching hold. The utter absurdity of entrusting the control of prisoners to unintelligent and untrained men is slowly becoming apparent. Inmates stay too short a time in prison for the functions of guards as "keepers" to be emphasized. Goods that are "kept" too long are likely to deteriorate. We can hardly afford to have these damaged goods returned to freedom worse than when they were impounded. The extreme dependency of prisoners upon the staff for every condition affecting their welfare in prison and their attitude towards the life they are approach-

[11] As John L. Gillin has pointed out, Japan apparently was the pioneer in this field. Her common course for lower prison officials was established in 1908. European schools, however, seem to have arisen independently of the Japanese program and perhaps without awareness of its existence.

ing outside determine the need for prison personnels both able and worthy of the highest respect.

THE NATURE OF PRISON DISCIPLINE

PRISON discipline is essentially arbitrary and childish. It reminds the observer of the sort of treatment meted out by ignorant parents to troublesome offspring. Its aim is to make the prison run smoothly and with as little trouble to the administration as possible. The management draws up a list of acts forbidden. The prisoners' task is one of avoidance. Goodness in prison consists in keeping quiet and doing what you are told to do. Since many inmates have never curbed themselves prior to their imprisonment it is often surmised that strict conduct requirements will teach them obedience to law as well as insure the orderly management of the prison. Uniformity is a high virtue. The test of fairness is that everybody is treated alike in spite of the obvious fact that everyone differs from his fellows in his problems and his needs. As in the courts outside, punishments are aimed to fit the crimes but not the criminals.

Printed lists of "Don'ts" prescribing in elaborate detail the conduct required of all inmates are generally issued to all prisoners upon their admittance. At their worst the directions are so minute that a prisoner literally cannot blow his nose or ask a question without considering the regulations. For example in the 28-page booklet containing 105 rules for the direction of the inmates of the Iowa State Penitentiary appear the following:

Rule 49 : Strict silence and decorum must be observed during the meal. Talking, laughing, grimacing or gazing about the room is strictly forbidden.

Rule 75 forbids : Altering clothing, bed not properly made, clothing not in proper order, communicating by signs, creating a disturbance, crookedness, defacing anything, dilatoriness, dirty cell or furnishings, disorderly cell, disobedience of orders, disturbance in cell house, fighting, grimacing, hands in pockets, hands or face not clean, hair not combed, having contraband article on your person or in your cell, impertinence to visitors, insolence to officers, insolence to foreman, insolence to fellow inmates, inattentive at work, inattentive in line, inattentive in school, laughing and fooling, loud talking in cell, malicious mischief, neglect of study, not out of bed promptly, not in bed promptly, not at door for count, not wearing outside shirt, not promptly out of cell when brake is drawn, out of place in shop or line, profanity, quarreling, refusal to obey, shirking, spitting on floor, staring at visitors, stealing, trading, talking in chapel, talking in line, talking in school, talking at school, talking from cell to cell, talking in corridor, throwing away food, vile language, wasting food, writing unauthorized letters.[12]

Violations of prison rules are punished by reprimands, loss of privileges such as the right to attend the movies, draw library books, receive visitors, write letters and so on, locking prisoners in their cells, locking prisoners in dark cells, solitary confinement, restriction of diets to bread and water, handcuffing men to cell doors, strapping them, and a variety of miscellaneous punishments such as turning the hose on a man while he is shackled to a post or making men walk around and around a small yard.

Punishments are assessed by the deputy warden after a talk with the prisoner who has been reported. In his judgment the inmate must trust. Often the deputy's judgment is reduced through practice to a habit. For example, the investigators for the Wickersham Commission one morning watched the disciplinary officer of a prison pass upon charges of loafing, eating before the signal, possessing contraband, insolence and threats, playing craps, fighting, being a queer fellow, and one voluntary request to be put in solitary confinement. Every man on the list was sentenced to solitary confinement.[13]

On the other hand, in some states prisoners who do not violate the rules are rewarded by credits of "good time" which may shorten their terms of imprisonment. A man sentenced for ten years, for example, may earn his release by good behavior in about eight. Prisoners who misbehave may lose such credits.

[12] National Commission on Law Observance and Enforcement, *op. cit.*, p. 25.
[13] National Commission on Law Observance and Enforcement, *op. cit.*, p. 32.

Many states release most of their prisoners on parole under the continued supervision of the state before the expiration of their maximum sentences. Nearly half of all the prisoners now released from state institutions go out by this method. In considering the parole of a prisoner parole boards usually place great weight upon his good behavior in prison as attested by his ability to keep quiet and do as he is told.

Fortunately a few institutions are pointing the way towards improvement, replacing endless petty rules by a straightforward explanation of the essential character of the prison routine and a statement that the prisoner is expected to conduct himself like any decent person in the circumstances. One or two prisons are now giving credits for positive action. Norfolk in Massachusetts, for example, rates its inmates upon their constructive achievements. It gives credits for such accomplishments as maintaining satisfactory relations with families outside of prison, earning more than the equivalent of $10 a week under the prison wage scale, and keeping physically well. Only prisoners who maintain a grade A 1 rating are recommended for parole.

THE RESULTS OF PRISON DISCIPLINE

In the face of nine major prison riots in 1930-31, a large number of lesser disturbances, escapes, and reported infractions of prison rules literally running up into the tens of thousands, prevailing methods of discipline cannot be considered successful. The premium placed upon automatic obedience is without reference to the qualities that prompt it. Wise old-timers who want to get back to their criminal business as soon as possible shrewdly keep within the letter of the law submerging any contrary impulses in order to gain their freedom at the earliest possible moment. They are good prisoners because they do not trouble the administration. Young fellows, still with excellent possibilities for reform, less skilfully smother their inclinations and flare up in bitterness when compelled to suffer the consequences. They are bad prisoners because they question and resent ordained rules whose value they do not understand. "There are some rules" writes one prisoner in concurrence with others, "if you could look them over you would think they were made by some persons who weren't right in the head." [14]

Since shirking, answering improperly, grimacing, dilatoriness, inattention and like offenses can be seen with a little imagination by any guard the chances for a sadistic keeper to make life miserable for his charges are almost endless. On the other hand, guards not infrequently accept petty bribes to permit and aid in violations of some rules, as, for example, against obtaining morphine or procuring and smoking cigarettes. Little but cynicism and loss of respect can result from such practices. Less serious is the tendency good-naturedly to overlook infractions of minor regulations. However, even the conscientious right-minded keeper is often hard pressed to draw the line between reporting and not reporting a prisoner. Even the best of them stir up enmities among the men who disagree, often unwarrantably, with the fairness of their snap judgments. Less tolerant guards engender an atmosphere of bitterness that rather frequently finds expression in physical attacks by inmates upon their keepers in spite of swift, sure punishment.

THE PRISON WORLD

CONSIDERING the abnormalities of prison life it is not a wonder that serious behavior problems appear. Restriction of freedom breeds resistance and irritation in prison exactly as it does in a home that has been quarantined. It is a one sex world. Normal social relations with members of the opposite sex are checked.[15] Attractive, worthwhile interests are few. In every prison is a small but damaging quota of drug addicts and sex perverts. These abnormalities are intensi-

[14] From a letter in the author's possession.

[15] There is no good reason why some measure of normalcy should not be achieved through the employment of both men and women on the staffs of both the men's and the women's institutions. Home visits under the care of an officer, now infrequently permitted, to those to whom such visits will be of advantage, would also tend to relieve the abnormal social conditions of prison life. Under some circumstances it might be well to colonize prisoners with their families on penal farms.

fied by the prevailing disciplinary scheme that makes normal behavior impossible for both guards and convicts.

The strong and the weak, the stupid and the bright are all subject to the same routine. Equality is carried to the last degree. The drab sameness of prison routine intensifies the leveling process. Privacy is unattainable. Arbitrary externally imposed rules divide the prison community into two opposing camps : those who are to enforce the rules and those who are to obey them. Between the two there is a constant atmosphere of tension. Fear and suspicion are the constant accompaniments of all prison activity. Both guards and prisoners are jumpy.

Stripped of all individuality and placed on equal terms under the dictatorship of the warden and his staff the prisoners are welded together into a unit by the strongest ties of self-interest. Loyalty to the group is the paramount virtue ; disloyalty the most heinous sin. He who would turn informer risks death. The strongest prop that a convict has to lean upon is the moral support of his fellow-inmates. The most fearsome punishment is their condemnation.

The prison community is self-centered, introspective. Cut off from the world beyond it cannot be otherwise. In its isolation life becomes narrow. Its perspective is distorted. The trivialities are magnified as they are in a rural village. Happenings of little moment to the larger world outside are of absorbing interest within prison walls. Prisoners become hypersensitive. They are touchy about their prerogatives. Gossip and rumors are seized upon and mulled over until every possible meaning behind them has been examined and judged.

When resentments are expressed they are inevitably directed against the warden and his staff. They are the immediate and observable sources of all things good and bad that affect the prisoners. Work, food, cells, privileges, and punishments all hang upon the warden's will. He is the source of imminent power, certain and final. Against him and his emissaries anger is kindled whenever anything disturbs the prisoners' world. Regardless of what goes on the warden somehow is held accountable.

Here is the setting for prison riots. Not poor food, not

failure to install radios, but a basic pathological condition ; a highly unstable community ready to blow up with little provocation. Poor food is as distasteful in a boarding house as in a prison but it does not lead to riots. Prison outbreaks occur because prisons are always near the breaking point where any indignity, real or imagined, may be a spark that will set the entire prison community aflame. This condition of instability will remain as long as prisons remain as we now know them. It is a permanent attribute of abnormal institutional life.

Only with the growth of a completely new and mature conception of discipline can any other fundamental improvements in our prisons be brought about. Such a scheme of discipline would have to be pertinent to the actual needs of the individual prisoner rather than to the comfort of the management. It would require the same sort of understanding and ingenuity on the part of its administrators that wise parents and teachers have to exercise in dealing with conduct problems in their charges. It would be a type of discipline constructive rather than destructive in its emphasis. Conceived in its relation to the entire problem of prison management it would appear merely as a minor and incidental item in a broader program of positive achievement.

CHAPTER XXI

THE REORIENTATION OF PRISONERS

THE constructive possibilities of prison life center around those activities that help prisoners to get their social bearings. They have failed because they had a poor notion of their relations to their fellow men. They may have been loyal to their little world but not to the larger group of which they are also a part. They have lacked perspective. What they need is not rehabilitation but reorientation. They need to get a better sense of proportion in meeting their rights and duties in human society.[1] What we should like to have them achieve is not compulsory good behavior in confinement but voluntarily decent behavior when constraint is removed. This would often require basic changes in the attitudes and habits of prison inmates. Education, religion, recreation, medicine, and work are the factors in which we now place a somewhat shaky trust to further this socializing process.

THE AIMS OF PRISON EDUCATION

PRISON education has a threefold task: to combat the poor habits of thought and action that lie behind all criminal acts, to overcome the deteriorating influences in prison life itself, and to build a positive, constructive approach that will give prisoners a workable basis for successful living upon their discharge. The entire prison régime should contribute to these ends. In practice only the academic and trade schools,

---

[1] The same criticism applies to many other types of individuals who with equal sincerity and narrowness display a fervent and socially harmful loyalty to families, businesses, fraternities, political parties, religious denominations, and many other groups.

the libraries, and the religious exercises are consciously regarded as of educational value in most prisons. To them is relegated the constructive orientation of prisoners.

THE PROCESSES OF PRISON EDUCATION

A SENSE of social responsibility cannot be forced upon prisoners like a strait-jacket. It requires, in truth, the education (L. *e*, out, + *duco*, lead), the leading out of the possibilities that lie within. It accompanies the maturing of the personality. Incentives may stimulate its growth. Guidance may be a trellis for it to cling to. The dynamics of the situation remain within the person.

Sublimation is the process by which the education of adult prisoners may be advanced. Prisoners must be attracted by new interests, new outlets for their energies, new loyalties. Only the substitution of a more intriguing world than the one in which they live can induce them to leave the old one behind. Knowledge of new opportunities and an intellectual recognition of the advantages of forsaking crime are not sufficient for reformation. Criminals must begin to act differently, to build new habits of work and play that will be more satisfying than the faulty behavior patterns that led to crime.

Obviously the reformation of habitual criminals is no easy task either for the criminals or their teachers. Improvement rather than cure is the best that can be hoped for in many instances. Some are hopeless until we learn more about the control of human behavior. It is always necessary to remember that the habitual criminal's approach to life is a natural and obvious one. It is as easy and as difficult to convert him as it is to convert a Democrat, a Republican, an Atheist, or a Christian to an opposite viewpoint. And the criminal can see no more advantage or reason to make the change than would the worthies who represent definite political or religious attitudes.

A second difficulty is the conflict between punishment and reformation in prisons. So long as one set of workers within a prison goes on the assumption that confinement must be made painful teachers will have an uncomfortable time overcoming the suspicions of their students. The dentist who proves the importance of preventive oral hygiene to his patients by making his naturally unpleasant treatment as vividly painful as possible is more likely to impress them with his unskilfulness than with the evils of their neglect.

A third obstacle, now being somewhat overcome, is the lack of classification of prisoners. Where all are treated alike those who are most dangerous set the plan of treatment for all, since maintaining the custody of prisoners is the first thought of every warden. All must be hampered and restricted because a few require close confinement, and many valuable resources must remain unutilized for safety's sake.

THE PRISONERS AS STUDENTS

As educational subjects prisoners are not promising. They are the failures of other institutions that had them at an earlier age. A goodly proportion of them have found school distasteful and they left it as soon as they could. The mere idea of school in prison revives unpleasant associations for them. A very few are college graduates. About ten per cent of the prison population is totally illiterate and twenty-five per cent cannot write a letter unaided nor read a daily paper. Sixy per cent of them have come from the ranks of unskilled workmen. Dr. Abraham Myerson says that when he finds a prisoner who has attained the level of reading the *Saturday Evening Post* he feels like grasping him by the hand and calling him, "Brother."

Lest the prospect, which these figures present, seem too discouraging it must be sadly admitted that they fit nearly as well the average adult population outside of prisons. The difference between the two groups is not primarily a difference in schooling or intellectual ability but of behavior patterns and attitudes. Yet Peter Kropotkin's observation [2] that the Great Russian peasant perfectly understands the talk of an educated man if it is not stuffed with words taken from foreign languages applies also to prisoners. The prisoner, like the peasant, cannot follow a series of abstract conclusions unless they are illustrated by concrete examples.

[2] P. Kropotkin, "Memoirs of a Revolutionist," p. 105.

Yet generalizations from the whole range of science can be conveyed to persons of ordinary intelligence if the teacher understands them concretely.

Every prisoner is a prospective student. The few college men within the walls now have a leisure which many college students would envy. They have the background to improve themselves in their spare hours if the prison régime would grant them the necessary facilities. The typical prisoner, who has been less favored, needs education. Unfortunately the practice of penal administrators has been to provide schooling only for those who have not passed the third or fifth grades and to limit more advanced study to those who can afford to buy correspondence courses.

THE PRESENT STATUS OF PRISON EDUCATION

No penal institution in this country today has an adequately organized and manned educational program although they vary greatly in their attainments. Often progressive and backward features struggle side by side within the same walls.

Thirteen prisons make no pretense of having an educational program. A dozen others do make a pretense — and little more. A handful have developed or are now building prison school organizations under professional direction. San Quentin, with a capable educational and religious director assisted by the Extension Division of the University of Southern California, has become pre-eminent among prisons for its educational efforts. The Wisconsin State Prison has a less extensive but helpful scheme of instruction built up through the coöperation of prison officials, the University of Wisconsin, and the State Free Library Commission. Elmira Reformatory in New York has since 1931 completely reorganized its academic and trade schools under professional direction with the purpose of rehabilitating its inmates socially and industrially at the highest possible level.[3]

Few other prisons can approach even these modest achieve-

[3] F. L. Bixby, "A New Educational Program at Elmira Reformatory," The Osborne Association, *News Bulletin*, April, 1933.

ments. Such teaching as is done is carried on by part-time men without professional training, helped by inmate assistants. Yet the work needs exceptional rather than "pick-up" teachers. It calls for men and women of high personal qualities, who understand what they teach, are alive to the rushing world about them, and who have a genuine insight into the nature of human behavior.

Little money is available for prison schools. No attention is paid to lighting, teaching equipment or study facilities. The textbooks are generally antiquated and unsuited to the needs of adult beginners. Sophisticated but uneducated men are given primary instruction from ancient primers considered too naïve for modern kindergartners. Austin Mac-Cormick, who has a first hand acquaintance with every prison in the country, found a civics class presided over by an inmate instructor studying the origin and growth of communities from a lesson sheet like this:

"Watch the boys and girls as they arrive at your school and see how naturally they form little groups and begin to do things together. One group is enjoying a game of baseball, another is listening to an interesting story, while a third is working in the school garden."

Enlightenment about *Your Wonderful Body* was offered in these words:

"The flowers, butterflies, birds, squirrels, cats and dogs are all alive ; and life is after all, the most wonderful thing in the world ; but the most wonderful of all kinds of living things are men and women (and of course boys and girls)." [4]

Happily since the publication of Mr. MacCormick's book the educational work of this institution has been reorganized.

In his investigations of the educational progress of penal institutions throughout the country MacCormick has found:

"History being taught from texts that were published before the World War, and reading from primers published as far back as 1868 ; seventy-five men of all ages crammed into the only classroom in the prison, seated on backless benches without desks, taught

[4] Quoted in A. H. MacCormick, "The Education of Adult Prisoners," p. 289. The National Society for Penal Information (now the Osborne Association), publishers. Quoted by permission.

under the district school method by an earnest but untrained chaplain, and searched by guards on entering and leaving the classroom ; sixty reformatory inmates in a single room, taught by an untrained inmate under twenty years of age, with a sleepy, stupid-looking guard perched on a high stool in front of the classroom to keep order ; guards conducting classes with hickory clubs lying on their desks ; guard-teachers, after a hard day's work in the school, 'swinging a club' over their erstwhile pupils in the cell houses and mess hall ; a $130-a-month guard in charge of the educational work in a 3000-man penitentiary ; men studying in the prison of one of the wealthiest states in the country by the light of fifteen-watt bulbs ; rules forbidding prisoners attending school to have writing material of any kind in their cells ; educational 'systems' which consist of allowing prisoners, without guidance, to purchase correspondence courses far beyond their ability and to follow them without assistance ; schools that are nothing but dumping grounds for the industries, places of temporary sojourns for men who have not yet been assigned to work, or convenient roosting-places for yard gangs that are called on occasionally to unload cars of coal or other supplies ; libraries in which there are not more than a dozen up-to-date books possessing educational value ; and so on almost endlessly." [5]

PRISON LIBRARIES

LIBRARIES are usually in charge of chaplains and are incidental to their main work. The books are "hand-me-downs," out of date, few in number, and poorly classified. They represent an ill-assorted lot of reading matter, accumulated rather than selected, and consisting of any odds and ends available from annual reports to pseudo-science. Current magazines and trade journals are conspicuous by their absence. Reading guidance is seldom given and there is little correlation of shop work, academic instruction, and reading opportunities. General access to the book racks is forbidden. Books are selected from printed lists. Library appropriations are small or entirely lacking. One institution with a population of 1600 recently bought $34 worth of books in a year.

Considering the amount of time that prisoners have for reading and their persistent demand for books, the library

[5] A. H. MacCormick, *op. cit.*, pp. 42-43. Quoted by permission of the Osborne Association, publishers.

might well become one of the major educational factors in penal institutions. The need is for regular library appropriations, competent librarians, standard methods of classification, and perhaps most important of all the stimulation and guidance of inmate readers by book and magazine displays, printed reading courses, personal interviews, talks on books, and the correlation of reading suggestions with the other activities and interests of inmates.

Minnesota and Wisconsin have gone farthest in developing state prison libraries along these lines. Minnesota has an institutional librarian in charge of library work in every state institution, both penal and non-penal. She directs, helps, and encourages the inmate librarians. A fund is available for the purchase of new books.

Wisconsin through its State Free Library Commission offers prisoners the chance to get books from the state library at the expense of one-way postage. A representative of the Commission makes frequent visits to the state penal institutions, advises prisoners about reading matter, and interprets their needs to the Commission.

In 1930, John Chancellor was appointed supervisory librarian in the United States Bureau of Prisons to reorganize the antiquated libraries of the federal prison system and to make them genuinely useful agencies for the improvement of prisoners. Trained librarians were obtained to manage the several prison libraries. The book collections were overhauled and sixty per cent of the books on hand were discarded as so antiquated or so poorly and inappropriately written as to be useless. Readable modern non-fiction works to meet the needs of prisoners were carefully chosen from the 1929 list of "Readable Books in Many Subjects" published by the American Library Association. By 1933 approximately 31,000 volumes had been added to the federal prison libraries. A central loan library of 1500 volumes either too expensive or too limited in appeal for general circulation and partly for the use of staff members, was established in Bureau headquarters in Washington. Standard systems of charging and cataloging books were installed so as to make them easy to find and to obtain.

The installation of books and administrative machinery

has been accompanied by an intelligent and successful effort to arouse and guide the reading interests of prisoners. Book displays and annotated reading lists have made the books attractive. Open shelves have been provided at Lewisburg and Chillicothe and they will be introduced into the other institutions when space can be provided for them. Personal assistance has been given by librarians to prisoners in the form of suggestions for individual reading, planned reading courses, and help in the formation and guidance of study clubs.

The reorganization of the federal prison libraries has already markedly increased their usefulness. At Atlanta Penitentiary it was followed by an increase in the circulation of books of 133 per cent a month during the first ten months after the reorganization ; at Leavenworth Annex the circulation increased 141 per cent during the five months; and at Leavenworth Penitentiary during the same period the circulation increased nearly 400 per cent coincident with an increase in borrowers from 989 to 1928. By 1933 the book circulation in federal institutions ranged from 1 to 5.9 books per prisoner per month as contrasted with an average of .44 books per inhabitant per month in public libraries of cities of more than 200,000 population in 1930-31. Another interesting result of the changes in the prison library system was the increase in non-fiction circulation from 15 per cent of the total to 30 to 57 per cent of the total.[6]

VOCATIONAL TRAINING

VOCATIONAL training is not cared for in prisons any more satisfactorily than academic instruction. Reformatories make definite but limited attempts at trade instruction but in only a few of them are the courses well-organized or capably conducted. Prisons have done still less to prepare convicts to earn a living upon their discharge. Except in rare instances the only vocational training prison inmates get is whatever they learn in connection with their regular industrial work or through correspondence courses chosen and

[6] J. Chancellor, "Public Library Standards for the Federal Prisons," The Osborne Association, *News Bulletin*, April, 1933.

studied without guidance and paid for by themselves. The problem is complicated by the inability of many prisoners to profit by trade instruction. The New York Prison Survey Committee in 1920 after studying 1515 cases reported that a great deal might be accomplished vocationally with about 40 per cent of the prisoners, something might be done for another 40 per cent but the remaining 20 per cent offered little hope.

A broader interpretation of trade instruction to include any training that fits a person to hold a job would extend the range of teachable prisoners. Austin MacCormick's ingenious suggestion of a Jack-of-all-Trades course for handy men on farms is a sample of what might be done. It would include instruction in maintaining and operating farm machinery, in plumbing, electrical work, masonry, and carpentry, including the erection of small buildings. MacCormick suggests also that prisons might make contracts with outside concerns to do certain parts of their work ; for example, with a foundry to do rough casting, with a furniture factory to do finishing, or with a garage to do valve grinding, brakelining, or greasing.

Lack of funds for the purchase of trade school equipment and for the employment of capable teachers is one reason for the lack of vocational instruction in penal institutions. Another is eagerness to make prison industries profitable. Lack of diversity and training value in penal industries is a third. These are handicaps that are not likely to be overcome quickly. The chances seem fair, however, that an enlightened warden, aggressive enough to plan and begin a worthy program to teach prisoners to earn an honest living, might win an appropriation for that purpose.

No one supposes that the mastery of trade skills will turn convicts into model citizens. At best it may open up new possibilities for some prisoners and give them help in meeting the world squarely if they want to try. Within prison, men who are interested in trade instruction may unexpectedly become interested in other parts of the educational program when they find that reading, writing, and arithmetic have practical uses. Beyond question the atmosphere, the morale, of an institution would be lifted up by a wide-awake educational system.

If vocational training is to be honest it postulates, also arrangements with labor unions that will insure prisoners who have learned unionized trades, reasonable prospects of being able to use their newly acquired skills upon their discharge.

RECREATION

THE possibilities of wholesome recreation in the chain of prison resources must not be overlooked. Almost all institutions permit good conduct men to attend motion pictures or other entertainments about once a week. Prison bands orchestras and choirs are encouraged although few institutions have gone so far as to employ musical directors. Little use is made of the great possibilities in mass and group singing. Only on rare occasions do prisoners have the benefit of good music in spite of the inexpensive programs that could be given by phonograph or radio. Dramatics offer unused possibilities for both cultural and recreational development. Outdoor recreation averaging perhaps an hour a day may be a time for loafing and talking in the yard or, more rarely, an occasion for the genuine enjoyment of sports such as quoits, baseball, and track. Military drill has a recognized position in some reformatories.

Many inmates have never engaged in wholesome sport with their fellows and it is possible that the combined experience of coöperating wholeheartedly with teammates and competing with opponents for the sheer joy of the game itself, might lead some of the prisoners into new realms of experience, and, at the same time, contribute in some small measure to that training in the wise use of leisure time which is a vital necessity to men of this sort. In other words, many of them may learn for the first time the surprising fact that there is genuine fun in doing decent things.

Such play also offers an opportunity for the practical expression of the principles of square-dealing, self-sacrifice and general good sportsmanship which can be learned much more effectively here than in a classroom. Recreation also gives some opportunity for normal social relationships so lacking in prison life. Its general effect upon the mental no less than the physical health of prisoners suggests a more careful study of penal recreational possibilities than has yet been made. Organizing, teaching, and directing games of all sorts is now recognized as an occupation with its own definite techniques. It is fast becoming a specialized branch of the teaching profession, requiring a broad training and a guiding philosophy. Its aim is to find recreational opportunities for every person adapted to his physical, social, and economic condition. A recreational program of this sort that will have something to offer to all of the prisoners is needed in prisons.

RELIGIOUS WELFARE

RELIGIOUS instruction has been a part of prison life from the beginning of the penitentiary system. At one time Bibles were the only reading matter permitted to prisoners, and the only teaching they received was that given by the chaplain whose aim was to convert prisoners to a Christian way of life. As the uselessness of formal preaching became apparent chaplains began to busy themselves with the general welfare of the prisoners. The administration of prison libraries, the publication of prison papers, and to a lesser degree the administration of prison schools, is still in their hands.

When a newcomer arrives at the prison he is usually interviewed by the chaplain who tries to discover his religious interests and who invites him to attend religious services. Outside ministers, priests, and rabbis also have access to prisoners of their several faiths for whom they also conduct services of worship about once a week. The resident chaplain may conduct a general service, direct a Sunday School and in some cases teach an evening class in religion or social ethics. There is a marked tendency now for chaplains to do social work with the families of prisoners in an effort to help both the prisoner and his relatives to become adjusted to the problems that imprisonment has brought and to prepare both the prisoner and his friends outside against the day of release.

The value of a prison chaplain depends in great measure upon the caliber of the man rather than upon his creed. Many hardened prisoners are unconvinced that they are any worse than the majority of their fellowmen outside. They are willing to debate the point. They may be induced to change their opinions. However, no formal preaching, no recitation of theological dogmas nor of moral platitudes will suffice to turn the trick. Against conventional assumptions they are set. One who would unsettle their convictions must be absolutely straightforward and honest in talk and in action, tolerant, sincerely interested in the men, energetic, and able. A chaplain with these qualifications might become an example and an inspiration of no small value to those among whom he would work.

The office of chaplain suffers because it is a minor office not likely to attract men especially suited for it. Consequently it does not receive the respect and interest of the prisoners that might be aroused were the office adequately supported by church bodies outside. A step towards improvement might be taken if resident chaplains were selected by a committee representing the wardens and the governing bodies of the several church organizations in a state. It would then be the duty of that committee to make regular, perhaps quarterly, visits to each penal institution to inquire into religious work among the prisoners, to interpret their needs to the churches outside, and to gain support for the chaplain in his work. Such a plan would not only improve the quality of religious service within penal institutions but would serve to educate churchgoers outside to a better understanding of their responsibilities towards prisoners, particularly upon their release. The prison chaplain himself may contribute much towards this end by accepting opportunities to speak to groups outside of the institution.

PRISON LABOR

PRISON labor has served several functions. In the days of the wearisome crank and the treadwheel its aim was punishment of convicts. When the state thought it could make money out of its unpaid laborers prison work was organized for profit. Labor intended to train men to earn an honest living upon discharge is a third notion, stressed long ago by the Quakers, that has always hovered discreetly in the background. All of these factors, emphasized in varying degrees, are represented in the practices of modern prisons which somehow hope to punish men, teach them trades, and make money with them all at once.

The peculiar circumstances surrounding prisoners adds to the problem of how to use their labor. The prison does not choose its workmen but must take whom it gets. Men are sent not because they want work nor have desirable work abilities but because they have been convicted of crimes. Many of them have never held a regular job, do not know how to work, and would not be hired by a private employer in ordinary circumstances. They are unclassified, rugged and sickly, laborers and white collar men, stupid and bright. They are paid little in some places, nothing in many. They cannot strike, resign, nor be discharged. Essentially they are slaves. Labor turnover is independent of conditions within the prison industry. Their relations to free labor and to manufacturers outside of prison walls are difficult to settle satisfactorily. The possibilities of escape influence the kinds of work they may do and the tools that can be put into their hands.

From the economic angle the handicaps of prison industry have, except in special instances, proved insuperable. Only Minnesota, Mississippi, and West Virginia have money-making prisons. In most of the other states they are not even self-supporting. Instead they cost taxpayers a mint of money. Architecturally, few prisons are suited for manufacturing. Their industrial equipment is antiquated and insufficient. They are not staffed with business men although the prevailing state-managed systems of prison labor require a business ability not necessary when prisoners were leased to contractors. Some prisoners cannot be made to work. Soldiering on the job has become a fine art. In 1929 the New York Crime Commission reported that "Every penal institution in the state shows insufficiency of plant and a waste of opportunity that would not be tolerated in any going concern in the world of business." [7] In this respect New York's prisons are not unique.

Many prisoners, who recall the ponderous phrase "sentenced to hard labor," must afterwards laugh at the joke.

[7] "Report of the New York State Crime Commission, 1929," p. 134.

Wardens are hard pushed to find anything for them to do to keep them from sheer idleness. Often several men are set to do what one could easily accomplish. In 1928, sixteen per cent of the 36,798 men in 27 prisons were unemployed. Of a convict population of 10,401 in New York on December 31, 1928, it was reported that "more than 2500 are idle nearly the whole time, or occupied by time-killing chores, or doubled or tripled into what should be one-man jobs."[8] Without occupation moral and physical deterioration of convicts is rapid, their behavior is troublesome, and their rehabilitation impossible. ✓

In the face of these obstacles there have been six chief ways of organizing prison labor in the United States. These are known as the lease, contract, piece-price, public account, state-use, and public works systems. At present about three-fifths of our prison products are made under the three systems of public control last mentioned and two-fifths under the contract and piece-price systems. Each has advantages and disadvantages. Ultimately the choice of best methods can be made only when the functions of prison labor are agreed upon and boldly carried out.

THE LEASE SYSTEM

THE lease system, a modification of the old English practice of selling the jail concession appeared in this country in Massachusetts in 1798 and thereafter in several other states. It never came into prominence until Reconstruction days when the southern states, which were without prisons or money to build them, accepted it as a means of solving their prison problems. Prisoners were leased to contractors who carried them off to the lumber forests or turpentine camps from which they could not easily escape.

Under the lease system contractors had entire control over the labor, housing, feeding, and discipline of the men. The more work they could get out of them and the more cheaply they could maintain them the greater their profits. The state by transferring its responsibilities received an assured income. Economically the lease system has been the most

[8] "Report of the New York State Crime Commission, 1929," p. 138.

uccessful way discovered to use prison labor but its profit as come through literally driving convicts to death with rutal punishments. The scandals that leaked out of prison amps, where men were disposed of at the mercy of their essees, has caused the virtual abandonment of the lease system. Only in Louisiana, North Carolina, and Arkansas is t permitted by law. Its complete disappearance seems imninent.

THE CONTRACT LABOR SYSTEM

UNDER the contract labor system the labor of prisoners is old to contractors who use the prisons as their factories. They furnish the necessary machinery, raw materials, and upervision. They pay the state a fixed price for the labor of each convict. The prison officials retain the power to guard and discipline the inmate workers.

The contract labor system has so many serious faults that here has been a growing opposition to it. Some of its faults might be mitigated if government representatives were a bit more perspicacious in looking out for their interests when they bargain with contractors. However, unless contractors are given unusual advantages they are not apt to seek prison labor. At present contract labor is illegal in federal penal institutions and in those of seventeen states. Winthrop Lane has summarized the charges against the system based upon ample evidence as follows:

"1. The contractor's interest in profit leads him to exact as much labor as possible from the prisoners.

"2. If necessary, he employs the disciplinary machinery of the prison to enforce a task system which may be inhuman and cruel.

"3. To secure the support of the guards, he finds means to make them personally and financially interested in the amount of work done by the prisoners.

"4. This interest leads to corruption of guards and, not infrequently, wardens, of which there is evidence on record.

"5. The system gives the few contractors who have prison contracts an undue interest in the type of prison warden and prison guards employed in the prison and leads to the use of influence to eliminate those prison officials who are not desirable from the contractor's special point of view.

"6. It tends to place the interests of the contractor above the interests of the prisoners and to make the prison organization, which is a public institution charged with a public purpose, serve private ends.

"7. The existence of the contract system has led in many prisons to the introduction of contraband, and thus to corruption of prisoners and demoralization of the prison régime." [9]

On the other hand, contract shops, in addition to bringing in to the state a greater income, are apt to be more efficiently managed than state-supervised shops and more likely to be run at the same tempo as those outside. In some of them a system of bonus payments for exceeding minimum work requirements is proving an effective substitute for punishments.

At present twenty-five institutions use the contract system. Together they produce upwards of $18,000,000 worth of goods which is about one-quarter of the total prison production. Since these goods are sold in the open market in competition with the products of manufacturers who do not have a kindly state to provide them with factory buildings and cheap labor, unfavored manufacturers particularly in the garment, furniture, textile, cordage, and shoe industries have complained vigorously against the practice which they consider morally and economically indefensible. Their efforts have recently borne fruit in the passage of the Hawes-Cooper Act, effective in 1934, which, unless declared unconstitutional, will seriously restrict the contract labor system by giving states the power to prevent within their borders the sale of prison-made goods from other states.

Although the Hawes-Cooper Act may curtail it, it certainly will not destroy the contract system. It is merely a permissive law. Shipments of goods into the states, probably many, that will not take advantage of the act, will still go on. Many of the seventeen states, Connecticut, Delaware, Indiana, Iowa, Kentucky, Maine, Maryland, Nebraska, New Hampshire, Oklahoma, Rhode Island, Tennessee, Vermont, Virginia, West Virginia, Wisconsin and Wyoming that produce most of the contract and piece-work goods are not

[9] National Commission on Law Observance and Enforcement, "Report on Penal Institutions, Probation and Parole," pp. 83-84.

apt to pass such legislation. Even if every state should stop the entry of prison-made goods, contractors would still sell them in the state of manufacture. The likely result would be the displacement of larger manufacturers who rely upon an interstate business by smaller contractors contented with a local business.

However the Hawes-Cooper Act represents a tremendous, if selfish, victory for American labor since through it the federal government for the first time gives official national authorization to legislation aimed to curb prison industries. The American Federation of Labor has already begun to follow up its advantage by introducing into state legislatures amendments to the existing laws prohibiting the shipment of prison made goods into the state for sale or exchange. By 1933 four states had passed such legislation. Not only is the Federation working to limit prison industry to exclusive state use but it wants to exclude even from that system some of the more powerful trades such as the construction industry. The trend is obviously to squeeze the life blood out of prison labor schemes.

THE PIECE-PRICE SYSTEM

UNDER the piece-price system contractors furnish the raw materials and pay a fixed price for each piece of finished goods. The machinery is provided by the state. Full responsibility for the prisoners including supervision of their work remains in the hands of the prison staff. Some relief from excessive work pressure is achieved by this system since the contractor pays the same price per article regardless of how long it takes to make it. The chief incentive and opportunity of the contractors to drive prisoners is thus removed. In all other respects the piece-price method has the flaws of the contract system, including, from the standpoint of other manufacturers, unfair market competition.

THE PUBLIC ACCOUNT SYSTEM

UNDER the public account system private contractors are entirely blotted out of the picture. Instead the state turns socialistic and goes into business itself. The state develops its own prison industries, finances them, buys raw materials, manufactures the products, sells them in the open market, and receives any profit. Louis Robinson suggests that the chief value of the public account system over the piece-price system accrues to the politician who is able to tell the public that private interests neither control nor profit by prison labor.

Three serious objections are raised against the public account system :

1. It tends to destroy similar outside industries and throw free laborers out of work since they cannot meet the unfair competition of the state using unpaid or exceedingly cheap forced labor.

2. The tendency is to make it difficult for released prisoners to find work nearby for which they have been trained in prison since local outside competitors tend to be forced out of business in proportion to the success of the prison industry.

3. The emphasis upon building up a large, specialized, and profitable prison industry makes the training of inmates in line with their interests and potential opportunities after release unlikely.

At Stillwater, Minnesota, usually cited as successful with the public account system, the prisoners make binder twine and farm machinery for which, in that agricultural state, there is an ample demand. The absence of competitive manufacturers within the state precludes the chance of unfair local rivalry but limits the market of outside manufacturers to that part of the demand that is in excess of the state's capacity to supply. From the economic standpoint the $25,000 net annual profit is a commendable achievement. The inability of this system to prepare men to earn an honest living upon their release makes the public account policy questionable from the standpoint of social welfare including both the convicts and those among whom they are to be freed.

In practice the full force of these objections is not felt because prison managed industries are not sufficiently alert or efficient to drive manufacturers out of business although they may be a thorn in the flesh to them.

Just how harmful prison competition is cannot easily be ascertained. Although the total volume of prison made goods is less than 1 per cent of the free production except in the manufacture of linen goods (31.2%), binder twine (23.9%), shirts (5.1%), jute bagging (13.67%), and road contracts (3.27%), the prison goods may be an important factor in a local market especially if marketing methods are faulty.[10]

Moreover, prison lines are apt to be so concentrated that it is not safe to compare them with the more generalized production of free labor. The free production of men's shirts, for example, is twenty times that of the prisons, but the prisons confine their efforts to work shirts and in that specialized field they have apparently offered stiff opposition to outside manufacturers. Incidentally, the tendency of prisons to limit their work to making coarse goods because of the abilities of their labor supply must be kept in mind whenever it is suggested that prisoners should manufacture goods not made in the United States but imported. The idea is an old one and it was considered along with other suggestions by the Commissioner of Labor in a classic report[11] issued in 1886 in which he pointed out that our imports are of fine quality goods, that our prisoners, as a group, are not able to make.

THE STATE USE SYSTEM

UNDER the state use system prisons manufacture goods for the exclusive use of other state institutions. It is most common in the industrial East and Middle West. In principle it pleases manufacturers and laborers by limiting unfair and obvious competition with them although it reduces the size of their market since the state no longer is a purchaser of the goods that its prisoners can make. Also it makes price cutting unnecessary in meeting the competition of prison-made goods. The Associated Manufacturers and the American Federation of Labor have turned from hostility to friendliness towards the state use system as a policy. However, when specific cases arise the particular unions or

[10] See tables in L. N. Robinson, "Should Prisoners Work," pp. 55-58.
[11] U. S. Commissioner of Labor, 2nd annual report, 1886, entitled "Convict Labor," p. 388.

manufacturers affected are apt to rise up in opposition. Their delegates admit that prisoners must work — but not at their jobs. There is no doubt, however, that the difficulties arising between unions and prison managers could be lessened by an intelligent attempt at local coöperation initiated probably by the prison warden.

Another obstacle to the state use system lies in the hesitancy of state institutions to buy prison-made goods on the ground of inefficient service and sometimes because prison goods are of inferior quality. Department heads dislike to have their shopping restricted to one manufacturer. They like freedom to make their own choices. Sometimes their specifications for goods are so drawn that prisons cannot readily supply them. On the other hand, prisons lag behind commercial producers in adopting new styles.

Massachusetts has made headway under the state use plan by forbidding auditors to pass bills for goods purchased by public institutions without a release from the State Department of Correction. The state use market is fairly large but it has not yet been efficiently cultivated. With proper legislative support and a business-like manufacturing and sales management for prison industries there is reason to believe that the state use market could be considerably expanded.

Expansion would also require diversification which is an advantage from the standpoint of vocational training for prisoners. Recently the National Committee on Prisons and Prison Labor has been supporting a states use system as a modification of the state use system. Under states use the interstate sale of goods to public institutions would be fostered. If this were successful a broader market would result but at the expense of diversification since each state would tend to develop larger specialized industries. The states use plan also would require a degree of coöperation and stability now lacking among state governments.

THE PUBLIC WORKS SYSTEM

THE public works plan is a modification of the state use system. It applies to the use of prisoners on state construction jobs such as building construction, swamp drainage, re-forestation, land reclamation, and road building. It has in some measure escaped the hostility of labor for two reasons : it does not compete with men in organized trades or with manufacturers except in building construction, and its competition with free labor is kept dark by the absence of prison-made goods on the market. The chief limitations are that work can only be provided for those convicts who can be properly controlled outside of prison walls and that in some states weather conditions make all-year work on such projects difficult if not impossible. The first of these obstacles does not now seem so large as in the past.

There are undeveloped possibilities in the state use and public works systems. They have not yet had a fair trial anywhere although several states are now making progress with them. They stand before a market capable of expansion. New York optimistically reports a market that aggregates about twenty million dollars, for which two million dollars' worth of goods or ten per cent, are now manufactured and furnished by prison industries.[12] Massachusetts has by law extended her state use market by requiring her cities and towns as well as her state departments to buy prison goods manufactured in styles and qualities agreed upon by the purchasers at an annual meeting. The annual prison production in Massachusetts now reaches a million dollars in a market conservatively estimated at three million dollars. In three years Alabama has built six hundred miles of graded roads and twenty-nine miles of concrete surface roads of the first quality using about 1400 men a day with a monthly profit of $6.76 per convict. New Jersey has built from seven to ten miles of first quality re-enforced concrete roads a year since 1925 using 110 to 150 prisoners housed in barracks at the job. The opportunity for extending the public works system is right at hand. With little equipment and much benefit, road building, and reforestation projects and the like could be developed for minimum security prisoners in every state.

Yet in practice neither state use nor its modification, the public works system, have been altogether successful. The

[12] "Report of the New York State Crime Commission, 1929," p. 135.

disadvantages already recited have proved too great. The poor quality of prison-made goods, limited markets, lack of coöperation among state departments and absence of competent business management and salesmanship have made the state use scheme in fact a failure. New York has tried it for nearly four decades without success. Its state departments evade the law intended to induce the purchase of its prison-made goods while hundreds of its convicts remain idle. In Ohio and Pennsylvania a similar failure exists. In the East which places the greatest reliance upon it, only Massachusetts and New Jersey have made a barely passable go of it, and Massachusetts takes advantage of a law permitting its surplus production to be sold in the open market.

Some small states are economically unable to support well-run prison industries as state enterprises without placing an unwarranted burden upon their taxpayers. State managed industries have proved far less productive than those that are privately managed in prisons. As Howard Gill has pointed out in his analysis of the report of the United States Bureau of Labor Statistics on *"Convict Labor in* 1923,"[13] 9660 convicts under private management produced $30,-646,862 worth of goods as compared with $27,841,718 worth produced by 32,376 (three and a third times as many) convicts under state management. According to the 1932 report of the U. S. Bureau of Labor Statistics, 13,436 convicts under private management produced $16,582,262 worth of goods as compared with $33,628,057 worth (twice the value) produced by 50,143 (three and seven-tenths times as many) convicts under state management.[14] Even when productivity in the same trades under private and state management is contrasted, private control is nearly four times more efficient than public control.

Not only has the state use system proved productively inefficient but it has led to the displacement of men on productive work and an ever increasing number on maintenance

[13] H. B. Gill, "The Prison Labor Problem," *The Annals*, Vol. 157, p. 88. See also U. S. Bureau of Labor Statistics, "Convict Labor in 1923," Bul. 372.

[14] Analysis based on U. S. Bureau of Labor Statistics, "Prison Labor in the United States in 1932," table 2, p. 6.

work in semi-idleness. In view of these facts the supposed advantages in the training of prisoners offered by public control are apt to be more fanciful than real, even the advantages for those actually employed being offset by their slipshod methods of work.

The public works system employed most commonly in the South has been associated with the use of chain gangs in stripes under guard along the highways. The problems of portable housing, sanitation, discipline, and escapes have not been satisfactorily met. In the North selection of prisoners has made stripes and chains unnecessary on road workers. In the West, California has been able to use prisoners in highway camps under guard and the federal government is now expanding its program along similar lines.

There is ground for the belief that the failures under the state use and public work systems are due to poor management rather than to the plans themselves. It is probably true that under wise administrators many of the factors that now bring failure could be met and overcome. But any single rigidly outlined plan is inherently narrow. No matter how wise an executive might be he would be restricted by its principles.

On the other hand, every scheme that is outlined has advantages which might be useful in certain situations. Some prison goods might at times be sold in the open market without serious damage to outside laborers. The states use system has already been anticipated by some interstate sale of goods. New Jersey, Michigan, Iowa, Washington, and Oklahoma have all sold prison-made automobile registration plates to other states. Even the lease system, admittedly intolerable under ordinary circumstances, might find a modified application as in the placement of women prisoners as maids or house-servants.

Considering both humanitarian and economic needs it would seem most desirable to have a combination of systems under state management with power to manufacture goods for state or states use, to sell surplus goods on the market for the public account, to develop public works and ways, and to employ labor for farming, institutional construction and other maintainance work. Only with the flexibility inherent in such a scheme is there hope of keeping all able prisoners at work.

Many states operate under such a combination of plans now. Because of the obstacles encountered reformers have tried to pick out a better, a single, an ideal system. When its failure is pointed out they say it is due to the management and not to defects in the plan. But the failure of a combination of plans is also due chiefly to a lack of business acumen in prison wardens. The remedy is not to hamper them by restricting them to a single supposedly ideal system but to retain the broadness and flexibility of the combination and work towards an intelligent, courageous, and independent prison management.

PRISON WAGES

THE matter of wage payments to prisoners is one that cannot be dodged in any discussion of prison industries. Opposed at first and even declared unconstitutional, wage payments to prisoners have been authorized in some form by thirty-eight states and by the federal government. Penologists, both here and abroad, have agreed upon the practical value of the wage payment. It offers an incentive to work that is just as powerful in prisoners as in free men. It gives a sense of solid, measurable accomplishment that may be of no little importance in rebuilding a life.

No state grants a released prisoner a sum of money adequate to fit him out and tide him over until he can find a job. Yet in most cases the alternatives to work are starvation or a relapse into crime. Even a small savings account available upon release is a wise and practical provision for a successful new start. Many prisoners have dependents outside to whose aid they would gladly contribute and who need their help. The satisfaction of being able to care in some measure for their own families is a factor in the improved morale of prisoners that must not be overlooked.

On the other hand, the conventional state practice of caring for the dependents of prisoners is a substitute for wage payment without the spur of having the prisoner support his own. Instead it assures the lazy convict that his dependents will be fed whether he works or not. Payment of regular wages for daily work offers a positive opportunity for placing some responsibility in this matter safely upon the shoulders of prisoners. It is another step towards making the burdens of prison life comparable to those that convicts will have to face after prison. Such positive factors in their rehabilitation are too few to be lightly discounted.

Although the principle of paying prisoners the standard wage paid for their work outside has been tacitly recognized by labor and advocated by reformers there is little chance that prisoners will soon, if ever, be able to support themselves and their families by their prison wages. Our present naïve methods of prison accounting make it difficult to separate the expense of prison manufacturing that comes because the men are prisoners as well as workers from the purely industrial costs of production. Yet the inefficiency of ordinary institutional shops, restrictions upon the type of labor available and upon the expansion of prison industries all make it impossible for prisons to pay normal wages even if they are based upon the purely industrial costs of production.

Of course there is the possibility of making payment without regard to costs. Many prisons now pay their small wages on a sliding scale dependent upon the conduct grade that a man has attained and not upon his productivity as a worker. The difference goes into the cost of maintaining penal institutions and is charged up to the taxpayer. If these small wages now paid were increased to match the normal rate outside it is doubtful if the citizens would accept the inevitable burden.

Those institutions that pay wages do not follow a uniform system. Some pay wages by the hour, day, month, or piece ; others give a bonus for work done above a stated amount ; a few pay in "good time" ; [15] and some use combinations of these methods. Money wages are generally small, the range being from a few cents a week to the relatively munificent sum of $40 a month, reported by Robinson as paid to a prison dietitian in the Iowa State Penitentiary. Gen-

[15] A credit in time to be deducted from the minimum sentence in payment for work done.

erally wages do not exceed 10 to 25 cents a day. Even small amounts however have proved strikingly effective and not without economic benefit to the state. Robinson cites several instances in which there was a marked increase in morale and productive efficiency following the establishment of reasonable wage scales. At Sing Sing production increased on two separate occasions when new wage schedules were announced although they were not put into effect.[16]

THE FUTURE OF PRISON INDUSTRY

IMPROVEMENT in the organization of prison labor must be based upon a recognition of the pertinent realities. These are four in number: the prisoners are going to be released, their terms on the average are short, a heavy proportion of them are common laborers, about half of them can be controlled with minimum or medium security provisions. Therefore, it would seem that the primary object of prison work should be to join with every other phase of institutional training in a coöperative effort to fit convicts as well as possible for their inevitable freedom. Profits should be incidental to reformation. The primary job of a prison is to make men not money.

Financially it is unfair to expect prison industries to support the tremendous overhead of a penal establishment in addition to the normal charges of industry. As Howard Gill has pointed out the ideal of self-supporting prisons must be abandoned for one of self-supporting industries. Probably we ought also to abandon the notion that industries can be both vocational and productive. Training should be relegated to trade schools. Industries may then be run with financial benefit to the prisons. As in any normal business this would involve the aid of trained industrial engineers and shop assistants to relieve the warden of impossible tasks. Such a scheme is now having a trial in Massachusetts, New Jersey and Pennsylvania.

If under a plan of this sort, prison industries are established with due regard to the future opportunities of the

[16] L. N. Robinson, "Should Prisoners Work," p. 212.

men, they may tend to develop in the prisoners work habits and standards reasonably like those needed for holding similar outside jobs. Linked with a system of prison trade instruction, work in prison industries, so conceived, might be thought of as a period of trial employment for those who had been given vocational instruction in prison classrooms.

FITTING PRISONS TO THE PRISONER

In any discussion of prison problems there is always a tendency to forget the all-important central figure, the prisoner. Outside we have in theory accepted the concept of fitting the school to the child. In industry where work theoretically represents the free choice of workingmen they are expected to meet the demands of their jobs. Prisoners, however, like school children, do not choose the institutions in which they are confined. The concept of fitting the prisons to the prisoners is therefore applicable. It involves a broad analysis and classification of prison populations with reference to their educational, industrial, and reformative possibilities.

Many institutions now make use of psychiatrical examinations in placing individual convicts in work positions or classes. The psychiatric clinic at Sing Sing, for example, examines all prisoners upon their entrance and the federal government has begun to do likewise with its charges. Psychiatrical examinations, however, emphasize personality traits and problems and unless these findings are organized so as to show administrators what types of prison schools or industries to develop they will not be particularly effective in making over our prisons to fit the convicts who are in them. Where routine psychiatrical examinations are given, however, the facts that the administration needs to know are there waiting to be gathered together and focused.

Doctors V. C. Branham and Amos Baker have devised one such classification scheme for New York which may be cited as an illustration of a method of grouping prisoners in specialized institutions as a means of treating them more effectively:

ADMINISTRATIVE CLASSIFICATION [17]

(This classification is flexible — An inmate may readily move from one grade to another)

Grouping of Inmates	Type of Inmate Belonging to this Group	Type that should not be assigned to this Group
I — *Colony Group* (Placed in colonies, road camps and other *types of open prison construction*) (a) First choice (b) Second choice (2nd choice need more restriction — choice made upon basis of crime, unelapsed time and general conduct) (Colony Group housed in the medium and minimum security type of prison construction)	Young occasional offender who has served at least half of his time. Those who have short, unelapsed time to serve, and have had excellent conduct records while in prison. Middle-aged inmates with good family connections as evidenced by social investigation and active interest in inmate during his incarceration. Many of those men have served considerable time and now show evidence of reaching a stabilization period usually evidenced in the middle aged. Inmates who have shown ability to assume responsibility in various tasks assigned during prison stay. Many of the so-called trusties belong to this group. The accidental offender likewise falls in this category. The stable, high-grade feeble-minded type which has served sufficient time to be suitably studied.	Those having warrants pending. The repeated sex offender of vicious type. Drug addicts and alcoholics whose stay in prison has been comparatively short. The assaultive types. Many of these are also psychopathic. The infirm or physically unfit. No inmate should be released to a colony until at least one year has been served in the walled prison (except Reformatories). Lifers should be admitted to colony group with greatest caution. Long timers, especially, if possessed of a long record.

[17] Dr. V. C. Branham, "The Classification of the Prison Inmates of New York State." Reprinted by permission.

Grouping of Inmates	Type of Inmate Belonging to this Group	Type that should not be assigned to this Group
II — *Restricted Group* (Within prison proper)		
(a) *Temporarily Restricted* (Schooling and industrial training emphasized)	All new admissions are detained in segregation for classification and observation in the Reception Building for a period of 3 weeks to 1 month.	Psychopaths whose history shows instability of long duration. The infirm and physically unfit.
	Inmates are detained in prison population generally speaking, for at least half of their time but in special cases an inmate may be released for colony at an earlier date.	
(This group housed temporarily in maximum security type of prison construction)	The young, occasional or first offender with a moderately short sentence is especially suitable for this group (later to be advanced to the colony group with enlarged privileges).	
(b) *Prolonged Restriction* (In some instances temporary solitary confinement is necessary, but majority will be housed in modernized cell structures and be given opportunity for daily w o r k in industrial units)	Lifers and other long timers. Those over whom a warrant is pending. Troublesome types that refuse to adapt themselves to prison routine (care must be taken to eliminate the psychopathic from this group).	Psychopaths, even if they are troublesome. Young offenders who are anxious to keep up reputation of being "hard-boiled." (If prison regime is adequate these inmates rapidly move into the temporarily restricted group.)
(This group housed in maximum security type of prison construction)	In this group are included inmates guilty of inciting riots, those who have committed murder or other vicious assaults.	

ADMINISTRATIVE CLASSIFICATION—Continued

Grouping of Inmates	Type of Inmate Belonging to this Group	Type that should not be assigned to this Group
III — *Psychiatric Group* (Special psychiatric unit should be made available as a treatment and study center)		
(a) *Extensive Treatment Group*	Those showing marked mental upsets either temporary in nature, or prolonged. (The latter group, awaiting transfer to Dannemora State Hospital). Many in this group are excited for the time being and require sedative treatment, or use of continuous baths, etc. They are essentially bad cases.	
(b) *Observation Group* (Observation and day room facilities in psychiatric unit)	Those who do not require medication or bed treatment but because of peculiarities in conduct are in need of observation and study for a period of one week to a month.	
(c) *Out-patient Group* (This corresponds to the dispensary group in the hospital unit)	Inmates in the general prison population who may request interview with Psychiatrist. Inmates who are in need of further study or advice after being released from the admitting unit into the general prison population. A number of inmates requiring regular treatment for neuro-syphilis. This will be done under the direction of the Psychiatrist within the hospital unit, because other syphilitic types, not nervous in origin, will be also treated there.	

to this Group

IV — *Hospital Group*

(a) *Those physically ill*

Cases requiring bed treatment, convalescence from illness, dispensary types, minor and major surgery, etc. Contagious cases must be segregated.

(b) *Aged and Incapacitated*

The great majority of these cases never need active hospital treatment, since their incapacity consists largely of a missing arm, leg or other deformity, or advanced age. A number of infirm, however, need constant care for chronic illnesses, such as cardiac disease, leg ulcers, tumors, etc. Because of lowered resistance this group is more subject to minor afflictions than the average prison inmates.

(c) *Tubercular Group*

Arrested cases of tuberculosis (*i. e.,* tuberculosis is quiescent) should be carefully watched but kept in the general prison population. As soon as signs of an active process are noted (either in arrested or new cases of Tuberculosis) the inmate should be transferred to the Sanitarium in Clinton Prison.

V — *The Defective Delinquent*

(Housed in separate institution at Napanoch, N. Y., limited only to this type of males. A special institution is recommended for defective delinquent females)

Low-grade feeble-minded delinquents, higher-grade feeble-minded delinquents who are unstable mentally.

Recidivists who have deteriorated mentally. (In general, the feeble-minded recidivist who is mentally unstable.)

VI — *The Insane Delinquent*

Inmates obviously insane.

The insane delinquent.

Inmates of normal intelligence.

High grade feeble-minded delinquents who are stable mentally.

The psychopathic delinquent (*i. e.* disturbed mentally but not actually insane).

The psychopathic delinquent.

An actual examination of the male populations of Sing Sing, Auburn, Great Meadow, Clinton, Elmira, and Napanoch in the autumn of 1930, in accordance with this plan, showed that the prisoners should have been grouped for treatment as follows: [18]

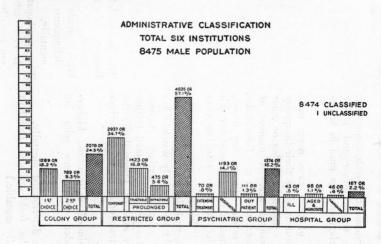

Although New York is well up in the van in providing specialized institutions for prisoners, the facilities for handling them properly in accordance with their classification were not available in 1930. Hospital care was inadequately provided except at Sing Sing and Napanoch. Less than half of those who could be kept under conditions of minimum security were being so kept. New York was therefore handling its prisoners less effectively and at greater expense than it might have done.

The implications of a classification of prisoners by this plan are far reaching. They suggest radical changes in methods of dealing with convicts. Very few states have gone so far as New York. Many of them send all of their adult prisoners to the one type of prison: a huge bastille of steel and concrete. Obviously that is a silly procedure if the prisoners are of such varied sorts as the New York study indicates. Furthermore it is economically costly. An old-time prison is the most expensive place in which a person can

[18] Dr. V. C. Branham, *op. cit.*, p. 18. Reprinted by permission of Dr. V. C. Branham.

be segregated from his fellows. Such prisons cost from $4000 to $6000 per cell to build and their maintenance costs are heavy. At this one point alone taxpayers are wasting a pretty penny for providing maximum security prisons for men who might just as well be kept in medium security prisons, inexpensive colonies, or permanent camps.

Classifications of this sort, when carefully done, should be most helpful. However, we must be on our guard against considering diagnosis and classification of prisoners as a "cure all." They are in fact merely the useful and necessary steps to the real business of a prison which is to do the constructive case work with convicts that is suggested by our understanding of them. Some of our largest prisons that are well administered have a tendency to lose sight of their charges as individuals and there is little likelihood that the reformation of prisoners can be brought about merely through the operation of an efficient prison machine.

Actually we are forced to confess that we know next to nothing about reformation as a process although we often use the term as freely and with as little meaning as some evangelists use the word "conversion." Apparently some prisoners who have reformed have simply bumped their heads against a stone wall so often that at last it has dawned upon them that they are not successful criminals. They intend to go straight thereafter, not because they have experienced a change of heart but because they have failed as criminals.

Undoubtedly the passage of time is an important factor in so-called reformation, for the underworld professions and the underworld business machine have their cast-offs as have the legitimate professions and industries. A man who has not practised his criminal trade and who has been largely out of touch with the developments in a rapidly moving world for the five or ten years of his imprisonment suffers a handicap, in competing with younger men, that is apt to make his continuance in crime difficult. The fact that he is older in years is an additional burden and if, as often happens, he has deteriorated physically and morally as well, his "reformation" may be assured by his sheer inability to carry on the only trade he knows. For some young criminals with reasonably good qualities, segregation from the world for a few years gives them an opportunity to reach the stability of maturity following the turmoil of adolescence of which their criminality was an expression.

Undoubtedly some prisoners leave their cells genuinely reformed in the sense that by painful reflection they have come to an inner acceptance of a socially higher set of ethical standards. They have in truth caught the glimmer of a new road. Why, we do not know. Probably, in many instances, it has been a single experience that has touched the convict at a time when he has been susceptible to it because of contiguous experiences. The shift may have to do with a crisis in the affairs of his family outside of the prison walls, to a chance remark of a fellow prisoner, the behavior of a shop foreman or the example of an officer.

An observer finds it difficult to disregard the notion that the chances of genuine reformation of psychologically normal prisoners are apt to be increased by the opportunities given to them for experiencing stimulating personal relations with competent and engaging leaders. Moreover these ought to be of both sexes. This implies a break in the ideal of a smooth-running machinelike prison routine that is so often the aim of the present managers of our prisons. We have already spoken of the manner in which the prison régime strips the newcomer of his individuality in that he loses his identity as a person and becomes a numbered cog in a machine. The Gluecks mention complaints on this score made by former prisoners at the Massachusetts Reformatory at Concord.[19] Some protest against the fact that no one took a personal interest in their problems during their stay in the institution. One of them has echoed the complaint of his fellows that psychiatrists have examined and classified them, have weeded out some who belong in other institutions, have used the materials so gathered for lectures and articles, but the prisoners have waited in vain for help with their individual difficulties.[20]

Since all of the problems of which the ordinary prisoner is conscious are personal, such criticisms merit serious con-

[19] S. S. and E. T. Glueck, "500 Criminal Careers," p. 324.
[20] V. F. Nelson, "Prison Days and Nights," p. 283.

sideration. After all, prisoners are not apt to concern themselves during their confinement with abstract ethical problems
nor to ponder their responsibilities towards society. Their
troubles are caused by matters much simpler and more immediate, such as their chances of getting transferred from a
factory machine to a teamster's job, and whether a younger
brother outside can be made to do his duty towards the
family, whether the girl friend is still faithful, and how
to get back at a guard who has the habit of riding prisoners.
Never have they been able to view such details with helpful
objectivity and perspective. To such persons the opportunity to express their opinions and to ask questions of a sincere neutral observer who is recognized by them as a qualified
advisor might be of inestimable value. The Gluecks, recognizing the need of this "personal touch," have suggested
that groups of inmates might be permitted to meet a few
times a week with a qualified personal advisor.

Much experimentation will doubtless be necessary to discover a workable technique for instituting the "personal
touch." Prisoners are exceedingly wary about giving any
information to persons having official relation to those in
authority. The writer's experience with a class of sixty
prisoners, with smaller groups of ten or fifteen and with individuals, leads him to believe that there might be some
advantages in using as tutors or advisors persons not directly
concerned with the administration of the prisons. If such
advisors kept a careful account of their methods so that
they could be correlated with the parole and post-parole
program of their charges, the results, regardless of difficult
problems of evaluation, in time would tend to be of inestimable value in the understanding and improvement of our
technique for the reorientation of prisoners.

WHAT PRISONERS THINK OF IMPRISONMENT

THAT prisoners derive many personal benefits from their
incarceration is attested by these men and women themselves.
A number of women prisoners at the Massachusetts Reformatory for Women have stated to the writer that they
have been helped in specific ways during their stay at Fram-

ingham. Some have received training in clerical work and stenography so that they feel that they could earn a living with these skills outside. Several have expressed their appreciation of the value to them of contacts with members of the staff. Many have received necessary medical care. Others have spoken of the advantages of the regularity of reformatory life.

In their recent study the Gluecks also found a recognition of definite advantages by the women.[21] Among them 67 were trained in homemaking, 52 were helped vocationally, 40 gained better ethical standards, 18 learned wholesome ways of using leisure, 10 habits of self-control, and 81 came to feel a deep fondness for Mrs. Hodder,[22] and 26 for the deputy superintendent.

In their study of Concord graduates, the Gluecks also found a spontaneous recognition of personal advantages. Among them 81 spoke of the deterrent effect of their imprisonment, 63 said they learned a trade or a skill, 60 mentioned the advantages of a regular routine and beneficial changes brought about in personal habits, 33 spoke of the beneficent effect of their contacts with certain officers, 17 said they profited by academic work, and 13 were benefited by medical care and exercise. Altogether, more than two-thirds of the 301 men who were willing to discuss the effects of reformatory life on themselves recognized personal benefits from their stay at Concord.[23]

On the other hand, nearly a third of the Concord men claimed that reformatory life harmed them in such ways as schooling them in crime, teaching them in bad habits, linking them with bad associates, or giving them the handicap of a prison record. Other parolees claim not to have been influenced in these ways. It is of some interest to notice that the number of favorable comments made by these men after their release from supervision overbalances the unfavorable more than two to one. Interesting also is the fact that the favorable comments were just about as numerous from prisoners who continued their criminality after supervision as

[21] S. S. and E. T. Glueck, "500 Delinquent Women," Ch. 12.
[22] At that time superintendent of the reformatory.
[23] S. S. and E. T. Glueck, op. cit., pp. 278-301.

from those who did not. Nearly 77 per cent of the unfavorable opinions however came from total failures, 12 per cent from partial failures, and 10 per cent from successes.

Some idea of the qualities of the reflections of prisoners may be gained from the following excerpts from inmates of a prison for adult males embodied in uncensored letters in the possession of the author:

Writes R. M.; "I have had time to think of what to do since I have been here and I have try to put my time in something that would show me and put me back in the world — when I get outside. I am not afraid to say I am not sorry that I was sent here for I think it has done me a lot and help me back in this world.

"My time is not so long 20 months I have put in and 9 more to go and I think that 20 months has done me good. First I have takeing up an instrument and I am a good player. But that is not what I am or care to do when I get out side. Second I was a hard guy when I fist came in here but it has show me not too be the hard guy. It has help me to control my self. I can now talk to a guy and keep my hands at my sides. That was one thing I could not to when I fist came in here. But after a boy gose down the can a few time in gets kind of hard and you seen too hate the place and then if a boy is lucky enught to go on bread and water a few time's then he knows what it is to do time. All I can say for this place is it has made a man of me. And I inten to go straight when I go out. I do not say like some of the boys when I get out I am not comeing back no for I do not know and no one knows what I may do when I do get out. But I am as far as things have gone and I say when I do get out I am going to try too to go straight. Now that I hve told what this place has done for me I am going to say a few things on things that are a hard a tuf deal to go with and the fist is. the privilege they give you it is the poorsit place I think in United States for privilege. Such as know papers no cigarettes tuf eats that three things are the hardest of all. Of course if we don't want to put up with that well don't come to a place like this leave things that don't belong to you alone and you won't have to say well why dont they give us papaers and cigarettes and better eats. But I fine this falt with the place. We have nothing to read about the boys get together and start to talk about what jobs they have put off and what one's they are going to put off when they get out. And the poor fish that liston to then gose out and trys what he was listioning to and come's right back. there for if they had papers to read they would not be talking about what jobs they are going to put off when they get out. And for cigarettes I do not smoke or drink I may be known as a crook but not a drinker or smoker. But there are young men who would give these three meals such they are away to get a fag to smoke. I think that that is one thing that is to hard on. . ."

Writes C. J. : "My profession, is breaking and entering, stores and business buildings. Does it pay ? Yes, if you are not caught. But easy come easy go, its gone almost as soon as you get it, and of course you go out and look around for another pull. You are bound to get caught though sooner or later, and when you do —, well, what's the use, you've got it coming to you. Five years and a day, don't sound like much does it ? but serve it !

"First thing you do is to start cursing the grub, no sugar in the coffee, sour hash, beef stew with a dirty rag in it, and several other things. It isn't the bunk. No cigarettes, no papers, nothing worth while to read (when you have the chance which isn't often) and plenty of work.

Then besides working from 7.30 to 4.30, to have an officer over you who thought the worst he treated you the more work and respect he got out of you.

No, I don't mean that all the officers are like that, but there sure are *some*, and they sure make a bad place hell. When I first arrived I was awful sore at myself for being such a fool as to get caught, but after I thought it over a while I decided that that wasn't the foolish part. No, not by a long shot. I have been here 7 months, have got 23 more before I see the board of parole. So far I haven't made head or tails out of my position.

If I see the board in '29 and get voted of course I would intend to go straight, but could I ? I don't know. A fellow has to have a lot of will power. Then again you might get out of the job, which by the way, was keeping your mind of other things. Broke, no place to go, without money. "Well, pull a job", one of the guys suggest. "Might just as well, won't get caught, just one and then lay off." One job leads to another, and then you find yourself back in jail.

Of course that dosen't include every fellow. Some go wrong right as soon as they are out. Some start to go straight and stick to it, others start straight, get hard up, and go wrong again."

Writes M. S. : "I think that some of the officers are not good enough to correct the men in here. And if the officers are not good them self, well then, I don't think that I have to say much more about that.

"As far as reforming goes. I think or I should say. A man can reform if he really wants to. He has hours and hours to think of both wrong and good that he has done. Therefor if, a man wants to reform all that is needed is a strong mind and a good will power. As for reading news papers, well I dont think it would make the mean any worst then they are. And it dose not help them any to reform. As for my self, I can not reform for I am reform, or rather was before I came in here. . .

"But there is one thing they do not teach a man a trade so when some or most of the men go out who did not have a trade go back to the old game, and by doing so came back or els where.

"What there should have is more scho ling in arithmetic and spelling and also in Grammar. And teach the men a good trade so that when they do go out can get a job. . ."

Writes C. O.: "The first night when I came to school to take examination to see wich class I should be put in, after I had finish Mr. Smith ask me to go to school I told him I did not want to go, he ask me why I told him it did not do me any good he ask me for an explanation did not want to tell him why because it might of ment truble for me. in the school room we could take up some interesting subjects such as civic and botany and a lot of other interesting thing to make us better instead of all the dryied up frection and spelling we get that does not show us how to be better we are no more down the stairs we forget it. the foremost thing they ought to teach us is law half of the men in here do not no a thing about law or their rights if these men new the law and their right then ten per cent of them would not be here there are too many narrow minded people who try to reform us.

"it is bad enough to be here they don't have to take everything away from us."

ARE OUR PRISONS USEFUL?

ARE prisons then successful? If by this question we mean to ask if they reform criminals and prevent the continuance of their criminality the answer is a slightly qualified, "No."

As nearly as we can judge four out of five persons who go through our state prisons and reformatories continue their delinquencies after their discharge. There is also the probability that, among the twenty per cent who stop their criminality, are some single offenders and others who may have deserved punishment, but who would not be apt to commit additional crimes even if they were not imprisoned. Very likely there are a few prisoners who cease their criminality chiefly as a result of their prison experience. The shock of imprisonment may bring some criminals for the first time to face the implications of their acts and lead to reformation. To others imprisonment may bring a helpful stability, a new and more satisfactory conception of life's values, a vocational training adequate to bring economic security, or an attachment to a prison officer that acts as a social gyroscope to keep the offender on an even keel after his discharge. The proportion of prisoners genuinely reformed by any of these methods however is obviously small and as an offset there are apparently some prisoners whose continuance in criminality is assured by their prison experience.

The one emphatic, though unpleasant, fact that remains is that most persons who are sent to prison continue their criminality for an indefinite time after their discharge from supervision. However, it is hardly fair to test the value of prisons solely by their success in reforming prisoners. Probably we should not expect a high ratio of this type of success with persons who must demonstrate their conduct failure as a prerequisite to admission ; at least not with our present meager knowledge of how to control human behavior.

There are, however, other possible services rendered to society by prisons. An obvious one is that they keep prisoners safely in custody and so protect society from their activities during the term of their incarceration. Another service is that society may be benefited by the cure of disease and the training in personal hygiene among prisoners. These values, however, hardly warrant the very great cost of maintaining prisons of the sort we now have. The real crux of the matter lies in the fact that criminal behavior is actually present in our society. No amount of wishful thinking can conjure it away. Something must be done with criminals who are caught.

Apparently we are not yet ready to make execution the one, inevitable punishment for most crimes. We must then imprison many offenders. If they all receive life sentences we must construct and maintain many more costly prisons to house these people. The economic burden entailed will be greater than we are willing to bear. The alternative to continuous building is to release prisoners at about the same rate as new ones are committed. That is what we do now. If we are to continue the process it would seem the part of wisdom to do the best we can to reform them while they are in prison. Presumably that is also part of what we try to do now, but with little success.

We may therefore resign ourselves to our present costly procedure as representing the best possible compromise with an irreducible evil or we may have sufficient confidence in the possibility of learning how to improve our ratio of success with these difficult subjects to be willing to adopt an experimental attitude in our treatment of them. If we do this all of our prisons should become experimental stations in which, with due regard for the immediate protection of society, we should turn the involuntary presence of prisoners into an opportunity for constantly improving our knowledge of how best to deal with offenders.

CHAPTER XXII

THE ABSOLUTE AND CONDITIONAL RELEASE OF PRISONERS

METHODS OF RELEASE

PENAL institutions are not permanent homes. They cater chiefly to transients who may check out by any one of four legal methods, viz:

1. They may serve the sentences named by the courts.

2. They may gain an earlier release through the commutation of sentences by governors or the president.

Such reductions are granted in view of extenuating circumstances warranting leniency. The guilt of prisoners is not thereby denied.

3. They may be freed by executive pardons, either absolute or conditional.

The courts have frequently held that a pardon removes guilt and restores the person to his status before conviction.

The pardoning power is variously placed. For federal prisoners it rests with the President. In 30 states it is in the hands of the governors advised, in 25 of them, by a board of pardons. In eighteen states the governor and council together have pardoning power. Mayors occasionally have limited authority to pardon offenders against municipal ordinances.

Pardons were originally used as a means of rectifying errors in justice. If it became apparent that an innocent person had been convicted a pardon would forthwith restore him to freedom and good standing among his fellows. In practice pardons have become a means by which mercy may be exercised towards those who seem to have been punished enough. The conditional pardon especially has lent itself to this function since liberty is granted only on condition that the person accept certain restrictions upon his behavior. Under a system of fixed sentences pardons may be necessary to relieve injustices. They have always been most numerous where sentences have been most severe. Unquestionably the pardoning power has been often abused for sentimental or political reasons. It has placed a heavy burden upon conscientious executives who have been subjected to great pressure to grant pardons into whose merits they have not had the time to make a thorough inquiry. As fixed sentences are replaced by those of variable length (limited indeterminate sentences) the use of pardons may decrease. Under truly indeterminate sentences (of no fixed length but depending upon the prisoners' readiness for freedom) pardons would be unnecessary.

4. They may be freed by administrative boards authorized to reduce the terms of sentences for good conduct as provided by good time laws, indeterminate sentence laws, and parole laws.

GOOD TIME LAWS

Good time laws allow a reduction in prisoners' sentences of so many days a year for good behavior. Prison boards are authorized to examine the conduct of prisoners and to release them in accordance with the schedule of reductions before the expiration of their full court sentences. Good time laws were originated here and abroad in the nineteenth century as an aid to prison discipline, prison labor production, and reformation.

Good time laws arouse little enthusiasm among modern penologists. As we have seen, good behavior in prison means unquestioning obedience to arbitrary rules. It is negative rather than positive. It often means mere outward compliance on the part of hardened crooks who want their freedom quickly. There is little correlation between good conduct in prisons and good conduct outside. The administration of good time rules has become little more than a matter of bookkeeping which leaves the prisoners out of account.

THE INDETERMINATE SENTENCE

An indeterminate sentence is one that sends a convict to a penal institution for a wholly indefinite period; presumably until he has reformed. No state has yet passed such a law. However, a move has been made in that direction by the passage of laws under which prisoners may be confined for a time that is indefinite but within limits prescribed by the legislature; for example, not less than five nor more than ten years. A few indeterminate sentence laws set only a maximum term.

Theoretically it is foolish to set limits to sentences in advance since it is impossible for legislators or judges to determine before or at the time of sentencing when a convict will be fit for release. Judges not in sympathy with limited indeterminate sentence laws have circumvented them by assessing penalties so restricted as to be in effect fixed sentences; for example, from nine to ten years. Those who insist upon a specified minimum period are afraid that either political influence or effective emotional appeals will gain the release of prisoners before they deserve or are fitted to go free. Those who insist upon a specified maximum point to the need of safeguards against arbitrary powers in the hands of prison boards who would otherwise be able to keep any offender behind prison walls for life.

Both of these objections are reasonable under present conditions. Political influence is exerted. Frequently cases are not settled on their merits. It is an unpleasant truth that in some states the office of parole commissioner is looked upon as offering one of the best opportunities to make money that politics affords. Usually the releasing board has neither the time nor the facilities to make adequate case studies. An investigator for the Wickersham Commission attended one board meeting at which 95 parole requests were studied and decided in four hours; an average of two and a half minutes to each case. The members of the board had no information about these cases before their meeting.[1] Fortunately this represents the extreme of poor practice, yet the fact remains that few release committees are in a position to do effective work. Another obstacle is our limited ability to say when a prisoner is fit for release. Psychiatrists and their aides have gone far in their understanding of human behavior in the last few years but they still fall short of being able to judge human nature with precision and confidence.

The principle of the wholly indeterminate sentence is excellent. The flaws are in our present organization and

[1] National Commission on Law Observance and Enforcement, "Report on Penal Institutions, Probation and Parole," pp. 306-307.

limited knowledge. It is an ideal system rather than one that is immediately practicable. We have already started towards it. Quite likely the future will see an indeterminate sentence coupled with a limitation of the function of the courts to the determination of guilt, the use of receiving and diagnostic prisons, modification of treatment under the direction of impartial experts, a graduated series of steps leading to re-entry into the community under supervision, and eventually into complete freedom. Towards some such scheme our efforts could profitably be directed.

THE NATURE OF PAROLE

PAROLE is the conditional release of a prisoner from a penal institution into the community under the authority and supervision of an official agency. Parolees are expected to behave themselves, but more specifically, to meet the definite terms of their paroles which may require that they work regularly, stay within the state, avoid drinking, report weekly to the parole officer and so on. Ordinarily parole boards have summary power to return parole violators to prison.

Parole substitutes a gradual re-entry of prisoners into the community for the otherwise inevitable abrupt discharge that would follow a completed sentence. It gives the state a chance to judge a convict's fitness for freedom under an approach to actual living conditions while the state still has a hold upon him. It also affords the state an opportunity to reduce crime by helping those who are released to adjust themselves to a new life. Release without parole makes a continuance in crime almost obligatory.

Many a man is turned out through prison doors with ten dollars or less in his pocket and a suit of prison clothes on his back. In the circumstances he can only pawn the suit, which every policeman recognizes, and try to get a living before he starves. Without references and with an ignorance of current events that betrays his recent imprisonment his chances of getting work are slim indeed. Only his friends can help him. If they are criminals the opportunities they offer him are almost certain to carry him back directly into crime.

Only hard-headed practical men fail to see the implication that parole is necessary to social protection. It is a means of assisting prisoners who want to go straight, and an additional and irksome check upon those who do not. It is a combination of prevention and punishment based upon facts instead of upon a sentimental fiction. It is not a reward for good behavior in prison. It is a stage through which all prisoners should be compelled to pass; an unavoidable appendage to every prison sentence. It should come to be the only way to get out of prison.

Although parole reduces the length of time that prisoners *might* spend in institutions it has generally been used in connection with indeterminate sentences which seem to be longer than the old fixed sentences of the courts. About half of the prisoners discharged from all state and federal prisons and reformatories are paroled or pardoned, the latter group being small. In 1926 the men who were paroled or pardoned served an average of 2.12 years as contrasted with an average of 1.75 years for those discharged at the expiration of their sentences. For paroled or pardoned women the average sentence served was 1.65 years as contrasted with 0.87 years for those who served their full sentences. The offenses in both groups covered the same range.[2] In 1930, 30 per cent of the men who completed their sentences served less than one year, but only 25 per cent of those who were paroled got out so early. Moreover, only 6 per cent of those who completed their sentences served more than five years whereas 10 per cent of those who were paroled actually served more than five years.[3] The conclusion is that parole has not made imprisonment shorter. Instead it has extended the period of state control and thereby increased the measure of social protection.

THE TECHNIQUE OF PAROLE

PAROLE is not an isolated procedure in the cure of criminals. It is a step in a stairway. Alone it is useless. Parole must

[2] Bureau of the Census, "Prisoners 1926," p. 51.
[3] Computed from data in Bureau of the Census, "Prisoners 1929 and 1930," table 35, p. 41.

rest upon prison life on the one side and lead to normal community living on the other. If prisons do not point their inmates definitely towards parole and if communities are not able or willing to give ex-prisoners a reasonable foothold the attempt to parole them is useless. It is therefore an absolute prerequisite of a good parole system that the state develop an educational and industrial program in prisons that will prepare inmates for successful conditional release.

Parole work proper is a specialized branch of social case work and should be so considered. Its technique should be comparable to that of grade A social agencies. Its field of operations has two major aspects. The first is the selection of prisoners to be paroled. This presumes a thorough and critical study of each case in order that prisoners who are fit for conditional release may promptly receive it and in order that dangerous and unsuitable persons may not be set at liberty. The second, is the supervision of those placed on parole. This involves continuous adequate and intelligent aid and control of parolees by a well-trained field staff. Obviously the success of the system rests in large measure upon the caliber and organization of those responsible for it. Good parole administration requires a full-time state parole authority and a sufficient number of skilled assistants all adequately paid and having a professional attitude towards their work.

These basic concepts underly the pattern of good parole organization the essential features of which have been clearly set forth by the Wickersham Commission's Advisory Committee on Penal Institutions, Probation and Parole as follows : [4]

1. An indeterminate sentence law, permitting the offender to be released conditionally at a time when he is most likely to make good, not at the end of a term fixed arbitrarily in in advance.

2. Preparation for parole in the institution. This means little more than preparation for normal social living. Specifically it involves, however :

[4] National Commission on Law Observance and Enforcement, *op. cit.*, pp. 324-326.

(*a*) Looking upon parole as the logical, natural way to terminate a prison term.

(*b*) Getting the offender to regard it in the same light.

(*c*) Instructing the offender, while he is still in the institution, in respect to the things that will be expected of him on parole — and not putting off such instruction until the last day.

(*d*) Bringing the offender and his parole officer into contact before the offender leaves the institution.

(*e*) Making sure that the parole officer is familiar with the home and environmental conditions of his charge before the latter leaves the institution.

3. Selection of persons to be paroled on the basis —

(*a*) Of all the competent information concerning him possessed by the institution, particularly the examinations and recommendations of the scientific members of the staff.

(*b*) Of supplementary information concerning his home environmental situation, etc., when this is necessary.

(*c*) Preparation, in advance, of a suitable environmental situation into which to release him, such as proper home surroundings, employment awaiting him, etc.

4. Supervision by trained, competent parole officers. This means :

(*a*) Maintenance of an adequate number of officers to insure that the number of parolees being supervised at any one time will not exceed 75, and, if much traveling has to be done, 50.

(*b*) Appointment of officers possessing, as nearly as possible, the following qualifications : A high-school education and, in addition, one of the following — (1) at least three years' acceptable experience (full time basis) in social-case work with a social agency of good standing or (2) a college education, with at least one year of satisfactory training either in a social-case work agency of good standing or in a recognized school of social service.

The parole officers should also be persons of tact and good address, possessing personalities making it likely that they will be effective in influencing the behavior of others.

5. Supervision should be careful and intensive, in the manner of social-case work.

6. Flexible arrangements for the release of offenders from parole, not automatic release at the end of a year or some other similar period. (When sentences carry maxima, it will probably be illegal to hold offenders on parole beyond the expiration of their maxima.) Supervision can be relaxed as the offender demonstrates his ability to do well.

7. Establishment of adequate standards and techniques for investigations and supervision.

8. An organization to supervise the work of parole officers and make sure that the foregoing standards are lived up to.

9. Payment of salaries to parole officers commensurate with their training, abilities, and duties.

10. Prompt return of offenders who commit further crimes or indicate that they are likely to become public menaces.

11. A record system which will include the keeping of full, useful and accurate case histories of all parolees.

12. Appropriations adequate to all these purposes.

THE PRESENT EXTENT OF PAROLE

PAROLE is an outgrowth of the ticket-of-leave system developed in the English penal colonies in the 1820's from whence it spread to Europe and America. In its modern form it was introduced into New York by Brockway and adopted by the legislature in 1869 as part of the reformatory program to be used at Elmira. Between 1884 and 1898 it was extended to state prisons and accepted as a progressive scheme by twenty-five states. Only two states, Virginia and Mississippi, now lack statutory provision for parole, and these states and Florida are the only ones in which prisoners are not paroled. The federal government first made provision for parole in 1910.

The proportion of prisoners released by parole ranges all the way from nearly 4 per cent in Texas and Missouri to 78 per cent in New Hampshire. For the entire country 47.8 per cent of the 61,653 prisoners discharged from state and federal prisons and reformatories in 1930, were paroled and 40.3 per cent completed their sentences.

Laws governing parole, of course, vary from state to state. Sixteen states permit parole after the minimum sentence has been served. Louisiana, Massachusetts, and New Hampshire require inmates to be released at the end of their minimum term if their records have been good. Other states leave the time to the discretion of parole boards. Some states forbid the paroling of repeated offenders or those guilty of certain specified offenses. The most generally accepted requirement found in 23 states is that parolees must remain under supervision for the maximum term of their sentences. Other essential statutory provisions deal with the organization of the parole system, the nature of the parole authority, and the type and extent of supervision.

The chief criticisms directed against parole laws apply to the rules by which eligibility for parole is determined. Parole is essentially a form of individualized treatment. It cannot wisely be restricted in advance by a legislature dealing with arbitrarily defined groups. On the other hand a capable parole board is in a position to consider each case on its merits and should have full power to do so without hindrance from long-distance meddlers. Such errors as they may make in releasing prisoners will not usually be irredeemable since parolees may always be returned to institutional care when that is necessary. The chief danger in putting responsibility upon the parole board may be in the extreme conservatism in releasing prisoners. However, it is assumed that proper safeguards against arbitrary and unreasonable use of the parole power will remain.

THE PRESENT ADMINISTRATION OF PAROLE

ADVOCATES of parole frequently answer its critics by saying that parole has never really been tried. The opponents condemn the practice of automatically reducing sentences masquerading under the authority of so-called parole laws. An honest application of a genuine system in accordance with the standards previously outlined is yet to be made. The principle of parole remains perfectly sound. The present practice of parole is a different animal.

The facts support this viewpoint. In twenty states so-called parole is simply an act of executive clemency. Only fourteen states place the parole function in charge of special boards or commissioners who are in most cases part-time or unpaid officials. Illinois, Massachusetts, New York, Ohio, Texas, and the federal government alone employ full-time paid parole boards. Fourteen states economize by having no parole officers; thirteen, less conservative, have one apiece. In most of the other states ill-trained and poorly qualified men attempt to supervise from 300 to 2000 parolees apiece. California, Illinois, Massachusetts, Minnesota, New Jersey, New York, Ohio and Pennsylvania alone have anything like an adequate field force.

Resting on such a basis, parole in practice is as far from parole in principle as darkness is from light. That the two will join hands is at present but a pious hope. Dr. Clair Wilcox, who has made a careful study of parole administration covering several states, reports that some parole authorities adopt the simple procedure of refusing all applications for parole, thereby nullifying the parole statutes and fostering resentment among prisoners who will later be given complete freedom without the right of re-incarceration. Other boards mechanically release all prisoners as soon as the law permits without reference to their fitness for conditional liberty.

Boards which attempt to select prisoners for parole are generally influenced by factors that are hardly safe to rely upon. The most important of these is the behavior of the applicant during imprisonment. Unfortunately good conduct in prison is not a sure sign that the inmate has been reformed although if wisely considered it may be of prognostic value. It may only mean that he wants to get out quickly and has enough self-control to walk the narrow path to freedom. A second major consideration is the offense for which the criminal was committed, which has been shown to be even less prophetic of his future than his prison conduct. A third point is the criminal's experience which is taken into account on the assumption that repeaters are poor parole risks. Unfortunately this also implies that supposed first offenders are entitled to early parole as good risks; which is a dangerous presumption. A fourth item that impresses parole boards is the prisoner's manner and appearance as he comes before them. The notion that an upright carriage and an unflinching eye betoken an honest man dies hard.

Yet on the assumption that they can read character at a glance parole boards send rascals out into the world and mayhap more worthy men back into prison.[5]

WEDGES OF IMPROVEMENT

HAPPILY there are signs that the true significance of parole is coming to be realized. New Jersey, which has made excellent progress in penology, has gone farther towards putting the principles of parole into practice than almost any other state.

Jurisdiction over public institutions in New Jersey[6] is vested in a State Department of Institutions and Agencies whose activities are directed by an unpaid State Board of Control and a paid Commissioner of Institutions and Agencies who is its executive officer. This state board has power to determine the policies and regulate the administration of the state's penal institutions and also the procedure and terms upon which parole may be granted. The government of each correctional institution however is in the hands of a local board of lay managers appointed by the state board of control. These managers are really local prison overseers who direct the separate institutions uniformly in accordance with the rules and policies of the state control board. It is with the local boards of managers that the final authority to grant paroles rests.

In New Jersey, however, the local prison managers *do not* try to *select* prisoners for parole as they do in so many states. That is done by classification committees in the several penal institutions. These comprise the major administrative officers of each institution, namely :

[5] Adapted and condensed from the report by Dr. Clair Wilcox, "Parole Principles and Practise," *Jour. of Criminal Law and Criminology.* Vol. 20, pp. 348-349.

[6] There is a question as to the authority of the State Dept. of Institutions and Agencies over the State Prison. Hence the relation between the Department and the Prison is one of voluntary coöperation rather than authority. The parole service of the prison remains independent of the State Department. The discussion of the New Jersey parole system in this chapter, therefore, does not apply to parole from the State Prison.

Superintendent — Chairman
Deputy Superintendent
Disciplinary Officer
Identification Officer
Physician
Psychiatrist
Psychologist
Chaplain
Director of Education
Director of Industries and Training
Field Social Investigator
Classification Secretary

Upon arrival at the institution a newcomer is examined by each member of the committee except the superintendent and his deputy, the social investigator and the secretary. Each examiner submits his findings in writing to the full committee which thereupon considers the case and draws up a tentative program for the individual prisoner with the aim of preparing him for release. A continuous record of the progress of each person is kept. Whenever a change of program appears necessary any case may be reconsidered. Every case not previously reviewed is brought up for a second examination six months after admission. At that time the committee examines the prisoner's progress carefully, tells him wherein he has failed or succeeded, makes it plain that release depends upon himself, and sets a date for further consideration of his progress or perhaps of his fitness for parole.

In the meantime the Central Parole Bureau of the Department of Institutions and Agencies has been preparing to receive each prisoner for parole supervision. When an inmate is received by a penal institution the Central Parole Bureau is notified so that its agents may investigate the home and environmental background of each convict. A second "pre-parole" examination of the home is also made by the parole bureau upon the request of a classification committee whenever an inmate is up for parole consideration. The parole bureau in turn receives full reports and recommendations from the prison about the person shortly to be supervised, based upon pre-parole re-examination by the prison staff.

In considering a prisoner for parole a classification committee completely reviews every available bit of information about him, paying particular attention to his health, industrial and educational fitness, social adaptability, and the conditions in his intended home. The recommendations of the classification committee are then submitted to the local board of managers which usually accepts but may reject them.

The Central Parole Bureau is notified when a prisoner is about to be paroled and the field worker who will supervise his conduct calls upon the inmate to become acquainted with him and to make sure that he understands his new obligations. At the men's reformatories at Rahway and Annandale prospective parolees are given a leaflet, *"Parole Duties,"* on which a written examination must be passed prior to release. The parole bureau intends eventually to establish routine parole classes in every institution where health instruction, budget making, motor laws, problems of citizenship and other useful information may be given. The New Jersey policy is not to release inmates until approved work is found for them by friends or by the parole agent.

The custom of the parole bureau is to supervise prisoners closely upon their release and gradually to relax its oversight as the parolees progress. A common practice is to give men a trial parole period of three months before they are placed on regular parole. Even prisoners who are finally excused from reporting are kept on parole until the expiration of their maximum sentences and may be recommitted if necessary.

Parole agents are appointed from civil service lists. Their qualifications, adopted in 1929, are unusually high including:

"Education equivalent to that represented by graduates from colleges or universities of recognized standing ; standard course in social investigation, or education and experience accepted as full equivalent by the Civil Service Commission. Knowledge of problems of delinquency, laws governing commitment, care and parole of delinquents ; knowledge of approved methods of social case work, investigation ability, thoroughness, accuracy, tact, leadership, fairness, good address."

Of the eighteen men and six women parole officers in New Jersey in 1933 only six have been appointed since this standard was set although a few of those already serving could meet or approximate these requirements. The chief handicap of the parole officers is the common one of overloading. In 1931, eight of the men were carrying from 103 to 255 active cases apiece. The appointment of additional men since then has relieved the situation somewhat. The loads of the women were within the acceptable limits of 50 to 75 cases.

No satisfactory check-up on the success of parole in New Jersey has yet been made. In 1929, 736 men (18.2%) out of 4046 were known to have violated their parole and 59 women (10%) out of 584 were also known failures. There is every likelihood that some violations are unknown to the parole officers and perhaps some who broke their parole and ran away may be otherwise successful in a new place. It would be exceedingly valuable to penology if New Jersey would make a study of parole and post-parole cases similar to that included in the Gluecks' study at Concord. In the meantime New Jersey's parole system looks good. It shows a rare understanding of the meaning and purpose of parole. It is carefully planned, uniform throughout the state, and integrated with the work of the penal institutions. It is probably the best example of parole planning that we have.

PAROLE IN NEW YORK

NEW YORK apparently intends to be not far behind her neighbor. In April 1930, New York discarded its heterogeneous and inefficient collection of five parole systems and unified and reorganized its parole plan in a grand manner befitting the Empire State. A division of parole having jurisdiction over the four state prisons and the men's reformatory has been set up within the State Executive Department. At its head is a full-time parole board of three men who must not be officeholders in any political party or association. The salary of parole board members is $12,000 a year. They are required to examine and dispose of all cases of prisoners eligible for parole. An executive director with a salary of $9000 is the board's administrative officer in charge of methods of investigation and supervision. The plan also calls for a field staff composed of a chief parole officer, three case supervisors, an employment director, ten investigating officers, thirty supervising officers, and an office force of fifteen including a chief clerk.

The present board of parole consists of a psychiatrist, a social worker and a layman. The parole officers are carefully selected on the basis of character, ability, and professional training. An attempt is made to get men of vivid personal influence. All prisoners are interviewed soon after their incarceration. A full social investigation of the prisoners' backgrounds, prison records, and prospective homes is made. An employment bureau under competent direction has been provided. Men are selected for parole with care and given positive supervision during their conditional release period. Unfortunately the use of fixed and partial indeterminate sentences in New York restricts the rational selection of parolees. It is the intention of the parole board to limit the load of each officer to seventy-five active cases in order that proper attention may be given to each parolee.

By January 1, 1931, the new Division of Parole had brought 4100 persons under its supervision and was preparing to supervise 2000 new cases and investigate 2500 possible admissions to penal institutions during the next twelve months. How well the reorganized parole unit of New York is meeting its tasks is too early to determine. The value of the plan does not yet lie in its accomplishments but in its striking recognition of parole as a highly important and necessary step in the treatment of prisoners.

THE EXTENSION OF PAROLE IMPROVEMENTS

In May 1930 Congress passed an act providing for a full-time Federal Board of Parole of three members to be appointed by the Attorney-General. This board, under the chairmanship of Judge Arthur D. Wood, is now building up the parole procedure of the federal government. Texas in 1929 placed parole power in the hands of an appointed paid board of three members who are required to make a complete study of all prisoners, determine their fitness for parole, help them to get work, and supervise them while on parole. Ohio in 1931 replaced its Board of Clemency with a paid parole board of four members within the Department of Public Welfare. The new board is given power to make a comprehensive examination of all prisoners and is required to use the information so acquired in passing upon cases brought up for parole. In 1927, Pennsylvania relieved its penal institutions of the supervision of their own parolees and centralized the work in its Board of Pardons.

These provisions, far less comprehensive than those of New York, will not result in the adequate practice of parole in the states affected by them. They do represent steps towards that end, however timid and feeble they may be. They are significant of an awakening interest in parole that may eventually make it a strong feature of American penal practice.

STATISTICAL AIDS TO PAROLE

In 1923 Hornell Hart, in a criticism of Warner's study of factors determining parole from the Massachusetts Reformatory, suggested the usefulness of applying to penology statistical methods of determining probability such as are commonly used by insurance companies.[7]

In 1928 Ernest W. Burgess, as one of a committee of three on the Operation of the Indeterminate Sentence Law and of Parole in the State of Illinois, attempted to use an analysis of the factors determining success and failure on parole as a basis for a table whereby success or failure on parole could be predicted. The records of 1000 men paroled from each of three institutions, Joliet prison, Menard prison, and the reformatory at Pontiac were studied to determine what factors were significantly related to their behavior on parole. Every man studied had been out of prison at least two and a half years. The usual parole period was one year.

---

[7] See S. B. Warner, "Factors Determining Parole from the Massachusetts Reformatory," *Jour. of Criminal Law and Criminology*, Vol. 14, p. 192, and H. Hart, "Predicting Parole Success," *Jour. of Criminal Law and Criminology*, Vol. 14, p. 405.

Twenty-two facts were noted about each offender, viz.:

1. Nature of offense.
2. Number of associates in committing the offense.
3. Father's nationality.
4. Parental status, including broken homes.
5. Marital status.
6. Type of criminal as first offender, occasional offender, habitual offender, or professional.
7. Social type as gangster, hobo ne'er-do-well.
8. County from which committed.
9. Size of community.
10. Type of neighborhood.
11. Resident or transient in community when arrested.
12. Statement of trial judge and prosecuting attorney with references to recommendation for or against leniency.
13. Whether or not commitment was upon acceptance of a lesser plea.
14. Nature and length of sentence imposed.
15. Months of sentence actually served before parole.
16. Previous criminal record of the prisoner.
17. His previous work record.
18. His punishment record in the institution.
19. His age at the time of parole.
20. His mental age according to psychiatric examination.
21. His personality type according to psychiatric examination.
22. His psychiatric progress.

When the relation of each of these factors to success or failure on parole was analyzed some sharp contrasts were discovered. For example, the average violation rate of 1000 men from Pontiac was 22.1% but professional criminals paroled from Pontiac had a violation rate of 52.4%, first offenders a violation rate of 15.8%; men from rooming house districts, 45.8%, from residential districts 17.8%; men who had served sentences of 5 to 8 years, 46.2%, under one year, 10.7%.

These and other significant differences suggested the possibility of building up a table which would show what the chances might be of successful or unsuccessful parole if the pertinent facts in any given case were to be summarized. Such a table actually was constructed by taking twenty-one facts in the history of each man paroled from Joliet and rating them one by one in comparison with the average score for the entire 1000 cases. Under this scheme a man might rank more favorably than the average on none of the twenty-one factors, on all of them, or any number in between.

The following table shows the way in which 1000 Joliet parolees compared with the average for their group together with the rate of parole violation or non-violation to be expected of them :[8]

EXPECTANCY RATES OF PAROLE VIOLATION AND NON-VIOLATION

Points for Number of Factors Above the Average	Number of Men in Each Group	EXPECTANCY RATE FOR SUCCESS OR FAILURE			
		Per Cent Violators of Parole			Per Cent Non-violators of Parole
		Minor	Major	Total	
16-21	68	1.5	....	1.5	98.5
14-15	140	.7	1.5	2.2	97.8
13	91	5.5	3.3	8.8	91.2
12	106	7.0	8.1	15.1	84.9
11	110	13.6	9.1	22.7	77.3
10	88	19.3	14.8	34.1	65.9
7-9	287	15.0	28.9	43.9	56.1
5-6	85	23.4	43.7	67.1	32.9
2-4	25	12.0	64.0	76.0	24.0

Of course it is not expected that these tables would give an absolute certainty in predicting the future of any one case. They merely indicate the mathematical chances in a series of cases. Moreover, they represent a beginning in the application of the statistical method to parole selection and not a refined and settled technique. Furthermore they are not expected to replace intensive individual case studies but only to be an additional diagnostic tool.

There are crudities in this pioneer study as might be expected. The social data upon which the tables were constructed were not altogether complete and verifiable. The factors upon which the expectancy table were built were not weighted. All were considered of equal influence ; a pro-

[8] Bruce, Burgess, Harno and Landesco, "Parole and the Indeterminate Sentence," p. 248. A report to the Hon. Hinton G. Clabaugh, Chairman, Parole Board of Illinois.

cedure, however, which does not appear particularly damaging to the Burgess' results in view of Vold's recent experiments with both weighted and non-weighted factors.[9] Finally, no attempt was made to study the behavior of ex-prisoners after their discharge from parole. Satisfactory conduct under supervision is quite different from good behavior without it. The tables constructed during this study were limited to the prediction of parole behavior and no attempt was made to extend the device for use by judges or parole boards in other connections.

The Gluecks recognized these defects and succeeded admirably in avoiding them in their own experiments[10] with prediction tables the first of which was based on their thoroughgoing study of 510 Concord men five years after their discharge from parole. They were concerned with the *post-parole* success of ex-prisoners which after all is the only real test of the efficiency of penal treatment. They were able to discover the relationship between more than fifty verified factors and the *post-parole* success of their men. Those that were found to have a *significant* relationship to success or failure *after* parole were used in the construction of prognostic tables.

The pre-reformatory factors that were indicative of later conduct were six in number:

1. Industrial habits preceding sentence to the Reformatory (Coefficient of correlation .42).
2. Seriousness and frequency of pre-Reformatory crime (Coefficient .36).
3. Arrest for crimes preceding the offense for which sentence to the Reformatory was imposed (Coefficient .29).
4. Penal experience preceding Reformatory incarceration (Coefficient .29).
5. Economic responsibility preceding sentence to the reformatory (Coefficient .27).

[9] G. B. Vold, "Prediction Methods and Parole."
[10] See S. S. and E. T. Glueck, "500 Criminal Careers," Ch. 18, their "500 Delinquent Women," Ch. 15, and their "Predictability in the Administration of Criminal Justice," *Mental Hygiene*, October, 1929. Also S. S. Glueck, "Individualization and the Use of Predictive Devices," *Journal of Criminal Law and Criminology*, Vol. 23, p. 67.

6. Mental abnormality on entrance to the Reformatory (Coefficient .26).

Only one factor in the behavior of the men while in the reformatory was found to have a usable relationship to *post-parole* success:

7. Frequency of offenses in the Reformatory (Coefficient .33).

These seven factors were used in constructing a prognostic table for the guidance of parole boards. The method used was to list the percentage of total post-parole failures for each class included under each of the seven factors, thus:

> Industrial habits preceding reformatory sentences
> Percentage of total failures during post-parole period
> among:
>
> | | |
> |---|---|
> | Good workers | 43% |
> | Fair workers | 59% |
> | Poor workers | 68% |

Percentages were similarly secured for the various items in the other six classes. The lowest percentages were then added together to give the lowest possible score that a man could have and be a total failure. The highest scores were added to give the highest possible total-failure score. Intermediate score classes were established and the chances of post-parole success or failure for each group established in a table such as the following: [11]

Total-Failure Score	PROBABLE STATUS AS TO POST-PAROLE CRIMINALITY (PERCENTAGES)			
	Success	Partial Failure	Total Failure	Total
274–325	71.5	21.4	7.1	100
326–425	40.6	18.8	40.6	100
426–475	11.6	15.2	73.2	100
476 and over	4.7	12.5	82.8	100
Total	20.9	15.8	63.3	100

Coefficient of contingency, .44

[11] S. S. and E. T. Glueck, *op. cit.*, p. 286, table 113. Reprinted by permission of and special arrangement with Alfred A. Knopf, Inc., authorized publishers.

From this table a parole board would learn that any prisoner who came before them with a total failure score of 274 to 325 would in seven cases out of ten be successful after his discharge from parole ; in two cases out of ten a partial failure ; and in less than one case in ten a complete failure. On the other hand, a man with a score of 476 would in more than eight cases out of ten be a total failure and would be successful in less than one case in twenty.

Similar tables, based upon the same factors plus those that were significant during and after parole were devised for the use of parole boards in the supervision of parolees and for the use of judges in dealing with criminals who have gone through all of these processes and are again before them for sentence. Similar tables could be constructed for the use of judges in sentencing new offenders and for probation officers in supervising probationers. They might serve not only to indicate the chances of success but also to permit intelligent discrimination among several possible types of treatment for offenders.

Those who are working with prediction tables would be the last to assume that we now have a mechanical device for disposing of prisoners. Prediction tables are intended to supplement experience and good judgment ; not to supplant them. Their originators realize fully that such tables will have to undergo extensive empirical tests before they can be adopted. At present they are merely illustrations of a promising method. They represent the application of a scientific method to the administration of justice ; a method that will not replace intelligence but will make its judgments wiser.

THE VALUE OF PAROLE

If parole is to continue as a penal instrument it must justify its existence by the way it answers these three questions :

1. What proportion of ex-prisoners avoid crime during their period of parole ?
2. What proportion of ex-prisoners avoid crime for a reasonable period after their discharge from parole ?
3. Would the successful ones be equally successful were they to be released from prison without parole ?

None of these questions can yet be answered with the degree of assurance that we should like. There are, however, shreds of evidence with which we shall have to make shift for the present.

Many states have casually reported their success with parole. Their figures naïvely indicate that from 70 to 97 per cent of their parolees make good while under supervision. It is not possible for us to accept their conclusions at their face value. These figures are invariably derived from the record of parole violators returned to prison, the hopeful assumption being that those who are not recommitted must be successful.

With parole supervision in its present undeveloped state we know that this is merely an over-optimistic guess. Of 401 Massachusetts parolees on parole one or more months, 215 (53.5 per cent) had never been personally visited while on parole and only three had actually been seen as often as once a month. Conditions can hardly be better, and probably are much worse in the forty states where nothing like an adequate force of parole agents exists.

It is inevitable under such conditions that many parole violations shall pass unnoticed. The Gluecks, in the course of their investigation, discovered 25 parole violators whose misconduct was unknown to their supervising agents. In addition the parole officers, themselves, knew 59 parolees guilty of serious misconduct whose parole permits had not been revoked. Cases like these all go into the success columns of our annual reports under the happy accounting system now in vogue. We need also to notice that even in the handful of cases that are actually kept under careful observation success means the observance of negative parole rules and does not imply positive social adaptation.

Therefore in answer to the first question "What proportion of ex-prisoners avoid crime during their period of parole" we can only say that :

1. *Known* parole violations range around 25 per cent, not all of which are crimes since they include failures to report, interstate trips, and other violations of parole terms.

2. In the most thorough studies of parolees that we have,[12] the percentage of parole violations was found to be 60 for the Concord group (men) and 55 for the Framingham group (women) ; an almost complete reversal of the usual poorly supported findings. The probabilities are that this is closer to the general state of affairs than the usual guesses.

More important to society than behavior on parole is the conduct of ex-prisoners after supervision has been removed. It has been the custom for prison superintendents, parole agencies, and writers on criminology to assume quite gratuitously that if 75 per cent of the parolees behave under supervision they may be considered as successful thereafter. We have seen that the assumption that three out of four succeed on parole is a naïve belief rather than a likely fact. To add to it a second wild guess that men who succeed on parole will succeed after parole is to place those who make them among the innocents. To be sure some statements of parole results are bolstered up by formidable attempts at research but with one exception these have been chiefly based upon unreliable annual reports and correspondence.

The Concord study alone actually traced the careers of 422 ex-prisoners for five years after their discharge from parole.[13] The results obtained are in sharp contrast to other reports on post-parole conduct : 78.9 per cent were found to have committed criminal acts totalling 1014 officially known crimes after their discharge from parole. Furthermore the percentage of both partial and total failures was greater after parole than during the parole period due to relapses of men who were able to behave while under supervision. Of the Framingham women, 76.4 per cent were known to have been delinquent during the five-year period following their release from parole.

Similar check-ups on the graduates of other types of penal institutions in different states under varying conditions of parole supervision are needed to augment this admirable beginning. Until such studies are made these stand as the

[12] S. S. and E. T. Glueck, "500 Criminal Careers," and "500 Women Delinquents."

[13] A forthcoming study by the Gluecks, "500 Young Criminals Revisited," will report the status of these same men ten years after their discharge.

only trustworthy research on what happens to ex-parolees. Insofar as it is representative it tells us that only one convict in five avoids crime after his discharge from parole.

This percentage is so small that it might well lead us to question whether the successful 20 per cent would not have been successful no matter how they were released. If one in every five can succeed without parole assistance why have parole at all? In 1828, long before the days of parole, Auburn reported that 77 per cent of its ex-prisoners had noticeably benefited by their confinement. Apparently prison officials had thus early adopted their slogan "Three out of four succeed."

The Concord alumni certainly were not much better after imprisonment and parole than before the commission of the offense that sent them to the reformatory if the extent of their criminal activity is a safe criterion. Seven-eighths of the men were total failures prior to their reformatory offense and nearly two-thirds of them continued their criminal careers after parole. In addition the number of partial failures jumped from one in twenty to one in six during this same period. When one considers the possible influence of the mere passage of time in reducing criminality it is difficult to escape the conclusion that the results would have been only slightly different in the case of these men had they been released without parole.

Is parole then of little or no value? Yes, if we mean our present form of post-prison supervision. After all it is not surprising that release by guess-work and supervision by correspondence should fail when applied to men who have already slipped at least once into crime. It is essentially the same outworn practice of abrupt release under an assumed name. The parole that penologists advocate, however, is neither a success nor a failure. It has never been tried. It is an experiment yet to be made. No one expects that it will complete the reform of all or even the majority of our prisoners. It will make possible an intelligent application to that problem of our increasing scientific knowledge of the dynamics of human behavior. Perhaps it will provide a degree of social protection from ex-prisoners considerably greater than that we now enjoy.

CHAPTER XXIII

THE PENAL SCIENCE OF TOMORROW

REVOLUTIONS in penal administration are not likely to occur. Improvement will come through the imitation of methods developed in the few progressive penal institutions, scattered throughout the world, in which the spirit of inquiry and the courage to experiment exists. Some prisons have already made themselves quite unlike the typical institutions previously described. They have not yet proved the value of their methods by results achieved. Furthermore a technique that works in Japan, Belgium or California may be of little value elsewhere. The important fact is that in some quarters there is imagination, inventiveness, life ; that in some institutions intelligence is supplanting force. Out of them by a process of natural selection and survival of the fittest will come the penal methods of tomorrow. For that reason, prophecy had best be based upon a glimpse at new trends in penology around the world.

THE NEW BASE AND THE NEW PURPOSE OF RUSSIAN PENOLOGY

FOLLOWING the lead of the Russian Socialist Federated Soviet Republic, the members of the Soviet Union have since 1926 adopted penal codes resting on a base fundamentally unlike that existing elsewhere. Our law assumes that freedom of will is a fact, and on that assumption holds men responsible for their acts. The Soviet codes discard freedom of will as a myth and hold that human behavior is the inevitable result of natural forces. Hence punishment is useless, but measures of social defense are essential. Therefore, if social protection entails the destruction of "socially dangerous persons" (no longer called criminals), they may be eliminated for that reason, but never out of a desire for revenge.

"Wrongs" (crimes), according to the Russian view, are an outgrowth of capitalistic economy. Even when that is displaced some persons are so fixed in their habits as to be incapable of making an easy adjustment to a new social order. Therefore, the state should apply the full resources of modern scientific knowledge to these unfortunates and try to bring about their satisfactory adaptation to a communistic society. Those who cannot be so helped must be permanently isolated.

Dangerousness has, of course, a new, a communistic measuring rod. Whatever may weaken the fundamental structure of the state must be wiped out. The old divisions of crime have been replaced by three new categories of "wrongs." The first and most serious group of offenses comprises all acts dangerous to the Soviet régime; the second, wrongs of individual self-seeking; and the third, wrongs against regulations, such as sanitary codes, designed to protect physical well-being and comfort.

Many of the "measures" taken against these wrongs are of the traditional sort. Political offenders receive short shrift. Execution is temporarily retained until communism is solidly established. Exile is permissible. Counterfeiting, sabotage, and rebellion may all be met by death. Yet wrongs against private property, such as embezzlement and forgery, are not serious and first degree murder is met by a maximum measure of confinement for not more than ten years. In addition to these traditional measures, three others have been created. The first is classification as an enemy of the working people plus banishment; the second is disbarment from certain industries or activities; the third, compulsory labor without confinement.

Prisons (called camps) of the familiar sort remain but the method of treatment in them follows logically the Soviet concept of the economic basis of wrongs and the definite ideal of social protection through reformation rather than through punishment. The application of these principles has introduced new features into Soviet prison camps. Their primary aim is to teach prisoners to take their proper place in a communistic workers' society.

Social solidarity is therefore stressed instead of isolation and social ostracism. Persons who are not prisoners may join the prison colonies. Trade instruction is an essential of every camp. It is accompanied by the constant vivid presentation of Soviet ideals through posters, literature, classes, clubs, plays, and every other available medium. Trade union men retain their affiliation with the national body and are made to feel that they are a part of it. Workers, who show satisfactory progress, may be given furloughs to go home to aid their families or to work in outside factories under the supervision of local workers' groups. Forms of inmate self-government have been developed within the camps to deal with the industrial, educational, health, and disciplinary problems affecting the prisoners. Planned production programs and the competition of camp units in industrial production are found within as well as without prisons. Prisoners, except those doing forced labor, are paid the regular wages of their trades less the expense of their maintenance.

Just how smoothly these schemes are working out it is impossible to say. The important fact is that features, heretofore advocated only by penal theorists, have been put into actual operation in Russia and however imperfectly they may at present be functioning they are apparently meeting with some measure of success. As the Soviet plan continues, its methods and results will warrant our careful study. It has already made noteworthy contributions in :

The setting up of an officially recognized, clear-cut, rational, penal objective, namely, social defense through readjustment wherever possible and in other cases through permanent isolation.

The recognition, both in law and in treatment, of modern sociobiological knowledge and theory relative to the causation and modification of human behavior.

The honest attempt to apply, and to experiment with the application of these principles in the actual treatment of prisoners in penal institutions and in the treatment of other offenders.

THE RATIONAL DETERMINATION OF TREATMENT IN MEXICO

MEXICO astonished the world and called forth bravos from criminologists when, in 1929, she promulgated a new penal code which dispenses with the jury, eliminates the traditional court sentence and provides instead for a diagnostic council, the Supreme Council of Social Defense and Protection, to prescribe treatment for the guilty. This reform has long been advocated by students of criminology, but Mexico alone has had the courage to relieve the courts of their traditional sentencing power. In so doing, Mexico, like Russia, formally recognized that men are the products of complex psycho-biological factors modified by environment and that a rational determination of treatment is dependent upon a study of these factors in the person to be treated. The Mexican code also recognizes social protection as the single aim of treatment.

SPECIALIZED FACILITIES FOR TREATMENT IN BELGIUM

BELGIUM with a unified prison system capably directed, has pioneered in the scientific case study and classification of individual prisoners and in the development of specialized institutions for their care. The insane, the psychopathic, dangerous recidivists, and pathological sexual criminals are considered essentially irreformable. Through examinations these are detected and separated from other prisoners who are potentially reformable. For them permanent segregation without useless suffering in institutions for abnormal offenders is the program. Other prisoners are assigned after careful study to the institutions for normal offenders whose régime is likely to benefit them the most.

For example, normal boys between sixteen and twenty-one are sent to a cottage settlement having progressive stages leading from punishment up through an active adjustment to a free life. Upon arrival a newcomer is isolated for a few days in a room of the receiving cottage. This procedure is specifically intended to bring the offender up sharply and make him feel the seriousness of his position. During his solitary confinement the boy is examined by the receiving officers who thus gain a glimpse of the personality they must deal with. Thereafter the boy is assigned to a cottage of the family type, governed by a house master who serves as a father to the boys. He is helped by social assistants who have charge of the groups of ten to which the newcomers are assigned.

In this house the supervision and guidance of the boys is firm and continuous. In the third stage of treatment which follows in Cottage C, the house officers become more and more self-effacing and the inmates more self-dependent. They appoint their own managing committee which organizes a savings fund and directs the expenditure of money for poverty-stricken mothers of inmates and for discharged prisoners who need help until they can make a satisfactory community adjustment.

In the final stage before release, the boy is permitted to work in the village but must return to his cottage in the evening, obey the rules, keep regular hours, and pay for his board as a civilian might at a private school.

In order to classify and segregate offenders in its specialized institutions Belgium has developed a *Service d'Anthropologie Pénitentiare* which makes thorough routine sociobiological studies of all repeaters and of all other offenders sentenced to more than three months' imprisonment. The examinations serve as the basis for assignment to the proper institutions and for directing the course of treatment to be followed. In addition to this examination the Belgium system also provides as an essential feature of each of its ten larger prisons a psychiatric annex for discovering and treating the mental and nervous defects of prisoners.

CLASSIFICATION, PREVENTIVE DETENTION AND THE USE OF LAY WORKERS IN ENGLAND

ENGLAND, whose prisons are centrally controlled, has devised an elaborate system of classification of criminals and assignment to special institutions. Prisoners are grouped according to the legal nature of their offenses, their ages, length of sentences, and recidivism. Special institutions for the aged and the insane are provided. In addition, Liverpool and Wandsworth are used for troublesome local cases that are mentally abnormal but not certifiably psychotic or feeble-minded. Progressive stages are recognized within the convict prisons through which advancement is made by good conduct and industry. But the whole scheme is of doubtful value and falls far short of the Belgium practice. It is based upon the old notion of preventing contamination of the good by the evil and the somewhat newer idea of using a grading system as an incentive to reformation. These objectives, while worthy, are far less important than classification as a basis for intelligent individualization of treatment.

England, like most other countries, has been a victim of the necessity of releasing dangerous unreformed criminals at the end of their terms. Opposed to this practice were a few penologists who believed habitual offenders should not be released until they had reformed. A modification of this idea became law in 1908. It provided for a preventive detention period of not less than five nor more than ten years after the completion of the regular sentence for unreformed offenders who had been convicted three times since the age of sixteen. Convicts undergoing preventive detention are confined under a progressive mark system at Camp Hill. So far it has had a limited use in England. The plan, like that of the habitual offender laws recently popular in the United States, is intended only to protect society. It is not reformative. Similar schemes of preventive detention, forecasting the eventual coming of wholly indeterminate sentences, are now found in Italy, Sweden, and Holland.

England's prison system also includes the Borstal[1] Institutions which are modified adult reformatories for offenders between the ages of 16 and 21. The sentences to Borstal range from two years to three with provision for release on license (parole) to the Borstal Association after six months for boys and three months for girls. Licensed offenders are kept on parole for the duration of their sentences plus one year. No one is sent to a Borstal institution until the court has considered a report on his health, mentality, and

[1] So-called because the first of these institutions was set up in what was originally a convict prison in the little village of Borstal in Kent.

social circumstances and has decided that he can profit by Borstal treatment. Borstal offenders are clinically examined at the receiving prison at Wandsworth. After assignment they are organized into house groups intended to number sixty, under a house master and five assistants. A strenuous fifteen hour day of work and study is required. An offender enters Borstal under rigid penal conditions and gradually works up through successive stages until he reaches the Special Grade. In this last stage he is on his honor. He works outside of the walls with little or no supervision. Occasionally special class inmates attend local technical schools or are permitted a brief vacation at camp. Outdoor sports are stressed. In recent years the Borstal Institutions have increasingly emphasized and broadened the educational aspects of their work. Their aim is to adapt treatment to individual needs through an intimate understanding of each boy or girl. The personal influence of staff members is stressed as an essential element in this scheme of reform.

The semi-official Borstal Association assumes responsibility for boys and girls released on license. It has been particularly successful in helping them to get work. In the opinion of the Prison Commissioners and the Borstal Association, from 65 to 75 per cent of those receiving Borstal training are not subsequently reconvicted. How trustworthy these figures may be is conjectural.

The Borstal Association is but one example of the use of a private organization by the Prison Commissioners. The after care of prisoners is quite generally carried on by subsidized private agencies. These are linked in service with 600-odd men and women who are appointed prison visitors. Their service is to visit prisoners, not as officials nor investigators, but as friends from the world beyond the walls. Each visitor assumes the task of building up a genuine acquaintance with ten or twelve inmates through frequent visits. By this means prisoners are saved from the demoralizing thought of being forgotten men. Contacts made between inmates and visitors are often continued with helpful results after the offender's release. Through this system communities also gain a more realistic appreciation of penal problems and of their responsibilities towards them than they would otherwise have. Probably this scheme savors too much of paternalism to fit the traditions of the United States.

PROFESSIONALIZING PRISON SERVICE IN JAPAN

JAPAN, in spite of her geographical isolation, has simply adapted the Western fortress prisons to her own needs. Nothing original appears in her penal system. Yet with characteristic energy and with a marked interest in discipline Japan has built up the world's most thorough training courses for prison officers. We are indebted to the sociologist, John L. Gillin, for an outline of Japanese prison organization based upon observations made during a recent tour of foreign penal institutions.[2]

The semi-official Japanese Prison Association with a membership of 11,000 prison officials and somewhat less than 3000 lay persons has conducted the training school since 1908. A two months' course required of chief warders is given annually. Lower officers and guards attend training school for six months. A special two months' course is offered for prison physicians. All officers are required to practise fencing and jiu-jitsu. In addition monthly lectures on penal science are open to all members of the Association.

The Association publishes monthly and biweekly professional journals. It also serves as a center for penal information which it collects, publishes and distributes. It has established scholarships to train students in criminology. Another venture of the Association is a relief fund to help officers who are injured or become sick while on duty and to provide fitting recognition for those who are honorably retired. It has also banded the officers together in a Mutual Aid Association of their own supported by monthly contributions amounting to one per cent of their wages.

The effects of the Prison Association's work may be seen in the type of men who enter the Japanese prison service. They are alert, capable and professionally minded. Dr. Gillin was particularly impressed by the varied inquiries made of him by prison officials who wanted to know how

[2] J. L. Gillin, "Taming the Criminal."

things were done in the United States. He characterizes Shirosuke Arima, until recently governor of Kosuge Prison at Tokio, as "one of the highest types of prison officials I have seen anywhere in the world," a man whose prisoners refused to flee when the earthquake of 1924 liberated them, because he might suffer if they escaped.

In two other respects the Japanese penal system is outstanding. One is a highly refined system of classification of prisoners comparable to that of England, and like England's scheme, of doubtful value. The other is her unsurpassed facilities for the care of prisoners who are physically or mentally ill. Her examining stations, clinics, isolation wards, and special hospitals are an adaptation of approved western methods. Staffed by physicians with special training for their work they carry the best practices of modern medicine into prisons with a thoroughness nowhere else to be found.

SOCIALIZING THE ANTI-SOCIAL AT IWAHIG

At Iwahig in the Philippine Islands, also, Dr. Gillin found a unique prison colony. It is a transfer settlement for selected offenders originally sentenced to Bilibid Prison in Manila. The colonists sent to Iwahig are not misdemeanants. Their minimum sentence is twelve years; their maximum, life. Their offenses cover the gamut of serious crimes including banditry, murder, and insurrection. The sole basis of their selection is their demonstrated likelihood of reform. They become eligible for transfer after they have served one-fifth of their sentences at Bilibid if they have not previously been convicted and maintain a conduct grade of 95 per cent for a year.

The Iwahig Colony occupies 100,000 acres on Palawan Island. It is administered by a superintendent assisted by twenty-two officers, some of them former colonists. In their charge are 2000 persons including the families of some prisoners. Two types of residents are recognized: settlers who live in villages in charge of an elected convict sheriff, and colonists who are assigned to designated areas in groups of thirty to sixty.

The work of the colony is carefully organized. One group of prisoners comprises the department of animal husbandry which is responsible for the cattle and fowl, the dairy, and the slaughterhouse. A construction division erects and maintains all buildings. Another builds bridges and roads. One transportation group maintains and runs all land vehicles, the other runs and repairs the boats. In the outlying districts are colonists engaged in cultivating fruit trees and cereals and in fishing. Other divisions include the engineers and mechanics, farmers, musicians, foresters, horticulturalists, sanitary service, information service, and the police. The police, like all other workers, are colonists.

Since the prisoners are being trained to become good citizens they must learn to live at Iwahig the sort of normal life that will be expected of them when they are released into the community outside. Colonists are expected to face their responsibilities squarely rather than to avoid them. They are trained to do their jobs well. What they have depends upon what they earn. They receive credit for half the net value of their work. The other half belongs to the government. Colonists maintain a coöperative store through which they sell their products and purchase supplies. In the settlement are schools, churches and a community recreation hall built by prisoners. The children of settlers and officers attend school together. The staff and their families mingle freely with the settlers at church and at the community concerts and dances. Discipline is maintained by an inmate police and court organization which prosecutes offenders and sentences them subject to the superintendent's approval.

Apparently the prisoners profit by the training, the problems, and the normal routine of the life at Iwahig. They become skilled workers and trained agriculturists. They learn how to handle money. They appreciate the advantages of good conduct. Often they settle on neighboring islands after their discharge. Because of their training at Iwahig they become more successful workers than their untrained neighbors. In spite of the bias of the provincial officials at Puerto Princesa against the Iwahig administration one of them has characterized the ex-prisoners among them as the most substantial citizens and the best settlers they have.

EXPERIMENTS WITH SELF-GOVERNMENT IN PRISONS

SELF-GOVERNMENT as a means of developing responsibility in unruly and delinquent children has been the subject of experiments ever since the eighteenth century. The best known attempts were at the New York House of Refuge in 1824 during the year of Joseph Curtis' superintendency and for a much longer period at the Boston House of Reformation beginning in 1828 under the direction of the Rev. E. M. P. Wells. Again self-government appeared at the George Junior Republic at Freeville in 1895. Calvin Derrick, an associate of William George, carried its practice into the California State Reformatory at Ione in 1912 where it proved so satisfactory that it was given official sanction by the state. It remained for New York, under the inspiration of Thomas Mott Osborne, to introduce self-government among adult offenders in 1914.[3]

Osborne was born and brought up in the shadow of Auburn Prison and for fifteen years after his graduation from college he was chairman of the board of trustees of the George Junior Republic at Freeville. It was probably William George who first suggested to him that a plan of self-government might work with adults. Osborne was then frankly skeptical about the idea. In 1913, Governor Sultzer appointed him chairman of a prison inquiry commission. Taking his appointment seriously, Osborne decided to gather facts by spending a week in prison as an ordinary convict. In the face of criticism and ridicule by the press he carried out his plan. His experiences and conversations with prisoners, particularly with his working partner, Jack Murphy, during his confinement convinced him of the utter hopelessness of the prison régime and the possibilities and desirabilities of change.

[3] The writer is indebted to Frank Tannenbaum for much of the information in this section. See the references to his writings in the bibliography.

SELF-GOVERNMENT INAUGURATED AT AUBURN PRISON

AFTER pondering over the ideas born of his brief but vivid prison experience, Osborne held a conference with Warden Ratigan and a little group of inmates to consider Jack Murphy's suggestion of a Good Conduct League. Osborne's informal committee believed such an organization to be feasible and, with the consent of Warden Ratigan, took steps to bring the scheme before the inmates. Guards carried ballots through the prison and the convicts elected 49 representatives as a sort of constitutional convention. These met without guards, under the chairmanship of Osborne.

Laboriously and earnestly they worked out the principles of their organization. Good conduct, as far as the League was conceived, was to be determined by the men and not by their keepers. The powers of the League would be whatever the Warden might grant it and would probably have to be earned by proof of ability. Government was to be vested in an elected house of 49 representatives who in turn were to choose an executive board of 9. The remaining 40 were to serve on committees. A sergeant-at-arms was to be appointed by the executive committee as chief inmate police officer.

When the plan was finished the prisoners met under guard in the assembly hall, discussed it, and adopted it. The next day 1350 prisoners joined the new Mutual Welfare League. A Brooklyn gangster was made sergeant-at-arms. Many points of friction between the old and the new systems had to be ironed out. The men were at first unwilling to assume the responsibility for discipline but eventually they did in all cases except assault on an officer, homicidal attack on a prisoner, strike, and attempted escape.

The effects of the Mutual Welfare League at Auburn were soon apparent. The men had to prove themselves responsible to hold their privileges. They were hurt if individuals broke the rules. Discipline was in their hands. Prisoners, who became martyrs in the eyes of their fellows when reported by their keepers and punished by the deputy, found no glory in being disciplined by fellow-convicts.

League rules were not arbitrarily set down by the warden. They were made by the men themselves and there could be no merit in breaking them.

SELF-GOVERNMENT AT SING SING

OSBORNE's work at Auburn was barely a year along when he was appointed warden of Sing-Sing Prison, one of the "hardest" in the country. There he, and Warden Kirchwey who took his place for a time, carried inmate self-government to its highest point. Osborne's predecessor had blindly and vaguely tried to copy developments at Auburn by imposing unrequested privileges without responsibilities, upon his men. Osborne proceeded as he had at Auburn. The customary fires and mutinies that usually accompanied administrative changes were absent. Osborne, unarmed and alone, presided over the prisoners' meeting which established the Mutual Welfare League of Sing Sing.

Its organization was patterned upon that at Auburn. One representative was elected for each twenty-five members. These delegates, and eventually other members as well, formed numerous committees. These expressed the men's wishes to the warden and were the means by which the warden secured the voluntary coöperation of the prisoners. It was through their committees, which at one time had a membership of 200, that the real work of the League was carried out.

The judicial committee, for example, tried the cases of prisoners accused by their fellow convicts of misconduct. Those found guilty were suspended from the League and deprived of all privileges, including that of becoming martyrs. The sanitary committee did excellent work in removing conditions conducive to ill-health. The employment committee studied the aptitudes and experience of prisoners and carried on a job of placement service by correspondence with the outside world. Noteworthy was the refusal of this committee to recommend unsatisfactory candidates.

An ambitious and energetic convict, "Doc" Maier, asked and received permission to run an educational institute. His enthusiasm to have every man learning something eventually brought between 70 and 80 per cent of the prisoners into study classes. When the regular classroom space became inadequate the men themselves built a new schoolhouse in the prison yard.

Warden Osborne, a capable musician, personally trained a choral society of 250. A prison musician developed a band. Both of these units provided a constructive form of expression to relieve irritation. More than that, their influence extended throughout the prison, resulting in an improvement of the general morale.

As a means of making the men responsible for an income and expenses Osborne issued token coins which he hoped eventually to redeem in standard coinage by means of subscribed funds. The prisoners were paid nine dollars for a week's work and charged for their board and clothes. The men at once began to save money. So did the state. Men who were not hungry at breakfast did not eat. They became less wasteful. Soon they asked permission to open a bank. Within seven months after it was opened the prison bank held $31,424.41 to the credit of 1030 depositors.

Sing Sing was a changed institution under the League. Never was discipline better. Civilian shop foremen, who saw the effects upon the men when the guards were withdrawn from the shops, were opposed to their return. Sing Sing became a real community whose members were working together for the common good. There were malcontents as in any community, but they were few and they were disciplined by the League staff. The League could not run automatically. It had work to do and its members had to puzzle over its problems; problems that in other prisons were shucked off onto the warden. Through the League, convicts learned the difficulties of government. They learned, also, to think beyond their own lives, to consider their neighbors not only in prison but outside. During 1915 and 1916 they knitted 64,800 garments for the Polish Relief Committee. The graduates of Sing Sing, instead of forgetting it as soon as possible formed a sort of alumni league outside to encourage released men to go straight — and to express their faith in Osborne's work through an annual dinner in his honor.

The results of the League within the gray walls are not

subject to exact measurement, yet it is noteworthy that under Osborne and the League hospital cases due to fighting dropped 60 per cent, escapes decreased from 19 and 17 prisoners in the two preceding years to 3 during the League's first year, while transfers for insanity were cut 50 per cent. The narcotic trade was all but stamped out.

Another illustration of the change that came over Sing Sing is found in an incident that happened when the entire prison body was attending a meeting. No guards were present; most of them were off duty. Suddenly all the lights went out. An inmate discovered the cause, fire. With the men out of their cells and the prison in darkness nothing but a wild rush to escape could be expected. But nothing of the sort happened. Under their own officers the prisoners marched back to their cells—all except the fire company. It went down and put out the fire.

Unfortunately inmate self-government at Sing Sing was not permitted to prove itself more fully. Determined efforts by politicians to frame Osborne led through a series of dramatic events to his indictment and acquittal on a charge of perjury. While Osborne was fighting this charge, his friend Dr. George W. Kirchwey, served as warden of Sing Sing. During the trying period the loyalty of Osborne's friends, from President Charles W. Eliot of Harvard to the convicts at Sing Sing, was an astonishing tribute to the man and his work. A mass meeting called at Carnegie Hall by 250 prominent New Yorkers in Osborne's support was matched by another mass meeting in the same place called and led by ex-prisoners.

Osborne resumed his office in July 1916 but political opposition to his work continued. The Superintendent of Prisons issued orders to the warden through the newspapers. Governor Whitman was not in sympathy with Osborne's régime. He resigned and the Mutual Welfare League was left in unsympathetic hands.

In 1917 Osborne was appointed Commander of the Portsmouth Naval Prison, and again he introduced self-government, after trying out the old system a week as a voluntary prisoner. His success there in placing responsibility upon the men can best be judged by an incident that occurred when

Osborne took 100 prisoners without guards 43 miles over the road to Manchester to give a theatrical performance. A snowstorm came up as the cavalcade was returning to prison just before midnight and one car containing several long-term prisoners took the wrong road and got lost. Then followed the amazing spectacle of a life-prisoner with companions whose sentences totaled 386 years driving around all night in an eight-cylinder Cadillac trying to find their way back to prison.

Osborne resigned in 1920. The League continued for a while under Osborne's successor, but was replaced by the old régime when the Marines were placed in charge of Portsmouth in President Harding's administration ; and inmate self-government, as Osborne conceived it, disappeared from the prisons of the country.

No doubt much of Osborne's success was due to his personal characteristics. He was a most persuasive man and he knew how to win the loyalty of convicts. Because his program of socialization lumped prisoners together without reference to the studied capacities and needs of individuals we cannot call it adequate today. Osborne's critics who complained of the lack of order in his prisons were no doubt witnessing the results of this omission along with a disturbing contrast between a new and a traditional régime. It is unlikely that all men would respond satisfactorily to the ideals of a Mutual Welfare League and doubtful if Osborne was as successful as he and his ardent supporters thought he was. Yet regardless of these flaws Osborne's work precipitated a useful crisis in penology in the United States. It stands at the dividing line between regimentation and repression on the one hand and individualization and socialization on the other. Osborne's supreme achievement is that he broke the backbone of the old system.

THE NORFOLK PLAN

OUT in the country at Norfolk, twenty-odd miles from the archaic bastille of Charlestown in Boston, Massachusetts began in 1927 the erection of a new state prison destined to be more than just another penal institution. Behind it lay a definite intention to develop a thoroughgoing individual program of rehabilitation for every Norfolk prisoner. Reversing the usual procedure the buildings at Norfolk were designed to fit the plan of treatment.

Penologists have long recognized the inefficiency of our oversized prisons. Norfolk is therefore limited to 1200 inmates, the maximum number for effective handling. These are to be carefully studied, classified and then divided into dormitory groups housed and fed as separate units. To further the program of individualized treatment each unit is in charge of a house officer and an assistant serving as resident case workers. The size of the dormitory groups is limited to fifty prisoners as the maximum case load that can be effectively handled by the house officers. So, in order to make this scheme possible, Norfolk is planned with living quarters in eight buildings, each comprising three wings for fifty men. The houses are designed so that they might be varied in arrangement and strength to meet the needs of different types of prisoners. The prison wall surrounding the entire plant can be mounted only from the outside, and it is guarded by men housed outside. There are no weapons within the walls and teachers, shop foremen and house officers are not expected to be guards nor do the prisoners look upon them as such. A safety line within the grounds a hundred feet from the wall makes a deadline which no prisoner may cross.

This prison houses a genuine community and not a group of hopeless wretches housed in isolated cells. Every Norfolk prisoner becomes a member of that community. He works a five and one-half day week. He joins evening classes to study woodworking, automobile repairing, welding, rug-making, modeling or other subjects for which he has the aptitude and the inclination. He plays basketball, raises chickens, reads books or follows other interests in his free time. He votes for council delegates and may himself serve his house in that capacity. So far as it is possible within the limitations of a prison, Norfolk is a community ; abnormal to be sure, comprising only adult males, but nevertheless a community. That is one element of the Norfolk plan.

The Norfolk plan is secondly to make an individual diagnosis of each prisoner and prescribe for him a definite but adaptable physical, mental, social, vocational and avocational program to be carried out during his term of imprisonment in the prison community under the immediate direction of his house master. Even progressive institutions are apt to think of case work largely in terms of diagnosis. Norfolk stresses the imperative need for treatment case work, a definite but modifiable course for every prisoner. Reversing the old scheme of treating every man alike, Norfolk is treating each prisoner differently and in accordance with his needs. It is surprising that we have so far been unable to see that all prisoners will no more respond to similar treatment than all non-criminals. Out of their studies of individual cases the Norfolk staff has already come to recognize at least five different classes among their criminals for purposes of treatment.

There is first the custodial case which includes men whose crimes are primarily due to senility, feeble-mindedness and the like. Their fundamental difficulty is irremovable. They will always need institutional care.

There is the medical case. A physical condition due to accident, disease, dissipation or war service makes normal living difficult or impossible. They need medical treatment primarily.

Defects of personality are major factors in some cases. Faulty habits of thinking and acting may be based upon neurotic or psychotic tendencies. These constitutional weaknesses must be met by psychiatric treatment to correct faulty mechanisms before the criminal behavior can be checked.

Other cases are definitely situational. Men have been overwhelmed by storms too strong for them to weather. Domestic maladjustment, financial burdens have bowled them over. The treatment of situational criminals involves aid in vocational training, sex education, budget-making, family readjustments and the like. It is frankly a social work problem.

Social cases are probably the most difficult of all to handle. They are the professionals in the field of crime, the men who have made it their careers. Nothing short of a complete reorientation will suffice to cure them. Upon that task every resource of the prison community must be concentrated in the effort to socialize those who have hitherto been outside of the pale.

To meet the differing needs of all of these individuals the varied facilities of a hospital, a school, industrial shops, a social center, and a jail are required. Adequate provision for farm work and an honor camp on the thousand acres of woods and fields outside of the prison wall is necessary. All of these needs are being intelligently met. The hospital is a thoroughly modern plant with operative, laboratory and psychiatrical facilities. The school is planned specifically for the teaching of adult male prisoners. The workshops are equipped with technical classrooms. The social center serves the specific religious and recreational needs of a prison community. The disciplinary and receiving building is properly designed for the study and segregation of different classes of offenders.

The third important aim of the Norfolk plan is to socialize the inmates. The government of the Norfolk prison community is an honest *joint undertaking* of prisoners and staff. They share the work and responsibilities of the community. It is *not an experiment in self-government*. The residents of each house hold weekly meetings with their house officer present. Delegates from each house form a prison-wide advisory council which has its own organization of committees. The prisoners' council and the staff meet weekly to consider matters affecting the institution as a whole. Suggestions may originate in either group and must be considered by both before final action is taken, although in case of disagreement the decision of the staff becomes effective. Committee service by the prisoners is considered a vital element in their socialization. House matters are settled between the house officers and the men. Individual problems are settled between individuals.

These three items then constitute the Norfolk plan: a prison designed for community life instead of isolated confinement, treatment for each man based upon a study of his particular case, and the attempt to socialize prisoners through an approach to normal privileges and responsibilities. Every one of these elements has been tried elsewhere but always with the handicap of standing alone. Cottage prisons have been built without provision for individual study or socialized treatment. Osborne's self-government was an experiment in socialization without individual study or proper plant facilities. The staff of the Western Penitentiary at Pittsburgh has made extensive individual case studies but has been handicapped in treatment by its cellular plant. It is the combination of all three phases that makes the Norfolk plan unique and alluring.

Summarizing the working of the scheme during the first two years of the Colony, Superintendent Gill in his first annual report to the Commissioner of Correction of Massachusetts said, "In general the plan has worked, although it is neither an 'honor system' nor 'self-government,' because it is founded frankly on a basis of results for both staff and men. In several crises the question of whether the Council should continue or not has been raised and each time it has been answered in the affirmative solely on the basis that both the staff and the men can operate more satisfactorily with it than without it. Neither officers nor men give up their independence or their responsibilities, and each continually checks the other to insure square dealing ; but both agree that coöperation works better than opposition where men must work and eat and live together, whatever the circumstances.

"To date the success of the plan is evident, both in the morale of the men and in the results achieved. Not only have grievances been aired and ironed out before they became acute, but constructive measures initiated either by the staff or by the inmates have been carried out with much greater success than would otherwise have been possible. During the first six months, production on construction was doubled by actual record due to the coöperation of the committees on construction, and the entire program of the institution in all its activities has been given an impetus and a vitality not otherwise possible. Coöperation and constructive service, instead of opposition and destructive enmity, on the part of both inmates and officers, continually break through the traditional prejudice of keeper and convict. And it is through such rifts in the old armor that one glimpses the normal, human, living body, the restoration of which is the aim of our whole endeavor."

PENOLOGY TOMORROW

The realm of penology as we have seen it through this and the preceding chapters is a realm of chaos. There is no certainty in it. All is bewilderment. In spite of forceful pronouncements or ostrich-like complacency the stark fact remains : we have yet no rational penal system. To be sure we have moved forward a little way. The evil of wanton physical cruelty has in large measure been outgrown. The utter futility of our penal measures, however, remains. Fortunately, as we have seen, there has appeared in a few quarters a brave willingness to question the traditional penal order. It is the growth of this spirit of critical inquiry rather than the present accomplishments of progressive penologists that gives us hope for the future. Slowly penology is becoming a profession rather than a steady job. It is beginning to make use of the knowledge which the social sciences have gathered. The trend of the new penology is already unmistakable. Its essential elements can be foreseen.

The first requisite is an agreement upon the fundamental aims of treatment. We cannot take vengeance on the criminal and reform him at the same time. We cannot strip him of all responsibility and at the same time train him to assume responsibilities. We can not confine him for five years under conditions unlike any that he will find outside and at the same time fit him to return to a normal life. We try to do these things at present and our efforts are as ludicrous as those of the novice who mounted his unruly horse and rode rapidly in all directions. Soon we shall have to resolve the conflict between emotion and reason and decide just what we do want to do with our criminals.

The answer is already becoming obvious. The penology of the future will find no place for vengeance ; no reason for inflicting unnecessary pain.[4]   Vengeance is a luxury that we cannot afford.   Its aim, instead, is two-fold:

(*a*) To protect mankind from the ravages of criminals with such minimum restrictions upon human freedom as are consistent with the social good.

Self-protection is an essential function of the social organism.   It is an inherent condition of social existence.   Yet it is conceivable that safety might be secured at too great a cost.   It would be unwise, for example, to make prison sentences mandatory for all persons caught driving without a license.   The penologist must be able to envisage the entire range of social values in order that his contributions to social welfare may be nicely balanced with those of other agencies.   It would do us no harm to reconsider just what sorts of behavior we wish to treat as criminal.   It is conceivable that in a more enlightened era many acts now labelled criminal will be known simply as symptoms of a maladjustment requiring treatment by non-penal agencies.   We must recognize that even now it is frequently chance that determines whether a person shall be punished as a criminal or aided as an unfortunate.   It is worth noting also that a prison is the most expensive institution in which to keep a human being who needs to be restrained.

(*b*) To develop the personal assets of the criminal to the highest point consistent with the primary aim of social protection and social efficiency.   Talents that might be developed and used for the social good should not be wasted simply because they are held by a criminal.   To do so is like throwing away a good suit of clothes because a vest pocket has been ripped.

To accomplish these ends it might be necessary for us to pain criminals more or less severely than we do now.   It is conceivable that the lash, the stocks, and the ducking stool might be revived.   Punishment will persist, but as a well-considered means to an end and not as an end in itself.   It will be retained as one perfectly sound method of treatment. No doubt new types of treatment should be developed. Amputation is a sound surgical operation but it is not wise to cut off every infected leg.   It would be equally foolish

---

[4] *Cf.* Prince Peter Kropotkin's remark based upon sad personal experiences, "For an active and independent man the restraint of liberty and activity is in itself so great a privation that all the remainder — all the petty miseries of prison life — are not worth speaking of."   P. Kropotkin, "Memoirs of a Revolutionist," p. 468.

to rub a bit of liniment on a leg when amputation is indicated, on the ground that to cut it off would be unpleasant. Moreover, only a quack doctor would prescribe the same patented remedy for every type of leg ailment. Yet judges all carry one patented medicine for every type of faulty conduct.

The moral is obvious : treatment should be based upon individualized study and diagnosis so that every method used whether old or new would be applied intelligently and purposefully rather than blindly as at present. Whether this is painful or pleasant to the criminal is beside the point. The criminologist should cater neither to the sentimentalists who would coddle the criminal nor to the sadists who would coddle themselves.

Such scientific individualization of treatment would require :

(a) Limitation of the power of the courts to the determination of guilt and to the rendering of a wholly indeterminate sentence therefor.

It is obviously silly for legislators to prescribe in advance or for judges to fix at the time of trial the amount and type of punishment which will make a convict safe to receive his freedom. The present scheme makes the release of a prisoner obligatory within specified limits of time whether he is still a social menace or not. The only rational plan is to commit offenders for a wholly indefinite period and make their release contingent upon their demonstrated fitness to return to freedom. Effective means would need to be devised to prevent the arbitrary and unwarranted detention of prisoners fit to be released. There is no reason, however, why the individual's rights in this respect could not be safeguarded as well in a penal institution as in a hospital for the mentally ill.

(b) The establishment of a receiving and diagnostic prison which should be a clearing house for all prisoners.

After all, it is the criminal, not a crime, who is sent to prison and eventually released therefrom. It is the prisoner, not his crime, that we must deal with. The only way to handle that prisoner effectively is to find out what manner of man he is. Is he intelligent or stupid, psychopathic or normal, satisfied with himself or dissatisfied, and so on? What are the causes of his criminality? Is he safe or dangerous at present? What are the chances for improvement? Could he earn an honest living if he wanted to or has he no trade? Is he physically sick or is he well? What should be done with him now? What steps will probably be necessary later?

It would be the function of the receiving prison to make this thorough individual case study of each prisoner, to make a diagnosis and prognosis of each case, and to outline a tentative plan of treatment to be carried out in the institution to which the prisoner is assigned. The progress of each prisoner would thereafter be reviewed from time to time and his plan of treatment would be revised whenever the actual results obtained made a change of program advisable.

(c) A coördinated group of specialized state penal institutions designed to carry out the types of programs tentatively devised at the receiving prison.

These might include institutions for mentally diseased, defective, and psychopathic criminals, industrial prisons, farm colonies, public works camps, maximum security prisons for the permanent segregation of irreformable prisoners, and so on. Only the latter type would cost as much to build as our "modern" fortress-like structures built at a construction cost of $4000 to $6000 per cell, and they ought not to be gigantic institutions of the sort to which we have been addicted. Prison architecture in fact needs to undergo a radical change in which buildings will be adapted to the types of prisoners that they are to house and the types of programs to be carried out in them. They will be relatively small. They will be more varied in form than now. Fortresses will become obsolete. After all it is a bit silly to spend $3,000,000 for a fortress when only 25 per cent of the men who are going there need to be so elaborately guarded and when 50 per cent of them could safely be housed in ordinary dormitories if they were surrounded by a guarded wall and 25 per cent could be safely kept in custody in inexpensive colonies.

All penal institutions should be under centralized state control, preferably through a division of rehabilitation of prisoners within a state department of criminology.

(*d*) The recognition of penal institutions as educational agencies primarily concerned with the social adjustment of criminal offenders.

Even if the percentage of life prisoners should increase under the proposed indeterminate sentence law the chances are that most offenders would some day be released. The proper segregation of dangerous incorrigible criminals in maximum security prisons would make it possible for wardens to concern themselves primarily with training rather than the prevention of escapes. Our present prison régime is devised to control the few dangerous men who would escape and gain a temporary freedom at the expense of the majority who could profitably assume responsibilities not now permitted them.

Socialization of prisoners through a broad educational program requires penal officers of high social character, that is, persons whose own social relationships are wholesome and successful, and not persons who are simply honest, just or devout. Graduation from high school plus a carefully planned training course for prison keepers might be the minimum educational base for any prison job. The requirements for staff officers should of course be much higher and comparable to the qualifications of staff members in a good state hospital.

In order to attract the right type of men and women into prison work their jobs will have to be made more attractive than they are now. Emphasis upon reëducation in penal institutions will go far towards changing the type of prison employee. But more than that is needed. The public will have to insist that political interference be reduced to a minimum. The hours of work and of pay for line men must be reasonable and standardized. The organization of penal employees in a prison association would lift their morale, stimulate the interchange of ideas, and give them the machinery for maintaining and improving their standards and conditions of work.

The organization of any penal community would depend upon its type. An industrial prison could hardly be administered like a state farm for misdemeanants or like an institution for defective delinquents. Every penal unit, however, would find use for a personnel department designed to assist prisoners and their families with family problems. It is foolish to attempt the social adjustment of prisoners without reference to the social units of which they are parts, and shortsighted to disregard new problems of social importance that are often created in the families of offenders by their imprisonment. Every institution or group of institutions could profit by the work of a permanent research bureau to criticize its methods and suggest improvements.

Educational methods would also vary with the type of prisoners and institutions. Academic, vocational and industrial training would follow approved lines but be adapted to the particular needs of prisoners. There seems no reason why the state department of education should not organize academic and vocational work in prisons in coöperation with the department of criminology. This is education in its narrower sense. More broadly, the essential business of penal institutions is to fit men for social living. They must be taught to accept normal responsibilities. This can only be learned through practice. It is useless to teach prisoners a trade if they are neither paid wages nor required to support themselves. It is hopeless to teach them civics without giving them some voice in their own government. Some of them might well be colonized with their families on a prison farm where they can be helped to solve their domestic difficulties. Others might be permitted occasional home visits as is now done in one or two progressive institutions. Some would work in the community during the day, but return to the prison at night, a practice which also is now being tried out in at least one women's reformatory. Under the conditions previously enumerated, therefore, there should be ample latitude for experimentation with schemes like the Mutual Welfare League and the Norfolk plan. With the professionalization of the prison staffs the desire and the ability to further such experiments would be present. Prisoners should progress through these institutions gradually and in accordance with their achievements so that their re-entry into society would be gradual rather than abrupt.

(e) An adequately manned, professionalized parole serv-

ice designed to assist prisoners to make their adjustments
to community life upon their discharge. Every prisoner
should be on parole after his discharge from an institution.

This service would naturally fall within the province of
the division of rehabilitation. Its work with prisoners would
begin before they are discharged. Ideally, it should be extended thereafter as long as they need its assistance. This
period, obviously, would not be alike for all offenders.
Hence, the parole period should be a part of the original
indefinite sentence.

Parole work as here conceived means more than periodic
checks upon the whereabouts of ex-prisoners. It means a
positive and aggressive service to parolees and their communities by which both would gain the maximum benefit
from the return of tested men to society. The methods of
this type of parole service are yet to be developed. They
offer a challenge to the ingenuity of a personnel with a professional viewpoint. Perhaps a major aspect of their work
will be the reëducation of the general population so that it
may come to have a realistic view of the qualities and problems of ex-prisoners. This may be a necessary preliminary
to the success of their work. Even if a taxi company is
willing to employ safe ex-prisoners it dare not do so if the
people who ride in its cabs are afraid. And what use is
reformation to a freed convict if no one will trust him?
Parole service therefore faces the task of assisting in a
process of mutual adjustment between parolees and the
community.

By some such methods as these the reconstruction of our
penal system must go on. Both reason and experimentation
say so. At some points the suggested revisions are drastic.
Temporizing will only continue the evils that we are so
anxious to cure. Perhaps we shall never find a way to deal
with convicted adult criminals that is wholly or even passably
successful. But until crime preventive agencies achieve
perfection the prisoner will remain with us. We cannot
dodge that fact. Our happiest course is to learn how to
meet it face on with the same rational, experimental technique of science that we have applied so successfully to
problems less charged with emotion than those of penology.

APPENDIX

SUGGESTIONS FOR RESEARCH IN CRIMINOLOGY

So much useful work waits to be done in the field of criminology that every effort should be made to direct the energies and intelligence of competent research students towards genuinely productive channels. To this end a group of active and able administrators in the field of applied criminology have contributed a list of real problems for research which they believe to be in actual need of study. The overlapping of suggestions from different sources is convincing evidence of a genuine need. Beginnings have already been made in the study of some of them. Criminological Research Bulletin, No. 4, published by the Bureau of Social Hygiene in May 1934 lists 300-odd research studies in criminology now in progress in the United States. This bulletin should, of course, be consulted by any persons intending to do research in this field.

The prime value of the following suggestions lies in this : they have come out of the experiences of those who are actively dealing with the problem of criminal behavior. Competent students with a sincere interest in criminological research would no doubt find the contributors of these suggestions willing to amplify and discuss them with those who can make a legitimate demand upon their time.

The Hon. Sanford Bates, Director of the Federal Bureau of Prisons, writes, "There are a host of problems, only a few of which I can list here, which need much study and research before a satisfactory solution can be arrived at. Here are a few :

1. To what extent should penal institutions aim to secure an exact equality of treatment among their prisoners ?
2. To what extent does this attempt collide with the working out of a wise program of individualized treatment for each prisoner ?
3. Admitting the hopeful possibility of reconstruction work with juveniles and first offenders, to what extent is the outlay of money justified to bring about a re-education of adult or confirmed types of offenders ?
4. Should prisoners be permitted or compelled to work at productive industries while unemployment exists on the outside to such degree as at present ?

519

5. In what circumstances should prisoners be permitted or encouraged to govern themselves while undergoing enforced segregation from their communities?
6. When, if ever, is the dark solitary cell justified?
7. Should military drill be made a regular feature of prison discipline?
8. To what extent should the diagnosis of the psychiatrist or scientific man control the actions of the warden or his deputy in administering discipline?
9. In what circumstances and to what extent should prisoners in a penitentiary be permitted to congregate?

"I also refer you to an issue of the Annals of the Academy of Political Science issued in September 1931 [Vol. 157] entitled 'The Prisons of Tomorrow.' You will find therein an article by myself which takes up one after the other some of the outstanding problems presented in the supervision of a group of prisoners or penal institutions."

Austin H. MacCormick, until December 1933 Assistant Director of the Federal Bureau of Prisons and now Commissioner of Correction of New York City, writes: "We need research work in the field of predictability of crime and predictability of success on probation, on parole after imprisonment, and in any other post-institutional status. This was the original approach which the Gluecks made in their '500 Criminal Careers.' A good deal of work has been done in this field but we have not got very far yet. We even lack reliable statistics showing what percentage of parolees actually straighten out. Institutions continually claim 80% to 90% of successes while at the same time their institution records show 50% or more of recidivism.

"The criminologists want to know what factors may be taken as fairly reliable signs that a given individual will later commit criminal acts or at least that the scales are heavily weighted on that side. The penologist wants to know what types of institutional treatment and post-institutional placement and supervision are most likely to bring about success on parole. Obviously, the probation authorities want to know what factors indicate that an offender is a reasonably good probation risk.

"I have no specific suggestions as to the exact lines that such studies should follow. In practically all research of this sort I am inclined to believe the case study method is the best."

Dr. Vernon C. Branham, Deputy Commissioner of Correction for the State of New York suggests: "A careful study of a selected series of parolees from a prison to see what adaptation has taken place over a period of not less than five years after leaving prison. This would be along the lines that Dr. Sheldon Glueck has done for the reformatory in his excellent book entitled, 'Five Hundred Criminal Careers.' The main idea back of such a research project is that we are releasing many men from prison who are improperly prepared for return to the community. The history of their lives after they leave prison indicates in many instances severe struggles to adapt themselves to situations which are at entire variance with the prison régime. In spite of these handicaps, in many instances their parole is successful and the individual does not come into contact with the law again. Of course, in these times of depression the situation is somewhat artificial and present circumstances should not be used as a measuring stick for the normal adjustment of inmates released into the community. Some adjustment to the situation, however, can be made in a research study even in these times. That is to say, a certain per cent of error or certain allowances could be made in the study, which would then give it the significance of parole under approximately normal conditions. For example, one could limit the study to those who had secured positions at the time of parole. Or one could make other adaptations which reduce present abnormal conditions in these cases to a minimum."

Dr. Branham says that the chief purpose of such studies would be to "check up on the actual efficiency of the machinery devised by the community for the arrest, conviction, and penal servitude of the criminal. Such data would be of tremendous importance to those who are dealing with the criminal because it would indicate clearly whether present methods are ringing the bell, so to speak."

In a paper on "Research Work in Prisons," read before the American Prison Congress, October 1931, Dr. Edwin R. Sutherland makes the valuable suggestion that there should be a study of escaped prisoners, their characteristics, their methods, and the conditions under which they escaped. Such a study would be of use to states in the establishment of medium and minimum security prisons and in the proper segregation of prisoners therein.

Bennet Mead, Statistician of the United States Bureau of Prisons has consistently emphasized the usefulness of an evaluation of the results of correctional treatment with a selected group of offenders. This involves the selection and measurement of significant facts concerning the prisoners treated, the treatment itself, and significant environmental factors. Possible methods for use in such a study are discussed in Bennet Mead's "Evaluating the Results of Probation" in the proceedings of the National Probation Association for 1932, and in a paper "Evaluating the Results of Correctional Treatment," presented at the annual conference of the American Statistical Association, December 1931.

The Honorable Joseph N. Ulman, Judge of the Supreme Bench of Baltimore City, writes, "The greatest problem of applied criminology from the point of view of the bench is the imposition of sentence. This problem becomes particularly acute in the jurisdictions where a number of judges sit on the criminal bench either simultaneously or consecutively. . .

"In every branch both of criminal law and civil law in America the earnest student is blocked by the absence of reliable statistical information. General impressions reënforced by prejudices take the place of objective information.

"Therefore I should say that any project likely to unearth exact information concerning the actual happenings in court procedure would be worth while. For example, does it help or hurt a defendant's chance of acquittal if he is represented by counsel? In jurisdictions where provision is made for a public defender, what are the results as compared with cases in the same jurisdiction where private counsel are employed and as compared with cases in other jurisdictions where traversers are not represented by counsel? What is the actual effect of pre-sentence investigation following conviction, measured in the use of probation, measured in the length of sentence, measured in selection of place of incarceration?

"I might extend this list of questions indefinitely. Almost every judge and interested lawyer is ready with an answer. My own conviction is that none of us know."

For those who are interested in the problems involved in probation work, Joel R. Moore, Chief of the Federal Probation Service, suggests for study the following questions :

1. To what extent do judges participate in the process of probation in the long established city, county and state systems?

2. Should control of probationary treatment be transferred from the judicial to the executive branch of the government? (Wisconsin plan.)

3. Is it proving to be compatible with the main objectives of probation for probation officers to collect from probationers the fines and costs incident to prosecution and conviction? The costs of probationary oversight? Reparation and restitution? Family support?

4. What is the percentage of probationers who at time of discharge actually show evidences of improvement in attitude and conduct? What is the persistence percentage during the two-year period thereafter (or whatever period is thought reasonable)? What percentage of these were subsequently convicted within two years?

5. What percentage of probationers were discharged as having completed term of probation without being surrendered for violation but during

the period not evidencing improvement in attitude and conduct? What percentage of same were convicted again within two years?

6. What percentage of probationers were discharged by revocation for violation of terms of probation? What percentage of these were convicted subsequently within two years?

7. Does the use of probation effect an increase or a decrease in the number of offenders? The number of offenses?

8. Does the use of probation on the whole effect an increase or a decrease in the cost of correctional treatment of offenders?

9. In the analysis of the effectiveness of probation, what are the comparative weights to be accorded to:

a) Selection of those to be treated by probation by pre-sentence, probation-officer investigations, diagnosis, tentative plans of probationary treatment.

b) Systematic family case-work, oversight — that is, method and technique.

c) Personalities of probation personnel.

d) Formal education, experience and training prior to entry on probation duty.

e) Influence of central supervision.

f) Coöperation of public officials and social betterment agencies.

g) Influence of public opinion.

In the same field, Irving W. Halpern, Chief Probation Officer of the Court of General Sessions of New York City, believes that the following topics are in need of careful examination:

1. A survey of the factors which make for probation success and failure with a view of ascertaining whether through an evaluation of such findings, practical criteria can be developed which will measure predictability.

2. A study to determine whether state control of probation departments possesses the merit claimed; and whether or not real results have been achieved, or has state control served to antagonize local authorities and judges and hampered rather than advanced the cause of probation.

3. Should the age limit in the Children's Court be raised to eighteen?

4. The use of Mental Hygiene Clinics in probation work — how best to correlate their services.

5. Methods for adapting probation practice to an unemployment emergency situation, maintaining morale, etc.

6. Should a probation department handle relief? According to the Milford Conference, social agencies should handle such relief as is incident to their function.

7. A study of methods of assigning cases in probation departments — the district plan, case problem method, etc.

8. Methods of selecting probation officers, training methods and ways to improve standards.

9. Integrating probation work with the other social services of a community. Why is this so seldom done ? How might it be carried out ?

10. How can the public be better informed as to what probation work is ? Should probation departments carry on publicity work or should this be the function only of private agencies such as the National Probation Association ?

11. Should probation departments handle financial matters such as collecting restitution, fines, family support, or should this be assigned to another department of the Court ?

12. A study of record-keeping. What type of records are best adapted for purposes of investigation, supervision, research into causes of delinquency, etc.

13. An evaluation of reporting as a probation requirement.

14. A study of probation ethics — maintaining a proper balance between the officer's duty to society and to his individual probationer.

Miss Katherine F. Lenroot of the Children's Bureau of the United States Department of Labor, writes: "Among the projects which we consider especially important are studies of results of various types of treatment as exemplified by the Glueck study of '500 Delinquent Careers' and by a study of the results of institutional care which the Children's Bureau now has in preparation. Studies of the relationship between the economic depression and delinquency would be very interesting." She also suggests as of interest to research students that "The Committee on Juvenile Protection of the National Congress of Parents and Teachers, of which Miss Alida Bowler of the staff of the Children's Bureau is Chairman, in its plan for 1932-33 projects outlines the following :

(a) The individual truant — intelligent understanding of his antagonism to school and discovery of how to apply constructive social treatment for the solution of his difficulties.

(b) Vocational guidance and job placement — as constructive factors in the prevention of anti-social attitudes and conduct.

(c) The problem child — at home and in school.

(d) Leisure-time activities of children and young people — recreation facilities, public, private, and commercial."

DISCUSSIONS, REPORTS, AND EXERCISES

CRIMINALS AND THE CRIMINAL LAW

TOPICS FOR DISCUSSION

1. What is your conception of the function of the criminal law ?
2. What is the common law ?   How did it come into being ?
3. What is a crime ?
4. How would you distinguish between a crime and a tort ?
5. What are the essential elements of a crime ?
6. What does the law mean by intent ?
7. What is the distinction between a felony and a misdemeanor ?
8. How do you explain the law's lack of interest in the criminal person ?
9. What are the advantages of having relatively inflexible legal boundaries of crimes ?   Do they outweigh the disadvantages ?
10. How did the law determine what acts should be made crimes ?

SUBJECTS FOR REPORTS

1. The Concept of Crime in Primitive Societies.
2. Crime in its Relation to the Folkways.
3. The Common Law.
4. Criminal Law in Relation to Social Progress.
5. The Nature of Crime.
6. The History of the Concept of Murder.
7. Noteworthy Decisions in Criminal Cases.
8. A Critique of the Criminal Law.
9. Fictions in the Criminal Law.
10. Insanity, Mental Disorder and the Criminal Law.
11. Ignorance and Mistake in the Criminal Law.
12. Defenses to Crime.

EXERCISES

1. Look up the statutory definitions of arson, burglary, larceny, murder, rape, and robbery in your state.   Compare them

with the common law definitions of these crimes. Give
the reasons for any changes noted.

2. Devise a brief questionnaire to discover what the layman knows
about the nature of certain common crimes and the penalties which the law assesses against them. Try it out on your
acquaintances.

3. Keep a record of all the crimes that you see committed during
a week's time. What conclusions can you draw from this
record ?

4. For what offenses in your state can a man be sent to prison
for life ? For what offenses can he be executed ?

THE ECONOMIC COSTLINESS OF CRIMINALS

Topics for Discussion

1. What is the distinction between the ultimate and the immediate cost of crime ?

2. What are the ultimate costs of crime ?

3. Are the insurance premiums we pay to be classified as losses
due to crime ?

4. Should stolen property be classified as lost ?

5. What do you think is the most destructive type of criminal
activity ?

6. Is it important to know the annual aggregate economic cost
of crime ?

7. What is the purpose of the recommendation that studies of
municipal costs of administering criminal justice be continued ?

Subjects for Reports

1. The Objectives of Economic Studies of Crime.
2. What Crime Costs Me.
3. The Non-Economic Costs of Crime.
4. The Dividends of Crime.
5. The Economics of Racketeering.
6. Getting Our Money's Worth in Police Work.
7. Private Expenditures for Crime Protection.
8. Homicide in the United States.
9. The Division of Costs in the Administration of Criminal
Justice.
10. Unwise Criminal Statutes.
11. The Economic Profits of Crime.

EXERCISES

1. Figure out the immediate money cost of crime to your family for the past year showing clearly what items are included and how their costs were determined.
2. Try to devise a scheme for bringing before every family head in the United States a vivid conception of the tribute that he pays to criminals.

THE MORAL AND SOCIAL COSTLINESS OF CRIMINALS

TOPICS FOR DISCUSSION

1. What is meant by the statement that the criminal person is the "locus of criminal infection"? Is it true?
2. Are there any particular types of persons to whom a criminal career would appeal?
3. In what ways do honest citizens encourage crime? Why do they do it?
4. Why do people vote for the servants of the underworld?
5. Is a man like Al Capone another Robin Hood?
6. Is a legitimate business that uses methods of the sort described by Donald Richberg less a public menace than one engaged in rum running or the white slave traffic?
7. Are we fundamentally too selfish to combat crime effectively?
8. Is it necessary to understand criminals in order to control them?
9. Do you think that the public's conception of the criminal is sufficiently near the truth to warrant opinions about controlling them?
10. Why do crimes of physical violence arouse us more than crimes of deceit?
11. What effect do honest differences of opinion about moral standards have upon criminality?
12. In what sense are criminals by-products of social change?

SUBJECTS FOR REPORTS

1. The Contagion of Criminality.
2. How Criminal Influences Touch the Layman.
3. The Beginnings of the Standard Oil Company.
4. Criminal Activities Among Legitimate Business Enterprises.
5. The Ramifications of Underworld Big Business.

6. The Relations Between Criminals and Politicians.
7. The Career of Alphonse Capone.
8. The Teapot Dome Case.
9. Tutors in Crime.
10. Night Clubs As Centers of Criminality.
11. Criminal Types in the Works of Charles Dickens.
12. Shakespeare's Criminals.
13. Characteristics of Moving Picture Gangsters.
14. Criminal Stereotypes.
15. Legislative Responses to Crime Waves.
16. Criminal Heroes.
17. Epidemics of Crime.

Exercises

1. List the suggestions to commit crimes that you have received during your lifetime. Classify them as to their sources, nature, attractiveness and any other qualities that may appear important to you. Note the facts about yourself affecting your attitude towards these suggestions ; your age, family, background and so on. What conclusions can you draw from this brief study ?
2. Look about your community and list the attempts to induce others to commit crimes of which you have reliable knowledge. Have you observed any such attempts ? If so, who made them ? By what means ? Why ?
3. Study the newspapers of several cities to discover the reported effects of police clean-up campaigns during the past year. Comment upon your findings.
4. Study the editorial comments of newspapers during the past year on the crime situation in the United States. Write a critical statement upon your findings.

THE EVOLUTION OF THE CONCEPT OF A BIOLOGICAL CRIMINAL TYPE

Topics for Discussion

1. Can you detect criminals by their appearance ? Have you ever done so ?
2. Do you think that the concept of the criminal as "born so" is decreasing among the population at large ? Are there any influences tending towards this end ? Are there any opposing factors ?

3. What do you think of the concept of criminals as persons who are mentally sick?
4. If criminals are not different in appearance from non-criminals why are they conventionally pictured as having "hardened faces"?
5. What is your present estimate of Lombroso's work?
6. Are the author's assumptions about the characteristics of uncaught criminals valid?
7. How much of our present confusion is due to varying connotations of the word "criminal"?
8. What is your present conception of the physical and mental characteristics of criminals?

Subjects for Reports

1. Newspaper Descriptions of Criminals.
2. Character Reading.
3. The Life and Work of Cesare Lombroso.
4. A Critique of Goring's "The English Convict."
5. The Intelligence of Criminals.
6. The Physical Characteristics of Some Famous Criminals.
7. Clarence Darrow's Conception of Criminals.
8. The Census Bureau's Picture of Criminals.
9. The Place of Franz Gall in Criminal Anthropology.
10. Ernest Hooton's Studies in Criminal Anthropology.

Exercises

1. Visit any available penal institution and also the criminal courts. Examine the rogue's gallery at police headquarters if possible. Write out your observations.
2. Compare the physical characteristics of criminals as pictured by Shakespeare, Dickens, Dostoyevsky, Conan Doyle, and S. S. Van Dine.
3. Question a number of your acquaintances about the characteristics of criminals.

FACTORS CONDITIONING CRIMINAL BEHAVIOR

Topics for Discussion

1. How important are technic factors among the forces influencing human conduct? Can you think of any technic factors whose influence has been markedly conducive to criminality?

2. Would it be worth while to pursue further the type of investigation made by Johannes Lange?

3. What bearing has physical over-development upon delinquency?

4. Is mental defect conducive to criminality? Does it lead to any particular types of crime? Is it to any extent a preventive of crime?

5. What types of crime are associated with drunkenness? To what, if any, extent does chronic alcoholism make criminal behavior impossible?

6. What are the characteristics of criminals who are drug addicts?

7. What do you think of the theory of "our lawless heritage" as an explanation of criminality in the United States? Ought it to be applicable also to Canada?

8. What are your conclusions about the effect of business cycles in causing criminality?

9. Do you agree that formal education is "a neutral force neither conducive to delinquent behavior nor preventive of it"?

10. What is a "bad home" from the standpoint of the criminologist?

Subjects for Reports

1. A Critique of the Whittier Scales for Grading Home and Neighborhood Conditions.

2. Criminal Behavior and The Ductless Glands.

3. Case Studies of Psychopathic Criminals.

4. The Newspapers and Crime.

5. The Relations Between Moving Pictures and Delinquency.

6. An Analysis of Crime Causation in the Career of "The Jack-Roller."

7. A Critique of the Case Study Method for Understanding the Causes of Criminal Behavior.

8. A Freudian Looks at Criminals.

9. It's the Weather.

10. What We Do Not Know About the Causes of Criminal Behavior.

Exercises

1. (*a*) Rate several homes with which you are acquainted as very poor, poor, fair, good, and very good from the criminologist's viewpoint, using any information at your disposal.

(*b*) Grade these same homes by the Whittier score card.

    (*c*) Analyze the personalities of members of these families whom you know well. Try to list all of the major factors that have made them the sort of persons that they are.

    (*d*) Write out your conclusions and a critique of your experiment.

2. Analyze your own behavior pattern using if possible some such aid as Allport's "North Carolina Rating Scale for Fundamental Traits." Compare the judgment of other persons with your own. Then try to evaluate the influences biological, geographical, technic, and social that have made you what you are.

    Of what importance is such an exercise to the student of criminology?

CHILDHOOD AND THE FOUNDATIONS OF BEHAVIOR

Topics for Discussion

1. How soon does a baby begin to behave consciously?
2. How soon does a baby begin to interpret the attitudes of others towards himself?
3. How soon may he practice conscious deception to achieve ends that he knows are forbidden?
4. Are the forces that give rise to misbehavior necessary to its continuation?
5. Is it true that the habits of early childhood have an important influence upon adult character?
6. What are some of the reasons for temper tantrums, jealousy, pilfering, and destructiveness in children under six years of age?
7. Should pre-school children be punished? If so, what should be the purpose of the punishment? What types of punishment are there? What principles should govern the infliction of punishment?
8. What is your conception of ideal parent-child relationships?

Subjects for Reports

1. The Use of Rewards in Establishing Good Habits.
2. The Experiences of Habit Clinics with Pre-School Children.
3. Habit Clinic Procedure.

4. Cases of Disobedience, Lying and Stealing in Pre-School Children.
5. The Emotional State of the Mother as a Factor in Childish Misbehavior.
6. Examples of Wise and Unwise Discipline.
7. The Effects of Physical Surroundings Upon Unwholesome Habit Formation in Children.
8. Problem Parents.
9. Sex Curiosity in Young Children.
10. Emotional Starvation in Children.

EXERCISES

1. Visit a nursery school and compare its régime with that of homes that you know in which there are children of the same age. Note the advantages and disadvantages of each, particularly with reference to the establishment of habits that you think may have a bearing upon later delinquency.
2. Visit the waiting room of a habit clinic, a kindergarten on its opening day, the waiting room of a hospital clinic for little children or some similar institution and record the behavior of the children towards each other and their parents in accordance with a scheme previously devised that will relate your observations to your knowledge of early habit formation.
3. Tell the story of the nine-year-old-boy recorded on Page 115. "A little boy nine years old . . . of poor mental balance," to several parents of your acquaintance, and ask them what they would do if one of their children became such a problem.

EXPANDING HORIZONS : MISADVENTURING INTO COMMUNITY LIFE

TOPICS FOR DISCUSSION

1. In what ways may teacher idiosyncrasies influence the behavior of pupils ?
2. What new forces start to play upon the child when he begins to go to school ?
3. Should the school be interested in the behavior of children who are able to do their school work satisfactorily ?
4. What are the evils of truancy ? Has it any compensating advantages ?

5. What are the evils of street begging by children?
6. What attitude should an adult observer take towards running away, begging, or impromptu street entertaining by children?

SUBJECTS FOR REPORTS

1. Recruiting tramps.
2. The activities of boy gangs.
3. Precocity as a factor in delinquency.
4. Adult responsibility for juvenile delinquency.
5. The problem of the native born child of foreign parentage.
6. The school as a disciplinary agency.
7. Slum children who have "made good" compared with those who have not.

EXERCISES

1. Make several walking trips about your city and observe the type, location and frequency of occurrence of irregular behavior in street children. Compare your findings with the statements made in chapter seven.
2. Observe what street trades are engaged in by children in your city. What effects does the work seem to have upon them? Do certain kinds of work attract children of particular types? What dangers do you find in such work? What is the law with reference to street trades in your city? How well is it enforced?
3. Make a study of conditions in a rural school taking into account the school factors mentioned in chapter seven and any others that seem important to you. Is there any connection between behavior problems in that school and the conditions that you have observed?
4. Talk with college students who have attended rural schools and those who have come from city schools about the forms of misbehavior that appeared most commonly among them while they were in the lower grades.

ADOLESCENCE AND THE DIFFICULTIES OF A CHANGING LIFE

TOPICS FOR DISCUSSION

1. Do you agree that the chief interests of adolescents are money, girl (boy), and a thrill? If not, what are their major interests?

2. Are adolescent interests more likely to lead to delinquencies than the interests of adults? Than those of grammar school children?

3. What part does love play in checking delinquent careers? In inducing criminality?

4. What is the relation between the use of automobiles and delinquency?

5. Are the family crises of adolescents factors in their delinquencies?

6. Should commercial amusement enterprises assume more responsibility than they do for their influence upon their youthful patrons?

7. What work conditions of adolescents do you consider to be most likely to breed delinquencies?

8. What is the rôle of advertising in the misbehavior of young people? Does it play any part in maintaining good conduct?

SUBJECTS FOR REPORTS

1. Adolescent Mental Conflict and Crime.
2. Community Responsibility for Adolescent Offenses.
3. The Pre-Reformatory Background of the Gluecks' 500 Cases.
4. Instalment Buying By Adolescents.
5. The Pleasure Philosophy of Youth.
6. Why Thrills?
7. "Con" Games and Sales Talks.
8. Publicity Stunts of Young Offenders.
9. Sex and Delinquency.
10. Delinquencies and Parental Failures.

EXERCISES

1. Make a survey of the number of commercial and non-commercial opportunities for adolescent recreation in your community. Visit a few of these amusement places and observe conditions therein.

2. Make a list of specific present-day juvenile offenses that could not have been committed in your community fifty years ago.

THE CRIMINAL HABIT

TOPICS FOR DISCUSSION

1. Are there any adult first offenders ? If so, what would you expect their characteristics to be ?
2. Of what value are attempts to classify criminals ?
3. Are criminals by avocation as much of a social menace as criminals by vocation ?
4. Why are there relatively few women criminals ?
5. Is it possible for a habitual criminal to reform ?
6. Are the requirements of criminal occupations changing ? If so, in what ways ?
7. Where is the underworld ? What are its relations to society ?
8. Are criminals younger than they used to be ? If so, why ?
9. What is the nature of "honor among thieves" ?
10. In what ways are criminals and non-criminals alike ?
11. Could "Two-Gun" Crowley's career have been averted ? By what means ?

SUBJECTS FOR REPORTS

1. Feudal Organizations in the Underworld.
2. The World of the Tramp.
3. Caste Among Criminals.
4. Classifications of Criminals.
5. Female Offenders.
6. The Influence of Modern Protective Devices Upon Criminal Occupations.
7. Social Conformity Among Criminals.
8. A Critique of Criminals' Autobiographies.
9. Criminal Occupations.
10. The Private Life of a Criminal.
11. The Role of the Fence in the Underworld.

EXERCISES

1. A man walked into a speakeasy and after wheedling drinks from others flaunted a roll of bills. Two farm hands who saw the proceedings suddenly decided to get his money. They waylaid the man and robbed him on his way home.

    Reconstruct the most likely history for these two men that might have made it possible for them to think and act as they did.

2. Read the autobiography of Charles L. Clark (Clark and Eubank, "Lockstep and Corridor"). List in parallel columns the viewpoints expressed that you consider peculiar to the criminal world and those that you commonly find among non-criminals.

THE PREVENTION OF CRIMINAL BEHAVIOR: GENERAL METHODS

TOPICS FOR DISCUSSION

1. What is meant by "crime prevention"?
2. Is there any danger that stricter marriage requirements may increase crime?
3. Assuming proper educational qualifications what faults have you most commonly found in your teachers? Do you think that such flaws are important factors in the misbehavior of school children?
4. What do you consider to be the ideal traits of personality in school teachers?
5. What part does your church play in preventing crime? Could it do more? How?
6. What improvements in industrial relations do you think might decrease crime?.

SUBJECTS FOR REPORTS

1. The visiting teacher movement as a preventive of crime.
2. Possibilities of crime prevention through Americanization classes.
3. The United States Children's Bureau as an agency for crime prevention.
4. Degenerate communities and their elimination.
5. The boys' club and the boys' gang.
6. Housing reforms as preventives of crime.
7. A eugenic program of crime prevention.
8. The relation between marriage reform and criminality.

EXERCISES

1. Talk with ministers, Y.M.C.A. secretaries, scout masters and other leaders of young people in your community to discover:
   (a) Whether they consider any part of their work from the standpoint of crime prevention.

(*b*) The effectiveness of their methods in preventing crime.
2. For one week keep parallel lists of any outstanding evidences of social responsibility and irresponsibility bearing upon crime that you notice, with your comments on each.

THE PREVENTION OF CRIMINAL BEHAVIOR: SPECIFIC METHODS

TOPICS FOR DISCUSSION

1. When crime is prevented in one field do criminals simply shift to another ? If this is so, is there any justification for crime prevention work ? If so, what is the fundamental problem in crime prevention ?
2. Is there any essential difference between individualization of treatment and *scientific* individualization of treatment ? If so, what is it ?
3. Can juvenile courts rightly be thought of as crime prevention agencies ?
4. What are the merits of foster homes for problem children as compared with institutions manned by specialists in child training ?
5. Ought the police to stress prevention of crime much more than they do ? What could the American police do in the field of crime prevention ?
6. What could a permanent state criminal research bureau accomplish that would justify its great cost ?
7. What do you think of the junior republic plan ?

SUBJECTS FOR REPORTS

1. The treatment of delinquents in foster homes.
2. Preventive police work in Europe.
3. Juvenile court theory and procedure.
4. The policewoman's movement.
5. The treatment of defective delinquents.
6. Cases illustrating the successful treatment of juvenile delinquents.
7. The big brother movement.
8. Judge Ben Lindsey's work with delinquents.
9. The work of Healy and Bronner with problem children.
10. Junior Republics.

EXERCISES

1. By talking with them or reading their writings, get the opinions of lawyers, psychiatrists, social workers, ministers, policemen, penal administrators, and criminals about the best ways of preventing crime. What conclusions can you draw from the results of your work?

2. Draw up a practical program of crime prevention for a community with which you are familiar, indicating specifically the part that each welfare agency will be expected to assume in carrying it out.

THE POLICE

TOPICS FOR DISCUSSION

1. Should the state give police power to employees hired by private concerns to protect their property? If not, how else may companies owning extensive property gain protection for it?

2. What do you think the functions of a state police force should be?

3. Why are the police and political groups so closely allied?

4. Do you favor the fingerprinting of all school children between thirteen and fifteen in the United States? Could it be done successfully? What obstacles would be in the way of such a program?

5. Should the police of the United States be given greater authority than they now have? What authority?

6. Should police commissioners be promoted from the police ranks?

7. What do you think should be the essential qualifications of a policeman?

8. Should the police be expected to carry on a program of crime prevention?

SUBJECTS FOR REPORTS

1. European police training schools.
2. Dactyloscopy.
3. Police journalism in the United States.
4. The Metropolitan Police of London.
5. The work of Arthur Woods as police commissioner of New York.

6. The police force of Berkeley, California.
7. The policewoman in the United States.
8. Policeman and public in Europe and America.
9. Theodore Roosevelt as police commissioner of New York.
10. The mechanical equipment of the police in the United States.
11. The Canadian Northwest Mounted Police.

EXERCISES

1. Devise a detailed plan for properly patrolling your town or district which shall include a statement of the duties of the men required to carry it out. Critically compare your plan with the one that the police now have in operation.
2. Make a critical analysis of the latest annual police report of your city.
3. Consider the possibility of preventing payroll robberies through the payment of wages by checks.
4. Consider the possibilities in crime prevention by means of the talking pictures.

THE ADMINISTRATORS OF CRIMINAL JUSTICE

TOPICS FOR DISCUSSION

1. Does our present court system generally result in justice?
2. Are appointed judges likely to be more satisfactory than elected judges?
3. Do you think it wise to permit a defendant to choose whether he will have his case heard by a jury or simply by a judge?
4. What can be done to minimize the influence of the fundamental difficulties in legal administration pointed out by Dean Roscoe Pound?
5. What is the relative importance of the municipal court magistrate and the trial court judge?
6. Can lay citizens be charged with any direct responsibility for the conditions surrounding our court system?
7. What would be the difference in function between a state judicial council controlling a unified court system and a state ministry of justice?
8. Would you limit the function of the trial court to the determination of guilt?
9. Should the state provide a public defender in criminal cases to aid all defendants who can not afford an attorney?
10. Are there any objections to the establishment of a commercial agency to act as surety for defendants admitted to bail?

Subjects for Reports

1. The Development of Criminal Procedure in England.
2. The Nature of the Judicial Mind.
3. The History of the Public Defender Movement.
4. A Critique of the Rules of Evidence in Criminal Cases.
5. The Use of Psychiatry by Our Courts.
6. The Influence of Journalism upon the Courts.
7. The Psychology of Testimony.
8. The Future of Juries.
9. The Need and Functions of a Ministry of Justice.
10. Famous Criminal Trials.
11. The Use of the *Nolle Prosequi* in Criminal Cases.
12. The Strategy of the Trial.
13. The Reform of Criminal Procedure.
14. The Training of the American Lawyer.

Exercises

1. Visit a magistrate's court and analyze your impressions. Try to put yourself in the place of a first offender charged with a petty crime in that court: what effect would the procedure have on you? What would be the effect on you if you were the magistrate? An innocent alien? The victim of a criminal?
2. Visit a criminal trial before a jury and analyze your impressions. Note particularly the tactics of the prosecuting and defending attorneys. If you were a juryman would you feel competent to reach a just verdict?

MINOR PUNISHMENTS

Topics for Discussion

1. Should a fine be adjusted to the economic status of an offender?
2. What should be done with money collected in fines?
3. What types of potential offenders are apt to be deterred by fines?
4. What types are not likely to be deterred by fines?
5. What place would you give to fines in our system of punishment?
6. Is the loss of civil rights a handicap to reformation?
7. What practical effects would the loss of civil rights have upon you if you were convicted of an infamous crime?

SUBJECTS FOR REPORTS

1. The Payment of Fines in Instalments.
2. Fines and Restitution.
3. The Fine System in Europe.
4. Infamous Crime as a Ground for Divorce.
5. Fines and Community Protection.
6. Fines as a Source of Municipal Revenue.

EXERCISES

1. Visit a magistrate's court and observe the assessment of fines. Are the fines varied with the offense or with the offender? On what basis do they seem to be assessed? Do you think that the persons who are fined are apt to be deterred from repeating their offenses because of their fines? Do most of them pay their fines and depart? What happens to those who do not?

2. Do you know persons who have been fined? If so, for what were they fined? Talk with them to discover how they felt about the whole affair and more particularly to find out how the penalty has effected their conduct since their conviction.

PROBATION AND ITS ADMINISTRATORS

TOPICS FOR DISCUSSION

1. What are the chief obstacles to the success of probation at present?
2. What are the most important qualifications of a good probation officer?
3. Should probation departments be independent of the courts in the sense that prisons are?
4. Should probation be limited to misdemeanants?
5. Should probation be limited to juveniles?
6. What restrictions should be placed on the use of probation?
7. Have community welfare agencies any responsibility for the success of the probation service?
8. Is success on probation likely to be followed by success after discharge from probation?
9. What are your chief criticisms of probation?

Subjects for Reports

1. The Spread of Probation Throughout the World.
2. The Development of the Federal Probation System.
3. John Augustus, Bootmaker and Volunteer Probation Officer.
4. The Qualities of a Good Probation Officer.
5. Probation as a Deterrent of Criminals.
6. The Relation of Religion to Probation.
7. The Possibilities in Coöperation between Probation Officers and Boys' Club Leaders.
8. Probation and the Big Brother Movement.
9. Opportunities for College Graduates in Probation Work.
10. The Place of Probation in Penology.
11. Probation as a Form of Punishment.
12. Contemporary Opinion about Probation.

Exercises

1. Examine the probation laws of your state and write a critique of them.
2. Draw up an ideal course of studies intended to be taken during the last two years of college by men and women desirous of becoming probation officers. Compare your ideal program with the courses and opportunities actually available at present in your institution.

CORPORAL PUNISHMENTS: THE BLOOD-LETTING STAGE

Topics for Discussion

1. What are the purposes of punishment?
2. What factors have determined the forms of the death penalty?
3. How effective is capital punishment as a deterrent of crime?
4. What is the future of capital punishment?
5. Is flogging an effective punishment for certain types of crimes or criminals? What types?
6. Would you revive exposure as a punishment?
7. In what ways did transportation to America differ from transportation to Australia?
8. Would floating prisons be worth-while today?
9. Is corporal punishment apt to be a more severe penalty than imprisonment?
10. Is exile a successful type of punishment?

Subjects for Reports

1. Crimes and Punishments in Primitive Societies.
2. The History of Capital Punishment.
3. Colonization by Prisoners.
4. Crimes and Punishments of Colonial Days.
5. The History of Sterilization Laws in the United States.
6. The Advantages of the Whipping Post.
7. Punishment by Ridicule.
8. The Era of the Hulks.
9. Devil's Island.
10. The Right to Punish.

Exercises

1. What corporal punishments are now legal in your state? For what crimes may each be imposed? How frequently are they used? Why are they used?
2. If you are at a port of call of the convict ship *Success* visit it and write a report of your visit with critical comments.

HUMAN IMPRISONMENT: A HISTORY OF CONFLICTING PRACTICES

Topics for Discussion

1. What were the chief influences leading to the replacement of corporal punishment by imprisonment?
2. What advantages, if any, has imprisonment over corporal punishment?
3. What good do you think was done by imprisonment as carried out during the nineteenth century?
4. What in your opinion are the relative merits of the Pennsylvania and Auburn systems?
5. Should prisons be made comfortable?
6. What are the purposes of imprisonment? What should be the purposes of imprisonment? Are these aims mutually compatible?
7. What are the most striking facts about the evolution of the idea of imprisonment?

Subjects for Reports

1. Ancient Prisons.
2. The Life and Work of John Howard.

3. The Part of the Quakers in Prison Reform.
4. Jeremy Bentham's Panoptican.
5. The Life and Work of Elizabeth Fry.
6. Prison Problems and Management During the Nineteenth Century.
7. The Early Jails of England.
8. San Michele.
9. The Influence of the Pennsylvania System Abroad.
10. A Critical Comparison of Eighteenth and Twentieth Century Jails.
11. The History of the Parisian Bastille.
12. Famous Prison Wardens of the Nineteenth Century.
13. Newgate of Connecticut.

Exercises

1. When was your local jail built? How many prisoners can it accommodate? How many are now confined there? How are the sexes separated? What sanitary provisions are there? What is the daily food allowance? How many prisoners are there because they have been sentenced to jail? Why are the others there? Are any of them innocent prisoners? How do these conditions compare with those described by John Howard?

2. Examine the annual reports of your state prison and any other sources of information about its history. What are the most important changes that have been made in its equipment? Its routine? Its administrative policies? Are they in line with the general evolution of prisons in this country? Is yours a typical United States prison?

THE REFORMATION OF PRISONERS: THE GROWTH OF AN IDEA

Topics for Discussion

1. What sorts of persons are now sent to our reformatories?
2. Are reformatory inmates reformable?
3. Is it worth while to spend time and money in the attempt to reform them?
4. What means of reformation do we have at our disposal?
5. What does reformation involve? When is a person reformed?
6. How do you account for the decline of adult reformatories in the United States?

7. Has the adult reformatory any place in a modern penal system? If so, what is it?
8. Has the juvenile reformatory any place in a modern penal system? If so, what is it? What would be the characteristics of such an institution?
9. In what ways do the tasks of men's and women's reformatories differ?
10. What, in your opinion, is apt to be the future of the adult reformatory?

SUBJECTS FOR REPORTS

1. Early Houses of Refuge.
2. Modern Correctional Institutions for Juveniles.
3. The Mark System of Alexander Maconochie.
4. The Irish System.
5. Elmira.
6. Adult Reformatories of the United States Today.
7. A Critical Review of the Gluecks' study of "500 Criminal Careers."
8. The Trend of the Reformatory Movement.

EXERCISES

1. Is there an adult reformatory in your state? Read its annual reports. Visit it if possible. What sorts of prisoners does it receive? How does it handle them? What does it do to reform them? Is it successful? Does its régime differ from that in your state's prison? If so, how? What does the "Handbook of American Prisons and Reformatories" have to say about it? What do your taxpayer friends know about it? What do they think of it?

JAILS AND THE JAILED

TOPICS FOR DISCUSSION

1. How important are jails?
2. Why are jail inmates different in type from prison and reformatory inmates?
3. Should jails be made sanitary? Comfortable? What should a jail be like?
4. Should persons detained in jail, who are subsequently found "not guilty," be entitled to recompense?
5. What are the reasons for idleness in jails?

6. What is accomplished by sentencing a man to jail?
7. Should all county jails be abolished? If so, what should take their places?
8. What are the advantages and disadvantages of state farms for misdemeanants?
9. What should be done with the chronic drunkards who make up a considerable portion of our jail population?
10. What is your estimate of our present jail system?
11. What are the chief obstacles to its improvement? How can they be removed?

SUBJECTS FOR REPORTS

1. The History of the County Jails.
2. State Control of County Jails.
3. The Sheriff as a Jail Keeper.
4. Chain Gangs in the South.
5. Handling the Vagrant.
6. Making Misdemeanants Work.
7. The Belgian Colony at Merxplas.
8. The Treatment of Chronic Drunkards.
9. The Penal Farm at Witzwil.
10. The Detention of Juvenile Prisoners.

EXERCISES

1. Visit a county jail and observe:
   (a) The physical conditions within.
   (b) The types of prisoners.
   (c) The characteristics of the guards.
   (d) The employment of inmates.
   Write down your observations accurately immediately after the visit and contrast them with the related statements in the text.
2. Set down the fundamental facts that you think every voter should know about the county jail. Question as many voters as you can to see how closely their actual knowledge approaches the ideal.

REFORMATORIES, PRISONS AND THE IMPRISONED

TOPICS FOR DISCUSSION

1. What principles should govern the construction of prisons?
2. What should be the qualifications of a prison warden? Of prison guards?
3. Why are women's reformatories in general more progressive than men's?
4. What should be the primary objectives of prison management?
5. Should prison life be made as nearly as possible like life outside of prison walls? In what ways would the attempt to do this change present conditions?
6. What is your explanation of prison riots?
7. What should be done with psychopathic prisoners, drug addicts, and sex perverts?
8. Are fortress-type prisons an extravagance? How would you economize?
9. What relation do you think exists between the efficiency of prison administration and the number of escapes?
10. Should prisoners be given any part in prison management?

SUBJECTS FOR REPORTS

1. The Prison Farms of the South.
2. Women's Reformatories in the United States.
3. The Life and Work of Jessie D. Hodder.
4. The Prison as a Community.
5. Training Schools for Prison Guards.
6. The Diversification of Penal Institutions.
7. Prison Life as the Prisoners See It.
8. Sing Sing Prison.
9. If I Were A Prison Warden.
10. If I Were Imprisoned.

EXERCISES

1. Visit a state prison or reformatory and:
   (a) Observe the architectural features of the plant.
   (b) Step inside of a cell and measure it with your arms.
   (c) Note and inquire about the arrangements for heat, light, ventilation, toilet purposes, eating.
   (d) Note and inquire about the arrangements for receiving visitors to prisoners.

(*e*) Get a copy of the rules given to new prisoners.

(*f*) Note the characteristics of the guards and prisoners.

(*g*) Are the guards armed?   What are their relations with the prisoners?

Write down your observations accurately immediately *after* the visit and contrast them with the report on that same institution in the latest "Handbook of American Prisons and Reformatories."

2. Examine in some detail the news reports of riots in several penal institutions throughout the country.   Look up the conditions in these institutions at that time as reported in the "Handbook of American Prisons and Reformatories." Write down your diagnosis of the cause of each disturbance.

THE REORIENTATION OF PRISONERS

TOPICS FOR DISCUSSION

1. What systems of prison labor do you favor?   Why?
2. Should prisoners be paid wages?
3. Should prisons attempt to become self-supporting?
4. Should prisoners be permitted to work and live under supervision outside of the prison walls?
5. How should prison schools be organized?
6. What subjects should be taught in prison schools?
7. In 1931 Sing Sing prison was represented by an inmate football team that played several games within the walls with non-convict elevens.   What do you think of the idea? Should such teams ever be permitted to play outside of the walls?
8. How should the religious requirements of inmates be met?
9. How could the services of chaplains be improved?
10. What should be the objectives of the prison régime?

SUBJECTS FOR REPORTS

1. The Employment of Prisoners on Public Works.
2. The Management of Prison Industries.
3. Unemployment in Prisons.
4. The Attitude of Trade Unions Towards Prison Labor.
5. The Correctional Aspects of Prison Labor.
6. Prison Journalism.
7. Convict Literature.
8. Prisons and the Church.

9. A Health Program for Prisons.
10. Coddling Prisoners.

EXERCISES

1. Try to discover the sentiment of business men you may know with reference to prison labor questions. Should prisoners work? Should they be paid for it? What should be done with the products of prison labor? What do you think of their views? Do they show a reasonable understanding of the facts to be considered?

2. Examine the reports in the latest "Handbook of American Prisons and Reformatories" on the following institutions:
   Federal Industrial Institution for Women, Alderson, West Virginia.
      United States Penitentiary, Atlanta, Georgia
      California State Prison, San Quentin
      Massachusetts Reformatory for Women, Framingham
      New Hampshire State Prison, Concord
      Minnesota State Prison, Stillwater
      New York State Reformatory for Women, Bedford Hills
      Kentucky State Penitentiary, Eddyville
      Texas State Penitentiary and State Farms
   What do you consider to be the outstanding features, good and bad, of these penal institutions, insofar as they can be judged in this manner?

THE ABSOLUTE AND CONDITIONAL RELEASE OF PRISONERS

TOPICS FOR DISCUSSION

1. Should the pardoning power be abolished?
2. Is the wholly indeterminate sentence desirable?
3. Should prisoners be paroled under the supervision of private agencies?
4. Are there any essential differences between the problems of probation and parole?
5. What are the chief obstacles to the improvement of parole?
6. Are prediction tables useful in selecting men for parole?
7. What qualifications would you require of a man whom you would be willing to place on parole?
8. Who should select prisoners for parole?

9. What should be the attitude of the public towards ex-prisoners?
10. What should be the qualifications of a parole agent?

SUBJECTS FOR REPORTS

1. Prisoner's Aid Societies.
2. Illustrative Parole Cases.
3. The Ex-prisoner's Opportunities to Work.
4. The Parole of Juveniles.
5. The Rules Governing Parolees.
6. The Elements of an Ideal Parole System.
7. The History of Parole.
8. The History of the Indeterminate Sentence.
9. Parole as the Prisoner Views It.
10. The Preparation of Prisoners for Parole.

EXERCISES

1. Study the organization of parole in your state and contrast it with what you would consider an ideal system.
2. Talk with your neighbors, policemen, lawyers, ministers and other available persons to get their opinions on parole. What is their conception of the purpose of parole? Of its practice? Of its possibilities?
3. Talk with business men about the employment of ex-prisoners. Would they employ an ex-prisoner? Why, or why not? Would it make any difference to them what kind of work the ex-prisoner wanted? Would they care what his offense had been?

THE PENAL SCIENCE OF TOMORROW

TOPICS FOR DISCUSSION

1. What should be the objectives of penology?
2. Should we be concerned with developing the personal assets of prisoners?
3. What is the difference between Osborne's idea of "self-government" and the Norfolk practice of "joint responsibility"?
4. Will "treatment" be less of a crime deterrent than "punishment"?
5. Should prisoners be made to suffer for the pain they have caused others?

6. How would a receiving and diagnostic prison function?
7. Should we follow Russia in discarding the concept of freedom of the will? If so, what effect would it have upon our penology?
8. What do you think of England's use of prison visitors? Should we develop a similar practice?
9. Just what is meant by "professionalization of the prison service"?
10. What are the prospects for a rational penal system in the near future?

SUBJECTS FOR REPORTS

1. Recent Progress Towards a Rational Penology in the United States.
2. The Present Status of Self-Government in our Prisons.
3. The Place of Thomas Mott Osborne in Penology.
4. The Belgium Penal System.
5. Preparing Prisoners for the Normal Life by Practice.
6. Fitting the Community to Receive Ex-Prisoners.
7. The Russian Penal System.
8. Prisons and Sentimentality.
9. The Treatment of the Incorrigible Offender.
10. The Practice of Penology Around the World.

EXERCISES

1. Look up the penal institutions of your state. How many are there? What types? What are their relations? Are they under centralized control? Visit as many of them as you can. Where does your state keep its defective delinquents? Its criminal insane? Its chronic drunkards? Its psychopathic offenders? The babies of convict mothers? Its professional criminals? Its juvenile delinquents?

   Write a constructive criticism of your state's penal organization.

2. Get your friends who are leaders of community thought (ministers, teachers, journalists et al.) to state concisely in writing what they consider to be the objectives of penology. *After* you have their statements sound them out on the ideas advanced in this chapter. Write up your own conclusions.

SELECTED REFERENCES

BIBLIOGRAPHIES

STUDENTS of criminology will find the following bibliographies of assistance :

Kuhlman, A. F.   A Guide to Material on Crime and Criminal Justice.

Conner, C.   Crime Commissions and Criminal Procedure in the United States Since 1920. *Jour. Criminal Law and Criminology*, Vol. 21 : 129-144.

National Commission on Law Observance and Enforcement.   Report on the Causes of Crime, Vol. 1 : 143-161.

New York Public Library.   List of Works Relating to Criminology.

McCarthy, K. O.   Racketeering, A Contribution to a Bibliography. *Jour. Criminal Law and Criminology*, Vol. 22 : 578-586.

Wigmore, J. H.   One Hundred Legal Novels. *Library Journal*, Vol. 52 : 189-190.

Campbell, D.   Bibliography on Training of Police. *Jour. Criminal Law and Criminology*, Vol. 24 : 591.

Glueck, S. (Director) and others.   Annotated Selected Bibliographical Digest of Crime-Causation Literature Since 1900, in Gries and Ford, Housing and the Community.

Wire, G. E.   Index of Celebrated Cases, Crimes, Criminals, Detectives, Escapes, Homicides, Mysteries, Swindles, Trials, etc., Described in General Books (Not in Volumes Specifically Devoted to the Particular Case or Person). *Jour. Criminal Law and Criminology*, Vol. 21 : 339-361.

Reviews of the more important new works in criminology are to be found in the current issues of the *Journal of Criminal Law and Criminology*.

Among the journals in English carrying useful articles are :

> *Journal of Criminal Law and Criminology.*
> *Journal of Juvenile Research.*
> *Journal of Social Hygiene.*
> *Mental Hygiene.*
> *The Survey.*
> *American Prison Association Proceedings.*
> *Journal of the American Judicature Society.*
> *National Probation Association Proceedings.*

National Conference of Social Work Proceedings.
American Bar Association Journal.
Sociology and Social Research.
Birth Control Review.
The News Bulletin of the Osborne Association.

The references marked "especially recommended" will serve together as a minimum reference library for those who are giving a course in criminology for the first time. Students who wish to add a section on criminology to their libraries might well purchase selections from the same list. The following books chosen primarily because they are interesting as well as informative might also find a place in the layman's library:

Alexander and Staub. The Criminal, the Judge, and the Public.
Bjerre, A. The Psychology of Murder.
Borchard, E. M. Convicting the Innocent.
Drucker and Hexter. Children Astray.
George, W. The George Junior Republic.
Gillin, J. L. Taming the Criminal.
Glueck, S. S. and E. T. 500 Delinquent Women.
Gordon, M. Penal Discipline.
Howard, J. The State of the Prisons in England and Wales.
Lawes, L. E. 20,000 Years in Sing Sing.
MacDougall, E. D. (Ed.). Crime for Profit.
McAdoo, W. G. Guarding a Great City.
O'Hare, K. In Prison.
Tannenbaum, F. Osborne of Sing Sing.
Tannenbaum, F. Wall Shadows.
Ulman, J. F. A Judge Takes the Stand.
Wembridge, E. R. Life Among the Lowbrows.
Woods, A. Policeman and Public.

PRISON JOURNALISM

STUDENTS desirous of gaining a hint about the interests and attitudes of prisoners may find it helpful to read critically some of the papers and magazines published by inmates of penal and correctional institutions. Among those most useful for this purpose are the following:

The New Era. U. S. Penitentiary, Leavenworth, Kansas.
The Island Lantern. U. S. Penitentiary, McNeil Island, Wash.
Good Words. U. S. Penitentiary, Atlanta, Ga.
The Beacon. U. S. Industrial Reformatory, Chillicothe, Ohio.
The Bulletin. California State Prison, San Quentin.
The Monthly Record. Connecticut State Prison, Wethersfield.
The Golden Rule. Kansas State Penitentiary, Lansing.
The Mentor. Massachusetts State Prison, Charlestown.
The Colony. Massachusetts State Prison Colony, Norfolk.
The Seed (an occasional collection of verse). Massachusetts Reformatory for Women, Framingham.

The School News. Michigan State Prison, Jackson.
The Prison Mirror. Minnesota State Prison, Stillwater.
The Advance. New Jersey State Home for Boys, Jamesburg.
The Summary. Elmira Reformatory, Elmira, N. Y.
The Prison News. North Carolina State Prison, Raleigh.
Ohio Penitentiary News. Ohio State Penitentiary, Columbus.
The Question. Rhode Island State Prison, Howard.
The Utah Penwiper. Utah State Prison, Salt Lake City.
The Beacon. Virginia Penitentiary, Richmond.
Agenda. Washington State Penitentiary, Walla Walla.

Of these the San Quentin *Bulletin* and the McNeil Island Penitentiary's *Island Lantern* are unusually well edited with the Washington State *Agenda* and the Rhode Island *Question* not far behind. Among the papers published in juvenile institutions, *The Advance* of the New Jersey State Home for Boys is outstanding.

Among the more important institutions that do not have any inmate publications are the following:

Illinois State Penitentiary.
Maryland Penitentiary.
Nebraska State Penitentiary.
New Hampshire State Prison.
New Jersey State Prison.
Auburn State Prison, New York.
Sing Sing Prison, New York.
Oregon State Penitentiary.
Eastern State Penitentiary, Pennsylvania.
Western State Penitentiary, Pennsylvania.
Wisconsin State Prison.

CRIMINALS AND THE CRIMINAL LAW

SELECTED BIBLIOGRAPHY

Especially Recommended

Kenny, Courtney S. Outlines of Criminal Law, 12th Edition. Cambridge University Press, 1926.
A readable, scholarly, one volume introduction to the principles of criminal law with stimulating comments upon its sociological implications.

BOOKS AND PAMPHLETS

Beale, J. H. A Selection of Cases and Other Authorities Upon Criminal Law.
Bishop, J. P. New Commentaries on the Criminal Law, 9th Ed.
Glueck, S. S. Mental Disorder and the Criminal Law.
Holdsworth, W. S. A History of English Law, 4th Ed., Vol. 3, Ch. 2.
Holmes, O. W. The Common Law.

Jenks, E.   The Book of English Law, Part 4.
Malinowski, B.   Crime and Custom in Savage Society.
Myers, G.   Ye Olden Blue Laws.
Phillipson, C.   Three Criminal Law Reformers : Beccaria, Bentham, Romilly.
Pollock and Maitland.   History of English Law, 2nd Ed., Vol. 1, Ch. 2, and Vol. 2, Ch. 8.
Pound, R.   Readings on the History and System of the Common Law.
Pound, R.   The Spirit of the Common Law.
Pound, R.   Criminal Justice in America.
Sayre, F. B.   A Selection of Cases on Criminal Law.
Smith, E.   Criminal Law in the United States.
Stephen, J. F.   A History of the Criminal Law of England.
Wharton, F.   A Treatise on Criminal Law, 11th Ed.
White, W. A.   Insanity and the Criminal Law.
Williams, E. H.   The Insanity Plea.
The Laws and Liberties of Massachusetts.   Reprinted by Harvard University Press, 1929.

ARTICLES

Baker, N. F.   The Organization of a Course of Study in Criminal Law. *Jour. Criminal Law and Criminology*, Vol. 22 : 833.
Kirchwey, G. W.   Criminal Law, Encyclopedia of the Social Sciences.
Kirchwey, G. W.   The Future of the Criminal Law.   *Proceedings National Conference of Social Work*, 1921.
Levitt, A.   Origin of the Doctrine of Mens Rea, *Illinois Law Review*, Vol. 17 : 117.
Lobingier, C. S.   Customary Law, Encyclopedia of the Social Sciences.
Myers, G.   Blue Laws, Encyclopedia of the Social Sciences.
O'Brien, T. C.   Crime and the Criminal Law, *Mass. Law Quart.*, Vol. 11 : 33.
Pound, R.   Common Law, Encyclopedia of the Social Sciences.
Pound, R.   The Future of the Criminal Law, *Columbia Law Review*, Vol. 21 : 1.
Radcliffe-Brown, A. R.   Law, Primitive, Encyclopedia of the Social Sciences.
Riddell, W. R.   Bygone Phases of Canadian Criminal Law, *Jour. Criminal Law and Criminology*, Vol. 23 : 51.
Sellin, T.   Crime, Encyclopedia of the Social Sciences.

THE ECONOMIC COSTLINESS OF CRIMINALS

SELECTED BIBLIOGRAPHY

Especially Recommended

National Commission on Law Observance and Enforcement.   Report on the Cost of Crime, Government Printing Office, 1931.
A fairly comprehensive, recent and critical analysis of the problem of crime costs resting upon basic statistical material and original investigation.

Books and Pamphlets

Bower, L. F.   The Economic Waste of Sin.

Bruce, A. A.   The Administration of Criminal Justice in Illinois.   Published as Part 2 of the *Jour. Criminal Law and Criminology*, Vol. 19, No. 4.

Cantor, N. F.   Crime, Criminals and Criminal Justice.   Ch. 24.

Flynn, J. T.   Graft in Business.

Gillin, J. L.   Criminology and Penology.   Ch. 3.

Haynes, F. E.   Criminology.   Ch. 1.

MacDougall, E. D. (Ed.).   Crime for Profit.

National Commission on Law Observance and Enforcement.   Report on Criminal Statistics.

Reeves, M.   Training Schools for Delinquent Girls.   Chs. 4, 6, 8.

Sutherland, E. H.   Criminology.   Chs. 2, 3.

Terrett, C.   Only Saps Work.

Articles

Bulger, J. E.   Automobile Thefts, *Jour. Criminal Law and Criminology*, Vol. 23 : 806.

Carter, C. F.   The Carnival of Crime.   *Current History*.   February 1922.

Crowther, S.   Invisible Government, *Ladies' Home Journal*, February 1931.

Davies, A. M.   Criminal Statistics and the National Commission's Report.   *Jour. Criminal Law and Criminology*, Vol. 22 : 357.

Duffus, R. L.   Function of the Racketeer.   *New Republic*, March 27, 1929.

Flynn, J. T.   The Betrayal of Cleveland, *Harpers*, January 1934.

Gunther, J.   The High Cost of Hoodlums, *Harpers*, October 1929.

Hoover, J. E.   Bankruptcy Frauds, *Jour. Criminal Law and Criminology*, Vol. 23 : 1073.

Keliher, T. T.   Freight-Car Robberies, *Jour. Criminal Law and Criminology*, Vol. 23 : 1080.

Loesch, F. J.   Crime and Your Balance Sheet, *Magazine of Business*, April 1929.

MacDougall, Knight and Bowman.   Report of Committee on Mercenary Crime, *Jour. Criminal Law and Criminology*, Vol. 23 : 94.

Pound, R.   The Limits of Effective Legal Action, *Amer. Bar Ass'n Jour.*, Vol. 3 : 55.

Renaud, R. E.   The Kidnapping Profession, *Forum*, June 1932.

Saunders, R. C.   Syndicated Bank Robbery, *Jour. Criminal Law and Criminology*, Vol. 23 : 797.

Sayre, J.   How to Run a Speakeasy, *Outlook*, April 1932.

Sellin, T.   The Basis of a Crime Index, *Jour. Criminal Law and Criminology*, Vol. 22 : 335.

Spaulding, W. F.   The Cost of Crime, *Jour. Criminal Law and Criminology*, Vol. 1 : 86.

Warner, S. B. Crimes Known to the Police — An Index of Crime?
Harvard Law Review, Vol. 45 : 307.

THE MORAL AND SOCIAL COSTLINESS OF
CRIMINALS

SELECTED BIBLIOGRAPHY

Especially Recommended

Landesco, John. Organized Crime in Chicago, being Part 3 of the
Illinois Crime Survey, Illinois Association for Criminal Justice, Chicago,
1929.
A vivid and illuminating history of organized crime in Chicago and
vicinity over a twenty-five year period. It shows effectively the ramifications of underworld business and the extent to which it can contaminate
a great community.

BOOKS AND PAMPHLETS

Adamic, L. Dynamite.
Beals, C. The Crime of Cuba.
Black, J. You Can't Win.
Bruce, A. A. The Administration of Criminal Justice in Illinois. *Jour.*
Criminal Law and Criminology, Vol. 19, No. 4, Part 2.
Chase, S. A New Deal.
Clark and Eubank. Lockstep and Corridor.
Flynn, J. T. Graft in Business.
Healy and Bronner. Judge Baker Foundation Case Studies, Series No. 1.
Hostetter and Beesley. It's a Racket.
Howard, S. The Labor Spy.
League of Nations. Report of the Special Body of Experts on Traffic
in Women and Children, Parts 1 and 2.
Lindsey and O'Higgins. The Beast.
Lowenthal, M. The Investor Pays.
Lynd, R. S. and H. M. Middletown, Ch. 24.
MacDougall, E. D. (Ed.). Crime for Profit.
Merriam, C. E. Chicago, Chs. 2 and 4.
Merz, C. The Great American Bandwagon, Ch. 6.
National Commission on Law Observance and Enforcement. Report on
the Enforcement of the Prohibition Laws of the United States, Ch. 2.
Reckless, W. C. Vice in Chicago.
Shaw, C. R. Delinquency Areas.
Shaw, C. R. The Jack-Roller.
Simkhovitch, M. K. The City Worker's World, Chs. 6 and 9.
Steffens, L. Autobiography, Parts 2 and 3.
Tarbell, I. M. The History of the Standard Oil Company, 2 vols.
Thrasher, F. The Gang.
Thomas and Blanshard. What's the Matter With New York.

ARTICLES

Bent, S. Newspapermen — Partners in Crime ? *Scribner's*, November 1930.

Chase, S. You and I and the Big Idea, *Survey*, March 1, 1932.

Conner, E. Crime Commissions and Criminal Procedure in the United States Since 1920 : A Bibliography, *Jour. Criminal Law and Criminology*, Vol. 21 : 129.

Everett, R. H. International Traffic in Women and Children, *Jour. Social Hygiene*, May 1927.

Holt, A. E. Bos, *The Survey*, August 1, 1928.

Kellog, P. U. Silence Coerced by Law, *The Survey*, January 1, 1928.

Lippmann, W. The Underworld: A Stultified Conscience, *Forum*, February, 1931.

Merriam, C. E. The Police, Crime and Politics, *Annals*, Vol. 146 : 115.

Moley, R. A Study of the Relation of the Daily Press to Crime and the Administration of Criminal Justice, in the *Report of the New York Crime Commission*, 1927.

Moody, P. D. The Age of Lawlessness, *Bookman*, January 1925.

Murphy, J. P. Hawaii Needs a Friend, *The Survey*, April 1, 1932.

Pearson, E. Trial by Tabloid, *Vanity Fair*, October 1927.

Richberg, D. The Spoils of Normalcy, *Survey*, July 1, 1929.

Sprague, J. R. Big Business and Banditry, *New Republic*, June 10, 1931.

Sutherland, E. H. Public Opinion as a Cause of Crime, *Jour. Applied Sociology*, September 1924.

Wallace, T. Caught in the Power Net, *Survey*, July 1, 1929.

Watts, H. M. The Fourth Estate and Court Procedure as a Public Show, *Jour. Criminal Law and Criminology*, Vol. 19 : 15.

Wile, I. S. Two-Gun Crowley *vs.* The People, *Survey*, February 1, 1932.

Worthington, G. E. Night Club Girls, *Survey*, January 1, 1929.

THE EVOLUTION OF THE CONCEPT OF A BIOLOGICAL CRIMINAL TYPE

SELECTED BIBLIOGRAPHY

Especially Recommended

De Quiros, C. Bernaldo. Modern Theories of Criminality. Tr. Alfonso De Salvio. Little, Brown and Co., 1912.

A brilliant historically accurate review chiefly of European contributions to criminology that faithfully reflects the many shades of opinion that have gone into the making of criminal science. Sections 1 to 15 are especially pertinent as a background for this chapter.

BOOKS AND PAMPHLETS

American Academy of Medicine. Physical Bases of Crime, A Symposium.

Bjerre, A. The Psychology of Murder.

Darrow, C.   Crime, Its Cause and Treatment.

Ellis, H.   The Criminal.

Ferrero, G.   Lombroso's Criminal Man.

Ferri, E.   Criminal Sociology, Part 1.

Goddard, H. H.   The Criminal Imbecile.

Goddard, H. H.   Juvenile Delinquency.

Goring, C.   The English Convict.

Healy and Bronner.   Delinquents and Criminals, Their Making and Unmaking, Chs. 7, 8, 14, 16.

Hoag and Williams.   Crime, Abnormal Minds and The Law, Part 1.

Lange, J.   Crime and Destiny.

Lombroso, C.   L'Uomo Delinquente or the French Edition L'Homme Criminel.

Lombroso, C.   Crime, Its Causes and Remedies, Introduction by Maurice Parmelee.

Lombroso and Ferrero.   The Female Offender.

Murchison, C.   Criminal Intelligence.

Osborne, T. M.   Society and Prisons.

Osborne, T. M.   Within Prison Walls.

Parmelee, M.   The Principles of Anthropology and Sociology in Their Relations to Criminal Procedure, Chs. 1-3.

Slawson, J.   The Delinquent Boy.

Stearns, A. W.   The Personality of Criminals.

Thomas, W. I. and D. S.   The Child in America, Chs. 3, 8, 10.

White, W. A.   Crime and Criminals.

ARTICLES

Bryant, E. K.   The Will-Profile of Delinquent Boys, *Jour. Delinquency*, Vol. 6 : 294.

Doll, E. A.   Mental Types, *School and Society*, Vol. 14 : 482.

Glueck, B.   A Study of 608 Admissions to Sing Sing Prison, *Mental Hygiene*, Vol. 2 : 85.

Karpman, B.   Psychoses in Criminals, *Jour. Nervous and Mental Diseases*, Vol. 64 : 331 and 482.

Pitkin, W.   The Intelligent Criminal, *Forum*, Vol. 73 : 466.

Sheffield, A. D.   The So-Called Criminal Type, *American Jour. Sociology*, Vol. 18 : 381.

Wallace, G. L.   Are the Feebleminded Criminals? *Mental Hygiene*, Vol. 13 : 93.

FACTORS CONDITIONING CRIMINAL BEHAVIOR

SELECTED BIBLIOGRAPHY

Especially Recommended

Burt, Cyril.   The Young Delinquent, D. Appleton and Company, 1925.
A judicious, keen exposition of the part played by the elements associated with juvenile misbehavior.   The chief basis of the work is the

author's own clinical case studies. It has the happy advantage of a pleasing literary style.

Books and Pamphlets

Alexander and Staub. The Criminal, The Judge, and the Public.

Anderson, N. The Hobo.

Aschaffenburg, G. Crime and Its Repression.

Black, J. You Can't Win.

Bonger, W. Criminality and Economic Conditions.

Blumer and Hauser. Movies, Delinquency and Crime.

Breckinridge and Abbott. The Delinquent Child and the Home.

Cantor, N. Crime, Criminals and Criminal Justice, Chs. 5-8.

Clark and Eubank. Lockstep and Corridor.

Drucker and Hexter. Children Astray.

Ferri, E. Criminal Sociology, Parts 1 and 2.

Furfey, P. The Gang Age.

Gault, R. H. Criminology, Part 1.

Glueck, S. S. and E. T. One Thousand Juvenile Delinquents.

Glueck, S. S. and E. T. 500 Criminal Careers.

Glueck, S. S. and E. T. 500 Young Criminals Revisited.*

Glueck, S. S. and E. T. 500 Delinquent Women.

Harris, F. Presentation of Crime in Newspapers.

Healy and Bronner. Delinquents and Criminals, Their Making and Unmaking.

Healy and Bronner. Judge Baker Foundation Case Studies, Series No. 1.

Healy, W. The Individual Delinquent.

Lange, J. Crime and Destiny.

Lombroso, C. Crime, Its Causes and Remedies.

MacDougall, E. D. (Ed.). Crime for Profit.

National Commission on Law Observance and Enforcement. Report on the Causes of Crime, Vols. 1 and 2.

President's Research Committee. Recent Social Trends, 2 vols.

Schlapp and Smith. The New Criminology.

Shaw, C. Delinquency Areas.

Shaw, C. The Jack-Roller.

Slawson, J. The Delinquent Boy.

Southard and Jarrett. The Kingdom of Evils.

Thomas, D. Social Aspects of Business Cycles.

Thomas, W. I. The Unadjusted Girl.

Thrasher, F. The Gang.

White, W. A. Crime and Criminals, Chs. 1-7.

Zorbaugh, H. The Gold Coast and the Slum.

Articles

Adams, J. T. Our Lawless Heritage, *Atlantic Monthly*, December 1928.

Brown, F. A Practical Study of Some Etiological Factors in Theft Behavior, *Jour. Criminal Law and Criminology*, Vol. 22 : 221.

* To be published.

Cantor, N.　The Search for Causes of Crime, *Jour. Criminal Law and Criminology*, Vol. 22 : 854.

Hayes and Bowery.　Marihuana, *Jour. Criminal Law and Criminology*, Vol. 23 : 1086.

Holmes, J.　Crime and the Press, *Jour. Criminal Law and Criminology*, Vol. 20 : 6 and 246.

Kellogg, A.　Minds Made by the Movies, *The Survey*, May 1, 1933.

Leighton, G. R.　In Search of the NRA, *Harpers*, January 1934.

Sandoz, C.　Report on Morphinism in the Municipal Court of Boston, *Jour. Criminal Law and Criminology*, Vol. 13 : 40.

CHILDHOOD AND THE FOUNDATIONS OF BEHAVIOR

SELECTED BIBLIOGRAPHY

Especially Recommended

Thom, Douglas A.　Everyday Problems of the Everyday Child.　Appleton, 1928.

The origins and treatment of behavior problems in young children discussed on the basis of clinical experience by the founder of our first successful habit clinics for pre-school children.

Books and Pamphlets

Blanchard, P.　The Child and Society, Chs. 1, 2, 13, 14.

Blanton, B. S. and M. G.　Child Guidance.

Burt, C.　The Young Delinquent.

Campbell, C.　The Neurotic Child (Pamphlet reprinted from the *Amer. Jour. Diseases of Children*, Vol. 12 : 425-44).

Gesell, A.　The Mental Health of the Pre-School Child.

Groves, E. R.　Personality and Social Adjustment.

Groves, E. R.　Social Problems of the Family, Ch. 13.

Groves, E. R. and G. H.　Wholesome Childhood.

Groves, E. R. and G. H.　Wholesome Parenthood.

Healy, W.　The Individual Delinquent.

Healy, W.　Mental Conflicts and Misconduct.

Healy and Bronner.　Delinquents and Criminals.

Healy and Bronner.　Judge Baker Foundation Case Studies, Series No. 1.

O'Shea, M. V. (Ed.).　The Child : His Nature and His Needs.

Piaget, J.　The Moral Judgment of the Child.

Piaget, J.　The Child's Conception of the World.

Piaget, J.　Judgment and Reasoning in the Child.

Sayles, M. B.　The Problem Child at Home.

Stein, W.　The Psychology of Early Childhood.

Thom, D. A.　Child Management (U. S. Dept. of Labor, Children's Bureau Publication, 143).

Thom, D. A.　Habit Clinics for the Child of Pre-School Age (U. S. Dept. of Labor, Children's Bureau Publication, 135).

Thomas, W. I. and D. S.   The Child in America, Chs. 1 and 2.

Truitt, R. P.   Team Work in the Prevention of Crime (Pamphlet, Joint Committee on Methods of Preventing Delinquency under Commonwealth Fund Program).

White, W. A.   The Mental Hygiene of Childhood.

ARTICLES

Armstrong, C. P.   The Gestalt of the Delinquent Child, *Jour. Abnormal and Social Psychology*, Vol. 28 : 87.

Bond, E. D. and P. G. E.   The Post-Encephalitic Behavior Disorders in Boys and Their Management in a Hospital, *American Jour. Psychiatry*, Vol. 6 : 26.

Campbell, C. M.   The Experiences of the Child : How They Affect Character and Behavior, *Mental Hygiene*, Vol. 4 : 314.

Kenworthy, M.   Mental Health in Childhood, *Mental Hygiene*, Vol. 10 : 242.

Owens, C.   Family Adjustment to the Demands of Community Life, *Jour. Social Hygiene*, Vol. 14 : 385.

Preston, G. H.   Mental Hygiene Factors in Parenthood and Parental Relationships, *Mental Hygiene*, Vol. 12 : 751.

Williams, J. H.   The Whittier Scale for Grading Home Conditions, *Jour Delinquency*, Vol. 1 : 271.

Woodill, E. E.   Psychiatric Examination of a Child, *Mental Hygiene*, Vol. 10 : 300.

Woolley, H. T.   Agnes : A Dominant Personality in the Making, *Pedagogical Seminary*, Vol. 32 : 569.

EXPANDING HORIZONS : MISADVENTURING INTO COMMUNITY LIFE

SELECTED BIBLIOGRAPHY

Especially Recommended

Thrasher, Frederic M.   The Gang.   University of Chicago Press, 1927. The social world of the city boy as seen during a field study of the structure and activities of 1213 children's gangs in the city of Chicago.

BOOKS AND PAMPHLETS

Addams, J.   The Spirit of Youth and the City Streets.

Blanchard, P.   The Child and Society.

Burt, C.   The Young Delinquent.

Drucker and Hexter.   Children Astray.

Furfey, P.   The Gang Age.

Furfey, P.   The Growing Boy.

Glueck, B.   Some Extra-Curricular Problems of the Classroom, ·Publication of the Joint Committee on Methods of Preventing Delinquency.

Hartshorne and May.   Studies in Deceit.

Healy, W.   The Individual Delinquent.

Healy and Bronner.   Delinquents and Criminals : Their Making and Unmaking.

— Judge Baker Foundation Case Studies, Series 1, Nos. 1-20.

Shaw, C.   Delinquency Areas.

Thom, D.   Normal Youth and Its Everyday Problems.

Thomas, W. I. and D. S.   The Child in America.

U. S. Children's Bureau, Pub. 197.   Child Labor Facts and Figures.

Van Waters, M.   Youth in Conflict.

White, W.   The Mental Hygiene of Childhood.

Wickman, E. K.   Children's Behavior and Teachers' Attitudes, Publication of the Joint Committee on Methods of Preventing Delinquency.

Yeomans, E.   Shackled Youth.

ARTICLES

Anderson, N.   The Juvenile and the Tramp, *Jour. Criminal Law and Criminology*, August 1923.

Cleveland, G.   Schoolroom Hazards to the Mental Health of Children, *Mental Hygiene*, Vol. 12 : 18.

Henry, M.   Near Delinquents in the Public Schools, *Jour. Delinquency*, Nov. 1921.

Landesco, J.   The Life History of a Member of the 42 Gang, *Jour. Criminal Law and Criminology*, Vol. 23 : 964.

Mason, F. V.   A Study of Seven Hundred Maladjusted School Teachers, *Mental Hygiene*, Vol. 15 : 576.

Menninger, W. C.   The Mental Hygiene Aspect of the Boy Scout Movement, *Mental Hygiene*, Vol. 13 : 496.

Moxon, C.   Antisocial Attitudes, Their Formation and Reformation, *Mental Hygiene*, Vol. 13 : 542.

Van Waters, M.   Why Hickman Hangs, *Survey*, Oct. 1, 1928.

Williamson, C.   The Origin and Cure of the Bad Boy, *Sociological Review*, Spring 1920.

Youmans, Z.   Opportunity Night, *Survey*, Sept. 1, 1927.

Young, P. V. and E. F.   Getting at the Boy Himself, *Social Forces*, Vol. 6 : 408.

ADOLESCENCE AND THE DIFFICULTIES OF A CHANGING LIFE

SELECTED BIBLIOGRAPHY

Especially Recommended

Van Waters, Miriam.   Youth in Conflict. Republic Publishing Co., 1926.

A thoughtful interpretation of the nature and causes of adolescent maladjustments delightfully written by one who has dealt with offenders as criminologist, juvenile court referee and as superintendent of penal and correctional institutions.

Books and Pamphlets

Addams, J., *Editor*. The Child, The Clinic and The Court. Articles by A. L. Jacoby, Miriam Van Waters, Nels Anderson.

Blumer, H. Movies and Conduct.

Blumer and Hauser. Movies, Delinquency and Crime.

Clark and Eubank. Lockstep and Corridor, Chs. 1-4.

Cooley, E. J. Probation and Delinquency, Ch. 14.

Cressey, P. G. The Taxi-Dance Hall.

Glueck, S. S. and E. T. 500 Delinquent Women.

Glueck, S. S. and E. T. 500 Hundred Criminal Careers.

Glueck, S. S. and E. T. 500 Young Criminals Revisited.*

Glueck, S. S. and E. T. One Thousand Delinquents, Their Treatment by Court and Clinic.

Hall, G. S. Adolescence, Vol. 1, Ch. 5.

Healy and Bronner. Delinquents and Criminals.

Healy and Bronner. Judge Baker Foundation Case Studies, Series 1.

Le Mesurier, L. Boys in Trouble.

Park and Burgess. The City, Chs. 5, 8, 9.

Reckless and Smith. Juvenile Delinquency.

Thom, D. Normal Youth and Its Everyday Problems.

Thomas, W. I. The Unadjusted Girl.

Van Waters, M. Parents on Probation.

Wile, I. S. The Challenge of Childhood.

Williams, F. E. Adolescence, Studies in Mental Hygiene.

Articles

Anonymous Autobiography. Girl Delinquent, Age Sixteen, *Harpers*, April 1932.

Eastman, F. What's To Be Done With the Movies? *Christian Century*, Jan.-Feb. 1930.

Holmes, J. L. Crime and the Press, *Jour Criminal Law and Criminology*, May and August 1929.

Kellogg, A. Minds Made by the Movies, *The Survey*, May 1, 1933.

Moore, E. H. Public Dance Halls in a Small City, *Sociology and Social Research*, January and February 1930.

Pearson, G. H. J. What the Adolescent Girl Needs in Her Home, *Mental Hygiene*, Vol. 14:40-53.

Roberts, M. Italian Girls on American Soil, *Mental Hygiene*, Vol. 13 : 757-768.

Seagrave, M. Causes Underlying Sex Delinquency in Young Girls, *Jour. Social Hygiene*, December 1926.

Stephens, H. B. The Relation of the Motion Picture to Changing Moral Standards, *Annals*, November 1926.

Van Waters, M. Nineteen Ways of Being a Bad Parent, *Survey*, January 1, 1927.

* To be published.

Wembridge, E. R. The Girl Tribe, *Survey*, May 1, 1928.

Wile, I. S. Francis Crowley *vs.* The People of the State of New York, *Survey*, February 1, 1932.

Woodbury, R. F. The Seamy Side of Carnivals, *Survey*, October 15, 1928.

Worthington, G. E. Night Club Girls, *Survey*, January 1, 1929.

Young, D. Social Standards and the Motion Picture, *Annals*, November 1926.

THE CRIMINAL HABIT

SELECTED BIBLIOGRAPHY

Especially Recommended

Clark and Eubank. Lockstep and Corridor. University of Cincinnati Press, 1927.

The unadorned autobiography of a professional criminal who has spent over 35 years of his life in prisons and reformatories ; with appended comments by the head of the Department of Sociology at the University of Cincinnati.

BOOKS AND PAMPHLETS

Allen, T. Underworld : The Biography of Charles Brooks, Criminal.

Amer. Medical Ass'n. Nostrums and Quackery, 2 vols.

Anderson, N. The Hobo.

Bjerre, A. The Psychology of Murder.

Black, J. You can't Win.

Chase and Schlink. Your Money's Worth.

Darrow, C. Crime, Its Cause and Treatment.

Felstead, S. T. Famous Criminals and Their Trials.

Flint, J. Tramping With Tramps.

Flynn, J. T. Investment Trusts Gone Wrong.

Flynn, J. T. Graft in Business.

Garofalo, Baron R. Criminology, Chs. 1 and 2.

Glueck, S. S. and E. T. 500 Delinquent Women.

Glueck, S. S. and E. T. 500 Criminal Careers.

Glueck, S. S. and E. T. 500 Criminals Revisited.*

Gray, F. The Tramp.

Hapgood, H. The Autobiography of a Thief.

Hostetter and Beesley. It's a Racket.

Illinois Crime Survey. Part Three.

Lange, J. Crime and Destiny.

Lowrie, D. My Life in Prison.

Lynch, D. T. Criminals and Politicians.

MacDougall, E. D. (Ed.). Crime for Profit.

Osborne, T. M. Within Prison Walls.

Reckless, W. C. Vice in Chicago.

* To be published.

Shaw, C. R.   The Jack-Roller.
Steffens, L.   Autobiography, Parts 2 and 3.
White, W. A.   Crime and Criminals.

ARTICLES

Anderson, V. V. and L. C. M.   Drunkenness as Seen Among Women in Court, *Mental Hygiene*, Vol. 3 : 266.
Anonymous.   Professor's Progress, *Harpers*, November 1932.
Baker, A. T.   Vagrancy, *Mental Hygiene*, Vol. 2 : 595.
Black, J.   A Burglar Looks at Laws and Codes, *Harpers*, February 1930.
Bolitho, W.   The Psychosis of the Gang, *Survey*, Feb. 1, 1930.
Flynn, J. T.   Inside the R. F. C., *Harpers*, January 1933.
Karpman, B.   Criminality, the Super Ego and the Sense of Guilt, *Psychoanalytic Review*, April 1930.
Kolt, L.   Drug Addiction in Its Relation to Crime, *Mental Hygiene*, Vol. 9 : 74.
Lawes, L. E.   The Life of an Ex-Convict, *World's Work*, October 1928.
Perkins, F.   The Cost of a Five Dollar Dress, *Survey*, Vol. 22 : 75.
Reckless, W. C.   The Distribution of Commercialized Vice in the City, *Publications Amer. Sociological Society*, Vol. 22 : 164.
Sutherland, E. H.   Crime and the Conflict Process, *Jour. Juvenile Research*, January 1929.
Van Waters, M.   Why Hickman Hangs, *Survey*, October 1, 1928.

THE PREVENTION OF CRIMINAL BEHAVIOR : GENERAL METHODS

SELECTED BIBLIOGRAPHY

Especially Recommended

Thomas, W. I. and D. S.   The Child in America.   Alfred Knopf, Inc., 1928.
A description and critical evaluation of the many methods now used in America for understanding, treating, and preventing behavior maladjustments in children.

BOOKS AND PAMPHLETS

Batten, S. Z.   The Social Task of Christianity.
Bloomfield, M.   The School and the Start in Life.
Cantor, N. F.   Crime, Criminals and Criminal Justice, Ch. 25.
Chase, S.   A New Deal.
Ellis, M. B.   The Visiting Teacher in Rochester.
Ferri, E.   Criminal Sociology, Part 2, Chs. 4-6.
Gault, R. H.   Criminology, Ch. 21 and Appendix C.
Glueck, B.   Some Extra-Curricular Problems of the Classroom, reprint No. 5, Joint Committee on Methods of Preventing Delinquency.

Goodsell, W.   Problems of the Family, Parts 2-4.
Groves, E. R.   Social Problems of the Family, Chs. 8-16.
Hall, F. S. (Ed.).   Social Work Year Book, 1933.
Haynes, F. E.   Criminology, Ch. 26.
Kulp, D. II, Educational Sociology.
Lee, J.   Constructive and Preventive Philanthropy.
Mass. Society for Mental Hygiene.   A Mental Health Primer.
Oppenheimer, J. J.   The Visiting Teacher Movement.
Peters, C. C.   Foundations of Educational Sociology.
Richmond and Hall.   Marriage and the State.
Sutherland, E. H.   Criminology, Ch. 25.
Tawney, R. H.   The Acquisitive Society.
Thom, D. A.   Habit Clinics for the Child of Preschool Age, U. S. Dept. of Labor, Publication No. 135.
Todd, A. J.   Industry and Society, Chs. 18, 21, 23-31.
Wickman, E. K.   Children's Behavior and Teachers' Attitudes.
Yeomans, E.   Shackled Youth.

Articles

Addams, J.   The Social Deterrent of Our National Self-Righteousness, *Survey*, February 1933.
Amidon, B.   Ivorydale, a Payroll That Floats, *Survey*, April 1, 1930.
Couzens, J.   Long Wages, *Survey*, April 1, 1930.
Culbert, J. F.   The Visiting Teacher, *Annals*, November 1921.
Smith, E. D.   Potent Leisure, *Survey*, May 1, 1930.
Wood, A. E.   The Place of the Community in Sociological Studies, *Publications Amer. Sociological Society*, Vol. 22 : 14-25.
Rogers, G. C.   Mental Hygiene in the Public Schools, *Mental Hygiene*, January 1930.
Van Waters, M.   Why Hickman Hangs, *Survey*, October 1, 1928.

THE PREVENTION OF CRIMINAL BEHAVIOR: SPECIFIC METHODS

SELECTED BIBLIOGRAPHY

Especially Recommended

Healy, Bronner, et al.   Reconstructing Behavior in Youth.   Alfred Knopf, Inc., 1929.
An incisive and illuminating discussion of the techniques and possibilities of modifying unsatisfactory behavior through an exploration of the bases of conduct deviations followed by placement in foster families. Conclusions are based upon actual experiences with the placement of 501 difficult delinquents.

Books and Pamphlets

Addams, J. (Ed.).   The Child, the Clinic and the Court, Parts 2 and 3.
Brockway, A. F.   A New Way With Crime.

Bruner, E. D.   A Laboratory Study in Democracy.

Davies, S. P.   Social Control of the Mentally Deficient, Chs. 6-18.

George, W. R.   The Junior Republic.

Glueck, S. S. and E. T.   One Thousand Juvenile Delinquents, Their Treatment by Court and Clinic.

Hamilton, M. E.   The Policewoman.

Healy and Bronner.   Delinquents and Criminals, Their Making and Unmaking.

Healy and Bronner.   Judge Baker Foundation Case Studies, Series 1.

Hoffman, C. W.   The Juvenile Court, the Community and the Child Guidance Clinic in The Child Guidance Clinic and the Community.

Howe, M. A. Dewolfe.   The Children's Judge : Frederick P. Cabot.

Hutzel, E.   The Policewoman's Handbook.

Joint Committee on Methods of Preventing Delinquency.   Three Problem Children.

Lou, H. H.   Juvenile Courts in the United States.

New York State Crime Commission.   A Study of Crime and the Community in the Report of the Crime Commission, 1930.

Owing, C.   Women Police.

Reeves, M.   Training Schools for Delinquent Girls.

Thomas, W. I. and D. S.   The Child in America, Ch. 2.

Thrasher, F. M.   The Gang, Ch. 22.

U. S. Children's Bureau, Pub. 193.   The Child, The Family and the Court.

Van Waters, M.   Youth in Conflict, Part 2.

Waterman, W. C.   Prostitution and Its Repression in New York City.

Woods, A.   Crime Prevention.

ARTICLES

Additon, H.   City Planning for Girls, *Social Service Review*, Vol. 2 : 234.

Adler, H.   The Prevention of Crime, *Jour. Criminal Law and Criminology*, Vol. 23 : 81.

Bates, S.   Criminal Records and Statistics, *Jour. Criminal Law and Criminology*, Vol. 19 : 8.

Calligan, C. I.   The Rural Court and the Clinic, *Mental Hygiene*, Vol. 14 : 137.

Cress, G.   A Sheriff Tries Crime Prevention, *Jour. Criminal Law and Criminology*, Vol. 22 : 422.

Dickson, V. E.   The Berkley Coördinating Council, *Mental Hygiene*, Vol. 13 : 514.

Dobbs, H. A.   Institutional Care for Delinquent Children : A New Appraisal, *Annals*, Vol. 151 : 173.

Healy, W.   The Prevention of Delinquency and Criminality, *Jour. Criminal Law and Criminology*, Vol. 24 : 74.

Hutchins, R. M.   An Institute of Human Relations, *Amer. Jour. Sociology*, Vol. 35 : 187.

Merrill, M. A.   The Care of the Psychopathic or Defective Delinquent, *Jour. Juvenile Research*, Vol. 14 : 165.

Rademacher, E. S. Treatment of Problem Children by Means of a Long Time Camp, *Mental Hygiene*, Vol. 12 : 385.

Raphael, Labine, Flinn and Hoffman. One Hundred Traffic Offenders, *Mental Hygiene*, Vol. 13 : 809.

Scott, R. H. Modern Science and the Juvenile Court, *Jour. Juvenile Research*, Vol. 14 : 77.

Shulman, H. M. Social Agencies and Crime Prevention, *Jour. Criminal Law and Criminology*, Vol. 22 : 545.

Swackhamer, G. V. The Advantages of Coöperation Between Justices of the Peace and a Social Agency, *Jour. Criminal Law and Criminology*, Vol. 20 : 122.

Woods, E. L. The School and Delinquency : Every School a Clinic, *Proceedings National Conference of Social Work* for 1929.

THE POLICE

SELECTED BIBLIOGRAPHY

Especially Recommended

The Police and the Crime Problem, Vol. 146 of the *Annals* of the American Academy of Political and Social Science, November 1929.

A symposium that touches every major phase of modern police work. It includes contributions from five foreign countries.

BOOKS AND PAMPHLETS

Annals, The. Vol. 125, Part 3.

Cahalane, C. F. Police Practice and Procedure.

Chandler, G. F. The Policeman's Manual.

Cleveland Association for Criminal Justice. Criminal Justice in Cleveland, Part I, Chs. 1-8.

Dilnot, G. The Story of Scotland Yard.

Fosdick, R. B. American Police Systems.

Fosdick, R. B. European Police Systems.

Gillin, J. L. Criminology and Penology, Ch. 30.

Graper, E. D. American Police Administration.

Hamilton, M. E. The Policewoman.

Hutzel, E. The Policewoman's Handbook.

Illinois Association for Criminal Justice. The Administration of Criminal Justice in Illinois.

Kuhne, F. The Finger Print Instructor.

Larson, J. A. Lying and Its Detection.

Lavine, E. H. The Third Degree.

McAdoo, W. G. Guarding a Great City.

Missouri Association for Criminal Justice. The Missouri Crime Survey.

National Commission on Law Observance and Enforcement. Report on Police.

National Commission on Law Observance and Enforcement. Report on Lawlessness in Law Enforcement.

Moylan, J. F.   Scotland Yard.

Owings, C.   Women Police.

Robinson, L. N.   The Relation of the Police and the Courts to the Crime Problem — A report submitted to the National Crime Commission.

Savage, E. H.   Police Records and Recollections.

Sayre, F. B.   Cases on Criminal Law, pp. 567-94.

Shore, W. T. (Ed.).   Crime and Its Detection, 2 vols.

Smith, B.   The State Police.

Steffens, L.   Autobiography, Chs. 4-14.

Sutherland, E. H.   Criminology, Ch. 9.

Thompson, B.   My Experiences at Scotland Yard.

Train, A.   Courts, Criminals and the Camorra.

Woods, A.   Crime Prevention.

Woods, A.   Policeman and Public.

ARTICLES

Baker, R. E.   Factors in Law Enforcement, *Social Forces*, Dec. 1929.

Best, H.   Why the Police Fail, *Harpers*, January 1933.

Black, J.   What's Wrong With the Right People, *Harpers*, June 1929.

Bolitho, W.   The Natural History of Graft, *Survey*, May 1, 1930.

Bowler, A. C.   A Police Department's Social Hygiene Activities, *Jour. Social Hygiene*, Vol. 15 : 528.

Chafee, Z., Jr.   Remedies for the Third Degree, *Atlantic Monthly*, November 1931.

Crawley, F. J.   Observations of American Police Systems, *Jour. Criminal Law and Criminology*, Vol. 20 : 167.

Fosdick, R. B.   The Passing of the Bertillon System of Identification, *Jour. Criminal Law and Criminology*, Vol. 6 : 363.

Hoover, J. E.   The United States Bureau of Investigation in Relation to Law Enforcement, *Jour. Criminal Law and Criminology*, Vol. 23 : 439.

Knoles, F. A.   The Statistical Bureau — A Police Necessity, *Jour. Criminal Law and Criminology*, Vol. 19 : 383.

Ostrander, J. M.   One Hundred and Fifty Policemen, *Mental Hygiene*, Vol. 9 : 60.

Smith, B.   Future Development of State Police, *Jour. Criminal Law and Criminology*, Vol. 23 : 713.

Vollmer, A.   A Practical Method for Selecting Policemen, *Jour. Criminal Law and Criminology*, Vol. 11 : 571.   The Third Degree, *Harvard Law Review*, Vol. 43 : 617.   Coördinated Effort to Prevent Crime, *Jour. Criminal Law and Criminology*, Vol. 19 : 196.   Police Progress in the Past Twenty-Five Years, *Jour. Criminal Law and Criminology*, Vol. 24 : 161.

Wilder, H. E.   The Japanese Police, *Jour. Criminal Law and Criminology*, Vol. 19 : 390.

THE ADMINISTRATORS OF CRIMINAL JUSTICE

SELECTED BIBLIOGRAPHY

Especially Recommended

Moley, Raymond. Our Criminal Courts. Minton, Balch and Co., New York, 1930.

A vivid, realistic picture of the courts in action by a law professor who has had official relations with many recent factual surveys in nearly a dozen states. One of its virtues is that it helps to correct common false perspectives.

BOOKS AND PAMPHLETS

Barnes, H. E. The Repression of Crime, Ch. 9.

Beeley, A. L. The Bail System in Chicago.

Brasol, B. The Elements of Crime, Ch. 8.

Bruce, A. A. The American Judge.

Callendar, C. N. American Courts, Their Organization and Procedure.

Cardozo, B. N. The Nature of the Judicial Process.

Cardozo, B. N. Law and Literature.

Ferri, E. Criminal Sociology, Part 4.

Gillin, J. L. Criminology and Penology, Ch. 31.

Glueck, S. S. Mental Disorder and the Criminal Law.

Glueck, S. S. (Ed.). Probation and Criminal Justice, Part 3.

Goldman, M. C. The Public Defender.

Gross, H. Criminal Psychology.

Haynes, F. E. Criminology, Ch. 6.

Howard, P. Criminal Justice in England.

Illinois Association for Criminal Justice. The Administration of Criminal Justice in Illinois.

Maguire, J. A. The Lance of Justice.

Missouri Association for Criminal Justice. The Missouri Crime Survey.

Moley, R. Politics and Criminal Prosecution.

Munsterberg, H. On the Witness Stand.

National Commission on Law Observance and Enforcement, Report on Criminal Procedure.

National Commission on Law Observance and Enforcement, Progress Report on the Study of the Federal Courts.

Parmelee, M. The Principles of Anthropology and Sociology in Their Relations to Criminal Procedure, Chs. 8-12.

Reports of the Crime Commission of the State of New York, 1926, 1927, 1928, 1929, 1930.

Sayre, F. B. Cases on Criminal Law.

Smith, R. H. Justice and the Poor.

Sutherland, E. H. Criminology, Ch. 12.

The Cleveland Foundation. Criminal Justice in Cleveland, Part 3.

Train, A. The Prisoner at the Bar.

Ulman, J. N. A Judge Takes the Stand.

Willoughby, W. F. Principles of Judicial Administration.

Zelitch, J. Soviet Administration of Criminal Law.

ARTICLES

Aumann, F. R. The Public Defender in the Municipal Courts of Columbus, *Jour. Criminal Law and Criminology*, Vol. 21 : 393.

Baker, N. F. The Prosecutor, *Jour. Criminal Law and Criminology*, Vol. 23 : 770.

Cardozo, B. N. A Ministry of Justice, *Harvard Law Review*, Vol. 35 : 113.

De Long and Baker. The Prosecuting Attorney. *Jour. Criminal Law and Criminology*, Vol. 23 : 926.

Gaudet, Harris and St. John. Sentencing Tendencies of Judges. *Jour. Criminal Law and Criminology*, Vol. 23 : 811.

Glueck, S. S. The Ministry of Justice and the Problem of Crime, *American Review*, Vol. 4 : 139.

House, V. Are American Juries at Fault? *Atlantic Monthly*, August 1928.

Levy, N. The Judges and the Legislature, *Jour. Criminal Law and Criminology*, Vol. 19 : 557.

Lippmann, W. The Popular Dogma of Law Enforcement, *Yale Review*, Autumn 1929.

Miller, J. The Report on Criminal Procedure, *Amer. Bar Ass'n Jour.*, July 1932.

Overholser, W. Use of Psychiatric Facilities in Criminal Courts, *Mental Hygiene*, Vol. 13 : 800. Psychiatry and the Courts in Massachusetts, *Jour. Criminal Law and Criminology*, Vol. 19 : 75. Two Years' Experience with the Brigg's Law of Massachusetts, *Jour. Criminal Law and Criminology*, Vol. 23 : 415.

Pendleton, H. Trial by Jury, *Century*, April 1929.

Ploscowe, M. Development of Inquisitorial and Accusatorial Elements in French Procedure. *Jour. Criminal Law and Criminology*, Vol. 23 : 372.

Pound, R. Causes of Popular Dissatisfaction with the Administration of Justice, *Report of the American Bar Association*, Vol. 29 : 395. Law in Books and Law in Action, *American Law Review*, Vol. 44 : 12. Juristic Problems of National Progress, *American Jour. Sociology*, Vol. 22 : 721.

Schroeder, G. The Psychological Study of Judicial Opinion, *California Law Review*, Vol. 6 : 89.

Schultz, O. T. Medical Science and Criminal Justice, *Jour. Criminal Law and Criminology*, Vol. 23 : 736.

Seagle, W. Too Many Laws, *New Freeman*, March 22, 1930.

Stevens, E. R. Crime and Criminal Justice, *Jour. Criminal Law and Criminology*, Vol. 21 : 325.

Tulin, L. A. The Problem of Mental Disorder in Crime, *Columbia Law Review*, Vol. 32 : 933.

Walker, M. L. Fitting Law to Life, *Survey*, June 1, 1930.

Watts, H. M. The Fourth Estate and Court Procedure as a Public Show, *Jour. Criminal Law and Criminology*, Vol. 19 : 15.

MINOR PUNISHMENTS

SELECTED BIBLIOGRAPHY

Especially Recommended

Seagle, William. Fines. *Encyclopedia of the Social Sciences*, Vol. 6 : 249.

Books and Pamphlets

Best, H. Crime and the Criminal Law in the United States, Ch. 39.
Ferri, E. Criminal Sociology, pp. 509-515.
Fox, J. C. The History of Contempt of Court, Ch. 8.
Garofalo, R. Criminology, Appendix A.
Gault, R. H. Criminology, pp. 354-356.
Robinson, L. N. Penology in the United States, pp. 269-282.
Schofield, H. Essays on Constitutional Law and Equity, Vol. 1 : 421-456.
Sutherland, E. H. Criminology, pp. 376-389.

Articles

Dickinson, J. Civil Rights, Encyclopedia of the Social Sciences, Vol. 3 : 513.
Hale, R. W. The Twenty-Nine Million Dollar Fine, *United States Law Review*, Vol. 41 : 904.
Oppenheimer, R. Infamous Crimes and the Moreland Case, *Harvard Law Review*, Vol. 36 : 299.
Potter, Z. Fines and Community Protection in Illinois, *Jour. Criminal Law and Criminology*, Vol. 6 : 675.
Spalding, W. F. The Legislative History of a "State Prison" Sentence as a Test of "Felony" and "Infamous Punishment," *Mass. Law Quarterly*, Vol. 7 : 91.
Worthington and Topping. Summary and Comparative Study of the Special Courts in Chicago, Philadelphia, Boston and New York, *Jour. Social Hygiene*, Vol. 9 : 348.

PROBATION AND ITS ADMINISTRATORS

SELECTED BIBLIOGRAPHY

Especially Recommended

Glueck, Sheldon, Editor. Probation and Criminal Justice, New York, The Macmillan Co., 1933.
A series of thoughtful essays on probation broadly conceived and admirably organized so as to give consideration to the theoretical and legal implications of probation as well as to the details of its administration.

Two challenging discussions from the viewpoints of a judge and a psychiatrist are included. Part 5 is a panoramic picture of the growth and use of probation and its analogues in the United States, England, France, Belgium, and Germany.

BOOKS AND PAMPHLETS

Addams, J. (Ed.). The Child, the Clinic, and the Court, Part 3.

Cooley, E. J. New Goals in Probation.

Cooley, E. J. Probation and Delinquency.

Cushman, R. M. and others. Harvey Humphrey Baker, Upbuilder of the Juvenile Court.

Flexner and Baldwin. Juvenile Courts and Probation.

Gillin, J. L. Criminology and Penology, Chs. 34-35.

Haynes, F. E. Criminology, Ch. 15.

Johnson, F. R. Probation for Juveniles and Adults.

Lou, H. H. Juvenile Courts in the United States.

Moran, F. A. Where Are We in Probation Work ?

National Probation Association Year Books.

Report of the Commission of Probation on an Inquiry into the Permanent Results of Probation. Massachusetts Senate Document No. 431.

Robinson, L. N. Penology in the United States, Ch. 10.

Sutherland, E. H. Criminology, Ch. 23.

Trought, T. W. Probation in Europe.

Webster, Jr., B. M. The Federal Probation System.

ARTICLES

Brown, C. L. Coördinating the Work of Public and Private Agencies in Probation Service, National Conference of Social Work Year Book 1920.

Chute, C. L. The Progress of Probation and Social Treatment in the Courts, *Jour. Criminal Law and Criminology*, Vol. 24 : 60.

Grinnell, F. W. Probation as an Orthodox Common Law Practice in Massachusetts Prior to the Statutory System. *Mass. Law Quarterly*, August 1917.

Houston, J. W. The Right Selection of Probation Cases, *Jour. Criminal Law and Criminology*, Vol. 12 : 577.

Korcourek, A. An Unconsidered Element in the Probation of First Offenders, *Jour. Criminal Law and Criminology*, Vol. 6 : 9.

Parsons, H. C. A Confidential Exchange for the Court, *Survey*, August 15, 1926.

Perkins, N. L. Mental and Moral Problems of the Woman Probationer, *Mental Hygiene*, April 1924.

Raphael, T. et al. Socio-psychiatric Delinquency Studies from the Psychopathic Clinic of the Recorder's Court, Detroit. *Amer. Jour. Psychiatry*, April 1924.

Starr, H. E. John Augustus, *Dict. Amer. Biography*, Vol. 1 : 429.

Mead, B. Evaluating the Results of Probation, *Jour. Criminal Law and Criminology*, Vol. 23 : 631.

Moore, J. R.   The United States Probation System, *Jour. Criminal Law and Criminology*, Vol. 23 : 638.

CORPORAL PUNISHMENTS : THE BLOOD-LETTING STAGE

SELECTED BIBLIOGRAPHY

Especially Recommended

Ives, George C.   A History of Penal Methods, London, Stanley Paul and Co., 1914.

A review of the methods of treating criminals, witches, and lunatics in the English speaking world from Anglo-Saxon times to the beginning of the twentieth century.

Books and Pamphlets

Barnes, H. E.   The Repression of Crime.
Bleackley, H.   The Hangmen of England.
Borchard, C. M.   Convicting the Innocent.
Bye, R. T.   Capital Punishment in the United States.
Calvert, E. R.   Capital Punishment in the Twentieth Century.
DeFoe, D.   Moll Flanders.
Dostoevsky, F.   The House of the Dead.
Dostoevsky, F.   Crime and Punishment.
Earle, A. M.   Curious Punishments of Bygone Days.
Gillin, J. L.   Criminology and Penology, Chs. 14-17.
Howard, J.   The State of the Prisons in England and Wales.
Lawes, L. E.   Man's Judgment of Death.
Malinowski, B.   Crime and Custom in Savage Society.
Oppenheimer, H.   The Rationale of Punishment.
Pike, L. O.   History of Crime in England.
Robinson, L. N.   Penology in the United States, Ch. 12.
Sutherland, E. H.   Criminology, Chs. 15-16.
Webb, S. and B.   English Prisons Under Local Government.
Wines, F. E.   Punishment and Reformation, Revised Edition, Chs. 1-5, 9.

Articles

Barnes, H. E.   The Case Against Capital Punishment, *Current History*, Vol. 24 : 365.
Barnes, H. E.   Corporal Punishment, Encyclopedia of the Social Sciences, Vol. 3 : 196.
Barton, R. F.   Ifugao Law, Kroeber and Waterman.   Source Book for Anthropology, Revised Edition, Selection 35.
Faris, E.   The Origin of Punishment, *International Jour. of Ethics*, Vol. 25 : 5.
Kirchwey, G. W.   Capital Punishment, Encyclopedia of the Social Sciences, Vol. 3 : 192.

Riddell, W. R. Bygone Phases of Criminal Justice in England, *Jour. Criminal Law and Criminology*, Vol. 22 : 517.

HUMAN IMPRISONMENT: A HISTORY OF CONFLICTING PRACTICES

SELECTED BIBLIOGRAPHY

Especially Recommended

Barnes, Harry E. The Repression of Crime. Doran, 1926.

A clearly etched picture of the evolution of penology in the United States. An incidental chapter of value to the student is a critical survey of some important recent literature on crime and prisons.

BOOKS AND PAMPHLETS

Adshead, J. Prisons and Prisoners.

Barnes, H. E. The Evolution of Penology in Pennsylvania.

Bentham, J. Works, Bowring Edition, Vol. 4.

De Beaumont and De Toqueville. On The Penitentiary System in the United States.

Dickens, C. American Notes, Ch. 7.

Dix, D. L. Remarks on Prisons and Prison Discipline in the United States.

Dixon, H. The London Prisons.

Dostoevsky, F. The House of the Dead.

Fishman, J. E. Crucibles of Crime.

Howard, J. The State of the Prisons in England and Wales.

Ives, G. A History of Penal Methods.

Phelps, R. H. Newgate of Connecticut.

Robinson, L. N. Penology in the United States.

Smith, G. W. A Defense of the System of Solitary Confinement of Prisoners Adopted by the State of Pennsylvania.

Webb, S. and B. English Prisons Under Local Government.

Wines, F. E. A History of Penal Methods.

Wines and Dwight. Report on the Prisons and Reformatories of the United States and Canada.

ARTICLES

Barnes, H. E. Elizabeth Gurney Fry, Encyclopedia of the Social Sciences, Vol. 6 : 511. John Howard, Encyclopedia of the Social Sciences, Vol. 7 : 521.

Bruce, A. A. One Hundred Years of Criminological Development in Illinois, *Jour. Criminal Law and Criminology*, Vol. 24 : 11.

Moore, E. H. The Livingston Code, *Jour. Criminal Law and Criminology*, Vol. 19 : 344.

Sellin, T. Don Jean Mabillon — A Prison Reformer of the Seventeenth Century, *Jour. Criminal Law and Criminology*, Vol. 17 : 581. Imprisonment, Encyclopedia of the Social Sciences, Vol. 7 : 616. The

House of Correction for Boys in the Hospice of Saint Michael in Rome, *Jour. Criminal Law and Criminology*, Vol. 20 : 533.

THE REFORMATION OF PRISONERS: THE GROWTH OF AN IDEA

SELECTED BIBLIOGRAPHY

Especially Recommended

Allen, Fred C., Editor. Extracts from Penological Reports and Lectures Written by Members of the Management and Staff of the New York State Reformatory, Elmira. The Summary Press, 1926.

Writings on various aspects of the work done at Elmira. Useful as a sample of the efforts and attitudes of persons actually concerned with the management of the type reformatory for adults in this country.

BOOKS AND PAMPHLETS

Brockway, Z. R. Fifty Years of Prison Service.

Carpenter, M. Reformatory Prison Discipline as Developed by the Rt. Hon. Sir Walter Crofton in the Irish Convict Prisons.

Clark and Eubank. Lockstep and Corridor, Chs. 2 and 5.

De Beaumont and De Toqueville. On the Penitentiary System in the United States, Part 3 and Appendix, pp. 216-223.

Garrett and MacCormick (Editors). Handbook of American Prisons and Reformatories.

Gillin, J. L. Criminology and Penology, Chs. 26-28.

Glueck, S. S. and E. T. 500 Criminal Careers.

Glueck, S. S. and E. T. 500 Delinquent Women.

Gordon, M. Penal Discipline, Ch. 10.

Henderson, C. R. (Ed.). Penal and Reformatory Institutions, Chs. 5-7.

Hobhouse and Brockway. English Prisons Today, Ch. 26.

Lekkerkerker, E. Reformatories for Women in the United States.

Maconochie, A. The Mark System of Prison Discipline.

Reeves, M. Training Schools for Delinquent Girls.

Robinson, L. N. Penology in the United States, Chs. 6-7.

Ruggles-Brise, E. The English Prison System, Chs. 8 and 10.

Snedden, D. S. Administration and Educational Work of American Juvenile Reform Schools.

Wines, F. H. Punishment and Reformation, Revised Edition, Ch. 10.

Wines and Dwight. Prisons and Reformatories of the United States and Canada, Chs. 3-4 and Appendix, pp. 399-457.

ARTICLES

Brockway, Z. R. American Reformatory Prison System, *Amer. Jour. Sociology*, Vol. 15 : 454.

Cleghorn and Canfield. Miss Ross' Girls, *Survey*, August 1, 1931.

Davis, K. B. The Laboratory and the Woman's Reformatory, *Proceedings of the American Prison Association*, 1920.

Fernald, G. G. The Laboratory and the Men's Reformatory, *Proceedings of the American Prison Association*, 1920.

Glueck, S. S. Sir Walter Frederick Crofton, Encyclopedia of the Social Sciences, Vol. 4 : 602.

Hodder, J. D. The Next Step in the Correctional Treatment of Girl and Women Offenders, *National Conference of Social Work Yearbook*, 1918.

Lane, W. D. Zebulon Reed Brockway, Encyclopedia of the Social Sciences, Vol. 3 : 7.

Rodgers, H. W. A Digest of Laws Establishing Reformatories for Women in the United States, *Jour. Criminal Law and Criminology*, Vol. 13 : 382.

Rodgers, H. W. The History of the Movement to Establish a State Reformatory for Women in Connecticut, *Jour. Criminal Law and Criminology*, Vol. 19 : 518.

Smith, C. W. The Elimination of the Reformatory, *Proceedings National Conference of Social Work*, 1921.

Van Waters, M. The True Value of Correctional Education, *Proceedings of the American Prison Association*, 1921.

Sellin, T. Paley on the Time Sentence, *Jour. Criminal Law and Criminology*, Vol. 22 : 264.

Coggeshall and Menken. A Woman's Reformatory in the Making, *Jour. Criminal Law and Criminology*, Vol. 23 : 819.

JAILS AND THE JAILED

SELECTED BIBLIOGRAPHY

Especially Recommended

Fishman, J. F. Crucibles of Crime. Cosmopolis Press.
A vivid description of jail conditions in the United States by a former inspector of prisons for the United States Government.

Books and Pamphlets

Gillin, J. L. Criminology and Penology, Ch. 25.

Gillin, J. L. Taming the Criminal, Chs. 6-7.

Gordon, M. Penal Discipline.

Gray, F. The Tramp.

Hart, H. H. Plans for City Police Jails and Village Lockups.

Haynes, F. E. Criminology, Ch. 9.

Kelly, E. The Elimination of the Tramp.

National Commission on Law Observance and Enforcement. Report on Penal Institutions, Probation and Parole, pp. 271-279 and 329-344.

Pennypacker, Fairbank and Draper. Convict Labor for Road Work, Bulletin 414, U. S. Department of Agriculture.

Queen, S. A. The Passing of the County Jail.

Robinson, L. N. Penology in the United States, Chs. 3-4.

Ruggles, Sir E. J. The English Prison System.
Steiner and Brown. The North Carolina Chain Gang.
Tannenbaum, F. Darker Phases of the South.
Warner, F. M. Juvenile Detention in the United States.

ARTICLES

Bates, S. The Care of Defective Delinquents at Bridgewater, Massachusetts, *Mental Hygiene*, Vol. 8 : 530.

Bates, S. What Should Be the Relation of the State to the County Prison System, *Proceedings American Prison Ass'n*, 1924.

Booth, E. A Texas Chain Gang, *American Mercury*, November 1927.

Buckler, H. Attack the County Jail, *Good Housekeeping*, August 1930.

Butler, A. W. The County Jail and the Misdemeanant Prisoner, *Proceedings American Prison Ass'n*, 1923.

Falconer, M. P. The Jail as a Perverter of Womanhood, *Proceedings American Prison Ass'n*, 1921.

Fishman, J. F. The American Jail, *Atlantic Monthly*, Vol. 130 : 792.

Robinson, L. N. The Relation of Jails to County and State, *Jour. Criminal Law and Criminology*, Vol. 22 : 396.

Kinsella, N. County Jails and the Federal Government, *Jour. Criminal Law and Criminology*, Vol. 24 : 428.

Kinberg, O. On So-called Vagrancy. A Medico-Sociological Study. *Jour. Criminal Law and Criminology*, Vol. 24 : 409 and 552.

REFORMATORIES, PRISONS AND THE IMPRISONED

SELECTED BIBLIOGRAPHY

Especially Recommended

Nelson, Victor F. Prison Days and Nights. Little, Brown and Co., 1933.

A vivid, frank, informative, and apparently straightforward account of life in our penal institutions today by an alert, intelligent ex-prisoner who has spent twelve and a half of his thirty-four years in them.

Garrett and MacCormick, Editors. Handbook of American Prisons and Reformatories, National Society for Penal Information, Inc. (now the Osborne Association).

A factual report on the organization and equipment of each of our federal penal institutions and of the prisons and adult reformatories of the forty-eight states. The "Handbook," based upon field investigations, is so arranged that it offers students the means of making useful comparisons.

BOOKS AND PAMPHLETS

Barnes, H. E. The Evolution of Penology in Pennsylvania.
Berkman, A. Prison Memoirs of an Anarchist.
Brockway, Z. R. Fifty Years of Prison Service.

Clark and Eubank. Lockstep and Corridor.

Gillin, J. L. Criminology and Penology, Ch. 22.

Gillin, J. L. Taming the Criminal, Ch. 9.

Glueck, S. S. and E. T. 500 Criminal Careers, Ch. 3.

Haynes, F. E. Criminology, Chs. 10-11.

Hart, H. H. Plans and Illustrations of Prisons.

Hopkins, A. Prisons and Prison Building.

Lawes, L. E. Life and Death in Sing Sing.

Lawes, L. E. 20,000 Years in Sing Sing.

Lekkerkerker, E. C. Reformatories for Women in the United States.

Lowrie, D. My Life In Prison.

Mountain, T. W. Life in London's Great Prisons.

National Commission on Law Observance and Enforcement. Report on Penal Institutions, Probation and Parole, pp. 5-80.

O'Hare, K. In Prison.

Osborne, T. M. Within Prison Walls.

Osborne, T. M. Society and Prisons.

Robinson, L. N. Penology in the United States, Chs. 5, 7, 13.

Smith, M. H. The Psychology of the Criminal.

Stutsman, J. O. Curing the Criminal.

Sutherland, E. H. Criminology, Chs. 18-20.

Tannenbaum, F. Wall Shadows.

ARTICLES

Baker, A. T. The Psychiatric Clinic of Sing Sing Prison, *Psychiatric Quarterly*, Vol. 2 : 464.

Cass, E. R. Responsibility for Prison Conditions, *Jour. Criminal Law and Criminology*, Vol. 22 : 586.

Cleghorn and Canfield. Miss Ross' Girls, *Survey*, August 1, 1931.

Editorial. Honoring Human Nature in Prisons, *Jour. Criminal Law and Criminology*, Vol. 22 : 323.

Growdon, C. H. The Mental Status of Reformatory Women, *Jour. Criminal Law and Criminology*, Vol. 22 : 196.

Jackson, H. F. Prison Labour, *Jour. Criminal Law and Criminology*, Vol. 18 : 218.

Jensen, C. C. Our Convict Slaves, *Atlantic Monthly*, May 1926.

Liepmann, M. American Prisons and Reformatory Institutions. Tr. C. A. Fiertz. *Mental Hygiene*, Vol. 12 : 225.

Lewisohn, A. Prisons and Prison Labor, *Century*, July 1923.

Schwartz, I. H. Welcome to Our Chain Gang, *New Republic*, April 8, 1931.

Sellin, T. A Quarter Century's Progress in Penal Institutions for Adults in the United States, *Jour. Criminal Law and Criminology*, Vol. 24 : 140.

THE REORIENTATION OF PRISONERS

SELECTED BIBLIOGRAPHY

Especially Recommended

MacCormick, Austin H. The Education of Adult Prisoners. National Society for Penal Information, 1931. (Now the Osborne Association.)

A first-hand survey of educational facilities in our prisons plus an attempt to formulate a broad and adequate program for the education of adult prisoners. The author was formerly assistant director of the United States Bureau of Prisons, and is now Commissioner of Correction for New York City.

Books and Pamphlets

Annals, The. Vol. 46.
Annals, The. Vol. 157.
Barnes, H. E. The Repression of Crime.
Berkman, A. Prison Memoirs of an Anarchist.
Bjerre, A. The Psychology of Murder.
Bureau of Foreign and Domestic Commerce. Prison Industries, Domestic Commerce Series No. 27.
Bureau of Labor Statistics. Convict Labor in 1923, Bulletin No. 372.
Ferri, E. Criminal Sociology, Ch. 5.
Gillin, J. L. Criminology and Penology, Part 4.
Glueck, S. S. and E. T. 500 Criminal Careers, Ch. 3.
Glueck, S. S. and E. T. 500 Delinquent Women.
Haynes, F. E. Criminology, Ch. 13.
Hobhouse and Brockway. English Prisons Today.
Jaffray, J. K. The Prison and the Prisoner.
Lekkerkerker, E. C. Reformatories for Women in the United States.
Nelson, V. F. Prison Days and Nights.
Rector, F. L. Survey of Health and Medical Service in American Prisons and Reformatories.
Reeves, M. Training Schools for Delinquent Girls.
Robinson, L. N. Penology in the United States.
Robinson, L. N. Should Prisoners Work.
Ruggles-Brise, Sir E. J. The English Prison System.
Shaw, B. Preface to Webb, English Prisons Under Local Government.
Sutherland, E. H. Criminology, Ch. 18.
Tannenbaum, F. Darker Phases of the South.
Tannenbaum, F. Wall Shadows.
Tasker, R. J. Grimhaven.
Topping, C. W. Canadian Penal Institutions.

Articles

Alger, G. W. Behind the New York Mutinies, *Survey*, September 1, 1929.
Bates, S. Architectural Environment in Relation to Prisoners, *Jour.*

Criminal Law and Criminology, Vol. 22 : 536. Have Our Prisons Failed ? *Jour. Criminal Law and Criminology*, Vol. 23 : 562.

Butler, A. W. Prisons and Prisoners, *Jour. Criminal Law and Criminology*, Vol. 20 : 182.

Hart, H. H. Penology, An Educational Problem, *Proceedings Amer. Prison Ass'n*, 1922, p. 33.

Lane, W. D. Prisons at the Breaking Point, *Survey*, September 1, 1929. Prisons Where Trouble May Come, *Survey*, August 1, 1930.

Wilcox, C. State Organization for Penal Administration, *Jour. Criminal Law and Criminology*, Vol. 22 : 51.

Willebrandt, M. W. The Federal Prison System, *Proceedings of Amer. Prison Ass'n*, 1925, p. 300.

THE ABSOLUTE AND CONDITIONAL RELEASE OF PRISONERS

SELECTED BIBLIOGRAPHY

Especially Recommended

Glueck, S. Sheldon and Eleanor T. 500 Criminal Careers. Alfred A. Knopf, Inc., 1930.
An original and painstaking study of the life histories of 510 criminals from childhood to five years after their discharge from parole. The facts uncovered serve as the basis of an attempt to construct an objective prognostic table for use in criminology. The entire study is an admirable illustration of the use and value of the scientific method in sociology.

Books and Pamphlets

Alger, G. W. Report on the Board of Parole and Parole System of the State of New York, 1926.

Booth, M. B. After Prison — What ?

Bramer, J. P. Parole.

Bruce, Harno, Burgess and Landesco. The Workings of the Indeterminate Sentence Law and the Parole System in Illinois.

Burleigh and Harris. The Delinquent Girl.

Gillin, J. L. Criminology and Penology, Ch. 29.

Glueck, S. S. and E. T. 500 Young Criminals Revisited.*

Glueck, S. S. and E. T. 500 Criminal Careers.

Glueck, S. S. and E. T. 500 Delinquent Women.

Haynes, F. E. Criminology, Ch. 14.

Hobhouse and Brockway. English Prisons Today, Ch. 28.

Lowrie, D. My Life Out of Prison.

Missouri Crime Survey, 1926, Ch. 11.

National Commission on Law Observance and Enforcement. Report on Penal Institutions, Probation and Parole, pp. 127-145 and 297-326.

Robinson, L. N. Penology in the United States, Ch. 11.

Sutherland, E. H. Criminology, Chs. 21 and 22.

* To be published.

Vold, G. V. Prediction Methods and Parole.

Wilcox, C. The Parole of Adults from State Penal Institutions, Part 2, Report of the Pennsylvania State Parole Commission, 1927.

Wines, F. H. Punishment and Reformation (New Ed.).

ARTICLES

Anonymous. Ten Dollars and Make Good, *Nation*, September 1928.

Butler, A. W. What the Courts, the Prisons, the Employer and the Public Should Know of the Released Prisoner, *Jour. Criminal Law and Criminology*, Vol. 21 : 504.

Cantor, N. Councils of Patronage, *Jour. Criminal Law and Criminology*, Vol. 24 : 768.

Glueck, S. S. Individualization and the Use of Predictive Devices, *Jour. Criminal Law and Criminology*, Vol. 23 : 67.

Glueck, S. S. and E. T. Predictability in the Administration of Criminal Justice, *Mental Hygiene*, October 1929, and *Harvard Law Review*, January 1929.

Hart, H. Predicting Parole Success, *Jour. Criminal Law and Criminology*, Vol. 14 : 405.

Kirchwey, G. W. Parole, *Survey*, March 14, 1925.

Lane, W. D. Parole Procedure in New Jersey, *Jour. Criminal Law and Criminology*, Vol. 22 : 375. A New Day Opens for Parole, *Jour. Criminal Law and Criminology*, Vol. 24 : 88.

Lawes, L. E. The Life of an Ex-Convict, *World's Work*, October 1928.

Social Work Year Book, 1933. Articles on : Parole for Adults, Prisoners' Aid.

Tibbitts, C. Success or Failure on Parole Can Be Predicted, *Jour. Criminal Law and Criminology*, Vol. 22 : 11.

Tsheltrow-Bebutow, M. A. Indeterminate Sentence and Soviet Penal Law, *Jour. Criminal Law and Criminology*, Vol. 19 : 408.

Warner, S. B. Factors Determining Parole from the Massachusetts Reformatory, *Jour. Criminal Law and Criminology*, Vol. 14 : 192.

Wilcox, C. Parole : Principles and Practise, *Jour. Criminal Law and Criminology*, Vol. 21 : 345.

Witmer, H. L. The Development of Parole in the United States, *Social Forces*, Vol. 4 : 318.

Witmer, H. L. The History, Theory and Results of Parole, *Jour. Criminal Law and Criminology*, Vol. 18 : 26 and 384.

THE PENAL SCIENCE OF TOMORROW

SELECTED BIBLIOGRAPHY

Especially Recommended

Prisons of Tomorrow, Vol. 157 of the Annals of the American Academy of Political and Social Science.

A symposium on progressive penal practises here and abroad written by the men who are responsible for their introduction or applications.

Books and Pamphlets

Brockway, A. F.   A New Way With Crime.

Cantor, N.   Crime, Criminals and Criminal Justice, Ch. 13 and the Appendix.

Ferri, E.   Criminal Sociology, Chs. 5 and 7.

Gillin, J. L.   Criminology and Penology, Ch. 23.

Gillin, J. L.   Taming the Criminal.

Gordon, J. W.   Borstalians.

Haynes, F. E.   Criminology, Ch. 12.

Hobhouse and Brockway.   English Prisons Today.

Le Mesurier, L.   Boys in Trouble.

Osborne, T. M.   Within Prison Walls.

Osborne, T. M.   Society and Prisons.

Osborne, T. M.   Prisons and Commonsense.

Ruggles-Brise, E.   The English Prison System.

Sen, P.   From Punishment to Prevention.

Shervindt, E.   Russian Prisons.

Wines, F. H.   Punishment and Reformation, Revised Edition, Ch. 14.

Jour. Criminal Law and Criminology, Century of Progress Number, Vol. 24, No. 1, May-June 1933.

Articles

Coggeshall and Menken.   A Woman's Reformatory, *Jour. Criminal Law and Criminology*, Vol. 23 : 819.

Robinson, L. N.   Institutions for Defective Delinquents, *Jour. Criminal Law and Criminology*, Vol. 24 : 352.

Glueck, S.   The Ministry of Justice, *American Review*, Vol. 4 : 139. Significant Transformations in the Administration of Criminal Justice, *Mental Hygiene*, Vol. 14 : 280.   Principles of a Rational Penal Code, *Mental Hygiene*, Vol. 13 : 1.

Lane, W.   The Sing Sing Stabbings, *Survey*, Jan. 22, 1916.

Margolin, A.   The Soviet Way With the Criminal, *Current History*, February 1932.

McCartney, J. L.   Introducing the Offender to Institutional Routine, *Jour. Criminal Law and Criminology*, Vol. 24 : 583.

Mendoza, S.   The New Mexican System of Criminology, *Jour. Criminal Law and Criminology*, Vol. 21 : 15.

Tannenbaum, F.   The Vision That Came to Thomas Mott Osborne, *Survey*, Oct. 1, 1930.   When Osborne Came to Sing Sing, *Survey*, Nov. 1, 1930.   The Community That Osborne Built, *Survey*, Dec. 1, 1930.   The Ordeal of Thomas Mott Osborne, *Survey*, March 1, 1931.   Prison Democracy, *Atlantic Monthly*, Oct. 1920.

Tsheltrow-Bebutow.   Indeterminate Sentence and Soviet Penal Law, *Jour. Criminal Law and Criminology*, Vol. 19 : 408.

INDEX

Adultery, defined, 16-17.

Age. See Criminality, Factors conditioning : age.

Alcoholism. See Criminality, Factors conditioning : alcoholism.

Argentine system, 249-250.

Arrest, authority to, 255; ratio of to certain crimes, 258.

Arson, defined, 18.

Assault, defined, 16.

Augustus, J., 303.

Babies, significance of their behavior, 105-111.

Bad homes. See Criminality, Factors conditioning : homes.

Bail system, 287-291.

Beccaria, C. See Criminology, classical school.

Belgian prison system. See Prisons, Belgian.

Berkeley Coördinating Council. See Crime prevention, by coordinating councils.

Bertillon system, 245-246.

Birth control, 172-173.

Bondsmen, professional. See Bail system.

Borstal Institutions. See Prisons, English.

Brockway, Z., 373-375.

Burglary, defined, 17-18 ; ratio of arrests to crimes known, 258.

Business cycles, 94-95.

Causes of Crime. See Criminality, Factors conditioning.

Chain gangs. See County convict road gangs.

Children, significance of delinquencies, 111-121 ; sex delinquencies, 115-118 ; lying, 118-119 ; stealing, 120-121. See Clinics, child study ; Courts, juvenile ; Detention homes ; Houses of Refuge.

Church, 186-188. See Prison personnel, chaplains.

Classical School. See Criminology, classical school.

Clinics, child study, 209-214 ; psychiatric classification, 453.

Common law. See Law, common.

Contract labor system, 441.

Correctional schools. See Reformatories, juvenile.

County convict road gangs, 385-388.

Courts, juvenile, 198-209 ; organization, 264-265 ; procedure, 265-268 ; municipal, 273-276 ; trial, 276-279 ; unification, 293-294 ; limitation of functions, 295, 495.

Crime, definition, 6-8 ; elements of a, 12-14 ; financial costs, 20-27 ; profits, 27-29 ; rural, 75-76 ; infamous, 299-300. See Burglary, Crime prevention, Felony, Larceny, Law, Homicide, Misdemeanor, Rape, Treason.

Crime prevention, importance, 169 ; in families, 170-176 ; in schools, 176-183 ; in industries, 183-185 ; government, 186, 191-194 ; community, 186-188 ; coördinating councils, 194-197 ; police, 218-226. See Clinics, child study ; Courts, juvenile.

Criminality, Factors conditioning : geographic, 70-72 ; wealth, 72-75 ; biological, 77-81 ; alcoholism, 81-84 ; drug addiction, 84-

587